The Fisherman's Catalog

Other books by Vlad Evanoff

Best Ways to Catch More Fish in Fresh
   and Salt Water
Fishing with Natural Baits
Make Your Own Fishing Lures
Surf Fishing
Another 1001 Fishing Tips and Tricks
1001 Fishing Tips and Tricks
The Freshwater Fisherman's Bible
How to Fish in Salt Water
Spin Fishing
A Complete Guide to Fishing
Modern Fishing Tackle

The Fisherman's Catalog

compiled by Vlad Evanoff

DOLPHIN BOOKS
DOUBLEDAY & COMPANY, INC.
GARDEN CITY, NEW YORK 1977

The author wishes to thank the many fishing-tackle manufacturers and companies making fishing accessories for supplying information and photos about their products and for permission to use them in this catalog. He would also like to thank the many boat manufacturers for supplying information and photos. Thanks are also due to the book publishers for sending information, review copies, and photos of the fishing books they publish. The fish and game and conservation departments of many states were extremely helpful in supplying lists of brochures, folders, booklets, and other publications that can be obtained from them. Thanks are also due to many other organizations for sending along information and photos.

DESIGNED BY LAURENCE ALEXANDER

Library of Congress Cataloging in Publication Data

Evanoff, Vlad.
   The fisherman's catalog.

   Includes index.
   1. Fishing tackle—Catalogs. 2. Fishing boats—Catalogs.
3. Fishing—Bibliography. 4. Fishing—Directories. I. Title.
SH447.E95   338.4'7'6887902573
ISBN 0-385-12196-2
Library of Congress Catalog Card Number 76–23806

Copyright © 1977 by Vlad Evanoff
ALL RIGHTS RESERVED
PRINTED IN THE UNITED STATES OF AMERICA
FIRST EDITION

Contents

Part I

FRESHWATER TACKLE AND FISHING

Rods, reels, lines, lures, baits, hooks, sinkers, snaps, swivels, floats, other terminal gear, tackle boxes, vests, clothing, fishing boats, outboard motors, electric motors, fish finders, other accessories, fishing tips and hints, fishing facts, fishing feats and oddities, fishing spots, clubs and organizations, fishing books, booklets, guides, catalogs, brochures, and other publications

Pages xii–234

Part II

SALT-WATER TACKLE AND FISHING

Rods, reels, lines, lures, baits, hooks, sinkers, snaps, swivels, floats, other terminal gear, tackle boxes, clothing, fishing boats, outboard motors, fish finders, other accessories, fishing tips and hints, fishing facts, fishing spots, clubs and organizations, fishing books, booklets, guides, catalogs, brochures, and other publications

Pages 236–384

The Fisherman's Catalog

How to Use This Catalog

This catalog was compiled as a source of information pertaining to almost everything having to do with fishing. Here you will find the latest and best in fishing rods, reels, lines, lures, and accessory equipment. It also lists and describes fishing boats, outboard and electric motors, fish and depth finders, and other electronic gear. And throughout the catalog there are reviews of the latest freshwater and salt-water fishing books on the market, and many other booklets, brochures, catalogs, and other publications dealing with fishing.

Most of the items covered in this catalog have photos or illustrations. As you flip through the pages you will notice photos of rods, reels, lines, lures, boats, accessories, and books. Below the photo or illustration you will find a description of the product. Following that will be the name of the firm making or selling the product and the address where you can write for their catalog or more information.

Many of the catalogs and publications listed are free, but some require a nominal fee, and this amount is listed in this catalog. Some prices of products and items are also listed to give you an idea of what they cost. But this catalog was never meant for ordering any of the items directly. It is strictly a reference book on where you can get additional information or facts about the product featured. So before you order any of the items in this catalog, first write to the company for information about the latest price, and additional facts about the product. After all, the company could have gone out of business or might no longer make or sell the product mentioned.

The same is true with the fishing books reviewed in this catalog. Try your local bookstore or dealer to see if they have a copy of the book in stock. If not, you can usually place an order for the book with them and they will obtain a copy for you. If there is no book dealer in your area, you can order a copy of the book from the publisher.

Throughout the book you will also find short "how to do it" articles about fishing, fishing tips, fishing oddities, feats, and records that make interesting reading and also offer fishing tips that will help you to catch more fish.

Please do not write to the author or publisher of this catalog for additional information. Write directly to the manufacturer, company, or supplier whose address is given in the catalog.

Part One

Freshwater Tackle and Fishing

Rods, reels, lines, lures, baits, hooks, sinkers, snaps, swivels, floats, other terminal gear, tackle boxes, vests, clothing, fishing boats, outboard motors, electric motors, fish finders, other accessories, fishing tips and hints, fishing facts, fishing feats and oddities, fishing spots, clubs and organizations, fishing books, booklets, guides, catalogs, brochures, and other publications

Reading for Better Fishing

There is no substitute for experience when it comes to fishing. The best way to learn how to fish or become a good fisherman is to go out as often as possible and fish hard and long, observe and learn by actually catching fish. If you can get an expert or old-timer to take you out fishing and teach you the ropes, you will get a good start. But unfortunately, not many beginners know such veteran anglers, and even if they do, the beginners rarely get invited out on fishing trips.

But another excellent way to learn how to catch fish is by reading magazines, fishing guides, catalogs, books, and other literature dealing with the sport. Just reading alone won't make you a good fisherman, but it will help shorten the learning period necessary to acquire the skills and know-how. Without such reading it may take you years to learn a certain method, technique, tip, or trick that has been discovered or perfected earlier by other anglers and is now available in print. This catalog is filled with fishing magazines, fishing guides, catalogs, books, booklets, and other publications that will help you to become a better fisherman faster if you read them.

EXPERT ANGLERS' COLLECTION

These are handy booklets written by several fishing experts on different kinds of freshwater fish and fishing. The books include the following titles:

New Guide to Salmon and Trout Fishing by ERWIN BAUER
New Guide to Panfish Fishing by GEORGE LAYCOCK
New Guide to Walleye and Sauger Fishing by PARKER BAUER
New Guide to Black Bass Fishing by HOMER CIRCLE

The price of these books is $2.00 each, and they are published by:
Lowrance Electronics, Inc.
12000 E. Skelly Dr.
Tulsa, Okla. 74128

THE LARGEST FRESHWATER FISH

How big do freshwater fish grow? In this country a muskie going over 50 lbs. is considered big, and they may reach 80 or 100 lbs. in weight. Our catfish have often reached over 100 lbs. in weight, with some blue catfish reaching 150 lbs. or more in early records. There are catfish in Guyana that still reach more than 200 lbs. And the Wels, a catfish found in European waters, is said to reach over 500 lbs. in weight. The alligator gar may reach close to 10 ft. in length and a weight of over 300 lbs. And the arapaima, which is found in the rivers of South America, is said to reach 500 lbs. or more.

But the biggest fish found in fresh water are the sturgeons. In this country, sturgeon found in our Pacific Coast rivers have been caught up to 1,285 lbs. and a length of 12½ ft. But the biggest sturgeon have been found in Russia, where one monster weighed 2,250 lbs. and had a length of 14 ft.!

PIKE ON A FLY ROD

Pike provide great sport on a fly rod if you use big bass bugs, streamers, and bucktails. You also need a heavy monofilament leader next to the lure or a short length of wire leader. Work your lures fairly fast for pike in coves with weeds, along the edges of lily pads and the shorelines where there are stumps, logs, driftwood, or fallen trees. And you don't have to fish early in the morning or late in the evening for the pike. They usually bite better during the middle of the day.

SMELT MEAN LANDLOCKS

If you are fishing for landlocked salmon, try to find the spots where smelt are concentrated. These small fish are often found in the same waters as the landlocked salmon and form a major part of their diet throughout the year. In the spring as the ice leaves the lakes, look for smelt at the mouths of streams emptying into the lake. Then smelt run up such rivers to spawn and congregate at the mouths. And the landlocked salmon move in to feed on them. Later on, when the water and weather get warm, the smelt head for deeper water, and if you can find the depth where they are hanging out, you'll usually find landlocked salmon there too.

LURES THAT SMELL

Many anglers fishing for carp or catfish in freshwater use various flavors or scents in their doughball baits. Or they let minnows, fish, or meat baits ripen for a few days so that they give off a strong odor. But more and more anglers are beginning to use various scents on fishing lures too. Such scents may not be too important when fishing with metal, wood, or hard plastic lures and reeling them in fast. Then fish usually strike by sight without getting a chance to taste the lure. But such scents could make a big difference when the slower-moving, soft plastic worms and eels are used. Many of these lures already have a scent that has been added at the factory. But it is also a good idea to carry a small bottle or tube of some kind of scent and smear it on the lure before you start fishing.

METEOR BASS BOAT

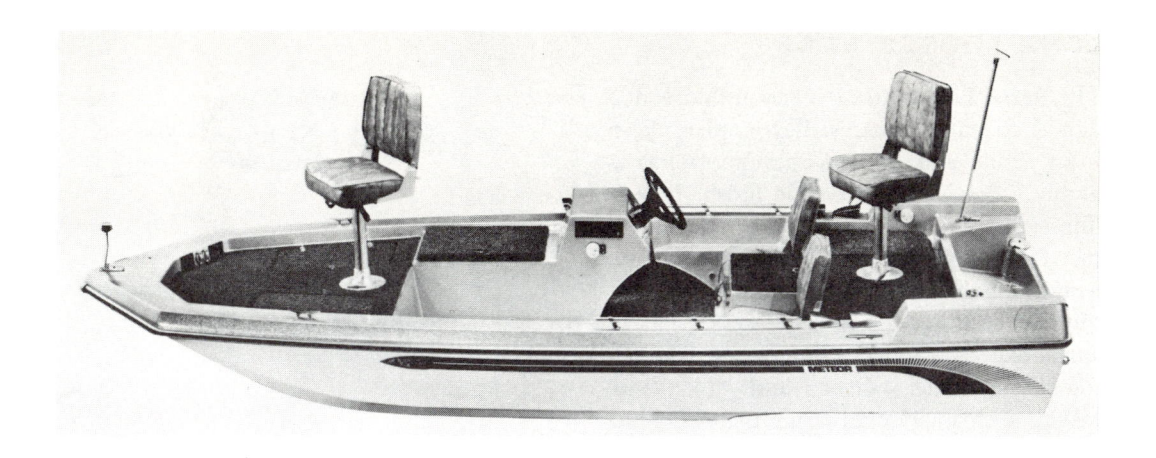

The Meteor bass boat is a trihull-type 15-ft., 6-in.-long craft with a beam of 74 in. and a depth of 24 in. It has positive foam flotation, safety kill switch, mechanical steering, aerated livewell, icebox, 18-gal. tank with electric gauge, bilge pump, forward control panel with voltmeter, duplex receptacle, outboard tilt switch and cigarette/chart lighter, twin folding swivel seats with storage pouches, horn, telescopic seat pedestals fore and aft, and rod storage. For their catalog showing this and other fishing boats write to:
Arrow Glass Boat & Mfg. Corp.
931 Firestone Blvd.
Memphis, Tenn. 38107

NYLORFI LINE

The Nylorfi monofilament line is imported from France and sold in this country by Cortland Line Company, its sole agent in this country. It has been one of the most popular lines in France because of its small diameter, great strength, flexibility, controlled elongation, and amazing invisibility in the water. It is available in tests from 4 lbs. up to 30 lbs. For more information write for the catalog showing this and other fishing lines to:
Cortland Line Co.
Cortland, N.Y. 13045

ACME LOOTER LURE

The Acme Looter lure is a spoon that is designed to catch bass, walleyes, pike, lake trout, coho, and chinook salmon. It has a highly reflective fishlike scale finish. It is a thin spoon, which makes it effective for either fast or slow trolling. It can be cast and worked slowly so that it rises, sinks, and flutters, or it can be reeled fast so that it darts like a crippled minnow or fish. It comes in nickel, silver, and gold and nickel, with fluorescent stripe or neon blue stripe. For their catalog of these and other lures they make write to:
Acme Tackle Co.
69 Bucklin St.
Providence, R.I. 02907

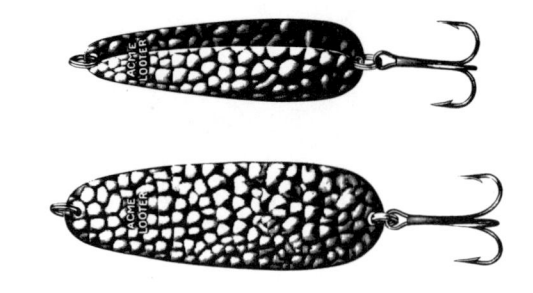

PERRINE AUTOMATIC FLY REELS

The Perrine free-stripping automatic fly reels have been made for many years and are well known to fly fishermen. They make several models with vertical or horizontal mounts. They weigh between 8 ozs. and 9 ozs. and come in brown, green, or blue. Each reel will hold several fly line sizes up to No. 9 or No. 10. All Perrine reels are guaranteed for life, and the factory will replace or repair them at no charge. For their color folder showing these reels and also the fly boxes they make write to:
Aladdin Laboratories, Inc.
620 S. Eighth St.
Minneapolis, Minn. 55404

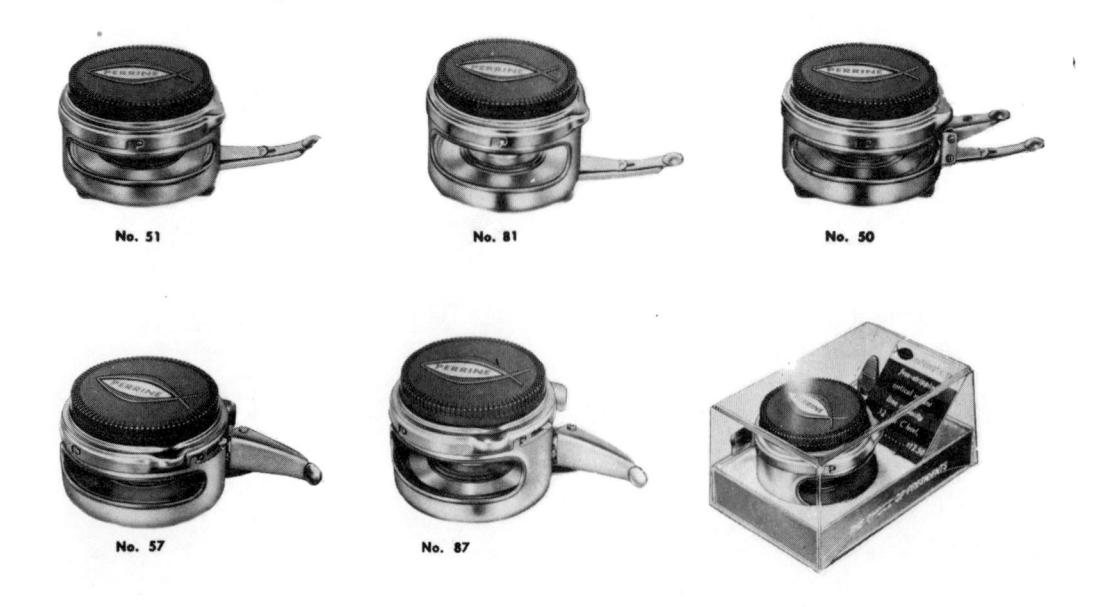

No. 51   No. 81   No. 50

No. 57   No. 87

BIG SALMON ON FLIES

Some big chinook salmon have been caught on fly rods and flies by such anglers as Bob Nauheim, especially in such rivers as the Smith in California. Here the king salmon run during the fall months and can be made to take hair flies tied with silver or gold tinsel bodies or Mylar piping. These are usually tied on No. 2 to No. 6 hooks. The secret in this fishing is to cast your high-density or lead core fly line with plenty of monofilament running line into spots where the big salmon lie. You may have to use a small boat to reach the best spots. And the fly should be cast 10 to 20 ft. above where the fish are lying and allowed to sink and drift so that they pass in front of the salmon. Chinook salmon in the 50-lb. class have been taken this way!

TELESCOPIC FISHING RODS

The Powerscopic Corporation makes a complete line of telescopic fishing rods. They make spinning rods, spin-casting rods, bait-casting rods, fly rods, and spin and fly combination rods. These can be collapsed to a short length anywhere from 17 in. to 11 in., depending on the model. This makes them ideal for fitting into tackle boxes, coat pockets, attaché cases, suitcases, and travel bags, and also makes them handy for backpackers who want to tote a rod into wilderness waters. Only the finest materials are used in making these attractive rods, which also perform well while casting or fighting a fish. For their catalog showing the complete line of telescopic fishing rods write to:
Powerscopic Corp.
P.O. Box 278
Westwood, N.J. 07675

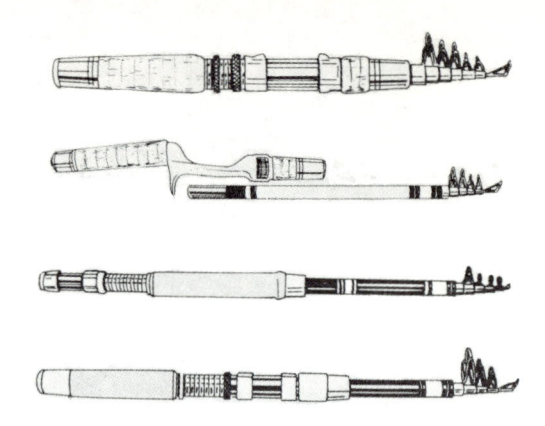

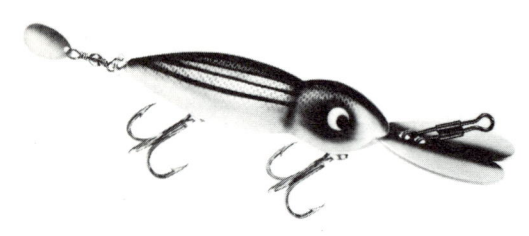

HELLBENDER AND HELLRAISER LURES

The Hellbender lure is a deep-diving fish-getter that is used when casting or trolling. It has a big, heart-shaped lip that makes it go down anywhere from 8 to 35 ft., depending on the size of the lure you use. It is at its best when cast and reeled or when trolled so that it just runs above the bottom and even bumps it every so often. It comes in many colors and four sizes.

The Hellraiser is a surface plug that is best when fished in short twitches, causing it to sputter, bounce, and dart. This can be done slow or fast, depending on what the fish want that day. This lure comes in a $3/8$-oz. size for spinning and light tackle and a $1/2$-oz. size for casting tackle or heavy spinning tackle. For their catalog showing these and other lures write to:
Whopper Stopper, Inc.
P.O. Box 1111
Sherman, Tex. 75090

ZEBCO REELS

The Zebco Division of Brunswick Corporation has been making closed-faced spinning reels and spin-casting reels from way back when these reels first showed up on the market. Since then they have added many other open-faced spinning reels for fresh-water and salt-water fishing. Now they manufacture dozens of spinning and spin-casting reels in all sizes and price ranges for all kinds of fishing. For a color catalog showing their reels, rods, and other fishing products write to:

Zebco Division of Brunswick Corp.
P.O. Box 270
Tulsa, Okla. 74101

WEEDLESS "ARROW-LOCK" HOOK

One big trouble with many weedless hooks is that the plastic worm or bait slides down the hook when cast or after you hook a fish. The "Arrow-Lock" hook was designed to avoid this by adding a tiny arrow on the shank of the hook. You thread the head of the worm over the arrow and it stays in place because of the two barbs on the arrow. These hooks come in Nos. 1, 1/0, 2/0, 3/0, and 4/0 sizes and are made by:

The Boone Bait Co., Inc.
P.O. Box 571
Winter Park, Fla. 32789

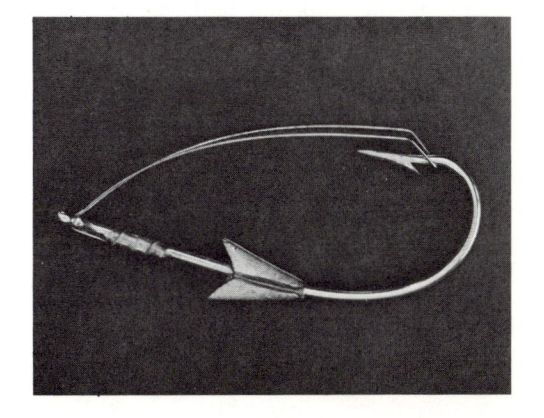

JIFFY ICE DRILLS

This company makes Jiffy Hand and Power ice drills for drilling holes fast through ice when you want to go ice fishing. Their Jiffy Hand Ice Drill has a durable drop forge steel auger that cuts through ice in a "jiff." It is lightweight and has a detachable handle that breaks down into two sections for compact storage and portability. The 5-in. blade drill sells for $29.95, and the 7-in. blade sells for $35.95.

The Jiffy Power Ice Drill has a 3-hp. gasoline engine that drives the bit through the thickest ice in seconds and ends the difficult and tedious job of hole chopping by old-fashioned methods. It provides easy ice chip removal with the spiral auger. They make several models with 7-, 8-, or 9-in. bits and ranging in price from $139 to $155. For more information write to:
Feldmann Engineering & Mfg. Co., Inc.
P.O. Box 153
Sheboygan Falls, Wis. 53085

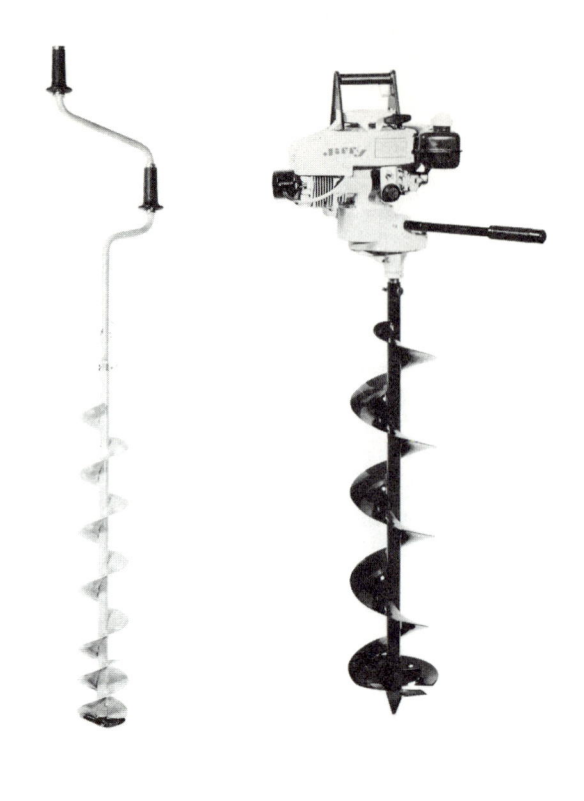

BUILD YOUR OWN FISH POND

The book *Creative Fishing* by Charles J. Farmer tells you in detail how to build your own pond and enjoy better fishing than ever in just two years and at surprisingly little cost. In fifteen chapters Farmer describes every step of pond creating, from purchasing the land and building the dam to what species of fish to stock, where to get help, how much it will cost, and how to maintain it in top condition year after year.

Farmer tells you what to look for in a pond site, the pond and its features, filling and stocking, costs, recent trends in pond construction, ecology and conservation, and pond management. You can obtain the help of several state and federal agencies, and he tells you who to contact. *Creative Fishing* sells for $5.95 and is published by:
Stackpole Books
Cameron and Kelker Sts.
Harrisburg, Pa. 17105

SUICK LURE

The Suick Lure has been a longtime favorite for muskellunge; one angler caught thirty muskies in thirty days on this lure. The larger-size Suick is 9 in. long and weighs 2¼ ozs. This lure is used by casting out and reeling and then pulling it sharply for 3 feet, after which you follow the line back to the start of the pull, avoiding slack. Then pull sharply again and repeat this all the way up to the boat. The smaller Suick, which is 7 in. long and weighs ¾ oz., can be worked the same way and will catch muskies, pike, and bass. For more information write to:
Suick Lure Co.
P.O. Box C
Antigo, Wis. 54409

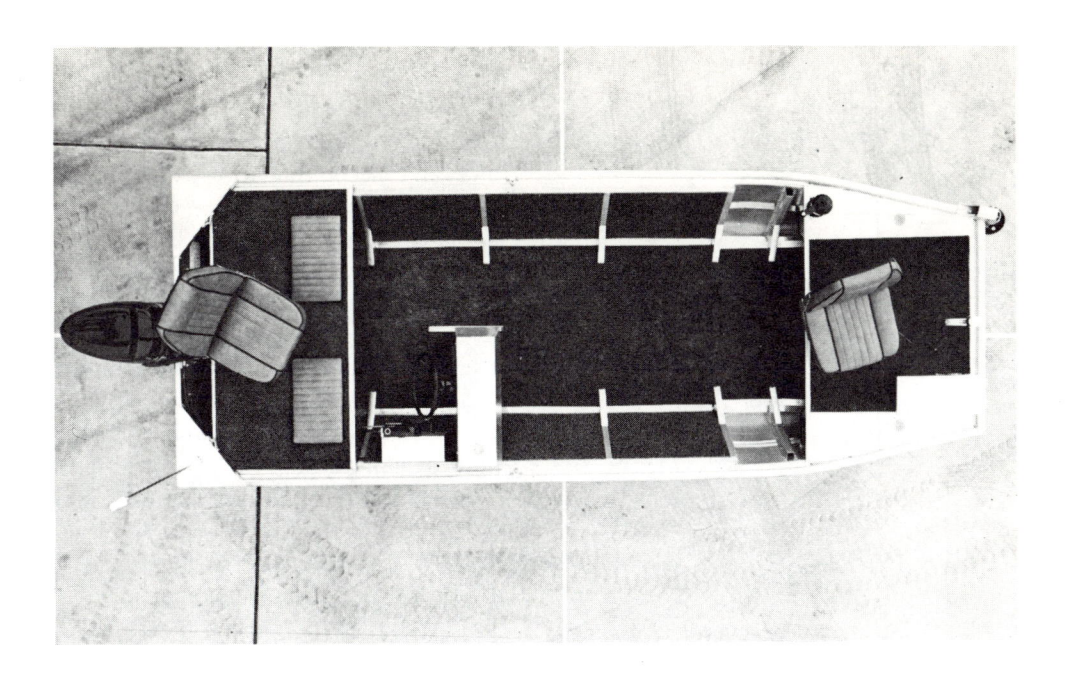

FISHER MARINE BOATS

The Fisher Marine line of lightweight aluminum boats are designed for the fisherman who wants his boat to be stylish, roomy, comfortable, practical, safe, and efficient to operate. They run quietly and inexpensively on relatively low-horsepower motors. They troll in deep water and shallow water and can go into vegetation or inches of water where other boats hang up. And they are economical compared to Fiberglas boats of the same size.

Light but strong, the unitframe construction and longitudinal hull torsioning are applied to Fisher Marine boats. Each model boasts triple-sized rivets, compression-type transom, full length, angled spray rails, and BIA and federal flotation requirements. Adjustable seats high in the boat allow the utmost in fishing convenience and comfort and are standard in the Bateau, Netter, and Scow models. The Water Strider DDC shown above features casting decks fore and aft, and console steering. For a brochure showing all of their boats write to:
Fisher Marine, Inc.
P.O. Box 1256
West Point, Miss. 39773

FISHING IN CLEAR WATER

Fish are much harder to catch when the water is clean, clear, and calm. Then they can see you at a distance, and every disturbance is magnified and so are the lures, leaders, swivels, hooks, and lines. Under such conditions use tiny lures, smaller baits, and light lines, and long, thin leaders and small hooks. And make longer casts and fish a good distance away from where you think the fish are. It is also a good idea to fish at dawn, dusk, and during the night at those times when the water is clear, clean, and calm.

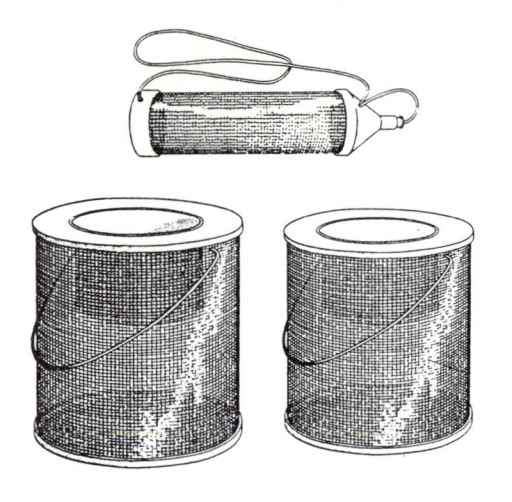

LIVE BAIT CAGES

Hubs Chub Lures makes several live bait cages. The cage is of 8-in.-by-8-in. mesh steel wire cloth, and is rust-resistant and attractive. It is galvanized after weaving to provide a heavy zinc coating. The top and the bottom of the cage are made of the new "high-impact styrene," which will withstand hot, cold, and wet weather and will take a severe shock without breaking. The larger cages will hold 100 to 150 crickets, grasshoppers, or roaches. The smaller cages hold fewer baits but can be worn around the shoulder or waist while fishing. For more information write to:
Hubs Chub Lures
103 S. West St.
Arcadia, Ind. 46030

MFG'S SUPER BASS 17 BOAT

When fishing big impoundments and lakes, bass anglers appreciate both the performance and accommodations of a boat like MFG's Super Bass 17. The top of the line of MFG high-performance bass boats, the Super Bass 17 has a broad, 75-in. beam and a hull design that makes it rated for up to 120-hp. outboard motor. Yet it weighs only 900 lbs., making it easier to maneuver with any electric trolling motor connected to the boat's standard prewired motor terminals.

Other standard fishing features include bow and stern live wells with aerators, six lockable storage compartments, a 7-ft. lockable rod storage compartment, two comfortable folding fishing chairs, two running seats, an insulated, molded-in beverage cooler, and molded-in lure trays.

Other features include navigation lights, fully fused switch panel, bilge pump, and a built-in, ventilated 18-gal. fuel-tank system with an electric gauge. Color options include an ivory hull and deck with deep tan, red or blue hull stripe, centennial yellow hull and deck; or surf-green hull and deck with forest-green hull stripe. MFG's family of Super Bass boats also includes a 14-ft. boat and a 15-ft. boat. For a catalog or more information write to:
MFG Boat Co.
55 4th Ave.
Union City, Pa. 16438

COREN'S ROD & REEL SERVICE

This is a unique rod and reel service, which repairs nearly all models of popular domestic and imported reels. If the fishing reels are not discontinued or are too old or too rare and they can get parts for it, they can repair it. They also sell fishing reel parts. And they repair fishing rods to a certain extent and sell rod-making blanks, rod handles, reel seats, ferrules, grips, spinning-rod rings, guides, winding thread, cement, varnish, and rod-making kits. They issue a catalog showing and describing all these services and products. Write for it to:
Coren's Rod & Reel Service
6619 N. Clark St.
Chicago, Ill. 60626

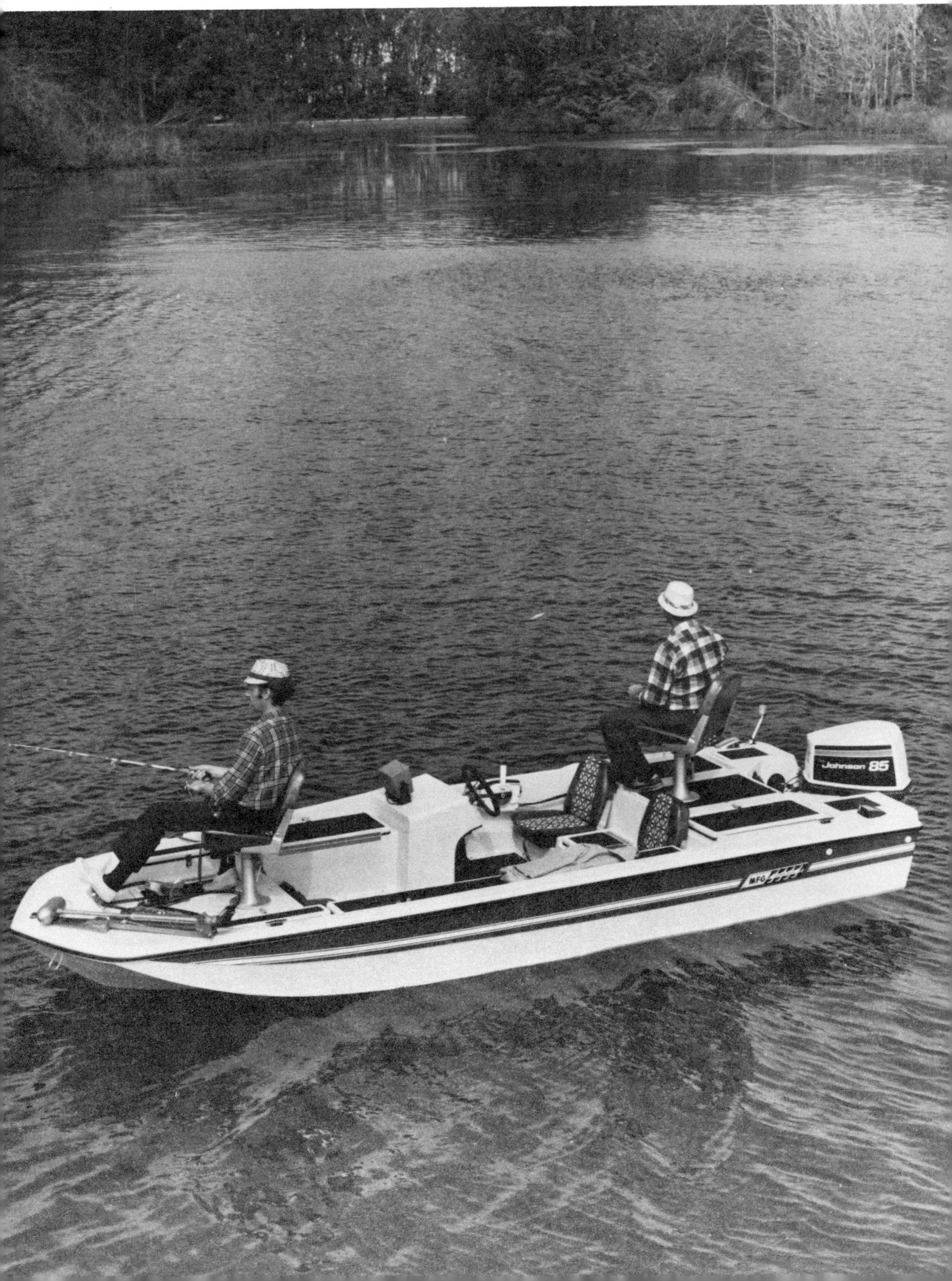
Johnson 85
MFG

SINGLE CARLISLE

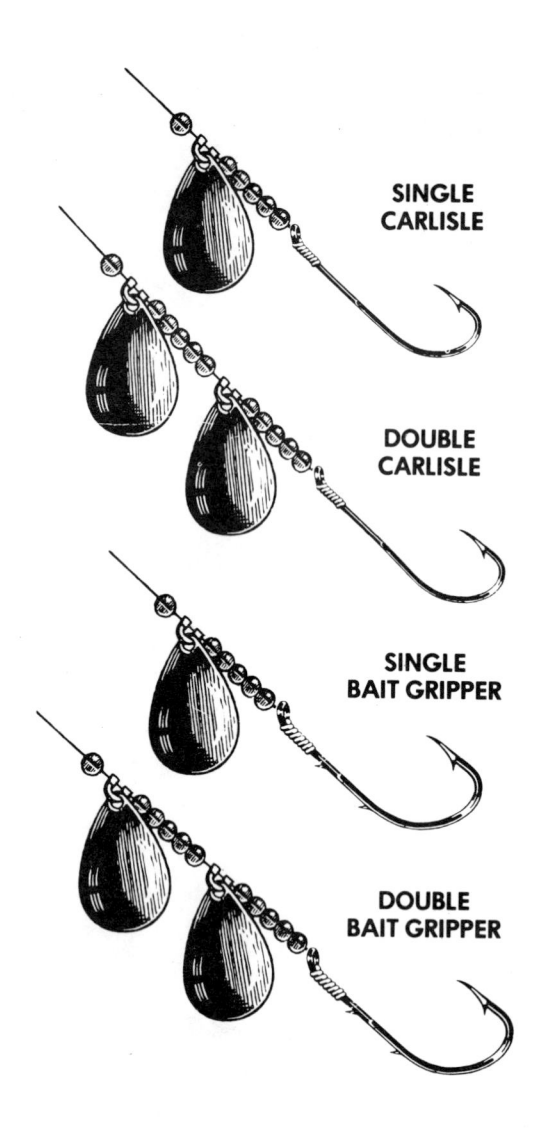

DOUBLE CARLISLE

SINGLE BAIT GRIPPER

DOUBLE BAIT GRIPPER

SNELLED HOOK SPINNERS

Weller's Bob-It spinners are made with transparent nylon or Steelcore—nylon plastic-coated stainless-steel wire cable. Each spinner is decorated with red fluorescent beads and a flashing single- or double-spinner blade. They are designed for use in lakes, rivers, and streams for trout, bass, walleyes, pike, and panfish. For their catalog showing these and other lures send $.50 to:
Erwin Weller Co.
P.O. Box 3204
Sioux City, Ia. 51102

TROLLING BAIT BUCKET

This polyethylene bucket is designed for automatic water changing to keep minnows lively. It has two built-in flotation chambers that eliminate the need for lifting the bucket out of the water and into the boat when moving from spot to spot. Just tie a rope to the handle and tow it behind the boat. For more information write to:
Woodstream Corp.
P.O. Box 327
Lititz, Pa. 17543

AMERICAN FISHING TACKLE MANUFACTURERS' ASSOCIATION

This organization has a membership of fishing tackle companies and allied products. It has an annual trade show in August and conventions twice a year. It also publishes and distributes some helpful booklets and literature on sport fishing. These include:

How to Catch Fish in Fresh Water
How to Catch Fish in Salt Water
All About Fishing Rods
All About Fishing Reels

These booklets are *free*, but you have to send a self-addressed stamped envelope size No. 10 or business-size for each booklet. Send this to:
American Fishing Tackle Manufacturers' Assn.
20 N. Wacker Dr., Suite 2014
Chicago, Ill. 60606

THIN-FIN LURES

The original thin-fin Silver Shad was designed to provide the most realistic simulation of a natural shad. The Silver Shad has the characteristic swayed belly and extremely thin body that is shared by all members of the shad family. It comes in floating diving and sinking models and three sizes. Other lures made by this company include the "Shiner Minnow," "Hot 'N' Tot," "Wiggle Wart," "Chug Bug," "Whiz Bang," and "Fatso." They also make spinner baits. Most of the plugs and spinner baits are available in a wide variety of colors. For their catalog showing these lures write to:
Storm Mfg. Co.
P.O. Box 265
Norman, Okla. 73069

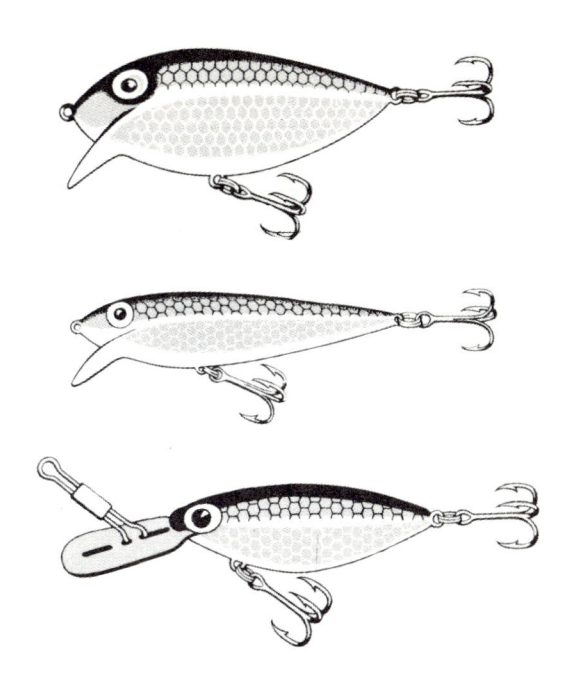

THE FRESHWATER FISHERMAN'S BIBLE

The book *The Freshwater Fisherman's Bible* by Vlad Evanoff has been widely read by many freshwater anglers and is a complete guide to this fishing. It covers freshwater fishing tackle such as rods, reels, lines, lures, and baits. It gives methods for rigging the natural and artificial baits, and it tells how to catch a wide variety of freshwater species. The *Bible* covers large-mouth bass, small-mouth bass, Atlantic salmon, landlocked salmon, brown trout, brook trout, rainbow trout, steelhead, lake trout, muskellunge, pike, pickerel, walleyes, yellow perch, bluegills, crappies, white bass, white perch, rock bass, catfish, bullheads, eels, shad, carp, suckers, and even lesser-known species such as whitefish, sheepshead, buffalo fish, chubs or fallfish, and sturgeon. There's a complete chapter devoted to each fish, giving its habits, distribution, and the best tackle, lures, baits, and rigs to use for them and how to fish for them. Each fish is illustrated, and there are numerous photos showing fishing scenes. *The Freshwater Fisherman's Bible* sells for $2.50 and is published by:
Doubleday & Co., Inc.
501 Franklin Ave.
Garden City, N.Y. 11530

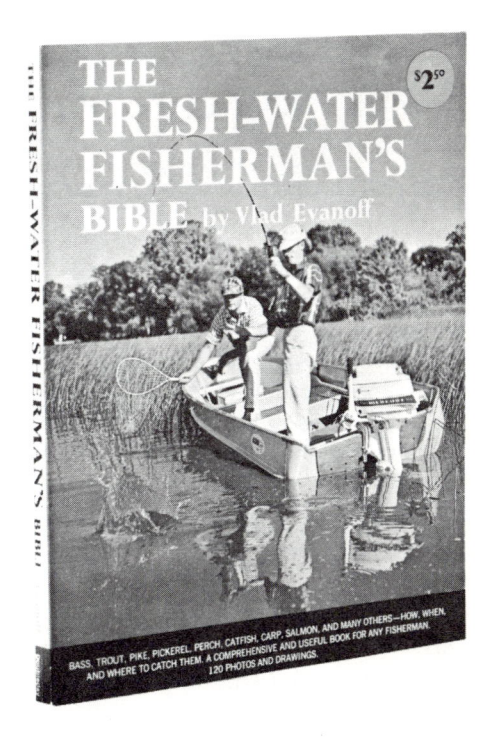

13

WEIR & SON BAMBOO RODS

Weir & Son still make fine bamboo fly rods for the most exacting fly fishermen. They make the entire rod except the guides and rod case. They use the finest Tonkin cane available. The hook keeper, in sterling silver, is mounted on the cork handle to spare the windings, finish, and bamboo from damage. It is also placed so that the fine hackles on a dry fly will not be crushed. The ferrules are hand-drawn and fully hand-made from nickel silver. They are mounted and then pinned with tapered nickel silver pins. The location of the pin in the male ferrule is such that it is encased in the female ferrule when mated, giving double assurance that you won't lose the tip and the fish in action. They now make eleven models of hand-made fly rods, ranging from 6 ft. to 8½ ft. and designed for line weights of 2L to 9WF. For a price list and more information about their split-bamboo rods write to:
Weir & Son
P.O. Box 1518
Los Gatos, Calif. 95030

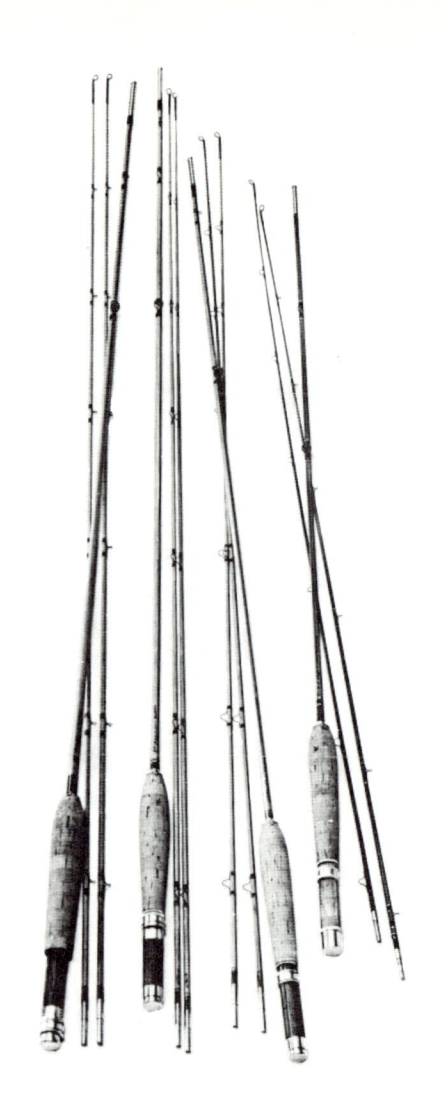

THE MONTANAN'S FISHING GUIDE

The Montanan's Fishing Guide by Dick Konizeski is a complete directory to that state's fabulous fishing waters. It comes in two volumes. Volume 1 covers the waters west of the continental divide, while Volume 2 covers the waters east of the divide. Both volumes appraise accurately and in detail the various streams, rivers, ponds, and lakes. They contain contour maps and detailed instructions on reaching the waters, and tell what kind of fish are found there. There are also color plates of the most popular fish and photographs throughout the books. The author drew on the experiences of the Montana State Fish and Game Department, U. S. Forest Service personnel, and professional guides, packers, trappers, and sportsmen to come up with the most detailed guides to Montana's fishing waters. Each guide sells for $6.95, and they are published by:
Mountain Press Publishing Co.
287 W. Front St.
Missoula, Mont. 59801

FISH FILLET KNIVES

The Olsen Knife Company offers handmade fish fillet knives of top-quality Swedish high-carbon tool steel. They have both flexibility and maintain a fine and lasting edge. They come with a safety sheath, and their Coho knife comes with a hone for sharpening. This company also makes many other knives for the kitchen, and for hunting, camping, and general use. They also have pocket knives, including the Swiss Army knife. And they also have a complete line of pocket compasses. For their catalog showing these knives and products write to:
Olsen Knife Co.
Howard City, Mich. 49329

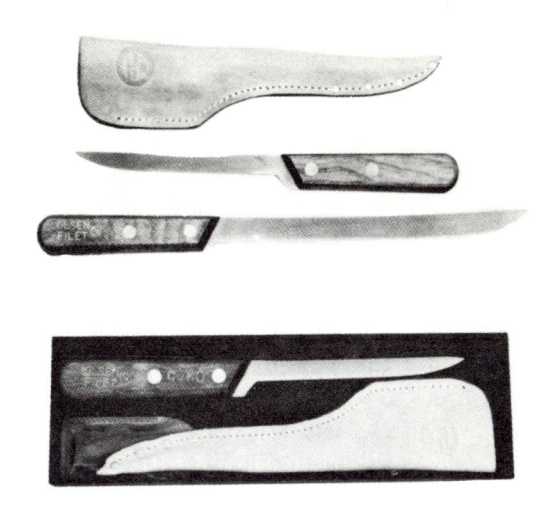

LINDY TAILS

These plastic worms are preferred by professional and expert anglers because of their texture and excellent flotation qualities. The long, thin tail, which literally breathes in the water, not only attracts fish but also influences the entire worm action. These worms are available in eleven popular colors and four lengths up to 9 in. Although used mostly for large-mouth bass, they are also effective for small-mouth bass and walleyes. For their catalog showing these and other lures, rigs, tackle, and accessories write to:
Ray-O-Vac Fishing Tackle Division
ESB, Inc.
P.O. Box 488
Brainerd, Minn. 56401

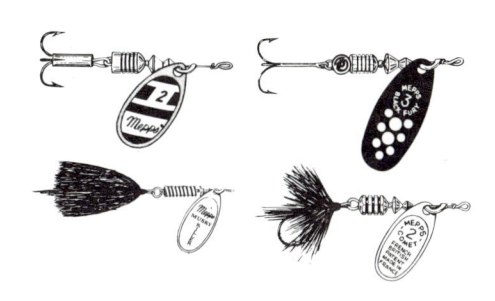

MEPPS SPINNERS

The Mepps spinners are well known to freshwater anglers all over the world as great lures that will catch anything from panfish and trout up to big salmon and muskies. They are used in salt water for many species. The original French spinner Aglia is made in many different sizes, finishes, and models. Other spinners such as the Comet, Black Fury, Musky Killer, and Giant Killer are also made by this firm. They also make a Plastic Mino and Kriss Spoon and Trolling Fly. Their catalog showing these and other lures in color is $.50 and is available from:
Sheldon's, Inc.
P.O. Box 508
Antigo, Wis. 54409

SPINFISHING

The book *Spinfishing*—the system that does it all—is written by two expert anglers, Norman Strung and Milt Rosko, and covers all phases of this method, from basic tackle selection and casting to the delicate nuances of hair-lining for trout and stalking bonefish on sparkling tidal flats. Spinfishing is the most popular form of fishing in the world. As the authors of this book illustrate, no other system does so many jobs so well as spinning nor lends itself to such a variety of species.

Each technique—including stream and lake fishing, surf casting, boat casting, bottom fishing, chumming, and trolling—is taken up individually, so that you can use this book as a guide, knowing what to do, step by step.

Spinning rods and reels are capable of tempting ½-lb. grayling and whipping 50-lb. striped bass. They can cast a wisp of a worm or a 6-oz. sinker. They're equally at home with bait or lures and even flies. "What's more," the authors continue, "spinning is a simple form to master."

With 150 black-and-white photographs that illustrate spinning, casting, and lures, plus a helpful discussion of the gamefish a spin fisherman can expect to catch, this is "a book written for modern fishermen, a book for all species, a book for all waters and a book for all seasons." It sells for $8.95 and is published by:
Macmillan, Inc.
866 Third Ave.
New York, N.Y. 10022

BOTTOM FISHING RIG

This fishing rig is designed to take live baits down to the bottom where such fish as crappies, yellow perch, white perch, white bass, and bluegills often feed. It has long arms that keep the hooks and snelled hooks away from the line. It is made of highly rust-resistant nylon-covered stainless-steel wire. It has brilliant red fluorescent beads. It comes without the snelled hooks, and you can add whatever size or length you need for the fish you are after. The hooks can be baited with worms, crickets, grasshoppers, meal worms, minnows, or any other bait. For more information or a brochure write to:
Bear Paw Tackle Co., Inc.
Bellaire, Mich. 49615

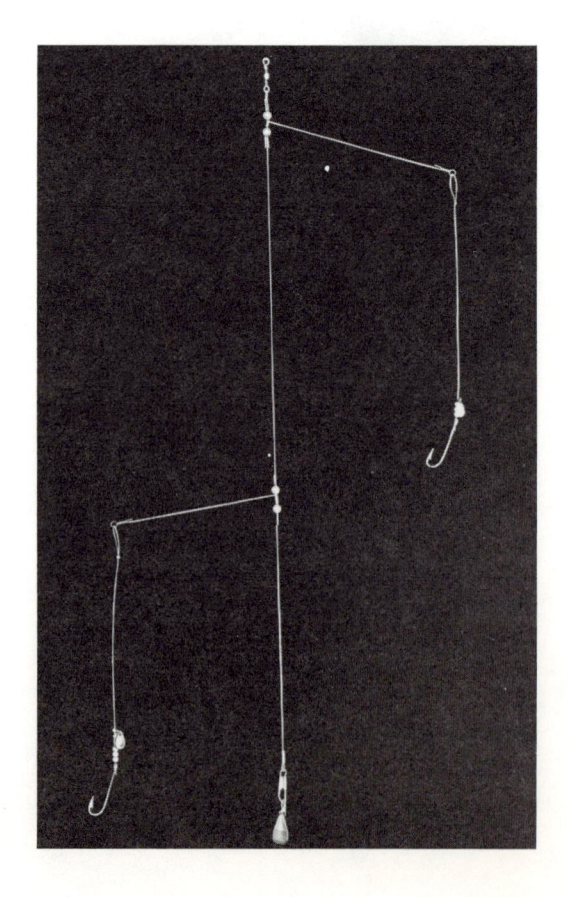

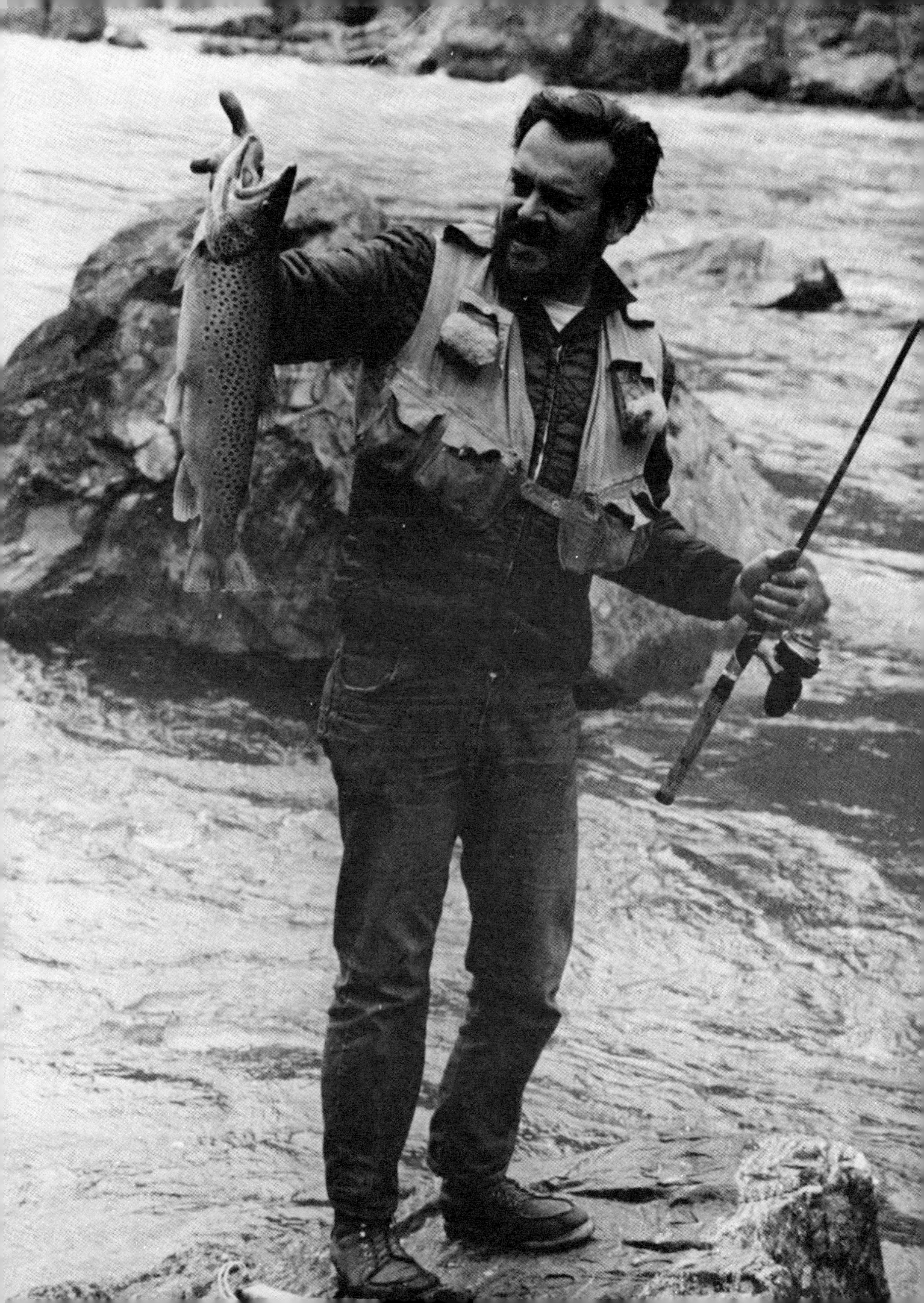

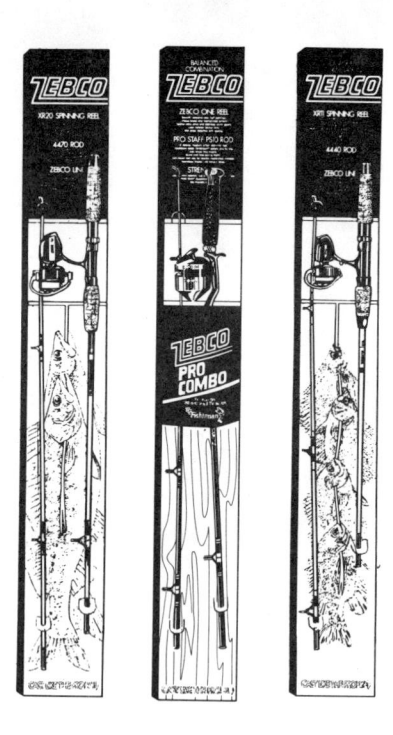

ZEBCO ROD-REEL COMBINATIONS

Zebco has packaged many of their most popular freshwater spinning and spin-casting rods and reels together in one neat container. They've also included a fishing line in each package. Each combination is performance-balanced and labeled according to the kind of fishing for which the "combo" was designed. For their complete line of combination rods and reels and other tackle write for their catalog to:
Zebco Division—Brunswick Corp.
P.O. Box 270
Tulsa, Okla. 74101

OKLAHOMA FISHING

You can get the following leaflets about Oklahoma fish and fishing:

Fishing Facts
Sport Fish of Oklahoma
Trout Streams of Oklahoma

They can be obtained from:
Dept. of Wildlife Conservation
1801 N. Lincoln
Oklahoma City, Okla. 73105

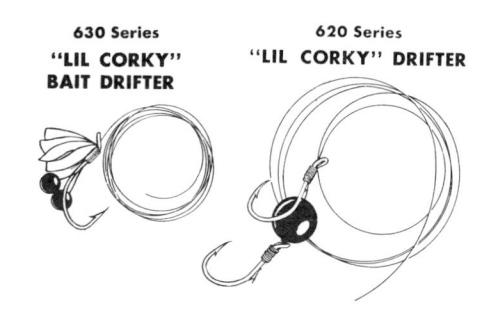

"LIL CORKY" DRIFTER

The "Lil Corky" drifter and bait drifter are popular steelhead lures that come in a wide variety of sizes and colors. They are available in such colors as Flame, Flame and White, Flame and Chartreuse, Pearl Red, Light Green Fluorescent, Pink, Pearl Luminous, Lime, Pearl Peach, Nickel Plate, Rocket Red, and Coral. They can be used as is, or you can add salmon eggs, worms, or other baits on the hook. The same company also makes a wide variety of other lures for freshwater and salt-water fishing. For a catalog write to:
Yakima Bait Co.
Granger, Wash. 98932

FRESHWATER FISHING IN HAWAII

Most fishermen think of Hawaii as a salt-water fishing area, but there is also excellent freshwater fishing in many of the ponds, lakes, and streams there. They also have reservoirs and public fishing areas where you can catch many of the species you are familiar with in the rest of the United States. Many of these waters contain large-mouth bass, small-mouth bass, rainbow trout, bluegills, and channel catfish. There's a booklet called *Freshwater Fishing in Hawaii* that tells about these fish and where they are found in Hawaii. For a copy write to:
Hawaii Dept. of Land and Natural Resources
Div. of Fish and Game
1179 Punchbowl St.
Honolulu, Hawaii 96813

WILLIAMS SPOONS

This company makes several types of spoons that are widely used for shallow and deep trolling for landlocked salmon, lake trout, pike, muskellunge, coho salmon, and Pacific salmon. They come in different shapes and sizes and finishes. Some have a hammered or rinkle finish that looks like fish scales. The spoons come in silver, gold, and half-and-half finishes. Most of them are rigged with strong treble hooks and barrel swivels up front. They range from small 1- and 2-in. models weighing $\frac{1}{16}$ oz. up to big 4- and 6-in. models weighing $1\frac{1}{2}$ ozs. They put out a small folder called *Deep Trolling by Williams,* which tells how to use these spoons on wire lines for deep trolling. For this folder and more information about their spoons write to:

Williams Gold Refining Co. of Canada Ltd.
30 Courtwright St.
Fort Erie, Ont.
Canada L2A 2R7

LEONARD FLY-FISHING SCHOOL

The H. L. Leonard Rod Company offers three-day fly-fishing school sessions at Roscoe, New York, where a beginner can learn how to present a fly and take a fish properly. And more advanced fly fishermen can sharpen their skills. The illustrated classroom instruction will cover such topics as balanced tackle, basic entomology and insect observation, fly selection, leader design and knot tying, proper wading techniques, reading a trout stream, and other information needed to catch trout. Each three-day session emphasizes extensive individual casting instruction and practice under the watchful eyes of Leonard personnel. The highlight of your stay will be access to private as well as public water on the famed Beaverkill River. The $150 registration fee includes your room, meals, fishing school tuition, the use of Leonard rods, reels, and lines, and your New York State fishing license. The three-day sessions are held in May and June on weekends. For specific dates and more information write to:

H. L. Leonard Rod Co.
25 Cottage St.
Midland Park, N.J. 07432

PRACTICAL BLACK BASS FISHING

The book *Practical Black Bass Fishing* by Mark Sosin and Bill Dance is a complete course on fishing for large-mouth and small-mouth bass. It covers spinning, bait casting, fly rodding, and the lures, baits, and tactics needed to get results. And it deals with fishing over all kinds of structure in lakes, ponds, rivers, and creeks. These are the methods and techniques used by most of the pros and especially bass master Bill Dance. *Practical Black Bass Fishing* sells for $7.95 in hard-cover and $5.95 in soft-cover. It is published by:

Crown Publishers, Inc.
419 Park Ave. S.
New York, N.Y. 10016

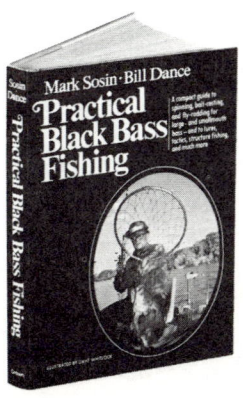

BASS ANGLERS SPORTSMAN SOCIETY

The Bass Anglers Sportsman Society claims to be America's largest fishing organization, with close to a quarter of a million members. It is dedicated to the bass fishermen of America, and while the members fish for many kinds of fish, they concentrate mainly on the large-mouth bass and to a lesser extent on the small-mouth bass. If you join this organization you receive a membership packet, which includes complete identification for the BASS member, including a handsome, silk-embroidered BASS emblem, membership card, colorful decal for boat or car, and a BASS member handbook. You also get six issues of the *Bassmaster Magazine* and a special *Bassmaster Fishing Annual*. You also get special information on the best bass fishing lakes and spots, and discounts on fishing tackle, car rentals, fishing clinics, and invitations to BASS fishing tournaments. Membership in the organization is $12 a year, and you can get more information and an application blank from:

Bass Anglers Sportsman Society
P.O. Box 3044
Montgomery, Ala. 36109

FISHING

The large book *Fishing* by Joseph D. Bates, Jr., is an encyclopedic guide to fishing tackle, lures, flies, and tactics for freshwater and salt-water fishing. It runs 736 pages, and between its covers it deals with almost everything you need to know to catch fish almost anywhere. There are complete chapters on spinning, spin casting, bait casting, fly fishing, trolling, still fishing, and every other angling method. There are other chapters on freshwater lures, flies, rigs, hooks, baits, leaders, and lines. Then there are still other chapters on the importance of water temperature, how seasonal changes affect fishing in lakes, how to find fish in streams and brooks, and fishing for all kinds of trout, including fly fishing, spinning, and the use of dry flies, wet flies, nymphs, streamers, and bucktails. There is a chapter on fishing for Atlantic salmon, another one on shad fishing; and still other chapters on the pike family and panfish. Even ice fishing is covered in Chapter 29.

The rest of the book deals with salt-water fishing, and here the author covers tackle, lures, baits, fishing from piers, bridges, breakwaters, and surf, and inshore and offshore fishing for all the popular gamefish such as striped bass, bluefish, channel bass, weakfish, cod, mackerel, snook, tarpon, bonefish, sailfish, marlin, dolphin, amberjack, and many others. *Fishing* sells for $14.95 and is available from the author:

Joseph D. Bates, Jr.
45 Prynnwood Rd.
Longmeadow, Mass. 01106

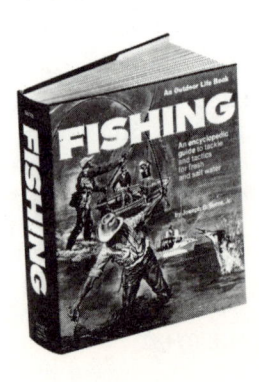

20

POLAR CRAFT FISHING BOATS

This company makes a line of aluminum fishing boats in various sizes and types. They have a semivee, which is a new series with the bottoms and sides redesigned for additional stability and rigidity. All SV-L boats of this series are constructed from a single aluminum sheet, eliminating long lines of rivets on the sides and bottoms. The new extended C-type rib and heavy-duty extruded runners allow easier planing and a truer trim, which help cut through rough water. These semivee-bottom boats range from 11 ft., 10 in. to 15 ft., 10 in.

They also make a variety of wide-bottom aluminum boats from small 10-footers up to long 20-footers suitable for big-river fishing and float trips. For their catalog showing these boats write to:
Polar Craft Mfg. Co.
P.O. Box 708
Olive Branch, Miss. 38654

FISH HAWK 550

More and more anglers are discovering that the oxygen content of the water, the water temperature, and the light intensity all have a bearing on fishing. Lakes and other bodies of water have different levels of oxygen in different areas, because of plant life, wind, inflowing streams, underwater springs, and other factors. And each species of fish lives in water of a specific —often very limited—temperature range, and a fish seldom will venture out of the temperature level where, scientists presume, its body functions most comfortably and effectively. And even if all other conditions of structure and environment are "right," fish cannot take your lure unless they can see it. This obvious fact has led to the study of underwater light intensity and how it affects lure colors as seen through the eyes of most fish. Under ideal conditions, red colors cannot be seen at depths much beyond 15 ft., while blue may be visible to fish as deep as 180 ft.

Now the Waller Corporation has come up with a meter called the Fish Hawk 500, which measures oxygen content of the water, plus light intensity as a guide to lure-color selection, plus temperature at varying depths, plus constant, positive digital read-out depth with no color-coded line to count or interpret. For a catalog and more information write to:
Waller Corp.
4220 Waller Dr.
Crystal Lake, Ill. 60014

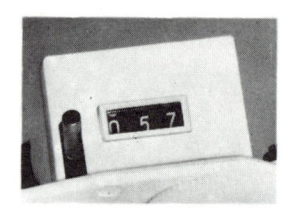

Built-in Digital Counter

Model 550

FISH SCOUT DEPTH FINDER

The Vexilar Fish Scout depth finder is designed for small boats having the best performance with under 10 hp. motors or nonmotorized craft. This latest addition to the Vexilar line is approximately 4 in. deep by 5 in. wide by 4 in. high. It measures depths to 60 ft. and is totally enclosed in a durable 16-gauge anodized aluminum case to protect the precision meter and all solid-state electronics. It is powered by an 18-v. system (two common 9-v. transistor batteries) and is easy to operate. Just plug in the transducer, mount the bracket, flip a switch, and you're ready to go get 'em. For more information or catalog write to:
Vexilar, Inc.
9345 Penn Ave. S.
Minneapolis, Minn. 55431

OREGON FISHING BOOKS

The Caxton Printers have three books that cover Oregon fish, fishing, and spots. One of these is *Fishing the Oregon Country* by Francis H. Ames, who has spent a lifetime fishing in Oregon waters. He covers fishing for trout, steelhead, shad, sturgeon, salmon, and panfish. He also covers salt-water fishing for salmon, striped bass, flounders, sea perch, and rockfish. This book sells for $6.95.

Another book is *101 Best Fishing Trips in Oregon* by Don Holm, who covers that number of lakes, ponds, streams, and rivers in Oregon. He tells about fishing for trout, steelhead, shad, salmon, and other species found in Oregon waters. This book sells for $3.95.

Still another book, also written by Don Holm, is *Pacific North* and this covers many Oregon hot spots for freshwater and salt-water species, but also ranges up and down the coast from the Channel Islands off Southern California all the way up to Alaska. This is a big, beautiful volume illustrated with many black-and-white and some color photos. It sells for $12.50.

All of the above books are published by:
The Caxton Printers, Ltd.
Caldwell, Id. 83605

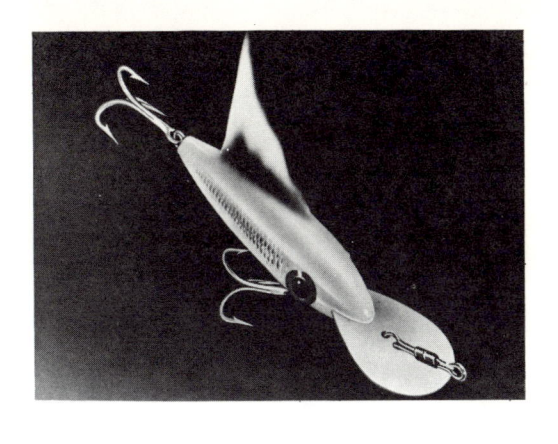

GUDEBROD FIREBACK LURES

It is a well-known fact that fish will often strike at the wildest and gaudiest colors that don't seem to match anything in nature that they feed on. Yet it is possible that such wild colors actually transmit themselves to the fish with a more natural look than we think and thus are not wild to them at all. So the Gudebrod Company has added fluorescent colors to their popular Maverick and Bump 'N' Grind plugs. Such colors as fiery red, super orange, and wild yellow have been added to the backs of these lures. Of course, these plugs are still available in the more natural, minnowlike colors too. For more information write to:
Gudebrod Fishing Tackle
12 S. 12th St.
Philadelphia, Pa. 19107

SCALING FISH

As every angler (and wife) knows, scaling fish inside a house can be a mess if the scales fly all over the place. There are two ways you can avoid this. One way is to scale the fish in a sink filled with enough water to cover the fish. The other way is to get one of those big clear plastic bags and scale the fish inside it. That way the scales remain in the bag too and can be disposed of by rolling up the plastic bag and dumping the whole thing in the garbage can.

FOOLING A MUSKIE

Muskellunge are notorious for following a lure but refusing to take it. One trick you can try to get a strike in such a situation is to use a floating underwater plug that travels just below the surface when it is reeled in steadily. Then when you reel it in a good distance below the surface, let up or slow down so that the plug rises to the surface and creates a commotion. This often excites the musky following the lure, and he hits it hard.

1001 FISHING TIPS AND TRICKS

This book is entirely different from most fishing books. It actually contains 1,001 lesser-known tips and tricks used by the top experts to catch most freshwater and salt-water fish. Many of these tips are illustrated with "how to do it" drawings showing how to make or use rigs, baits, lures, and other tackle. There are many tips and tricks on the best techniques and methods used in fresh water and salt water. There are twenty chapters covering freshwater tackle, lures, rigs, natural baits, trout, black bass, muskellunge, pike, pickerel, walleyes, panfish, and other freshwater fishes. The salt-water section covers tackle, rigs, lures, natural baits, striped bass, channel bass, bluefish, weakfish, tuna, swordfish, marlin, sailfish, dolphin, wahoo, albacore, bonito, tarpon, snook, sea trout, bonefish, salt-water bottom fishes, and other salt-water species. The book is simply written and illustrated and easy to read, but even expert anglers will discover tips and tricks they never knew. *1001 Fishing Tips and Tricks* by Vlad Evanoff is published by:
Harper & Row, Publishers, Inc.
10 East 53rd St.
New York, N.Y. 10022

WONDERTROLL ELECTRIC FISHING MOTOR

The WonderTroll 603 electric fishing motor—a new lightweight motor—has been added to Shakespeare's motor product line. Weighing only 9 lbs., the 603 operates quietly on 6-v. or 12-v. batteries. The three-speed motor has low, medium, and high settings in addition to the forward and reverse operating control. The "O" ring-sealed lower unit produces 3 lbs. of thrust at low speed, 6 lbs. of thrust at medium speed, and 10.5 lbs. of thrust at high speed.

The WonderTroll 603 operates quietly and efficiently, with a permanent-magnet motor unit. A sturdy, single screw holds the motor securely to the transom of fishing boats. For further information contact:
Fishing Tackle Div.
Shakespeare Co.
P.O. Box 246
Columbia, S.C. 29202

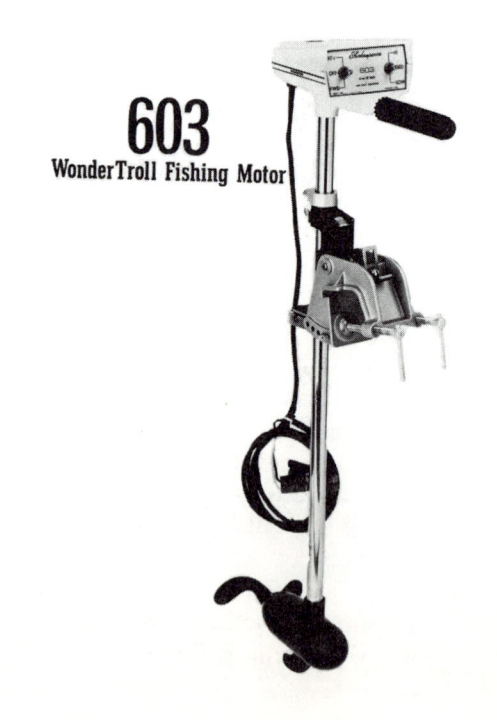

THE TEXAS FISHERMAN

The Texas Fisherman is a newspaper-type monthly publication which calls itself the "Voice of the Lone Star Fisherman." Every month it covers a wide variety of freshwater and salt-water fish and fishing in Texas. Such well-known and expert anglers as Russ Tinsley, A. C. Becker, Al Eason, L. A. Wilke, and others contribute to this fishing paper. A yearly subscription is $5.00, and a single copy can be obtained for $.50 from:
The Texas Fisherman
5314 Bingle Rd.
Houston, Tex. 77018

NEW MEXICO FISHING WATERS

The New Mexico Department of Fish and Game has a colorful booklet called *New Mexico Fishing Waters* that anglers planning to fish in that state will find helpful. It has detailed maps showing the various sections of the state, and it tells which streams, rivers, lakes, and reservoirs contain fish and what species and how to find these waters. Send for it to:
New Mexico Dept. of Fish and Game
State Capitol
Santa Fe, N.M. 87503

TIPS ON ROD BUILDING

Tips on Rod Building by Gene Bullard is a very helpful booklet that tells how to choose a rod blank, how to trim it, how to install butt ferrules, how to select and place guides, how to wrap them, how to cement and add grips, how to fit reel seats, and how to finish the rods. *Tips on Rod Building* is available for $1.00 from:
Gene Bullard Custom Rods, Inc.
10139 Shoreview Rd.
P.O. Box 38131
Dallas, Tex. 75238

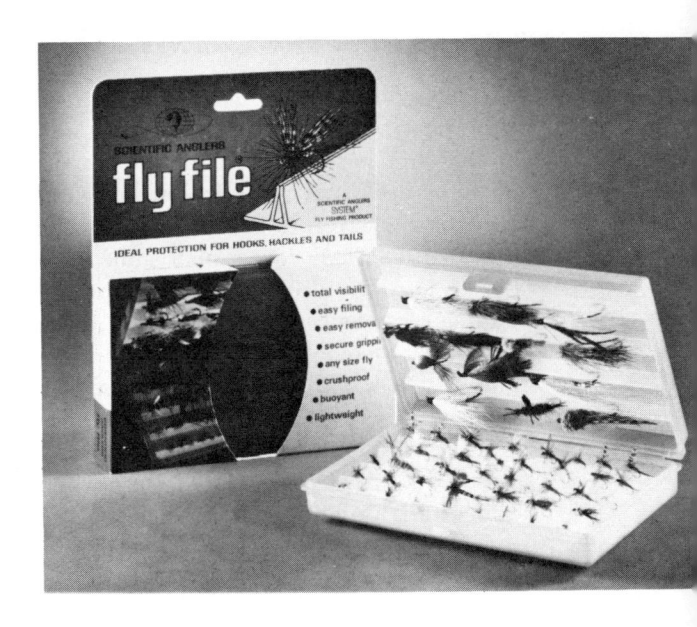

FLY FILE

The Fly File by Scientific Anglers is a pocket-size organizer for your collection of flies. It is of durable rustproof construction and has removable inserts that grip flies tightly without damaging fragile hackles or tails. It also floats and is available in orange, yellow, or blue.

Scientific Anglers also publishes two helpful booklets for fly fishermen. One is called *To Cast a Fly,* which has thirty-six pages of "how to" information on the theory, methods, and techniques employed by contemporary professionals. The price is $.50 for this booklet.

The other booklet is called *Fly Fishing for Bass and Panfish,* and it gives all the know-how on how to lure bass and panfish into striking a fly. It covers tackle, methods, and techniques that get results. This one sells for $.25. For more information about the Fly File or to obtain the booklets write to:
Scientific Anglers
P.O. Box 2001
Midland, Mich. 48640

THE BASS FISHERMAN'S BIBLE

The Bass Fisherman's Bible by Erwin A. Bauer deals with both the large-mouth and small-mouth bass, giving a description of their characteristics and life histories. But the book quickly goes to the practical side of bass fishing and covers such subjects as how to find bass, four steps to casting, fly rodding for bass, fishing from shore, float fishing, cane poling, trolling, and lead-line fishing. It tells you where to catch the biggest bass, how to catch them at night, the best live baits to use, which lures to use, and the best tackle and outfits to use when fishing for bass. The author then covers the best bass-fishing states and spots in the East, Midwest, Southeast, Southwest, West, and Canada. *The Bass Fisherman's Bible* sells for $2.50 and is published by:
Doubleday & Co., Inc.
501 Franklin Ave.
Garden City, N.Y. 11530

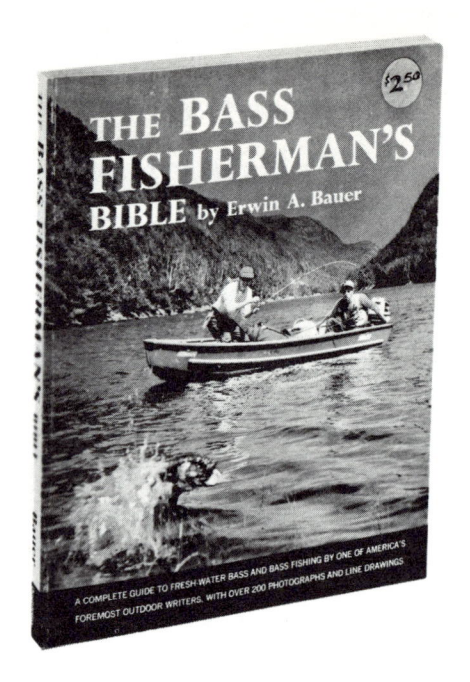

EARLY BIRD WORM BEDDING

Early Bird Worm Bedding is a specially blended mixture of ingredients necessary to keep worms alive and healthy for long periods of time. Each pound of bedding will nourish and sustain four dozen night crawlers and twice as many small worms. This worm bedding mixes easily with water and can be "squeezed out" if too wet without packing or balling up. Moisture evaporates from the bedding and keeps it cool. Worms thrive in cool temperatures ranging from 30 to 60 degrees. Early Bird Worm Bedding is available in 1-, 2-, and 5-lb. packages for fishermen and in 25-lb. bulk packages for the professional worm grower. For more information write to:
Early Bird Co.
P.O. Box 1485
Boise, Id. 83701

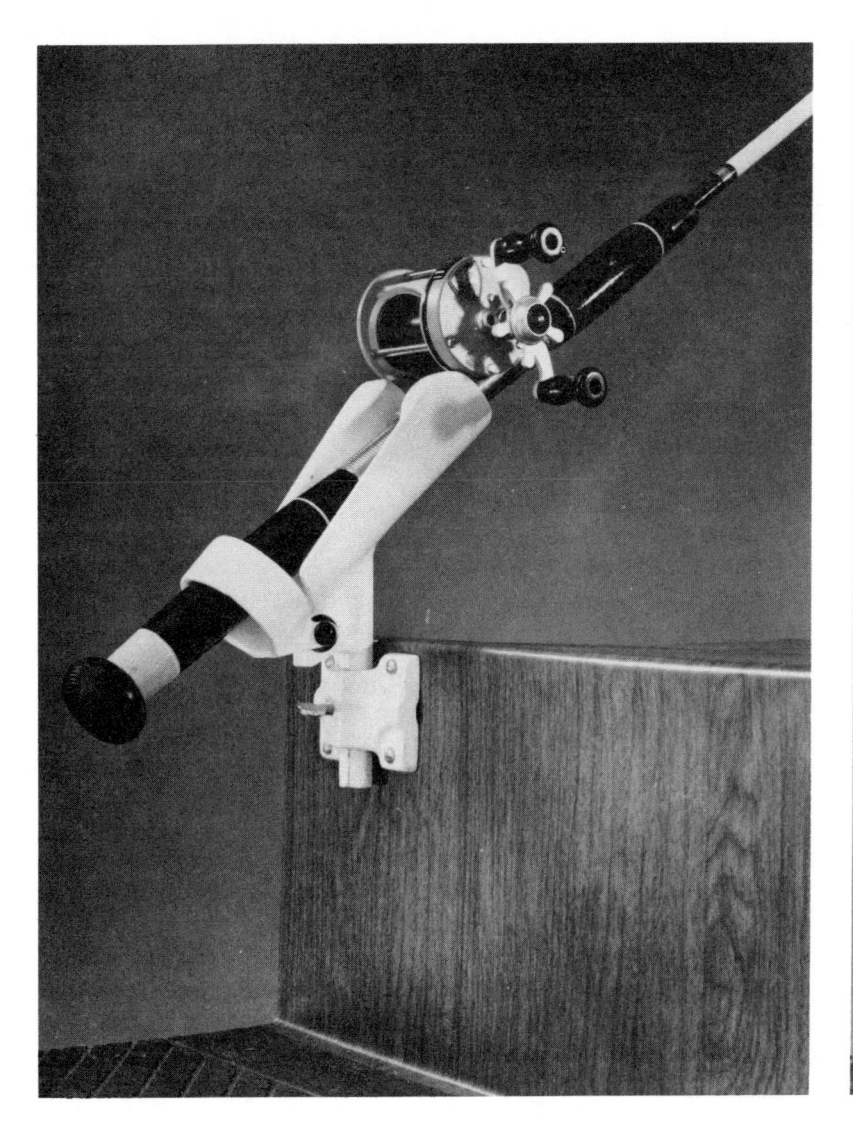

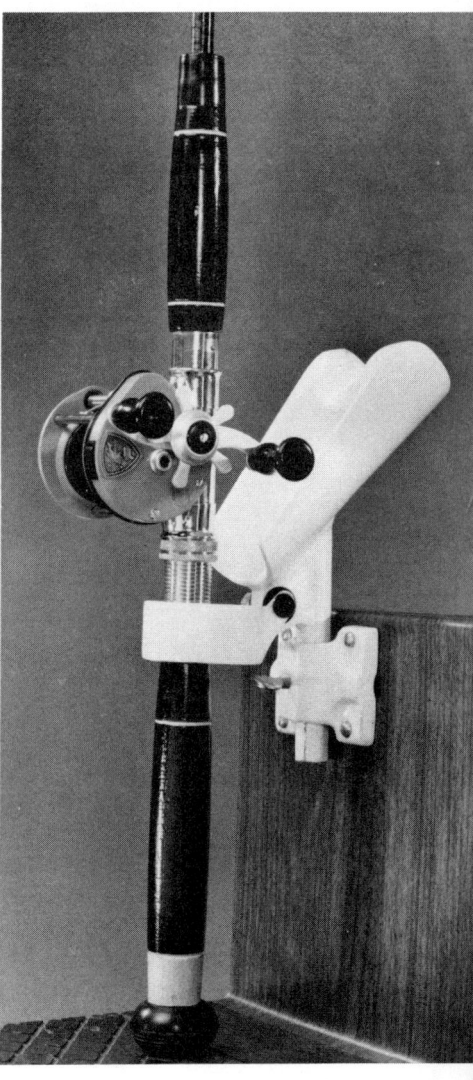

VERSATILE RING ROD HOLDER

Here is a rod holder for sport fishing that does it all. When there is a strike, the angler is able to set the hook simply by pulling back on the rod while it is still in the holder. The holder's open design and a pivoting "drop-back" ring at the base make this possible. When baiting, the rod can be tilted into a vertical position—the drop-back ring then functions as a retainer, leaving both hands free to handle bait. Other tube-type rod holders require the fisherman to remove his rod completely before the hook can be set, losing valuable seconds during which the fish very often is lost while running with the bait.

Made of durable lightweight aluminum alloy, the rod holder can be mounted easily with four screws or bolts fastened to a bulkhead, coaming, or other vertical surface. It is removable for safekeeping when not in use and is adjustable to three different positions. An extremely durable coating keeps this noncorrosive angling accessory looking sharp and serviceable indefinitely. Suggested retail price of the Ring Rod Holder is $12.95. It is made by:
**Tempo Products Co.
6200 Cochran Rd.
Cleveland (Solon), O. 44139**

27

CONVERTIBLE FISHING CHAIR

This three-in-one convertible fishing chair is of light, tubular steel construction and has many features that are handy for a fisherman. There's a beverage holder on one side and a rod holder on the other side. Underneath there's a small box that can be used for lures and other fishing tackle. But if you want to remove these items and convert it to a picnic chair or camp stool you can quickly do this. All the hardware is included. For more information write to:
Emco Specialties, Inc.
P.O. Box 853
Des Moines, Ia. 50304

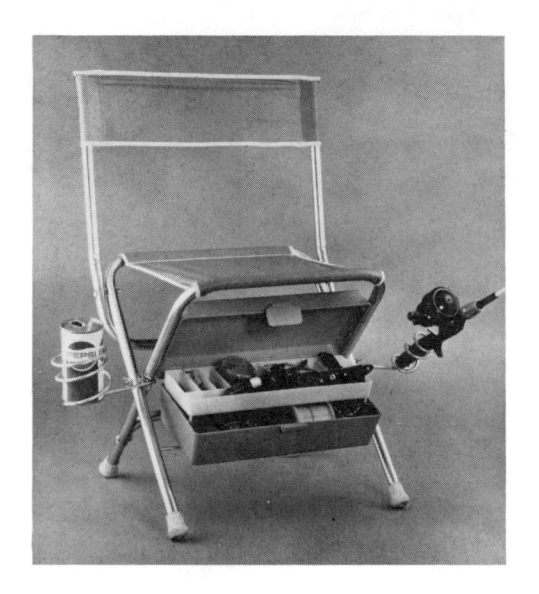

ELECTRIC-POWERED PIROUGE

Here is the newest in a two-man shallow-draft boat with electric power built into it that lets anglers silently poke into stump-, weed-, or rock-infested shallows and other favorite haunts of lunkers impossible to approach with conventional boats.

The 12-ft.-long Electric Feather Pirouge, pronounced "pee-row," is powered by a custom, heavy-duty electric trolling motor built into the stern of the boat and operated by remote controls. Although installed to operate like an inboard, the motor can be easily removed for maintenance. Any standard 12-v. car battery can be used for power, which will give from 8 to 12 hrs. running when fully charged.

An exciting and versatile boat, it is ideal for fishing and hunting as well as just all-around fun. It is simple to operate. A flip of a switch provides instant power in forward or reverse directions. A second switch permits low, medium, or high speeds, with a maximum of 10 mph. Slight pressure on the tiller gives a change of direction almost instantly as the lightweight (67 lbs.) sleek hull glides silently through the water. The boat can turn in its own length.

Ruggedly built of hand-laid Fiberglas with a wide, flat bottom and wrap-around gunwale, the Electric Feather Pirouge offers a high degree of stability and safety because of a low center of gravity and foamed plastic flotation in the floor.

The boat is light enough to be carried by one person and can be easily cartopped. Its beam is 38 in.; bow height, 8 in.; and depth amidships, 12 in. Its load capacity is 540 lbs. It is available in these colors: hunter green, cobalt blue, yellow and camouflage olive drab overspray. Optional accessories included are a seat and propeller weed guard. Suggested retail price is $369 without battery. For more information write to:
Fin & Feather Mfg. Co.
P.O. Box 179
Marshall, Tex. 75670

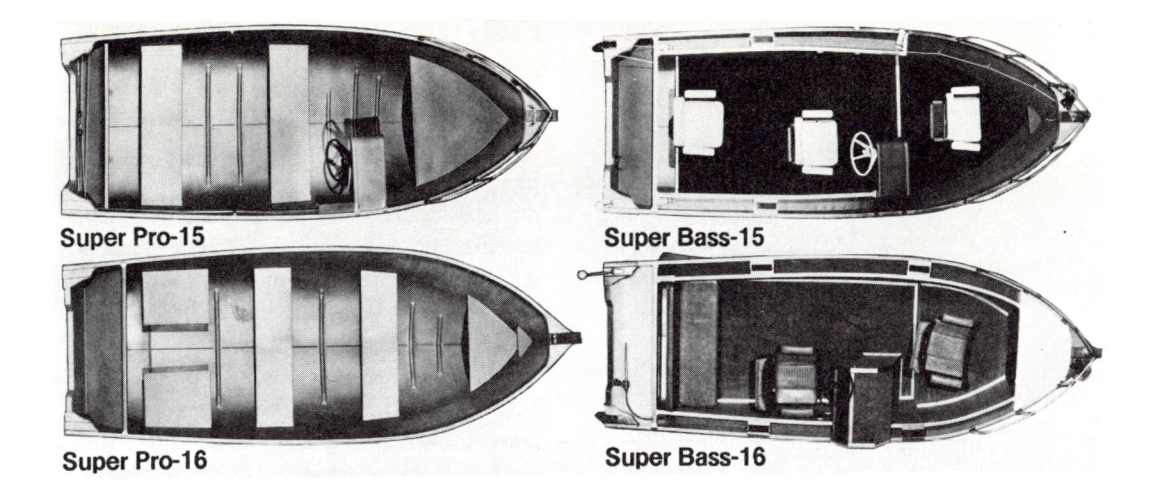

Super Pro-15   Super Bass-15
Super Pro-16   Super Bass-16

MEYERS ALUMINUM BOATS

A new line of lightweight all-aluminum boats designed especially for fishing and recreation use has been introduced by Meyers Industries, Inc. The twenty new boats in the Meyers line range from an 8-ft., flat-bottomed, square-bowed Jon boat that is ideal for solo sportsmen to a sophisticated 16-ft. bass boat that comes complete with upholstered seats and carpeted floors.

The Meyers line offers six different series, with each series designed to satisfy the special needs of different boaters. A selection of sizes is available in each series. Top of the line is the new Meyers Super Bass series. Boats in this series feature all-aluminum construction, which not only makes them much lighter in weight than comparable Fiberglas bass boats, but they are also less costly both in initial investment and in maintenance. Meyers Super Bass boats, which are available in 15-ft. and 16-ft. sizes, have flotation built in under their flat floors. They include as standard equipment the bow rail, bow and stern lights, step plates, rod racks and holders, three upholstered seats, carpeted floors, bow and stern anchors and anchor mates, and a choice of console or stick steering.

Meyers Super Pro Series gives the fisherman a choice of three sizes—14 ft., 15 ft., and 16 ft.—in all-aluminum boats especially designed for navigating in heavy seas, including the Great Lakes. They feature a special flare hull design that minimizes splash and spray, vee bottoms with three keels for stability, and 20-in. transoms. Cable or mechanical steering bow rails, anchors, anchor mates, and 15-in. transoms are optional in the Super Pro series. Complete information about these and other boats they make is available from:
Meyers Industries, Inc.
Tecumseh, Mich. 49286

NEW HAMPSHIRE FISHING

The New Hampshire Fish and Game Department issues a little booklet called *New Hampshire Fishing & Hunting*. This tells about the fishing in that state and lists some of the best waters, telling where they are located, the acreage, and what species are prevalent. It is free. Send for it to the address below.

Another book is called *Freshwater Fishes of New Hampshire* by John F. Scarola. It sells for $2.50 and is available from:
New Hampshire Fish and Game Dept.
34 Bridge St.
Concord, N.H. 03301

PLASTIC MINNOWS

These small, silver, plastic minnows come in many sizes, from a fraction of an ounce up to ½ oz. The smallest one is barely 1 in. long, and the biggest is about 5 in. in length. They come in two types. The plain minnow, which is rigged with a single hook, or the other type, which is rigged with a red jig head and single hook. The plain minnows can be cast with a fly rod or behind a float or weight for panfish such as bluegills, crappies, white perch, and white bass. The plastic minnows with a jig head can be cast with a spinning rod for the same fish when using the smaller minnows. The larger minnows can be used for bass, walleyes, and pickerel. The minnows come packed in blister packages, with one rigged minnow and several spare minnows. For more information write to:
Falls Bait Co., Inc.
1440 Kennedy Rd.
Chippewa Falls, Wis. 54729

FISHING FACTS MAGAZINE

The magazine *Fishing Facts* calls itself "the magazine of today's freshwater fisherman," and it lives up to that slogan by printing all the latest information and facts on how, when, and where to catch fish. It is extremely practical and informative, and it takes the scientific approach, with no details spared or overlooked. It has a regular staff of experts or contributors who supply all the information and facts needed to catch bass, trout, walleyes, pike, muskies, lake trout, salmon, steelhead, and panfish. A subscription to this monthly magazine is $12 for twelve issues, and it is published by:
Northwoods Publishing Co., Inc.
P.O. Box 609
Menomonee Falls, Wis. 53051

CATCHING BIG MINNOWS

Although most minnows used for fishing are bought from bait dealers or are caught in nets, seines, or minnow traps, you can easily catch your own big minnows on hook and line. Just carry some tiny No. 14 or No. 16 hooks and bait them with a bit of worm, bread, or doughball.

REED TACKLE

If you like to tie your own flies, make lures, or make up your own rods, this is the place where you can obtain all the materials and component parts for this work. They carry a complete line of fly-tying materials and tools, rod-making blanks and reel seats, grips, handles, guides, and wrapping materials. They also carry spinner blades, spoons, jig heads, and beads for making finished lures. For their catalog write to:
Reed Tackle
P.O. Box 390
Caldwell, N.J. 07006

ORVIS FLIES

The Orvis Company of Manchester, Vermont, has been selling flies for as long as we can remember. Their flies are tied by a distinguished group of individual famous tiers, and each one of the Orvis fly tier group is not only dedicated to top-quality workmanship and materials, but also is himself a creative artist with sound knowledge of entomology and with long, expert, practical fishing experience. Orvis has divided-wing flies, hackle flies, thorax-type dry flies, parachutes, terrestrials, hair-bodied flies, hair-wing flies, variants, midges, spinners, wet flies, nymphs, streamers, salmon flies, and bass bugs. They also have salt-water flies and bugs. You can buy these individually, by the dozen, or in special selections. For their catalog showing these flies and other tackle they make and sell write to:
The Orvis Co., Inc.
Manchester, Vt. 05254

KEEP HOOKS SHARP

Sharp hooks will hook and catch more fish than dull ones. Yet many anglers neglect this small but important part of their fishing gear. Always examine your hook point after hooking and fighting a big fish or after hanging up in a tree or on the bottom, or if you hit a rock during a cast. Even new hooks right out of a box usually need some touching up. Use a small sharpening stone or file to sharpen your hooks. A fingernail file used by women is a good hook sharpener and doesn't take up much room in a vest or pocket.

FLOAT AND FISH

One of the most pleasant and productive ways to catch fish is by "float fishing," where you drift with the current and fish a river along the way. This can be done from almost any kind of boat, but the flat-bottomed aluminum john boats are best suited for this purpose. You can have one man handling the boat while the other casts lures or flies toward likely spots. Or you can haul the boat up on an island or shore and fish from land. Trout, steelhead, bass, walleyes, pickerel, and panfish can all be caught when float fishing.

Of course, you should do your float fishing on the quieter, safer rivers and leave the rapids and rough water to the experts or fishing guides. And you should not try to cover too many miles in one day. Fish only a few miles of a river thoroughly. If you want to fish a longer stretch, break the trip down into two or three days or longer.

You can use fly fishing tackle, spinning, spin-casting, or bait-casting outfits on a float-fishing trip. Flies, spinners, spoons, small plugs, jigs, and plastic worms can all be brought along and tried along the way.

The great thing about float fishing is that you fish stretches of a river that cannot be reached in any other way. And along the wilder stretches of a river you'll enjoy scenery that alone will make the trip worthwhile.

RAMBLER 12/24 ELECTRIC MOTOR

The Rambler 12/24 electric motor has a new, powerful, permanent-magnet motor that develops up to 24 lbs. of quiet thrust and draws only 19 amps on 24-v., high-speed operation. It has full three-speed operation on both 12 v. and 24 v., with low battery-drain circuits. It is designed for comfortable operation and convenient touch-of-the-toe control. It has a super-tough epoxy powder-coated finish that resists chipping and scratching. It has a stainless-steel shaft, Lexan power prop, and a unique, single-action bow-mount bracket system of heavy-gauge extruded and bar-stock aluminum. For more information write to:
Plastics Research & Development Corp.
3601 Jenny Lind—P.O. Box 1587
Fort Smith, Ark. 72901

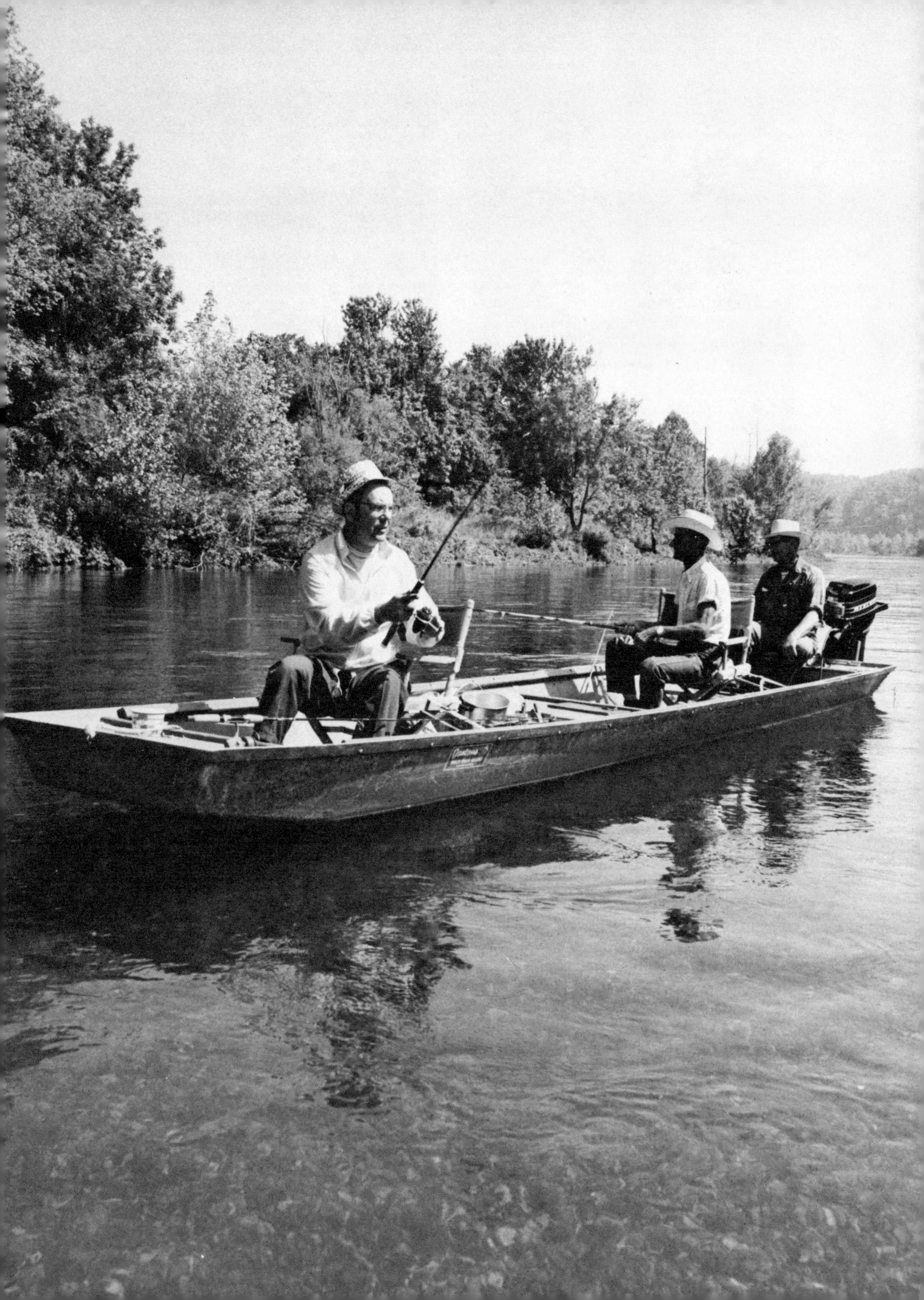

LISK LURES

The Lisk-Fly Manufacturing Company makes many different flies, nymphs, jigs, plastic worms, and grubs. Many of these are rigged behind weighted heads or behind nymphs or spinners. Some are also used with tiny plastic worms cut into sections. Their "Skunk Nymph," "Pole Kat," and "Tar Heel Ant" are well known among panfishermen who seek bluegills, crappies, perch, and white bass. Many of their flies and lures are also used for trout and bass. For their catalog or more information write to:
Lisk-Fly Mfg. Co.
P.O. Box 5126
Greensboro, N.C. 27403

HIGH COUNTRY FLIES

This is a small establishment run by Jay Buchner and his wife, Kathy, who personally tie flies and sell them by mail. They tie the standard and well-known patterns such as dry flies, wet flies, streamers, bucktails, and nymphs. They will also tie any pattern you request if you send a sample of the fly you want. They also sell fly rods, reels, lines, leaders, vests, and fly boxes. For their catalog write to:
High Country Flies
P.O. Box 1022
Jackson, Wyo. 83001

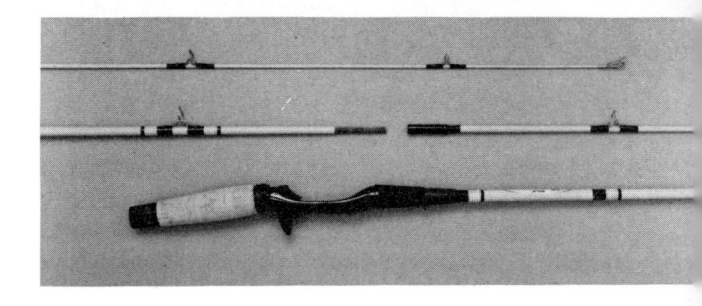

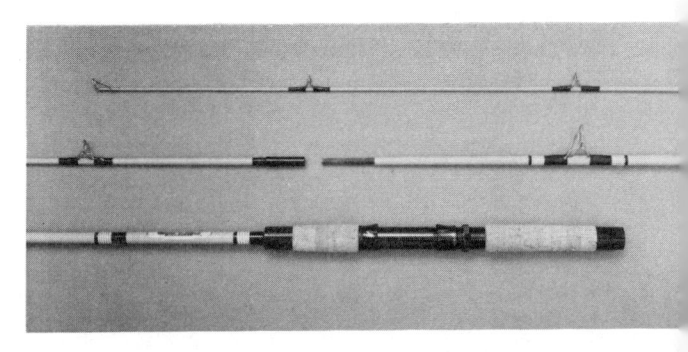

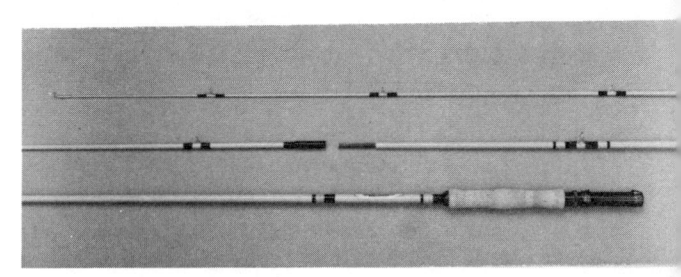

BERKLEY FISHING RODS

Berkley and Co. makes a full line of spin-casting, bait-casting, spinning, and fly rods for freshwater fishing. These are offered in three series: the Para/Metric, the Cherrywood, and the Buccaneer. Their top-grade rod, the Para/Metric, is for the angler who takes his fishing seriously, and it comes in a rich, mahogany finish. The Cherrywood is the mid-priced rod, while the Buccaneer is the lower-priced series. The spinning and spin-casting rods range from 5 to 7 ft. in length and come in different actions. The fly rods range from 6 ft., 3 in. to 8½ ft. in length. For their catalog or more information showing these and other rods and tackle write to:
Berkley and Co.
Spirit Lake, Ia. 51360

ESKA MOTORS

This company makes several outboard motors designed with the fisherman in mind. The Power Loop Engine Design incorporates a revolutionary engine design into all its fishing motors, even the small-horsepower models. The Power Loop engine offers the ultimate in fuel economy and low operating costs. The engine operates on a noncontaminating charge of fresh fuel, delivers more power for the same amount of fuel, and reduces maintenance. Fuel is brought in and exhaust pushed out in one continuous power loop through a series of matched intake and exhaust ports. Results: more horsepower, more miles per gallon, and no increase in motor size. They make outboard motors in all the popular sizes from 3 hp. to 15 hp. They also make 10-speed and 20-speed Travel-Troler electric motors. For a brochure showing all these motors write to:
Eska Co.
2400 Kerper Blvd.
Dubuque, Ia. 52001

FLY-TYING MATERIALS

The book *Fly-tying Materials* by Eric Leiser is a thorough, complete guide to the sources, treatment, and uses of fly-tying materials. It fills the gaps in the other manuals and contains priceless information never before published; chapters on bleaching and dying, cleaning animal and bird skins, special sources for hard-to-get materials, new uses for natural materials, and much more. *Fly-tying Materials* sells for $7.50 and is published by:
Crown Publishers, Inc.
419 Park Ave. S.
New York, N.Y. 10016

HEDDON REELS

James Heddon's Sons have been making fine fishing tackle for many years and offer a complete line of rods, reels, and lures. They make several spin-casting and spinning reels for freshwater and light saltwater use. Their spin-casting reels handle lines from 6 to 30 lbs., depending on the model. The spinning reels handle from 4- to-25-lb.-test monofilament, also depending on the size of the reel and whether used in fresh water or salt water. For their catalog or more information write to:
James Heddon's Sons
Dowagiac, Mich. 49047

WORMS ARE BIG BUSINESS

With millions of fishermen in this country, the demand for worms as bait is great, especially during the fishing season. So hundreds of worm farms or ranches have sprung up all over the country to meet this demand. And the wonderful thing about going into the worm farm business is that you don't have to make a big investment to get started. Two women who started with a mere $12 investment four years ago now have a $150,000 worm business and even have other worm farmers or sharecroppers raising worms for them. Besides selling worms for bait, they also do a big business with organic gardeners and nurseries, who find the worm castings very rich for the soil.

You can start a worm business with a few thousand worms and build boxes, bins, or big containers to keep them in. Then you provide a rich soil with plenty of manure and the worms will grow fast and breed and multiply in numbers until you have millions of the wigglers. You can sell the worms to bait dealers, tackle shops, or to individual fishermen in person or by mail. To obtain your first supply of breeder worms and information on how to raise them, look in the classified sections of such magazines as Outdoor Life, Field & Stream, and Sports Afield. You'll find many worm farmers advertising here, and you can write them.

SPLIT-SHOT SINKER

ADDING WEIGHT TO A MINNOW

One good way to add weight to a live minnow so it sinks below the surface and still swims around freely is to put a BB shot or split-shot sinker inside the minnow's mouth. Just insert the weight and then run a hook through both lips of the minnow to keep the shot in place.

FISH NAMED AFTER ANIMALS

Hogfish	Bullhead	Catfish
Boarfish	Alligator	Parrotfish
Dogfish	gar	Horsefish
Porcupine	Lionfish	Tiger shark
fish	Tigerfish	Toadfish
Sea raven	Rabbit fish	Cowfish
Sheepshead	Sea robin	Ratfish
Batfish	Spider fish	Oxfish
Goosefish	Butterfly fish	Fox shark
Wolffish	Pigfish	Buffalo fish
Squirrel	Elephant fish	Dog
fish	Eagle ray	salmon
Frogfish	Sea dragon	
Houndfish	Raccoon	
Sea mink	perch	

BUILD YOUR OWN DEPTH/FISH FINDER

The Heath Company offers several models of depth/fish finders and fish spotters and an electronic fish thermometer in kit form so that you can assemble your own. They claim that it is easy and that you will not fail if you follow their directions. Of course, you can also have fun and save some money by assembling your own fish/depth finder. For more details and the models they offer, write for their catalog to:
Heath Co.
Benton Harbor, Mich. 49022

USLAN RODS

This company makes the unique five-strip split bamboo rod, which it claims has distinct merits over the standard six-strip split bamboo rod made by most rod builders. In the manufacture of fishing rods, it is not possible to utilize a single stalk of cane. Instead, several strips are cut from the hard, outer portion of the bamboo. These strips are mitered with exacting care, according to the purpose to which the rod is to be put, and then glued together under considerable pressure. In the case of ordinary woods, the glued seam is stronger than the wood itself. Bamboo, on the other hand, is many times stronger than the common hardwoods—enough so, in fact, that but few glues in existence can equal its strength. The tendency of one element to slide over the next, while the rod is bent, is most pronounced along a line joining opposite corners of a rod built of an even number of strips. Therefore the glue line is called upon to resist the strongest internal stress, a situation precisely the reverse of proper arrangement. The simple expedient of substituting five slightly wider strips restores order. No continuous straight glue line extends through the center of the five-strip rod action. The heavy sliding stresses are then borne by the bamboo rather than the glue. The Uslan rod is made in several models, from a 7-ft. model weighing 2½ ozs. up to a 9-ft. model weighing 5¾ ozs. For a booklet telling more about their rods and giving the prices write to:

Uslan Rods
18679 W. Dixie Hwy.
N. Miami Beach, Fla. 33160

THERE HE IS!

The book *There He Is!* is subtitled *Bill Dance's Book on the Art of Plastic Worm Fishing*. Everyone who has fished for black bass seriously or in tournaments knows about Bill Dance. He has been the top money winner in many of these tournaments, and his favorite lure is the plastic worm. In this book he gives complete details about plastic worms, how to choose them, how to rig them, the best colors, odors, and the best ways to fish them over various bottoms and structures. *There He Is!* sells for $3.95 and is available from:

Bass Anglers Sportsman Society
P.O. Box 3044
Montgomery, Ala. 36109

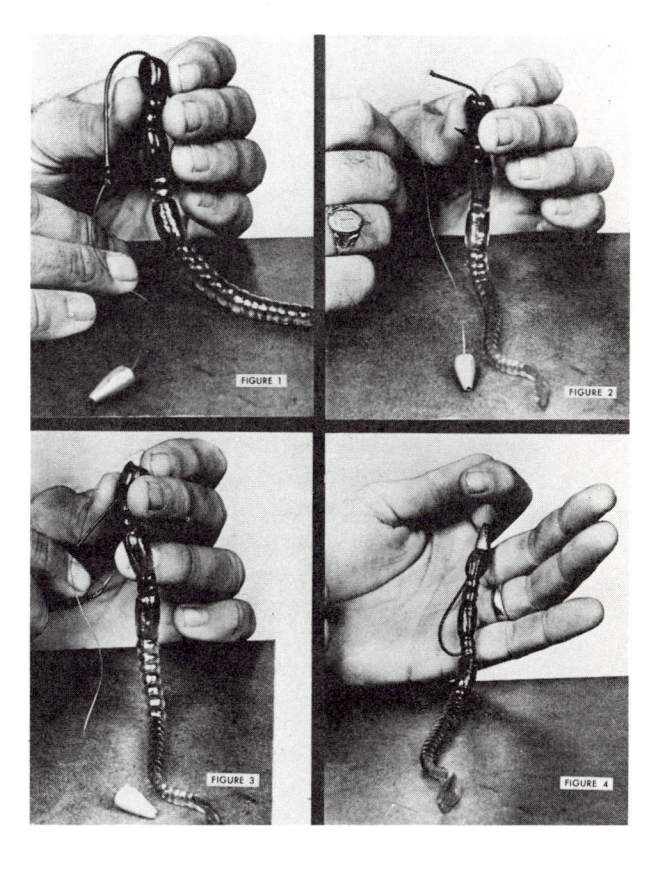

CRIPPLED KILLER LURE

This was one of the first surface spinning lures produced in this country, and thousands have been sold and used through the years. Its counterrevolving blades rattle and splash, bringing gamefish to the surface. It weighs ¼ oz. and comes in several colors, including the new Moon Glow pattern, with a phosphorescent body that glows at night. This company also makes other lures such as plugs, popping bugs, bass bugs, and flies. For their catalog showing all these lures write to:
Phillips Fly & Tackle Co.
P.O. Box 188
Alexandria, Pa. 16611

MAINE FISHING BOOKLETS AND MAPS

The Maine Department of Inland Fisheries and Game puts out many interesting and helpful booklets and maps on fish and fishing in that state. There are booklets and papers on brook trout, brown trout, salmon, small-mouth bass, pickerel, lake trout, whitefish, and Maine lakes and rivers. They also have made a survey of fifteen hundred Maine lakes and ponds showing water depths, fish present, and management suggestions. For a list of these publications and maps send for the booklet *Publications Catalog* to:
Maine Fish and Game Dept.
Information and Education Div.
284 State St.
Augusta, Me. 04333

FIRESIDE ANGLER

The Fireside Angler shop specializes in fly-fishing tackle and accessories and sells these by mail. They carry fly rods, reels, lines, leaders, flies, rod-making blanks, and components. They also have a complete line of fly-tying tools and materials. And they also sell fly-fishing books. For their catalog write to:
Fireside Angler, Inc.
P.O. Box 823
Melville, N.Y. 11746

SUPER THREADFIN

This lure will swim so that it makes a blooping noise on the surface, but it can also be fished at any depth by using the countdown method. It is a deadly lure for use in the winter in our southern states. Then you drop this lure straight down in anywhere from 15 to 40 ft. of water, then lift it up 1 ft. or so, then swim it slowly back to the bottom, repeating this three or four times, then reel up 3 or 4 ft. and let it swim back to the end of the line. Along steep banks cast and let the lure swim to the bottom, retrieve, and repeat as you work your way along the bank. Also fish it along creek- and riverbanks the same as the Threadfin Shad. The Super Threadfin comes in ¼- and ½-oz. sizes and in many colors. For a catalog showing these and other lures write to:
Ranger Tackle Co., Inc.
P.O. Box H
Greenwood, Ark. 72936

38

LFP 300 FISH LO-K-TOR

Lowrance Electronics pioneered electronic fish-finders with the original, portable "green box" sonar unit. The model LFP 300 FISH LO-K-TOR has come a long way since then. Many recent changes and added features have been added to the new FISH LO-K-TOR.

The unit has a battery level indicator to give instant readings as to battery strength. Additional features are an adjustable interference suppressor, which eliminates interference from air bubbles passing over the transducer and electrical interference from bilge pumps, bilge blowers, bait tanks, or any electric motor and C.D. ignitions.

Accurate readings are possible at depths in excess of the 100-ft. dial, and fish can be located singly or in schools with the portable LFP 300. The original "green box" is still in compact size with a 6-in. width and height and a 9-in. depth. For a brochure or more information write to:
Lowrance Electronics, Inc.
12000 E. Skelly Dr.
Tulsa, Okla. 74128

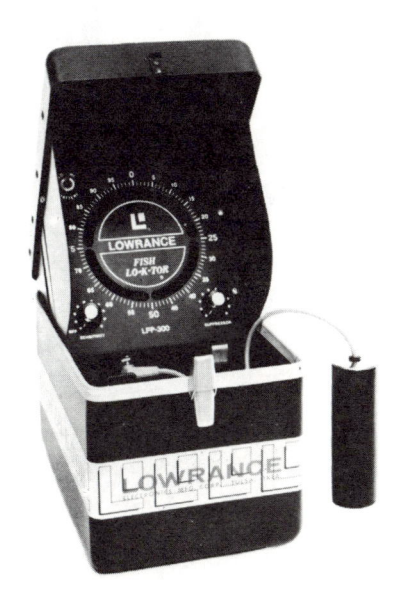

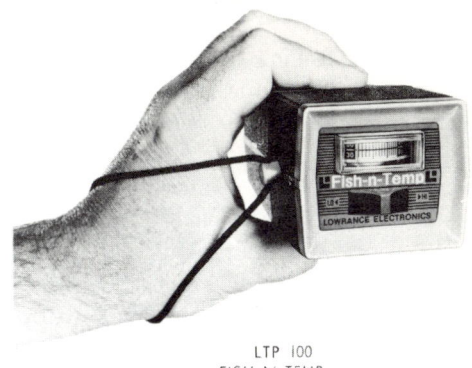

LTP 100
FISH-N-TEMP

LTP 100 FISH-N-TEMP

The Lowrance Fish-N-Temp will indicate the preferred temperature between 30 and 90 degrees Fahrenheit and depths of the water for all gamefish. Completely portable, the solid-state Fish-N-Temp is easy to carry in the smallest of tackle boxes. The unit indicates electronically temperatures at depths up to 100 ft. Handy footage markers are stamped into the cable for depth and temperature reference as the sensor is lowered in the water. A chart showing the temperatures preferred by different species is located on the back of the case. For more information write to:
Lowrance Electronics, Inc.
12000 E. Skelly Dr.
Tulsa, Okla. 74128

TASTY PORK RIND

You can make pork rind strips and chunks taste better and smell better to the fish by adding a few drops of anise oil in the jar containing the rind. Then put them on your lures and you will find they are more effective for black bass and other fish.

39

LUHR-JENSEN DOWN-RIGGER

Hauling a trolling weight up with two hands rather than one makes fishing a little more effortless. This is one of the key features of the new King "Auto Track II" Down-Riggers from Luhr Jensen & Sons. With a crank handle on each side, it also makes one-handed cranking easier in installation locations where one handle on the wrong side might be difficult to operate.

Easier cranking is also due to Delrin bearings that virtually eliminate side thrust and radial load friction, sure-grip tapered handles that revolve freely, and elimination of a fixed cable guide for less cable drag.

The King Auto Track II also has a built-in depth indicator, a heavy-duty plastic reel that insulates the cable and prevents electrolysis corrosion in salt water. For positive locking, there is a swing-away lock bar that secures the reel at any depth. When the weight is cranked up, the lock bar automatically swings out of the way.

A quick-mount base plate permits instant setup and removal by simply sliding the Down-Rigger into place and tightening the lock screw. All steel parts are heavily chrome plated, and the base is strong cast aluminum. Guaranteed for two years, the Auto Track II comes in two models—a Short Arm model with 250 ft. of 135-lb.-test cable, counter, mounting base and hardware for $52, and a Long Arm model with the same accessories, plus a swivel base that locks at 90-degree intervals, for $77. For more information write to:

Luhr Jensen & Sons, Inc.
P.O. Box 297
Hood River, Ore. 97034

MISTER TWISTER'S SIN-SATION

Mister Twister's new SIN-SATION is producing good catches of large-mouth and small-mouth bass, crappie, trout, bream, perch, speckled trout, and many other species of both freshwater and salt-water gamefish.

The "triple" living lure action incorporates the ribbonlike tail of the original Mister Twister with two super action legs. Deadly alone, on a jig head, or Texas rigged, the SIN-SATION is great as an added attractor on a spinnerbait or bucktail jig. The SIN-SATION comes in 3-, 4-, and 6-in. sizes in fourteen proven producer colors. It comes unrigged in a snak pak or rigged on $\frac{1}{16}$-oz., $\frac{1}{8}$-oz., $\frac{1}{4}$-oz., and $\frac{3}{8}$-oz. jig heads or on a spinner rig in $\frac{1}{16}$-oz., $\frac{1}{8}$-oz., and $\frac{1}{4}$-oz. sizes. For further information contact:

Mister Twister, Inc.
P.O. Drawer 996
Minden, La. 71055

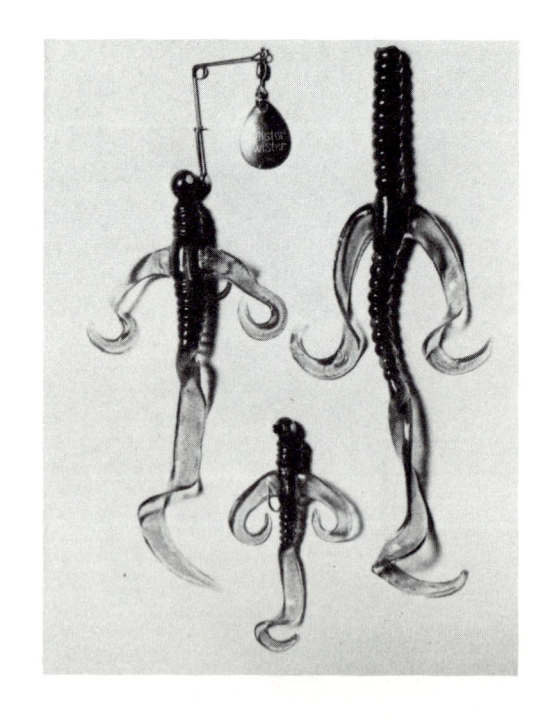

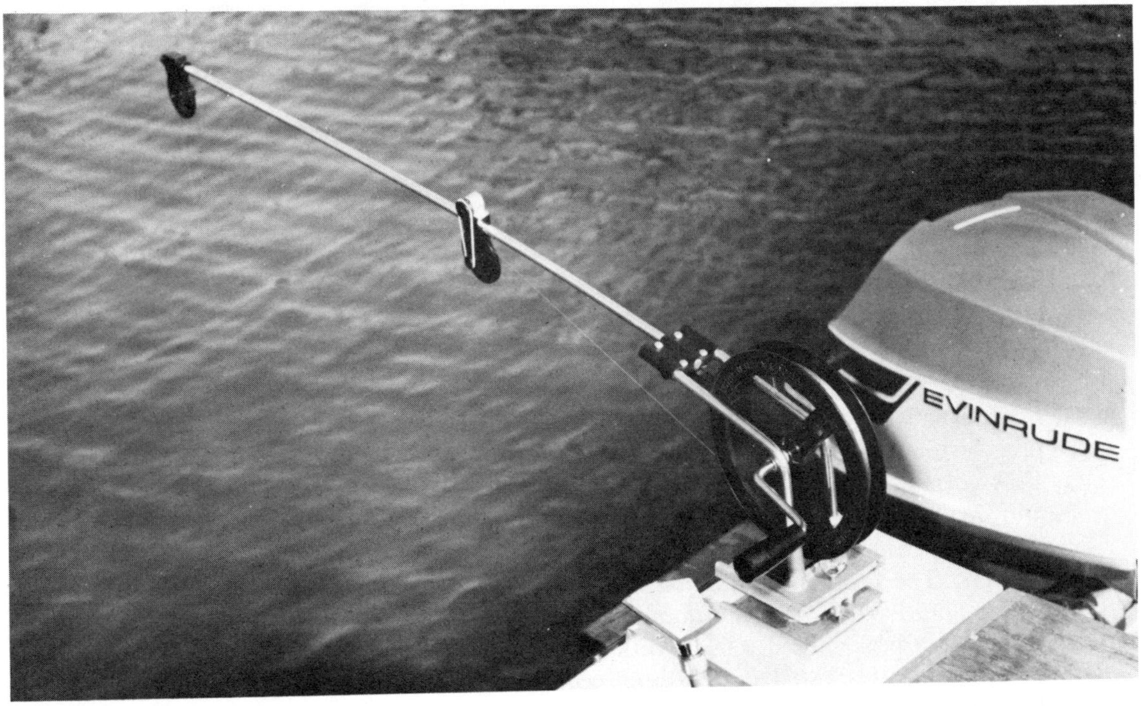
EVINRUDE

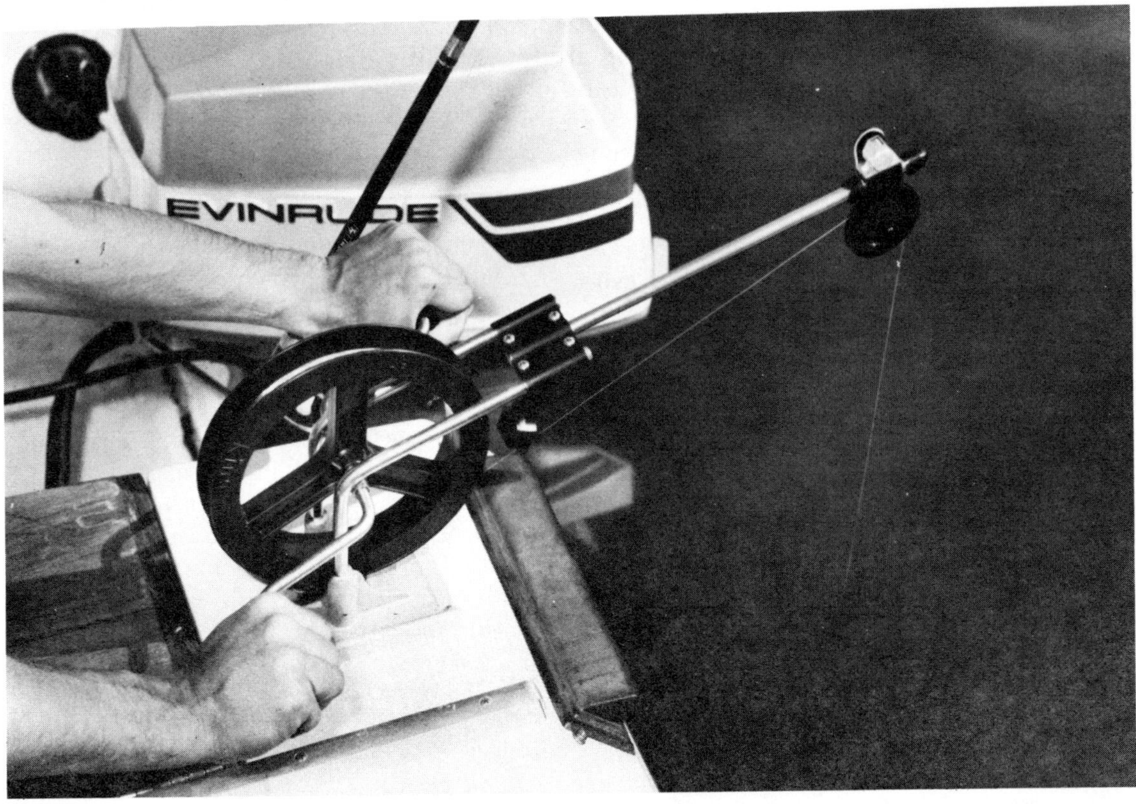
EVINRUDE

GARCIA BASS FISHING SCHOOL

Recognizing the growing number of bass fishermen who are eager to learn the techniques and methods of the tournament pros, Garcia and the American Sportsman's Club are now joining their talents in presenting the Garcia Bass Fishing School. The chief instructor is Garcia pro Dick Gasaway. Dick is an outstanding instructor and has given seminars as far away as South Africa. He is a bass fisherman's bass fisherman, with a direct, no-nonsense approach to both fishing and instructing. Dick currently holds both the large-mouth and small-mouth bass records for Colorado and is president of the Denver Bass masters. The location is Bullfrog Marina on fabulous Lake Powell, in Colorado.

This is a personalized school, with only twelve students allowed per class, specializing in teaching the "Garcia Touch System." The school curriculum includes bass biology, utilizing and understanding the latest electronic gear, reading structure, techniques with crank baits, worms and lures, casting instructions, and much, much more.

The school runs in three-day sessions beginning in May. The tuition price is $260 per individual, exclusive of travel expense and fishing license. Each session lasts three days and three nights. Lodging is on a shared basis in new 45-ft. mobile homes overlooking beautiful Lake Powell. There are eight home-cooked meals, use of tackle, bass boats, guides, etc., included in the above price.

Openings will be limited and reservations accepted on a first-come, first-served basis. For reservations and further information contact:
Garcia Bass Fishing School
c/o American Sportsman's Club
650 S. Lipan
Denver, Colo. 80223

WORTH JACKET PATCH

An attractive new four-color jacket patch for fishermen is available now from The Worth Company, manufacturers of terminal tackle. The 3-in.-by-3-in. embroidered patch is Worth's new logo or trademark. It illustrates a white-colored fish jumping in aqua-color water and silhouetted against a night sky. Northern pine trees in the background are silhouetted by a large gold moon. The patch is available for $.50. Along with the patch, fishermen will receive a copy of Worth's attractive new sixteen-page booklet "Worth Your Time," which is printed in rich colors on high-grade-paper stock. The tacklebox-size booklet illustrates many of the more popular Worth lures and fishing accessories, plus some of the large fish caught on Worth lures. To get the patch and booklet send $.50 to:
The Worth Co.
P.O. Box 88
Stevens Point, Wis. 54481

WORTH'S FLUTTER-FIN

Combining the attraction of a rattle with fluttering action of an injured prey, Worth's Flutter-Fin is a new lure for bass anglers to try. The hollow round body of the lure has small beads that rattle on retrieve, while the patented fluttering action is created by a pair of scissorlike blades on the head that make a popping sound as they open and close, leaving bubbles in the lure's wake. A color-matched dressed hackle streamer conceals the 2/0 ringed eye treble hook.

The Flutter-Fin is made of strong plastic that cannot become waterlogged. The hardware is solid brass, heavily nickel-plated against corrosion. The lure weighs ¼ oz. and also comes in a weedless model. It is available from:
The Worth Co.
P.O. Box 88
Stevens Point, Wis. 54481

STREN FLUORESCENT LINE

This is the monofilament line that is used by many expert anglers to make record catches on light tackle. It is also an excellent line for day-in-and-day-out fishing that will enable the average angler to catch more and bigger fish. The patented fluorescent glow of the Stren lines lets you keep track of them for better control. It's activated by the sun's ultraviolet light, even on cloudy days. Underwater, where ultraviolet is filtered out, Stren's glow deactivates or "switches" off. In addition, the line has a small diameter, superior knot strength, limpness, controlled stretch, and is resistant to abrasion. Stren is available in three fluorescent color systems—clear blue, golden, and orange. The line comes in different strengths and packages of various sizes and lengths. For more information write to:
Public Relations Dept.
E. I. du Pont de Nemours & Co.
Wilmington, Del. 19898

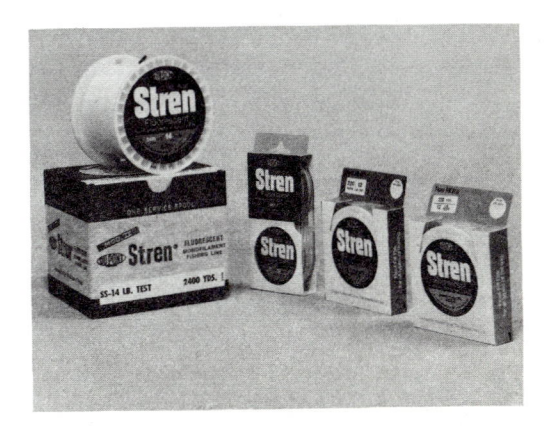

PLANO 777 TACKLE BOX

The new Plano 777 Tackle Box will hold more large lures than most other boxes of comparable size. It occupies only 14¾ in. when fully open because of the unique drawer arrangement. The front panel opens and is hinged to slide under the bottom drawer. Part of the front panel then becomes an additional work surface. Drawers pull out, and baits are readily accessible to the fisherman. The standard box consists of five 1¼-in. depth drawers and one 3¼-in. depth drawer, with a total of 57 spacious compartments, available to meet the needs of the specialty fisherman. Two compartments are provided in the 3¼-in. bottom drawer to securely hold pork rind or salmon egg jars. ABS construction resists most plastic baits and withstands most rugged use. It has a big, easy-grip handle, Sta-Dri ribs that dissipate moisture, and bail-type latch. The colors are beige and saddle leather brown. For a catalog showing this and many other tackle boxes they make write to:
**Plano Molding Co.
Plano, Ill. 60545**

THE AMAZING FISHES

Man takes pride in his many inventions and accomplishments, but fish have been doing things for ages that we have only learned to do in recent times. The flying fish has been gliding through the air long before man every dreamed of doing the same thing. The archer fish of Thailand has its own built-in gun and shoots drops of water with its mouth to knock down insects for food. The electric eel, electric catfish, and electric ray have been producing and discharging electricity long before man even suspected such a power existed. Most of the fish found in the dark depths of the ocean have their own lights and never have to worry about batteries or the electric bill. And a small African fish was found to have a built-in radar system that sends out electric waves that enable it to avoid obstacles.

BASS IN A FARM POND

When fishing for bass in farm ponds during the hot summer months, look for the deepest part of the pond where the water is coolest. Then cast and work your lures along the bottom slowly. But you can fish closer to shore at dusk, daybreak, and during the night when the bass often come into the shallows to feed.

WATCH THE SWALLOWS

When fishing on lakes or reservoirs toward evening, look for swallows flying and dipping for insects that are hatching from the water. Head toward that area and cast a fly or small bass bug under the birds. The chances are good that you'll find a school of trout, bass, or panfish also feeding on the insects.

STREAMER FLY TYING AND FISHING

Streamer Fly Tying and Fishing by Joseph D. Bates, Jr., has been a classic for many years and is the only book devoted entirely to streamer flies. As most trout fishermen, bass fishermen, and many salt-water fly rodders know, streamers and bucktails catch bigger fish in fresh water and salt water than other types of flies. They imitate minnows or small fish or big bugs and offer a good mouthful, which attracts the lunkers. Joe Bates tells you all about the streamers and bucktails in this book. It provides complete, authentic dressing instructions for more than 300 flies, and 119 of these are reproduced in full color. These are the most popular, proven and famous and productive patterns. Joe then goes into detail on how to use the streamers and bucktails near the surface or deep down, in fast or slack waters, in lakes, ponds, streams, rivers, bays, and other salt waters. *Streamer Fly Tying and Fishing* sells for $7.95 and is available from the author:

Joseph D. Bates, Jr.
45 Prynnwood Rd.
Longmeadow, Mass. 01106

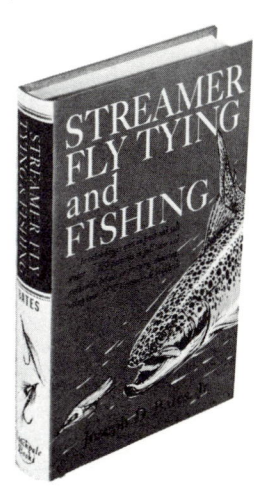

FLORIDA FISHING BOOKS

The Great Outdoors Publishing Company has several inexpensive fishing books and guides, mostly about Florida fishing, that anglers will find helpful and useful. They are:

The Book of Florida Fishing by Gordon Lewis. Tells where, when, and how to fish in all of Florida. Price, $1.75.

Rube Allyn's Fishermen's Handbook by Rube Allyn gives many tips, hints, and information on how to catch fresh-water and salt-water fish. It covers rigs, knots, hooks, baits, lures, methods, and techniques. Price, $1.00.

How to Fish for Snook by Earl Downey. This book covers the methods, tackle, baits, and lures used to catch snook, and even mentions some of the best spots in Florida. Price, $1.00.

How to Fish for Bass by A. Paul Smith. This book tells you how to catch black bass, with information on locations, licenses, and regulations, as well as baits, lures, methods, and techniques. Price, $1.00.

Florida Fishes by Rube Allyn. This handy book describes the most popular fish caught in Florida waters, with line drawings and color reproductions of the fish. Price, $1.50.

Florida's Fishing Grounds by Martin Moe. The author spent two years researching this book to give you over two hundred salt-water fishing locations. This book is used by many boat captains and guides and expert anglers to locate the best fishing areas. Price, $1.95.

These books are sold in many bookstores, tackle shops, and gift shops in Florida. They can also be obtained from the publisher if you enclose $.35 for postage and handling. The publisher is:

Great Outdoors Publishing Co.
4747 28th St., N.
St. Petersburg, Fla. 33714

CORTLAND GRAPHITE FLY REELS

The Cortland Line Company now offers the C-G graphite fly reels, which are 30 per cent lighter than comparable aluminum reels. They make an excellent companion to the new graphite fly rods or very light bamboo and glass rods. They are light but strong and maintenance-free and lubricate themselves. And the gears and other internal parts are made of high-density graphite material. There are two models available—the C-G graphite fly reel No. 1, which is 2⅞ in. and 2½ ozs., and the C-G graphite fly reel No. 2, which is 3¼ and 2¾ ozs.

Extra spools are available for these fly reels. For more information contact:
Cortland Line Co.
Cortland, N.Y. 13045

LOCATING FRESHWATER FISH

The angler arriving for the first day of fishing on a strange lake faces a common challenge and a puzzling one. Serious fishermen everywhere know the importance of studying the waters they fish. Even the fisherman returning to a well-known lake may have dry periods of several hours before he learns again where the fish are. The fisherman capable of cutting time from his preliminary search has a remarkable advantage over his fellow angler who casts blindly on the strange waters.

For example, three fishermen from Indiana arrived at Kentucky Lake, oldest of the giant TVA impoundments, for a week of bass fishing. They had been there many times. They knew some of the productive places from previous trips. But during their first half day they had only slight success. Then they began to produce. Their boat soon began bringing in the biggest bass weighed that week at Sportsman's Marina, where they were fishing.

Their success was anticipated by marina owner Carl Hamilton. "They do it every time," he said. Part of their secret is found in the electronic device carried in their boat to show them the nature of the bottom and the location of fish over which they pass. Their Lowrance Fish Lo-K-Tor runs constantly, pointing out dropoffs where bass, crappie, sauger, and channel cats concentrate. These Indiana anglers troll with deep-running plug, nothing else. Once they find where the fish are, they work that area repeatedly. They have one other thing going for them: They fish hard, often twelve hours a day.

In addition to the fish locator, there are other less sophisticated ways to study a new lake. A good set of topographic maps can give you locations of ledges, dropoffs, and deep holes where the fish may be living. Talking with local fishermen and guides can also produce valuable tips. Sooner or later the exploring angler begins to understand the lake and its choice fishing holes. Then the action picks up and those first hours of study and experimenting pay off.

WALTON'S THUMB KNIFE

The Walton's Thumb is a beautifully designed specialized folding knife made entirely of 100 per cent stainless steel. This practical and unique knife has many uses for not only the fisherman but also for any outdoorsman. Measuring only 3 in. overall when folded and just over 4 in. fully extended, it weighs only 2 ozs. With its flat shape and light weight, it fits comfortably in the pocket. It is precision hand-fitted and -crafted to watchlike tolerance to provide a smooth operating knife of exceptional quality. Some of its features are knife blade, long pincer nose or tweezers, line clipper, split-ring opener, screwdriver, scissors, stiletto or hook eye cleaner and knot picker, and split-shot opener. All blades and parts on this knife are replaceable. The price of each knife is $25, and it is available from:
Hank Roberts
P.O. Box 171
Boulder, Colo. 80302

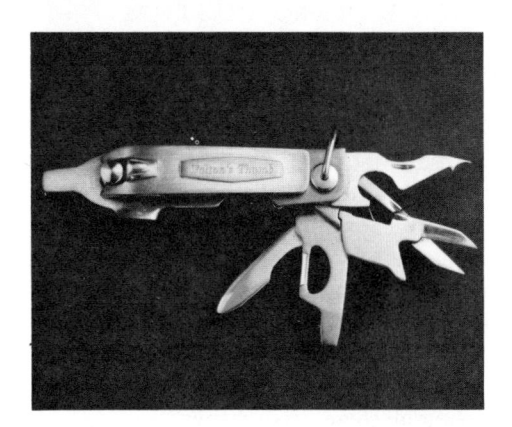

SPORTSMAN'S GUIDE TO GAME FISH

The book *Sportsman's Guide to Game Fish* by Byron Dalrymple covers 138 freshwater and 190 salt-water species. There are color and black-and-white illustrations of each fish so that it can be identified easily. Dalrymple also gives identifying features in the text so that you can tell the differences among the fish. He also includes their characteristics, feeding habits, likes and dislikes, weight, geographical distribution, even the best time of day and year to catch the fish. The book also gives specific suggestions on the tackle, lures, and baits to use for each species under various conditions and the best methods for taking each fish, including depths, speed of retrieve, and many other fine points. *Sportsman's Guide to Game Fish* sells for $6.95 and is published by:
Thomas Y. Crowell Co., Inc.
666 Fifth Ave.
New York, N.Y. 10019

WYOMING FISHING GUIDE

A booklet called *Wyoming Fishing Guide* gives all the important lakes, reservoirs, ponds, and rivers in that state. It tells what kind of fish are caught in each body of water, where it is located, the public-access or boat-launching sites, and whether there are boat rentals, outfitters, or fishing camps located there. It can be obtained from:
Wyoming Game and Fish Commission
P.O. Box 1589
Cheyenne, Wyo. 82001

Another good Wyoming fishing folder and map is called *Family Waters Sports in Big Wyoming*. It has a big map showing the various lakes, reservoirs, ponds, rivers, and streams in the state and tells what kind of fish are caught there. It gives the public fishing areas and boat-launching sites. It can be obtained from:
Wyoming Travel Commission
Cheyenne, Wyo. 82002

DALE CLEMENS CUSTOM TACKLE

This is a mail-order house that sells all the component parts you need to make your own fishing rods for both fresh water and salt water. They carry graphite and Fiberglas blanks for spinning, spin casting, bait casting, and fly fishing, and for boat, pier, surf, and offshore trolling. They have various types of handles, butts, cork grips, reel seats, ferrules, guides, winding thread, cements, and sundry items. For a catalog showing all these products write to:
Dale Clemens Custom Tackle
P.O. Box 415, Rte. 3
Allentown, Pa. 18104

HANK ROBERTS FISHING TACKLE

Hank Roberts has been a leading fly specialty house for more than thirty years. They carry a complete line of fly-tying tools such as vises, hackle pliers, bodkins, whip finishers, scissors, bobbins, forceps, half-hitch tool, and tweezers. They also carry fly-tying materials, including feathers, hair, chenille, wax, thread, cement, and hooks. And they have a complete selection of finished flies such as dry flies, wet flies, nymphs, streamers, bucktails, steelhead flies, and bass bugs. These are available by the dozen or in special selections in clear, rigid plastic boxes. Their catalog showing all these flies, fly-tying tools, materials, and vests costs $1.00 from:
Hank Roberts
P.O. Box 171
Boulder, Colo. 80302

TEMPTING WALLEYES WITH LEECHES

In walleye fishing circles, "Lindy Rigging" means plain hook/slip sinker fishing. It's the surest method for presenting leeches, the hot live-bait phenomenon that has everybody talkin' in walleye country. Here are some worthwhile tips for fishing with leeches on Lindy Rigs:

Make sure you have "ribbon" leeches, not the soft mud leech or blood sucker. Bait dealers trap the kind you need from nonfish lakes and sloughs. Chances are the leeches you find near your dock will fail to tempt walleyes.

Choose the large or "jumbo" leeches, but be prepared to try the smaller ones, especially when fish are finicky. Sometimes it pays to trail several small leeches from a single hook.

Hook a leech through the sucker end, impaling it only once.

Troll or drift slowly. This allows the leech to swim with a natural, undulating action. Going too fast causes the leech to spin or to pull "straight" through the water.

Periodically check the leech to make sure it's trailing properly. Once in a while a writhing leech will "ball up" in a hopeless tangle with hook and leader.

With leeches, use your Lindy Rig method of feeding line to a biting fish, as you would with minnows or night crawlers. At the first sign of a bite, release line toward the biting fish. With large leeches, or when fish seem cautious, allow plenty of time before setting the hook. With smaller leeches, or if the fish strikes hard, simply lower your rod tip toward the fish and set the hook.

Never hesitate to reuse a fresh-looking leech after catching a fish. Leeches are more resilient and tear less easily than night crawlers. Store leeches in cold water. Feeding them is unnecessary.

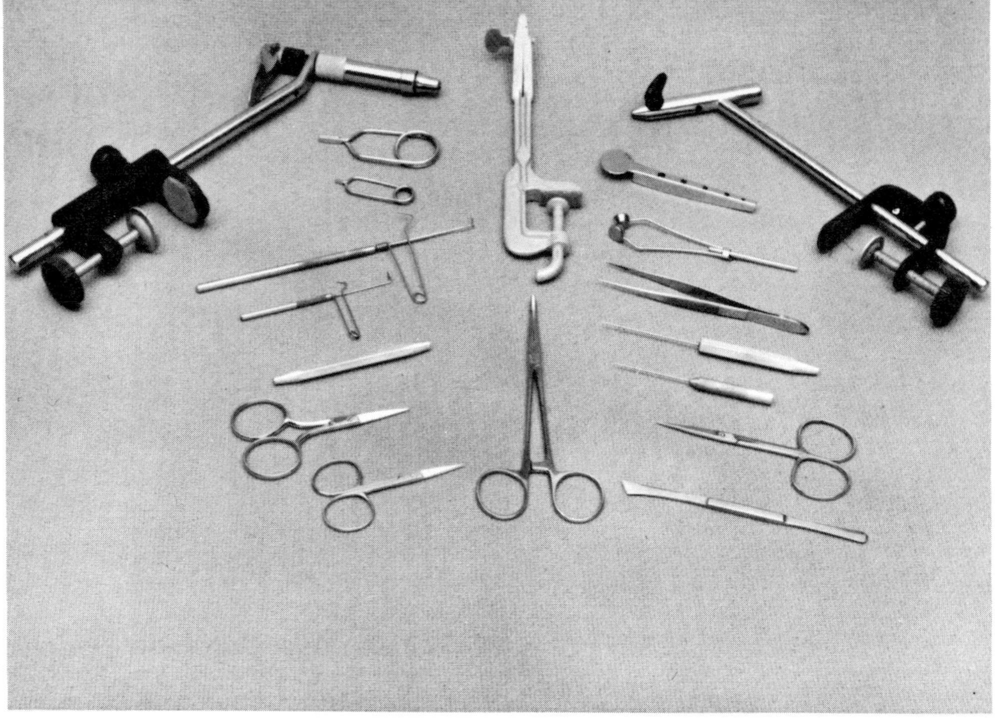

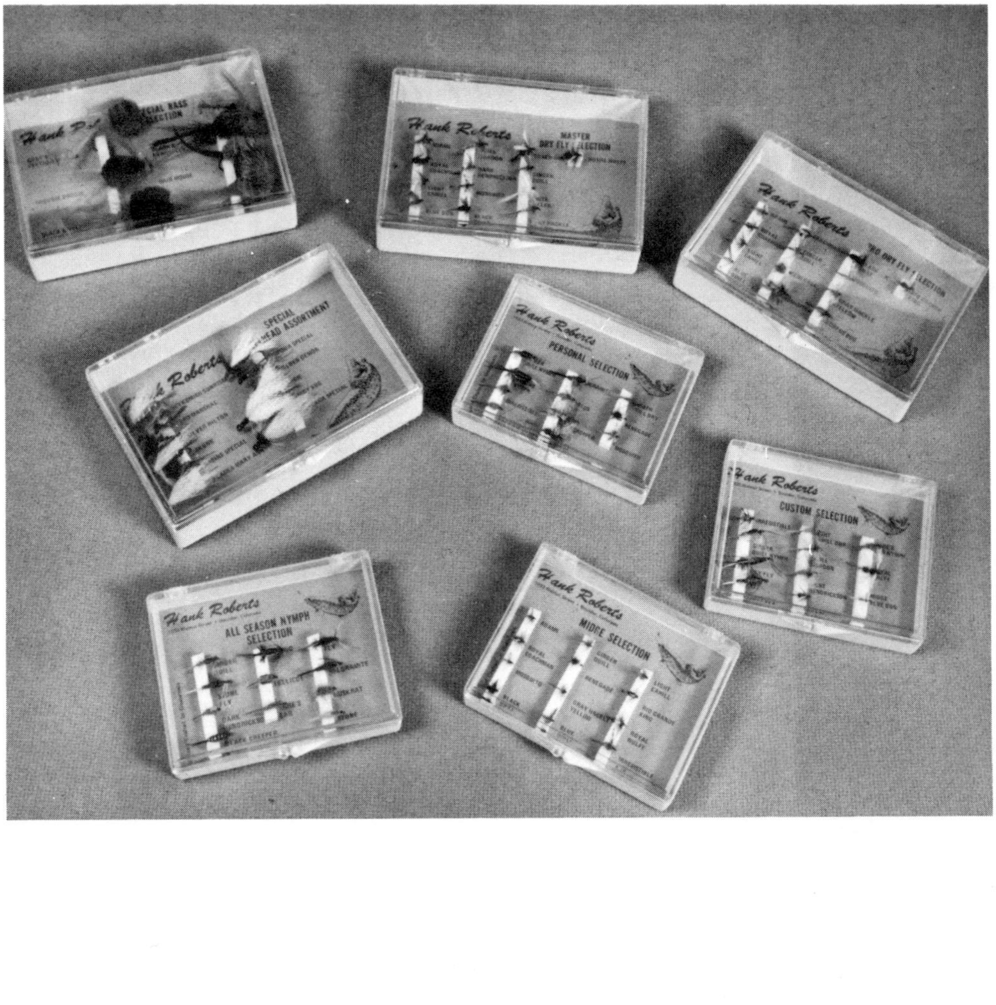
Hank Roberts
MASTER DRY FLY SELECTION
Hank Roberts
Hank Roberts
PERSONAL SELECTION
Hank Roberts
CUSTOM SELECTION
Hank Roberts
ALL SEASON NYMPH SELECTION
Hank Roberts
MIDGE SELECTION

BASS BOSS TACKLE BOXES

The Bass Boss tackle boxes are a new line of tackle boxes introduced by Old Pal/Woodstream in conjunction with fishing expert Jerry McKinnis, star of "The Fishing Hole" TV program. This is a matched set of Bass Boss tackle boxes, each one specifically designed for ease in handling bass plugs, grubs, plastic worms, or spinner baits in a bass boat. All four boxes combine the best-selling features of Old Pal's "Famous Fish" series, with a number of tray innovations specifically designed for bass fishing. For more information write to:
Woodstream Corp.
P.O. Box 327
Lititz, Pa. 17543

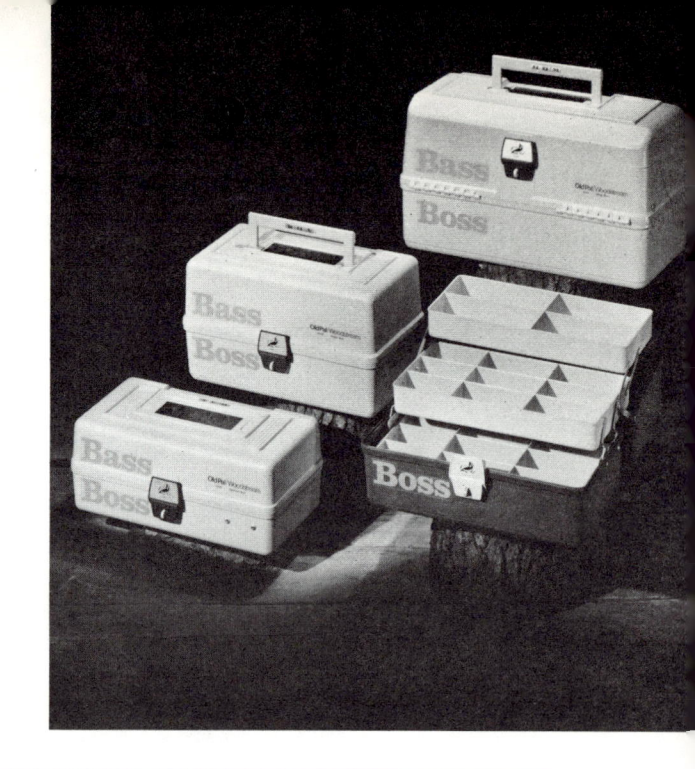

ROGERS LURES

This company makes lures such as the Hawg Hunter, Sr., and the Hawg Hunter, Jr., which are surface plugs with propellers available in two sizes—3/8 oz. and 1/2 oz.—and in twenty-two colors. Another plug they make is the Deep Jim, which is a diving underwater type that travels down to 6 ft. or 10 ft., depending on the size you get. Other plugs include the Little Jim, Middle Jim, and Big Jim, which can be bobbed along the surface or cranked well below the surface. These three sizes come in twenty-five different colors. For their catalog showing these and other lures they make write to:
Rogers Lures—G&R Industries, Inc.
P.O. Box 18
Purdy, Mo. 65734

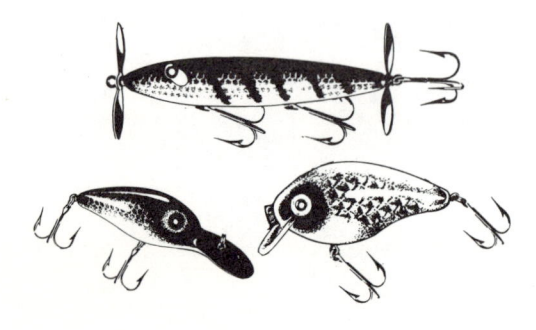

SEBAGO TROLLS

Sebago Trolls are multiple-spinner blade rigs that are used for deep trolling for landlocked salmon, lake trout, and coho salmon. They are made of jewelry-finished nickel- or gold-plated blades, glass or metal beads, and in a variety of combinations. This same firm makes and sells the well-known Al's Goldfish Spoon and other spoons in a variety of shapes, finishes, and colors. They also sell spinners, plugs, ball-chain swivels, trolling weights, trolling keels, spreaders and rigs, and other tackle. For their catalog or more information write to:
Al's Goldfish Lure Co.
P.O. Box 13
Indian Orchard, Mass. 01151

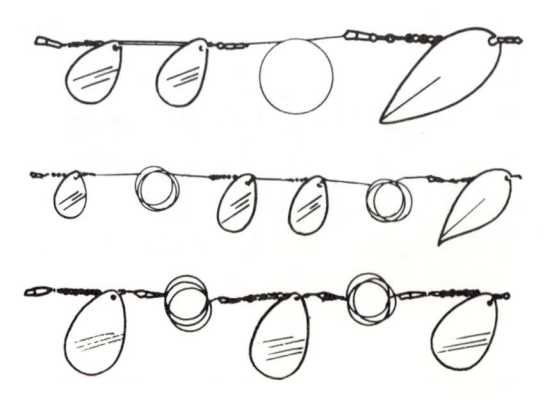

FISH CLEANING BOARDS

The Rapala fish cleaning and skinning boards are just the thing for anglers who catch a lot of fish and have to do a lot of fish cleaning. Two sizes of the Fish n' Fillet fish cleaning boards (7 in. by 36 in. and 6 in. by 24 in.) are available to make cleaning and filleting easier. There's a rust-resistant, deep-jaw clamp that holds fish firmly in place. Deep-ribbed grooves keep the fish from sliding back and forth, freeing both hands for faster cleaning or filleting. The boards come in hardwood or plastic. They also make a Rapala skinning board, which has a clamp that holds a bullhead or catfish you want skinned in a hurry. For more information write to:
Normark Corp.
1710 E. 78th St.
Minneapolis, Minn. 55423

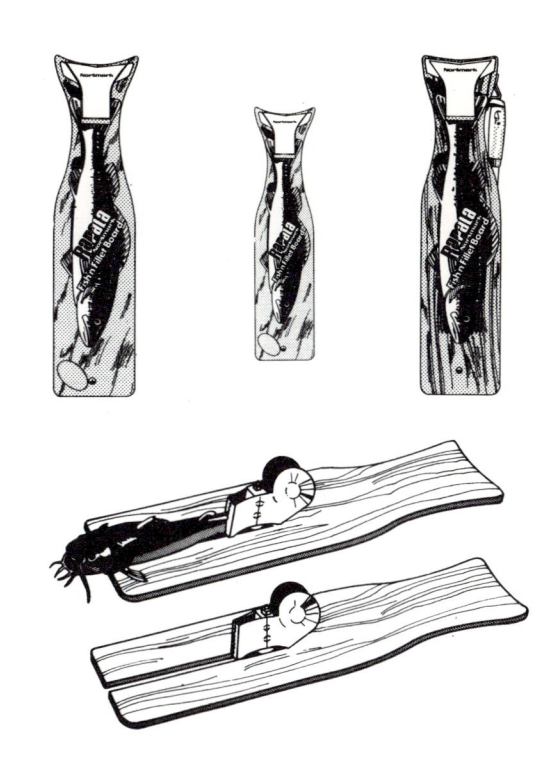

SPOON-FEED WINTER BASS

For many years fishermen and biologists believed that when cold weather arrived, bass fishing had to stop because fish weren't active. A few hardy anglers finally put this myth to rest by experimenting during winter and catching enough fish to prove their contention that bass fishing is a year-round sport, especially in our southern states.

Cold-weather fishing for bass does require different skills, a fact the angling experts at Mercury Marine learned while on a late-winter expedition to a major southern impoundment. Jigging with spoons was the method used, and they discovered that a healthy dose of patience, a feel for light taps on the line, and a liking for cold weather play important roles in winter bass-fishing success.

As the water cools in the fall, bass form into schools that will stay together until early spring. Many times the fish in these schools are large bass that were in deep water during summer and escaped capture by anglers. These fish prefer to spend their winter in suspended cover.

Look for long, underwater points of land that have an abundance of flooded trees and brush. Begin fishing in about 10 ft. of water, working out the point on both sides until the depth is 30 ft. It's doubtful if you'll find many fish beyond this.

Using ¾-oz. spoons, jig the trees and brush by free-spooling the spoon to the bottom of the lake, then jerking the spoon upward about 2 ft. and letting it drop to the bottom again. A second technique calls for casting over brush, letting the spoon flutter to the bottom, then retrieving in long, upward sweeps, with intermittent flutters to the bottom again. Either way calls for a delicate touch on the fishing line. Bass will tap the lure, perhaps mouth it, and run for a few feet, and it takes continual vigilance to tell when a fish has the spoon.

AMBASSADEUR BAIT-CASTING REEL

This Garcia bait-casting reel is the latest addition to the well-known Ambassadeur series of freshwater and salt-water casting reels. Called the 2500 C, it is small enough to nestle right in the palm of your hand. It has two stainless-steel ball bearings supporting the spool. It has a fast 4.7 to 1 retrieve ratio for reeling in those crank baits fast. The spool is featherweight—it starts quickly for easy casts. There's a smooth, adjustable star drag and two sets of brakes for backlash control. Their *Fishing Annual and Catalog* combined costs $1.50, and it tells more about this and other reels and tackle they make. Write for it to:
The Garcia Corp.
329 Alfred Ave.
Teaneck, N.J. 07666

THE DORADO

The new Arbogast Dorado is a second-generation "banana" type lure with a unique, slow, sweeping subsurface swimming action. The Dorado floats at rest. On a steady retrieve, it swims to approximately 2 ft. and runs with an injured natural minnow action. When fished with quick, short jerks, it resembles an injured fish. Both actions obtain hard sticks from bass, pike, and big panfish. It's ideal for fishing calm, clear water when fish are spooky or over underwater weedbeds. The Dorado can also be effectively slow-trolled in shallow, shore water. The weight is $3/8$ oz. for use with spinning, spin-casting and light bait-casting equipment. It comes in six finishes for most light conditions. For more information or their catalog write to:
The Fred Arbogast Co.
313 W. North St.
Akron, O. 44303

MUSKIES ON SPOONS

When muskies do not hit a spoon cast or trolled in the regular manner, try casting the spoon out and letting it sink toward the bottom. But watch your line carefully while the spoon sinks. Muskies (and pike) will often hit such sinking spoons as they flutter toward the bottom, and you have to set the hook at the slightest indication of a hit.

BIG MUSKIE FROM DOCK

Many freshwater anglers fish for years and catch few muskies or no big ones even though they spend days, weeks, and months fishing from boats in the best waters. So you can imagine their reaction when one angler fishing from a dock in Chautauqua Lake in upstate New York cast out and hooked and landed a 54-lb. muskellunge!

RUSHTON PACK CANOE

For the avid outdoor enthusiast who is compelled to wet a line on those untried waters of a remote mountain pond, hunt the impossible backwaters of a beaver flow, or just plain get where people ain't—Old Town's new pack canoe may be just the answer.

The lines of Wee Lassie, a delightful model developed in the mid-1880s by J. Henry Rushton of Canton, New York, have been re-created in light, tough Fiberglas, resulting in a beautiful little canoe that weighs an amazing 18.5 lbs. and is 10½ ft. long!

It is not a craft one jumps into and out of with reckless abandon, nor is it a boat for the exhibitionist who prefers to be seen standing in a canoe. When used as intended, it will prove itself to be an excellent companion on the water and a light, highly efficient pack canoe ashore. The one-handed ease with which it can be tossed about is a never-ending wonder both in and out of the water. It will run straight as an arrow and responds to the paddle like a fallen leaf in a breeze.

Old Town also makes the Carleton and Chipewyan models, which are two-man pack canoes weighing 35 and 38 lbs. and are 12 ft. in length. Additional information is available by writing to:
Old Town Canoe Co.
125 Beaver St.
Old Town, Me. 04468

IPCO FILLETING BOARDS

This company produced the first fillet board, and now they offer a varied line of filleting boards. Their original fillet board was made of wood, and they still offer this model with a heavy-duty "chopping block" board. There is a sharp V-ribbed cleaning surface that keeps fish from slipping sideways during filleting and cleaning. And a steel power jaw clamp grips the fish firmly by the head or tail. They also have plastic boards and other wooden boards in different sizes to take most of the fish caught in fresh water and the smaller species caught in salt water. For a catalog showing their complete line of filleting boards write to:
IPCO, Inc.
331 Lake Hazeltine Dr.
Chaska, Minn. 55318

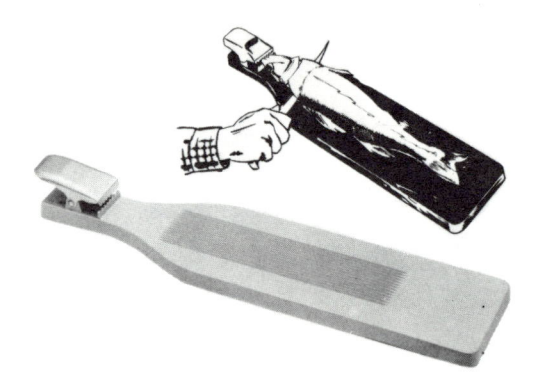

MOST POPULAR FISH

Someone once said that the most popular fish in a lake has to be the one on the end of your line. And that's certainly true, but in a larger sense there is one species of fish that has captured the interest of more anglers than any other —the black bass.

Dr. James A. Henshall, an early enthusiast of bass angling in this country, predicted their popularity in his book Book of the Black Bass, written in 1881, when he said that bass would "become the leading gamefish in America. . . ."

An informal survey of fishing equipment in any local sporting goods store will tend to confirm that statement, and the current data from the fishing tackle industry also show that Dr. Henshall was correct in his assessment of the bass's future. According to the fishing department at Mercury Marine, the variety of lures, rods, reels, boats, and related equipment built especially for bass fishermen is at an all-time high. Never before, they point out, has there been so much specialized gear for the pursuit of one species of fish.

A major reason for the bass's popularity is their ability to live in almost any water, as long as it is clean. Once found only in eastern waters, bass have been stocked, and have reproduced naturally, in streams and lakes from coast to coast.

They're fun and fairly easy to catch. You don't have to be an expert fisherman to take black bass, although the more experience you have the better angler you will be. But kids, mothers, others too busy to really learn the skills of fishing—in fact, almost anyone who wants to—can catch bass.

And they grow large. Six- and 7-lb. fish aren't uncommon, and the world record bass weighed more than 22 lbs. So your chances of catching a big fish are greater with bass than with most other popular gamefish found in the same waters.

With so many good points in its favor —availability, fun to catch, and the chance of getting a large fish—it's no wonder the black bass is our most popular gamefish.

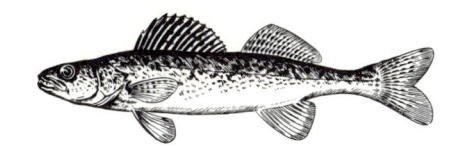

MICHIGAN FISHING GUIDES

The Michigan Natural Resources Department publishes some booklets on fishing in that state that would be helpful for anglers planning to fish there. They are as follows:

Catching Great Lakes Salmon and Trout tells about the lake trout, coho and chinook salmon, and steelhead and rainbows and gives methods, techniques, seasons, and rigs and baits to use to catch these fish.

Michigan Fish and How to Catch Them tells how to catch most of the fish such as trout, bass, walleyes, panfish, pike, and muskies found in Michigan waters.

These two booklets are available from:
**Michigan Dept. of Natural Resources
Stevens T. Mason Bldg.
Lansing, Mich. 48926**

Another good booklet on Michigan fishing is *Fishing in Michigan*. This is in color and tells how to catch the various species in that state, together with some of the best waters and rigs, lures, and baits used to catch them. This can be obtained from:
**Michigan Tourist Council
Suite 102, 300 S. Capitol Ave.
Lansing, Mich. 48926**

OHIO FISHING PUBLICATIONS

The Ohio Department of Natural Resources publishes many helpful and informative leaflets and reports on fish and fishing in that state. They put out such publications as the following:

Baitfish
Muskellunge Fishing in Ohio
Public Fishing Waters in Central Ohio
Public Fishing Waters in Northeastern Ohio
Public Fishing Waters in Northwestern Ohio
Public Fishing Waters in Southeastern Ohio
Public Fishing Waters in Southwestern Ohio
Brook Trout in Ohio
Brown Trout in Ohio
Rainbow Trout in Ohio
Bullheads in Ohio
Carp in Ohio
Coho Salmon in Ohio
Large-mouth Bass in Ohio
Pickerel in Ohio
White Bass in Ohio

There are many more, and they also publish public fishing maps of various lakes and reservoirs. To get their complete list write to:
**Publications Center
Ohio Dept. of Natural Resources
Fountain Sq.
Columbus, O. 43224**

IZAAK WALTON LEAGUE OF AMERICA

This organization has been in the forefront for many years in combating pollution and helping to restore our soil, forest, and water resources. They not only fight the battles against those who would spoil our waters and resources, but also join forces with other conservation groups, both local and national, to combat the threats to our environment. The organization is now more than fifty years old and has over fifty thousand members. There are various classes of membership, from regular to life membership. If you want to join or find out more about their goals and projects write to:
**Izaak Walton League of America
1800 N. Kent St.
Arlington, Va. 22209**

55

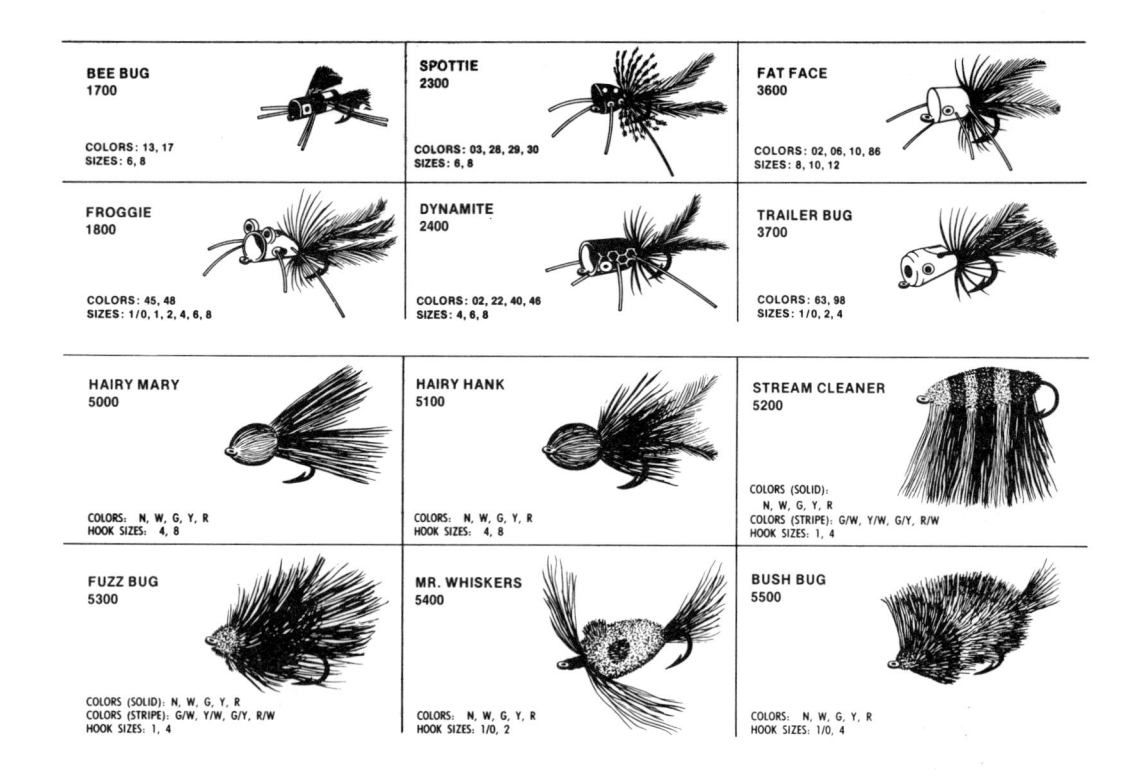

BEE BUG 1700 COLORS: 13, 17 SIZES: 6, 8	**SPOTTIE** 2300 COLORS: 03, 28, 29, 30 SIZES: 6, 8	**FAT FACE** 3600 COLORS: 02, 06, 10, 86 SIZES: 8, 10, 12
FROGGIE 1800 COLORS: 45, 48 SIZES: 1/0, 1, 2, 4, 6, 8	**DYNAMITE** 2400 COLORS: 02, 22, 40, 46 SIZES: 4, 6, 8	**TRAILER BUG** 3700 COLORS: 63, 98 SIZES: 1/0, 2, 4
HAIRY MARY 5000 COLORS: N, W, G, Y, R HOOK SIZES: 4, 8	**HAIRY HANK** 5100 COLORS: N, W, G, Y, R HOOK SIZES: 4, 8	**STREAM CLEANER** 5200 COLORS (SOLID): N, W, G, Y, R COLORS (STRIPE): G/W, Y/W, G/Y, R/W HOOK SIZES: 1, 4
FUZZ BUG 5300 COLORS (SOLID): N, W, G, Y, R COLORS (STRIPE): G/W, Y/W, G/Y, R/W HOOK SIZES: 1, 4	**MR. WHISKERS** 5400 COLORS: N, W, G, Y, R HOOK SIZES: 1/0, 2	**BUSH BUG** 5500 COLORS: N, W, G, Y, R HOOK SIZES: 1/0, 4

GAINES LURES

This company makes a wide variety of popping bugs, hair bugs, Grubby bugs, bass bugs, and panfish bugs. They also make lead-bodied jig lures and darts with tiny spinners on the hook. Their popping bugs are made from cork, and they have twenty-two different bugs in various sizes and a hundred colors to choose from. The sizes range from No. 14 up to 1/0.

They also have added a new line of hair bugs and these are highly effective lures for big trout and bass. Their Grubby bugs and Softie Crickets are small panfish bugs with soft sponge bodies or with chenille bodies. They are used for bream or bluegills and crappies. And the Kinzua Country Lures, which are lead-bodied jig lures and darts with tiny spinners on the hook, can be used for trout, bass, and panfish. For their catalog showing these lures write to:
The Gaines Co.
P.O. Box 35
Gaines, Pa. 16921

WOOD FRAME TROUT NET

This wood frame trout net is sold by the Rangeley Region Sports Shop. It has an ash and mahogany hoop with a walnut handle, a hand-rubbed gunstock finish, and small mesh with a wide-bottom bag. This shop in Maine also sells many other items for trout, salmon, and bass fishermen such as rods, reels, lines, fly boxes, flies, lures, sportswear, and books. For their catalog write to:
Rangeley Region Sports Shop
28 Main St.
Rangeley, Me. 04970

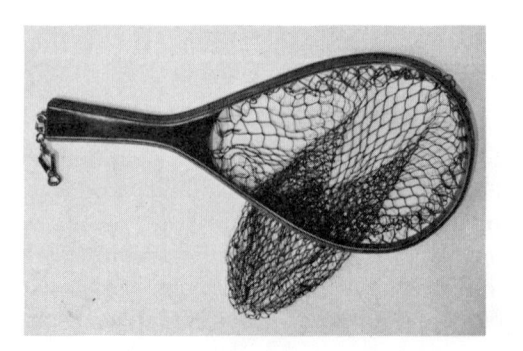

THE ANGLER'S CALENDAR AND FISHING HANDBOOK

The Angler's Calendar and Fishing Handbook is a thirty-two-page, quality-coated calendar with sixteen full-color photographs capturing the artistry and beauty of fly fishing. It features fishing scenes and fish. There are articles by Ron Cordes, Lefty Kreh, Nick Lyons, Bob Nauheim, and Ernie Schweibert. The calendar also lists the opening-season fishing dates, flies, and a list of angling conservation organizations. *The Angler's Calendar and Fishing Handbook* sells for $4.95 plus $.80 for postage and handling each. It is available from:

**The Angler's Calendar
P.O. Box 4576
Berkeley, Calif. 94704**

SKATING A SPIDER FLY

A highly effective way to fish a spider dry fly for trout is to cast across and slightly upstream. Then as it drifts down, strip in about 1 ft. of line with your left hand, twitch the rod tip, and then strip in line again. This causes the spider fly to skate forward a foot, then stop, then dart forward again. This often raises trout from deep water on hot, bright days when other flies or lures bring no response.

TRY SKITTERING

This is an old fishing method used to catch pickerel in weeds or lily pads that still works. Get a long cane or glass pole and tie a line of about the same length as the pole to the end. Then take a surface lure or pork chunk or pork rind or a strip cut from the belly of a fish and move or "skitter" it on top of the water. This can be done by moving the lure or bait back and forth or in circles or in figure 8's.

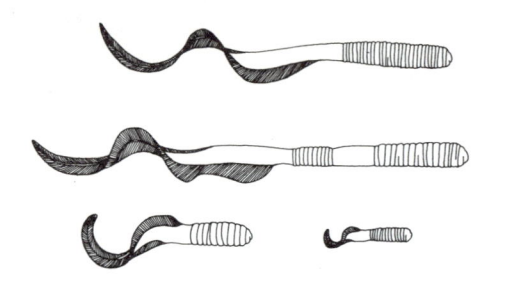

BURKE WIG-WAG WORMS

Burke Wig-Wag plastic worms have scorpionlike tails that swim and wiggle at the slightest movement with amazing lifelike action. The tail is blade thin and moves even at very slow speeds, enticing strikes. The worms come in many colors, from tiny 2-in. sizes up to 9-in. jumbos for the lunkers. The big worms can be rigged Texas style or with just a weedless hook. The smaller ones can be used with sliding sinker weights or jig heads. For a catalog about these and other Burke fishing lures, write to:
**Burke Fishing Lures
1969 S. Airport Rd.
Traverse City, Mich. 49684**

STUMP KNOCKER BOAT

This is a unique, compact fishing boat designed by David Livingston for one-man operation. He had always wanted a small fishing boat that was light, easy to transport, and could be used in ponds and small streams. The boat has slightly squared off ends, making it easier to maneuver in small bodies of water.

The Stump Knocker is 11 ft. long and weighs about 65 lbs. It is made of Fiberglas, but has foam flotation sandwiched in the deck fore and aft of the seat. It even has a small live well for keeping fish or bait alive. And it also has a storage compartment, which is located immediately behind the live well. Between the live well and storage compartment there's a removable back rest. The back rest comes in mighty handy for long trips, but can easily be lifted out when it isn't needed or for cartopping the boat. On the side there are small wooden blocks to which you can attach rod racks. For more information about this boat write to:
**David Livingston
Stump Knocker Boats
P.O. Box 26
Headland, Ala. 36345**

UNCLE JOSH SALMON EGGS

The Uncle Josh Bait Company is well known for its pork rind and pork lures. But they also pack salmon eggs for bait from single eggs to clusters for lake, river, and stream fishing. Salmon eggs are a natural fish food. They attract by feel or texture, odor, and color. They are gulped down by fry and fingerling and consumed in vast quantities by mature fish of many species, including the trout. Hordes of trout and char follow salmon runs as they pour into the natal streams from the ocean and the Great Lakes to feed on loose eggs swept by the current from the spawning beds. Salmon eggs can be fished singly on tiny hooks, or two or three eggs on a bigger hook, or in clusters consisting of many eggs. For a catalog showing their salmon egg baits and tips on how to use them, send $.25 to:
**Uncle Josh Bait Co.
Fort Atkinson, Wis. 53538**

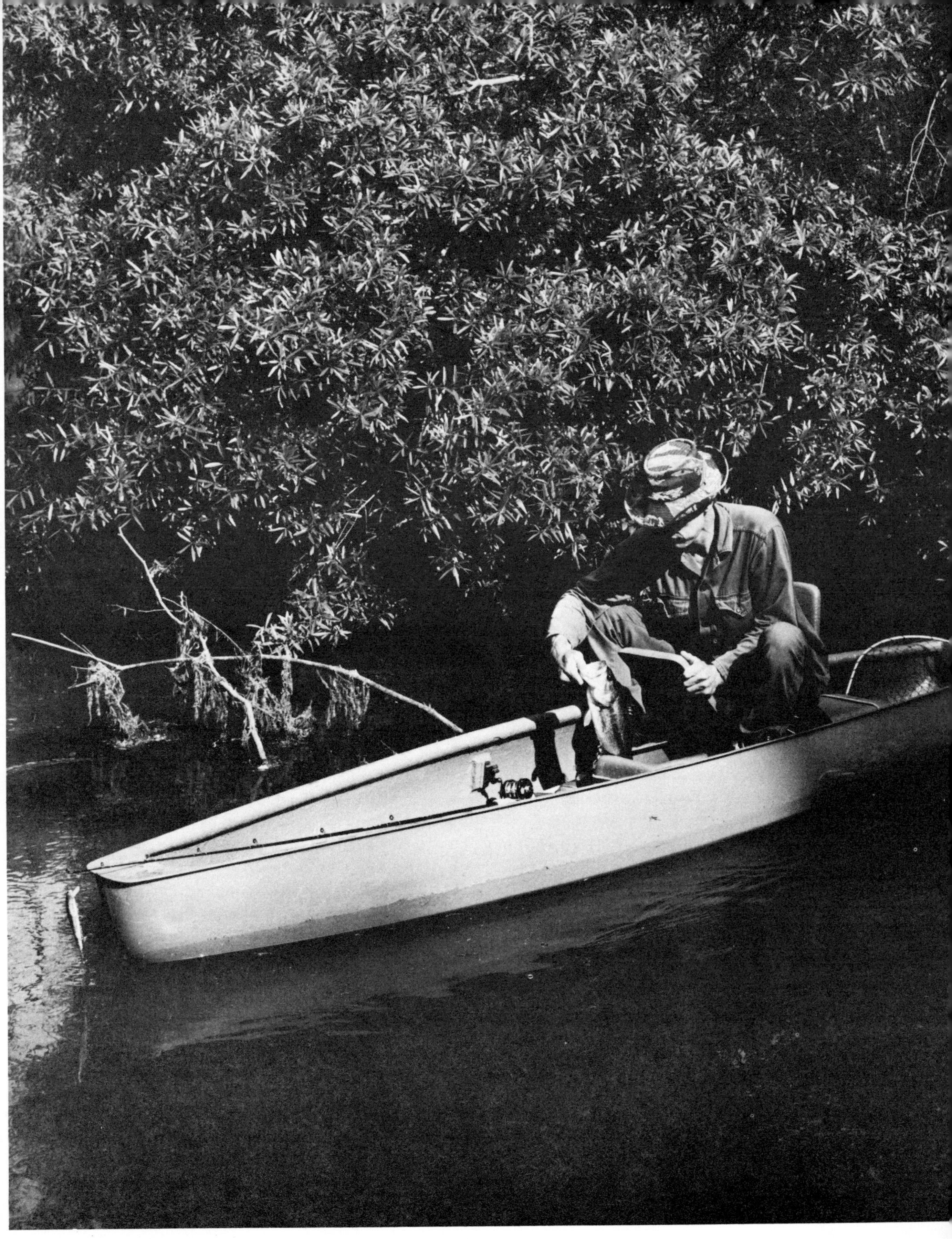

ROD AND REEL HOLDER

The IPCO Hold-a-Rod rod and reel holder stores rods in the correct vertical position. It is a handsomely finished 6-in.-by-18-in. fish-shaped select-grain hardwood wall mounting plaque. It stores five freshwater rods and reels and can also be used as an all-purpose utility rack to hold knives and tools. It can be mounted on a wall in a rec room, cabin, den, basement, garage, or workshop. For a catalog or more information write to:
IPCO, Inc.
331 Lake Hazeltine Dr.
Chaska, Minn. 55318

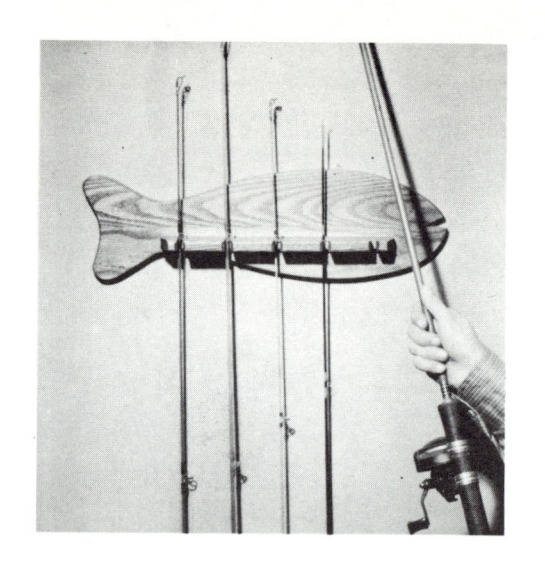

WOE TO THE BACHELOR FISH

Although spring may turn a young man's thoughts to matters of the heart, it signals a return to bachelorhood for male members of the white crappie family. These prolific fish spawn in late spring, with the female laying as many as fourteen thousand eggs. Since it becomes the male's duty to baby-sit the nest, he has earned the nickname of "bachelor perch" in many areas.

Crappie, both white and black, are sought by eager anglers just as soon as the ice opens and the water warms enough to move the fish toward shore. Their popularity is easy to understand, say the fishing experts at Mercury Marine, since crappie are excellent table fish and provide outstanding sporting action as well.

Crappie feed on other fish and on insects. They usually school around protective cover and forage from there. Fishermen look for brush and sunken trees, and anchor their boats near the cover. Minnows and small shad are usually used as bait. Crappie also take small jigs, spinners, and sometimes flies tied behind a surface plug.

Large crappie are often caught by trolling a minnow or spinner-and-minnow combination. Use a fly rod or cane pole and work the bait near the shore along brush banks and around underwater cover. Slow the outboard engine so the trolled lure is working just as close to the cover as possible. Limit the length of the fishing line to no longer than the pole being used. This makes it easy to swing the fish aboard, flip it off the hook, and return to the action.

Don't worry if spring rains muddy the water a little, as the Mercury fishermen have found that white crappie prefer some turbidity. Black crappie like clear water and will move to feeder streams when a lake becomes too muddy.

ADVANCED BASS FISHING

This practical, insightful book gives the angler all the advanced know-how and sophisticated techniques he needs to consistently land large numbers of big bass under all conditions. Based on recent scientific discoveries about bass behavior, it explodes misconceptions and shows exactly how to locate and catch trophy bass of all species. Step-by-step, John Weiss, nationally known angling writer and tournament fisherman, reveals revolutionary strategies, methods, equipment, and lures for pursuing these most popular of freshwater game fishes. *Advanced Bass Fishing* sells for $11.95 and is published by:
E. P. Dutton & Co., Inc.
201 Park Ave. S.
New York, N.Y. 10003

ALABAMA FISHING

The Alabama Department of Conservation and Natural Resources offers several folders and reprints on fishing in that state. Two of these are *Public Access Areas* and *State-owned and -managed Public Fishing Lakes*. They also have reprints on fishing Alabama streams, speck fishing, fishing Alabama's large impoundments, and similar literature. For these and others write to:
Alabama Dept. of Conservation and Natural Resources
Montgomery, Ala. 36130

VERMONT GUIDE TO FISHING

This little booklet is a guide to fishing Vermont's waters. The map shows all the important lakes, ponds, rivers, and streams in the state. It covers stream fishing, bow and arrow fishing, fish hatcheries, camping, and canoeing. Another booklet published by them is called *Vermont Fisheries Annual*, which tells about the research and fish management programs taking place. Both *Vermont Guide to Fishing* and *Vermont Fisheries Annual* can be obtained from:
Vermont Fish and Game Dept.
Montpelier, Vt. 05602

MARATHON RUBBER PRODUCTS

This company makes and sells all kinds of clothing, suits, parkas, fishing shirts, hats, boots, and waders that can be used by fishermen. The company's garments are pressure-welded and cemented and joined, making them waterproof and extremely durable. For a catalog showing all these outerwear products and boots and waders write to:
Marathon Rubber Products
510 Sherman St.
Wausau, Wis. 54401

FISHING AND SPORTING BOOKS

If you are looking for a new, used, or rare book about fishing or hunting, this is the place for you. They have over one thousand fishing and hunting books in their current catalog. Send $1.00 for the latest catalog, and this will be refunded on the first order of $10 or more. Write to:
Gary L. Esterbrook
P.O. Box 23898
San Jose, Calif. 95153

WORTH'S CHROMA-GLO WATER DEMON

Worth's Chroma-Glo Water Demon was introduced on the market less than two weeks before a major coho salmon tournament on Lake Michigan and caught many of the coho and lake trout. Since then the Chroma-Glo Water Demon has proven effective on a number of other species, particularly walleyes, which hit consistently on the 2-in.-size Water Demon.

The original Water Demon, which set records for lake trout catches on Lake Superior in the 1930s, has the same minnow shape, but the new Chroma-Glo series has a section cut out of the nickel-finished body and a colorful prismatic plastic panel riveted over it. The translucence of the panel permits light to shine through for greater underwater light penetration, which simulates additional action to the lure's inherent carting characteristics.

The Chroma-Glo Water Demon is available in orange, red, and yellow fluorescents and in blue, white, and gold panels. Because various colors appear to turn black at different depths, the range of colors provides maximum effectiveness at different depths, fluorescents being effective closer to the surface and the blue at depths to 100 ft. Available in single- or treble-hook models, the Chroma-Glo Water Demon retails for $1.40 for the 2-in. size, $1.85 for the 3⅜-in. size, and $1.95 for the 4½-in. size. For more information write to:

The Worth Co.
P.O. Box 88
Stevens Point, Wis. 54481

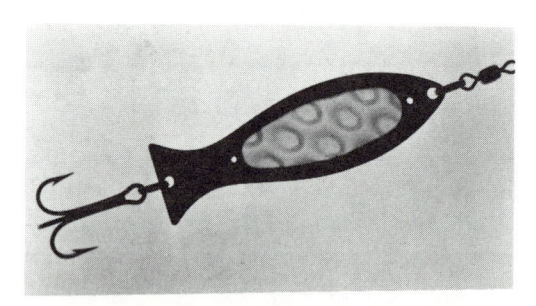

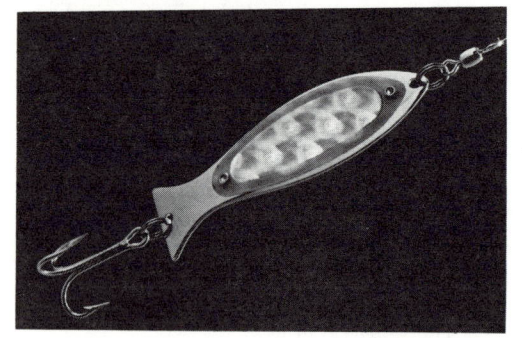

PELICAN CANOE

This 12-ft. squareback canoe manufactured by Eksay Plastics is a real catch for any weekend fisherman who hooks into it. The EPP-12-SB weighs only 55 lbs., yet its sturdy crossbar and ribs give it real strength. Ethafoam linings in the canoe and ethafoam strips on either side of the hull make this thoroughly practical craft almost unsinkable! For those who prefer their canoeing paddle-free, the EPP-12-SB's square stern will easily handle outboards up to 3½ hp. For more information about this canoe write to:

Berger, Tisdall, Clark, and Lesly, Ltd.
630 Dorchester Blvd., W.
Montreal, Canada H3B 1N8

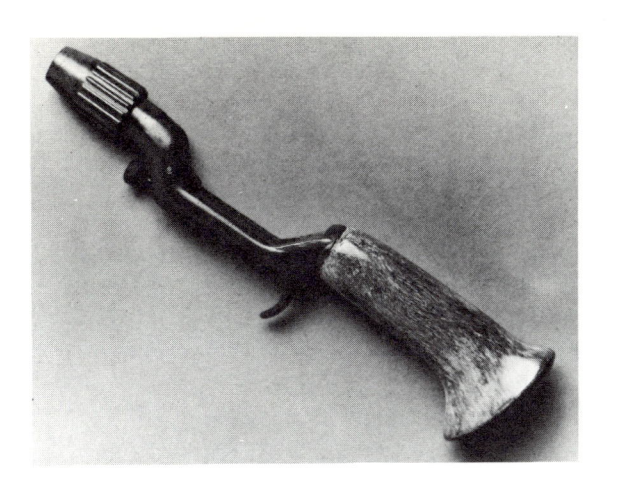

CUSTOM CASTING ROD HANDLE

For those who aren't satisfied with the standard rod handles found on most fishing rods, the Boone Bait Company people designed a tough, reliable rod handle that provides many hours of comfortable fishing. It is made of supertough, multicellular Tuf-Stuf, that is impervious to solvents such as gasoline and is not affected by the hot sun. The custom handle is lightweight and smooth, without the "textured" look and feel that can cause blisters on a long fishing trip. It has a flared butt with a positive nonslip grip. For more information write to:
The Boone Bait Co., Inc.
P.O. Box 571
Winter Park, Fla. 32789

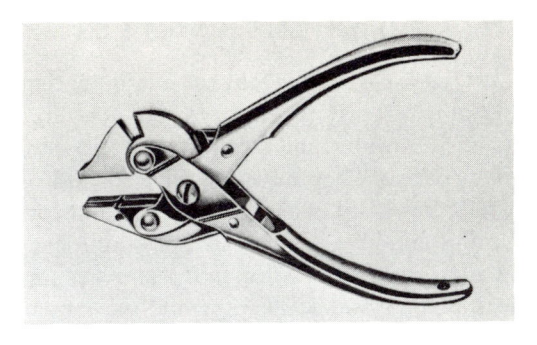

SPORTMATE PLIERS

Many fishermen are already familiar with these pliers, which are so versatile that all you need is one pair of pliers to do a wide variety of jobs. These pliers cut heavy wire, nails, and hooks. They can be used as pliers or a wrench and have five times the normal cutting or holding power. They can be used to straighten bent lures, hooks, nails, and wire. They also act as a small vise for tying flies, snells, or working on lures. After you catch a fish you can use the pliers as a hook disgorger to remove hooks or lures from a fish's mouth. And when you clean a fish you can use the pliers to grip the fish skin and pull it loose from the meat. These multipurpose pliers are only 5 in. long and can be carried in your pocket, tackle box, or in a special leather holster. These pliers are sold in most fishing tackle, sporting goods, and hardware stores. For more information you can write to:
Sargent & Co.
New Haven, Conn. 06509

HANDY FISH SCALER

If you can't locate your regular fish scaler or forgot to bring it, use a soup spoon or tablespoon as an emergency scaler. If you want to make a permanent fish scaler, just file some teeth on one side of the spoon.

JIG-A-DO WORMS AND EELS

The Jig-A-Do worms and eels made by the Burke Company have been popular for many freshwater and salt-water species for many years. They have a weighted and a plastic head cup, which provides weight for casting and gives them a lively action. The smaller sizes are best for freshwater fishing such as bass and walleyes, while the larger ones can be used for pike and muskies. The larger eels are also very good for striped bass in salt water when casting or trolling for these fish. For a catalog and more information write to:
Burke Fishing Lures
1969 S. Airport Rd.
Traverse City, Mich. 49684

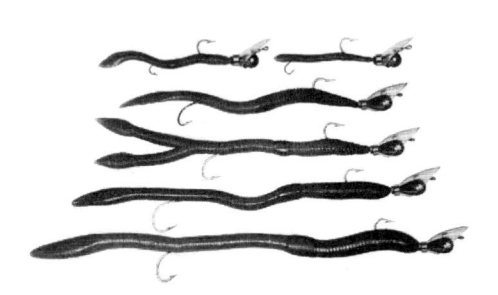

FISHING IN THE EVERGLADES

Just thirty minutes from Miami or Fort Lauderdale, Florida, will find you in the wild Everglades, miles from the traffic, congestion, and crowds of the more popular Gold Coast resort areas and cities. Here you have access to 750,000 acres of beautiful waters filled with fighting fish such as bass, pickerel, crappies, catfish, and bream. There are two jumping-off points where you can rent a boat with or without a fishing guide, launch your own boat, or just fish from shore along the canals. One is the Everglades Holiday Park, and the other is the Sawgrass Recreation Park. They are open all year 'round from daylight to dark. There are campsites near the water. There are also stores that sell fishing tackle, bait licenses, gasoline, groceries, and ice. You can even go for an air boat ride to thrill your family. For more information and maps about these fishing spots write to:
Sawgrass Recreation Park
P.O. Box 22755
Fort Lauderdale, Fla. 33315

THE COMPLETE BOOK OF CASTING

The Complete Book of Casting by Rex Gerlach is a comprehensive explanation of both the theoretical and the practical aspects of all types of casting. It offers a complete course in all forms of casting, both for anglers and tournament casters, with more than two hundred rapid-sequence photographs illustrating every step. Most of these were taken right on the fishing scenes, in or near the water. The author covers fly casting, spinning, spin casting, bait casting, and surf casting. The paperback edition sells for $5.95 and is published by:
Stoeger Publishing Co.
55 Ruta Ct.
South Hackensack, N.J. 07606

MISSISSIPPI FISHING

You can obtain the following leaflets about Mississippi fishing:

Fishing in Mississippi gives the latest sport fishing laws and regulations.

Mississippi Game Fish tells about the most important game fish caught in Mississippi fresh waters. There are illustrations of each fish.

Mississippi Commission Lakes tells about the twenty prime fishing lakes owned or leased by the state. It tells about the various facilities available for fishing, boat launching, picnicking, and other activities. These leaflets can be obtained from:
Mississippi Game and Fish Commission
P.O. Box 451
Jackson, Miss. 39205

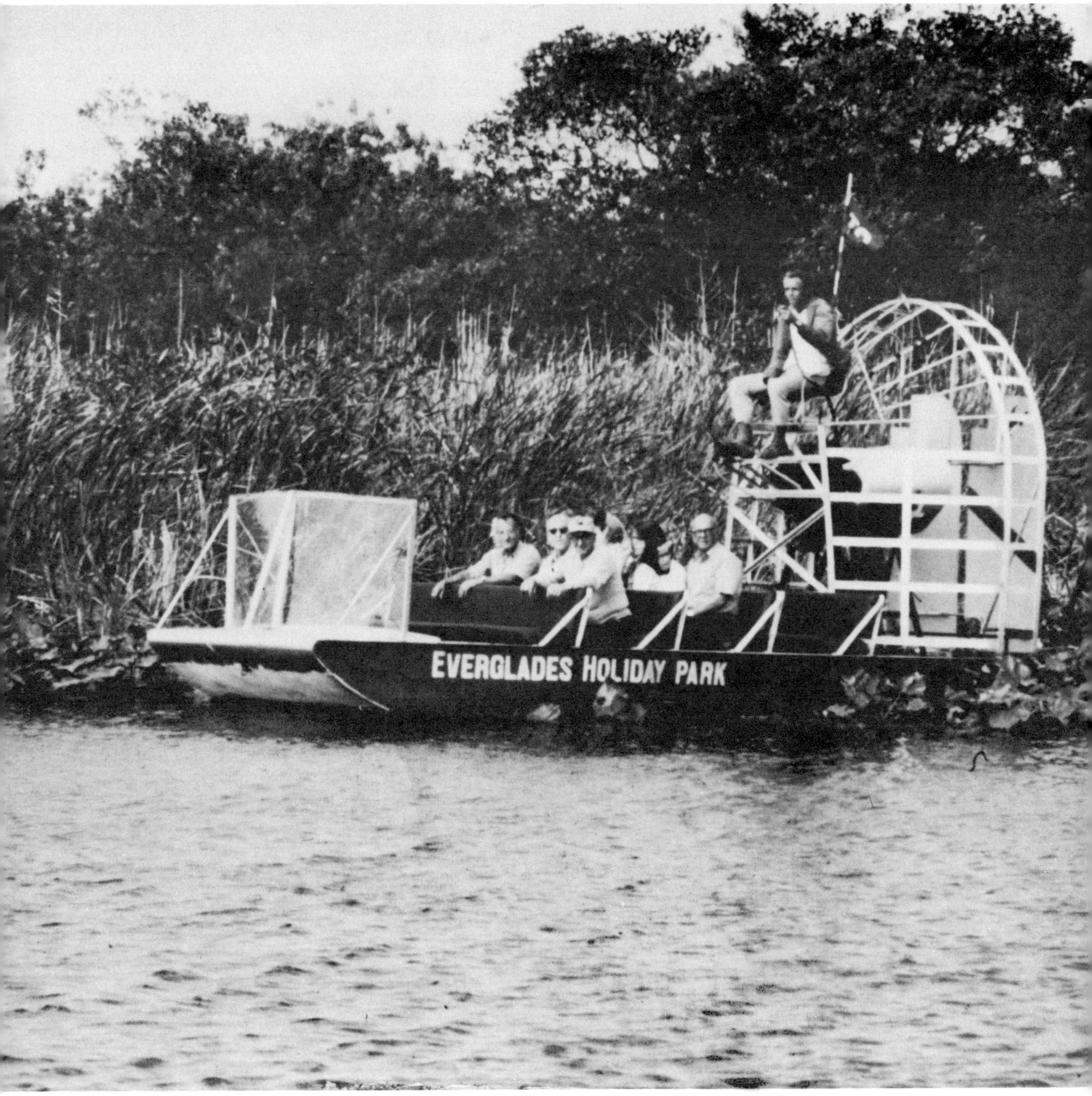
EVERGLADES HOLIDAY PARK

FISH FARMING

In recent years more and more fish are being hatched and reared artificially both for sport and commercial use. Catfish farms are springing up in many of our southern states. But such fish farming or fish culture is not a new idea. The Chinese were hatching and raising fish artificially way back in 2100 B.C. The early Romans used to construct pools and piscines where they raised mullet and other fish. And during the Middle Ages the Germans raised carp in ponds, and this soon spread to other countries in Europe. In our own country the first attempts at fish culture begin in 1864, when Seth Green set up the first trout hatchery in Mumford, New York.

FLORIDA BASS IN CALIFORNIA

When biologists stocked some Florida-strain black bass in the warm-water lakes owned by the city of San Diego Recreation Department in Southern California, they had no idea that the bass would find conditions ideal and reach monster proportions. But that's what happened when they planted some of the Florida bass in 1959 as an experiment. The bass were caught in the 9-to-11-lb. class in only seven years of growth. In ten years a 15-lb. bass was caught. Then a 16½-lb. and 17-lb., 14-oz. fish were taken in 1971. Finally, all of these were topped by a 20-lb., 15-oz. monster bass caught by David Zimmerlee. He caught the record bass in Lake Miramar on a live night crawler!

WHAT DID YOU CATCH?

Fishermen are supposed to catch fish, but they often bring in some weird and strange objects. Anglers have caught their own and other people's fishing tackle, eyeglasses, watches, diamond rings, and false teeth. One kid pulled in a bicycle, and all he had to do was wipe off the mud and ride home. And another angler fishing a lake in Tennessee hooked something, and when he reeled it in he saw it was a bundle wrapped in old cloth. When he opened it, he discovered $685 inside!

HOOKING BASS ON PLASTIC WORMS

When using plastic worms for bass, hold your rod tip high when reeling in. When you feel a tap or peck, drop the rod tip quickly to give some slack line. Then reel in the slack line while holding the rod low over the water. When the line tightens, raise the rod fast and hard to set the hook.

CLOTH AND PLASTIC STRIPS

Carry some cloth or plastic material in various colors such as white, yellow, red, pink, blue, green, brown, and black when you go fishing. You can cut these strips into various widths and lengths and add them to spoons, spinners, plugs, and jigs. Or you can cut really short and narrow strips and put them on a bare hook and use it with fly rod or cane pole to catch panfish.

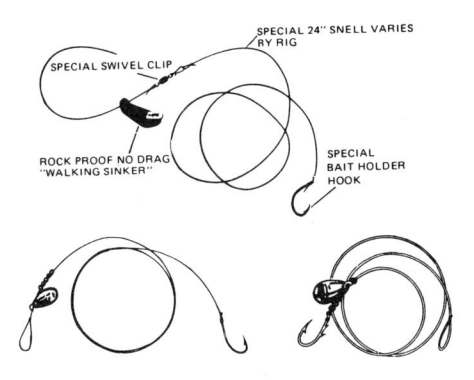

LINDY RIGS

Standard original Lindy Rigs come in a multitude of forms. Each type is made for a special fish or fishing condition. Lindy Rigs, depending on type, can be fished either on the bottom, suspended off the bottom, or free-floated in the current. Some can be fished with minnows, night crawlers, or leeches, while others utilize spawn sacks or egg clusters. This company also makes snells and spinners to use with Lindy Rigs or their Flikker Rig. They also carry a full line of tackle and accessories for all kinds of freshwater fishing. For their catalog write to:
Ray-O-Vac
Fishing Tackle Div.
ESB, Inc.
P.O. Box 488
Brainerd, Minn. 56401

FLY ROD FISHING BOOKLET

The Cortland Line Company has a little booklet called *Fly Rod Fishing Made Easy* that tells all about how to get started in fly fishing. It tells you about the fly rod, fly reel, line, and how to choose one to suit your purposes. It gives the basics of fly casting and tells you about catching trout, bass, and panfish. The booklet costs $.25 and can be obtained from:
Cortland Line Co.
Cortland, N.Y. 13045

BUD LILLY'S TROUT SHOP

This is a shop run by Bud and Greg Lilly in West Yellowstone, Montana, which specializes in tackle, flies, and equipment for the western trout angler. They also sell fly-tying tools and materials, rods, reels, lines, leaders, waders, vests, clothing, and various other items used by fly fishermen. They will send you their catalog and booklets on fishing waters in Yellowstone National Park, Montana, and Idaho on request. Write to:
Bud Lilly's Trout Shop
P.O. Box 387
West Yellowstone, Mont. 59758

ICE FISHING TACKLE

The Arnold Tackle Company specializes in making tools, tackle, lures, and accessories for ice fishing as well as for general fishing. It makes a complete line of ice drills, spuds, tip-ups, skimmers, jigging rods, and assorted jigs or lures for panfish. For more information write to:
Arnold Tackle Co.
100 Commercial Ave.
Paw Paw, Mich. 49079

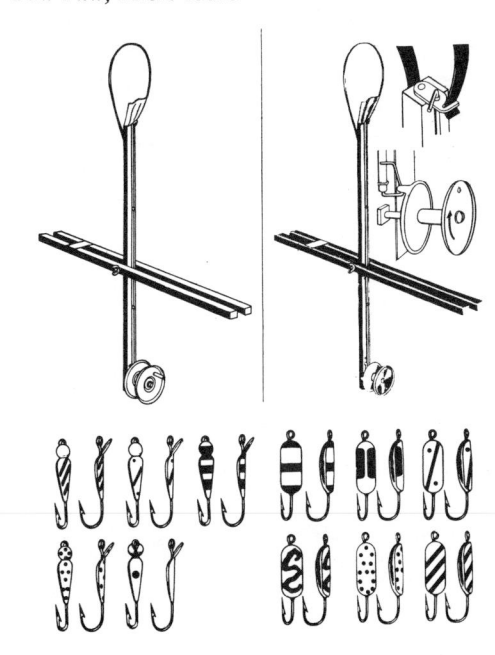

PIKE THE EASY WAY

A fisherman in Illinois cast long and hard for hours trying to catch a fish, but had no luck. He decided to try once more and tossed the plug out. He worked the lure with skill and plenty of action, but not a single fish was interested in it. Finally he decided to head for home and reeled in the plug up to the boat and lifted it out of the water. At that moment a pike leaped for the plug and missed, but landed right in the bottom of the boat! Later, when weighed, it went 13½ lbs.

COLOR, SIZE, OR ACTION?

Which is most important in a fishing lure—color, size, or action? This is a question that has been debated by freshwater and salt-water anglers ever since they began using lures for fishing. Trout fishermen feel that the flies they use should imitate the insect the trout are feeding on closely in color and size. But the fly should also move on top or under the water in a lifelike manner, like a natural insect does. Lures such as streamers, spoons, and plugs that imitate minnows should be close to the size of the baitfish the larger fish are feeding on. And they should be worked or manipulated so that they look like a crippled minnow or small fish.

Actually, in the final analysis the color, size, and action of lures are all-important and have a bearing on your fishing success. When fishing is slow, the smart angler keeps changing the color and size of the lure and experiments with different actions until he finds what the fish want on a particular day and in the waters he is fishing.

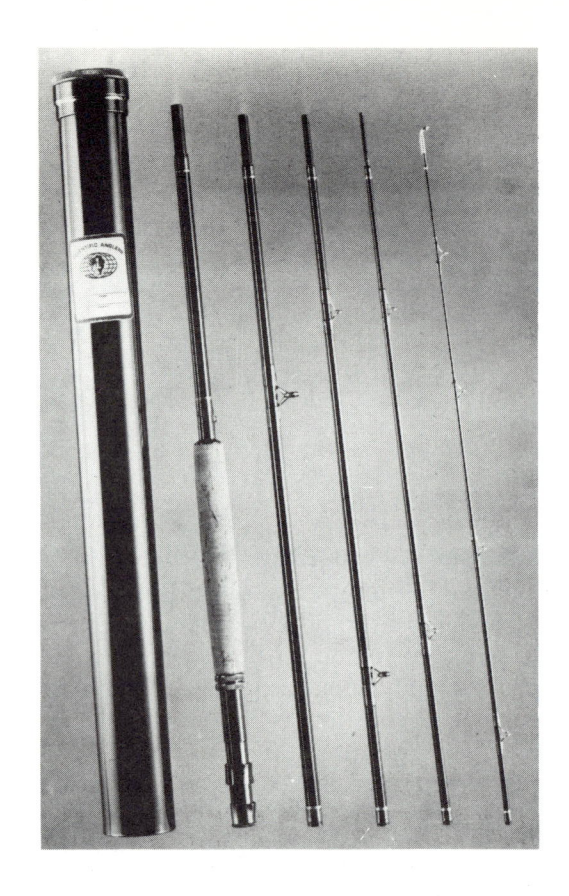

PACK FLY ROD

The Scientific Anglers have the System 6 Pack Rod, which is just the thing for the backpacker who wants to tote a fly rod and try those wilderness and mountain streams and lakes. It is also handy for the traveling salesman or businessman who flies a lot and wants to have a fly rod that doesn't take up much space in a suitcase. The rod is designed to handle No. 6 fly lines and is 8 ft., 1 in. long, weighs 4 ozs., and sells for $100. For their catalog showing this and other rods, reels, fly lines, and tackle write to:
Scientific Anglers
P.O. Box 2001
Midland, Mich. 48640

FISHING MUSEUM

The Gladding International Sport Fishing Museum in upstate New York is dedicated to the preservation of our sport fishing heritage and is committed to the promotion of sensible conservation measures. It was chartered as a nonprofit corporation to preserve, restore, and conserve the relics and historical objects of recreational and sport fishing. The Gladding Corporation, which manufactures fishing tackle and accessories, is sponsoring and helping to finance the museum but will have no commercial connection with the museum corporation. They helped to restore and renovate the 147-year-old "octagon house" that houses the institution. Inside, the museum contains and exhibits a valuable collection of antique rods, rare reels, lures, historic fishing catalogs, famous paintings and original prints of fishing scenes, and a library of old and new books on angling and related subjects. The museum welcomes donations of fishing equipment from the general public if such equipment is antique or unusual. Admission to the museum is free, and it is located at:
**Gladding International Sport Fishing Museum
South Otselic, N.Y. 13155**

TROUT OF CALIFORNIA

Trout of California is a little booklet that covers all the trout found in California. It has color and black-and-white plates showing brook trout, rainbow trout, steelhead, golden trout, cutthroat trout, Dolly Varden trout, lake trout, and other kinds of trout. It tells their distinguishing characteristics, distribution in California, and interesting facts about each species. The booklet is available from:
**Conservation Education Div.
Dept. of Fish and Game
1416 Ninth St.
Sacramento, Calif. 95814**

ROD KEEPER

The Rod Keeper is the ideal way to store valued fishing rods. Adjustable for the thinnest fly rods to the heaviest trollers, it protects rods and provides positive support on the rod instead of the guides. It makes a decorative wall piece in the study, den, or office. There are three sizes to select in the practical and decorative stained pine. They are as follows:

Model RK-4	Supports 4 rods	$5.75
Model RK-6	Supports 6 rods	$8.50
Model RK-8	Supports 8 rods	$10.95

If you order by mail you also add $1.25 for postage and handling. The Rod Keeper is available from:
**Chelsea Products Co.
127 Sea Flower Rd.
Milford, Conn. 06460**

FISHING NEBRASKA

This is a large-format booklet in color that describes the best fishing waters in Nebraska. It gives the location of the lake, pond, reservoir, creek, or river, telling what kind of fish are caught there. It also tells if camping is allowed and if power boats are permitted on the body of water. *Fishing Nebraska* can be obtained from:
**Nebraska Game and Parks Commission
P.O. Box 30370
Lincoln, Neb. 68503**

THE PRACTICAL FLY FISHERMAN

The book *The Practical Fly Fisherman* by Al McClane was a pioneer when it was first published in 1953 and is an acknowledged classic in its field, definitive in its treatment of fly fishing both as a way of living and as a method of fishing. In this new, updated edition the book is a complete course in fly fishing between two covers. It covers the fly rod, fly reel, fly line, leaders, how to cast, fishing the nymph, fly fishing for bass, dry flies, wet flies, streamers, and bucktails, and even covers fly fishing for panfish. There are many popular patterns of flies listed, with descriptions and color photos. McClane has added some new material to each chapter to cover the changes that have occurred in the twenty-four years since its first publication. Al McClane, of course, is well known as the editor and author of other fishing books and as the fishing editor of *Field & Stream* for many years. *The Practical Fly Fisherman* sells for $10 and is published by:
Prentice-Hall, Inc.
Englewood Cliffs, N.J. 07632

FISH STRINGERS

The Plastilite Corp. makes several fish stringers of heavy Poly Rope and Braid, and also a chain-type stringer with nine individual snaps. The metal parts, such as the needle and ring, are either from brass or plated metal. They range in length from 6 ft. to 25 ft. For more information write to:
Plastilite Corp.
Box 12235, Florence Sta.
Omaha, Neb. 68112

HARDWARE CAN RUIN THE ACTION

When using surface lures, especially the smaller, lighter types, tie the leader or line directly to the lure. Don't use a snap or snap-swivel because the weight will tend to give it less buoyancy and also kill the action.

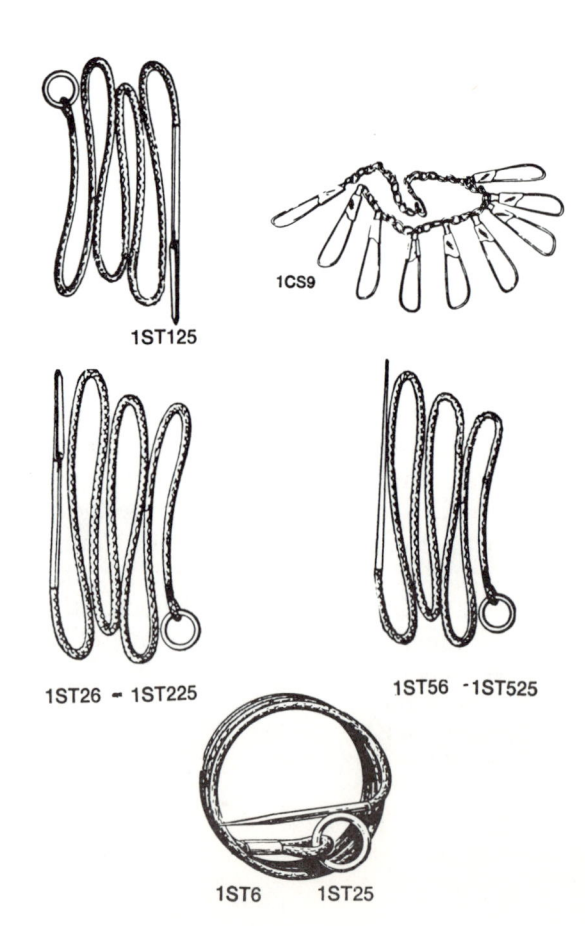

MERCURY'S BIG OUTBOARD MOTORS

With more and more serious anglers and pro bass fishermen demanding fast, powerful outboard motors to get to distant fishing grounds or for fishing many spots miles apart, the Mercury people have responded to these demands. They offer their Black Max in the 115-hp. Merc 1150, with 6-cylinder smoothness for performance and dependability. The other motor is the Merc 1500, in 150 hp., also a 6-cylinder job with a factory-installed Power Trim Option for faster accleration and level ride. For more information and details about these motors and others in their line write to:
Mercury Marine
Fond Du Lac, Wis. 54935

EAGLE CLAW REELS

The Wright & McGill Company carries several types of fishing reels for freshwater and salt-water fishing. Their Mediterranean line of spinning reels includes models from ultralight to heavy salt water. Their Blue Pacific spinning reels include models from ultralight to heavy salt water. They also have several spin-casting reels and a Freline all-purpose spinning reel. And they also have several fly reels from single-action to automatic models. Their catalog showing these reels and other fishing tackle costs $.25 from:
Wright & McGill Co.
P.O. Box 16011
Denver, Colo. 80216

71

DARDEVLE SPOONS

The Dardevle spoon is the most famous of its type and is the lure that has been copied more than any other through the years. This company also makes many types of spoons for freshwater and salt-water fishing, ranging from the tiny $\frac{1}{32}$-oz. sizes up to 3 ozs. for pike, muskies, and salt-water fish. The spoons come in a wide variety of finishes and colors, although the red and white has been most popular for many years. For more information on how to fish their spoons and information about the lures themselves send $.50 for their *Fishing Annual* to:
Lou J. Eppinger Mfg. Co.
6340 Schaefer Hwy.
Dearborn, Mich. 48126

PORTABLE ELECTRIC SMOKER

This compact, portable electric smoker can be used to smoke fish, game, and meat. Just place the fish or meat inside, put hickory chips in a container, and plug the smoker into a standard 120-volt AC outlet. The electric heating element toasts chips in the receptacle to produce a pungent hickory smoke without a flame. It can be used on the patio, in the garage, or in the yard. Small pieces of meat or fish can be smoked on racks, or they can be removed to smoke a larger fish or ham or turkey up to 20 lbs. For more information write to:
Mit-Shell Co.
640 S. Fifth St.
Quincy, Ill. 62301

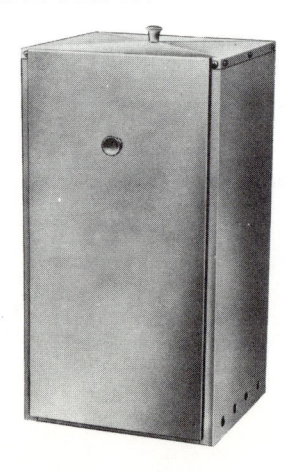

NATIONAL MUSKIE ASSOCIATION

If you are a muskie enthusiast or would like to learn how to catch more of these fish, then the National Muskie Association can help you. It covers muskie fishing in all the states and parts of Canada where this fish is found. If you become a member you will receive a membership card, club decal, patch, and a subscription to six issues of *Man vs. Muskie* per year. The Association also offers its members discounts at member resorts where muskies are caught. Special forms are provided, on which you can procure information on specific muskie lakes, rivers, guides, and the general habits and traits of the muskellunge. They also sponsor or participate in muskie tournaments and award plaques, certificates of merit, honorable mentions, and various fishing-tackle prizes. For more information about this association and an application form write to:
The National Muskie Assn.
2922 N. Pulaski Rd.
Chicago, Ill. 60641

EVINRUDE ANGLERS CLUB

The Evinrude Anglers Club is an organization designed to reward the fisherman for his efforts and to promote national tournaments on a local level. While Evinrude Motors sponsors its national fishing club, it is not necessary to own or operate an Evinrude outboard motor in order to participate. Anyone is eligible to become a member regardless of age, sex, race, creed, or color. All memberships are individual and remain in effect one year from the time of application. Once you join you'll receive a membership card, boat decal, patch, newsletter, and tournament listings. And you'll get recognition if you catch any of the fifteen popular freshwater and salt-water game species over a certain weight. Membership is $4.00 a year. For more information send for club rules and application form to:
Evinrude Anglers Club
Evinrude Motors
P.O. Box 663
Milwaukee, Wis. 53201

FISHING IN MANITOBA

There are two publications you can get if you plan to do any fishing in Manitoba, Canada. One is called *Fishing in Manitoba,* a beautiful, large-size color booklet telling about the fish you will catch there. The other is called "Manitoba Stocked Waters Angling Map." This is a folder with a series of maps showing the main waters in Manitoba and also listing the waters that are stocked with brook trout, brown trout, kokanee, lake trout, rainbow trout, splake, large-mouth bass, small-mouth bass, muskellunge, pike, walleyes, and yellow perch. Both publications can be obtained from:
Manitoba Government Travel
200 Vaughan St.
Winnipeg, Man.
Canada R3C 1T5

MCCLANE'S FISHING ENCYCLOPEDIA

McClane's New Standard Fishing Encyclopedia is a huge, 1,172-page volume of fish facts, fishing lures, and techniques that has been completely revised, expanded, and updated. It is beautifully printed, with more than 1,000 illustrations, many of them in full color. The book has over 6,000 entries in all and covers over 1,400 freshwater and salt-water species, which are described and shown in black and white and in color. There is a big section devoted to the best fishing spots in the United States and all over the world. There are 300 wet- and dry-fly patterns photographed in full color. A big section is devoted to preparing and cooking fish, with many favorite fish recipes by McClane. It is the biggest and most complete encyclopedia on fishing ever published. McClane's New Standard Fishing Encyclopedia sells for $40 and is published by:
Holt, Rinehart & Winston, Inc.
383 Madison Ave.
New York, N.Y. 10017

ATLANTIC SALMON FLIES AND FISHING

The book *Atlantic Salmon Flies and Fishing* by Joseph D. Bates, Jr., is, as the title implies, a complete guide to salmon flies and how to use them for this great gamefish. For fly dressers there are new, simplified instructions and historical notes for over two hundred modern Atlantic salmon fly patterns most popular in North America and in countries around the Atlantic. The book provides instruction so detailed that flies can be tied properly without seeing the originals. It covers dry flies, classic and modern feather-wings, the new hair-wings, nymphs, streamers, and unusual attractors. Over one hundred of these are illustrated in vivid, faithful color. Joe Bates also explains factually and interestingly where in streams to fish for Atlantic salmon under variable conditions, whether to fish top water or deeper down, and what sizes and types of flies to use under all circumstances, plus many new ways to cast and work them to induce reluctant salmon to strike. *Atlantic Salmon Flies and Fishing* sells for $14.95 and is available from the author:

Joseph D. Bates, Jr.
45 Prynnwood Rd.
Longmeadow, Mass. 01106

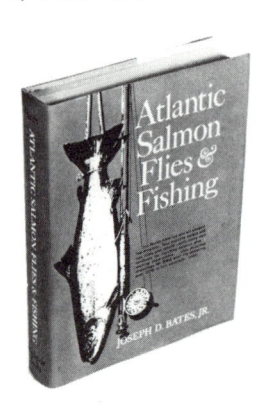

FISH TRACKER DEPTH SOUNDER

For the budget-minded boatman and angler, Allied Sports Company now offers the new Fish Tracker series of depth sounders. Built with the same high-quality components as Allied's popular Humminbird line of depth sounders, the new economy-priced Fish Tracker models have comparable high-performance features, including a superbright flasher, high-speed transducer, and Allied's unique Night Light Panel for easy night reading.

The Fish Tracker has an attractive high-impact plastic case and built-in automatic positive noise-rejection circuitry without the separate adjustment knob standard on Humminbird models. A sturdy aluminum bracket is included for vertical, horizontal, or overhead mounting, and a high-quality transducer with an adjustable transom-mounting bracket.

The Fish Tracker 60 is designed to give accurate depth readings, even at high speed. Large, easily read numbers and widely spaced 1-ft. calibration marks around the outside of the dial provide a reading range of 0 to 60 ft. Smaller numbers around the inside of the dial face record depths up to 120 ft. with a second turn around the dial. Suggested retail price for the Fish Tracker 60 is $99.95. For more information write to:

Allied Sports Co.
Two Humminbird Lane
Eufaula, Ala. 36207

FABUGLAS PRO FISHERMAN

The Fabuglas Pro Fisherman is available in two sizes—the 146 and the 160. Both feature lots of storage space and still leave plenty of room for active fishing. They have two foam-padded armchairs on full adjustable bases, and a folding driver's chair mounted on a storage compartment base. There are twin fish boxes in the rear of the cockpit with padded lids for seating, the lids clamp shut on a seal strip, and the boxes are foamed in for use as iceboxes. There is a fully upholstered rod locker with rod holders on the port side of the cockpit. There's also an electric bilge pump and electric combination circulator and aerator installed in the port side of the fish box. The console with mechanical steering has a plexiglas windshield. For their catalog or more information write to:
Fabuglas Co., Inc.
6401 Centennial Blvd.
Nashville, Tenn. 37209

WHITEFISH DO BITE

You can have great sport if you use light tackle and fish for whitefish. A fly rod and natural stonefly nymphs on a small hook can be used in many streams for mountain whitefish found along the western slopes of the Rocky Mountains. This fishing is usually best in the late winter months. Whitefish will also hit small wet flies, nymphs, and dry flies in many waters, especially in lakes in our northern states. The lake whitefish, which is very common in the Great Lakes region, for example, can often be caught on rod and reel. They'll hit tiny spoons, spinners, jigs, and natural baits such as tiny minnows or cut fish. Some of the best fishing with dry flies takes place when the whitefish are feeding on top and dimpling the surface.

WADE FOR YOUR FISH

One of the most effective and sporting ways to catch freshwater fish, especially bass, is to wade in the water near shore and cast toward likely spots, such as this Florida angler is doing. Waders are handy for this, and an inner tube around your waist will enable you to reach deeper spots and keep you dry. You can use spinning, spin-casting, and bait-casting tackle for this fishing, especially if the cover is thick and the bass are big. But for most sport, use a fly rod about 8 to 9 ft. long with a bass bug taper fly line. Then get some bass bugs, poppers, and streamers, and you are in business. When wading, do so quietly and sneak up on the best spots such as edges of lily pads, hyacinths, sawgrass, rocks, logs, brush, and other cover where bass like to lurk. Then cast a popper as close as you can to these spots and work it very slowly. In fact, a good way to fish is to cast your popper and then let it lie still for a minute or so. Then twitch or jerk it a short distance and let it lie again. Keep doing this during most of the retrieve. You can't fish a bass bug or popper too slowly, especially for the bigger fish. Besides bass, you can also catch pickerel and panfish when wade fishing the lakes and rivers.

HEDDON LURES

In 1897 James Heddon whittled the first artificial bait out of wood. And in subsequent years Heddon has been responsible for many other major innovations in artificial, hard lures. They now have a complete line of plugs and spinners, including surface, underwater, deep-diving, and sinking lures. Such lures as the River Runt, Sonar, Sonic, Punkin Seed, Torpedo, Zara Spook, Tadpolly, Chugger Spook, and Dying Flutter are well known to expert bass fishermen who carry them in their tackle boxes. The lures are made in many sizes, weights, and colors. Their catalog showing these and other lures they make can be obtained from:
James Heddon's Sons
Dowagiac, Mich. 49047

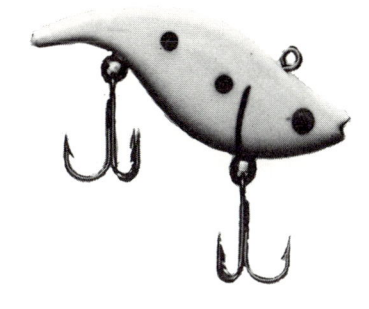

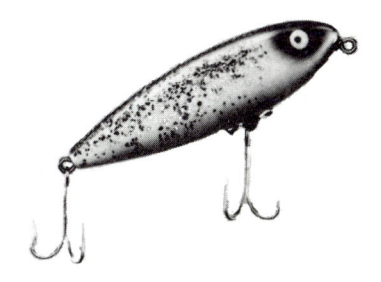

BERKLEY FISHING LINES

Berkley and Co. has been making and selling fishing lines for many years, and their Trilene line is popular with freshwater and salt-water anglers. It comes in many different types, grades, and colors, and it tests from 2 to 80 lbs. They come packaged in various containers and different-sized spools up to bulk sizes holding many yards. They also make braided nylon lines and fly lines. For their catalog or more information about these lines and other tackle, write to:
Berkley and Co.
Spirit Lake, Ia. 51360

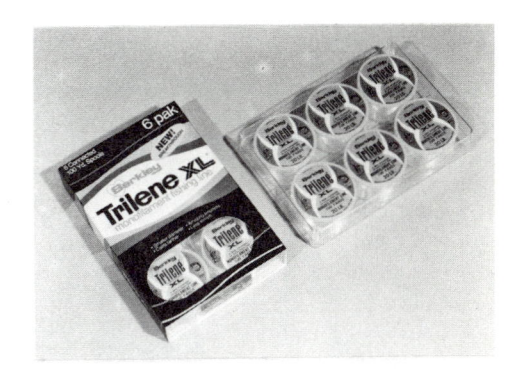

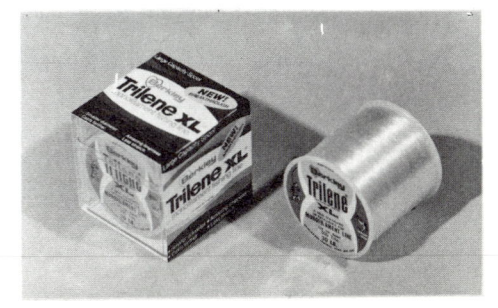

77

HEDDON RODS

James Heddon's Sons have been making fishing rods for more than seventy-seven years. They have many models for freshwater and salt-water fishing in all price ranges. They make fly rods, spinning rods, spin-casting and bait-casting rods, pack rods, and boat, bay, pier, and surf rods. Their custom line is called "Rod of Rods" and made step-by-step in limited quantities. Each Fiberglas blank is hand-selected by Harding and Hills, their master rod builders. Then it receives Heddon's unique Quartz Curing, and the wood-grain finish is hand-applied. The Fiberglas ferrules are hand-shaped and custom-fitted. The rods have gold-plated guides, and each rod is further enhanced by a hand-rubbed, permagloss coating, which makes it tough and waterproof. Other Heddon rods have stainless wire guide windings that cannot rot, fray, stretch, slip, or corrode. They have a catalog showing these rods if you write to:
James Heddon's Sons
Dowagiac, Mich. 49047

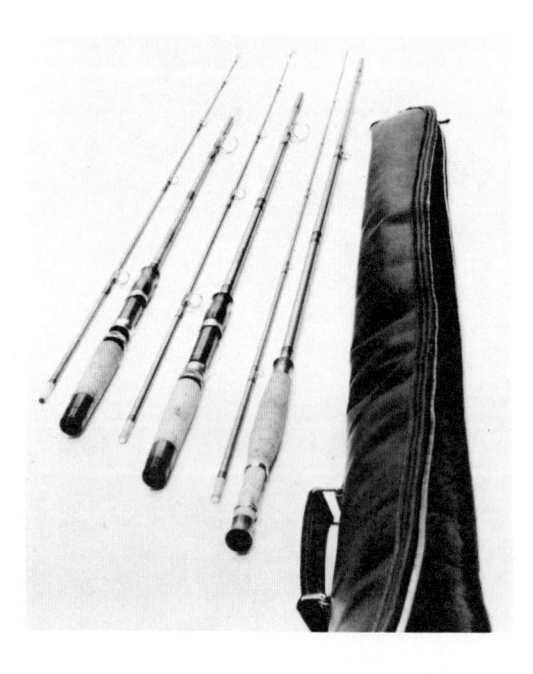

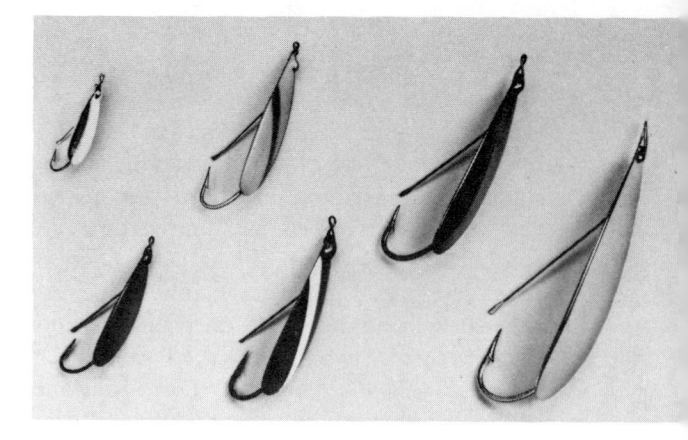

SILVER MINNOW SPOONS

Fishermen of all ages and with all types of tackle will appreciate the bulletlike casts, high underwater visibility, and attractive swimming ability of Louis Johnson Co.'s Silver Minnow weedless spoons, which have been used by freshwater anglers for over forty years. They can be used plain or with pork rind strips, pork frogs or chunks, rubber skirts, and plastic worms.

The Johnson Silver Minnow spoons come in various weights and sizes, such as $1/24$ oz., $1/8$ oz., $1/4$ oz., $1/2$ oz., $3/4$ oz., and $1 1/8$ ozs., and in such finishes as silver, gold, copper, red-and-white, yellow-and-red, purple, and black nickel. For a catalog or more information write to:
Louis Johnson Co.
1547 Old Deerfield Rd.
Highland Park, Ill. 60035

WEST VIRGINIA FISHING GUIDES AND MAP

If you fish or plan to fish in West Virginia, the following guides and maps will prove helpful and informative:

West Virginia Trout Fishing Guide
Special Catch and Release Trout Streams
"West Virginia Stream Map"

They can be obtained by writing to:
Dept. of Natural Resources
State Capitol
Charleston, W.Va. 25305

WORTH'S POP-UP AUTOMATIC TIP-UP

Ice fishermen can leave their lines unattended with Worth's Pop-Up magnetic tip-up, yet be able to tell at a distance when they've got a strike. With the line baited, the magnet-equipped spool is adjusted to hold the fluorescent orange signal rod and flag down inside the Pop-Up body.

When a fish strikes and the line begins to feed out, the magnet releases the spring-loaded rod inside the Pop-Up, signaling a strike. The spool has an exclusive finger socket for easy winding plus adjustable tension that permits the Pop-Up to be set light for panfish, medium for walleyes and pickerel, and heavy for lake trout or northern pike. On hard strikes, the spool winder acts as a brake to keep the spool from overrunning and fouling the line.

The Worth Pop-Up is made of space-age plastic that will not freeze, even in below-zero temperatures. Noncorrosive folding tripod legs keep the Pop-Up firmly in place, regardless of wind or snow. For more information write to:
The Worth Co.
P.O. Box 88
Stevens Points, Wis. 54481

LAND OF BIG PIKE

If you want to catch big northern pike, you can't go to a better place than Canada. Here in the provinces of Quebec, Ontario, Manitoba, and Saskatchewan you'll find most of the larger lakes and rivers filled with big pike. In the wilder areas these pike are so plentiful and unsophisticated that they'll grab almost any lure you cast, and you can catch as many pike as you want in one day. In fact, many anglers fishing these waters like to use spoons with a single hook because it takes too long and is too much trouble to remove treble hooks. Of course, even in Canada the smaller pike predominate, and most of those caught will run between 5 and 15 lbs., but pike in the 20- and occasionally 30-lb. class are taken from time to time.

STEELHEAD LIKE BRIGHT COLORS

When you are fishing for steelhead you can forget about matching insects or using the dull, gray, brown, black, and green patterns usually used for trout. Steelhead like their lures and flies on the gaudy side with their favorites the bright yellow, orange, pink, and red colors. Fluorescent colors that stand out in dark or murky waters are excellent. You can buy such fluorescent colors in paints in hobby or craft stores and paint your lures and fly bodies with them. Apply several coats, allowing each coat to dry before you apply the next. Even when using natural baits such as night crawlers or salmon eggs for steelhead, it's a good idea to tie bright-colored fluorescent yarn on the hook or leader right next to the bait.

DISAPPEARING LAKES

Some lakes in Florida drain away through large sinkholes, and then the local people scoop up thousands of bass, bream, and catfish left high and dry or in shallow pools. Such lakes may be dry for several seasons, then the water returns and fishing will start getting good again. Lake Jackson, located in the northern part of Florida, near Tallahassee, is such a disappearing lake. When it is filled it provides excellent fishing for big bass, with many of them weighing from 10 lbs. to 18 lbs.!

SMALLEST FISH

The smallest fish in the world is the pygmy dwarf goby (Pandaka pygmaea), which is found in Lake Buhi on Luzon in the Philippines. It reaches a length of about 10 mm., or $2/5$ in. You can hold a hundred of these tiny fish in the palm of your hand. Surprisingly, they make good eating if you make fishburgers out of them!

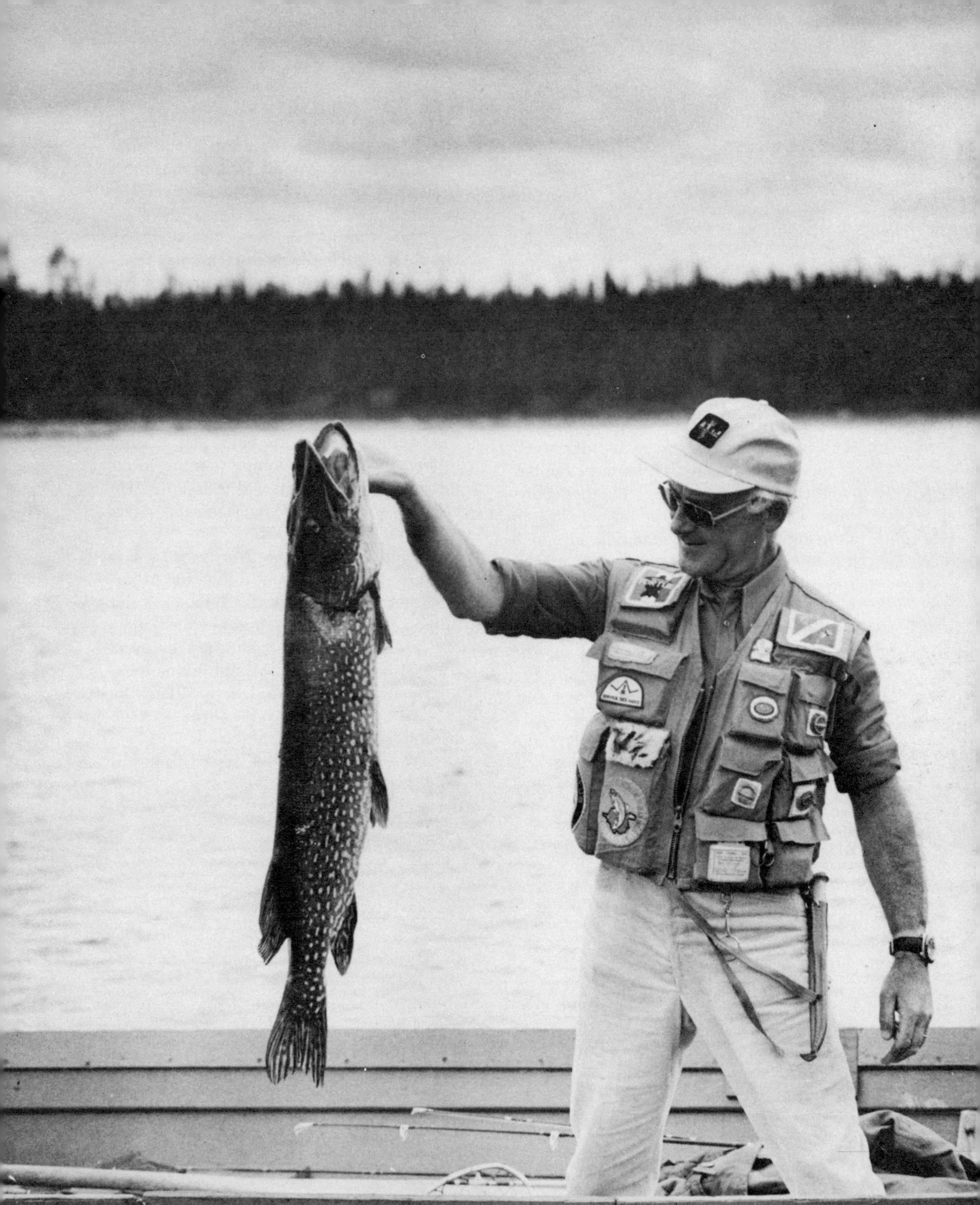

HERTER'S, INC.

This is one of the largest mail-order houses in the world catering to fishermen, hunters, campers, archers, boaters, and other sportsmen. They have one of the biggest stocks of fly-tying tools, fly-tying materials, lure-making parts, and components for making rods. They also carry many different kinds of hooks, lures, and various accessories used by fishermen. Their book on fly tying, spinning, and tackle making, and fly-tying dictionary is one of the most complete ever written on the subject. They put out a big catalog showing all these products, materials, and parts. The catalog costs $1.00, which is refundable if you order $10 or more from the company. For their catalog write to:
Herter's, Inc.
RFD 2, Interstate 90
Mitchell, S.D. 57301

NEW ENGLAND FISHING

Three paperback books have been published by the Stone Wall Press dealing with freshwater fishing in New England and the Northeast.

Trout Fishing in New England by Harold Blaisdell discusses techniques, tactics, and equipment as they apply to the streams, rivers, ponds, lakes, and coasts of New England in catching brook trout, rainbow trout, and brown trout.

Bass Fishing in New England by Bob Elliot covers fishing for small-mouth and large-mouth bass in New England waters. The author deals with baits and bottom fishing, fly fishing, spinning, casting, trolling, and other methods and techniques. He also lists some of the best lakes and rivers for bass in New England.

Salmon Fishing in the Northeast by Edward C. Janes tells about fishing for Atlantic salmon, landlocked salmon, coho salmon, and kokanee salmon in the waters of New England and Canada. He covers the best tackle, lures, flies, and fishing techniques and methods. And he mentions the best rivers and lakes where you can go salmon fishing.

Each of these books sell for $3.50 and is published by:
Stone Wall Press
19 Muzzey St.
Lexington, Mass. 02173

TRY THE "MINI" LURES

There are days when bass and other fish refuse to look at or hit the larger-sized lures or even regular-sized ones. On such days the fly rodder usually does best with his small flies and bugs. But if you use spinning or spin-casting tackle, try carrying an assortment of the smaller-sized plugs, spoons, spinners, and jigs, and even the shorter plastic worms. To cast these you will find an ultralight outfit best. But you can also carry an extra spool of line filled with 4-lb.-test and put this on your regular reel to cast the "mini" lures. You'll find such small lures best when the water is clean and clear and when the smaller fish are hitting. But don't be surprised if every so often a bigger bass grabs one of these small lures.

MIRRO-CRAFT 14 DEEP FISHERMAN

A good choice for anglers who want a rugged boat for big water is Mirro-Craft's 14 Deep Fisherman. With a tough .064-in.-thick hull bottom and .058-in.-thick sides, the 14 Deep Fisherman can take a real beating when the going gets rough. It has a broad, comfortable, 63-in. beam with a 30-in. bow depth and has an outboard rating for up to 35 hp. It weighs 202 lbs. and has a load capacity rating of 950 lbs. Standard features include four vinyl-coated aluminum unit seats, positive foam flotation, skidproof flecked-paint interior, oar sockets, transom handles, bow eye, and drain plug. For more information write to:
Mirro-Craft
Mirro Marine Div.
804 Pecor St.
Oconto, Wis. 54153

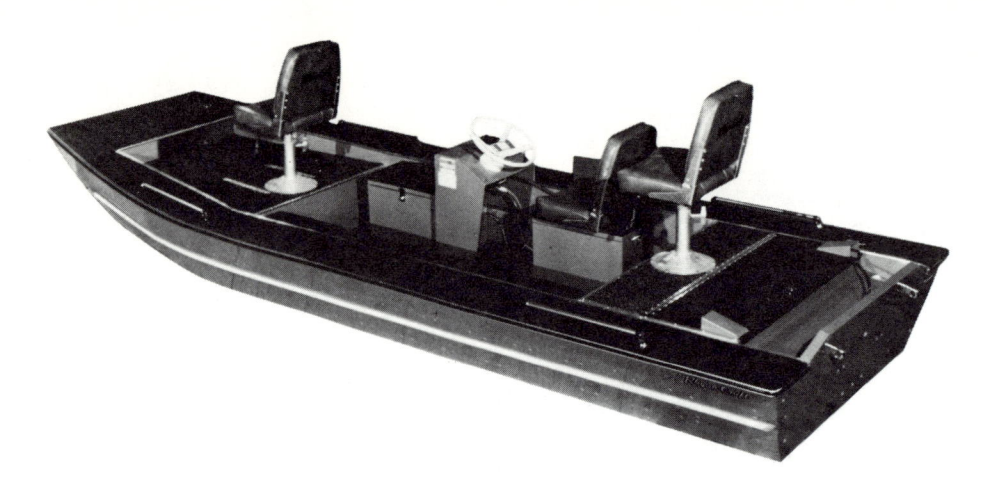

RHYAN-CRAFT ALUMINUM BASS BOATS

This company makes all-aluminum bass boats that are 16 ft. long and have a beam of 62 in. They offer two-seat and three-seat models with stick steering or mechanical steering. They have a 7-ft. rod box and two live wells. There are padded deluxe seats, turf carpets, running lights, handrails, bow storage, pedestal storage, and gas-resistant foam flotation. This company also makes a complete line of flat-bottomed aluminum boats from 10 ft. to 18 ft. in length. For their catalog showing all these boats write to:

Rhyan-Craft Boat Mfg. Co.
P.O. Box 1537
El Dorado, Ark. 71730

THE "N" FISHING LURES

Bill Norman has designed the "N" series of lures, which consist of the Little "N," the Baby "N," and the regular "N." This is a versatile lure with a true-to-life swimming action and a built-in fish-attracting rattle. It can be used as a top-water lure by letting it rest a few seconds after casting, then giving it a series of short, two-foot pulls with the rod, taking up the slack as it floats back to the surface. To make it run deep, you reel at a medium speed to get it down to 6 or 8 ft., and reel at a faster speed to make it reach 10 to 12 ft.

The "N" plugs are also made to run still deeper and are called Deep Little "N" and Deep Baby "N." These will dive to 10-to-20-ft. depths. Both plugs are available in many colors and finishes. For a complete catalog of lures and more information write to:

Norman Mfg. Co., Inc.
Hwy. 96 E., Drawer H
Greenwood, Ark. 72936

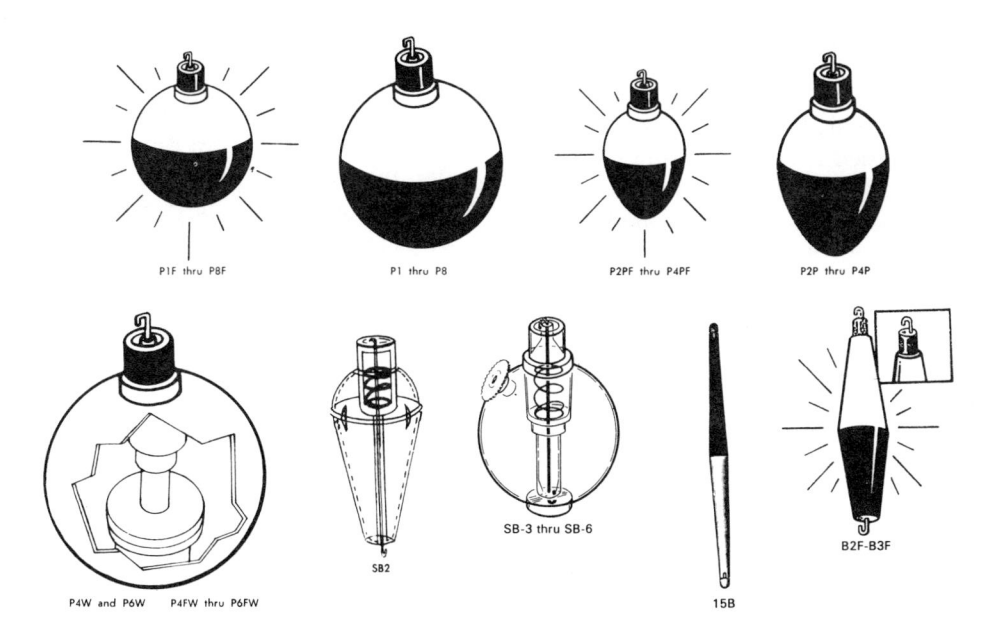

PLASTILITE FISHING FLOATS

This company makes many different kinds of fishing floats suitable for all kinds of fishing. They make round, brilliant red, and white floats, fluorescent floats, slim panfish-type floats, pencil-type floats, porcupine quill floats, clear plastic spinning and casting and still-fishing floats, and fillable spinning bubble floats. For a complete catalog or more information write to:
Plastilite Corp.
P.O. Box 12235, Florence Sta.
Omaha, Neb. 68112

JIFFY ICE SKIMMER

A new ice skimmer with easy ice-release feature is introduced by this manufacturer. For easy release of the ice buildup you simply tap the flat bottom of the Jiffy Ice Skimmer on the frozen lake surface, and the ice in the ladle of the ice skimmer will pop out to free all drain holes. It comes in two sizes: the Pike size with a 6-in.-diameter ladle and 20-in. handle, and the Bluegill size with 4¾-in.-diameter ladle and 18-in. handle. They are of all steel construction with a plated surface for long rust-free life. For more information write to:
Feldmann Engineering & Mfg. Co., Inc.
633 Monroe St.
Sheboygan Falls, Wis. 53085

TROUT UNLIMITED

Trout Unlimited was founded in 1959 by a group of Michigan anglers who were deeply concerned over the deterioration of trout fishing. It is a unique, national, non-profit, membership organization dedicated to the enhancement, preservation, and restoration of the nation's cold-water fishery resources. Tough, yet scientifically based, Trout Unlimited is geared for effective action. Today it has thousands of active members in chapters from coast to coast and in other countries. Trout Unlimited is organized on national, state, and local levels.

Trout Unlimited believes that what is good for trout, salmon, and steelhead is good for fishermen. It believes that wise management of our water resources is fundamental to the preservation and enhancement of our environment and fishery resources. It believes that sound land- and water-management practices and enjoyment of good fishing go hand in hand. It believes that only by preserving the kind of water quality vital to man can we preserve trout, salmon, and steelhead fishing.

If you wish to enroll as a member or find out more about the organization and the locations of the local chapters write to:
Trout Unlimited
4260 E. Evans Ave.
Denver, Colo. 80222

WALLEYES IN THE SUMMER

One of the most colorful fables circulated among the angling fraternity is that walleyes lose all their teeth in July and therefore are seldom caught. This is just not so, says the Nebraska Game Commission. Actually, the fishing gets a little tougher because the fish are on the move looking for a cool hangout during the hot weather. So the angler must use different techniques to cash in on the lunker walleye, but it can be done.

When the water turns warm in a reservoir, the walleyes cruise around in deep water and often settle in rocky areas that provide shade and coolness. The wise angler will move close in to a fairly steep, rocky shore and troll slowly in the moderately deep water. More lures will be lost and snags will be cussed, but as the old saying goes, "If you're not losing tackle, you're not catching fish."

If the reservoir lacks these prominent rocky areas, try sandy shoals late in the evening and after dark, which are feeding times for the popular walleye. Another favorite summertime trick is to locate a school by persistent trolling in likely areas until a walleye is caught. The spot of the catch should then be marked with an anchored float, and the boat passed repeatedly over the spot. Spoons and live bait with spinners are both good bets.

Walleyes congregate in small schools during certain parts of the year. Usually all fish in the school will be about the same size, and they will all have teeth—even in July.

Both Big and Super George can be fished over moss or weed beds very effectively. Hold rod tip high and buzz the lure over the weeds. Bass will dart from their ambush point and strike the lure as it passes over them.

TOM MANN'S "GEORGE" LURES

Tom Mann of Eufaula, Alabama, is a bass fishing expert who has also designed a variety of lures that he now makes in his own fishing tackle company. Among his most popular lures are the "Little George," "Big George," and "Super George." The "Little George" is the original lure, which has proven to be one of the world's great fishing lures. Over thirty different species of fish have been caught on this lure, and over five million have been sold. It comes in a wide variety of colors and in $\frac{1}{4}$-oz., $\frac{1}{2}$-oz., and $\frac{3}{4}$-oz. weights.

The "Big George" lure has proven to be one of the best vibrating baits of its kind. It is a perfect baitfish imitation and will catch bass and many gamefish species. This lure has excellent balance, can be cast a great distance, and has one of the best sound chambers of any lure. The "Big George" comes in a wide variety of colors plus a complete chrome series as well as a new crawfish series.

The "Super George" is recommended for stained or dingy water and will produce excellent catches when other lures will fail. The built-in sound chamber plus the vibrating tail spinner will attract bass as well as many other species of gamefish. This lure is designed to fish slowly and will produce well in cold water. It is excellent when fished over moss or weedbeds. It weighs $\frac{1}{2}$ oz.

A catalog and more information about these lures and other lures designed by Tom Mann can be obtained from:
Mann's Bait Co., Inc.
P.O. Box 604
Eufaula, Ala. 36027

PORTABLE TRANSOM MOUNT FOR DOWNRIGGERS

Downrigger fishing for the most part has been done on large, deep bodies of water from boats large enough to provide a mounting surface for downriggers.

Now, however, there is a way for fishermen to use downriggers on cartop aluminum and wood boats. Big Jon, Inc., offers a new Universal Transom Mount, which is predrilled and taped to fit all Big Jon downriggers and sideriggers.

Made of solid aluminum with anodized finish, the Big Jon Universal Transom Mount weighs 2¾ lbs. and fits transoms from ⅝ in. to 2¼ in. thickness. Angled to mount level on pitched transoms, the mount is secured by a ½-in.-diameter threaded rod with an easy-to-grip cast-aluminum knob and strong ⅜-in.-thick nylon clamp disk, which prevents damage to the inside of the transom. The mount also comes with four Big Jon knob screws to secure the downrigger to the universal mount. For easy transport from one boat to another or storage, the downrigger can be left right on the universal mount.

Available from leading marine and tackle dealers stocking Big Jon downriggers and deep trolling accessories, the Universal Transom Mount has a suggested retail price of $18. For more information you can write to:
Big Jon, Inc.
14393 Peninsula Dr.
Traverse City, Mich. 49684

EAGLE CLAW RODS

The Wright & McGill Company of Denver makes a complete line of freshwater rods for almost every kind of fishing. Their various brands include the Dencos, Favorites, Champions, Trailmasters and Packits, Deluxes, Sweethearts, Granger, and Pro Rods, with a wide variety at all price ranges. They make spin-casting and bait-casting rods, spinning rods, and fly rods. They also make many models for backpacking or easy carrying in up to six and eight sections. In all they have at least 250 different styles, sizes, lengths, actions, and function rods. For their catalog showing all these rods and other fishing tackle send $.25 to:
Wright & McGill Co.
P.O. Box 16011
Denver, Colo. 80216

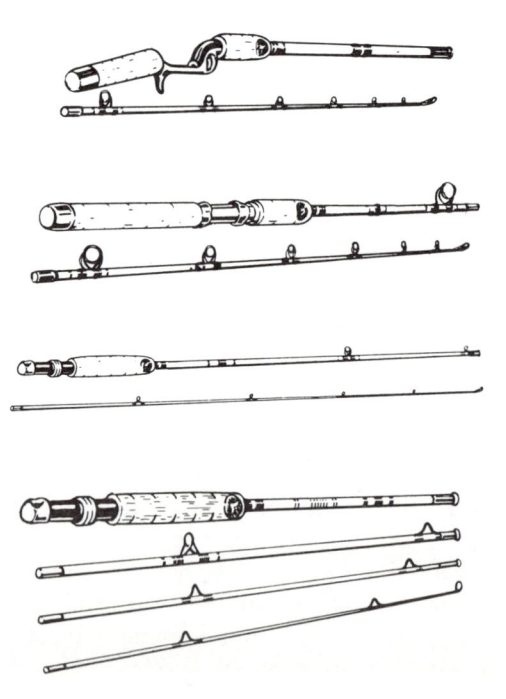

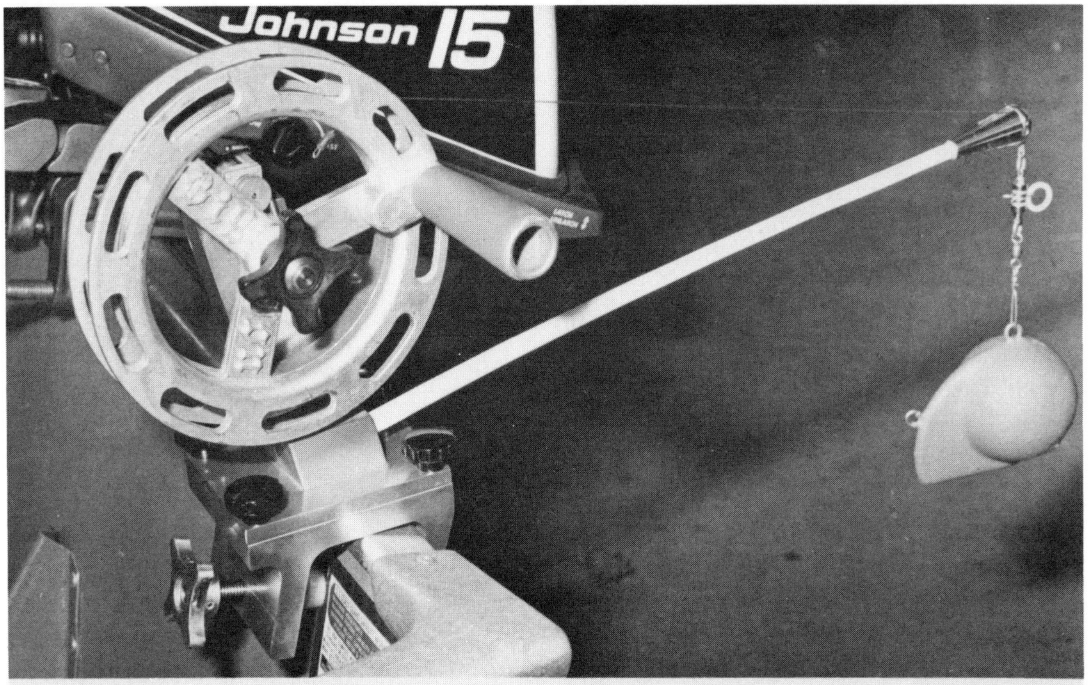
Johnson 15

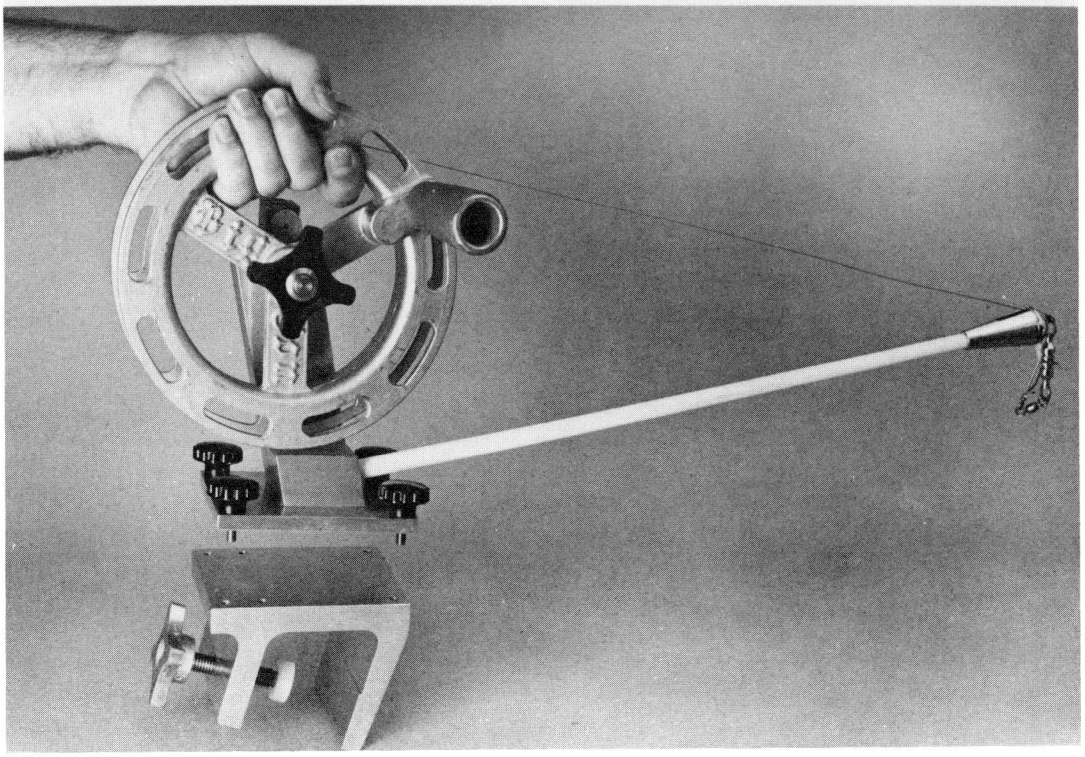

ADVENTURER TACKLE BOXES

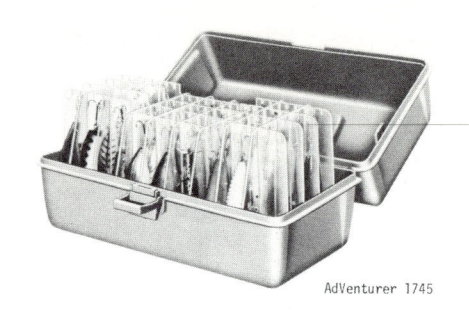

The Adventurer Tackle Boxes come in many models for freshwater and salt-water lures. The Adventurer 1745 has a clear plastic lift-out rack, which holds as many as forty-five lures. It is made in a raintight tongue and groove design and is rustproof. It is impervious to vinyl skirts and soft plastic lures.

The Adventurer 2233 comes with a front panel, which drops to permit use of three easy-sliding, interchangeable, removable drawers. The automatic cover latch guard prevents accidental spills. There is also space under the bottom drawer for reels and other tackle. For a catalog showing their complete line of tackle boxes write to:
Vlchek Plastics Co.
Middlefield, O. 44062

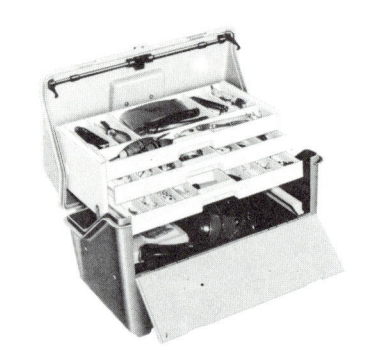

AdVenturer 1745

AdVenturer 2233

MCKENZIE DRIFT BOATS

There are two places where a white-water man needs a maintenance-free boat—in the river and out. He buys a boat for fun and fishing, not for work and worry. The McKenzie Alumaweld boats are designed and constructed for such care-free use. The structural integrity is based on years of professional experience and testing in whitewater rivers. There are no wooden seats or gunwales to deteriorate or require annual refinishing. Alumaweld boats are guaranteed against bottom and side puncture. There are more than five hundred of them in use, and none of them have been punctured, according to the company, mainly 6061-T6 Aluminum, a material used extensively in jet aircraft because of its optimum strength-to-weight ratio. The McKenzie drift boats come in 14-, 16-, and 18-ft. lengths and weigh from 195 lbs. to 325 lbs. For their catalog showing these and other boats they make write to:
Alumaweld
4665 Crater Lake Hwy.
Medford, Ore. 97501

"Candy Yazz" Curl Tail Worm

"Candy Yazz" Straight Tail Worm

"Floozy" Spinner Bait Featuring "Nasty" & "Feisty"

"Feisty" Tail

"Feisty" Liar Tail

Saltwater Jig-A-Lo and "Nasty" Skirt

"Nasty Spin"

"Nasty" Grub

Slip Sinker/Nasty/Candy Yass Worm

Saltwater Jig-A-Lo

Weedless Jig-A-Lo

Jig-A-Lo

"Shady Lady"

Nasty Slip Sinker

"Huzzy"

"Nasty" Skirt

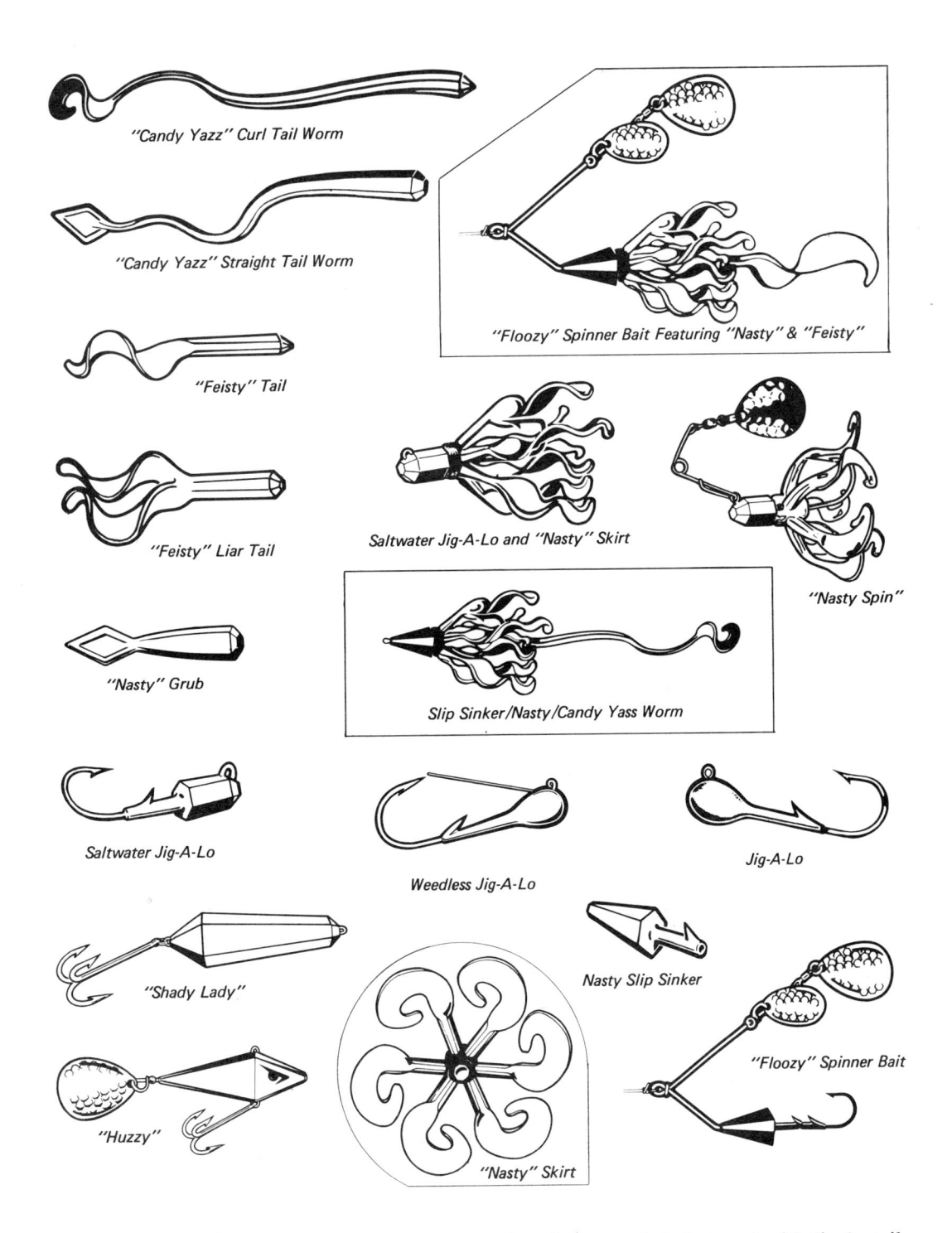

"Floozy" Spinner Bait

NASTY LURES

This company makes a variety of lures and has developed a special "Nasty" skirt, which can be added to spinner baits, jigs, slip sinkers, and plastic worms. This gives these lures more lively action, resulting in more strikes. They also make plastic worms in a hexagonal design and with lively tails. And they make special jig heads and slip sinkers, which can be used with skirts and plastic worms and lures. For their catalog showing all these and other lures write to:

Paducah Tackle Co., Inc.
P.O. Box 23
Paducah, Ky. 42001

SIBERIAN SALMON EGGS

The Siberian Salmon Egg Company is one of the biggest processors and packers of salmon eggs. Salmon eggs are an extremely effective bait for trout, steelhead, catfish, panfish, and other fish. The most popular salmon eggs are basically firm though not hard, and their processing has not changed much in thirty years. The biggest change has come with the advent of fluorescent dyes and the aromatic scents that can be incorporated into eggs during processing. Firmness is a quality that most fishermen like; the eggs thus processed have a good consistency that allows them to hang on the hook through casting and makes it possible to use them both in lakes and streams. Siberian in recent years has developed two heavily scented brands: the Cheezette eggs, which are both cheese-flavored and cheese-scented and have proved to be very popular, and the scented Giant brand, which is either dry- or oil-packed. For a little booklet *Catch More Trout!* and more information about their salmon eggs write to:
**Siberian Salmon Egg Co.
4660 E. Marginal Way S.
Seattle, Wash. 98134**

HUMMINBIRD MARK-IV DEPTH SOUNDER

The Humminbird Mark-IV depth sounder is designed to operate at boat speeds up to 55 mph., providing accurate depth readings without a loss of even the smallest target. The light, developed exclusively for Allied Sports, can be read in bright sunlight without a shade. The slim-line flash gives precise readings to as low as 1 ft., making the Mark-IV ideal for shallow-water use. Readings are guaranteed up to 200 ft. on a second sweep of the dial. Of special interest to the night fisherman is the Mark-IV's illuminated dial, with 0 to 100 ft. scale marked with wide-spaced 1-ft. calibrations for easy reading in the dark. Other features include waterproof connections, noise rejection, and an electrical-system monitor that incorporates a meter that shows at a glance if the unit's power source is sufficient to operate the depth sounder. Retail price of the Humminbird Mark-IV is $199.95. For more information write to:
**Allied Sports Co.
One Humminbird Lane
Eufaula, Ala. 36027**

KENTUCKY FISHING

With fifteen major impoundments, forty-two state-owned lakes, thousands of farm ponds, and rivers and streams with more miles of running water, Kentucky offers many fishing opportunities. The state has put out a little booklet called *Fishing in Kentucky,* which tells about the lakes, rivers, streams, farm ponds, crappie runs, white-bass runs, jump and jig fishing, float fishing, trolling, and other methods. The booklet also discusses the seasons, licenses, size limits, laws, facilities, and other fishing information. For your copy write to:
**Dept. of Fish and Wildlife Resources
Frankfort, Ky. 40601**

HUMMINBIRD
DEPTH SOUNDER
MARK IV
ALLIED SPORTS CO.
EUFAULA, ALABAMA

WATER GREMLIN SINKERS

The Water Gremlin Co. makes a full line of all kinds of sinkers for freshwater and salt-water fishing. Their Rubbercore sinkers, which are lined inside the slot with rubber, are popular with many freshwater anglers. They can be added to a leader or line in a jiffy and removed quickly too without damaging the leader or line. They come in sizes from $\frac{1}{16}$ oz. to $1\frac{1}{2}$ ozs. They also make dipsey or bell sinkers, sliding worm weights, egg sinkers, pinch-on sinkers, and split-shot sinkers. They also carry Bead Chain casting and trolling weights. Their sinkers can be bought in round, plastic sinker selector containers, which can be carried on your person or in a tackle box for instant use. For their catalog and more information about their sinkers and weights write to:
**Water Gremlin Co.
White Bear Lake, Minn. 55110**

SCIENTIFIC ANGLERS FLY LINES

Scientific Anglers offers one of the largest and most versatile selections of fly lines they have developed in recent years. Their wide choice of fly lines makes it possible for you to fit your rod with any number of different and helpful types of lines for every kind of fly fishing you will ever do. There are now, for example, sophisticated floating lines and sinking lines, floaters with sinking tips, shooting tapers and lines, weight-forward tapers, bug tapers, and also recent innovations such as the extrafast-sinking Wet Tip, Wet Belly, and Wet Head lines. For their catalog showing these lines as well as rods, reels, and tips on choosing the right fly lines and tackle write to:
**Scientific Anglers
P.O. Box 2001
Midland, Mich. 48640**

THE SOFT-HACKLED FLY

The book *The Soft-hackled Fly* by Sylvester Nemes is a trout fisherman's guide to a fly that is little known to the trout anglers in this country. The term "soft-hackled fly" is used generically throughout the book and applies to a class of wingless, sub-aqueous flies, the hackles of which come mostly from such birds as partridge, woodcock, grouse, snipe, and starling. The soft-hackled fly is not a new discovery. In fact, the author traces its history way back to Dame Juliana Berners, who included it on her list in 1496. Since then it has been used in England to the present day. The author has used soft-hackled flies on some of the finest trout streams in America. He gives detailed, step-by-step, illustrated instructions on tying the flies, advises how best to fish them, and offers highly reasonable explanations for their astonishing success, regardless of the season, geography, or local hatch. *The Soft-hackled Fly* sells for $7.95 in hard-cover and $4.95 in paperback. It is published by:

The Chatham Press
143 Sound Beach Ave.
Old Greenwich, Conn. 06870

TRIMARC FISHING RODS

The Trimarc Corp. makes both the regular two-piece fishing rods and the "Concealed Rods," which are telescopic fishing rods that slide down to short lengths. They make spinning, spin-casting, and bait-casting rods, fly rods, open-water rods, and combination rods. They also have still-fishing and ice and jigging rods. These vary in lengths and actions. For more information write to:

Trimarc Corp.
High Point Plaza
Hillside, Ill. 60162

95

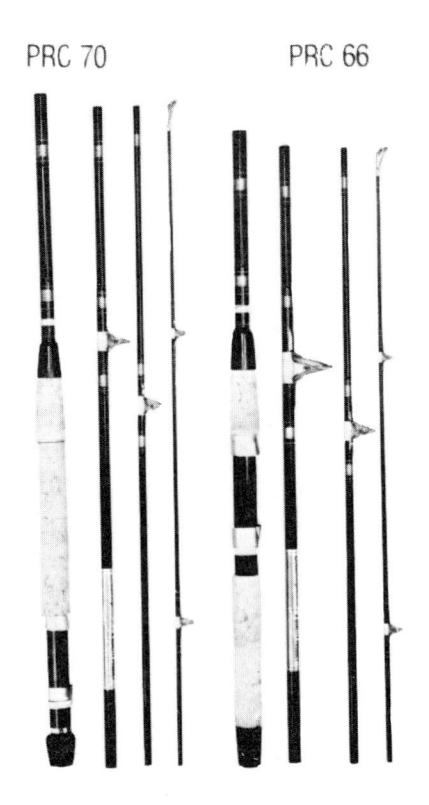

UMCO TACKLE BOXES

The Umco Corporation offers a tackle box for almost every fishing need. Some fishermen use only flies; others swear by plastic worms and jigs; and still others use plugs, spoons, and other freshwater and salt-water lures. Such a diversity among fishermen is one reason why many different kinds of tackle boxes are needed to fill specific needs and preferences. The Umco Corporation offers seventy-two different tackle boxes, one for virtually every fishing need. These are made of either rugged, lightweight Umcolite plastic or embossed aluminum. There are big and small boxes for plastic worms, spinner baits, and jigs, and larger boxes for plugs, big spoons, and salt-water lures. For their catalog showing all these tackle boxes write to:
Umco Corp.
P.O. Box 608
Watertown, Minn. 55388

SHAKESPEARE BACKPACKER RODS

Two new four-piece pack rods and a telescoping fly rod are available from Shakespeare. A 6-ft., 6-in. spinning rod, the PRS 66, has four guides and tip-top. The PRC 70 is a 7-ft. rod that has a convertible handle for using a spinning or fly reel. It has four guides and a tip-top.

Both rods are made of tubular rod blanks and are ferruleless. Guides and tip-top are of wire-framed stainless steel. The PRS 66 and PRC 70 have all-purpose action for casting 1/8-oz.-to-3/8-oz. lures or baits.

The new Shakespeare rods are only 18 in. when disassembled into four pieces for convenient backpacking or traveling. Both are dark brown with brown wraps over gold. For further information contact:
Fishing Tackle Div.
Shakespeare Co.
P.O. Box 246
Columbia, S.C. 29202

VIRGINIA FRESHWATER FISHING

There are two helpful guides available about Virginia's freshwater fishing and boating access to its water. One is called *Let's Go Freshwater Fishing in Virginia;* it tells where to go to fish the streams, rivers, reservoirs, and impoundments of the state. It also tells about the public fishing waters and when to go fishing in the various waters, and it has a map showing some of the most popular spots.

The other booklet is called *Boating Access to Virginia Waters,* and it has a large map showing all the major freshwater and salt-water boat-access points in the state. There's a listing giving the depth of the water, phone number, berths, storage, boats for rent, services, and fuel and repair facilities for boats at each spot. Both booklets are available from:
Virginia Game Commission
P.O. Box 11104
Richmond, Va. 23230

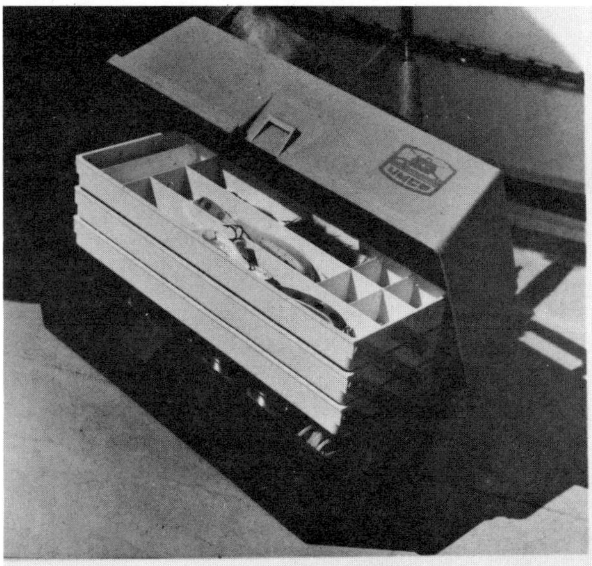

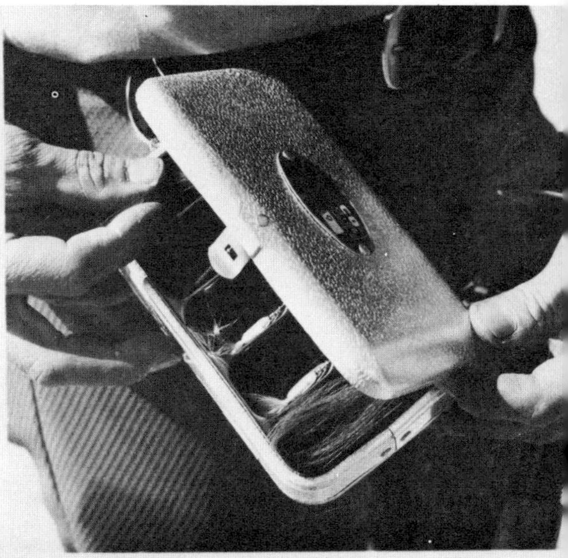

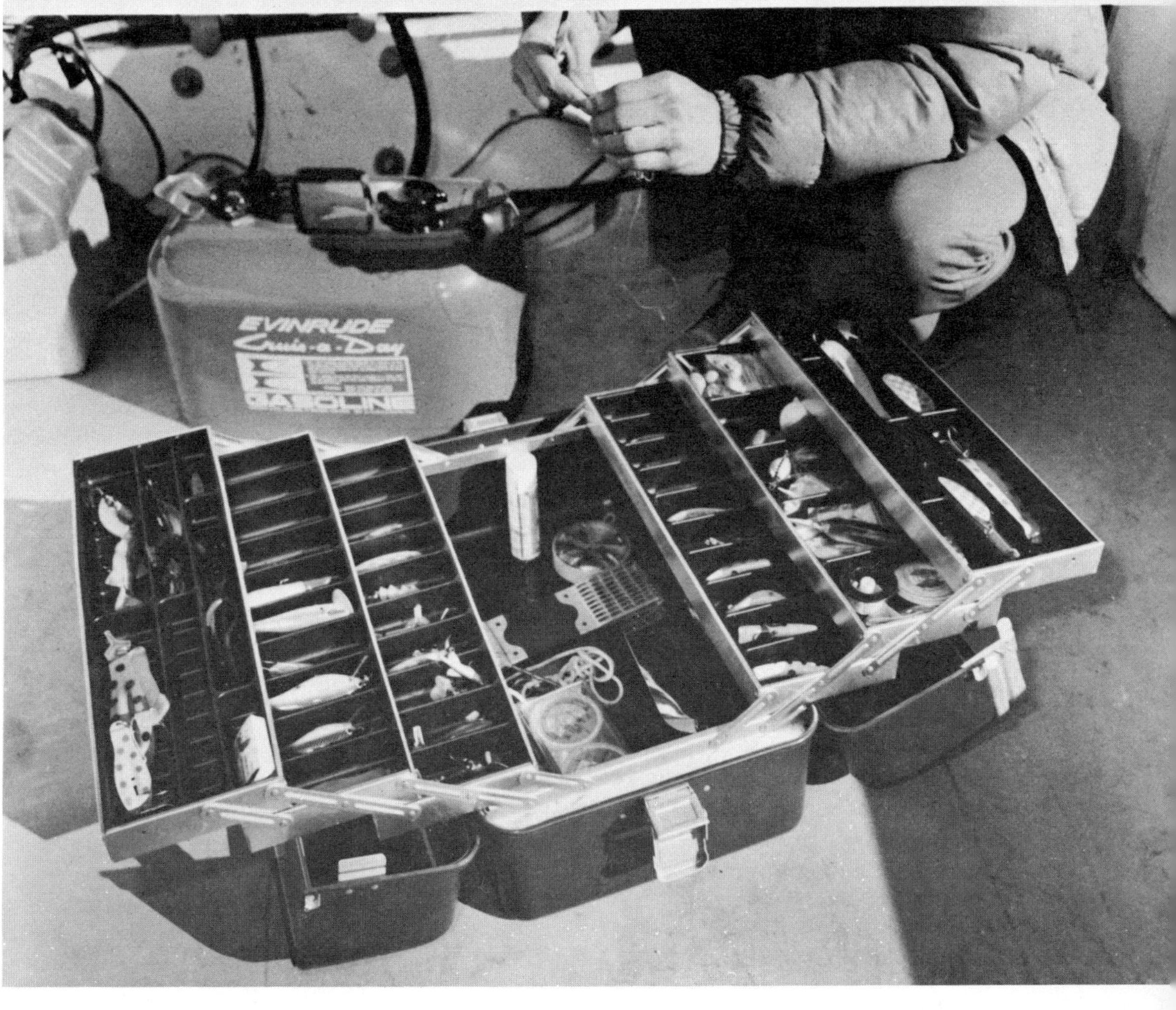
EVINRUDE
Cruis-a-Day
GASOLINE

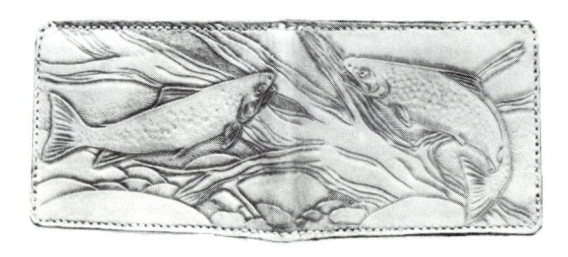

FISHERMAN'S LEATHER GIFTS

Sharon Weber makes handcrafted leather gifts especially created for anglers. She makes wallets, belts, key cases, key fobs, bookmarks, bookcovers, and many other items. These are engraved with hand-carved designs of flies, trout, ducks, game, and other wildlife. She uses top-grain cowhide and tools the leather so that it forms a relief. Some designs are also painted in colors. In fact, she will custom-make these leather goods and carve and paint your favorite fly or lure or other object if you send a sketch, illustration, or photo she can follow. For a booklet showing the leather gifts and products she makes write to:
Sharon Weber
P.O. Box 133
Weston, Vt. 05161

FREE FISHING FILMS

The Lou J. Eppinger Mfg. Co., makers of the famous Dardevle spoons, offers several fishing films that can be shown at fishing clubs and sportsmen's groups on meeting nights. They deal with such freshwater fish and fishing as walleyes, pike, grayling, lake trout, coho salmon, and Arctic char, and salt-water fish such as salmon, tarpon, and bonefish. The films are free, and you can obtain a list of them from:
Film Lending Dept.
Lou J. Eppinger Mfg. Co.
6340 Schaefer Hwy.
Dearborn, Mich. 48126

FISH FRESHWATER NOVA SCOTIA

A little booklet *Fish Freshwater Nova Scotia* is available listing the laws, regulations, seasons, and the best rivers, lakes, and brooks for the popular gamefish in that province. It covers Atlantic salmon, landlocked salmon, brook trout, rainbow trout, brown trout, lake trout, and shad. It is available from:
Dept. of Tourism
P.O. Box 456
1649 Hollis St.
Halifax, N.S.
Canada B3J 2R5

AQUABUG AND SUPERBUG MOTORS

These outboard motors are extralight in weight, with the Aquabug weighing only 11 lbs., and the Superbug going to 18 lbs. The Aquabug is a 1.2-hp. motor, while the Superbug develops from 2.5 hp. to 3 hp. Both motors have stainless-steel roller bearings on top and bottom of the crankshaft, another roller bearing on the drive shaft, and yet another on the prop shaft. This results in a smooth, easy-starting motor that reduces friction losses to a minimum. The Aquabug sells for $165, and the Superbug sells for $235. For more information and a brochure write to:
Aquabug International, Inc.
P.O. Box 61
Lawrence, N.Y. 11559

STINGRAY TROLLING SINKER

The Stingray Trolling Sinker is designed to take a bait or lure down to various depths with less weight. It has a hydrofoil design that makes it dive when it is trolled. Yet it offers less resistance while playing and landing a fish. It comes in six basic sizes, from $1/3$ oz. to $5\tfrac{1}{4}$ ozs. It can be utilized on many different kinds of rigs for both freshwater and salt-water fishing. For more information write to:
Ideal Fishing Float Co.
2001 E. Franklin St.
Richmond, Va. 23223

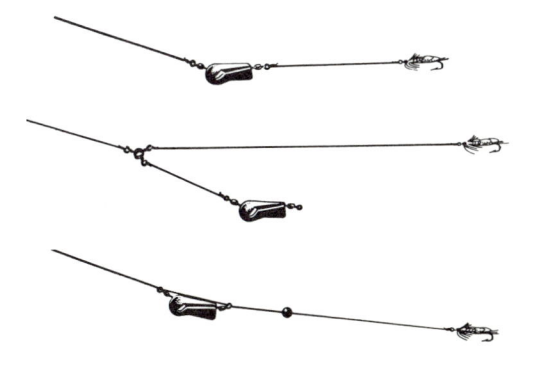

99

GARCIA MITCHELL 300

The Garcia Mitchell 300 spinning reel has been on the market now for more than twenty-five years and is still a popular choice with many freshwater anglers. Of course, dozens of improvements have been made through the years, such as two oilite bushings supporting the maingear shaft; a redesigned drag knob to make adjustments easier; an anti-inertia brake; and a Teflon drag. The 300 comes in several different models, including left-hand versions and a gold-plated-trim presentation model. Their combined *Fishing Annual* and catalog showing this and other reels and tackle costs $1.50 from:
The Garcia Corp.
329 Alfred Ave.
Teaneck, N.J. 07666

LEADER STRAIGHTENER

The D'Curl is a custom-crafted leather holder for two silicone-treated industrial rubber pads. When the leader is drawn between the two pads, heat and gentle stretching occurs. This heat and gentle stretching take the curl out of the leader and remove the high shine. All mono-type leaders have a built-in memory. When stored in a coil or on a reel, they stay in coils. Only by warming and stretching can you straighten out the coils. This leader straightener can be pinned to your vest for easy use and handling.

The same company also makes Hi & Dry fly flotant, which combines five chemicals into a permanent waterproof dressing for dry flies. It resists washing off and lasts for a long time. The bottle can be pinned to your vest in a leather holder for handy use. This same company also makes other interesting and unique items for the fly fisherman. For more information about them write to:
Laggies Fish Catching Co.
7059 Varna Ave.
North Hollywood, Calif. 91605

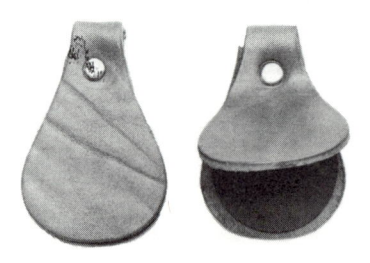

100

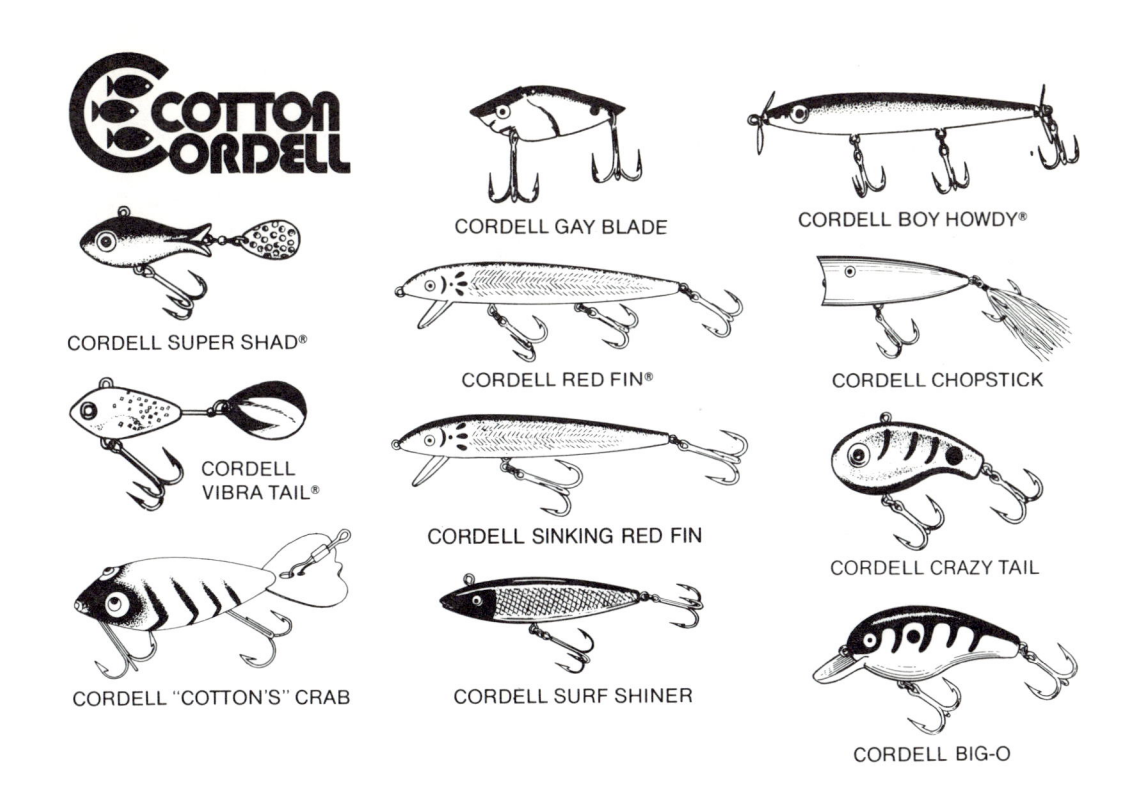

COTTON CORDELL LURES

The Cotton Cordell Tackle Co. makes a wide variety of fishing lures for both freshwater and salt-water fishing. They make plugs, spoons, metal lures, spinner baits, jigs, plastic worms, eels, and grubs. They also sell a spinner bait kit, with which you can make your own spinner baits. For more information write to:

Cotton Cordell Tackle Co.
P.O. Box 2020
Hot Springs, Ark. 71901

SUGAR WEIGHT

To cast a light bait out a good distance without having a sinker on the line, use an ordinary lump of sugar instead. Tie this lump of sugar near the hook and cast it out. It will sink a few feet but will then dissolve, and the bait will have a natural action in the water free from any weight. And when you hook a fish you can fight it on a free line.

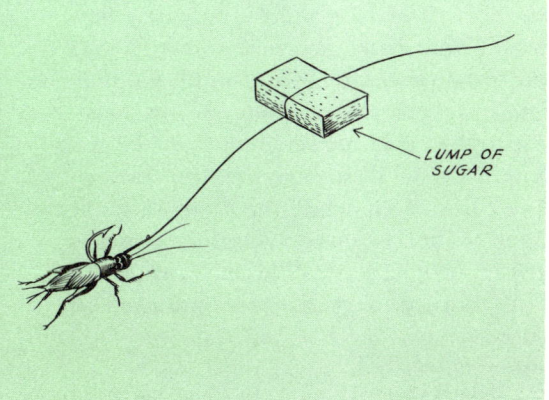

101

AVON INFLATABLE BOAT

For those who want the enjoyment of boating and fishing but have a storage problem, there is an Avon inflatable. Built for hard use, Avon inflatables offer advantages over rigid boats that have to be car-topped or trailered. Avon inflatables are compact enough to be stowed in a car trunk, a camper, aircraft, or larger boat, and they can be readied quickly for use. Though lightweight and easily carried to the water, Avon inflatables are ruggedly built, with nylon-reinforced fabric coated with a hypalon-based material that is particularly resistant to abrasion and the effects of gasoline, oil, and sunlight.

From small models to large ones that will handle an outboard motor powerful enough to ski behind, Avon inflatables are all designed with a minumum of three flotation chambers and come equipped with a repair kit, oarlocks, hand/foot bellows, and a heavy rubbing strake all around the boat.

Other features, either standard or optional, include mariné-ply floors, CO_2 emergency inflation, bowdodgers, oars, windscreen, remote steering controls, inflatable seats and backrests, pressure gauge, and transport wheels. Avon inflatables are so stable that standing on the buoyancy tube of even the smallest model won't capsize it.

Made in Great Britain, Avon inflatables are distributed throughout the United States and Canada. Information on the complete line is available from:
Inland Marine Co.
79 E. Jackson St.
Wilkes-Barre, Pa. 18701

LIVEWELL AERATOR KIT

The PAR Livewell Aerator Kit can be used in your boat to keep your minnows or fish alive by maintaining water temperature and oxygen content of the water in your livewell or bait tank. There is fast, simple installation, with a telescoping transom tube fitting included. There is ample capacity for two livewells, since the addition of a "Y" fitting in the hose from the pump allows you to aerate two tanks simultaneously. You have fully adjustable flow control—an easily accessible valve allows you to adjust the flow to control aeration. You have ease of maintenance—a twist-lock replaceable power unit can be removed without disturbing the thru transom installation, even while the boat is in the water. The Livewell Aerator operates quietly, without any vibration. Price of the aerator kit is $29.95. For more information write to:
Jabsco Products ITT
1485 Dale Way
Costa Mesa, Calif. 92626

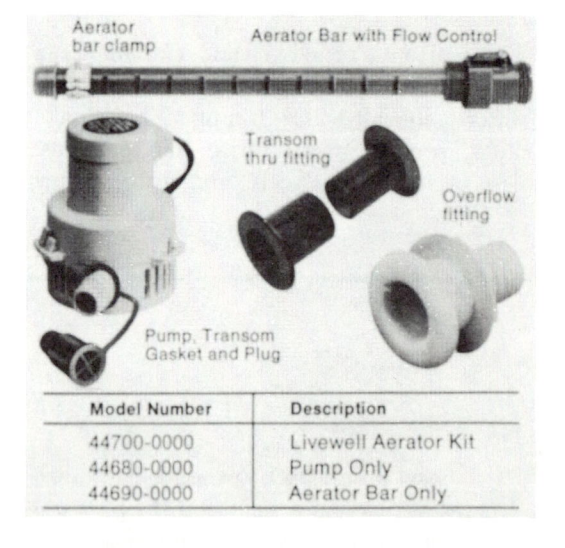

Model Number	Description
44700-0000	Livewell Aerator Kit
44680-0000	Pump Only
44690-0000	Aerator Bar Only

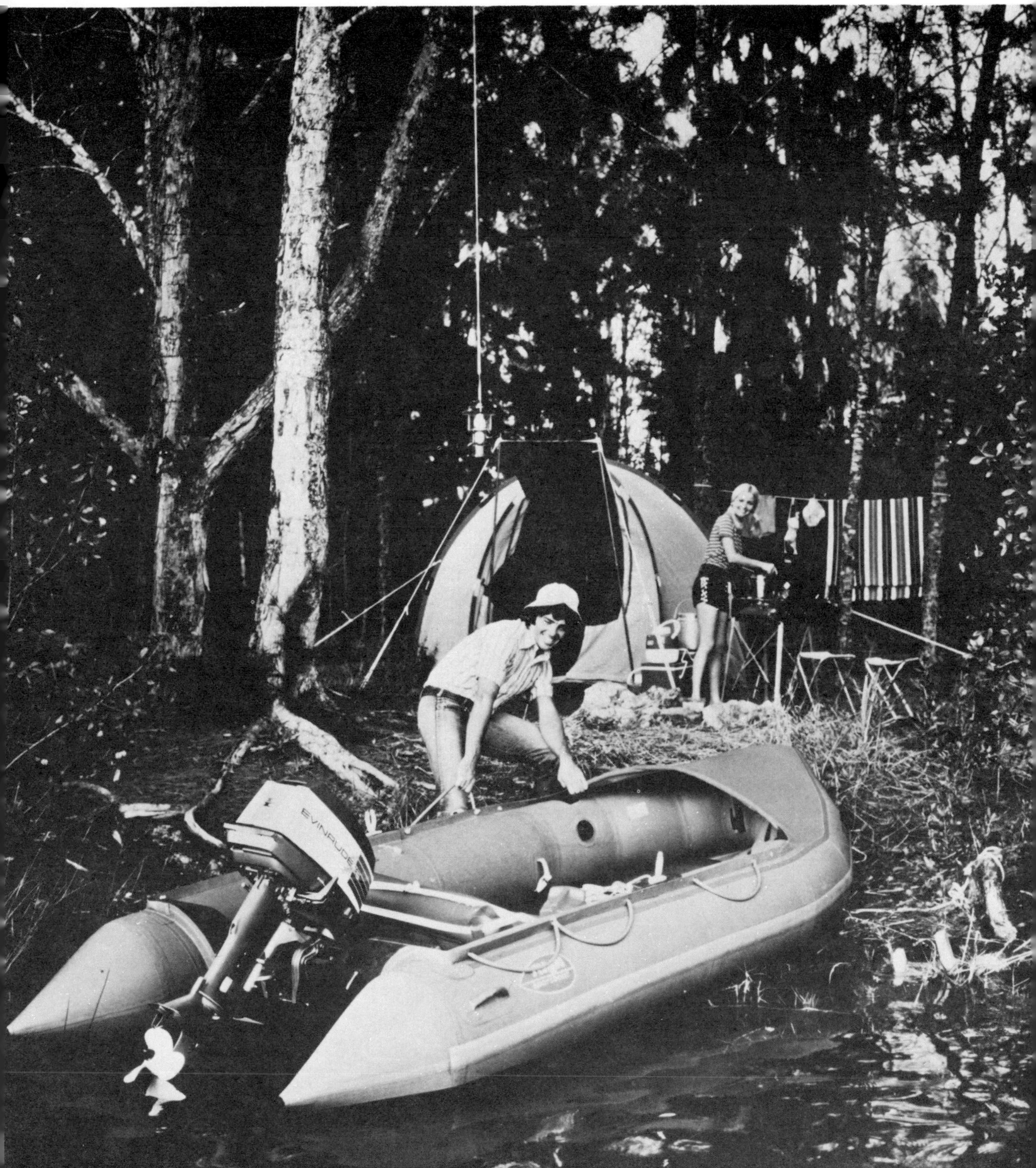
EVINRUDE

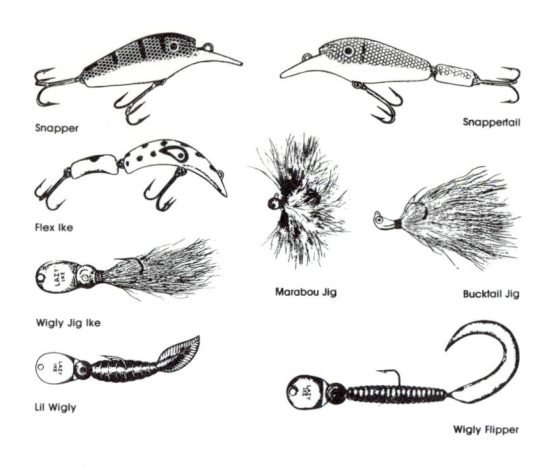

LAZY IKE LURES

Besides their famous banana-shaped Lazy Ike lure, this company also makes a wide variety of other lures for freshwater and salt-water fishing, including other plugs, spinners, jigs, and plastic worms and grubs. They come in various sizes, shapes, weights, and colors.

They have also published a small booklet called *The Lure of Fishing*, which tells how to use their lures; fish and their habits; fly-casting, spinning and bait-casting tackle; trolling; locating fish; freshwater world records; and other fishing facts and information. For a copy of this booklet and the latest catalog showing their lures send $.50 to:

**Lazy Ike Corp.
Fort Dodge, Ia. 50501**

BAIT CANTEEN

The Oberlin Canteen Co., makes several Bait Canteens for keeping worms, hellgrammites, soft-shelled crayfish, lizards, and other baits alive. The Bait Canteen works by having the moisture seep through the porous fiberboard walls. As it hits the air, it evaporates, taking with it heat from the interior of the box. This leaves the inside of the box cool and humid, which is the natural condition under which most baits live. Their Model E Bait Canteen shown here opens at either end, thus keeping the bait on top and easy to reach. For more information write to:

**The Oberlin Canteen Co.
Oberlin, O. 44074**

FISHING LURE HOLDER

Put a few small blocks of styrofoam in your tackle box. They make excellent fishing lure holders for small lures such as flies, spinners, spoons, and jigs. Just bury the hook in the styrofoam, and the lures will be ready for instant use.

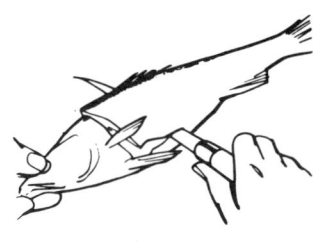

1. Make first cut just behind the gills. Slice down to the bone, then, without removing blade, turn it and slice straight along backbone . . .

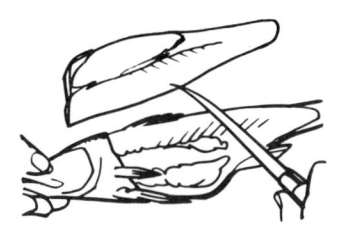

2. . . . to the tail. Note that the fillet has been cut away from the rest of the fish. After slicing fillet off at tail, turn fish over and repeat procedure on the other side.

3. With both sides removed, you have cut away both fillets without disturbing fish's entrails. This is the neatest and fastest way to prepare fish. Now to finish the fillets . . .

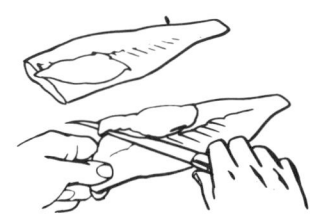

4. Next step is to remove the rib section. Again, a sharp, flexible knife is important to avoid wasting meat. Insert blade close to rib bones and slice entire section away. This should be done before skin is removed to keep waste to a minimum.

5. Removing the skin from each fillet is simply a matter of inserting the knife at the tail and "cutting" the meat from the skin. Start cut ½ inch from tail end of skin, allowing wedge for best grip. With the proper knife, like the "Fish 'N Fillet," it's easily done.

6. Here is each fillet, ready for the pan, or freezer. Note there is no waste. Remember not to overwash fillets. This will preserve tasty juices and keep meat in its firm natural state.

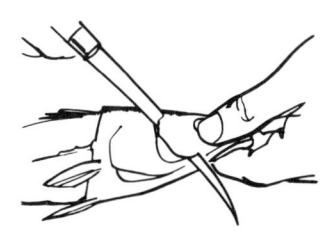

7. Cutting out the "cheeks" is the next important step. Few fishermen know that cheeks are the filet mignon of the fish. Though small, they're tasty and well worth saving.

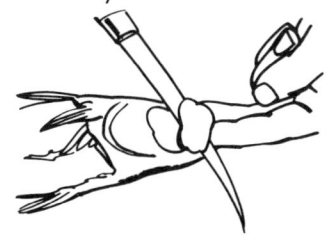

8. Slice into cheek where indicated then "scoop out" meat with blade, peeling away skin. Repeat on the other side. Many fishermen save cheeks until they have accumulated enough for a real gourmet's delight.

9. Here are all parts of the fish after you've finished. Note fish head, entrails, spine, tail and fins stay intact. This is the neatest way to prepare most game fish and, once you've mastered these few steps, the easiest.

HOW TO FILLET A FISH

The Normark Corporation, which sells the famous Rapala lures, also has fillet knives that feature the traditional Laplander knife design with curved flexible European stainless-steel blades hand-ground to stay razor sharp through long, hard use. Each knife comes with a fine tooled-leather sheath. The handles are reinforced birch. The Rapala Fillet knives come in 4-in., 6-in., and the new big-fish 9-in. models. To find out about these knives, how to use them, and how to use the Rapala lures, send $.25 for their booklet *Proven Fishing Methods and How to Fillet Fish* to:
Normark Corp.
1710 E. 78th St.
Minneapolis, Minn. 55423

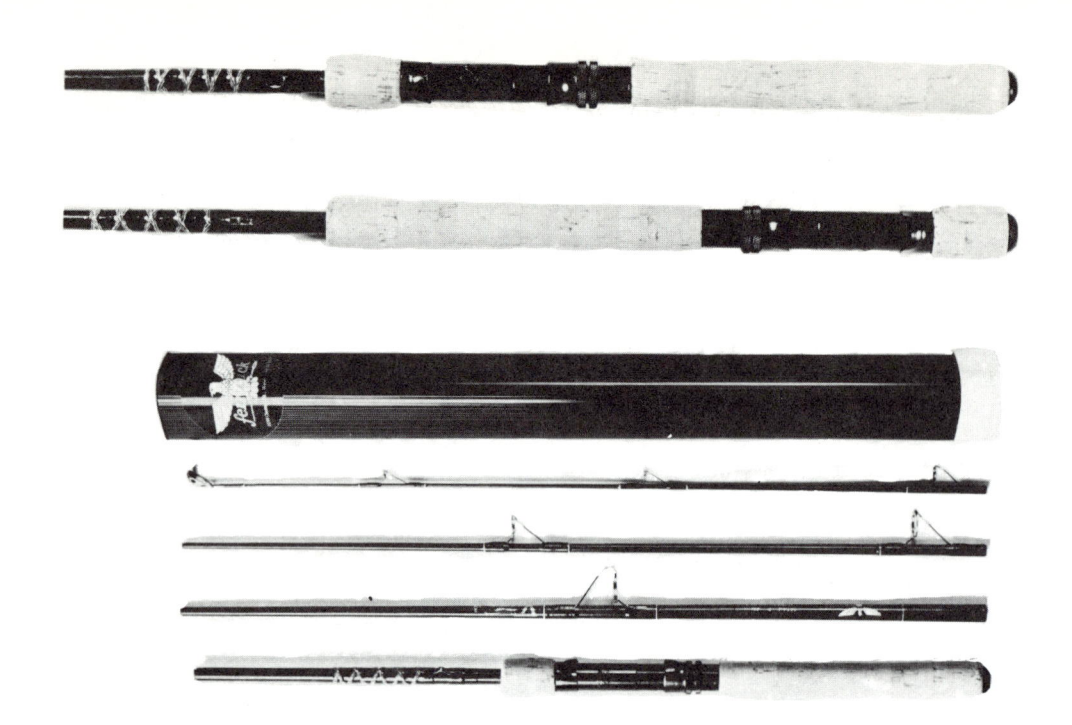

FENWICK VOYAGEUR RODS

Fenwick makes several Voyageur rods that slip easily into a backpack, a small canoe space, the family trailer or houseboat, or into airline luggage. Like most Fenwick rods, they have the Feralite ferrule design, which eliminates the heavy metal ferrules that add weight and interrupt the smooth power curve on most rods. The Voyageur fly rods range from 7½ ft. to 8½ ft. The spinning rods range from 5-ft., 9-in. to 7-ft. models or from ultralight to bass and light salt-water types. They also make two Fly/Spin Combo rods, each with a reversible handle so that it can be used for fly fishing or spinning. Their catalog showing these and other rods and tackle they make costs $.25 from:
Fenwick
P.O. Box 729
Westminster, Calif. 92683

SASKATCHEWAN FISHING

If you would like to fish in Saskatchewan, Canada, there are two publications which should help you. One is called *Fishing Saskatchewan;* this is a colorful pamphlet describing where to fish and what species are available. There is general information on licenses, maps, regulations, seasons, accommodations, and campgrounds, and fly-in fishing is included.

The other folder is called *Angler's Guide;* this gives the latest information on license fees, fishing rules, regulations, district offices, species of fish, where to fish, and management areas. Both publications can be obtained from:
Information Div., Extension Services Branch
Tourism and Renewable Resources
P.O. Box 7105
Regina, Sask.
Canada S4P 0B5

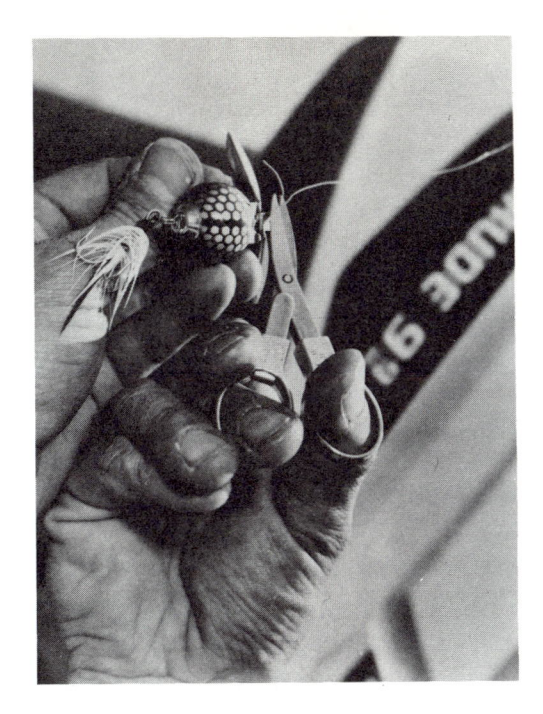

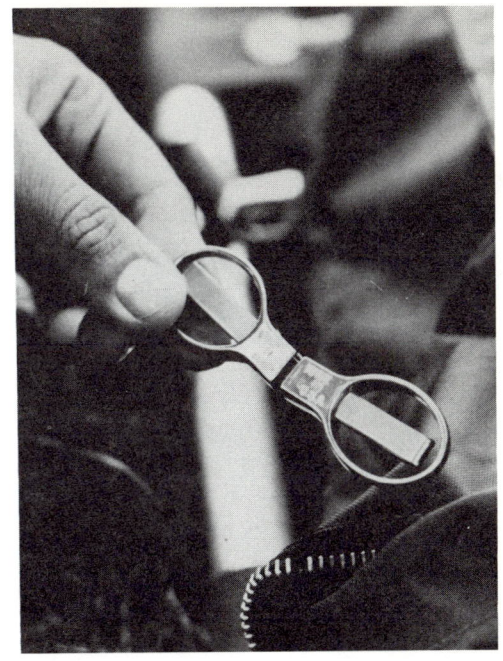

FOLDING SCISSORS

The fisherman who wants to carry a small pair of scissors that fold and take up little room will find the Slip-N-Snip folding scissors handy. They can be used for trimming flies, cutting leaders or lines, or for other uses. They are made of stainless surgical-steel blades, chrome-plated handles and can be obtained in a gift box. For more information write to:
K-Mac & Co.
15404 Dooley Rd.
Addison, Tex. 75001

SPEED SPOOL CASTING REEL

The Lew Childre Speed Spool casting reel was designed especially for the black-bass fisherman and the light-tackle salt-water angler. It has a low profile and knob-free end plate, which fit the fisherman's hand comfortably. It's a high-speed reel and very light in weight. The spool is narrow and has a greater diameter than ordinary reels. The spool starts fast and stops quickly to avoid overruns. The level wind on this reel disengages for the cast, and the level-wind guide itself is a Fugi diamond-polished Hard Speed Guide. It reduces line wear and allows longer casts than reels with conventional level-wind mechanisms. For more information write to:
Lew Childre & Sons, Inc.
P.O. Box 535
Foley, Ala. 36535

107

HANDY PLASTIC BOTTLES

The plastic bottles and containers used to hold detergents, cleaners, and other liquids can be used by fishermen in different ways. The larger ones with handles make good markers or buoys to mark a good fishing spot. Here you tie a line to the handle and a sinker or weight on the end of the line. Then wind the line around the bottle and keep it handy in your boat. When you find a good fishing spot while trolling, throw it overboard to mark the spot.

You can also cut the top off a plastic bottle and use the bottom half to hold sinkers, floats, lures, or even baits such as worms.

BIG CATCH BY LITTLE GIRL

Melissa Woodworth, who was only eight years old, was fishing in Muskegon, Michigan, with her brother and father when a big fish grabbed her line and she had her hands full. "I thought it was a whale!" the little girl said. "I heard it splash out there and it felt very heavy. I yelled out loud for Daddy."

Finally, after a terrific struggle, they succeeded in landing the big fish. It was a 28-lb., 14-oz. king salmon. "Look at it," Melissa cried. "You can see it's a whale!"

Both the brother and father could see the big salmon lying on the ground. But little Melissa could not. She lost her sight a year earlier when she had a brain tumor removed and is now totally blind. But that doesn't stop her from fishing, and according to her father she has the special touch of the blind person and knows how to hook and catch fish.

THE DEADLY MARABOU

There's something about the action and looks of a marabou streamer fly that drives freshwater and salt-water fish wild and makes them chase and hit it. Most likely it's the soft, fluttering movement of the stork feathers that makes it look alive and irresistible. But even big, educated trout will tear into a marabou when they refuse other flies or lures. The white and yellow and black marabou streamers are the most effective colors to use.

BLUEGILLS ON PLASTIC WORMS

You can catch big bluegills on plastic worms, but not the big ones you use for bass. Instead, you get the small, thin, plastic worms and cut the tail off to a length of 1¼ in. Then you run a No. 10 hook through the worm, leaving a bit of the tail to dangle. Use white, yellow, pink, orange, or light-green worms. Cast the worm out with a fly rod and let it sink deep, then retrieve it slowly in short jerks.

MACARONI CARP BAIT

You can have all the carp bait you want quickly and easily by using elbow macaroni. Bring a pan or pot of water to boil, then drop in a handful of the elbow macaroni. Boil them for about three minutes and then drain. Keep the macaroni in a plastic container until used. Then string two or three of the macaronis on the shank and bend of a hook.

ALABAMA FISHING

There are several booklets and reprints available telling about Alabama's fishing and its fishing spots. They are as follows:

Recreation on TVA Lakes
State-owned and -managed Public Fishing Lakes
Fishing Alabama's Small Streams
Float Fishing on the Sipsey River
Fishing Alabama's Bays and Tidal Streams

These publications are available from:
State of Alabama
Bureau of Publicity and Information
Montgomery, Ala. 36104

ROYAL BONNYL II LINE

This is the monofilament line sold by the Garcia Corporation. It has been improved in recent years with a tough new finish that makes it resistant to abrasion from rocks, submerged logs, and other abuse that a hard-working line is subjected to. It also stands up well to guide wear—a major cause of line wear and failure. But despite the tough exterior, the line is soft and limp to make it cast well and remain controllable. It has a thin diameter and comes in two colors—classic brown and high-visibility yellow. It is made in tests from 2 lbs. to 50 lbs. For more information write to:
The Garcia Corp.
329 Alfred Ave.
Teaneck, N.J. 07666

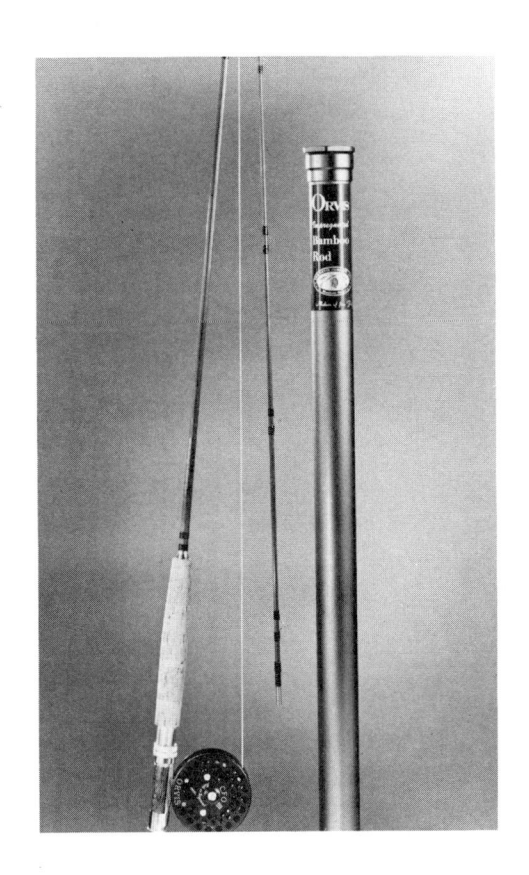

ORVIS FLY RODS

The Orvis Company of Manchester, Vermont, has been making fine fly rods for a long time. Their impregnated bamboo rods, such as the Battenkill series, range from 6½-ft. to 8½-ft. models to take Nos. 5, 6, 7, and 8 fly lines. They come in two and three pieces. They also make impregnated bamboo rods in other series and special-function rods for lightweight lines. These range from ultralight 5-ft., 9-in. models up to 7-ft., 9-in. rods. Orvis also has a line of glass rods and graphite rods for every kind of freshwater and salt-water fly fishing. And they make a complete line of spinning rods. You can also get rod kits to build your own rod. Their catalog shows all these rods as well as other fishing tackle, and clothing and accessories. Write to:
The Orvis Co., Inc.
Manchester, Vt. 05254

BYRD UNIVERSAL ROD HOLDERS

These rod holders hold different-size rods and can be mounted almost anywhere to hold fishing rods in a boat, camper, trailer, station wagon, or den. The tournament design lets you remove or store any rod instantly with one hand. The exclusive center-lock support secures the rod in the roughest running conditions. The rod racks are completely adjustable after mounting to accommodate almost any combination of rods and reels. They come in two-pack and four-pack models. For more information you can write to:
Byrd Industries, Inc.
201 Rock Industrial Park Dr.
Bridgeton, Mo. 63044

LAKE MICHIGAN COHO FISHING

When the coho salmon start running in Lake Michigan sometime in the spring, thousands of anglers descend on this lake to fish for the big, wild, silvery fish. Some anglers fish from shore and piers and docks, but most of the salmon are caught from boats by trolling at various depths.

The amazing thing about this sport fishery is that it is relatively new. Up until 1966 there were no coho salmon in Lake Michigan. In that year the first salmon were planted in creeks and rivers feeding into the big lake. Results were fast and dramatic—only 90 days from stocking, the 5-in. salmon had grown to 15 in. and weighed 1¼ lbs. Evidently the abundance of alewives and smelt in Lake Michigan provided plenty of food for the coho, and they ate and grew fast.

A year or two later the coho were so big and plentiful that they attracted anglers from all over Michigan and neighboring states and even from other parts of the country. They come in the spring when coho are caught in shallow water near shore and you can troll just below the surface down to 10 or 15 ft. Later on as the season advances during the summer and fall, coho follow the smelt and alewives into deeper water, and here trolling in depths from 40 to 100 ft. may be necessary a good distance from shore. Lead core and Monel wire lines and weights and downriggers are all used to get down to these depths. The best lures are spoons, spinners, plugs, jigs, and sewn-on natural baitfish such as alewives and smelt. If you want to find out more about this fishing write to:
Michigan Dept. of Natural Resources
Stevens T. Mason Bldg.
Lansing, Mich. 48926

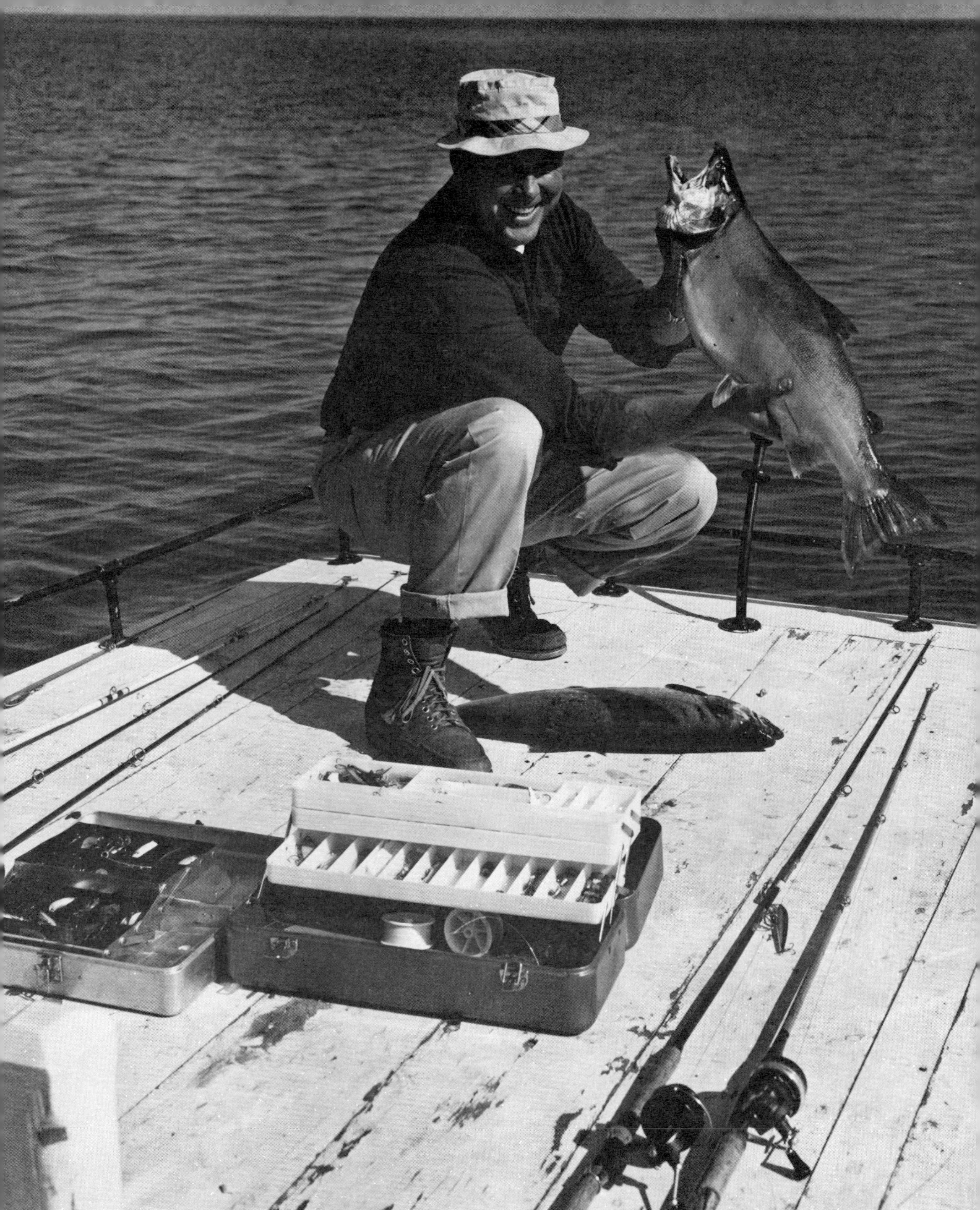

CISCO KID LURES

The Cisco Kid lures are designed for freshwater and salt-water fishing and come in top-water, underwater, shallow-running and deep-running models. The smaller sizes are used for bass, pickerel, and walleyes. The larger sizes are used for pike, muskies, lake trout, and salmon. These larger sizes are also widely used in salt water for sea trout, snook, tarpon, king mackerel, and other fish. For a booklet called *Fishing Tips* and a brochure showing their entire line of lures write to:
Cisco Kid Tackle, Inc.
2630 N.W. First Ave.
Boca Raton, Fla. 33432

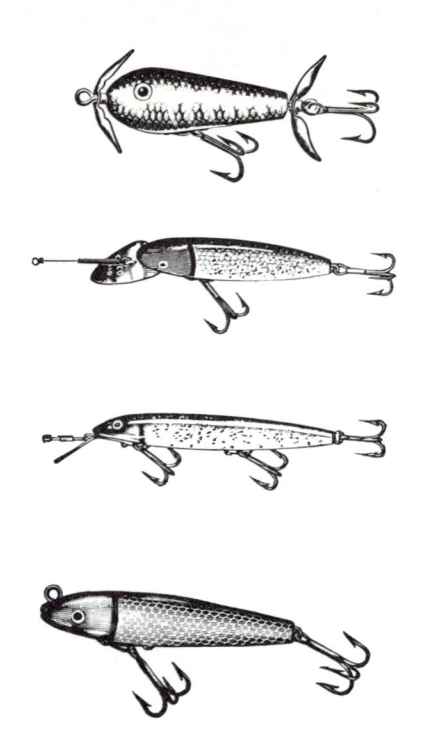

BEGINNER'S LUCK

Although most expert anglers are skillful and depend on know-how and experience to catch the most fish or the biggest fish, a bit of luck helps at times too. There was the father who bought his nine-year-old son a cheap rod and reel and took him fishing to Bull Shoals, Missouri, "just to keep him quiet." Then he tied a lure on the boy's line and left him to play while he went off to do some "serious fishing." He returned empty-handed to find his boy with an 8-lb. bass he caught while dangling the lure in the water!

JUMP FISHING

Freshwater anglers who do "jump" fishing search for schools of black bass or white bass feeding on the surface and chasing gizzard shad, minnows, or other small fish. This usually occurs on the larger lakes, reservoirs, and impoundments. You can look for the fish churning the surface of the water or for gulls or other birds hovering and diving over the school of fish. Then you can speed to the spot with your boat and shut off the motor within casting distance and then cast lures such as plugs, spoons, and jigs to the feeding fish.

FISH HAWK 204

The popular-priced Fish Hawk 204 fish finder is designed for any bass boat, any coho craft, and any sport runabout, and its combination of most desired features and realistic pricing makes it a popular permanent-mount fish finder. It has a Magnum Titanate Transducer System—with high-speed transducer for a wide-angle cone and best structure signals at any speed. There's a fine-line readout for detailed structure analysis, and it reads right through the hull in the bilge section of most bass boats. It has sensitive, interference-free electronics to locate single fish or schools. These are sealed from rain and spray. It has a strong gimbal mount with full tilt head for easy viewing. For a catalog or more information write to:
Waller Corporation
4220 Waller Dr.
Crystal Lake, Ill. 60014

Fish Hawk 204

TROUT FISHING

Trout Fishing is one of the best books written by the late, famous fisherman Joe Brooks. In this book he eloquently conveys in prose and pictures the drama of trout fishing, the ways of the trout, and the techniques and stratagems for taking these highly prized gamefish in streams and lakes. The book gives the history of trout fishing, recounting the contributions of Berners, Walton, Halford, Gordon, La Branche, Hewitt, and other famous trout fishermen and authors of the past. There's a big section on fly casting, covering over twenty different casts and how to handle the line, leader, and presentation of the fly so that the fish will take it.

Then Joe Brooks covers all the different kinds of flies, such as dry flies, wet flies, nymphs, streamers, and bucktails. He explains how to work upstream and down, how to deal with tricky currents, and how to match the hatch for the cruisers. He covers the fine points of fishing skating spiders on stream or lake, terrestrials between and after the hatches, and large streamers and bucktails in big water holding lunker trout. And after you hook the trout, Joe Brooks tells you how to fight and land it. In all, it is a complete course in fly fishing for trout under all conditions and in all kinds of waters all over the country. *Trout Fishing* sells for $8.95 and can be obtained from:
Harper & Row, Publishers, Inc.
10 East 53rd St.
New York, N.Y. 10022

RUBBER BANDS HOLD BAIT

It's a good idea to carry a good supply of thin rubber bands in your tackle box or on your person when you go fishing. They come in handy for keeping baits on a hook and alive for long periods. You can hold grasshoppers, locusts, caterpillars, and big beetles on a hook with a rubber band. And a good way to put a hard-shell or soft-shell crayfish on a hook is by using rubber bands. Just place the hook shank along the underside of the crayfish and snap the rubber bands around the bait and hook.

LIGHT UP FOR NIGHT FISHING

Freshwater anglers have been turning more and more to night fishing to escape daytime anglers, water skiers, boaters, and crowds in general. They have also discovered that some of the best fishing can take place after sundown. Of course, some anglers have fished for trout, bass, walleyes, and catfish at night for many years. But in recent years anglers have found that even panfish such as crappies and white bass can provide fast fishing after dark.

The "secret" here is to bring along some kind of light, such as a gasoline lantern, floodlight, or lamp. Then, after the boat is anchored over a good spot, you light the lanterns and hang them over the gunwales, close to the water so that the light is directed downward. Reflectors made from tin or foil can be used for this purpose.

The light will soon attract insects and then minnows, and these in turn will attract the panfish and even some gamefish. Then you lower a hook baited with live minnows into the water, and the action is usually fast and furious, because crappies and white bass are school fish and gather below the light in large numbers.

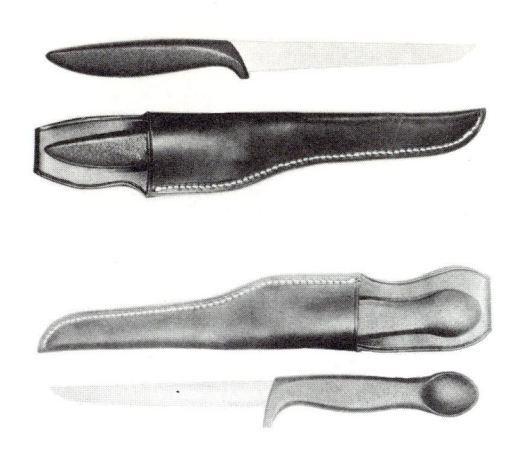

GERBER FISHING KNIVES

This company makes several fine knives for fishing, including models for sportsmen and commercial fishermen. The sports fishing knives are fitted with Gerber's all-aluminum Armorhide coated handles for firm, nonslip control when hands are wet and slippery. The sportsmen's fishing knives come in their own belt scabbards. Two basic filleting and fish-cleaning knives are made—the Coho and the Muskie. Both are slightly over 11 in. in length. This company also makes a varied line of hunting and special-purpose knives. A catalog is available, and if you want their folder *How to Field Dress Game & Fish* send $.25 to:

Gerber Legendary Blades
14200 S.W. 72nd Ave.
Portland, Ore. 97223

RAISING EARTHWORMS FOR PROFIT

The little book called *Raising Earthworms for Profit* by Earl B. Shields is one of the best on the market telling how to raise earthworms on a large scale. It is a completely illustrated working manual for one of the most fascinating and profitable of home money-making or full-time business projects—one that requires no special skill or training and that can be launched with the smallest of investments and built up to imposing proportions within the limits of a basement, garage, or lot. It's a business that any man, woman, or partially handicapped person may conduct successfully as a part-time or full-time project.

In the book the author tells you about the different kinds of worms, how to obtain your "starter" worms, types of containers, pits, and bins needed to keep and raise them, how to prepare the soil and what to feed the worms, how to harvest them, and how to pack, ship, and sell the worms. *Raising Earthworms for Profit* sells for $2.00 and can be obtained from the following address. They also sell other books and booklets on raising worms. Write for their free list.

Shields Publications
P.O. Box 472
Elgin, Ill. 60120

HILDE'S SPINNERS

The John J. Hildebrandt Corp. has been making spinners for seventy-seven years and still turns out a wide variety of spinners such as the Idaho, Indiana, Colorado, Willow Leaf, June Bug, Flicker, Shad-King, Swing-King, and other types. They come in nickel, copper, brass, and gold finishes. They also make many combination spinners with flies or plastic tails. For their catalog or more information write to:

John J. Hildebrandt Corp.
P.O. Box 50
Logansport, Ind. 46947

CASE FISHING KNIVES

The Case knives are well known to all those who like fine cutlery that is well made, holds an edge, and does the job it is intended to do. The company makes several knives for fishermen, including a 6-in. fish fillet blade glazed stainless steel with a rosewood handle and spoon end for cleaning fish; another 6-in. fillet, flexible, mirror-finished, chrome-plated blade with a Pakkawood handle; and an 8-in. fish fillet flexible glazed stainless-steel blade with a walnut handle and guard. All of these fillet knives come with leather sheaths.

They also make a fly fisherman knife with a glazed, stainless-steel handle with cutting blade and scissors on one side and a pick and file on the other side. There is a screwdriver on one end, and a scale in inches on the opposite side. Still another fisherman's pocket knife made by Case has a cream-colored composition handle, nickel silver bolsters, brass lining, and stainless-steel blades and springs. A stainless disgorger and scaler come on another blade, and there's a fish hook sharpening stone on one side of the handle.

The Case Company also makes many other knives, such as hunting knives, pocket knives, riggers knives, special-purpose knives, and various kinds of butcher, carving, steak, paring, trimming, bread, and professional knives. For more information or a catalog showing their entire line write to:

W. R. Case & Sons Cutlery Co.
20 Russell Blvd.
Bradford, Pa. 16701

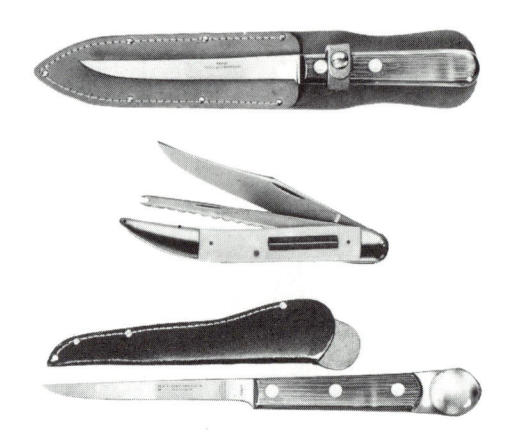

MY BUDDY TACKLE BOX

The new No. 9314 My Buddy Tackle Box is molded of ABS CO-POLYMER, which is a new plastic that is chemical-resistant. It cannot be damaged by plastic worms or other plastic lures. In fact, it's impervious to almost everything, and can be used in fresh water or salt water. The recessed luggage-type handle folds flat, allowing the box to be stored under the boat seat and has an interlocking bottom in the handle well for positive stacking. Overall box size is 14¼ in. by 8½ in. by 8 in. For their catalog showing this and other tackle boxes they make send $.25 to:

Falls City Div.—Stratton & Terstegge Co.
P.O. Box 1859
Louisville, Ky. 40201

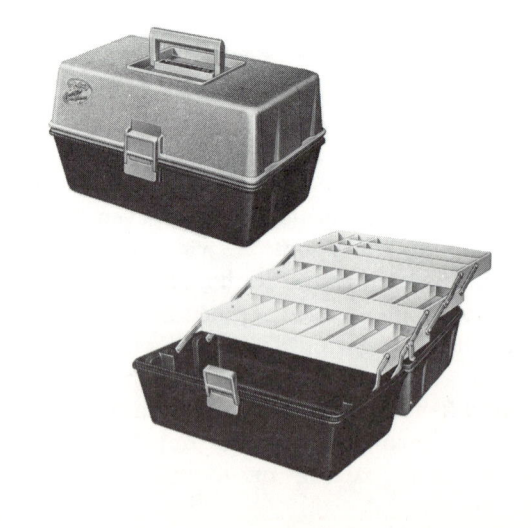

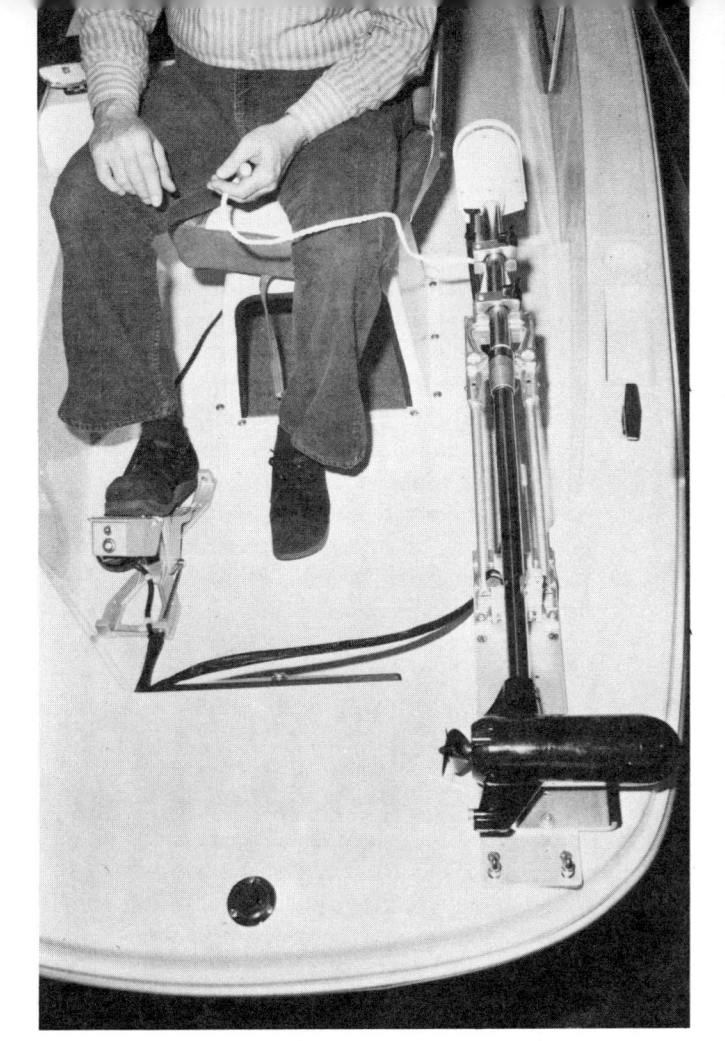

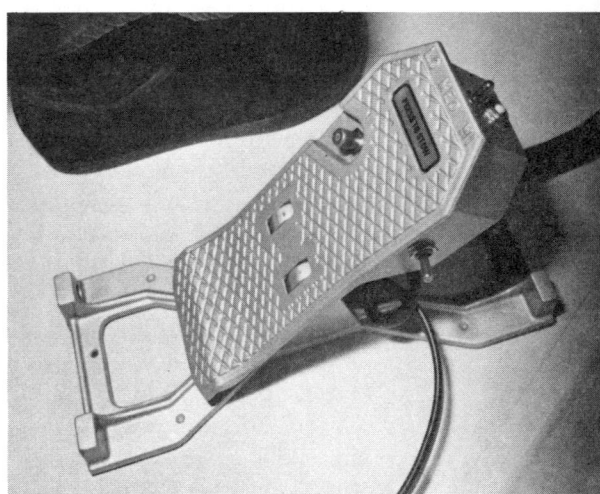

WONDERTROLL 924

Designed for big bass boats, Shakespeare's new WonderTroll 924 delivers up to 22½ lbs. of thrust from its 24-v. permanent-magnet motor, yet draws only 18.5 amps of current. With three preselected trolling speeds, the WonderTroll 924 also features a 12/24-v. selector switch for operation on either voltage. In the stowed position, the low-profile unit locks flat and vibration-free. A pull on the lanyard will swing the motor down into a locked running position. Another pull on the lanyard unlocks the motor and returns it to the stowed position. A 54-in. control cable, shielded with a braided nylon sleeve, connects the motor to a new one-piece foot pedal with a plunger-type on/off switch, the three-speed control switch, and nonskid rubber pad that prevents the control from slipping on the deck.

Strong die-cast steering gears, ball bearings, and self-lubricating bushings provide a smooth 360-degree turning range. The motor tube adjusts from 28 to 36 in. and is heavily chrome-plated to resist corrosion.

Other features of the WonderTroll 924 include Shakespeare's exclusive cooling system to dissipate heat, a reinforced Lexan propeller, a stationary weatherproof head with a lighted directional indicator and night light, and O-ring seals to protect moisture in the motor and switches. The new WonderTroll 924 is one of a complete line of 12- and 24-v. fishing motors made by:

Shakespeare Fishing Tackle Div.
P.O. Box 22517
Columbia, S.C. 29222

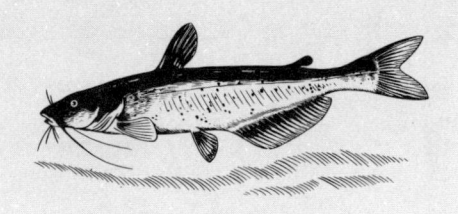

TRY JUGGING FOR CATFISH

One good way to fish a river for catfish is to go "jugging" for them, assuming it is legal to do so. In the old days they actually used old jugs with handles for this, but today they use old cans, plastic containers, or big chunks of styrofoam or floats from the same material. You tie a length of strong line and a hook on the end to the handle of these floats or attach it in any secure manner. Then you take them out in a boat, bait the hooks, and release the floats at intervals so that they float spaced well apart but within sight. Then you follow them in your boat, and when a float starts to bob up and down, you catch up with it and haul it out. Usually there will be a good-sized catfish on the end of the line.

FISHING LURES FROM CANS

You can make lures from old beer or soda cans by cutting them into small rectangles and folding these over a hook shank, then trimming the edges as shown in the drawings below. You can cut tiny rectangles for small hooks and for panfish, and larger ones for big hooks and bigger fish such as trout, bass, pickerel, etc. You can tie some feathers or hair on the hook at the bend before you bend the metal over the hook shank.

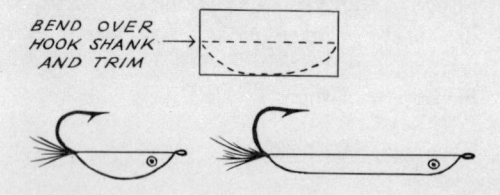

ONE THAT DIDN'T GET AWAY

When it comes to pursuing their sport, fishermen are a hardy, dedicated bunch, often risking life and limb to land that big one. Such as the New Hampshire angler fishing a lake on opening day for trout. He hooked a heavy fish, and just as he was landing it, the line broke. Without hesitation, the angler jumped into the icy water, grabbed the disappearing line, and pulled in his prize—a 5-lb., 14-oz. rainbow trout!

EVER CATCH A TIGER TROUT?

The tiger trout is a hybrid that is a cross between a female brown trout and a male brook trout. The result is a fish that has some of the qualities of both trout, such as the wariness of the brownie and the voraciousness of the brookie. The name "tiger" was given to this trout because it has faint vertical stripes like this big member of the cat family. Those who have caught these trout claim they are real gamefish and fight hard and make good eating.

WHY PROS CATCH MORE FISH

One of the main reasons why the freshwater bass fishing pros catch more fish is that they don't spend much time fishing spots that do not produce. They usually make a few casts in a good spot, and if there is no action they move on to the next spot. They use fast boats and big, powerful motors to move from one spot to another as quickly as possible. And, of course, they know how to work their lures and they fish hard, putting in many hours or even a whole day on the water.

FLORIDA BASS LAKES MAPS

The ten best big bass lakes in the state of Florida have been mapped, and these maps will prove a big help for those who want to nail a "wall hangin'" hawg bass. The Southern Guide Fishing Maps are designed not only to improve your chances of catching one of these big bass, but they also show camps, parks, public ramps and landings, major roads and highways, water depths, stump and lily pad concentrations, hot spots, and lunker holes. The following lake maps are available:

"Juniper Lake"   "Rodman Reservoir"
"Dead Lakes"   "Lake George"
"Lake Talquin"   "Lake Tohopikaliga"
"Lake Jackson"   "Lake Kissimmee"
"Orange/   "Lake Okeechobee"
Lochloosa"

Each of these maps sells for $1.75 plus $.15 for postage and handling and can be obtained from:
Southern Guide Fishing Maps
1325 E. Tennessee St.
P.O. Box 1106
Tallahassee, Fla. 32303

GENE BULLARD CUSTOM RODS

Gene Bullard sells all the parts needed to make custom fly rods, spinning rods, baitcasting and spin-casting rods, surf rods, and trolling and big-game rods. They handle Lamiglas, Fenwick, and Featherweight blanks in Fiberglas and graphite.

They also sell the other parts such as reel seats, ferrules, butts, grips, handles, guides, roller tip-tops, roller guides, butt caps, rings, winding thread, color preserver, rod varnish, epoxy and rod finish, and everything else you need to complete a rod. They also sell Quick spinning and casting reels, Gudebrod fishing lines, Cortland fly lines, Mustad hooks, Sampo swivels, and fighting belts and harnesses. A free catalog is available from:
Gene Bullard
10139 Shoreview Rd.
Dallas, Tex. 75238

UTAH FISHING GUIDES

The Utah Division of Wildlife Resources has books and booklets on fish and fishing such as the following:

Fishes of Utah
   Price, $2.00 (paperback)
   Price, $3.00 (hardcover)
Popular Utah Fishing Waters
   Price, $.50
Boulder Mountain Lakes Booklet
   Price, $.50
Utah Fishing and Hunting Guide
   Free

These books and booklets can be obtained from:
Div. of Wildlife Resources
1596 W. N. Temple
Salt Lake City, Ut. 84116

CALIFORNIA FISHING GUIDES

The following guides tell about fishing in California's lakes, streams, and rivers and are illustrated with photos and maps:

North Sierra Trout Fishing
How to Catch California Trout
Trinity River Fishing
Klamath River Fishing
California Trout Fishing
California Steelhead Fishing
Shasta Lake Fishing
Lake Berryessa Fishing
San Diego Bass Lakes Fishing

Each guide is an eighty-page paperback and sells for $1.95 per copy. They are published by:
Chronicle Books
870 Market St.
San Francisco, Calif. 94102

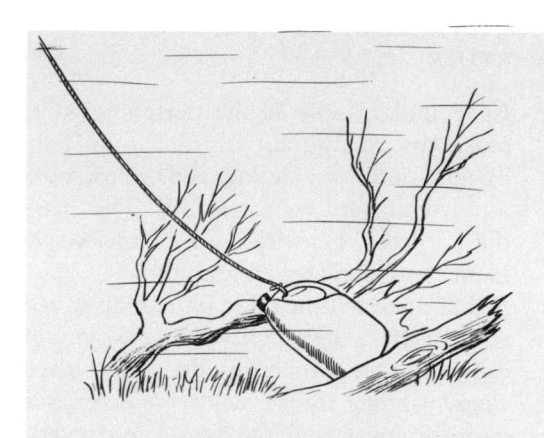

CHEAP ANCHOR

If you are fishing among submerged trees, stumps, or rocks, where you are apt to hang up and lose an expensive anchor, don't worry—your problem is solved! Just get one of those big plastic jugs with a handle and fill it with mud, sand, or pebbles. Then tie a fairly weak anchor line to the handle. When you get hung up in the obstructions below the surface, pull hard, and the handle will break off or the anchor line will snap, and you'll be free with little loss. Of course, it's a good idea to make up several such anchors if you plan to fish many spots.

HOOK MORE MUSKIES

It usually takes hundreds of casts or many hours of trolling to hook even one musky. So what happens? The angler often has a light, limber rod and a line that stretches too much and fails to hook the fish, or he loses it soon after it is hooked. More muskies would be hooked and boated if anglers used stiffer rods, nonstretch or little-stretch lines, and kept the hooks on their lures and baits needle-sharp at all times. It also helps to come back hard and fast with the rod when a fish grabs the lure.

CHEWING GUM BAIT

One angler claims that chewing gum can be used as bait, and he suggests that you carry a few sticks in case you run out of bait. Then all you have to do is chew a stick until it gets soft and then shape it around the shank or bend of your hook. You can chew several sticks and form a good-sized bait shaped like a minnow. Or you can shape it into a worm or grub or caterpillar. The bait may lose its shape after a hard strike or after a fight with a fish, but it can quickly be reshaped again.

FALL TROUT

During the late summer and early fall most of the mayfly hatches are about over. But trout still feed on terrestrial or land insects such as grasshoppers, crickets, beetles, and various bugs. Use flies that imitate these insects, and work them close to grassy or bushy banks where trout are lying and waiting for the land insects to fall into the water.

MAKE YOUR OWN FISHING SPOTS

If it is legal in the waters of your state, you can make your own fishing spots by sinking brush or trees or mats of limbs and logs in a lake to attract fish such as bass, crappies, and bluegills to the spot. All of these materials should be tied and weighted down with a rock or cement blocks or other weights to keep them in place. An easy way to place the piles or mats or brush in a lake is to slide them out on the ice during the winter months. Then, when the ice melts, the brush will sink to the bottom.

GLADDING SOUTH BEND LIFE VEST

The new Angler fishing life vest provides complete safety for the active outdoor sportsman without restricting his movement or burdening him with unnecessary weight. The wearer can easily cast as he works his lures through a hot fishing spot. And since the Angler can be adjusted at both sides and shoulders, the vest always fits properly, even if the sportsman is wearing heavy clothes. No matter how bulky the clothing, the Angler's Ethafome filling will keep the wearer afloat indefinitely. Four deep pockets hold a lot of flies or lures. Each pocket has a drainage hole to shed water, and the comfortable nylon mesh lining also dries out fast. The vest is available in camouflage, timber brown, forest green, or skipper blue in chest sizes 34 to 48. For more information write to:
Gladding Corp. Flotation Products Div.
P.O. Box 8277, Sta. A
Greenville, S.C. 29604

PORTABLE ICE-FISHING SHELTER

This company makes portable ice-fishing shelters that are compact and light and can easily be carried by one man out on the ice. They are collapsible and break down into a neat, flat package that can be carried on your back or in a car trunk. The floor and roof are heavy 18-oz. black-vinyl-coated polyester. The walls are 10-oz. black-vinyl-coated polyester. The special fabric used in the construction of the shelter has been tested in the Arctic and will withstand temperatures down to —40 degrees. They make three different sizes and models, weighing from 16 lbs. to 30 lbs. For more information write to:
Harmony Enterprises, Inc.
704 Main Ave. N.
Harmony, Minn. 55939

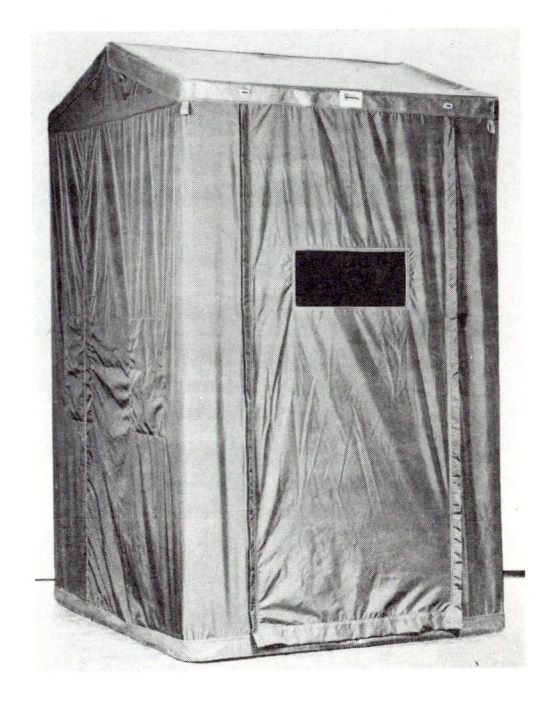

THE TROUT FISHERMEN'S DIGEST

The Trout Fishermen's Digest, edited by David Richey, is a big paperback-format book that contains numerous articles by various trout fishing experts. There are articles by such well-known fishing writers as Mark Sosin, Bill Browning, Jerry Gibbs, Jim Bashline, Nick Sisley, Norman Strung, S. R. Slaymaker II, and many others. The author also wrote some articles for the book. It covers trout fishing for brook, rainbow, and brown trout, lake trout, steelhead, golden trout, and other species. The authors cover almost every natural bait, lure, and fly used for trout and the best methods and techniques. *The Trout Fishermen's Digest* sells for $7.95 and is published by:

DBI Books, Inc.
540 Frontage Rd.
Northfield, Ill. 60093

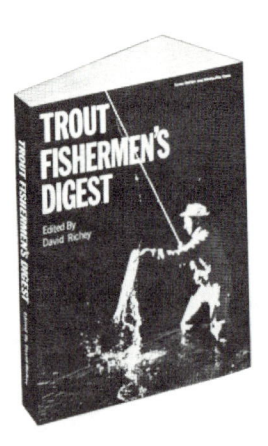

HOW MANY FLIES?

Some trout fishermen carry hundreds of dry flies in dozens of patterns and sizes and are continually changing them to match the hatch or find a fly the fish are interested in. They catch a lot of trout, but also spend a great deal of time changing flies. To simplify matters, many trout anglers have found that all you need is a half-dozen or so patterns each in about four different sizes and you can usually catch trout on most waters. A good choice, for example, would be such dry flies as the Light Cahill, Adams, Quill Gordon, March Brown, Brown Bivisible, and Royal Coachman.

If you get each of these flies in size Nos. 10, 12, 14, and 16 and add a few Wulffs in size Nos. 8, 10, and 12, you'll catch trout on most streams if you fish hard, cover a lot of water, and know how to present the flies naturally.

SPRING FISHING FOR TROUT

When the water is cold and often murky in the spring on most streams, the trout are usually down deep near the bottom. They are also sluggish and will not chase a lure or rise too far to grab it. Then you can still catch them on lures such as spoons, spinners, weighted nymphs, and streamers by getting them down deep near the bottom. With flies a sinking fly line is a must. One good technique used to get the lures down deep in a fast or heavy current is to wade upstream and cast your lure up and across stream into the current and let it swing downstream. By judging the speed of the current and the water depth correctly, you can take in slack line just enough so that the lure travels close to the bottom. For best results you should feel the lure touch bottom every so often.

ROD-WRAPPING HANDBOOK

How to Wrap a Rod with Gudebrod is a fully illustrated new manual designed especially for the amateur rod builder. The handbook teaches how to strip old guides, choose and wrap on new guides, how to apply a long-lasting finish, and even offers some ideas on creating special effects, including the intricate diamond pattern.

It relates to the use of Gudebrod's Rod-building Accessory Products, and takes the reader through rod-wrapping and -finishing processes in step-by-step instructions. Ninety-four sharp photographs and illustrations literally take you by the hand.

The authors reveal several unpublished time-saving techniques that simplify rod wrapping. Featured is a section on determining proper guide spacing, a task that formerly involved more guesswork than knowledge. Now Gudebrod has presented a method that makes it easy to arrive at optimum guide spacing.

How to Wrap a Rod with Gudebrod is a must addition to every rod builder's workshop. Gudebrod offers this twenty-four-page manual for only $1.00 at better tackle shops or by writing to:

Rod Wrap Handbook
Gudebrod Bros. Silk Co., Inc.
12 S. 12th St.
Philadelphia, Pa. 19107

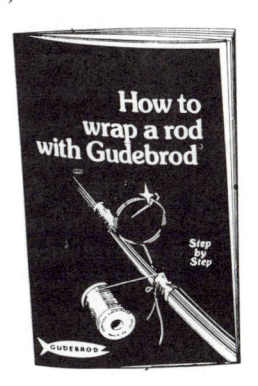

SOUTH DAKOTA ANGLER'S ALMANAC

This is a large-sized booklet called *South Dakota Angler's Almanac,* which tells about the fishing in that state. It has color photographs and black-and-white photos and drawings. It also has two pages of rigs and baiting methods that can be used for trout, bass, walleyes, catfish, and panfish. The *Almanac* also has maps and charts showing and describing the best waters such as streams, river, lakes, and ponds, giving their location, acreage, fish available, and access. *South Dakota's Angler's Almanac* can be obtained from:

South Dakota Dept. of Game, Fish, and Parks
State Office Bldg. No. 1
Pierre, S.D. 57501

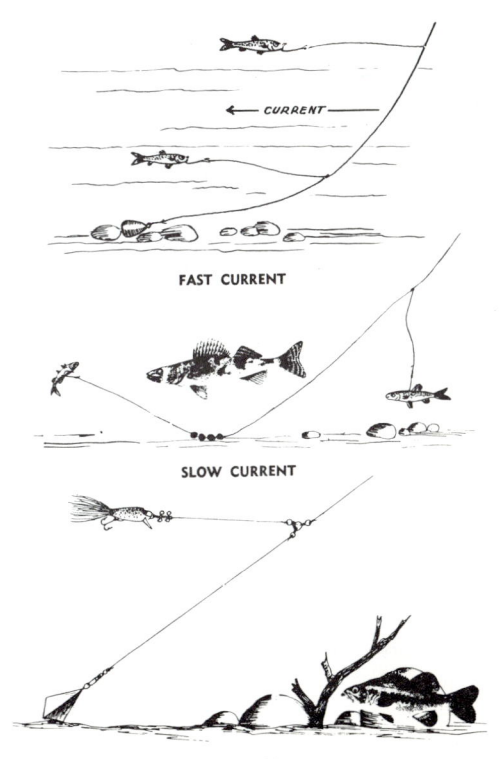

CATCHING SUCKERS

In the spring it doesn't take many warm days to start a fellow thinking about fishing. Fortunately there is a fish ready and waiting for the first worms to hit the water, according to the Pennsylvania Fish Commission. There are several kinds of suckers in Pennsylvania waters, but they all have the same forked tails and small, puckered, rubbery mouths. These mouths can be extended to press against the stream bottom and suck up small items of food, giving the fish its name.

In March, suckers begin moving up from lakes and larger streams and rivers into the smaller creeks to spawn. They often gather in large numbers in the deeper holes at the mouths of small streams, below riffles, or below obstacles such as dams or waterfalls. Here the early-bird fisherman can have a ball.

Sucker fishing doesn't take any special equipment. A regular casting or spin-casting outfit is usually used, and anglers who want a lot of sport are even using light spinning tackle. A few hooks, sinkers, and a can of worms complete the outfit.

The sinker, attached to the end of the line, should be large enough to hold the bait in the current. The baited hook is allowed to dangle on the bottom. The rod is placed in a rod holder (a forked stick is fine) and the slack is taken out of the line. A cigarette-sized piece of wood clipped to the line will indicate a nibble.

Now it's up to the fish. Since sucker fishing is often a waiting game, it's a good idea to dress warmly. A folding camp stool or box and hot soup or a hot drink in a vacuum bottle will make the waiting more enjoyable. A good sucker, however, is worth the wait, and you can have your hands full landing the tugging fish, rebaiting your hooks, and tossing them out again. Eating the catch is pretty enjoyable, too. Fried golden brown, they are a real treat.

TROUT ON OPENING DAY

On the opening day of the trout season most of the larger streams, pools, and lakes are usually crowded with wading anglers or fleets of boats—especially on the more popular streams and lakes, which are known to all trout anglers. To avoid such crowds you'll do better if you look for the smaller streams, ponds, and lakes and fish these. Such waters also warm up sooner in the spring and the trout are more active and hit better. And such small waters are cleaner and clearer than the bigger waters, which are often high and discolored on opening day.

BICARBONATE OF SODA

Anglers will find that a package of bicarbonate of soda is handy not only to keep at home but also to take along on a fishing trip. It can be used to polish spoons, spinners, metal squids, and other metal lures to make them shine and sparkle. You can also use it to wash the fish smell from your hands after handling and cleaning fish. You can also make a paste from the bicarbonate of soda and put it on insect bites to take the sting out. And, of course, if your stomach is upset from a recent meal, you can mix the bicarb in some water and drink it.

PRESIDENT 1980 CASTING REEL

Continuing the tradition of the famous President reels, Shakespeare has announced the introduction of the new 1980 President II casting reel. The new reel has been the subject of years of testing and designing. It was created to include the features that serious fishermen have been looking for and appreciate. Bass fishermen will appreciate the President II's rugged construction and power when fishing structures that attract lunkers.

A true free-spool reel, the level wind operates anytime the spool rotates. The easy-to-reach plunger-operated free-spool mechanism disengages the spool pinion from the spool shaft. There is no dead spot in the mechanism, and the trip force is constant.

Two cast-control systems are included in the President 1980. Shakespeare's patented Hydro-Film cast control insures accurate, trouble-free casting. A centrifugal braking mechanism controls spool speed during casting to prevent backlash. Extra centrifugal weights come with the reel so that different weight lures can be cast with ease. The reel's full five-to-one gear ratio uses a brass-drive gear and stainless-steel pinion. The large gear set reduces excessive friction loading and gives increased strength and longer gear life.

Two stainless-steel, shielded ball bearings are used at the spool pivots to make the 1980 operate smoothly. Each bearing utilizes seven balls in a ribbon separator for quiet operation and high loading carrying capacity. A superstar drag with large-diameter, heat-resistant, and chrome-plated brass washers provides a wide range of smooth, even drag pressure, from ultra-light to full lock-up.

The 1980 President II has a stainless-steel gear plate that resists corrosion and wear. The built-up aluminum spool has turned flanges and a stainless-steel back-up washer. A crankshaft nut retainer presents the nut and power handle from working loose. Three large screws permit quick take-down for cleaning. The reel is styled in anodized gun-metal black with a distinctive silver-finished eagle medallion and filled decorative engravings. For more information write to:

Fishing Tackle Div.—Shakespeare Co.
P.O. Box 246
Columbia, S.C. 29202

ALASKA SPORT FISHING GUIDE

There's a handy booklet called *Alaska Sport Fishing Guide,* which is a compilation of the current angling information available on fishing waters adjacent to the various highway systems in Alaska. Information on fly-in waters is also included in the guide. Air or boat charter service is available at those cities and villages listed for anglers with the desire to fish the more remote areas. The booklet has many maps pinpointing the spots and waters and listing what kind of fish are caught there. For a copy of this booklet write to:

Alaska Dept. of Fish and Game
Information and Education Sec.
Subport Bldg.
Juneau, Alaska 99801

AMBASSADEUR CASTING RODS

The Garcia Ambassadeur casting rods come in bait-casting, worm, and popping rods. They are made to be mates to the well-known Ambassadeur casting reels sold by the same company. They have light to stiff actions, with plenty of backbone for handling heavy lures, setting the hook, and holding big fish. They have ceramic Conoglide guides and tip-tops and come in lengths from 5 to 7 ft., depending on the model you choose. For more information write to:
The Garcia Corp.
329 Alfred Ave.
Teaneck, N.J. 07666

CATCH MORE BASS

Every bass man wants to put more large-mouth on his stringer, and the book *Catch More Bass* will help him to do it. Stan Fagerstrom, who wrote it, is outdoor editor of the *Daily News* in Longview, Washington, and his byline has appeared many times in national magazines. This volume is a distillation of a lifetime of bass angling experiences—Stan has been fishing for large-mouth ever since he got hold of his first level-wind reel in the 1930s. He lives right on the shore of the best bass lake in western Washington State, and has spent countless hours studying, catching, releasing, and writing about large-mouth bass.

Among the many subjects covered in the book are the benefits derived from modern technology. The author describes the way in which electric trolling motors—silent, no-hands substitutes for oars—assist the bass fisherman to increase his catch by giving him more time on the water and allowing him to boat fish he might otherwise have lost. Fish locaters, the best in bass boats, the use of water thermometers, and many other new products are discussed in detail.

Nothing pertinent to bass fishing is ignored. Stan Fagerstrom discusses his favorite plugs and how he uses them. For years Stan has been a lunker hunter, and he shares his knowledge of where to find them and how to bring them in. The proper way to fish pad fields, the advantages and use of the plastic worm, line weights, pork rind, and correct methods of casting with both casting and spinning outfits and fly-fishing rods for bass are just a few of the topics covered.

The book sells for $7.95, with $.50 for postage and handling from:
Catch More Bass
P.O. Box 27
Silver Lake, Wash. 98645

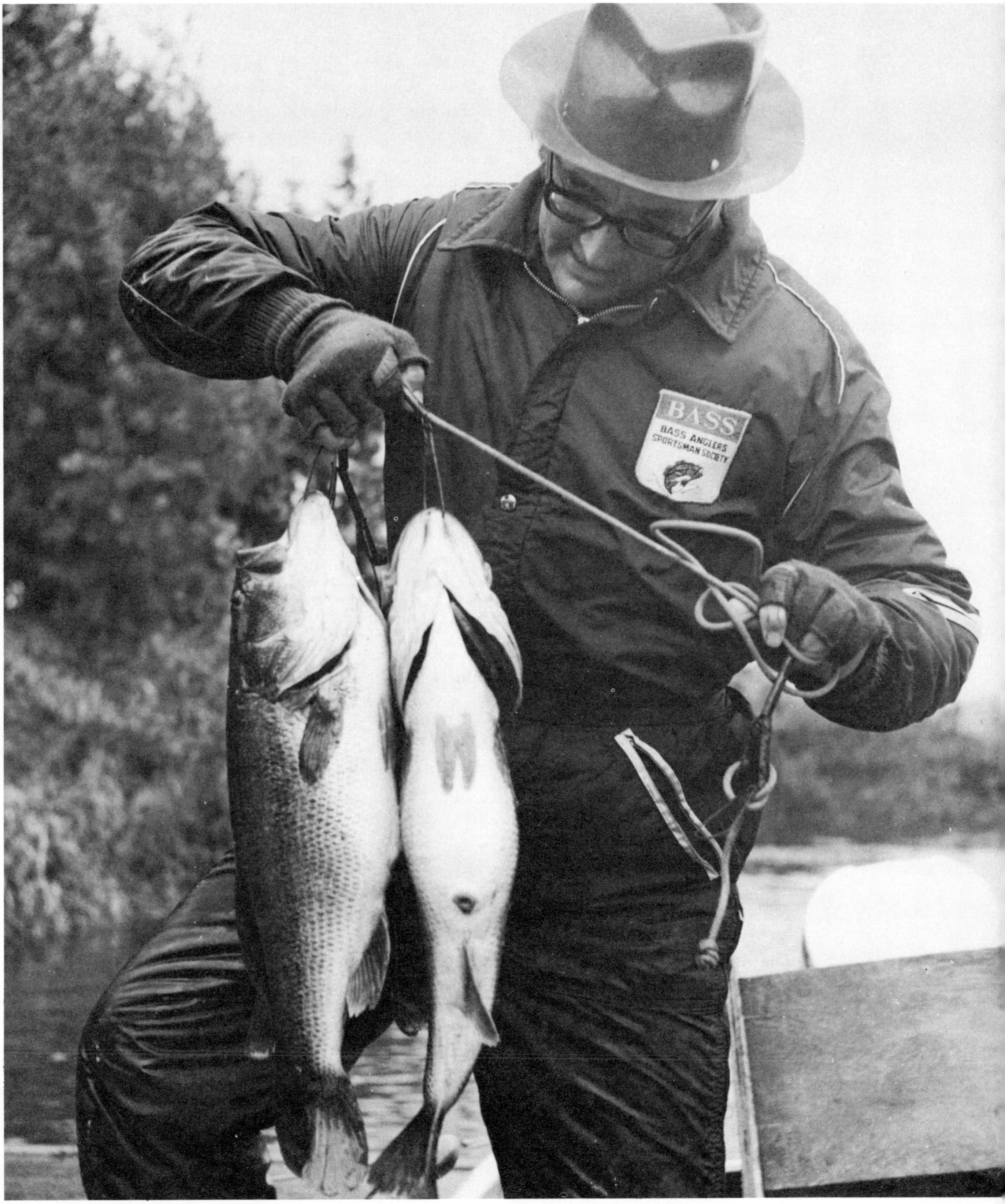
BASS
BASS ANGLERS
SPORTSMAN SOCIETY

TAKE TIME FOR BLUEGILL

How long has it been since you really caught a lot of fish? Most anglers, as they gain experience, spend their time pursuing large trout, bass, salmon, and similar good-sized fish. But just how often do you take a trophy-size fish? There are usually acres of empty water between catches.

If you've been devoting most of your energy to this kind of angling, perhaps it's time to stop and consider fishing for fun and action. Although they're not going to break any records, bluegill do rate on top when it comes to exciting and enjoyable fishing. Spring is the time to go after them, and the method used by the fishermen in Mercury Marine's outdoor department is guaranteed to put some fun into your fishing.

When water temperatures reach 67 degrees F., bluegill begin to spawn. With her tail, the female scoops out a shallow depression and lays the eggs. Male bluegill guard their nests from predator fish, which usually include other bluegill. Nests often overlap at this time, and the crowded conditions bring excellent fishing.

The technique favored by many anglers calls for simple tackle—a light-action, 7-ft. fly rod and a soft rubber cricket for a lure. If the fly rod isn't available, a limber cane pole works just as well. Fish from a boat and cast along the shore at various distances from the bank until the fish are found. Then anchor the boat and continue to fish in one spot until the action stops.

Let the artificial cricket (or a live one, if they are available) slowly sink beneath the surface over the multiple nests. The opportunity to feed is almost irresistible to bluegill in the area, whether they are guarding the nest or waiting to prey on one whose male fish is gone.

Don't worry about hurting the bluegill population. The female lays up to thirty-five thousand eggs, and since many of these live to become adult fish, there's no chance for a bluegill shortage.

FLY RODS FOR BASS

Fly rods are especially effective for bass in heavily fished waters where other fishing tackle has been used a lot. The bass get used to the loud splashes and seeing the big lures used on such outfits and after a while get wary or shy away. But something more delicate, different, and smaller—like a bass bug or streamer or bucktail—will often make them hit with abandon.

FISH LIKE A HOME

Most freshwater gamefish will feed in shallow water but not too far from deep water for a "home," where they can take cover and feel safe. So look for such hiding places as pools, holes, pockets, dropoffs, sunken rocks and trees, logs, tree roots, overhanging banks, branches, and brush that fish can reach quickly when threatened in the shallow-water feeding areas.

QUICK REELS

The Quick Reels are well known as quality products, with several models available for freshwater fishing. They make a Champion series of bait-casting reels featuring silent level-wind, push-button free-spool and extralong handle counterbalanced with a sure grip. They have star drags and fast no-tool take-apart.

They also make three models of fly-fishing reels, from a small 4½-oz. reel to a large, heavy-duty fly reel for salmon and steelhead. And they have a complete line of spinning reels, from their ultralight Microlite to the larger Finessa models, which hold 225 yds. of 12-lb. test for heavy freshwater or light salt-water fishing. Their spinning reels feature ball-bearing drive on the main shaft. They have stainless-steel bails with tungsten carbide line guides and all precision-machined gears. Their catalog showing these reels and other fishing tackle costs $.25 from:

Quick Corp. of America
620 Terminal Way
Costa Mesa, Calif. 92627

CREEK CHUB LURES

The Creek Chub Bait Company has been making freshwater and salt-water fishing lures from way back, and they are still among the most popular lures used by anglers. In their freshwater line they have such popular lures as the Injured Minnow, Jointed Darter, Viper, Plunker, Pikie, Nikie, Mouse, Tiny Tim, Streaker, and Cohokie, among others. Their catalog costs $.25 and it shows these and other lures in the many colors in which they are made. Write to:

Creek Chub Bait Co.
Garrett, Ind. 46738

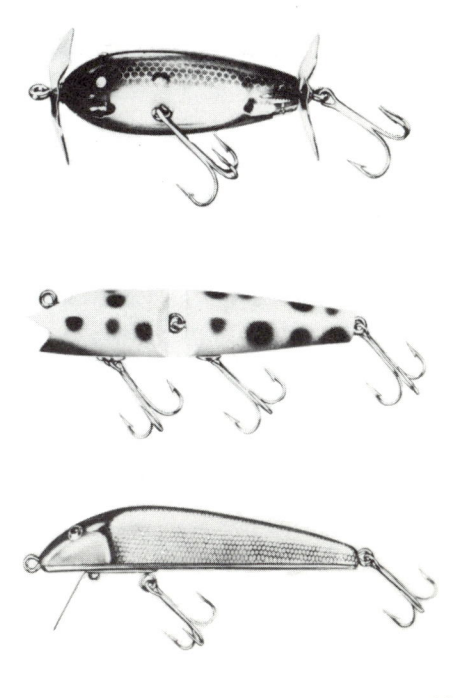

GREAT FISHING TACKLE CATALOGS OF THE GOLDEN AGE

The book *Great Fishing Tackle Catalogs of the Golden Age* by Sam Melner and Hermann Kessler is a collection of old fishing tackle catalog pages recalling the days when you could buy a split-bamboo rod for $15 and other tackle at equally low prices. Between the covers they have assembled catalog pages from L. L. Bean, Orvis, William Mills, Kiffe, Marshall Fields, Edward Vom Hofe, and many other old-time tackle firms. Here you'll find incredible gadgets—the African Steel Vine rod and the Weedless Struggling Mouse, brought to market with everything but the heraldic blast of trumpets. And the solid ideas that have withstood the test of time. The book *Great Fishing Tackle Catalogs of the Golden Age* sells for $6.95 and is published by:
Crown Publishers, Inc.
419 Park Ave. S.
New York, N.Y. 10016

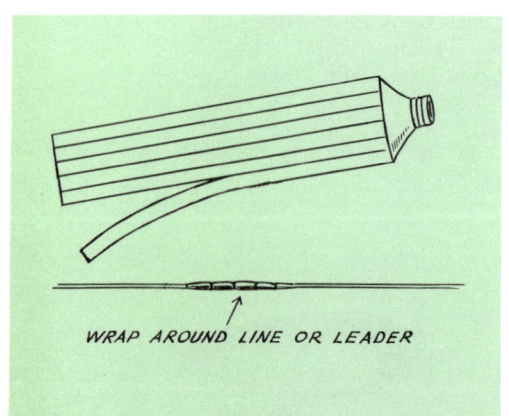

MAKING WRAP-AROUND SINKERS

You can make all the wrap-around sinkers you need quickly and cheaply from old toothpaste or shaving cream tubes. Just cut the tubes into strips and then wrap them around your line or leader. If you cut the strips on the tube on one end but leave the other end attached, you can carry the tube in your pocket or tackle box and just tear off a strip or two when you need it.

FISHERMAN BOOKS

Cordovan Corp., Publishers, has published a series of "Fisherman" paperback books that should prove very helpful, especially to fishermen in Texas and neighboring states. They are listed as follows:

Freshwater Fishing in Texas by Russell Tinsley $4.75

Panfishing in Texas by Russell Tinsley $5.50

Fishing Holes of Texas by L. A. Wilke $4.25

Topwater Fishing by Max Eggleston $4.25

Striper—The Super Fish by John Clift $4.75

How to Fish for Bass by Jerry Zuber $3.00

Know Your Fishing Baits by Jerry Zuber $2.50

Know Your Fishing Boats by Jerry Zuber $2.75

These books are available from:
Cordovan Corp., Publishers
5314 Bingle Rd.
Houston, Tex. 77018

SENTRY OXYGEN MONITOR

Ray Jefferson's all-new, compact Sentry Oxygen Monitor shows where the fish have to be by measuring where there's enough dissolved oxygen in the water to sustain fish life, eliminating bad fishing areas. Fish, like humans, need oxygen to breathe. By knowing there's enough oxygen to support fish life, the fisherman can concentrate on those spots, avoiding areas where fish couldn't be. The Sentry is a sophisticated electronic device that measures the dissolved oxygen content at any point in a body of water. The unit works in both fresh and salt water and in the atmosphere and uses the oxygen in the atmosphere as the standard against which underwater oxygen is measured. The monitor is easy to read at a glance and has a color-coded scale. As long as the needle is in the green area, there's enough oxygen in the area being surveyed to sustain fish life. Yellow means few fish, and red means no fish. For more information contact:

Ray Jefferson
Main and Cotton Sts.
Philadelphia, Pa. 19127

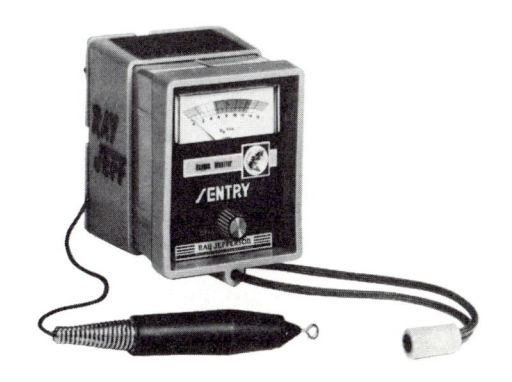

CALIFORNIA FISHING MAPS

The Angler's Guides to Lakes and Streams provide detailed information on trout fishing in specific, out-of-the-way places in California's mountainous regions or on special fisheries such as salmon and steelhead. They are as follows:

28. "Bear Creek"
29. "Crown Valley"
30. "Emigrant Basin"
32. "Lake Tahoe"
33. "French Canyon"
34. "Mono Creek"
36. "Granite Creek"
37. "Trinity Alps"
39. "Marble Mountains"
42. "Salmon and Steelhead"
43. "Upper Bishop Creek"
44. "Klamath River"

Each copy of the Angler's Guides above sells for $.40 and should be ordered by number and name. They can be obtained from:

Office of Procurement—Documents Div.
P.O. Box 20191
Sacramento, Calif. 95820

WORKING A DARTER PLUG

The darter is an old-time plug that still continues to take fish in fresh and salt water. It is especially good for bass in fresh water and for striped bass, bluefish, and snook in salt water. This plug was designed to run just below the surface of the water in a "darting" action from one side to the other. By reeling slowly you can work it a few inches below the surface. Faster reeling will make it dive and run about 2 or 3 ft. down. But you can also work a darter on top and make a commotion that will draw strikes from many gamefish. Then it becomes a top-water plug. Here you reel much slower, with pauses, but work your rod tip up and down quickly so that the plug skitters and skates on top of the water in a zigzag motion.

FISHING WITH NATURAL BAITS

The book *Fishing with Natural Baits* by Vlad Evanoff is the most complete guide to freshwater and salt-water fishing baits yet published. Millions of fishermen in both fresh water and salt water use live or natural baits when they go fishing. Sooner or later, every fisherman finds that he can catch more fish, bigger fish, and have more fun if he uses natural baits on many of his fishing trips.

But most books and magazine articles written about fishing deal with artificial lures. There is a common belief among fishermen who use artificial lures that using natural baits is too easy and requires little skill or study. But those anglers who have used natural baits for a long time soon discover that there are many things to learn about such baits. The use of natural baits often requires as much skill and know-how as the use of artificial lures.

Fishing with Natural Baits is a complete illustrated guide to the use of natural baits. Covering fresh water and salt water, it tells you everything you need to know about natural baits—how to find them, how to keep them alive or preserve them, how to rig or hook them, and how to use them for most gamefish. There are even chapters on how to raise and sell baits for profit and how to start a bait business. The book covers earthworms, minnows, water insects, land insects, prepared baits, sea worms, clams, mussels, snails, whelks, conchs, squid, crabs, shrimp baitfishes, eels, and other freshwater and salt-water baits.

Fishing with Natural Baits by Vlad Evanoff comes in a hard-cover edition, which sells for $8.95, and a soft-cover edition, which sells for $4.95. It is published by:
Prentice-Hall, Inc.
Englewood Cliffs, N.J. 07632

WORM BEDDING

Worm Bedding is a specially prepared pulp product with simulated soil ingredients and food supplements, which are put into boxes or bait containers with earthworms or night crawlers. They will stay alive for days and grow healthy and lively and make attractive baits for most fish. For more information write to:
The Oberlin Canteen Co.
Oberlin, O. 44074

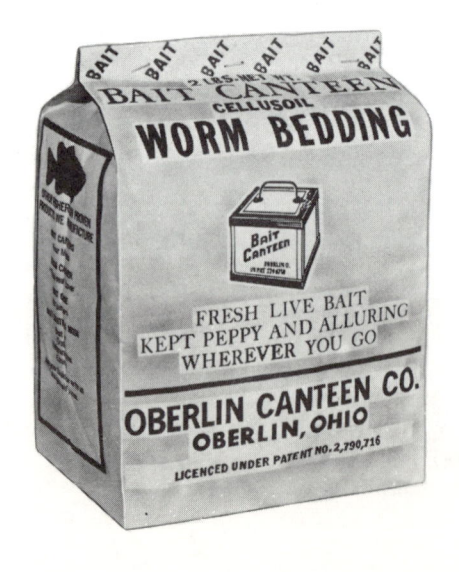

JOHNNY REB LECTRANCHOR

This electric device for raising and lowering an anchor is built to withstand the brutal punishment of tournament fishing, but is also a backsaver for the weekend or vacation fisherman who likes to try many spots. It has a quiet, powerful 180-lb.-pull permanent magneto motor with case-hardened steel gears capable of raising the anchor approximately 1 ft. per second. The compact stainless-steel reel has 50 ft. of special anchor rope. New up-and-down switches prevent anchor pulldown. The quick-release knob and composition clutch eliminate all springs. It offers through-the-deck mounting for decks from 1/4 in. to 1 1/4 in. thick. For more information write to:
Johnny Reb Mfg. Co.
P.O. Box 902
Clinton, Miss. 39056

SPORT FISHING U.S.A.

Sport Fishing U.S.A. is a beautiful book published by the Bureau of Sport Fisheries and Wildlife of the U. S. Department of the Interior. It covers both freshwater and salt-water fish and fishing and has numerous contributions from expert and well-known anglers, outdoor writers, and biologists. There are chapters on selective breeding, stocking, and intensive management programs. Also included are fishing tackle, lures, baits, accessories, methods and techniques, fishing experiences, and angling history. The book is illustrated with color photographs and paintings as well as black-and-white photos. This big 464-page hardcover book sells for $10 and can be obtained from:

Superintendent of Documents
U. S. Government Printing Office
Washington, D.C. 20402

GUIDE TO FUN IN FLORIDA

Now for the first time ever, maps of all Florida counties in one big 10¾-in.-by-16-in. colorful publication. The book includes finely detailed maps of the 67 Florida counties, facilities listed in detail for over 600 campsites, complete facilities for all Florida fishing camps, all official Florida canoe trails described and pinpointed on maps, points of interest and special attractions described and located in color, marine facilities, completely described water depths, and types of dockage. State parks are also described and detailed on county maps in color and special maps of the Everglades, The Keys, St. John's River Waterway, and Kissimmee River Waterway, and boat-launching sites and all coastal and inshore facilities are covered. *Guide to Fun in Florida* is 152 pages in all, is offered in co-operation with the Florida Wildlife Federation, and is available for $5.95 from:

The Bureau of Maps
Drawer No. 5317
Tallahassee, Fla. 32301

GLADDING SOUTH BEND FLY REELS

The Gladding South Bend fly reels come in three models, which are made in England by Gladding's Morrit Division. The unique free-turning roller prevents damage and excessive wear when stripping fly lines. The roller dismantles for thorough cleaning by removing two holding screws. Check Pawl position can be converted for left-handed use. For more information write to:

Gladding Corp.
South Otselic, N.Y. 13155

WISCONSIN FISHING INFORMATION

The Wisconsin Department of Natural Resources puts out some helpful booklets on the fish and fishing in that state. The following booklets on specific fish give their life history, ecology, and management. There are booklets on large-mouth bass, small-mouth bass, Wisconsin muskellunge, brook trout, brown trout, walleyes, lake sturgeon, white crappie, rock bass, and the white sucker.

They also have the following booklets:

Wisconsin Muskellunge Waters
Wisconsin Walleye Waters
Wisconsin Trout Streams
Wisconsin Streams

These booklets can be obtained from:
Dept. of Natural Resources
P.O. Box 450
Madison, Wis. 53701

WHY FISH CARP?

The book *Why Fish Carp?* answers the question and tells you everything you need to know on how to find, rig, and bait for this much-neglected gamefish. I say "gamefish" because the carp is a real tough scrapper on sporting tackle and especially on light tackle. This booklet points out the fun, thrills, and reasons why fishing for carp can be real sport. It takes you into the world of noted carp fishermen, including Fred Taylor from England, who has fished for these fish all over the globe. He reveals his secrets and fishing methods, which will enable you to catch more and bigger carp. There are also a dozen and a half excellent recipes on how to prepare carp at the end of this book, which sells for $1.25 and is published by:
Gapen Tackle Co.
Big Lake, Minn. 55309

SKEETER BASS BOATS

The Skeeter Company has been in the fishing boat business for a long time and was one of the first companies to start making "bass boats." They now have a wide variety of such bass boats in all sizes, hulls, seating arrangements, specifications, accessories, and standard and optional equipment. Most of their boats fall in the 15- or 16-ft. range. The boats have standard and optional equipment such as console steering, casting decks, padded seats, carpeting, live wells, rod boxes, bow and transom lights, storage compartments, and bilge pumps. You also have a choice of many colors. For a catalog showing their complete line of boats in detail write to:
Skeeter Products
1 Skeeter Rd., P.O. Box 1602
Kilgore, Tex. 75662

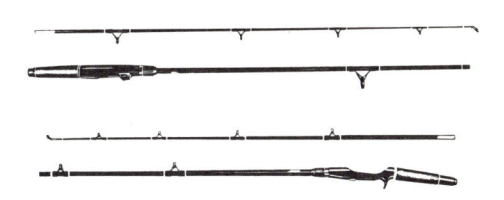

LEW CHILDRE SPEED STICKS

Lew Childre & Sons offers these Speed Sticks, which are made extralight throughout but of strong, durable materials that stand up and make casting easier. These rods enable a fisherman to feel the slightest vibration from hook to hand. The rods are equipped with Fuji Hard Speed Rings, which are lighter than carbide guides, and the frames are of one-piece, no-weld construction. The Speed Sticks are made in spinning and casting models in different lengths and actions to handle a wide range of freshwater lure weights. This company also sells rod blanks, component parts for making rods and fishing poles. Their catalog costs $1.00 and can be obtained from:
Lew Childre & Sons, Inc.
P.O. Box 535
Foley, Ala. 36535

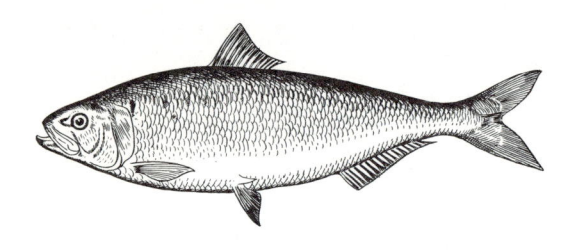

SHAD FISHING

If you haven't tried fishing for shad, you're missing out on great sport, for these fish fight hard and are fast and flashy when hooked on light tackle. They can be caught on light spinning tackle using small spoons, spinners, jigs, and shad darts. Or you can use a fly rod and small wet flies or streamers or special shad flies. They can also be taken by trolling with many of these same lures.

The secret in this fishing is to find out where the shad are concentrated in a river, and cast or troll there. And keep your lure down deep near the bottom for best results. There are many rivers from Canada to Florida on the Atlantic Coast that can be fished for shad. Most outstanding are the Connecticut River, Delaware River, Susquehanna River, and the St. John's River in Florida. They are also found along the Pacific Coast in many rivers such as the Russian River, Sacramento River, Feather River, Columbia River, and Umpqua River. If you want a good book dealing solely with shad fishing, get a copy of *Shad Fishing* by Boyd Pfeiffer; it sells for $8.95 and is published by:
Crown Publishers, Inc.
419 Park Ave. S.
New York, N.Y. 10016

NEVADA FISHING

The following booklets on Nevada fishing spots and areas are available:

Angler's Guide to Lake Tahoe
Angler's Guide to Eastern Nevada
Angler's Guide to Northeast Nevada
Angler's Guide to Lakes Mead, Mohave, and the Colorado River

Each booklet costs $.25 and can be obtained from:
Nevada Dept. of Fish and Game
P.O. Box 10678
Reno, Nev. 89510

STREAMSIDE ANGLERS

This company sells fly-tying materials and tools, hooks, feathers, hair, thread, and cement for the fly fisherman. They handle fly rods, fly lines, leaders, reels, vests, and various items used in fly fishing. They also carry fly-tying and fly-fishing books. For their catalog showing and describing all these items write to:
Streamside Anglers
P.O. Box 2158
Missoula, Mont. 59801

FISHERMAN'S BOAT CUSHION

The Gladding Aqua-Float fisherman's boat cushion features a resilient, extrabuoyant kapok filling for safety and comfort and rugged drill cover for durability. In fact, many boat rental and fishing camp businesses use these as rental cushions because of their long, safe use period. Strong stitching and securely fastened safety straps are other Aqua-Float features. The cushion is listed by Underwriters Laboratory and is Coast Guard approved as a Type IV personal flotation device. For more information write to:
Gladding Corp., Flotation Products Div.
P.O. Box 8277, Sta. A
Greenville, S.C. 29604

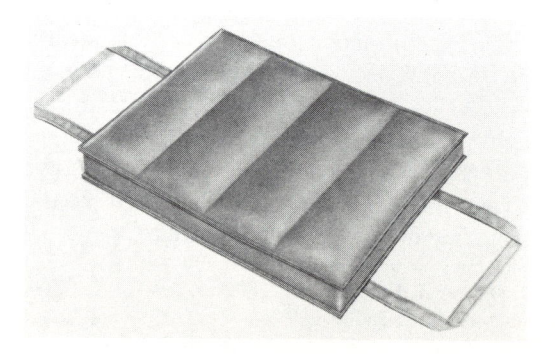

WORTH'S MUSKY LURES

Worth's Musky Fin (left), with a patented offset shaft that prevents line twist, is the lure that produced a world record 53¾-lb. musky. The nickel-fluted blade has a streak of red on the underside for added attraction and an abundantly dressed bucktail 6/0 treble hook. Bright red and nickel beads finish off this lure. It is available in ten bucktail colors and weighs 1⅛ ozs. It is also available in smaller sizes and hooks for pike, bass, salmon, and trout.

Worth's Musky Tiger (center) features tandem 2/0 treble hooks and has a genuine abalone pearl blade polished to a jewelry finish for the maximum iridescence that attracts muskies. For those who prefer a "French" style blade, the Musky Tiger also comes with Worth's "blitz" made in nickel, brass, or copper finish. The 1-oz. Musky Tiger comes in black, red, natural, or yellow bucktail colors.

Worth's Musky Mauler (right) has tandem 3/0 bronzed treble hooks and is dressed with either gray or fox squirrel tail or white or black northern deer hair. The Mauler has a No. 5 willowleaf blade, solid brass body, in nickel, brass, or copper finish and red and solid brass bead bearings. A 1/0 barrel swivel is used to help prevent line twist with this ¾-oz. lure. For their catalog or more information about these lures write to:
The Worth Co.
Stevens Point, Wis. 54481

FISHING IN KANSAS LAKES AND RESERVOIRS

The booklet *Fishing in Kansas Lakes and Reservoirs* is a colorful, well-illustrated guide to the waters of this state. It covers the major impoundments, reservoirs, and lakes, and has maps showing the nearby highways, boat ramps, marinas, parks, and other facilities. It has charts showing the acreage, boat rentals, swimming, drinking water, tables and grills, and concessions. It tells what kind of fish are caught in each reservoir or lake. The booklet can be obtained from:
Kansas Forestry, Fish, and Game Commission
P.O. Box 1028
Pratt, Kans. 67124

AMERICAN BASS FISHERMAN

The *American Bass Fisherman* is a bimonthly magazine that covers fishing for large-mouth and small-mouth bass all over the country. They have such field editors as Tony Mack, Nick Sisley, Larry Green, A. D. Livingston, Larry Williams, and others who contribute articles to the magazine. This magazine also sponsors bass tournaments each year with big-money prizes. You get the magazine if you become a member of their club, which offers various other benefits. For more information write to:
American Bass Fisherman
P.O. Box 908
Cocoa Beach, Fla. 32931

MAKING LURES AND OTHER TACKLE

The Limit Manufacturing Corporation carries a full and varied supply of various parts and components and materials for making your own fishing lures, rods, and other tackle. They sell rubber and plastic molds to make plastic worms and tell you in their catalog how to do it. They also carry jig and spinner molds. And they have spinner blades, wire shafts, clevises, beads, swivels, snaps, split rings, and tools for making lures and materials for tying flies. They also carry rod blanks, ferrules, reel seats, handles, cork grips, guides, and other parts needed to make complete fishing rods. And they also have a line of finished rods, reels, lines, hooks, lures, tackle boxes, vests, and other fishing accessories. Their catalog costs $1.00 and can be obtained from:

Limit Mfg. Corp.
P.O. Box 369
Richardson, Tex. 75080

MARKER BUOY

This Marker Buoy from N. A. Taylor offers an ideal way to mark favorite fishing spots (so you can return to them) and underwater hazards (so you can avoid them).

The Marker Buoys also can be used for setting up sail and power boat race courses, marking the location of a valuable item dropped overboard for later recovery, and for other uses.

Molded of solid puncture-proof plastic foam, the Marker Buoys are unsinkable and will not mar boats coming in contact with them. The buoy has a 24-in. mast with colorful pennant that's easy to spot from a great distance. An anchor ring is provided on the bottom of the buoy for easy securing of an anchor or drop line. It is galvanized for long, corrosion-free life. The buoys retail for $4.50 each. For more information write to:

N. A. Taylor Co., Inc.
Gloversville, N.Y. 12078

REBEL BASS'N BOX

This tackle box by Rebel is made to order for the serious bass angler who knows which lures he wants to use and doesn't need one of those big, heavy tackle boxes that get in the way and take up too much room. This new box is molded of high-impact PRADCO-lite plastic, and the single box has twenty compartments for holding plugs, jigs, plastic worms, spinners, weights, and hooks. The two-sided double box has twenty compartments on each side for a total of forty compartments. Both boxes are only 14 in. wide by 10 in. deep. The single box sells for $7.00, and the double box sells for $12. For more information write to:

Rebel Division—Plastics Research and Develop. Corp.
P.O. Box 1587
3601 Jenny Lind Rd.
Fort Smith, Ark. 72901

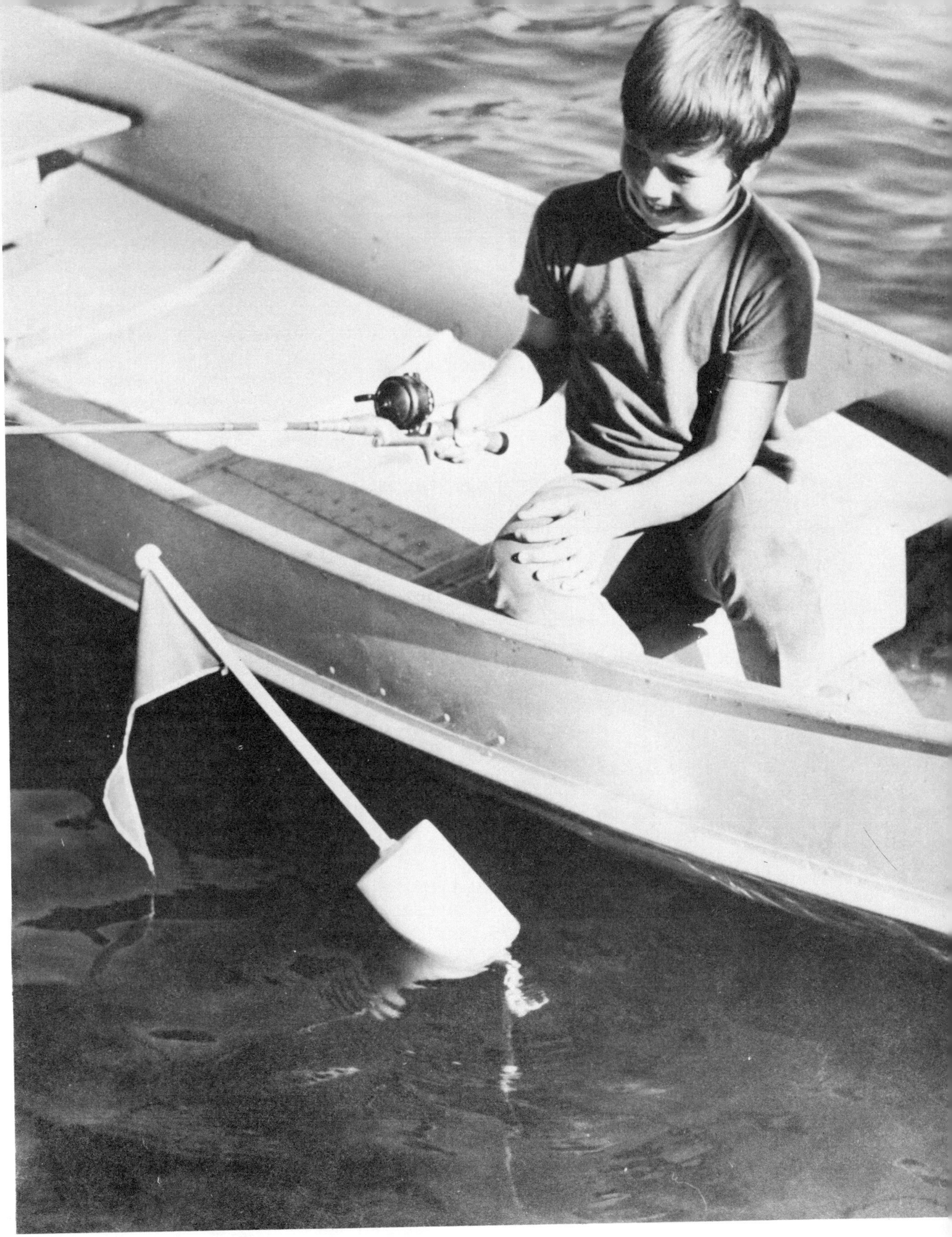

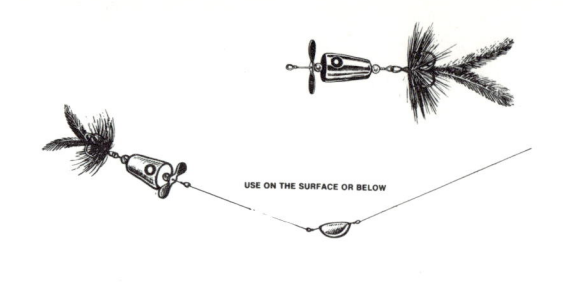

OLD PAL MINNOW BUCKETS

These oversize minnow buckets are made from polyethylene to resist corrosive conditions and eliminate boat noise. They float upright and are unsinkable and self-aerating. Baffle in inner pail makes it easy to pick up the bait. They have noncorrosive aluminum handles and are available in 8-qt. and 10-qt. sizes. For more information write to:
Woodstream Corp.
P.O. Box 327
Lititz, Pa. 17543

MARATHON SCRAPPY LURE

The Marathon Scrappy Lure is a fish-getter that floats and can be used without any weight on top to sputter and ripple and attract fish. If the fish aren't hitting on the surface, you just add a weight ahead of this lure and use it underwater off the bottom or at any depth you want. It comes in one size but with four different colors. For more information about this lure or others they make write to:
Marathon Bait Co.
Rte. 2, Hwy. XX
Mosinee, Wis. 54455

THE TROUT FISHERMAN'S BIBLE

The Trout Fisherman's Bible by Dan Holland is a complete guide to all the trout species and the best ways to catch them. It deals with the life history, habits, senses, foods, flies, fly tackle, fly casting, dry-fly fishing, wet-fly fishing, nymph fishing, streamer and bucktail fishing, spinner fishing, spinning, bait casting, bait fishing, lake fishing, lake trout fishing, and steelhead and sea trout fishing. It also tells where to go and how to take big trout and how to play and land them. The book is well illustrated with line drawings and photos, and it sells for only $2.50. It is published by:
Doubleday & Co., Inc.
501 Franklin Ave.
Garden City, N.Y. 11530

140

BEVIN-WILCOX FISHING LINES

The Bevin-Wilcox Line Company makes many different kinds of fishing lines for fresh water and salt water. They formerly made a monofilament line called Perlene, which was very popular with fishermen. This same line is now marketed under the name Perlex. It is available in tests from 4 to 50 lbs. and comes in a pearl-gray color. They also make other monofilaments, fly lines, braided nylon, squidding, and trolling lines. For their catalog describing these and other lines write to:
Bevin-Wilcox Line Co.
Moodus, Conn. 06469

LI'L TUBBY

The Li'l Tubby lure has a specially designed replaceable soft-plastic TubbyTail, which securely couples directly to its hardbait swimming body. Its weight and balance have been engineered to place its rattling ballast near the rear to give unmatched casting accuracy. Each Li'l Tubby is packed with a spare tail, and extra tails may be purchased in a variety of colors. This lure is 2 in. long and weighs ½ oz., and is made in several colors. For more information write to:
Tubby Tackle, Inc.
P.O. Box 426
Norman, Okla. 73069

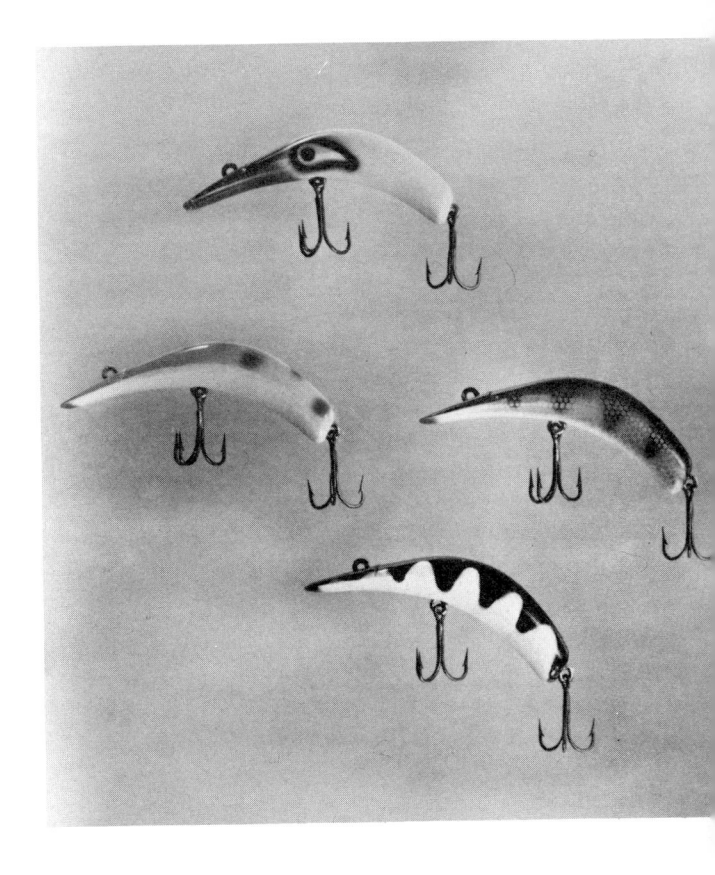

LAZY IKE LURES

A proven lure since the first one was hand-carved in 1938, the Lazy Ike KL series is effective for many freshwater gamefish and comes in seven different sizes, so there's a Lazy Ike length and weight for every angling situation. Ideal for casting or trolling, the Lazy Ike KL series creates a tantalizing, wobbling action during retrieve. Perfect for any fish that feeds on minnows, the 3-in. Lazy Ikes shown here weigh ⅓ oz. and come in twelve standard colors and twelve metallic colors, as do the others in the KL series of subsurface lures.

For bigger species such as muskellunge or pike, there is the 3½-in., ⅝-oz. Husky Ike and the 4½-in. (1-oz.) Musky Ike. For the spincaster and even the fly rod angler there are smaller Lazy Ikes. For more information about these and other lures they make write to:
Lazy Ike Corp.
Fort Dodge, Ia. 50501

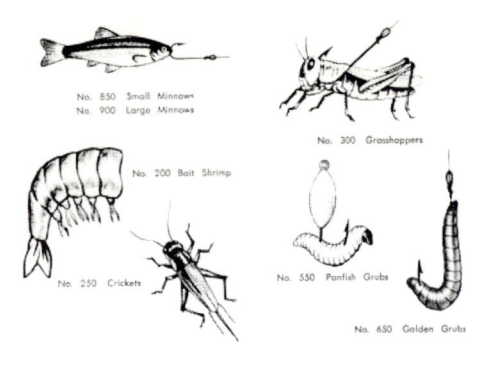

FIN NATURAL BAITS

The Fin processed baits are preserved natural baits packed in clear, plastic bags. They are treated with special fish-attracting oils and compounds and are processed to maintain a pliable, lifelike texture and natural appearance. They are clean and easy to handle and have no offensive odor. They package minnows, shrimp, crickets, grasshoppers, panfish grubs, and golden grubs. You'll find these baits for sale in many fishing tackle shops and sporting goods stores. For more information you can write to:
Arndt & Sons, Inc.
788 Evans St.
Akron, O. 44305

THE SMARTEST TROUT

Most experienced trout anglers rate trout in the following order. They say that the brook trout is easiest to catch on bait and lures. The rainbow trout is rated as the next easiest to fool. But the brown trout is considered the most difficult to catch—they are more wary and cautious, and long after the other trout are removed by anglers from hard-fished trout streams, great numbers of brown trout remain, even though they may not show or be hooked too often.

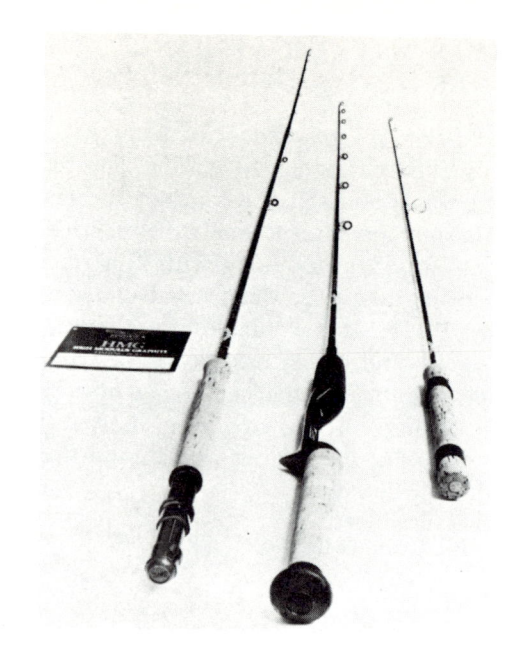

FENWICK HMG GRAPHITE RODS

Fenwick introduced the Graphite rod a few years ago and today makes a wide variety of these rods for both freshwater and saltwater fishing. These rods have met with instant acceptance in the fishing world because of their lightness, strength, and sensitivity. They also add distance to your cast and have a fast recovery with no rod vibration. Their fly rods range from short 6-ft., 3-in. models weighing only $1 \frac{7}{8}$ ozs. up to $10 \frac{1}{2}$-ft. models weighing $4 \frac{5}{8}$ ozs. They also make many freshwater spinning rods from ultralight $4 \frac{1}{2}$-ft. models up to 8-ft., 9-in. steelhead rods. And they also make casting rods in $5 \frac{1}{2}$- and 6-ft. lengths with varied actions. Their catalog showing these rods and other freshwater and salt-water rods costs $.25 and is available from:
Fenwick
P.O. Box 729
Westminster, Calif. 92683

MARTIN AUTOMATIC FLY REELS

The Martin Automatic Fly Reels are well known to anglers who have used them through the years. They feature push-button tension release and adjustable safety trigger. The solid-core spool provides extra strength. The patented, nonfriction brake stops the retrieve instantly and won't wear, slip, or need adjusting. The spools can be changed fast without using tools. For their catalog showing these and other fishing tackle write to:
Martin Reel Co., Inc.
P.O. Drawer 8
Mohawk, N.Y. 13407

INDIANA FISHING

The Indiana Department of Natural Resources has a helpful guide called *Lake and Stream Information,* which covers in detail some of the most important fishing streams and lakes in Indiana. It tells the county, nearest town, directions, public access, camping facilities, and what kind of fish are caught in each body of water. For your copy write to:
Dept. of Natural Resources
Div. of Fish and Wildlife
Rm. 607, State Office Bldg.
Indianapolis, Ind. 46204

FISHING LURE COMPONENTS

Lakeland Industries makes fishing lure components for making spinners, jigs, and other lures. They carry several kinds of spinner blades such as the Indiana, Colorado, Willowleaf, June Bug, French blades and beads, wire, swivels, snaps, clevises, split rings, and the hooks needed to assemble the finished lures. They sell mostly to dealers and manufacturers in large quantities. For more information write to:
Lakeland Industries
Isle, Minn. 56342

LOCATING STEELHEAD

As any steelhead angler knows, these highly prized fish of the Pacific Coast are often difficult to locate in a big river. They move upstream rapidly and stop or rest in certain spots. Most of these popular spots are heavily fished. You'll do better if you concentrate on the smaller tributaries and streams, which are not as crowded. It also pays to get maps of these tributaries and streams, and after fishing them a few times mark the best spots and note under what stream conditions they are most productive. After you have located at least a dozen good pools, runs, and riffles, fish these choice spots hard and avoid other stretches of the stream and river.

143

FISHING IN ONTARIO, CANADA

This is a very informative booklet telling about Ontario, Canada's, fishing and hunting. It is called *The Hunter's & Fisherman's Ontario/Canada,* and it tells you when to come, what you'll find, what to bring, and how to get there. It covers guides, licenses, regulations, maps, equipment, accommodations, and fly-in services. For your copy, write to:
Ministry of Industry and Tourism
Province of Ontario
Queen's Park
Toronto
Canada M7A 2E5

FRESHET PRESS BOOKS

The Freshet Press publishes new fishing books and also classics that have gone out of print. These are being brought back because of the demand by book collectors and anglers who want them to read or for their libraries and collections. They include such well-known and new titles as:

The Fly and the Fish by John Atherton $12.95
A History of Fly Fishing for Trout by John Waller Hills $8.95
The Lure and Lore of Trout Fishing by Alvin R. Grove $9.95
The Complete Fly-tier by Reuben R. Cross $7.95
This Wonderful World of Trout by Charles K. Fox. $9.95
Night Fishing for Trout by L. James Bashline $7.95
Fishing the Midge by Ed Koch $7.95
Fish the Impossible Places by J. Richard Pobst $9.95

For their brochure telling more about these books and others they publish write to:
Freshet Press
90 Hamilton Rd.
Rockville Centre, N.Y. 11571

LUNKER LAKERS

Although good-sized lake trout are caught in the United States, they can't compare to those caught farther north. If you want real "lunker" lake trout you'll find Canada your best bet, especially such waters as the Great Bear Lake in Canada's Northwest Territories, accessible by float plane from Yellowknife to the southeast. Beyond the tree line and surrounded by dramatic cliffs and hills, Great Bear is larger than Lake Erie and is brimming full with fighting "lakers" weighing up to 60 lbs. that challenge your skill and endurance. Anglers normally throw back anything weighing under 30 lbs.! A number of comfortable fishing lodges are strung along the shores, all equipped with good food and lodging, boats, guides, and a friendly atmosphere. Flights above the Arctic Circle can be arranged for those interested in spectacular Arctic scenery or fishing for Arctic char. But reservations should be made well in advance for the short summer season. For more information write to:
Canadian Government Travel Bureau
Kent Albert Building
150 Kent St.
Ottawa
Canada K1A 0H6

THE ANGLER

The magazine called *The Angler* is a beautiful all-color publication slanted toward all fishermen in fresh water or salt water. It has such contributing editors as Dan Blanton, Stan Fagerstrom, Michael Fong, Jim Grassi, Larry Green, Dave Meyers, Bob Nauheim, Lew Palmer, Andre Puyans, and Bernie Sherman. Other well-known anglers and writers also appear in its pages, often with articles on freshwater and salt-water fishing. *The Angler* is published bimonthly, and the subscription rate is $7.50 for one year. It is published by:
Angler Publications
P.O. Box 12155
Oakland, Calif. 94604

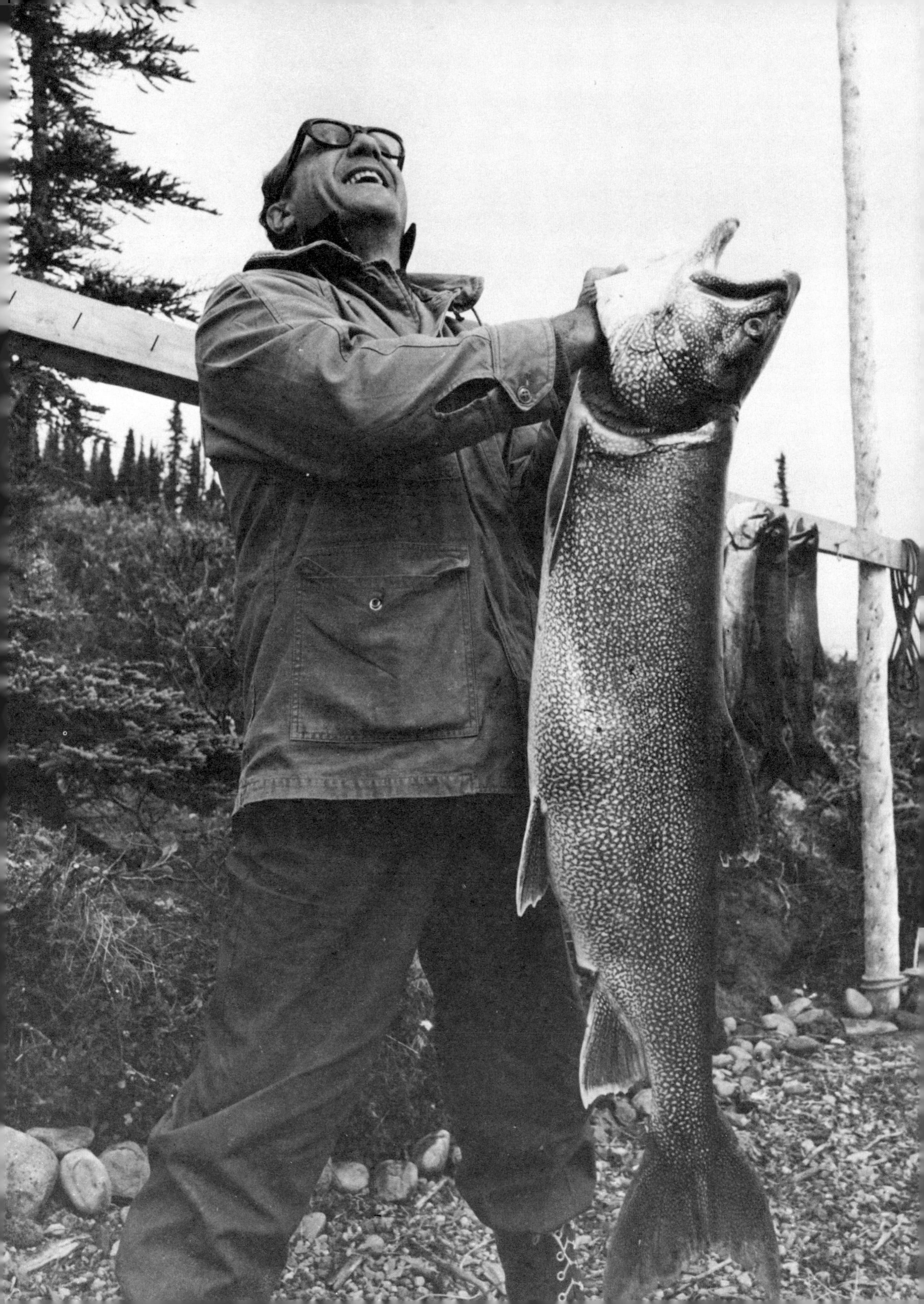

PLAN YOUR CAST

In fly fishing for trout it is usually the first cast that is important and counts the most. A sloppy cast or an unnatural presentation will alert or frighten a trout. So it pays to study the water, currents, and eddies and try to figure out where the fish is lying or even try to see it before you make the first cast. And get into a position where you won't be seen and your leader and fly line won't drift over the fish before the fly.

STURGEON ON HOOK AND LINE

Most sturgeon have been caught commercially on set lines or in nets or seines. A few anglers have hooked one accidentally while fishing for other fish. But more and more anglers along the Pacific Coast have been deliberately fishing for sturgeon with rod and reel, and some good catches have been made. Since sturgeon run big (up to several hundred pounds), you need sturdy, salt-water-type rods and big reels filled with strong lines testing from 20 to 100 lbs.

For bait the sturgeon anglers use smelt, herring, anchovies, lamprey eels, and other small fish or baitfish. These are impaled on big, strong hooks, and rigs with heavy sinkers are needed to hold bottom in the tide or strong currents usually fished.

This sturgeon fishing is done in California waters in the brackish bays of Suisan, San Pablo, Richardson, and San Francisco. Other sturgeon anglers fish in Oregon and Washington in such rivers as the Columbia, Rogue, and Umpqua.

LOOK, MA—NO HOOK!

Two anglers in Florida had fished the waters of Everglades Holiday Park hard for several hours without catching anything. So they quit, pulled up their anchor, and turned on the boat lights since it was pretty dark, and started the motor for the trip back to the dock. As the boat turned around, there was a big splash, and a 6-lb. bass leaped through the air and into the boat!

LUNCH FOR BAIT

What happens if you get to your favorite fishing hole and find out you forgot to bring the bait? Well, just do what two California anglers did in the same situation. They decided to use their lunches—salami and cheese sandwiches. And it worked, for they caught three big catfish—of 12 lbs., 13½ lbs., and 14 lbs.!

GO TO FISHING SCHOOL?

If you want to become a better angler in freshwater or salt water, go to a fishing school. Don't laugh—more and more anglers these days are going to a fishing school to get the know-how and skills that will enable them to catch more or bigger fish. There are now many such schools that teach fly fishing, spinning, casting, surf fishing, salt-water boat fishing, offshore fishing, and even shark fishing. Many of these fishing schools are listed and described in this catalog, and you can send away for information that gives the seasons, dates, tuition fees, and type of instruction you will receive.

ANGLER'S & SHOOTER'S BOOKSHELF

The Angler's & Shooter's Bookshelf is one of the largest dealers in new, used, and rare or out-of-print fishing and sporting books in the country. In fact, their list is so long that they have to issue their catalog in two parts. Part 1 lists the authors from A to K, and Part 2 lists those from L to Z. They charge $2.00 for the set, and it can be obtained from:
Angler's & Shooter's Bookshelf
Goshen, Conn. 06756

WATER CRICKET

Sponge rubber "bugs" have been a favorite with expert panfish anglers for years. The new Water Cricket from Fin comes in two colors and models. The white model is a floater; the black model sinks and fishes under water. Both are effective for big trout and panfish. The Fin Water Cricket is available in No. 8 and No. 10 hook sizes, and the hooks are securely tied and cemented to prevent slipping and twisting on the long-wearing body. Rubber legs add to the Water Cricket's "natural" insect appearance. It can be fished with a fly rod or with a spinning/bubble combination. For more information and a catalog of other baits and lures write to:
Arndt & Sons, Inc.
788 Evans St.
Akron, O. 44305

CORTLAND 333 FLY LINES

The Cortland 333 fly lines have been popular with fly fishermen in fresh and salt water for many years. They have been improved by research in materials and methods and are available in floating and sinking types and in level, double taper, rocket taper, bug taper, and sink-tip-rocket taper. They are available in weights from No. 4 to No. 11. For their catalog describing these and other fishing lines write to:
Cortland Line Co.
Cortland, N.Y. 13045

LAKE TROUT

If you can't obtain big minnows or run out of them when fishing for lake trout through the ice, try putting several small minnows on one hook and lower them to the bottom.

147

JIFFY LURE

You can easily and quickly make a jig-type lure by taking a couple of split-shot sinkers and a small, light-wire hook. Bend the hook up about ¼ in. from the eye. Then get some bucktail hair or feathers, insert these between the split shot, and clamp the shot to the feathers or hair and hook shank by using pliers. You can paint the split shot white, yellow, red, or any other color.

ANYONE FOR CAVIAR?

Genuine caviar, which comes from sturgeon, has always been expensive, even in Russia in the old days. Today it is out of sight, with a pound costing from $50 to $100 or more if it is the genuine Beluga, Osetra, or Sevruga sturgeon. The real caviar consists of the small dark or black eggs the size of BB shot, which are prepared and preserved with borax or salt. The best caviar still comes from Russia, Iran, and Europe. But sturgeon have become so scarce all over the world that many substitute caviars are produced from such fish as whitefish, chubs or ciscoes, paddlefish, cod, catfish, and mullet. These are dyed black to make them look like sturgeon caviar. There is also a "red" caviar, which is made from salmon eggs. All these substitutes for the genuine caviar, are, of course, cheaper, and this is what most people eat.

THE MYSTERIOUS EEL

The eel has been the subject of speculation and mystery for ages. The early Greeks such as Aristotle thought the eels were spontaneously generated from the mud on the floor of the ocean. Others thought that blades of grass suddenly developed into eels. It was not until the middle 1800s that the first larva of an eel was examined by Dr. Karp, a German naturalist. Then in 1906 a Danish scientist named Johannes Schmidt began a series of investigations that lasted more than fifteen years and finally proved that both American and European eels travel to the Sargasso Sea region near Bermuda to spawn.

But the eel still remains a creature of mystery by its nocturnal habits of hiding during the day and venturing out to feed at night. It is also claimed that on rainy nights or when a heavy dew wets the grass, eels will leave the water and travel on land for short distances. Whether true or not, eels bite best at night. However, if the water turns muddy from recent rains, they will also come out to feed and can be caught in good numbers then, even during the daytime.

Most eels are caught by still-fishing from shore, with the anglers casting out their lines with baited hooks and letting them lie on the bottom. Such baits as worms, minnows, pieces of fish, or meat can all be used for bait. And you'll do best if you use several lines in the water spaced along the bank at intervals.

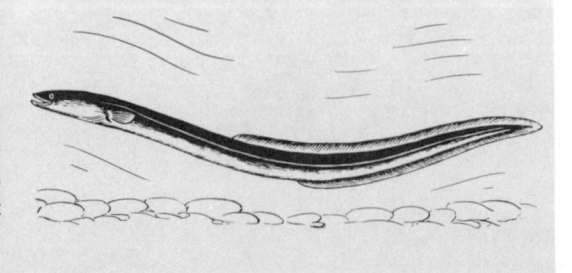

NIGHT FISHING

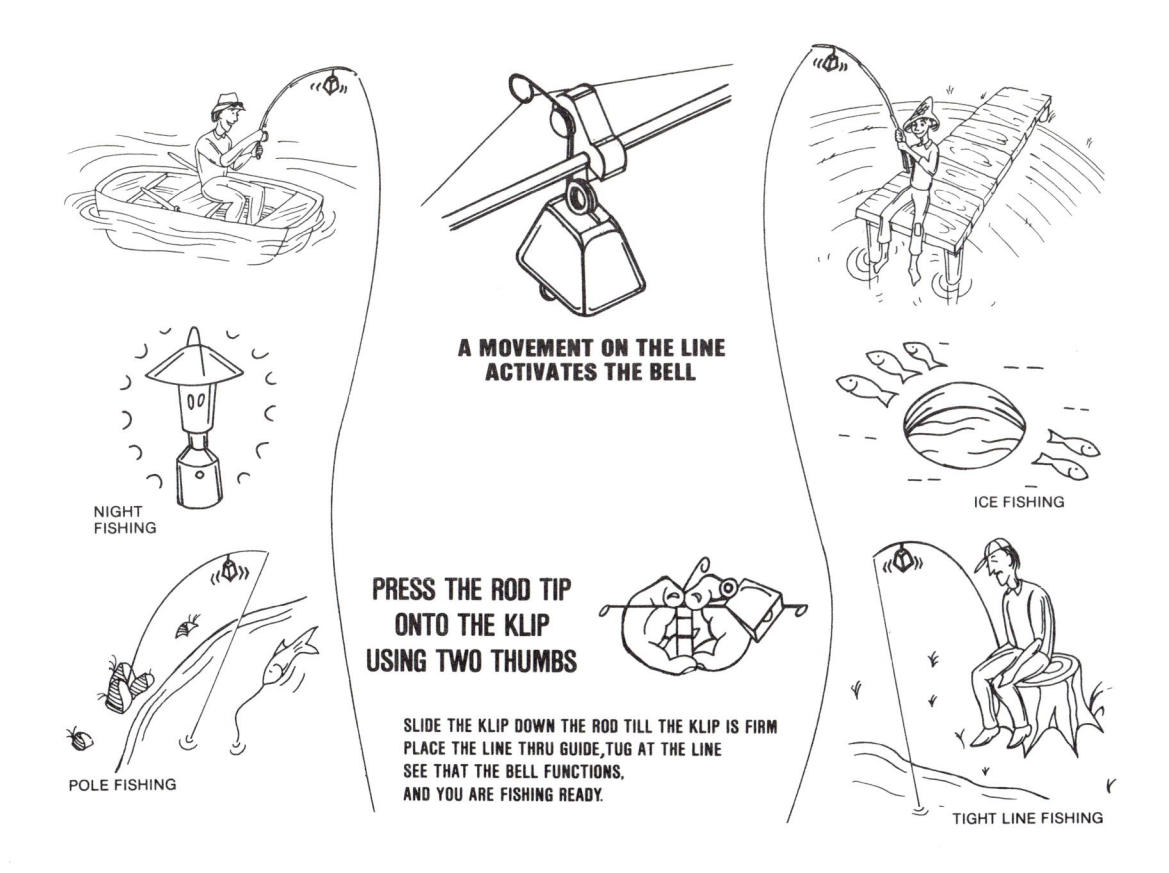

A MOVEMENT ON THE LINE ACTIVATES THE BELL

ICE FISHING

POLE FISHING

PRESS THE ROD TIP ONTO THE KLIP USING TWO THUMBS

SLIDE THE KLIP DOWN THE ROD TILL THE KLIP IS FIRM
PLACE THE LINE THRU GUIDE, TUG AT THE LINE
SEE THAT THE BELL FUNCTIONS,
AND YOU ARE FISHING READY.

TIGHT LINE FISHING

ROD KLIP BELL

The angler who does a lot of still fishing and wants to relax and wait for a bite will find this little bell with clip handy. It gives an alarm when a fish bites and can be especially useful when you spread out several lines or poles or rods along the bank, or if you do a lot of fishing at night for catfish, carp, or eels. The Rod Klip is attached to the rod, and the line is run through the guide. When a fish takes the bait, the line is pulled through the guide, moving the arm and bell and causing it to ring. For more information write to:
Rod-Klip
1627 Washington Ave.
St. Louis, Mo. 63103

WALKING FISH

There are fish that leave the water for long periods of time, and others that can survive out of the water for various lengths of time. The walking perch of Siam often leaves the water for long treks over dry roads and fields. One of these perch, which was removed from a pond and placed in a basket, escaped and walked back 300 ft. to the same pond from which it was removed. The mudskippers found in Asia can skip along the mud flats so fast that a man has difficulty in catching them. And the walking catfish, which was introduced not long ago into Florida, also walks on dry land from pond to pond.

LURE LIFE

Lure Life is a metallic, iridescent foil that comes in sheets and looks just like fish scales. It has silver, gold, and light blue finishes, and reflects a light and a scale pattern that looks remarkably like a minnow or baitfish. The sheets are small, and you simply cut out any shape or size you want, peel off the backing, and apply it to a lure. The powerful waterproof adhesive will stick and last for a long time.

This company also makes several rod and reel boots or protective cases with zippers that cover reels even when they are on a rod. These protect the reels from dust, dirt, sand, and weather conditions. For more information about these products write to:
Dart Mfg. Co.
1724 Cockrell Ave.
Dallas, Tex. 75215

THE MUSEUM OF AMERICAN FLY FISHING

The Museum of American Fly Fishing was founded in 1969 as a nonprofit, educational institution chartered by the state of Vermont. The Museum started with a magnificent collection of antique rods, reels, fly patterns, and a gift of monies from the Orvis Company. The Museum now has over one thousand items on display in its exhibit rooms. More than twenty-five thousand visitors now come annually to view the rare and famous fishing tackle. Rods formerly owned by Presidents Hoover and Eisenhower, Winslow Homer, and Ernest Hemingway are on display. There are reels as old as 1826 and many hundreds of items representative of the old-time tackle makers —Chubb, Abbey & Imbrie, Orvis, Shipley, Mills, Leonard, Edwards, Thomas, and Vom Hofe. Other unique items are in storage, and two libraries are in formation: A technical and a rare-book library are being used for research purposes. The Museum publishes the *American Fly Fisher,* a magazine that comes out quarterly; the articles deal with fly-fishing history and early fly-fishing tackle. You can become an associate member of the Museum for $10. Sustaining, patron, and life memberships range from $25 to $250. For more information write to:
The Museum of American Fly Fishing
Manchester, Vt. 05254

BIG PICKEREL

Most of the chain pickerel you catch along the Atlantic Coast will run from about 1 lb. up to 3 lbs. in weight. But in Maine, where pickerel are very plentiful in most lakes and ponds, many bigger ones are often caught in the spring, summer, fall, and through the ice during the winter. Here pickerel up to 6 or 7 lbs. have been taken. The world record on rod and reel for many years was the 9-lb. pickerel caught in Green Pond, New Jersey, by R. Kimble. This was beat by a 9-lb., 3-oz. pickerel caught by Frank McGovern in Aetna Lake, New Jersey. Then this fish was topped by a 9½-lb. pickerel caught at Homerville, Georgia, by Baxley McQuaig, Jr.

FISH THE FORESTS

Some of the best bass fishing takes place in the "forest" areas of lakes, where there are trees standing in the water. Such spots are especially common in our southern states, where cypress trees are often found growing in shallow water. But lakes that are newly formed or flooded may also have such standing "timber," even in our northern states. Old submerged creeks winding among such trees are good spots to try. You can fish these forests by casting your lure or bait as close to the base of the tree as you can. Trees that are submerged entirely are also hot fishing spots for bass.

THE ART OF PLUG FISHING

The book *The Art of Plug Fishing* by Homer Circle is a complete guide to using plugs in all kinds of situations, conditions, waters and for all kinds of fish. Homer Circle had a wide and varied experience in helping to design, test, and use plugs when he worked for a fishing tackle company. Since then he has become freshwater fishing editor of *Sports Afield* magazine and has traveled far and wide using all kinds of plugs and fishing with many expert and pro bass fishermen. This book covers almost everything you need to know about using plugs effectively to fool fish. Homer covers fishing tackle such as rods, reels, and lines. Then he goes into detail about the different kinds and types of plugs, their colors, weights, actions, and where they work best. He covers surface or top-water plugs, shallow runners, divers, deep runners, and sinkers. And he tells you where to use them to get the bass and other fish to hit. All in all, it is a very informative and helpful guide to plug fishing. *The Art of Plug Fishing* sells for $3.95 in paperback and is published by:

**Stackpole Books
Cameron and Kelker Sts.
Harrisburg, Pa. 17105**

BUCK KNIVES

This company is famous for its high-quality knives used by many fishermen, hunters, and campers. The company makes many different types of knives, including a filleting knife for cleaning fish. Send for their booklet *Knife Know-how*, which shows how to fillet fish with one of their knives, to:

**Buck Knives, Inc.
P.O. Box 1267
El Cajon, Calif. 92022**

SNAGPROOF LURES

The Snagproof lures are made of soft plastic materials and are weedless so that they can be fished in thick cover where the big bass lie. There are many different lures in this line, such as the popper, frog, hellgrammite, minno, spider, crawfish, worm, mouse, and leech. They come in different colors and in spinning or casting weights. For a catalog or more information write to:

**Snagproof Mfg. Co.
4153 E. Gailbraith
Cincinnati, O. 45236**

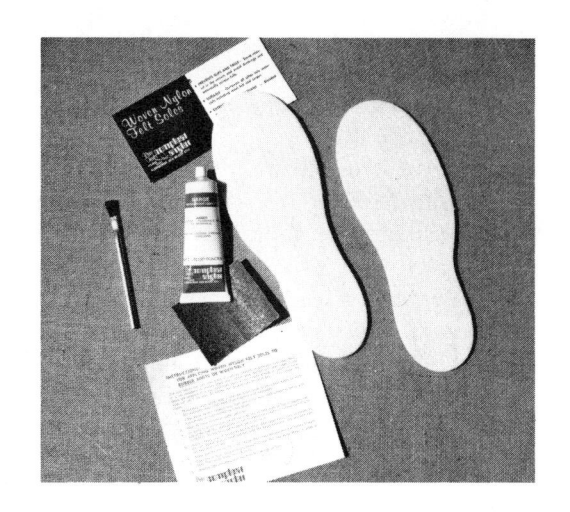

BODMER'S FLY SHOP

Bodmer's Fly Shop handles and sells all kinds of flies, fly-tying materials, rod blanks, and other component parts for making fishing rods. They also sell finished fly-fishing rods, fly reels, fly lines, fly boxes, fishing vests, and other fly-fishing tackle and accessories. Their catalog costs $1.00 and can be obtained from:
Bodmer's Fly Shop, Inc.
2400 Naegele Rd.
Colorado Springs, Colo. 80904

FELT SOLE KIT

This is a handy felt sole kit for installation of new felt or replacing worn felt on waders or hip boots. The woven nylon felt is a new synthetic material that is far more durable than any material now used on waders or boots. It outwears wool felt, carpet, polypropylene, and even heavy woven wool felt. It is a blend of nylon and polyester and is extremely slip resistant. The kit contains woven nylon felt, soles, waterproof cement tube, brush for applying the cement, abrasive for roughing the bottom of the boot, and complete detailed instructions for the best method of bonding felt to rubber boots. It sells for $8.50 and is available from:
Pete Test's Compleat Angler
P.O. Box 14442
Albuquerque, N.M. 87111

SYSTEM FLY REELS

These fly reels offered by Scientific Anglers are precision-made pieces of angling equipment. They have a modern functional design styled in traditional, classic lines by Hardy Brothers of England, internationally famous for their master craftmanship of fine fly-fishing reels since 1872. Every component in these reels is precision-machined of space-age materials, using advanced computer techniques. Each reel is hand-fitted, hand-assembled, and tested by Hardy's master craftsmen. Each of the eight fly reels is designed specifically for Scientific Anglers fly lines with the right capacity for line and backing. Each reel is provided with a handsome, padded, zippered carrying case. For more information about these reels write to:
Scientific Anglers
P.O. Box 2001
Midland, Mich. 48640

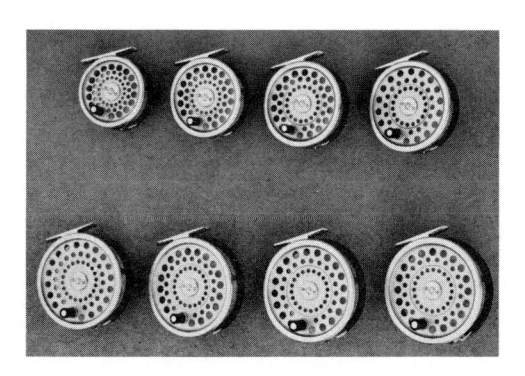

SPORT FISHING IN NEW YORK STATE

You can obtain a big map and information about New York State's freshwater fishing by writing for the *Sport Fishing in New York State* folder. It has license information, fish regulations, and other information an angler needs. Send for it to:
New York State Dept. of Environmental
  Conservation
Albany, N.Y. 12201

PREPARED SCENT BAITS

The Uncle Josh Bait Company has long been known for its pork rind and pork chunk baits. But now it is marketing prepared baits in jars that are handy and ready to use. They have a scent that attracts fish such as carp, catfish, panfish, and even trout. They can be used as they come right out of the jar, or you can add water to make a softer bait. And you can mold the bait around a small hook in a tiny ball or around a big hook into a large pear-shaped bait. For their catalog and booklet about these baits and their pork rind and chunks write to:
Uncle Josh Bait Co.
Fort Atkinson, Wis. 53538

CRESTLINER FISHING BOATS

This company makes several aluminum fishing boats from 12 ft. to 18 ft. Their Voyager Deluxe 18 and 16 are fashioned as "Northern Bass Boats." They have an underbow storage area and rod storage area. High-back swivel seats are an optional feature. These two boats have mechanical steering, side-steering console, and running lights. The other fishing models are the Sportsman 12, Super Seaman 14, Commodore 14, Admiral 16, and Voyager 18. They have aluminum enclosed motor mounts, nonskid flooring, laminated wood seating, and underseat flotation. The hulls are constructed from extra-thick marine aluminum and are welded, not riveted. They are finished with a baked acrylic enamel finish. For more information about these and other boats this company makes, write for their catalog to:
Crestliner Division of AMF
609 N.E. 13th Ave.
Little Falls, Minn. 56345

TEXAS FISH

The Texas Parks and Wildlife Department offers several booklets and bulletins on fish found in that state. They are:

Freshwater Fishes of Texas	Price $.60
Food and Game Fishes of the Texas Coast	Price $.55
Catfish and How to Know Them	Price $.30
The Texas Menhaden Fishery	Price $.55

Texas residents should include sales tax when ordering. The booklets can be obtained from:
Texas Parks and Wildlife Dept.
John H. Reagan Bldg.
Austin, Tex. 78701

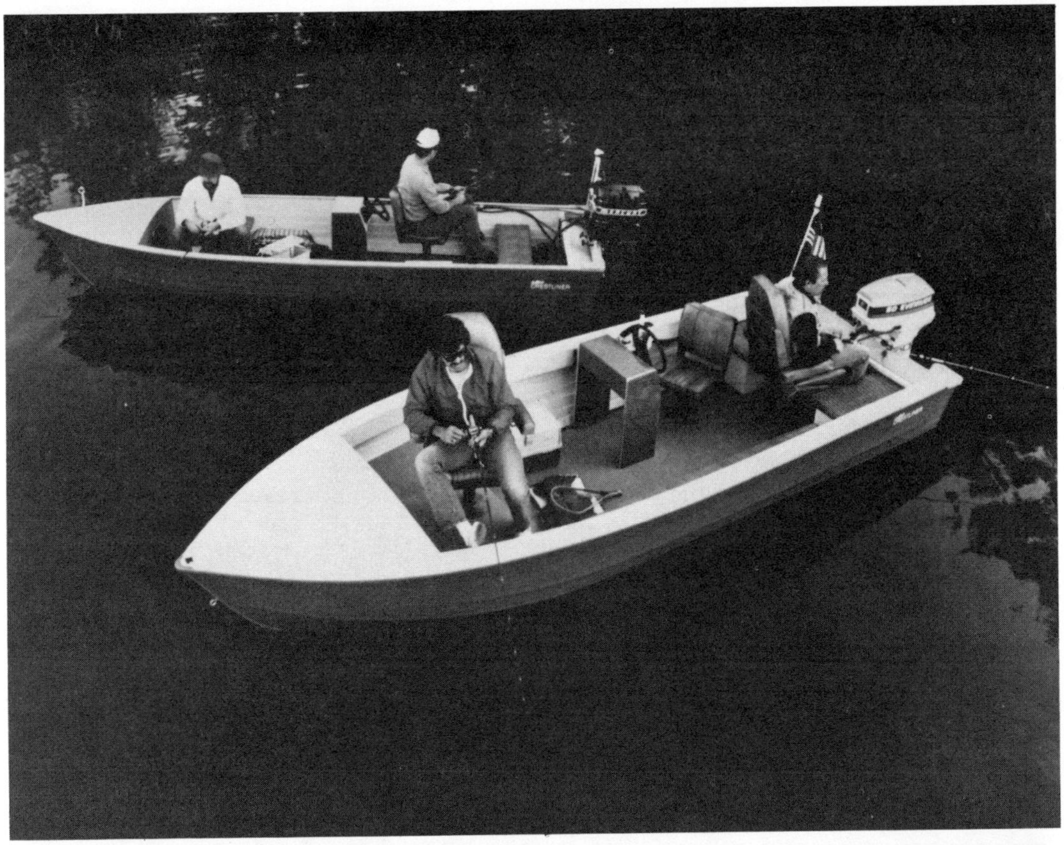

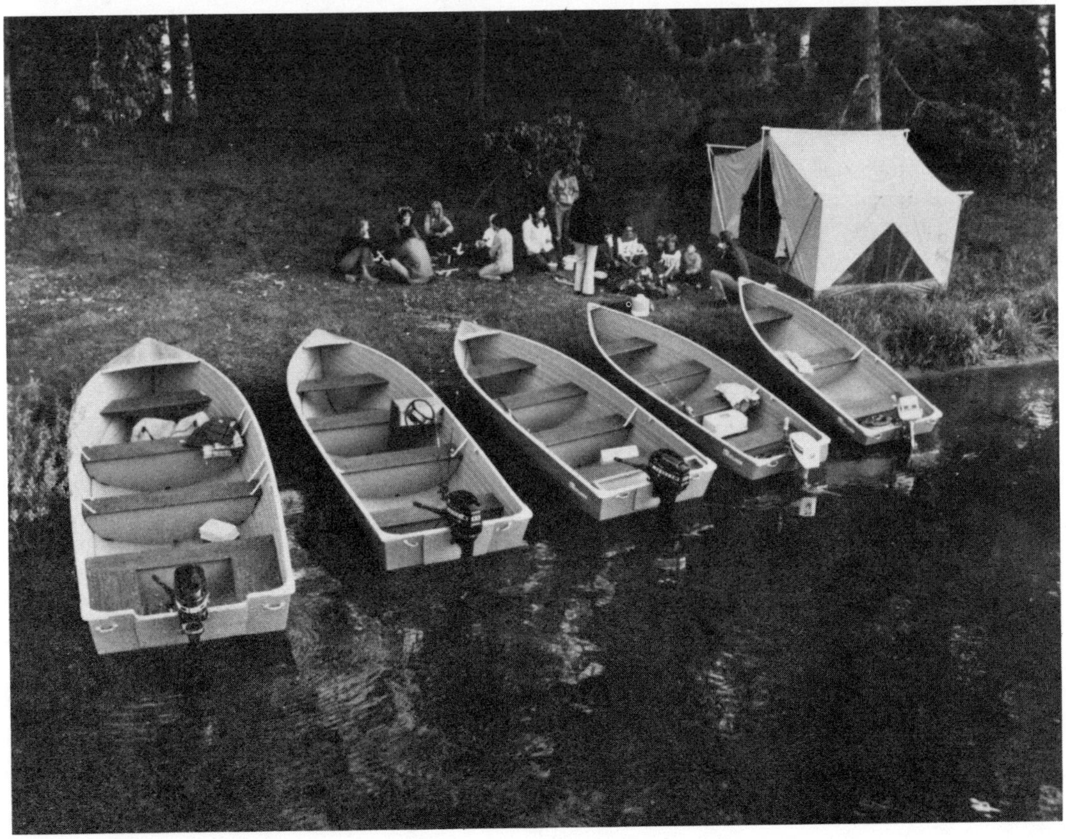

FISHING IN AMERICA

The book *Fishing in America* by Charles Waterman is a handsome volume that traces the history of angling in America from pre-Colonial Indian fishing to modern-day gamefish tournaments. The evolution of tackle, the distribution and habits of North American fishes, the ins and outs of angling techniques as they have developed over the span of our national life, the inland and coastal waters that bear our fish population—all are discussed and evoked in narrative that is at once enjoyable and authoritative. And throughout the book, on nearly every page, the eye is treated to superb illustrations, rare engravings, stunning four-color photographs and other drawings and illustrations. *Fishing in America* sells for $19.95 and is published by:
Holt, Rinehart & Winston, Inc.
383 Madison Ave.
New York, N.Y. 10017

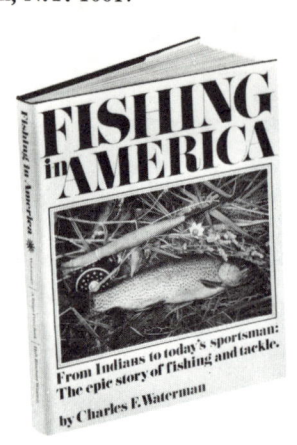

CHANGE LURES

If everybody has been using the same lures for days, weeks, or even months on a certain lake, try switching to something entirely different or even unusual. No matter how outlandish it looks, give it a try. The bass and other fish may hit it because it doesn't resemble the familiar lures everyone has been using.

BIG FLIES FOR TROUT

When fishing the larger western streams and rivers use the bigger dry flies on these waters. Big, bushy-hair flies tied on No. 8 or No. 9 hooks are best for the rough western rivers for rainbow or cutthroat trout. One good trick that can be used with the floating flies is to drag the fly directly upstream against the broken water, then let it drift back on the slack line that has been recovered.

CAMILLUS FISHING KNIVES

The Camillus Cutlery Company has been making knives for more than one hundred years. Their Deluxe Fisherman's Knife (No. 25) has a stainless-steel clip blade with serrated tip. The hook disgorger is specially ground to double as a fish scaler and bottle cap lifter. The genuine maize handles have a hook sharpener. The other model, the Angler's Knife (No. 31), features Indian Stag handles, and the rest of the features are the same as the other knife. This company makes a wide variety of other fishing knives, hunting knives, pocket knives, and special-purpose knives. For their catalog showing all these knives write to:
Camillus Cutlery Co.
Camillus, N.Y. 13031

L. L. BEAN

If you haven't heard of the establishment called L. L. Bean, you should know about it. Most fishermen, hunters, campers, and backpackers know L. L. Bean and order much of their equipment from this Maine store and factory. They are unique in that they stay open twenty-four hours a day, and you can drive in anytime and get a fishing license or hunting license or buy equipment for these sports.

They carry a wide assortment and variety of freshwater and salt-water rods, reels, lines, lures, vests, waders, boots, fishing knives, and other gear needed for fishing. But they are also noted for their fishing and hunting clothing such as shirts, sweaters, jackets, pants, shoes, boots, tents, camping equipment, and anything else needed to play or live outdoors. They do a big mail-order business. For their latest catalog write to:
L. L. Bean, Inc.
Freeport, Me. 04032

CARP ON ARTIFICIALS

Not many anglers fish for carp with trout or bass flies, but at certain times of the year when carp are close to shore feeding on mayflies or nymphs or other insects, the carp will hit artificial flies. Dry flies or small bass bugs can be used on top, and wet flies and nymphs can be used below the surface.

RAPALA LURES

The Rapala lures took the fishing world by storm when they were first introduced in this country. Created by Lauri Rapala of Finland, these balsa wood plugs go through as many as thirty painstaking steps before each lure is completed. Each lure is individually hand tank tested for the precise action necessary to simulate a swimming minnow. Such extreme attention to balance, contour, appearance, and strength is one reason these lures are used by many anglers and are copied by other manufacturers. The Rapala lures are now made in many floating, jointed, sinking, and diving models in many sizes and colors. They also make jigging models, which are used in the summer and also in the winter through the ice. For their catalog showing all these lures send $.25 to:
Normark Corp.
1710 E. 78th St.
Minneapolis, Minn. 55423

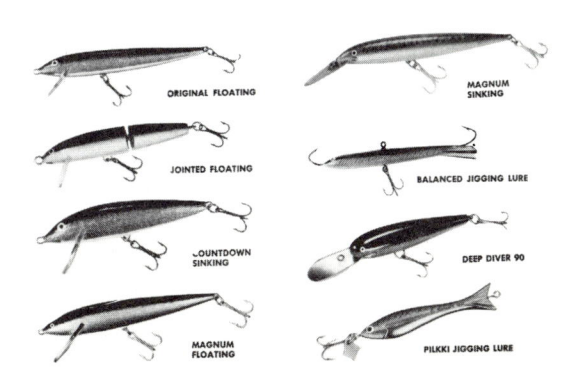

157

ELECTRIC WINCH ANCHOR BRACKET

Dutton-Lainson has developed a new bracket for stowing fishing anchors in a horizontal position when used with its electric anchor winch—a far superior way to the vertical stowing provided by many other anchor-handling systems.

As the photo indicates, a standard mushroom-type anchor that many fishermen use is pulled snugly into the bracket, where it is cushioned horizontally on a heavy rubber roller. Being firmly secured by the roller and outboard end of the bracket, the anchor cannot swing with boat movement or from waves slapping against it as with other bracket designs that hold the anchor in a vertical position when retracted.

The D-L bracket also can be used with other winches, both electric and hand-operated. Suggested retail price of the mounting bracket is $14.25. It is made of high-strength steel with a heavy chrome finish. For more information write to:

Dutton-Lainson Co.
Hastings, Neb. 68901

QUICK FINESSA RODS

The Quick Corporation of America makes a line of Finessa rods, including spinning, casting, and mooching models. Some of these feature Neo-Grip handles and Polygon guides. They have one-piece and two-piece rods from 5½ ft. to 7 ft. long suitable for worm fishing or lure casting with fresh-water spinning reels. The longer, heavier rods range from 6 ft. to 9 ft. and are designed for steelhead, coho salmon, and light salt-water fishing. For the catalog showing these rods and other fishing tackle they make, send $.25 to:

Quick Corp. of America
620 Terminal Way
Costa Mesa, Calif. 92627

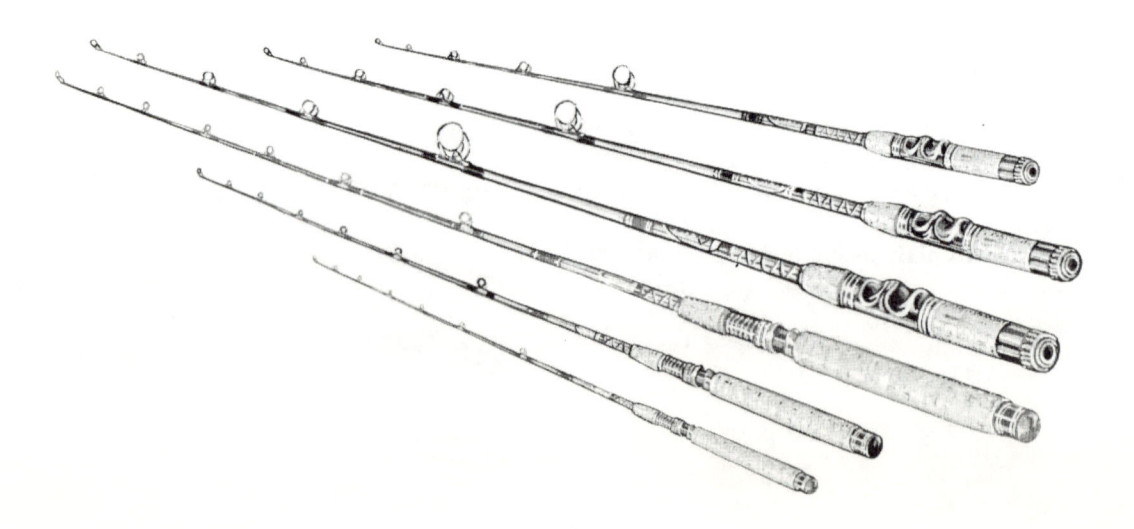

158

CHOOSING AND RIGGING PLASTIC WORMS

Bing McClelland, president of Burke Fishing Lures, whose firm makes the "Buckshot" plastic worms, feels that this worm is a great fish-getter because of its jewel-clear color; soft, floppy texture; and high-floating qualities. He also feels that the round ball segments act like a magnifying glass, creating more flash and glitter than with any other construction. Bing recommends some of the special hooks that have been developed for plastic worm fishing. To rig the "Buckshot" worm, you thread line through a slide sinker and tie the line to the hook eye. Then you start the hook point in the center of the worm head, and at a 30-degree angle push the point out through the worm body about 1/2 in. from the head. Then revolve the hook 180 degrees so that the hook point can stick in the worm body. But bend the worm slightly up the hook so when the point is imbedded the worm will be straight. Now push the point almost through the worm, and it is rigged for fishing. This makes the worm weedless, but the hook point and barb will emerge to hook a fish if you set the hook hard. For more information about the Burke line of worms and their catalog write to:

Burke Fishing Lures
1969 S. Airport Rd.
Traverse City, Mich. 49684

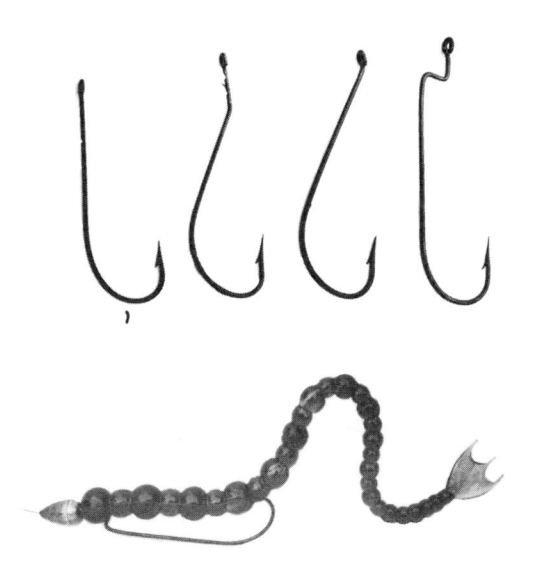

BASS BUDDY FLOAT

The Bass Buddy Float weighs just 21 lbs. but is suitable for fishermen up to 300 lbs. It is made of a tough polyethylene outside and flotation material inside, and is a virtually indestructible float that hooks and fins can't rip or tear. And it won't crack, rust, or corrode. It has shoulder straps to use when entering and leaving the water. It features comfortable sports-car style—no-sag seat and back rest—and has molded-in lure trays and rod holders. No inner tube is required for this float. It has a mounting bracket for an electric trolling motor and can also be used with paddle pusher foot fins. For more information about the Bass Buddy Float write to:

K-Mac & Co.
15404 Dooley Rd.
Addison, Tex. 75001

FLY FISHING STRATEGY

The book *Fly Fishing Strategy* by Doug Swisher and Carl Richards presents innovative and highly practical fly-fishing techniques—stalking, casting, stream strategy, lake fishing, salt-water fly fishing, and new patterns, including the revolutionary stillborn duns—that all fishermen can use in their everyday fishing. This new book emphasizes the techniques of proper presentation of the fly, which is equally as important as having the right imitation at the right time. They present a startling new theory of casting dynamics, give complete casting instructions for special stream situations, explore new fly-fishing frontiers, and offer tactics for fishing the rises and for fishing the water when no feeding is apparent; they evaluate new equipment, the latest developments in fly-tying tools, materials, and techniques, and they provide a whole chapter of Swisher-Richards patterns. *Fly Fishing Strategy* sells for $10.00 and is published by:

**Crown Publishers, Inc.
419 Park Ave. S.
New York, N.Y. 10016**

MARTIN TROLLS

Martin Trolls are multiple-spinner flexible-cable trolls with blades that revolve freely against red plastic bead bearings. The blades are made of brass with nickel or fire-orange nickel finishes. They all have rudders, which help prevent line twist. They are used when deep trolling for trout, lake trout, landlocked salmon, and coho salmon. For more information write to:

**Martin Tackle and Mfg. Co.
512 Minor Ave. N.
Seattle, Wash. 98109**

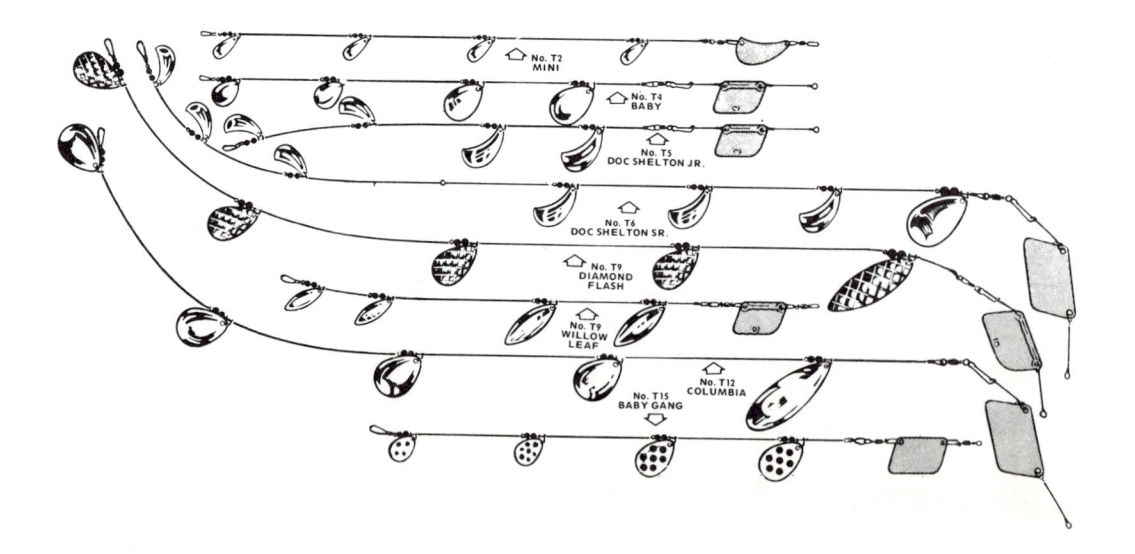

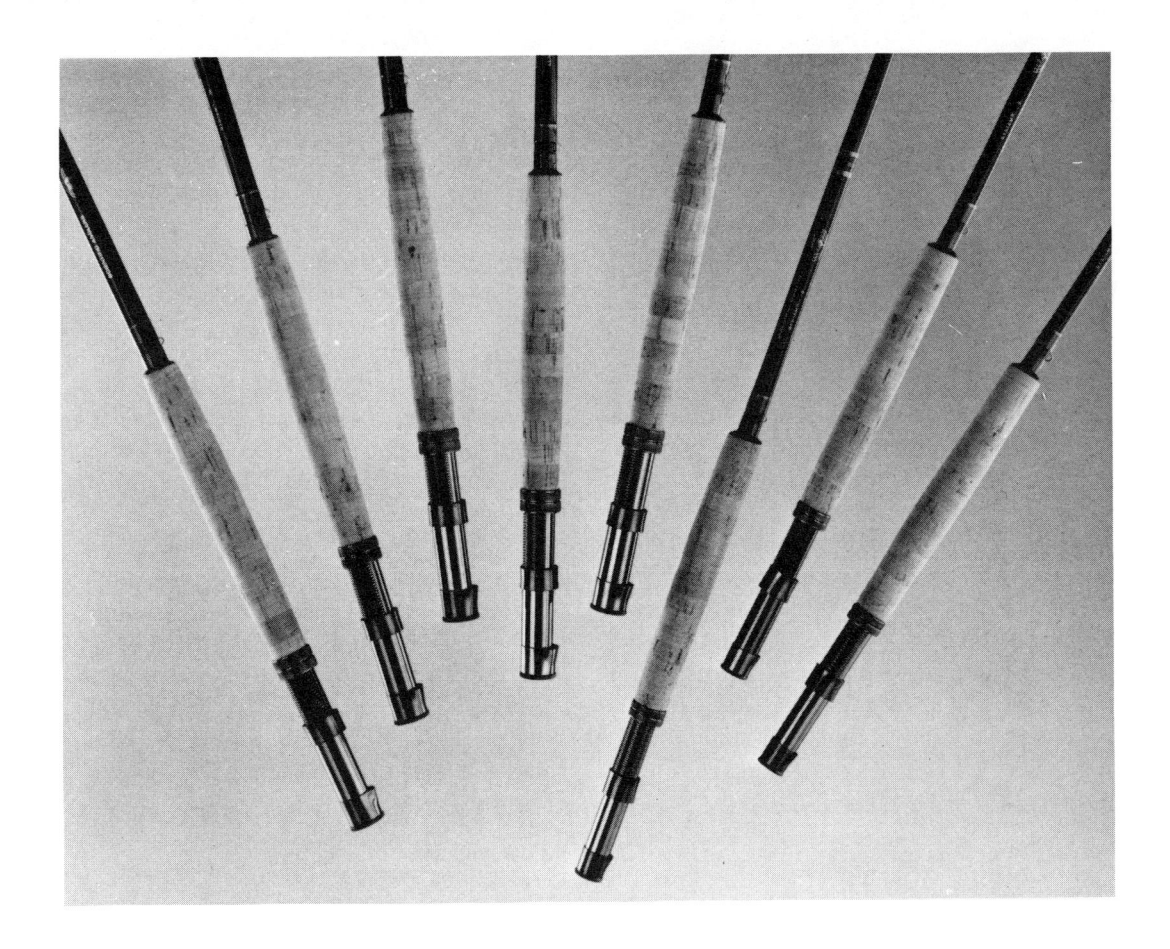

SCIENTIFIC ANGLERS SYSTEM FLY RODS

The Scientific Anglers System fly rods are designed to bring out the optimum performance of a particular fly line, from System 4 to System 11. This unique approach to rod building assures you of a perfectly balanced rod and line from the beginning. The rods are of precision-tapered, two-piece tubular Fiberglas construction, with a continuous-action zone from tip to grip. They have extra-hard, chrome-plated stainless-steel tip-top and snake guides and ceramic, stripping guides. They are packed in a tailored cloth bag and aluminum rod case. The rods range from 7 ft., 2 in. to 9 ft., 3 in. and sell for $90 to $95. For their catalog showing these rods and other fly tackle write to:
Scientific Anglers
P.O. Box 2001
Midland, Mich. 48640

MINN KOTA ELECTRIC MOTORS

The Minn Kota Manufacturing Company makes many different models of electric motors in both bow mount remote control and transom mount models. There are 12- and 24-v. units, with thrusts from 4 to 24 lbs. The motors vary in price, depending on the model. For their catalog or more information write to:
Minn Kota Mfg. Co.
201 N. 17th St.
Moorehead, Minn. 56560

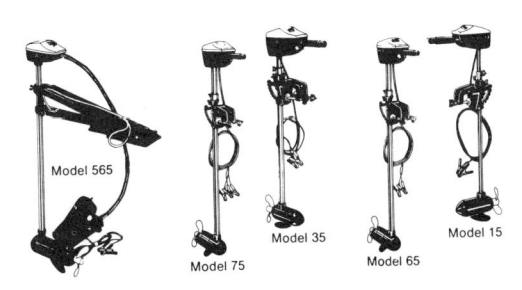

THE WASHINGTON STATE FISHING GUIDE

The Washington State Fishing Guide contains 352 pages and details over 2,000 of the best fishing lakes and streams, along with directions on how to reach them. It also covers in pictures and text the Northwest's major freshwater sport fish. How-to features include those about summer and winter steelhead, shad, bass, cutthroat trout, rainbow trout, salmon, whitefish, sturgeon, ice fishing, and much more. Recently added in the new fourth edition are listings of virtually every named lake (3,400) and stream (1,500) in Washington State, along with a listing of the 401 best bass and panfish waters. Also included are lists of hunting and fishing guides and horsepackers. *The Washington State Fishing Guide* sells for $3.95 and is published by:
Stan Jones Publishing Co.
3421 E. Mercer St.
Seattle, Wash. 98112

COLUMBIA FISHING VESTS

The Columbia Sportswear Company believes that color is extremely important in fishing clothes. So they make all their fishing vests from dark-colored fabric to blend with the streamside cover. The Furnace Creek vest shown in the photo is a superlightweight, which makes it applicable to many wilderness-fishing situations. It is constructed of tough 100 per cent nylon mesh, making it strong yet light, and it offers cool angling even when the fishing gets hot. Six oversize cargo pockets of coated nylon taffeta, plus a giant cargo pouch at back, keep gear readily available. It's made of forest-green fabric to keep you camouflaged when fishing in gin-clear high lakes and streams. It is available in S-M-L-XL sizes. This company also makes other fishing vests and clothing, and for their catalog or more information write to:
Columbia Sportswear Co.
6600 N. Baltimore St.
P.O. Box 03239
Portland, Ore. 97203

PACK ROD

Anglers who do a lot of hiking or backpacking into the wilderness fishing areas need a light, short rod that can be broken down in several sections and not take up a lot of room. Such a rod is also good for the traveling man who wants to put a fishing rod into his suitcase or luggage when flying on business or pleasure. The Berkley Cherrywood Pack Rod fills this need handily. It is a combination 7-ft. spinning or fly-fishing rod. The detachable butt grip can convert it to a fly rod from a spinning rod. It breaks down into five pieces and fits into a short metal rod case. For more information about this rod and other tackle they make write to:
Berkley and Co.
Spirit Lake, Ia. 51360

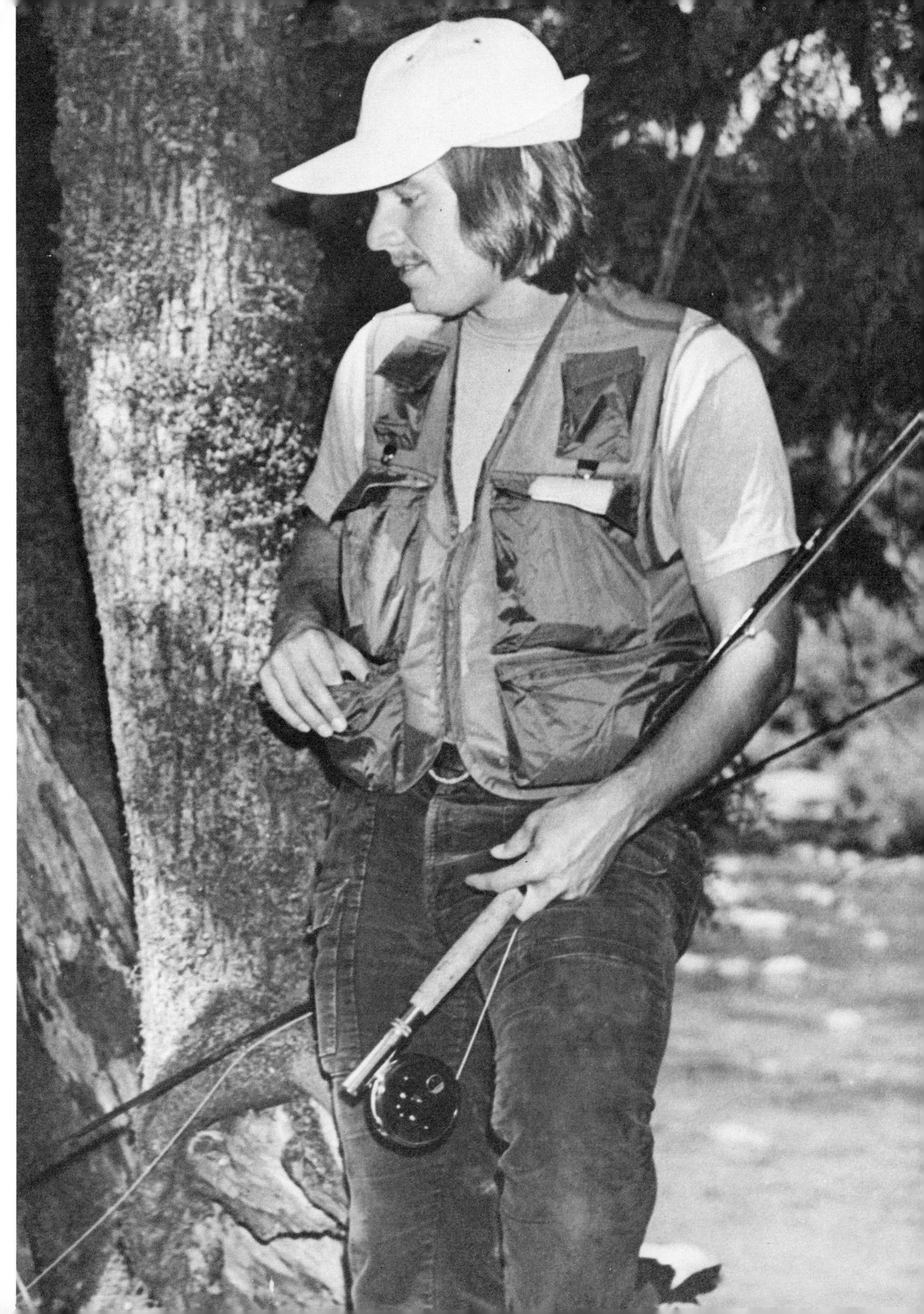

MODEL "90" FISHING THERMOMETER

Serious fishermen know that, as a rule, different species of fish prefer different water temperatures. By finding the depth where temperature matches the preference of his favorite gamefish, the fisherman knows about how deep he has to fish. Water temperature isn't constant; it varies at different depths and changes from season to season.

Ray Jefferson's new Model "90" Fish Thermometer is a precision electronic thermometer and visual depth-measuring instrument that gives readings of depth and temperature down to 100 ft.

The unit reads temperature from 30° to 90° F. and is exceptionally easy to operate. The fisherman simply turns the unit on and lowers the temperature probe and cable into the water. The cable is calibrated in 1-ft. increments and marked every 5 ft. for accurate readings. The Model "90" operates off of one 9-v. transistor-type battery with snap terminals. For reference, a chart on the top of the unit lists the preferred temperature ranges for the most popular gamefish.

The Model "90" is compact and weighs less than 1 lb. For safety and easy handling, a safety lanyard that wraps around the wrist is included to prevent it from falling overboard. The Model "90" can even be used while trolling. The unit carries a full one-year factory warranty. It is housed in a rugged, weather-resistant, virtually indestructible Cycolac case. It lists for $39.55 (less battery). For further information contact:
Ray Jefferson
Main and Cotton Sts.
Philadelphia, Pa. 19127

CRAPPIES IN THE SUMMER

When the weather gets hot in the summer, crappies leave their shallow-water haunts near shore and head for deeper water. Then it is important to find the exact level at which they are lying or feeding. This can be a narrow layer, and fishing above or below the school of fish will usually fail to produce positive results. If you are in a good spot, try fishing different levels, starting from the bottom and working up until you get action.

CRICKET RANCH

If you want to buy crickets for bait or to raise your own for fishing or profit you'll find the Selph's Cricket Ranch the place to contact. They have been in business for many years raising and selling crickets for fishing and for the bait business. They produce the famous "Gray Cricket" that is so popular as bait for bluegills or bream, bass, trout, and panfish. They also sell various kinds of equipment needed to raise and handle crickets in large numbers for fishing or for profit. For more information write for their booklet to:
Selph's Cricket Ranch
P.O. Box 2123
Memphis, Tenn. 38101

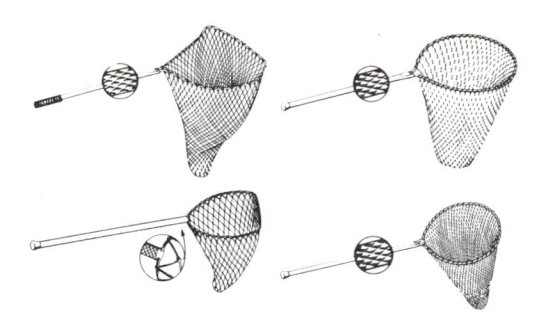

NETS

The Isaac Franklin Company specializes in making different kinds of nets. They have nets for landing all kinds of fish in fresh water and salt water. They also make nets for minnows, shrimp, crabs, and baits. They feature aluminum floating landing nets, but also make nets with wooden handles. For a catalog showing their complete line of nets write to:
Isaac Franklin Co., Inc.
630 N. Pulaski St.
Baltimore, Md. 21217

CLAUDIO CUSTOM FLY RODS

Ferdinand Claudio makes a series of custom Fiberglas fly rods. He makes trout rods from 7 ft. to 8 ft., 9 in., and steelhead and salmon rods from 8 ft., 9 in. to 9 ft. The rods are golden brown, of two-piece construction with hard chrome, stainless-steel snake guides, and Carboloy stripping guide. The wraps are antique gold with eggshell trim. The ferrule is interior Fiberglas. The grip is a top-quality cork designed by Claudio with a flare at the base and cigar-shaped at the tip. The reel seat is a machined, highly polished aluminum locking device. It has a fancy hardwood barrel with "piano finish." The rods come with a bag and rod tube with machined metal cap. For a color folder telling more about these rods write to:
F. M. Claudio Rod Co.
1482 38th Ave.
San Francisco, Calif. 94122

MERCURY FISHING OUTBOARDS

The Mercury people make two lightweight, low-horsepower motors popular with fishermen with small boats who want to have motors and boats that can fish in the thick weeds and go almost anywhere. They are also popular if you have to tote them any distance to get to the fishing river or lake. One is the 4-hp. Merc 40, which weighs only 36 lbs. and features a two-cylinder water-cooled powerhead.

The other motor is the electric-starting Merc 110, with 9.8 hp. and Flo Torq Safety Clutch, which protects the engine and drive train from impact damage. It has features that help you devote more attention to fishing, like steady slow running with "troll set" and the quick-responding twist-grip throttle when you want to get going. For a catalog or more information about these motors and other outboard motors in the Mercury line write to:
Mercury Marine
Fond Du Lac, Wis. 54935

165

TWO RODS BETTER THAN ONE

If you are fishing over or through sunken trees, bushes, or logs you may get hung up often with your lure. To avoid frightening the fish, use two outfits with the same lure on the end. Then if the first lure gets hung up, don't try to free it, but let it stay there. Then start fishing with the second outfit. If that one also gets hung up, you can row over to the fishing spot and try to free both lures.

FISHING—SKILL OR LUCK?

There's an old saying among fishermen that if somebody else catches more fish than you do or a big fish, then that angler was just lucky. But if you catch more fish or a big fish, then it was skill or know-how. Just what part luck or skill plays in fishing has been argued since anglers have been fishing for sport. Most surveys have shown that a small minority of skilled or expert anglers catch most of the fish. Some say they catch 90 per cent of the fish, but 60 per cent is more likely. At any rate, there are times and days when luck will enter the picture and an angler will catch many fish or a big fish. But day in and day out, skill and know-how will result in more and bigger fish than depending on just plain luck. So it always pays to keep learning, to be observant, alert, and to concentrate on what you are doing when fishing. Learn the best fishing spots and practice casting and working your lures until these become second nature. And fish as often and as long as you can. Someone once said, "You can't catch fish unless your line with lure or bait is in the water!"

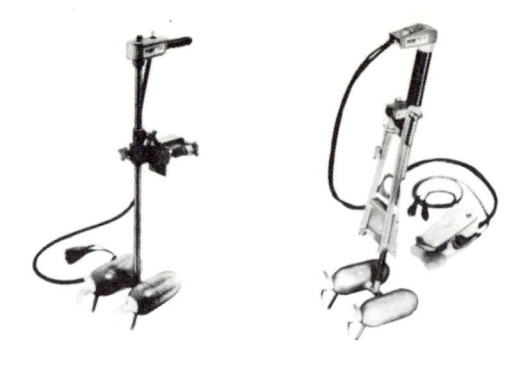

REBEL ELECTRIC MOTORS

The Rebel Company offers two twin-motor models—one of which is mounted on the transom. The twin 17-amp permanent-magnet motors provide 16 hrs. of quiet fishing maneuverability or auxiliary power from a fully charged 12-v. battery. It also offers a heavy-duty stainless-steel shaft, Lexan props, and instant-reversing and three-speed controls. The other dual motor is mounted on the bow and has a remote-control pedal. For more information write to:

Rebel Division—Plastics Research and Develop. Corp.
P.O. Box 1587
3601 Jenny Lind Rd.
Fort Smith, Ark. 72901

E. HILLE ANGLER'S SUPPLY HOUSE

E. Hille is a mail-order house that carries a big stock of materials and supplies for fly tying, making fishing lures, making rods such as rod blanks, kits, reel seats, ferrules, grips, guides, and other component parts. They also sell a complete line of fishing tackle including rods, reels, lines, lures, tackle boxes, terminal tackle, and various accessories. For their catalog write to:
E. Hille
P.O. Box 269
Williamsport, Pa. 17701

WORTH LURE-MAKING KIT

A Worth lure-making kit offers hours of productive winter-evening fun preparing for the time lunkers run again. It encourages creativity and is a good way for anglers to save money.

The Worth kit contains easy-to-follow illustrated instructions and material for twenty-five lures, including French- and reflex-style spinning lures, single and double spinners, Colorado and June bug spinners, jig spinners, and wire leaders.

Materials include Indiana, willow leaf, ripple, June bug, Colorado, French, and swing blades, clevises, snaps, and swivels, coil spring fasteners, wire shafts, hooks, split rings, lure bodies, beads, a wire former, paint, brush, and convenient plastic work tray.

The wire former is a precision instrument that enables the lure designer to make every kind of bend, loop, and eye in a professional manner. The instruction book is easy to read, complete, and packed with ideas. The kit makes an ideal gift for anglers as well as youngsters eight years and older. The price is $10.95. For more information write to:
Worth Fishing Tackle
Stevens Pt., Wis. 54482

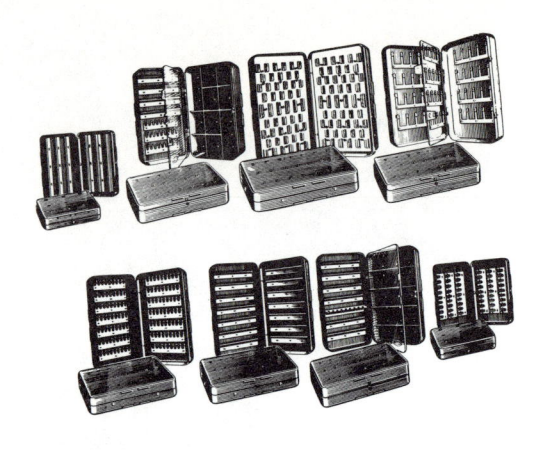

PERRINE FLY BOXES

This company has been making Perrine fly boxes for many years and has a complete line of ventilated aluminum fly boxes suitable for carrying all kinds of flies. Their latest box is lined with a special molded insert of polypropylene that will tenderly but securely hold one hundred wet or dry flies in an upright position. The hackle and wings are protected in this light, crushproof box. They now have twelve different vented aluminum boxes in various sizes and in three other basic styles. There are Perrine boxes to hold flies by coil clips, ten points, and magnetic attraction. For more information about these fly boxes write to:
Aladdin Laboratories, Inc.
620 S. Eighth St.
Minneapolis, Minn. 55404

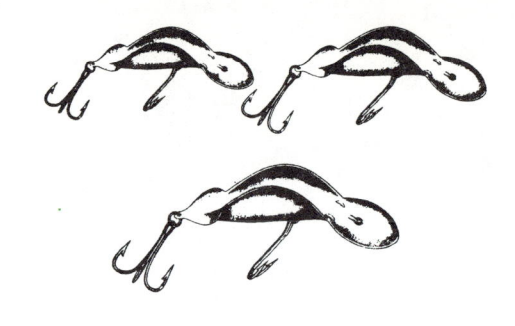

SPOONPLUG

The Spoonplug is the deep-running metal lure developed by Buck Perry, who is recognized as the father of "structure" fishing. In fact, spoonplugging is a system of fishing emphasizing the locating of fish and making them strike, the use of lures for testing various depths of water, how to find and work productive structure, how fish migrate, and the effects of weather and water conditions on fishing. The Spoonplugs are designed to be trolled at various depths from 2 to 25 ft., depending on the size and model of the lure. They come in different finishes and colors. Buck Perry has written a little booklet called *A Spoonplugging Lesson*, which sells for $1.00 and tells how to fish his lures. It can be obtained from:
Buck's Baits
P.O. Box 66
Hickory, N.C. 28601

HEDDON BRUSH POPPER

The new Heddon Brush Popper is both a surface and a sinking lure. The V-keel and parachute action lets the lure swim on top if you reel fairly fast. Slow down and it sinks and can be worked at different depths. It has a built-in rattle and weighs ½ oz. It comes in several colors with a plastic skirt. The Heddon Company also makes many other lures for freshwater and salt-water fishing. For their catalog or more information write to:
James Heddon's Sons
Dowagiac, Mich. 49047

TACKLE SATCHEL

The Tackle Satchel is for the sportsman on the go who needs a neat container that holds plenty of lures but is convenient to carry, store, and use. It has two sliding shelves and eight slide-out plastic boxes with compartments for lures, flies, and tackle. This satchel has also become popular as a fly-tying kit to carry all the fly-tying materials, tools and thread, and hooks and cements needed to tie flies at home, in the fishing camp, or even on the bank of a trout stream. The satchel can be personalized with gold initials on the handle. For more information write to:

Woodstream Corp.
P.O. Box 327
Lititz, Pa. 17543

SOLUNAR TABLES

This booklet gives the best feeding periods of fish and game during a given day and has been published for more than forty years. It was originally worked out by the late John Alden Knight, who was an expert fisherman and outdoor writer. The Solunar Tables are now being published by Mrs. Richard Alden Knight. By studying the tables and finding out the best fishing period during a given day you can be on the water when fish are apt to be most active. The Solunar Tables booklet sells for $1.50 plus $.15 for postage and handling from:

Mrs. Richard Alden Knight
P.O. Box 207
Montoursville, Pa. 17754

JOHNSON REELS

The Johnson closed-faced reels come in many models; the Guide 160 and 155—the full-size and compact models—both offer patented Double Drag Systems. This exclusive feature makes it virtually impossible for even the largest freshwater fish to break the line if the drag is correctly set.

The Sabra, Commander, and 710 reels feature exclusive automatic transmission in different size ranges. When you crank the retrieve handle forward, you're in direct-drive retrieve. When you release it, the reel automatically downshifts into drag to tire the fish as he runs.

The Century/Citation family offers unmatched versatility. These reels can be mounted up top on casting rods or underneath on spinning or fly-casting rods. And either way, they can be converted quickly and easily from right- to left-hand retrieve. For more information about these reels write to:

Johnson Reels, Inc.
1531 Madison Ave.
Mankato, Minn. 56001

FRED ARBOGAST LURES

Anyone who has done much fishing knows the Fred Arbogast lures, which go back many years and are still red-hot favorites with many anglers for freshwater and saltwater gamefish. The famous Jitterbugs, Hula Poppers, Sputterbug, Sputterfuss, Hawaiian Wiggler, and other Arbogast lures are used by anglers all over the country. They also make several kinds of saltwater lures for striped bass, tarpon, snook, bluefish, and other species. You can obtain a copy of their catalog and a "Fisherman's Diary," where you can record your fishing trips, by sending $1.00 to:

Fred Arbogast Co., Inc.
313 W. North St.
Akron, O. 44303

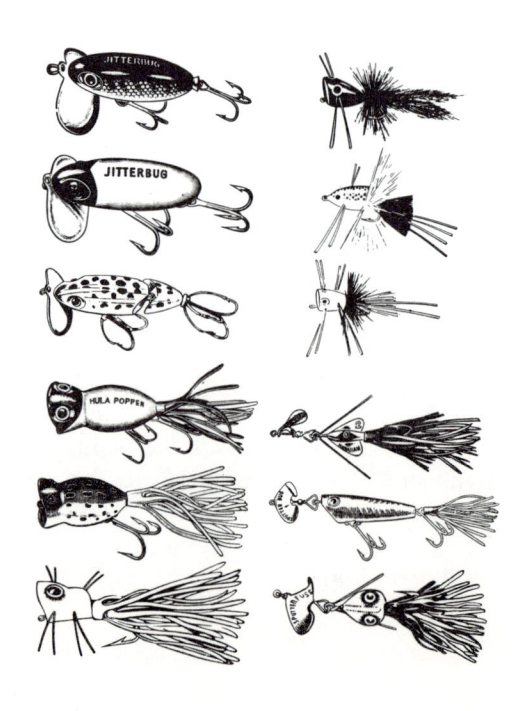

LOWE FISHING BOATS

Bass boats are a special kind of craft. They were born out of a need for a boat that will go just about anywhere, yet they must offer the angler the conveniences of modern fishing. Aluminum bass boats by the Lowe Line can be used in deep water in reservoirs, yet their shallow draft lets you slip over the flats and into the backs of coves where the fishing might be best. And less hull weight means you can use an outboard with less horsepower and still move out fast when it's time to change locations. And the strength and durability of marine aluminum provide years of worry-free use with little or no maintenance.

Lowe Line's Hustler is a 16-ft. boat with standard equipment that includes side console wheel steering, pilot seat, and two deluxe padded swivel seats that are mounted on sturdy, raised pedestals. There's room beneath each pedestal seat for storing accessory batteries. The pilot's seat folds, and the seat raises to a bait well.

Additional standard items are rod holders mounted on one sidewall, closed door storage underneath the front deck, and running lights that can be removed and placed in individual holders to clear the decks for fishing. The Hustler is rated for outboard motors up to 50 hp.

They also make two 15-ft. bass boats called the Stinger and the Darter. And they have other aluminum family fishing boats, flat-bottomed boats, and canoes. For a catalog showing all these boats write to:

Lowe Line Boats
Interstate 44
Lebanon, Mo. 65536

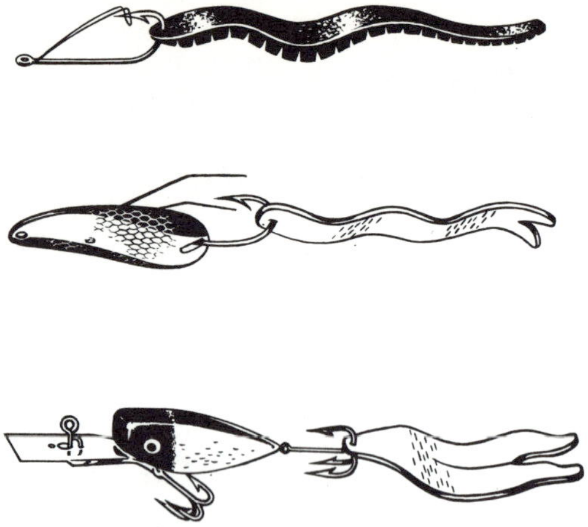

USING PORK RIND

The Uncle Josh Bait Company points out that there are many ways you can use pork rind or pork chunk or pork frog baits. They can be used alone on plain or weedless hooks. Or you can add them behind a spinner or spoon. Or you can add a strip or an eel on a jig. One of the deadliest combinations is a pork frog on a spoon with a weedless hook. You can even add small pork rind strips on a plug or a fly. And the Uncle Josh Bait Company makes pork rind baits in many sizes, shapes, and colors for use on all these lures. If you want to see their complete line and learn more about how to use their pork rind baits, send $.25 for their catalog to:
Uncle Josh Bait Co.
Fort Atkinson, Wis. 53538

RODERICK L. HAIG-BROWN BOOKS

These are old books by beloved fishing writer Roderick L. Haig-Brown, who writes about his native waters of the Pacific Northwest. They cover many titles that have been out of print for years and commanded high prices from collectors. They include such classics as *A River Never Sleeps, Return to the River, Fisherman's Spring, Fisherman's Summer, Fisherman's Fall,* and *Fisherman's Winter.* Each book sells for $7.50, and they are published by:
Crown Publishers, Inc.
419 Park Ave. S.
New York, N.Y. 10016

PIRANHAS

The man-eating piranhas found in South American rivers are often caught on hook and line, and make good eating. But you need thick, strong hooks and heavy wire leaders to hold them. Ordinary thin or soft hooks and lines are bitten through in a hurry. They'll bite a wooden plug in half in one snap!

HARTIG'S LURES

This company makes several spinning-type lures for use with a fly rod, spinning, casting, and trolling tackle. These range from small spinners for trout, bass, panfish, and walleyes up to their big "Muskie" special, with a big 5/0 treble hook. The lures come in different-colored tails or streamers. For more information write to:
Hartig's Lure Co.
56640 Garfield St.
Osceola, Ind. 46561

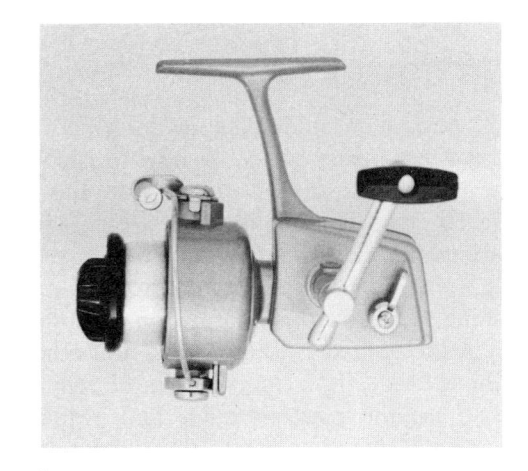

BERKLEY SPINNING REELS

Berkley and Co. makes several spinning reels, mostly for freshwater fishing or light salt-water fishing. The two models shown are light and ultralight spinning reels used with 4- and 6-lb.-test lines. They have lightweight bodies but large-capacity spools. They feature a double ball-bearing action and a 4.1 to 1 retrieve. For more information about these and other reels write to:
Berkley and Co.
Spirit Lake, Ia. 51360

BASS FISHING

The title of the book *Bass Fishing* by Bob Gooch is misleading because it does not deal with the black basses—the large-mouth or small-mouth, which most anglers think of when the word "bass" is mentioned. Instead, this book covers the true basses—the white bass, yellow bass, white perch, and the striped bass. It gives a detailed rundown on the fishing methods and techniques, tackle, lures, and baits used for these fish. There is also a detailed coverage of all the states where these fish are found, the best waters and spots and seasons. *Bass Fishing* is a paperback that sells for $5.00 and is available from:
Tidewater Publishers
P.O. Box 109
Cambridge, Md. 21613

EAGLE CLAW HOOKS

Anyone who has done a lot of fishing in fresh or salt water is familiar with Eagle Claw hooks. They are widely used for all kinds of bait fishing and even on lures, and for making jigs or tying flies. They have a variety of patterns made with plain, regular shanks, ringed eyes, turned-down eyes, short shanks, long shanks, bait-holder types, and worm-holder hooks. Besides the regular Eagle Claw patterns, they also make Aberdeen, Salmon Egg, Siwash, Steelhead-Salmon, O'Shaughnessy, Keel Fly, Sproat, Kirby, Tuna and Albacore, Carlisle, Wide Bend, and treble hooks. They also carry a full line of snelled hooks. Their catalog showing all these hooks and other tackle they make costs $.25. Write to:
Wright & McGill Co.
P.O. Box 16011
Denver, Colo. 80216

THE JOY OF FISHING

This recreation guide contains information that offers expert advice on how to choose the proper rod or reel and how to match the tackle to the angling job. It includes various fishing techniques such as fly casting, spinning, bait casting, trolling, and still fishing. There is also information on lures, baits, tackle boxes, fishing boats, and other fishing tackle. It includes charts of fishing locations, the seasons, rules, and regulations, and there are photos throughout the book. *The Joy of Fishing* sells for $3.95 in many bookstores and is published by:
Rand McNally & Co.
P.O. Box 7600
Chicago, Ill. 60680

T. H. E. FISHING VESTS

The T. H. E. Fishing Vests were originated by Stan Hui, assisted in design by experts such as Dan Bailey, John Bailey, and Ray Hurley. Field-tested by expert fishermen, professional guides, and outdoor writers, "The Vest" has fished exotic places from one end of the trout world to the other. The verdict was the same: "The best trout vest ever produced for the serious fly fishermen." The vests are made of various materials such as polyester/cotton fabric, tight-weave cotton poplin, and blue denim. They are available in S-M-L-XL sizes. For a brochure or more information write to:
T. H. E.
P.O. Box 998
Livingston, Mont. 59047

"T. H. E." LIGHTWEIGHT FISHING VEST

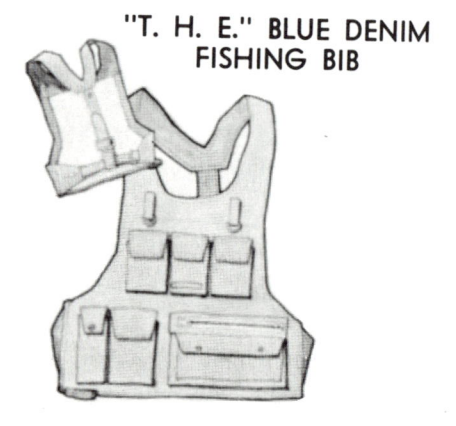

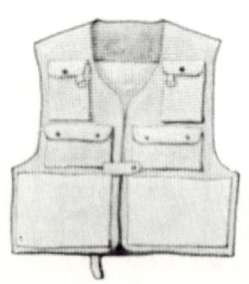

"T. H. E." BLUE DENIM FISHING BIB

"T. H. E." BLUE DENIM FISHING VEST

"THE VEST" DELUXE FISHING VEST

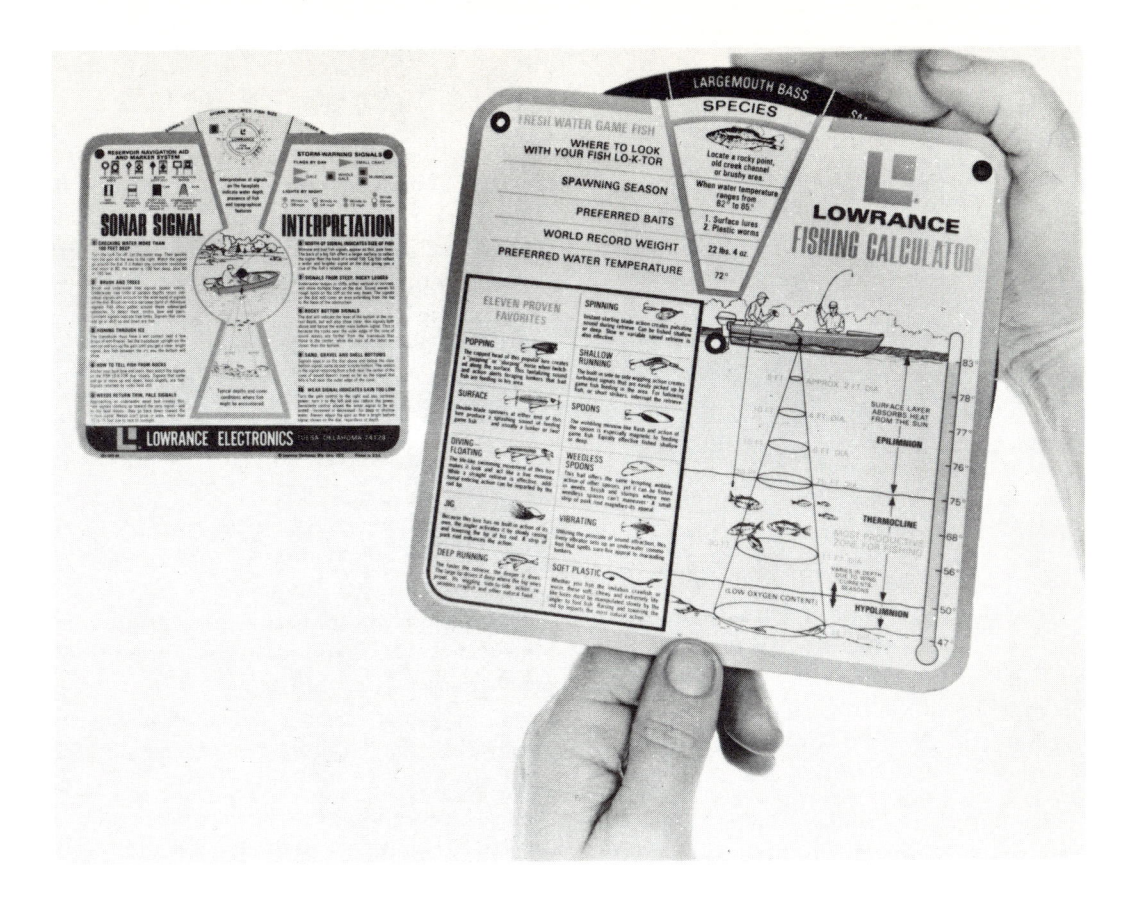

FISHING CALCULATOR

With the handy Lowrance Fishing Calculator you may use a dial to find a short biography including preferred temperatures, favorite baits, optimum spawning temperatures, and world-record weights of various species. On the other side, the same easy-to-read dial lets you match up specific bottom and cover conditions with the corresponding signals transmitted by all Lowrance Locator/Sounders. It costs $1.00 and can be obtained from:
Lowrance Electronics, Inc.
12000 E. Skelly Dr.
Tulsa, Okla. 74128

IDAHO FISHING

There's a booklet called *Idaho Lakes and Reservoirs* that many fishermen who plan to fish in that state will find very helpful. It gives the major fishing lakes and reservoirs in the six drainage units of Idaho. It gives directions on how to reach the lake or reservoir, and information about the facilities found there and what kind of fish are caught in each body of water. To get a copy of this booklet you can write to:
Idaho Fish and Game Dept.
P.O. Box 25
Boise, Id. 83707

LANDLOCKED SALMON

Instead of using a boat and outboard motor when trolling flies for landlocked salmon, try paddling a canoe as close to shore as possible. This places your lures closer to rocky points, gravel bars, reefs, and mouths of streams where smelt and minnows are found. It is also quieter and frightens fewer fish than a boat and motor, especially in shallow water.

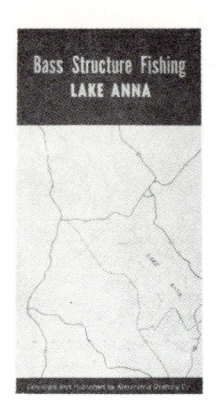

FISHING MAPS

These fishing maps are big 22-in.-by-34-in. sheet maps that give in detail the underwater contours, structures, water depths, and facilities available at each spot. The following maps covering mostly waters in Virginia and North Carolina are available:

"Bass Structure Fishing—Lake Anna"
"Bass Structure Fishing—Occoquan Reservoir"
"Bass Structure Fishing—Lake Gaston"
"Bass Structure Fishing—Smith Mountain Lake"

The fishing maps sell for $2.47 each and are published by:
Alexandria Drafting Co.
417 Clifford Ave.
Alexandria, Va. 22305

CRAPPIE BAIT

If you run out of small minnows when fishing for crappies you can still catch these fish. Just take one of the crappies you have caught and cut a small strip of meat from the back or side of the fish. Put this on a No. 6 hook with a tiny spinner in front of the bait. Then cast or flip this combination out, let it sink, and retrieve just fast enough to make the spinner blade revolve.

SPORT FISHING INSTITUTE

The Sport Fishing Institute was organized in 1949 when a group of farsighted fishing manufacturers met and set up a professionally staffed, nonprofit, fish conservation organization to help fishing and fishermen. The prime objectives of the Sport Fishing Institute are listed as follows:

1. To promote and assist in conservation, development, and wise utilization of our national recreational fisheries resources.

2. To advance and encourage the development and application of all branches of fishery research and management.

3. To collect, evaluate, and publish all information of value to advance fishery science and the sport of fishing.

4. To assist existing educational institutions in the training of personnel in fisheries science and management.

5. To encourage a wider participation in sport fishing through the distribution of information pertaining to its health and recreational values.

6. To assist and encourage co-operative effort among all existing conservation organizations.

To accomplish these aims, the Sport Fishing Institute devotes a good part of its budget to research in fishery biology. It grants fellowships and cash or equipment to fishery research works in many colleges, universities, and state and other agencies. The Institute also publishes a monthly bulletin, which goes to those interested in conservation and fishery research.

The objective of all this, of course, is to improve and maintain the sport fishery so that more and more people can enjoy fishing and find it worthwhile. If you are interested in becoming a member or learning more about the Sport Fishing Institute write to:
Sport Fishing Institute
608 13th St., N.W.
Washington, D.C. 20005

STEURY BASS BOAT

The Steury Bass Boat is a 16-ft. fishing boat that seats two and has adjustable swivel-arm chairs, a bench, and a wet box. It has custom upholstery, carpeting, glove box, storage under bench seat, large wet well, bow locker, built-in rod holders, side grab rails, courtesy light, and Hydro-lift spray rails. It sells for $1,950. For more information about this and other boats they make write to:
Steury Corp.
310 Steury Ave.
Goshen, Ind. 46526

ZEBCO OUTDOOR FILMS

The Zebco Company has several fishing films available without charge for showing at fishing clubs, sportsmen's clubs, and civic and business organizations. These feature fishing in lakes and streams of North and South America; the films are 16 mm. sound and color, and vary in length from 10 to 35 min. For a list of the films available write to:
Zebco Films
Modern Talking Picture Service, Inc.
1145 N. McCadden Pl.
Los Angeles, Calif. 90038

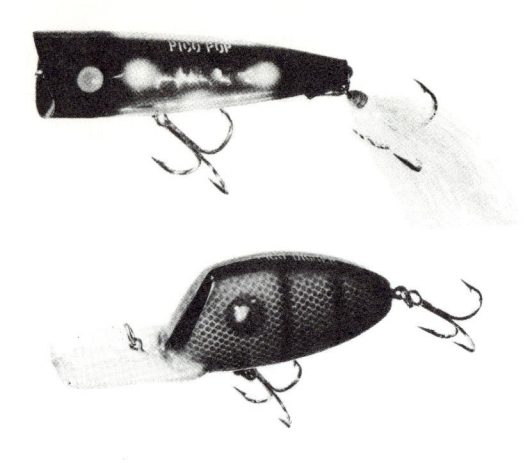

PICO LURES

The Padre Island Company has come out with two new Pico lures. One is the Pico Super Pop, which is a surface plug with the new psychedelic flash insert. It has a bucktail on the rear hook. This plug is 3¼ in. long and weighs ½ oz.

The other plug is the Pico Deep Digger, which is a floating-diving lure with a long, broad bill and which can be used for casting or trolling. The broad bill helps the lure jump over underwater obstacles. It is 3½ in. long and weighs ½ oz. Both plugs are available in various colors. For their color brochure showing these and other lures they make write to:
Padre Island Co.
P.O. Box 5310
San Antonio, Tex. 78201

RED EYE LURES

The Hofschneider Red Eye lures have been around for a long time and are still popular and effective for many freshwater species. They are spoons and spinners in various sizes and weights, but all of them have "Red Eyes," which are finely cut glass beads that are red in color. They make them in all sizes for spinning, casting, and trolling for various fish, from trout to muskies. For a brochure showing these lures write to:
Hofschneider Corp.
P.O. Box 4166
Rochester, N.Y. 14611

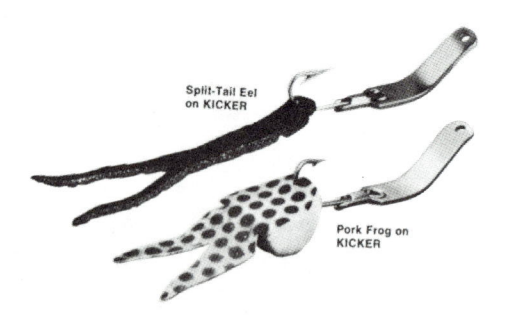

THE KICKER

This metal wobbler was designed by Uncle Josh for use with pork rind baits. But it can also be used with plastic worms, plastic or rubber skirts, and pork frogs or chunks. It comes in silver, gold, chartreuse, and red colors. It can be reeled slowly at a leisurely wobble or speeded up to dart and kick. It can also be skittered on the surface by reeling fast while holding the rod high. Or you can bounce bottom in a stop-and-go fashion or even jig it up and down under the boat. For their catalog showing this and their pork rind baits write to:
Uncle Josh Bait Co.
Fort Atkinson, Wis. 53538

HOT STRIKE

A man in Oregon was fishing from a boat when lightning hit the tip of his rod and the current circled his waist, went around his leg leaving red marks, and burned two holes in the side of the boat. The rod tip melted, the cork grip exploded, and his jacket and trousers zippers were fused shut. But he lived through the experience to tell about it. The strange part was that his two fishing buddies in the same boat didn't even realize what was happening.

MAKE YOUR OWN FISHING LURES

One of the most satisfying experiences a fisherman can have is catching a fish on a lure that he has fashioned with his own hands. The fly fisherman has plenty of good books on how to tie his own flies for fresh-water and salt-water fishing. But little printed information has been available for those who want to make their own plugs, spoons, spinners, metal squids, jigs, plastic worms and eels, tube lures, and other freshwater lures. That is why the book *Make Your Own Fishing Lures* by Vlad Evanoff was written.

As the book demonstrates, it is not necessary to be a skilled craftsman in order to make lures. Most anglers already possess the ability to handle the few necessary tools, and if they follow the directions and let the illustrations guide them, they can make good fishing lures. They may not be professionally perfect, but they will catch fish, and that's all that really counts.

And if you make your own lures, you will probably catch more fish in the long run. An angler who buys expensive lures avoids using them around logs, sunken trees, weeds, rocks, and similar hazards. He's afraid to lose them. But that's where the fish usually hang out. If you make your own lures cheaply you can afford to lose them, and you'll fish these productive spots.

Making fishing lures can be an enjoyable hobby, especially during the long winter months when fishing is slow. And you'll get a lot of satisfaction out of making your own lures. You can invent, create, and experiment, and maybe come up with a new lure that other anglers want. Many fishing lure companies started this way—in the workshop, basement, or kitchen. Then they sold so many lures that they went into business and are big companies today. *Make Your Own Fishing Lures* sells for $9.95 and is published by:
A. S. Barnes & Co., Inc.
P.O. Box 421
Cranbury, N.J. 08512

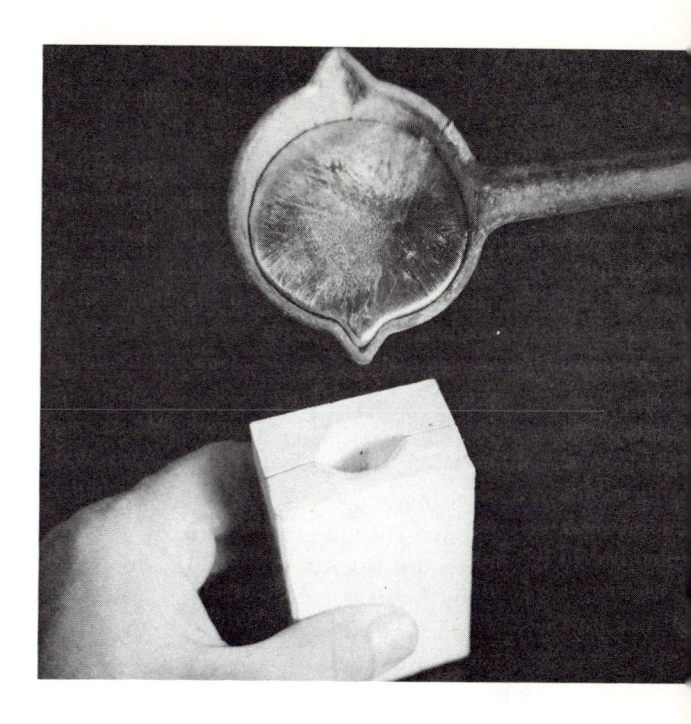

USING A BASS BUG

One of the most exciting ways to catch bass is on a fly rod using surface bass bugs. But you have to know how to use these bugs to obtain strikes and catch fish. You can scare a bass if you pop a bass bug too hard and too loudly. What usually happens is that a bass will swim away from a bug that hits the water with a splash. But he'll only swim a few feet away and then turn and keep an eye on it. If you pop the bug lightly or twitch it, the bass will usually move in closer. Then another pop or two and he'll be ready to take it. During hot weather you should cast the bug out and let it sit on the surface as long as a minute or two. Then give it a pop and another long rest and then a series of slow pops. And there are times when you can tease a bass into hitting your bug if you know where the fish hangs out and then keep casting repeatedly and popping the bug near his hideout.

BEST WAYS TO CATCH MORE FISH IN FRESH AND SALT WATER

The book *Best Ways to Catch More Fish in Fresh and Salt Water* by Vlad Evanoff goes right to the heart of fishing by concentrating on the methods and techniques rather than on theories or fishing tackle alone. It does cover rods, reels, lines and lures, and baits, but only briefly. Most of the book is devoted to the know-how and skills you need in actual fishing. After all, most anglers have little trouble buying a good fishing outfit that will catch fish. But they often encounter difficulties in learning how to use this tackle and the lures and baits in the most effective way. This book is a shortcut to learning how to use your tackle, lures, and baits so that you will catch more fish.

And the book covers not only freshwater fishing but also salt-water fishing, making it a miniature encyclopedia of fishing information that can be used no matter where you live. It covers such methods in freshwater as still fishing, spinning and spin casting, bait casting, fly fishing, trolling, drifting, jigging, float fishing, and night fishing.

In salt water it covers bottom fishing, pier and bridge fishing, surf fishing, inshore and offshore fishing, drifting, chumming, boat casting, fly fishing, wade fishing, jigging, and night fishing.

There are special sections dealing with the most popular freshwater and salt-water species and concise information on how to catch them. The book is illustrated with "how to" line drawings and photos. *Best Ways to Catch More Fish in Fresh and Salt Water* by Vlad Evanoff sells for $7.95 and is published by:
Doubleday & Co., Inc.
501 Franklin Ave.
Garden City, N.Y. 11530

BASS HANGOUT

A good spot to fish for black bass is over an area with sunken trees. Schools of bass will often hang out among the branches and over the sunken tree, and you can often catch several good fish in such a spot. The bigger the trees the more fish they will hold.

CONNECTICUT PUBLIC ACCESS

A small booklet called *Public Access to Connecticut Fishing Waters* tells the fisherman and boater where he can find public-access and boat-launching facilities on lakes, ponds, reservoirs, and rivers in Connecticut. It is available from:
Dept. of Environmental Protection
State Office Bldg.
Hartford, Conn. 06115

TROUT AND BASS FISHING BOOKS

These two inexpensive but valuable fishing guides provide information on trout and bass fishing. The first book, *Trout Fishing,* by Charley Dickey and Fred Moses, gives complete details on the short-cast method and the use of dry flies for catching brook, rainbow, and brown trout. It also gives the best trout-fishing locations, equipment, how to dress and prepare the catch, and other information about trout.

The other book, *Bass Fishing,* is by expert angler Jerry McKinnis, who has a nationally syndicated television show called "The Fishing Hole." In this book, McKinnis tells about bass and their characteristics, items to include in the tackle box, selection of the rod and reel, types of line, the bass boat, the depth finder, lures, worms, and top-water and stream fishing.

Each book is a large-sized paperback, and each one sells for $2.95 and can be obtained from:
Oxmoor House
P.O. Box 2262
Birmingham, Ala. 35202

DIAMOND RATTLER PLUG

This is a popular and highly effective surface plug that is used for large-mouth bass in the South and throughout the country. It is a crippled-minnow-type lure, with two propellers, which sputter and make a fuss on top to attract fish to the surface. It comes in two sizes—⅜ oz. for spinning and ⅝ oz. for bait casting. It comes in several colors, including the electromagnetic swirl finishes. For their catalog showing this plug and other lures write to:
Strader Tackle, Inc.
P.O. Box 708
Havana, Fla. 32333

DEEP TROUT

You'll catch more trout and bigger ones if you concentrate most of your fishing close to the bottom rather than fishing on or near the surface. Sure, it's nice to have a trout rise to a dry fly floating on top of the water. But trout spend most of their time where food is plentiful. And this means that they look for this food along the bottom more often than on the surface of the water. So scraping the bottom with a wet fly, nymph, or streamer is the most productive method not only in streams and rivers but also in lakes. For such fishing, of course, you have to use a sinking fly line and a weighted fly. This deep-fishing method is especially effective during the late summer, when the water is low and warm, and then again during the early spring and late fall, when the water is cold and the trout are hugging the bottom.

YUM-YUM WORMS

The "Yum-Yum" plastic worms have a unique spiral design that adds strength and gives them a shimmering light reflection that attracts bass. They are floaters and come in twenty-one colors, including solid and mixed shades. For a brochure and more information write to:
Factory Distributors
500 S. 7th St.
Fort Smith, Ark. 72901

WEBER FLIES AND BUGS

The Weber Tackle Company makes many kinds of flies and bugs for freshwater fishing. They make dry flies, wet flies, nymphs, streamers, bucktails, bass bugs and panfish bugs. They also make big hair lures for big bass, pike, and muskies, and many other kinds of lures, such as spinners, spoons, and jigs. Their catalog costs $1.00 and shows these and other fishing products they sell to fishermen. Write to:
Weber Tackle Co.
Stevens Point, Wis. 54481

COVEY'S FISH BOX

For the boat fisherman, Covey's new 80-qt. convertible chest cooler makes a versatile fish box. Since many fishermen use their boat for family cruises, this chest also is designed for vertical use as an icebox. One end has four small feet on which it rests in an upright position.

The smooth, easy-to-clean inner liner has precisely spaced ribs that support the large plastic box, food tray, and 1-gal. jug in either the upright or horizontal position. The removable plastic box is more than large enough to store a block of ice, but a handy feature for fishermen is that the box makes an excellent place to put fish. This eliminates the need for the fisherman to remove the entire chest from the boat for cleaning.

For anglers who fish with live bait, the plastic box can be used for this purpose, with the rest of the spacious 2.7-cu.-ft., 80-qt. convertible reserved for the catch.

The 1-gal. capped jug, which fits securely between any of the ribs, is designed so that water can be frozen inside to eliminate the need for loose ice.

And with space often limited inside many boats, the sturdy insulated hinged top of the chest is strong enough to double as an extra seat.

The rugged, pebble-grain-finished chest has polyurethane insulation for maximum cooling, recessed carrying handles on each end, and a drain plug. The 80-qt. convertible weighs 23 lbs., and is 33 in. long, 15¼ in. wide, and 15 in. high. It is made by:
Covey Corp.
P.O. Box 1317
Houston, Tex. 77001

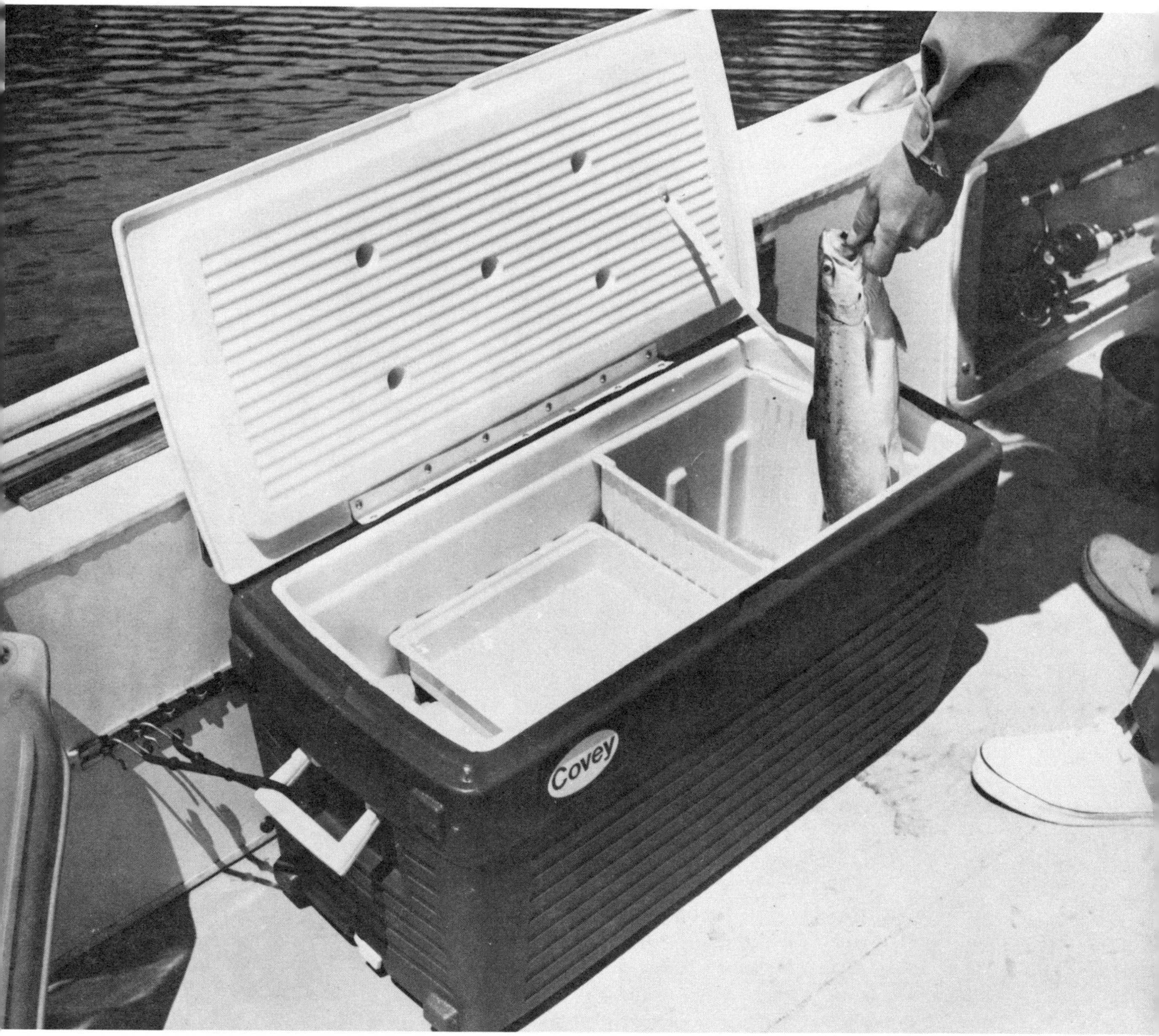
Covey

SINKING AND SINK-FLOAT FLY LINES

Sure it's fun to take trout on the surface with your floating fly line and dry flies—and we enjoy it every chance we get. But still it pays to remember that 90 per cent of a trout's life is spent feeding at varying depths below the surface. Successful fishing often calls for an eyeball-to-eyeball confrontation with these fish wherever they choose to roam or feed.

With this in mind, Cortland has opened up a whole new world of subsurface fishing with its development of sinking fly lines in three different densities—medium-sinking, fast-sinking, and extrafast-sinking. Naturally, if underwater snags or brush piles are present, you'll want a slower- or medium-sinking fly line to better avoid such snares. The fast-sinking fly line will get the call when the water is relatively clear of obstructions and the fish are feeding at greater depths, often at the very bottom. When swift currents or tides come into the picture, the extrafast-sinking line will get the job done. It sinks like a plummet and is designed to cope with large trout, salmon, or bass under extreme conditions.

The major difference in casting with the floating vs. the sinking fly lines is that the latter need to be retrieved farther in before the next cast. However, this allows your fly or lure more "fishing time."

A few seasons back, in an effort to give fly fishermen "the best of two worlds," Cortland created its now famous SINK-TIP taper fly line, which features a 10-ft. forward or tip section that sinks, while the balance of the line floats, for greater ease in retrieving and casting. This was a "natural" for nymph and wet fly fishing. Additionally, a 30-ft. forward-sinking section called the SINK-HED was developed to plumb even greater depths. Cortland's concept of the floating-sinking fly line is now gladly accepted in the industry as a basic tool for the fly rod angler. It provides more productive fishing time, better action for your wet flies and nymphs, and increased casting ease. That's the lowdown on subsurface fly fishing from Cortland.

DUMB FISH

As most anglers know, fish can be smart and hard to catch, but there are also dumb fish that never seem to learn. A 10-lb. lake trout landed by an angler had three hooks and five spinners in its stomach and another lure and leader protruding from its mouth. A catfish caught in Oklahoma had eleven fishhooks and 50 ft. of line in its stomach. And one rainbow trout caught in Ohio had thirteen fishhooks in its stomach!

FOLLOW-UP FOR BASS

When fishing the heavy growth, weeds, and sawgrass for Florida bass it's a good idea to bring along two rods. One rod can be rigged with a weedless spoon and a skirt or pork chunk. The other rod should be rigged with a plastic worm. Use the first rod with the spoon to raise and locate the bass. If he misses the spoon or refuses to take it, grab the second rod with the plastic worm and cast it out to the same spot. This will often result in a strike.

FISHING ATLASES

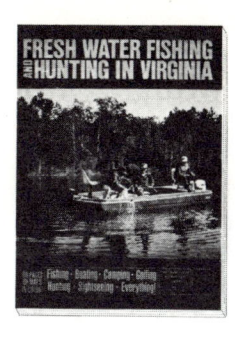

These fishing atlases are complete guides to fishing, with information collected from various sources, but primarily from the most experienced fishermen in each area. Articles provide specific information about each fish species found in the area covered as well as the seasonal aspects involved. They contain many pages of bottom-contour maps, giving the best fishing locations, public access, and telling what kind of fish are caught in each body of water. The following atlases are available:

Freshwater Fishing and Hunting in Virginia $7.44

Bass Structure Fishing—Santee-Cooper Lakes $5.93

Bass Structure Fishing—Kerr Reservoir $5.93

These atlases are published by:
Alexandria Drafting Co.
417 Clifford Ave.
Alexandria, Va. 22305

BOMBER BAITS

The Bomber Bait Company makes a wide variety of plugs and other lures for freshwater and salt-water fishing. They make surface lures such as the Popper and Spinstick and Stick plugs. Their Bomber is designed for deep-diving and fast wriggling. It has a broad diving bill, which makes it go down and also helps it from hanging up too often in weeds or brush. Their Pinfish bait is a fast-vibrating, slow-sinking lure that sends out high-frequency underwater sounds at the slightest movement. This company also makes spinner baits, spoons, and jigs. Their catalog showing all these lures in color costs $.25 and is available from:
The Bomber Bait Co.
326 Lindsay St.
Gainesville, Tex. 76240

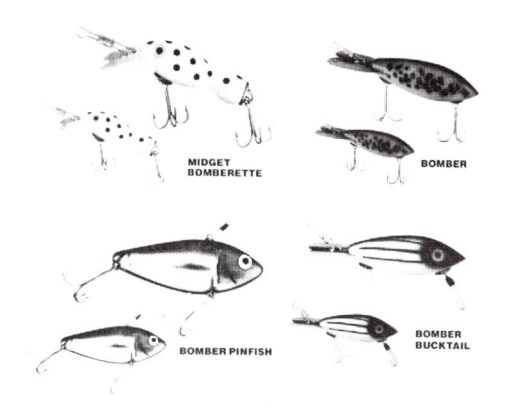

FISHING TENNESSEE

There are two booklets available from the Tennessee Wildlife Resources Agency. One is called *Fishing Tennessee* and tells about the fish caught in that state and where to catch them, listing the best streams, lakes, and reservoirs and the facilities available at each spot. There is also a map showing many of these waters.

The other booklet is called *Fishing and Camping in East Tennessee*. It covers the main fishing areas and campgrounds in East Tennessee, giving complete information about each spot as to the facilities available and even mentioning costs. Both booklets are available from:
Tennessee Wildlife Resources Agency
P.O. Box 40747
Nashville, Tenn. 37204

RECORD REELS

The Record spinning reels made in Switzerland were first imported into this country when spinning was just beginning to be accepted. Now they are once more available to a new generation of American fishermen. There are five models from the light No. 21 reel to the heavy-duty freshwater and surf-fishing models. The reels come with bails or finger pickups but can easily be converted to manual pickup. All the reels have the drag located in the rear where you don't have to grope through the line when fighting a fish. The gears are precision-machined of steel and brass. They have an aluminum alloy housing and spool. For more information write to:
**RedTack of America
P.O. Box 36
Downey, Calif. 90241**

THE FLORIDA FISHERMAN'S HANDBOOK

The Florida Fisherman's Handbook is a guide to the freshwater and salt-water fishing in Florida, with the emphasis on the northern part of the state and the southern part of Georgia. It has many articles, by such writers as Charles Waterman, Dick Busey, Paul Mains, Paul Ferguson, and Evelyn Long. Some of these writers have interviewed experts on fishing who give their views and know-how on catching many species. There is a lot of information on fishing spots, boats, fishing marinas, and fishing camps located in northern Florida and southern Georgia.

The book sells in many department stores, drugstores, fishing tackle stores, and sporting goods stores and newsstands in northern Florida, for $1.95. It is published by:
**Florida Publishing Co.
1 Riverside Ave.
Jacksonville, Fla. 32201**

186

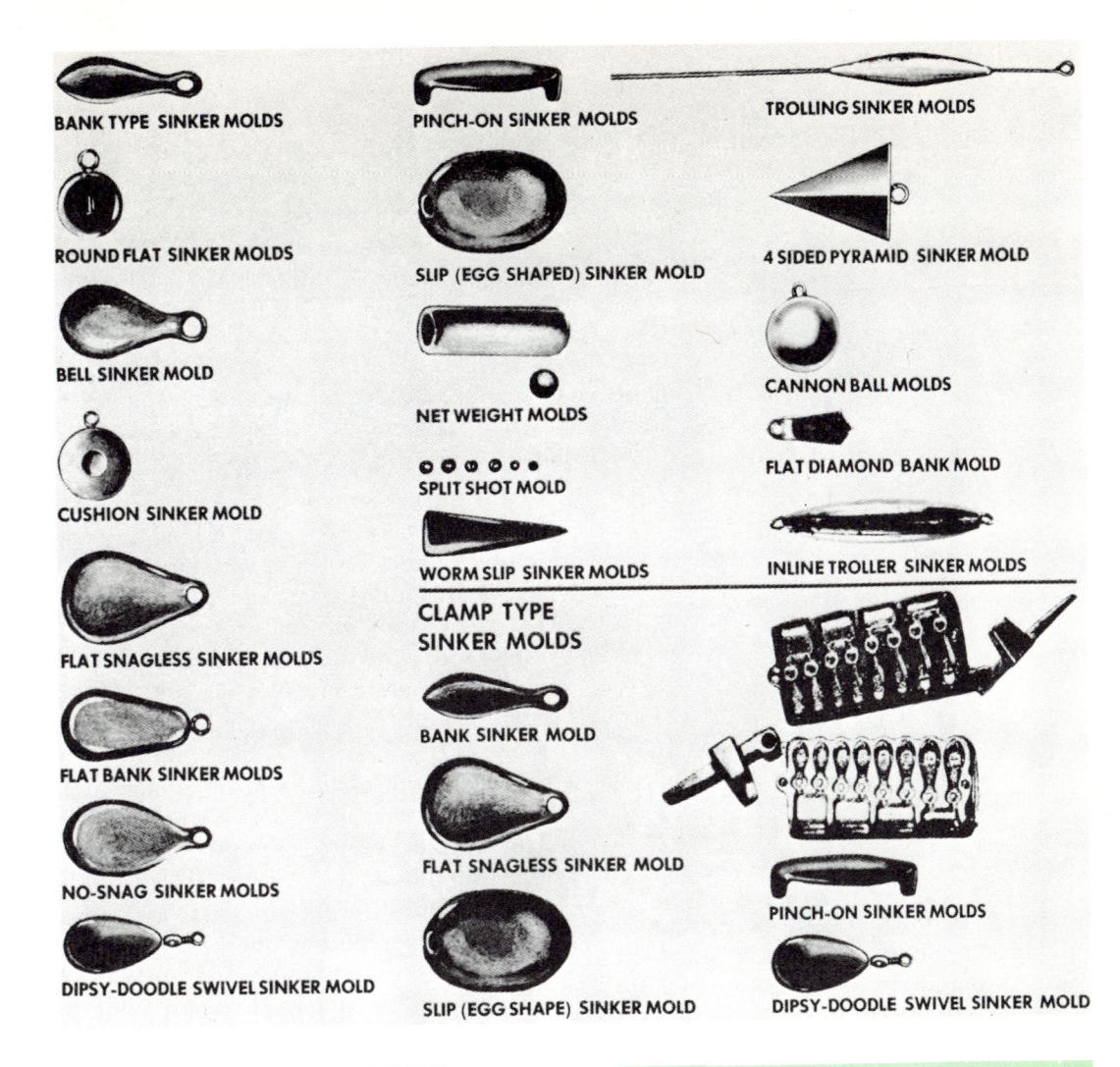

PALMER SINKER MOLDS

This company makes a wide variety of aluminum-hinged sinker molds for almost every kind of freshwater and salt-water fishing. They have bass casting, dipsy, round, pinch-on, snagless, split-shot, egg or oval, cannonball, worm slip sinkers, trolling sinkers, and bank and pyramid molds. These have anywhere from one to twelve cavities and make different weights and sizes of sinkers. They also sell hot pots and stands and ladles for heating and pouring the lead. And they have a variety of molds for making jigs too. For their brochure showing and describing all these molds write to:
C. Palmer Mfg.
P.O. Box 220
West Newton, Pa. 15089

USING CRIPPLED MINNOW PLUGS

Crippled minnow plugs that have propellers in front or in the rear or on both ends are among the best surface plugs you can use. At times the bass will hit them if you reel them fast along the surface. But most of the time you get better results if you cast the plug out, let it lie until the ripples die down, then twitch the rod tip, let it lie still again, then move it again a few inches and pause, and repeat this a few times. Then reel it back in all the way and repeat the process.

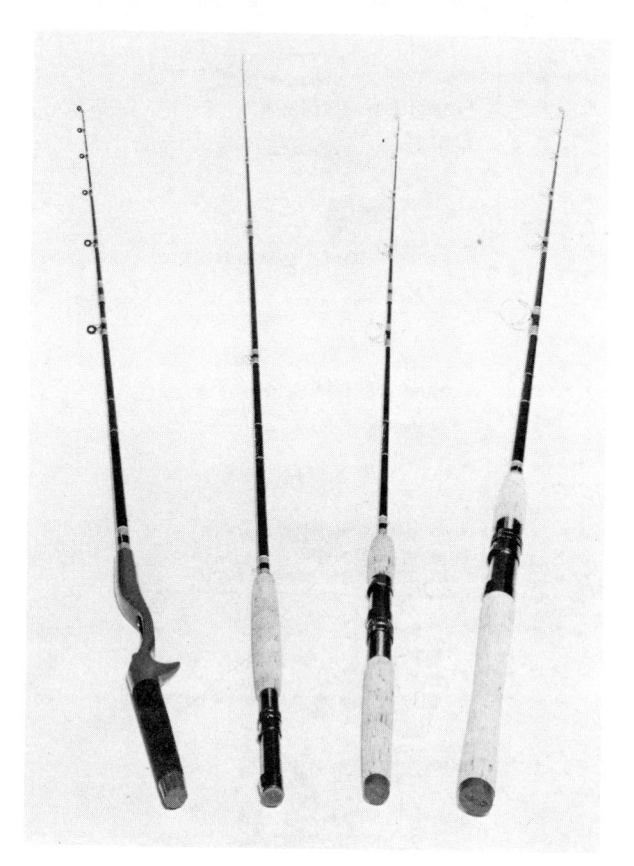

BROWNING RODS

Browning is noted for its guns, archery equipment, clothes, boots, and camping gear, but they also make and sell a fine line of fishing rods. Their Silaflex glass rods for fly fishing, spinning, casting, and salt-water fishing have been made for many years. The Magnum I Taper and the Magnum Progressive Taper are used in many of their rods to provide flexibility with power. The High Density Fiberglas is compressed into a very compact, lightweight wall lamination resulting in a light but tough rod made mostly of glass fibers and not resin. They now have a new line of rods called the STD Series, which are made the same way but sell at lower prices. So far these are being made in freshwater spinning and casting models, with one light salt-water spinning and another popping and jigging rod. Their catalog showing the entire line of fishing rods, guns, archery equipment, camping gear, clothes, and boots costs $1.00 from:
Browning
Morgan, Ut. 84050

THE WAYS OF GAME FISH

The Ways of Game Fish by Russ Williams and Charles L. Cadieux is a big book, beautifully illustrated, that covers the world of freshwater and salt-water fishing. Russ Williams describes and explains the rich and limitless pleasures of fishing the lakes, rivers, and streams in "Our Freshwater Heritage," the first section of this volume. He covers most of the important species from trout to muskellunge, with lesser known fish such as sturgeon in between.

The second section of the volume, dealing with salt-water fish and fishing, is written by Charles Cadieux, who has been associated with the sport and writing about it for many years. He deals with such glamorous species as bonefish, tarpon, sailfish, and the more commonly caught striped bass, bluefish, grouper, flounder, and other species.

The beauty of this volume is enhanced by the illustrations of such artists as Bob Hines, Fred Sweney, and R. H. Palenske, who did fifty-four color paintings of fish and seventeen etchings. There are also many photographs throughout the book showing fish and fishing. *The Ways of Game Fish* sells for $24.95 and is published by:
Doubleday & Co., Inc.
501 Franklin Ave.
Garden City, N.Y. 11530

PIKE AND WALLEYE BOOKS

Here are two fishing books about fishing for walleyes and pike that should have been written a long time ago. Many fishing books have been written about trout, bass, and even panfish, but the pike and walleye have been neglected in this field. Now two good books have been published about these fish. The first one is called *Walleyes and Walleye Fishing* by Joe Fellegy, Jr. It covers all you need to know to locate and catch these tasty fish in lakes and rivers. Joe Fellegy has been a guide who has fished more than fifteen hundred hours a year, and his favorite fish is the walleye. The book sells for $6.95.

The second book is called *Northern Pike Fishing* and is written by Kit Bergh. It is a complete guide to this much-neglected gamefish. The book includes scientific background material on all the pike species, as well as specific advice on how, when, and where to fish for the big northerns. Kit Bergh is an outdoor writer who has fished for pike himself and has also rounded up the best fishing methods and techniques of several experts. The book sells for $7.95. Both books are published by:
**Dillon Press, Inc.
500 S. Third St.
Minneapolis, Minn. 55415**

DAN BAILEY'S FLIES

Any angler who fishes with flies for trout, salmon, or salt-water fish probably has heard of Dan Bailey. He has been tying and selling flies as long as we can remember. Located in Montana not far from such famous trout streams as the Yellowstone, Madison, Gallatin, Boulder, and other waters, Dan Bailey's shop is the rendezvous of many trout anglers, tourists, and others interested in fly fishing. But you can also order his flies by mail, as well as other tackle items and even books from his catalog. For a copy write to:
**Dan Bailey Flies and Tackle
P.O. Box 1019, 209 W. Park St.
Livingston, Mont. 59047**

Lew's Fiberglass Telescopic Poles

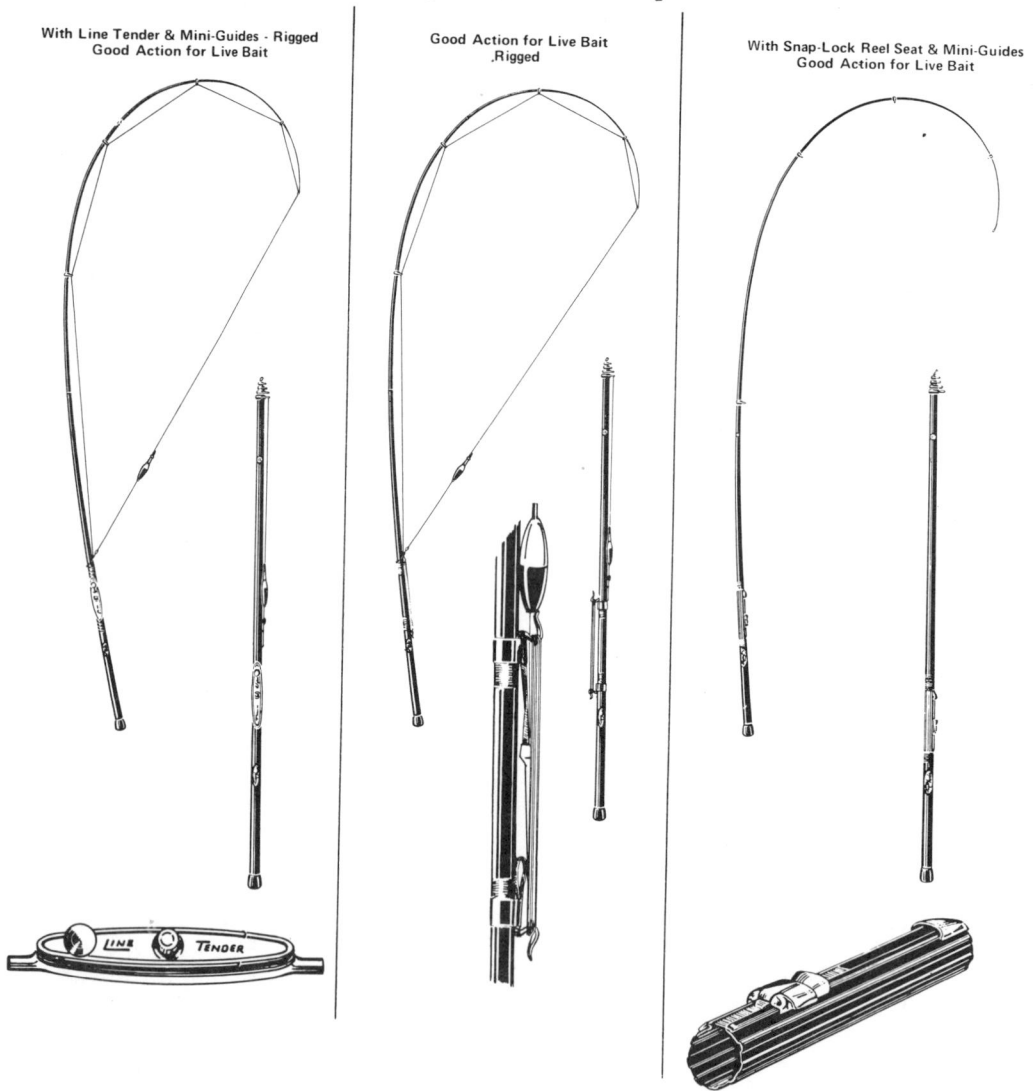

LEW'S FIBERGLAS TELESCOPIC POLES

These telescopic poles are tough and lightweight, being made from Dense Fiber Fly Rod quality Fiberglas with rubber butt cap and metal tip. They have a beautiful mahogany flint finish and come ready-rigged with line, hook, float, or sinker and guides. Or you can get the plain pole without the line, hook, and float, which comes with a reel seat to take a reel with line. The other rods have a Line Tender for winding on extra line. This company also makes other models of Fiberglas poles, regular fishing rods, and also offers rod blanks, rod-making components, fish spears, hooks, floats, and other fishing products. Their catalog is $1.00 and can be obtained from:

Lew Childre & Sons, Inc.
P.O. Box 535
Foley, Ala. 36535

BAIT CAGE

The Bait Cage has proven a boon to the wading fisherman for use along streams or edges of lakes because of its light weight and the fact that it may be carried on your shoulder or belt. It is convenient for keeping small frogs, hoppers, crickets, and other insects and baits ready for instant use. It is made of a heavy galvanized screen tube with stamped metal end covers held together with a long wire eye bolt. A long, elastic loop cord attached to one end permits slinging over your shoulder. The lower end has a rotating lid through which bait can be inserted or removed and placed on a hook in a jiffy. For more information write to:

The Oberlin Canteen Co.
Oberlin, O. 44074

DRY-FLY SPRAY AND LEADER SINK

Seidel's makes dry-fly sprays and leader sink in squeeze bottles and aerosol spray cans. Their "700" dry-fly spray is a fast-drying formula using the new CO_2 environment-safe propellant; it also comes in a squeeze bottle for easy carrying in your fishing vest. The new formula has been perfected to float even the smallest flies on rough water.

Seidel's "600" leader sink, when applied to fly leaders, puts the leaders and tippets down naturally and overcomes the flotation problem by sinking the leader and eliminating those fish-spooking shadows. It works equally as well on wet flies, nymphs, and streamers, and puts the flies down where the fish are feeding. One application lasts all day. For more information write to:

T. R. Seidel Co.
P.O. Box 268
Arvada, Colo. 80001

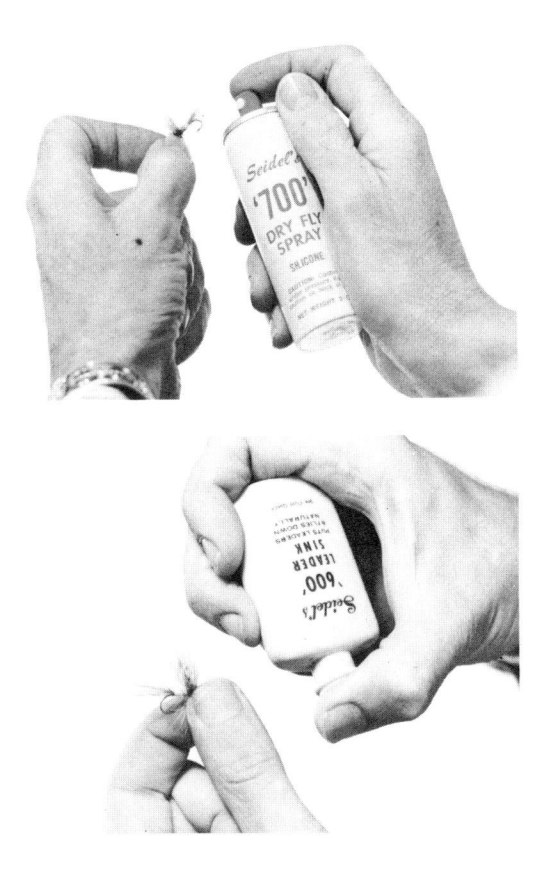

2-IN-1 GLOBE BOBBER

The new 2-In-1 Globe Bobber is designed for either still fishing or spin casting and has a mechanical device on one end that makes it easy to put on the line or remove when necessary. It has a slip slot on one side for spin casting and an instant lock that can be adjusted for various depths for still fishing. You can add or remove the float without cutting the line or removing the bait, hook, or sinker. It allows the line to slip freely when spin casting but locks the line securely when still fishing. The floats cost $.50 each. For more information write to:
Globe Float Co.
711 Iroquois Trail
Niles, Mich. 49120

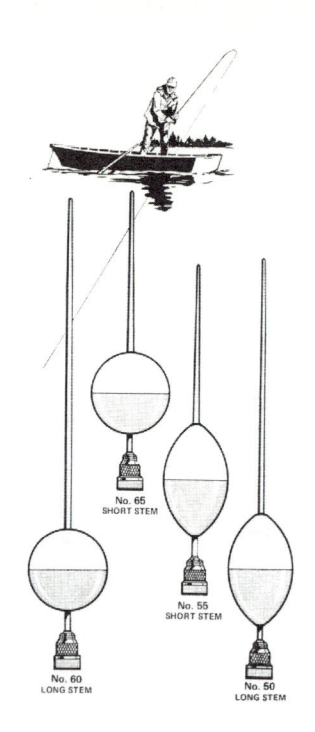

FLIPGUN FISH HOOK REMOVER

The Flipgun fish hook remover is a handy tool that removes hooks from fish fast and easily. It is specifically designed for the small "hard to remove" deeply imbedded hooks. There is no need to touch the fish or even see the hook. You get no injured hands from sharp fins, teeth, or hooks. It is made for use by bait fishermen where the hook and bait are swallowed deep on many occasions. The Flipgun fish hook remover sells for $2.00 and is available from:
Zak Tackle Mfg. Co.
235 S. 59th St.
Tacoma, Wash. 98408

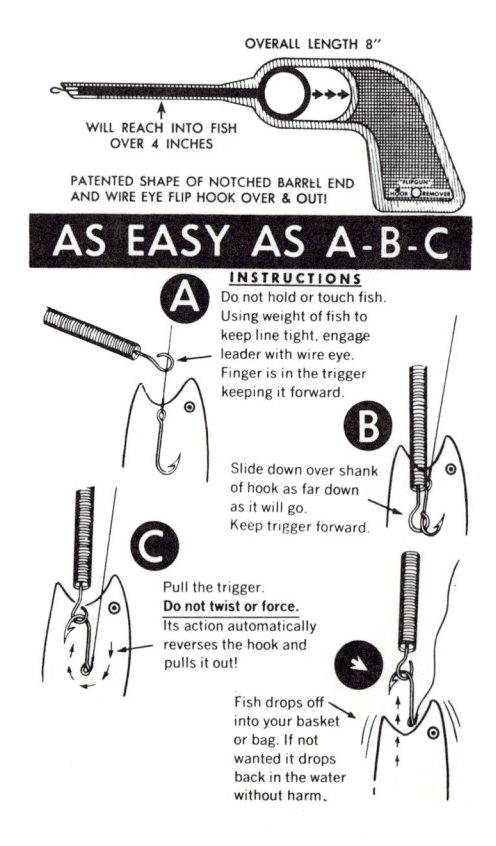

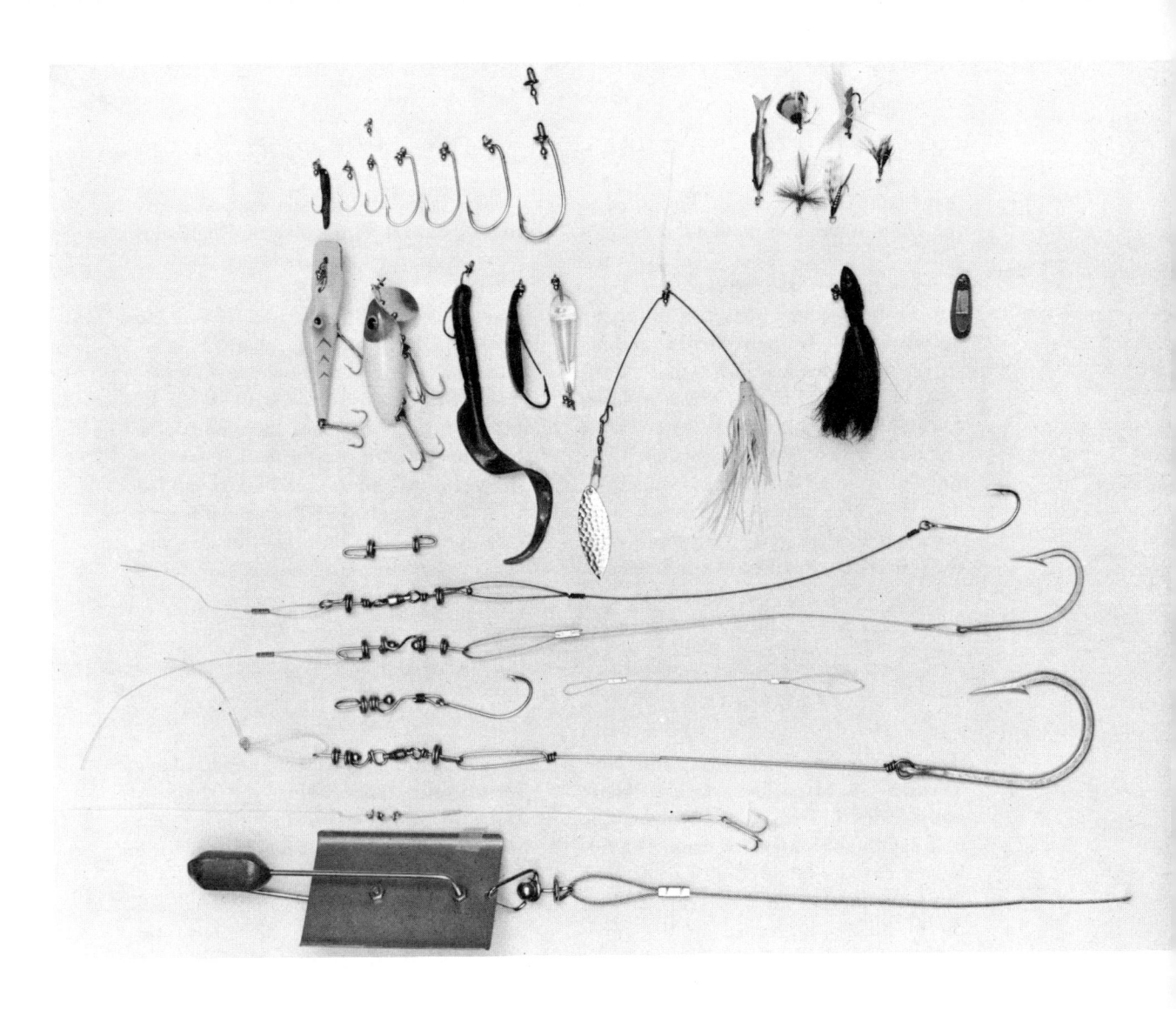

D.D.E. LOOP A LINE

This company makes a handy little eyelet that makes changing lure quick and easy. You simply tie a small loop on the end of your line or leader and slip this between the rings and around a little ball, and your line then moves up to the front eye. It can be removed just as quickly. They sell a small conversion kit with a set of these eyelets for different-size lures. You just remove the old screw eye from the plug or lure and screw in the new D.D.E. Loop A Line eyelet. The double eye can also be used when making up leaders and rigs. For more information write to:

Loop A Line
1896 Coolidge Ave.
Melbourne, Fla. 32935

NEW JERSEY TROUT GUIDE

This booklet is published by the New Jersey Council of Trout Unlimited. The money received from the booklet is used for stream improvement and creating better trout fishing. The booklet, which is seventy-five pages long, has a map that pinpoints the major trout waters in New Jersey. The waters are written up in detail, giving tips on which flies, baits, and lures are best to use and when to use them. There are other articles giving information on trout fishing. For your copy of *New Jersey Trout Guide* send $2.95 to:

New Jersey Council
Trout Unlimited
P.O. Box 581
Edison, N.J. 08817

HOW MANY FISHING LURES?

Some anglers tote a tackle box filled to the brim with lures holding dozens of different kinds, sizes, colors, and weights. If they are experts and know how to use all these lures and fish many different waters, then there's nothing wrong with carrying such a big assortment of lures. But if you are a beginner or casual fisherman who goes out only a few times a year, you're better off if you stick to a small number of lures. Use these few lures often and learn how to bring out the best action that appeals to the fish. Then you'll have confidence in the lures and catch your share of fish.

MUSKY ON A FLY ROD

Fishing is full of the startling and unexpected, as Bill Yurgealitis of Rochester, New York, found out one day. He was fishing in Black Lake with a softshell crayfish and an 8½-ft., 5-oz. fly rod. He hooked a bass weighing about 2½ lbs. and played it for a couple of minutes. Then the bass broke water, shook its head, and dropped into the mouth of a huge musky. Bill played the monster for the next two hours and finally landed it. It later weighed 49 lbs., and it wasn't even hooked! The bass was hooked, but the muskie was impaled on the dorsal spines of the bass.

GREEDY FISH

An angler fishing a lake in upstate New York saw a black bass close to shore and decided to feed it some worms. The first day the bass ate 56 worms. The following day it swallowed 62 worms. The third day the fish ate 84 worms, and on the fourth day it cleaned up 104, for a total of 306 worms in four days! Tired of digging worms, the man gave up the experiment.

BIG PERCH

If you want big yellow perch, don't waste your time fishing the shallows close to shore, especially during the middle of the day. You'll only catch the small perch in this shallow water. Instead, look for underwater weedbeds and holes and dropoffs in water from 10 to 50 ft. deep, depending on the time of year and the waters you are fishing.

FLIES FOR SMALL-MOUTH BASS

Small-mouth bass in lakes and rivers will often take dry flies, wet flies, nymphs, and streamers. Many of the same patterns that are used for trout can also be used for bass. But these should be larger, with stronger hooks and more heavily dressed. The bass are more apt to hit the larger, bulkier flies than the smaller, sparsely dressed ones.

CHANGE FISHING SPOTS

The main reason for changing fishing spots often, even if there are fish present, is because the fish soon get wise or frightened. Noise, splashing, or carelessness in casting, wading, or boat handling soon alerts the fish or makes them suspicious. If this happens, move on and try a different spot. After resting the former spot you can often return and catch more fish there.

REBEL DEEP-RUNNING "R" LURES

The new deep-running "R" series of lures by Rebel are deep runners designed to give a new, carefully balanced, slow, roving action. Their large, clear lip and carefully designed buoyancy balance makes them virtually snag free. These features are combined with Rebel's exclusive tuned sound chamber and light-reflecting cross hatching on the body. They come in three sizes and weights to run from 6 to 15 ft. deep. For more information about these lures write to:
Rebel Lures
P.O. Box 1587
Fort Smith, Ark. 72901

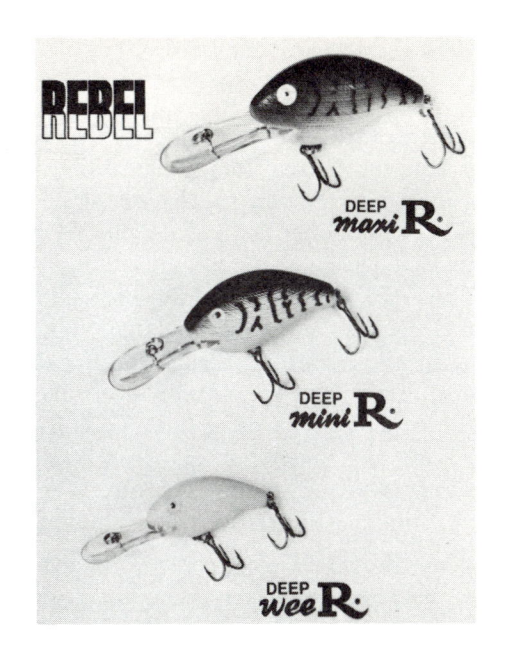

THE ATLANTIC SALMON

The book *The Atlantic Salmon* by Lee Wulff has been a classic for many years and is the result of years of fishing for this magnificent gamefish in almost all the waters where it is found. The name Lee Wulff is, of course, well known to most anglers who have seen this master angler in action on TV for many years. Lee fishes for most freshwater and salt-water species, but his favorite has always been the Atlantic salmon. In this book he details, from start to finish, the various advantages, pitfalls, equipment, and conditions the salmon fisherman must know before he even puts on a pair of waders. Lee Wulff goes into detail on the rods, reels, lines, leaders, and flies you need to catch salmon. He tells about the standard and special casting techniques, how and when to fish the dry and wet fly, playing the salmon, and how to fish various rivers, and he winds up telling where to go for the best Atlantic salmon fishing. The book sells for $12 and is published by:
A. S. Barnes & Co., Inc.
Box 421
Cranbury, N.J. 08512

SHELLCRACKERS

When searching for shellcrackers—a popular member of the sunfish family in our southern states—look for them on their spawning beds in shallow water. These can be located by the muddy spots that appear when the fish fan the bottom with their tails to form the beds, and this stirs up the mud and creates the muddy patches.

USING SPINNER BAITS

One highly effective way to use a spinner bait is to cast it out and engage your reel before the lure hits the water and start it coming back toward you even while it is still in the air. This way the blade of the spinner will trap a bubble of air. Then as the spinner blade turns underwater it will release a stream of air bubbles, which will attract fish.

AMERICAN INSTITUTE OF BASS FISHING

The American Institute of Bass Fishing is a new concept in bass fishing education and has stirred interest in the hearts of dedicated bass fishermen throughout the United States.

The AIBF has assembled five of the most knowledgeable and successful bass fishermen in the nation to instruct a five-day course that will detail virtually every technique devised for catching bass. They have lined up such instructors as Tom Mann, Roland Martin, Bobby Murray, Jerry McKinnis, and Bill Dance whose combined knowledge can insure the angler of taking fish anytime, anywhere, and under any conditions.

They choose sites in different parts of the country for these classes. And the tuition for the five-day course includes the cost of room, two meals a day, textbook and materials, use of launching and docking facilities, membership patch, and certificate of course completion. For more information and details about this course write to:

American Institute of Bass Fishing
P.O. Box 2324
Hot Springs National Park, Ark. 71901

FLY AND TACKLE BOOKS

This company makes a wide variety of fly and tackle books for keeping wet and dry flies, nymphs, streamers, bucktails, panfish bugs, bass bugs, and small spinning lures. They also make leader cases. Most of their "Common Sense" fly and tackle books have leaves or envelopes that open like a book and reveal the flies or lures so that you can pick out the ones you need. Some are lined with sheep shearling into which the hooks are inserted. The covers of these fly books are genuine cowhide, pigskin, or imitation leather. For a catalog showing their complete line of fly and tackle books write to:

A. J. Gallager
319 Delsea Dr.
Westville, N.J. 08093

CONVERSE WADERS

The Converse Rubber Company makes waders for fishermen and has three popular models. One is the nylon stocking foot wader, which has an extremely lighweight fabric surface and is an English-type wader. A sock both under and over the form-fitted stocking foot is suggested for maximum comfort and wear. It comes equipped with belt loops for safety, and this wader is worn with wading shoes.

Another fabric, surface cleated-sole wader is also lightweight and is made of nylon. The upper material affords comfort, and the seams are reinforced. The wader has convenient inside pocket and belt loops for safety.

Still another wader is the cleated or felt sole nylon wader with a nylon surface and two rubberized layers of nylon cloth fully vulcanized for complete protection. It has a boot fold guard and wide rubber chafing strip. There's a large inside chest pocket, reinforced crotch, adjustable draw cord, nonskid felt sole, steel shank, belt loops, and suspender buttons.

These waders are green in color and come in sizes 7 to 13. For a catalog or more information showing these waders and other boots, parkas, jackets, and protective clothing write to:

**Converse Rubber Co.
55 Fordham Rd.
Wilmington, Mass. 01887**

TUCKER FISH-N-FLOAT

The Tucker "Fish-N-Float" will help you reach those fish that cannot be caught by mere wading in the water or fishing from shore. You can go right after your fish in this float, since it buoys you up in any water, so you slip quietly as a floating leaf among rocks, weeds, lily pads, or brush to drop your plug, fly, or bait in the most inviting spots. You can tote a stringer, bait bucket, or net with you. Also there's a handy zipper pocket for extra lures and gear. The float comes in two sizes—one for medium-sized anglers and the other for large-sized persons. For more information write to:

Tucker Duck and Rubber Co.
P.O. Box 4167
Fort Smith, Ark. 72901

FISHING THE CALIFORNIA WILDERNESS

The book *Fishing the California Wilderness* by Mike Hayden is a personal account of fishing some of the wildest waters in California. This book will entertain and inform all those interested in fishing the streams, rivers, and lakes of the High Sierra and other California mountain areas from a 1,000-ft. elevation to well above the timberline. The author goes into detail on what to take when backpacking—the food, clothing, supplies, tackle, and lures you need to fish the wilderness waters. He feels that the success or failure of a mountain backpacking trip for trout is largely determined by the plans and preparations a hiker makes before leaving home. Mike Hayden covers bait, lure, and fly fishing for rainbow, steelhead, and cutthroat trout. *Fishing the California Wilderness* is a paperback that sells for $2.95 and is 128 pages long and is well illustrated with photos. It is published by:

Chronicle Books
870 Market St.
San Francisco, Calif. 94102

BURKE WIG-WAG MINNO

This new lure by the Burke Company, makers of many other well-known lures, has a "curly tail" and the profile of a true minnow, which gives it a lifelike appearance and action. You can fish it as a jig, crank bait, drop bait, or even troll it. It has been field-tested in salt water and caught many varieties of gamefish, including tarpon, sea trout, snook, grouper, and snapper. In fresh water it has caught trout, bass, walleyes, pike, lake trout, salmon, and panfish. The Wig-Wag Minno comes in $1/8$-, $3/8$-, and $5/8$-oz. weights and several colors. For a catalog or more information write to:

Burke Fishing Lures
1969 S. Airport Rd.
Traverse City, Mich. 49684

MARTIN TRAVEL SET

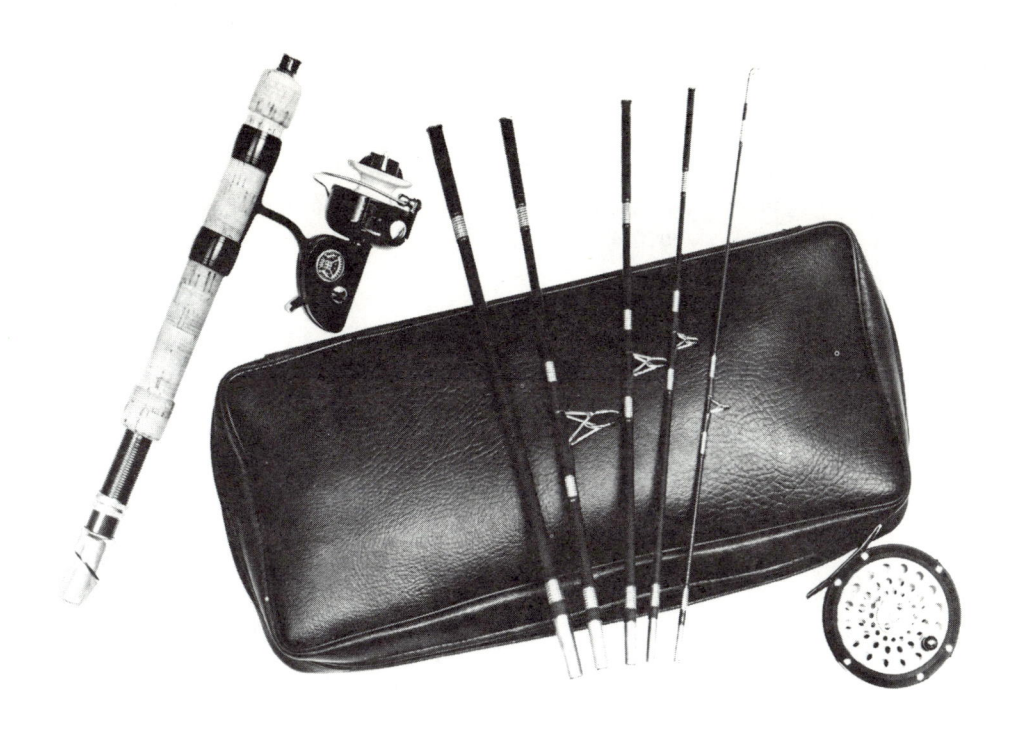

This Martin Travel Set is for the angler who wants to be prepared for fly or ultra-light spinning. The 6½-ft. tubular rod is equipped with spinning guides that handle a fly line too. There is a fixed reel seat for the fly reel and there are slip rings for the spinning reel. Model 66 single-action fly reel with on-off click comes with the set. The No. 104 spinning reel takes 150 to 200 yds. of 6-lb.-test line and is helically geared and ball-bearing mounted, with a five-to-one retrieve, with a smooth, spring-loaded multiple-disk star drag. All of these fit into the padded, lined, and zippered case, which itself will easily fit into an attaché case or backpack. For a catalog showing this and other travel sets and fishing tackle write to:
Martin Reel Co., Inc.
P.O. Drawer 8
Mohawk, N.Y. 13407

DELONG PLASTIC WORMS

Delong Lures, Inc., makes a wide variety of plastic worms and eels, spring lizards, frogs, tadpoles, minnows, crawfish, and insects for freshwater fishing. They have plain worms and outside rigged worms and weedless hook worms in different sizes, colors, and weights. For their catalog and information about these worms and the other lures they make write to:
Delong Lures, Inc.
85 Compark Rd.
Centerville, O. 45459

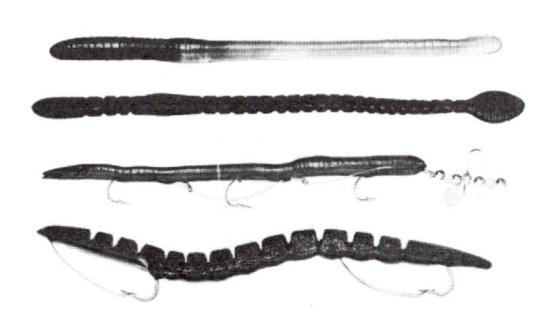

DON'T SCARE THE FISH

Most expert or veteran anglers are great believers in silence and stealth when fishing. You can shout, holler, scream, whistle, or talk all you want—but don't jump on the deck or floor of a boat or hit it with your tackle box, the anchor, or any other heavy weight. Some freshwater anglers go to such extremes as to cover the bottom of their tackle boxes and the deck or floor with rubber or mats or carpets. They lower the anchor gently without making any big splash. And they shut off their motors a good distance from the fishing spot and row or drift the rest of the way, or they use an electric motor to maneuver the boat quietly at the fishing spot.

Fish cannot hear sounds in the air very well, but they very quickly pick up noises or vibrations transmitted through the water. Sound waves travel underwater far and wide and are readily picked up by the fish.

Noises and wakes from boat engines will scare certain species but will attract others. Most fish in fresh and salt water in heavily populated or popular boating areas soon grow accustomed to powerboats scooting around over them, and they usually resume their normal living and feeding habits. But this may not hold true in wilderness areas, where the sound of the motor or a big wake will make the fish scatter and hesitate to feed or hit lures or baits.

Fish in shallow water are more readily "spooked" than in deep water. They seem to feel more insecure and exposed to dangers and are more alert, cautious, and ready to leave for deeper water if anything frightens them. So it pays to be quiet when fishing in shallow water near shore.

Fish are also more frightened when feeding or breaking on the surface. Trout are extremely cautious when rising to the surface for a fly. And bass, too, will hit a lure on top fast, then dive for deeper water. When approaching a school of fish feeding on top, cut the motor a good distance away and cast the rest of the distance or drift quietly toward the feeding fish.

Fish are more cautious in clean, clear water than in dark, murky water. And fish also hide and stay in deeper water during the bright, sunny days than they do when the day is overcast or during periods of dusk, daybreak, and at night. In fact, you can approach most fish closer at night than during the daytime.

FISHING THE SPIN-TAIL LURES

The spin-tail lures that have a lead minnow-type body and a small spinner blade on the tail are great fish catchers. They not only look attractive to fish, but the vibrating spinner also draws fish. This lure is easy to use because you'll get many strikes by just casting it out and letting it sink on a tight line. If you get no hit on the way down, let it sink all the way to the bottom, then raise your rod tip fast, making the bait rise a couple of feet, then let it drop back to the bottom. Keep doing this all the way in to the boat. The spin-tail lure can also be worked on top by reeling fast so that it sputters and makes a commotion on top for a few feet, then slowing down and letting it sink. Bass will often hit then. This method can also be used when you see bass schooling and feeding on top.

MONARK FLAT-BOTTOM BOATS

The MonArk Boat Company makes a full line of boats for fishing and general boating, including aluminum flat-bottom boats, which are so popular for float fishing or for shallow-water use. They have many models, ranging from a 10-ft. boat weighing only 75 lbs. up to their 18-ft. commercial-type boat weighing 322 lbs. They are available in aluminum or various colors. For their catalog and prices of these and other boats write to:

MonArk Boat Co.
P.O. Box 210
Monticello, Ark. 71655

KEEPING FISH FRESH

A sad truth of the fisherman's world is that fish served up at the family table are often not quite as good as they might have been. Frequently this is traceable to the fact that they were not given the best of care between the time of catching and cooking. The following tips on fish care are suggested by the folks at Lowrance Electronics, Inc., makers of the Fish Lo-K-Tor and other aids to anglers.

Freshness is all-important, and there are two good ways to keep fish fresh. The first, and one used by many fishermen, is to keep them alive. Either live wells or stringers serve this purpose.

Once a fish is dead, it should be kept cool and be cleaned as soon as possible. A cooler is a handy place for icing down crappies and other panfish when they are coming into the boat one after the other. Once cleaned, the fish should still be kept cool right up to the time of cooking, and they should not be stored in water. Keep them dry instead.

In any case, say the Lowrance fishermen, if you have to keep the fish more than twenty-four hours before cooking, the best plan is to freeze them. They should be cleaned and ready for cooking when they go into the freezer. One way to freeze fish is to first wrap them in aluminum foil or heavy wax paper, then wrap them again in heavy meat paper. Careful wrapping helps prevent freezer burn. Remember to label and date the package. Another method used for fillets and small fish such as bluegills is to freeze them solid in ice. Pack them in meal-sized portions in paper milk cartons and label and date them.

Fish can be stored frozen for about six months with no concern about spoiling except perhaps for very fat ones. They should never be refrozen. If you want to know whether or not your fish are still fresh when you bring them in, remember that the eyes should be bright and clear, the scales should be firmly attached, and the gills should have a good red color.

Follow these rules and the entire family will want you to go fishing more often.

TIDEWATER BLACK BASS

You can have some excellent fishing for black bass in the tidewaters along the Atlantic Coast, if you know your waters and watch the tide and seasonal changes. But fishing such brackish waters can be tricky, and you have to watch the tidal action with the constantly changing water level, which makes the bass move to different locations during different stages of the tide. They tend to spread out during the high tides and "spring tides" but are more concentrated in the deeper streams, channels, and holes during low tides.

The salinity of the water also controls the movements of the bass and the fishing. During the hot summer months and drought periods, the freshwater flow decreases and salt water moves farther inland, and the bass also go inland seeking the fresh water. Winds also affect the fishing because the tidewater bays and sounds are rather shallow, and storms or strong winds will dirty the water and ruin the fishing.

You can use the same bass lures when fishing these tidewaters as you use elsewhere and cast these lures along the shoreline cover and grass as well as into the underwater structure found some distance from shore.

FREE FISHING FILMS

You can obtain free fishing films to show at your club, group, gathering, or organization from the following source. But send in your order for them early, since they are popular and in great demand. Write for the list of films available to:
Solana Studios
4365 N. 27th St.
Milwaukee, Wis. 53216

FISHING WITH SMALL FRY

The book *Fishing with Small Fry* by Jim Freeman is a good book for parents who want to teach their children how to fish. Teaching a child to fish is an experience no parent should miss. Too many do because they don't know how, or when they try, the child doesn't catch any fish and is quickly discouraged. In this book Jim Freeman, outdoor columnist for the San Francisco *Chronicle*, gives shortcuts that help children understand the basics of landing fish from the first cast, how to catch pan- and gamefish in lakes and streams, and the proper equipment and tackle for the young beginner. *Fishing with Small Fry* is a paperback well illustrated with photos and sells for $2.95. It is published by:
Chronicle Books
870 Market St.
San Francisco, Calif. 94102

JOHNSON ROD-REEL COMBOS

The complete line of twelve Johnson reel and rod Combination Packs has been graphically modernized recently. Simplicity and boldness characterize the new green, black, and white packaging. Inside, each Johnson Reel, from the full-sized Guide to the compact Skipper, has been perfectly balanced to a color-co-ordinated rod of proper length and tip action to assure a proper match of rod and reel action. Each Combination Pack carries graphic instruction on: "How to spincast like a professional," "How to tie the angler's basic knots," "How to fillet fish," and "How to enjoy fish cooked to perfection." Also included is an instruction booklet covering the proper way to fish the reel plus a thirty-page booklet, *How to Catch Fish in Fresh Water*. All Johnson reels carry an exclusive lifetime service guarantee. For more information or a catalog showing their reels and other products write to:
Johnson Reels, Inc.
1531 Madison Ave.
Mankato, Minn. 56001

PRO FILLETING KNIFE

The Pro Filleting Knife made by IPCO is designed for filleting and cleaning fish. The 6-in. flexible high carbon tool steel blade is precision-made from the finest steel. The razor-sharp blade is tapered to resist dulling and keeps its edge through repeated use. The contoured checkered ebony molded handle has solid brass fittings and is designed to fit the hand comfortably. It comes with an embossed black all-leather sheath with a nonbinding swivel belt loop. For their catalog or more information about this knife write to:
IPCO, Inc.
331 Lake Hazeltine Dr.
Chaska, Minn. 55318

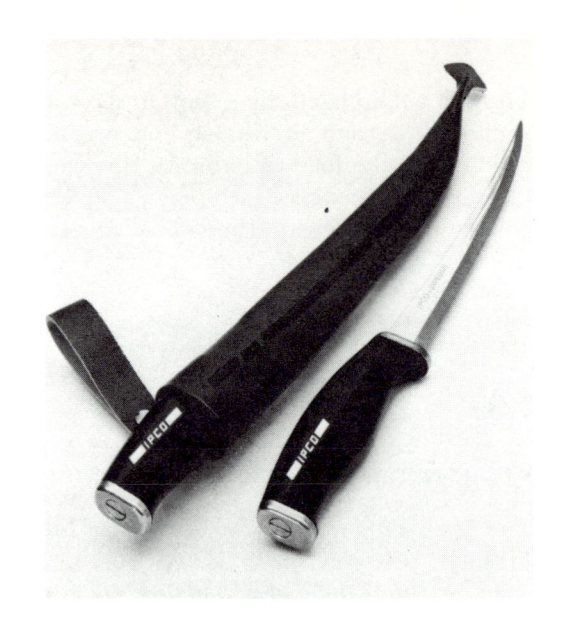

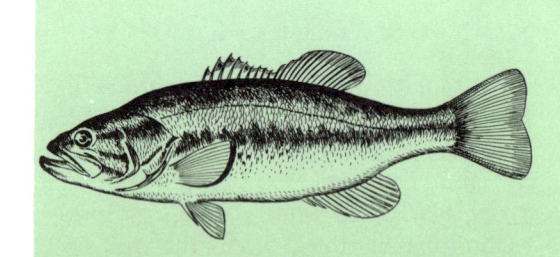

NIGHT FISHING FOR BASS

What's the music that makes big bass dance during the middle of the night? Experienced anglers will tell you it's the sound of something to eat—usually other fish, insects, frogs, or small animals moving about in the water.

Not able to see their prey at night too well, bass change their feeding technique to match the dark environment. They switch from visual hunting to using their two highly sensitive methods of detecting motion in water—the lateral line system, often called fish sonar, which detects vibrations; and the inner ear, which "hears" disturbances in the water. Both these senses are used at night to find, track, and attack prey.

To tempt the night-feeding fish into striking, the angling experts at Mercury Marine use a variety of noisy lures. These include popping plugs that chug their way on top of the water, shallow-running, double-bladed spinners that churn the surface, and sinking plugs that wobble violently as they are retrieved.

Night-fishing success can be bettered by remembering that the bass will "home in" on their prey by finding and following the noise and vibrations it makes.

Once you've found the lure rhythm to which the fish will respond by striking, it's important to maintain the same cadence throughout your retrieve, and follow the same pattern on each cast. A break in cadence will confuse the fish that are after your lure. They'll be thrown off track and are not likely to get interested in your lure again.

LEADER-KEEPER

The Leader-Keeper was designed to end fishing leader tangling and storage problems. It holds eight wire or monofilament leaders with or without hooks attached to leaders on a collapsible compartmented reel. It will also hold a few leaders with small lures such as flies or tiny jigs when locked, and bigger lures when open. Each leader is wound around the Leader-Keeper and locked by placing both ends of the leader or hooks in slots provided on the reel. The reel then collapses into a case for storage and easy handling in a tackle box or can be mounted on a boat in any convenient location. For more information contact:
Phil Bart Inventions
4844 N. E. 10th Terrace
Ft. Lauderdale, Fla. 33308

RABBLE ROUSER LURES

The Rabble Rouser lures come in many different types. Their top-water plug has a hollow mouth and large eyes, creating pops and gurgles and rolling darts and dives and even has a new clatter rattle. The other models are underwater divers and crank baits that work at various depths. They come in ¼-oz. and ½-oz. sizes and in different metallic and standard colors. For a color brochure or more information write to:
Rabble Rouser Lures
500 S. 7th St.
Fort Smith, Ark. 72901

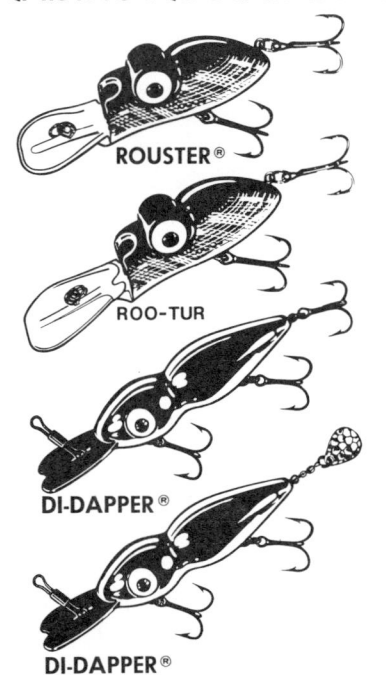

FRESHWATER STRIPERS

The striped bass has always been a popular fish in salt water, especially among surf anglers and boat anglers who seek these fish day and night along both the Atlantic and Pacific coasts. Many inland freshwater fishermen have wondered about striped bass after reading glowing accounts about these great game fish. Well, now they are beginning to find out because striped bass are being introduced and stocked in many freshwater lakes all over the country.

Of course, some striped bass have been found in coastal freshwater rivers as long as we can remember and have provided good fishing. Striped bass migrate up coastal rivers to spawn and spend a lot of time in fresh and brackish waters. Such fish have provided good fishing in the Hudson River, Delaware River, and Apalachicola and St. John's rivers in Florida. Stripers were also trapped and thrived in the Santee-Cooper Reservoir in South Carolina and have provided red-hot fishing there for many years.

But in recent years striped bass have been stocked in many freshwater lakes and rivers throughout the country. They can now be found in forty-two reservoirs in eighteen states in fresh water. When the Colorado River was dammed to form Lake Havasu, stripers were introduced and thrived, and the fishing for them has been excellent for several years. They are being stocked in Florida in such lakes as Talquin near Tallahassee and are showing up in the catches. And the Kerr Reservoir on the North Carolina-Virginia border also has good fishing for striped bass.

SNEAK UP ON THE FISH

One of the biggest mistakes many anglers make is to rush up to a fishing spot at full speed, creating noise, ripples, waves, and shadows, which frighten fish, especially in shallow water. But the smart anglers know better and always try to sneak up on the fish or stay a good distance away when fishing. When trying for trout in a stream, stay away from the water you plan to fish, keep low, and even cast from a kneeling position or from behind a bush when casting to a spot near shore. If you are wading, do so slowly and quietly, without disturbing the water. And when fishing from a boat, always shut off the motor a good distance from a fishing spot and then use an electric motor or row or paddle or drift toward the spot to be fished.

THE DEADLY SPINNER BAIT

Spinner baits have appeared in great numbers on the fishing scene in recent years and are deadly for big bass. These are the lures that have a lead head hook dressed with rubber, plastic, or feather skirts, and a single or double spinner blade revolving above it. They are versatile lures and can be fished fairly fast so that they travel and whirl on or near the surface. Or you can work them from 1 ft. or 2 ft. below the surface all the way down to the bottom. They are especially effective in weeds, over sunken brush, trees, logs, and along the dropoffs. In the spring, work the spinner bait over the spawning beds, and angry bass will attack it. In the hot summer months, work it deep along the bottom very slowly.

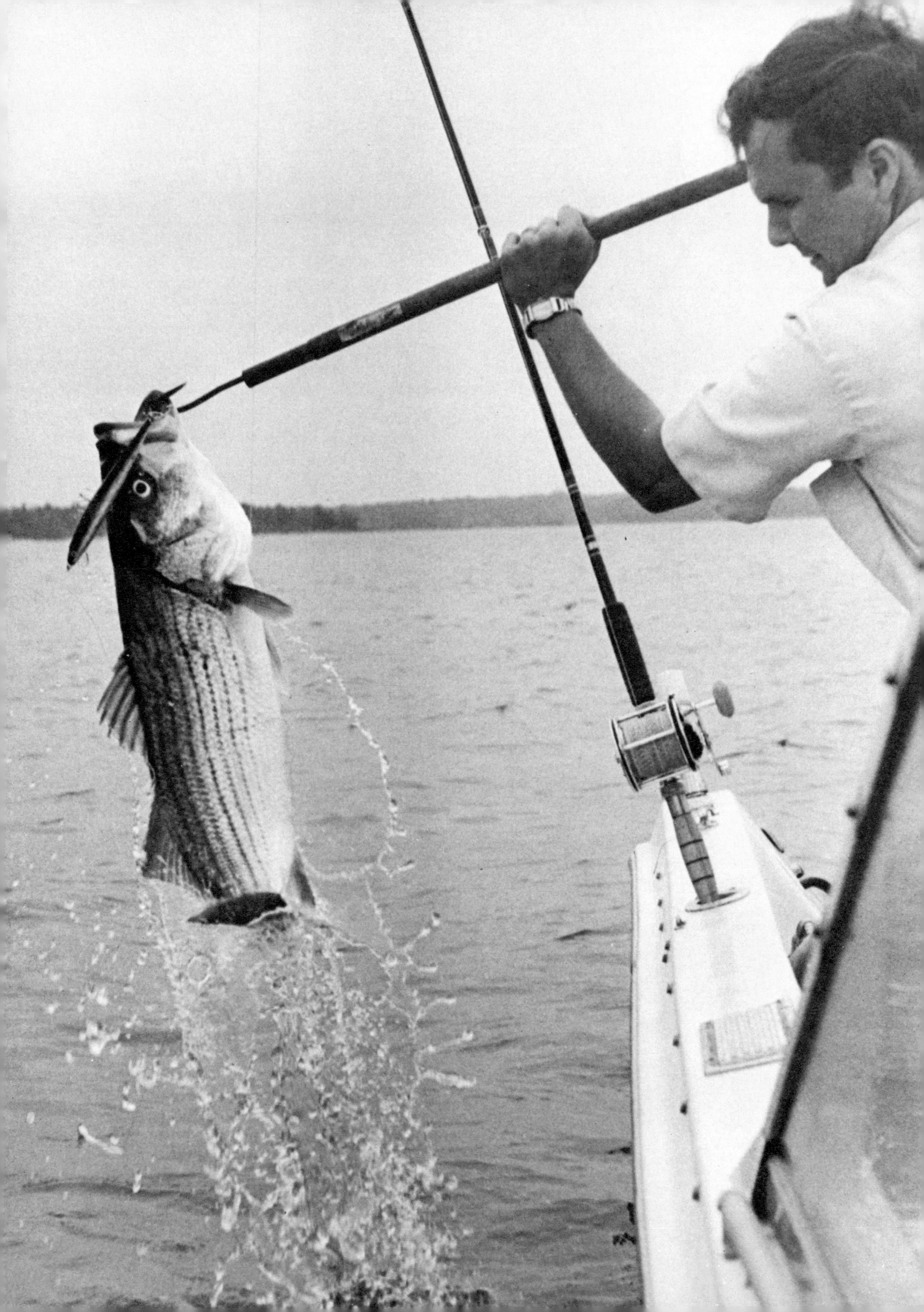

#123

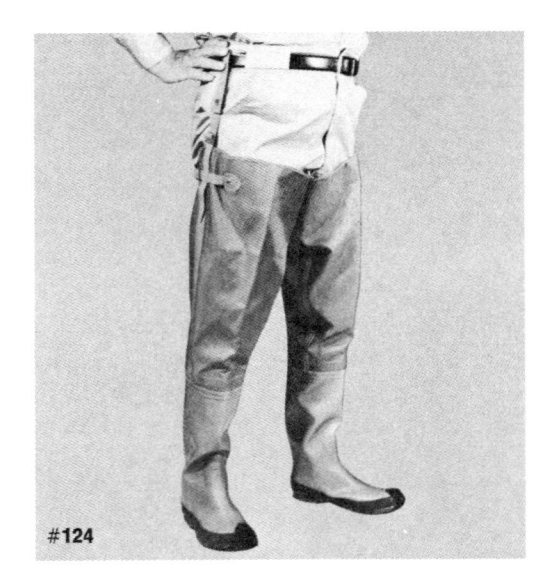

#124

CHEST AND HIP WADERS

Fritz Von Schlegell makes several chest waders and hippers for fishermen. They have nylon-laminated chest waders with rubber-cleated soles. And they also make insulated chest waders and lightweight chest waders. Their hippers are made like the chest waders but are only hip high.

The waders and hippers are available in sizes 6 through 13. They also make fishing vests, fishing shirts, creels, and fish and tackle bags. For more information about these products write to:
Fritz Von Schlegell
1407 Santa Fe Ave.
Los Angeles, Calif. 90021

CORTLAND FLY ROD OUTFIT

The Cortland fly outfit makes choosing and using a fly rod easy and convenient. This complete, professionally balanced fly-rod outfit eliminates all the problems of matching rod, reel, line, and leader. The outfit contains a tubular glass fly rod, single-action fly reel, a "333" fly line, tapered nylon leader, and even a little booklet called *Fly-rod Fishing Made Easy*. You have a choice between a 7½-ft. and 8½-ft. rod, and level, double-tapered, and bug-tapered fly lines. For more information write to:
Cortland Line Co.
Cortland, N.Y. 13045

RIVIERA DOWNRIGGERS

The actual idea of deep trolling is not really new, as all sport fishermen know that varied species of fish prefer certain water temperatures, water pressures, currents, feeding areas, and other changes made during a fishing season. These conditions determine the depth you will be fishing.

Once you know the particular habits of the fish you are going after, the next thing you need to know is how to reach them. Any depth for trolling is obtainable with enough weight. However, a number of variables have to be considered, such as trolling speed, water current, amount of trolling weight, and length of the line. And even then, how can you be sure of the exact level at which the lure is running, or whether the added weight is going to take all the fight out of the fish? These factors are eliminated by rigging with controlled-depth trolling equipment.

The trolling unit lowers a heavy trolling weight to an exact, predetermined depth—where the water conditions are most likely to produce the desired species of fish. Attached to the trolling weight is a release mechanism that is also attached to your rod line. When a fish strikes, your rod line snaps free from the trolling weight. At this point two important things have taken place: (1) You have been able to troll at a precise depth; (2) your fish is free from all trolling weight—giving you full fighting action.

The Riviera people have designed several such manual and electric controlled-depth trolling units for big-lake, deep-water freshwater fishing or for salt-water trolling. For more information write for their catalog to:
Riviera Mfg., Inc.
3859 Roger Chaffee Blvd., S.E.
Grand Rapids, Mich. 49508

GLADDING SOUTH BEND SPINNING REELS

The Gladding South Bend Spinning Reels are made in many models, from ultralight to heavy-duty freshwater and salt-water types. There are regular and fast retrieve reels, and they have multidisk drags for wide range and dependability. For more information or their color catalog showing these reels and other tackle write to:
Gladding Corp.
South Otselic, N.Y. 13155

CATCH MORE FISH ON JIGS

Unlike many artificial baits, leadhead jigs display little action of their own. A jig's appeal to fish is determined by the jig's appearance and by your particular method of "working" it. You can bounce or hop a jig, or swim it straight. Your retrieve can be fast or slow, near the surface or along the bottom. To help you catch more fish in jig time, here are important jigging tips from LINDY/LITTLE JOE:

When casting for walleyes and bass, variations of the simple "lift and drop" retrieve often work best. While retrieving your jig, repeatedly pull your rod tip forward and let it back. This pumping motion of the rod allows the jig to hop along the bottom. Sometimes you'll catch more fish by exaggerating this jigging action with sharp, sweeping strokes of the rod. On other occasions you'll score with short twitches or even a straight retrieve.

With jigs use monofilament line, as light as conditions permit. A useful guideline: The smaller the jig, the lighter the line.

For best results, tie your jig directly to the line. Avoid leaders, snaps, swivels, and sinkers. If more weight is needed—to cast against wind or to compensate for boat speed—go to a heavier jig.

When tipping jigs with small minnows or pieces of worm, sock it to them right away, especially when fish are hitting hard. But with large minnows and whole night crawlers, point your rod tip toward the fish for a moment before setting the hook. This brief hesitation allows the fish time to work the bait, and the hook into its mouth.

Fish sometimes scoop jigs right off the bottom! When tipping with minnows, pork strips, plastic worms, or other bait, you'll get more of these "bottom bites" with a Lindy Dingo. This jig literally stands on its head and elevates the hook, making your bait readily seen and easy to grab.

Slow trolling and drifting allow you to maintain your preferred jigging action without the usual casting and retrieving. How much line to let out will depend on the depth level of the fish, the weight of your jig, and the speed of your boat. Trolling and drifting methods are ideal for locating fish.

Fish very often hit jigs on the drop. An alert angler can detect these hard-to-notice strikes by closely watching the line for unusual behavior—such as a telltale twitch or "knock" on the line. Sometimes the line moves off to one side or stops while the jig is settling. If you suspect a fish, set the hook immediately.

Regardless of how you do it with jigs, you provide the action. That's what makes jigging such great fishing sport!

WEEDLESS MINNOW

When using a live minnow for bass, pickerel, or pike in heavy lily pads or weeds, tie a weedless hook on the end of your line and then run it through both lips of the baitfish. Now you can let the minnow swim around in and near the heaviest cover until a fish sees and grabs it.

FENWICK FLY FISHING SCHOOLS

The Fenwick Fly Fishing Schools are held in various states during the spring and summer months. Most of these are two-day schools, but some run up to three and five days. They are open to beginners and advanced students and give a short but fairly complete course in fly fishing. You'll learn rod, reel, and fly-line construction, how to choose the right tackle, and terminology. There are classes on insects covering their life cycles, what to look for, when, and where. Artificial flies and their construction are covered so you can identify, choose, and learn "how to match the hatch." Leaders and knots are also covered, as well as how to read a trout stream, where fish lie, and why they do. You learn how to approach them and present your fly. The instructors are all expert fly casters. For a brochure giving the location of these schools and what they offer and the cost write to:
Fenwick
P.O. Box 729
Westminster, Calif. 92683

BRETTON SPINNING REELS

The Bretton spinning reels are made in France and are imported to this country by the Martin Reel Company. They feature noiseless helical gears, stainless-steel shaft with quiet ball-bearing mounting. The seven-plate drag performs smoothly under the fastest run. They have a stainless-steel bait, carbide line roller, and folding stainless-steel handle. They have several models, from ultralight to heavy freshwater fishing. For their catalog showing these and other reels and tackle write to:
Martin Reel Co., Inc.
P.O. Drawer 8
Mohawk, N.Y. 13407

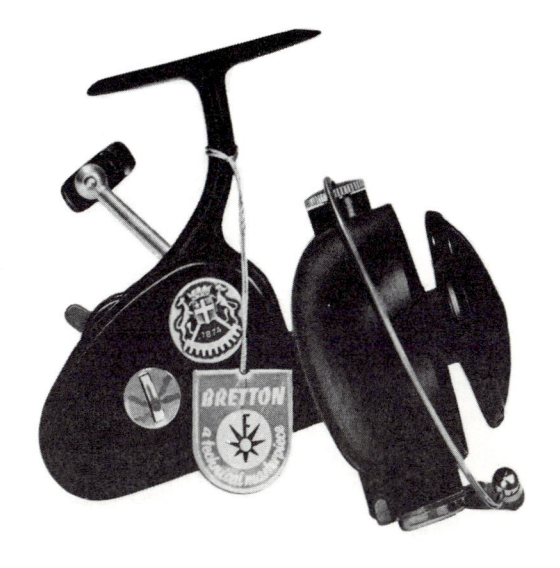

MOUNT YOUR OWN FISH TROPHIES

Doubleday & Co., Inc.
501 Franklin Ave.
Garden City, N.Y. 11530

In conversational style, illustrated with excellent drawings of all the processes and equipment needed, a dedicated taxidermist addresses himself to the fisherman who'd like to create his own trophy. He shows each step in skinning the fish, removing the body, adding a preservative, and inserting a foam or wood body. The fish can then be posed, the colors retouched, and mounted on a panel—and it's not complicated, expensive, or beyond the scope of any fisherman.

W. E. Moore is a taxidermist with his own studio. He also did the illustrations to accompany this book, which sells for $5.95.

FISHING BOOKS BY TWO PROS

These two fishing paperbacks between them have most of the fishing "how to's" and secrets used by the pros for black bass. The first book is *Tom Mann's Secrets of the Bass Pros* by Tom Mann, well-known bass fisherman and lure manufacturer. In the book he gives all the up-to-date methods and techniques of fishing with plastic worms, grubs, tail spinners, spinner baits, and the crank baits. He also shows you how to find bass, establish a pattern in fishing, how to fish shallow and deep, fishing structure, and how to choose the best tackle for bass.

The other book is *Al Lindner's Bassin' Facts,* and here pro angler Al Lindner tells Joe Fellegy how he locates bass and how he catches them. Lindner deals with bass boats, tackle, and accessories. He goes into his favorite lures and tells about the tactics, presentation, and retrieves he uses for plastic worms, jigs, spinner baits, tail spinners, crank baits, floater-divers, and swimming-jigging spoons. He also tells how to use live baits such as night crawlers, frogs, leeches, crayfish, salamanders, and minnows. All in all, it is a complete book on how to locate and catch bass in all types of waters.

Each paperback book is $4.95 and is available from:
Bass Anglers Sportsman Society
P.O. Box 3044
Montgomery, Ala. 36109

FLORIDA FISHING SPOTS

The Central and Southern Florida Flood Control District publishes a map and some folders of the areas they control that can be helpful to fishermen. They are:

"Recreational Map of the Everglades Conservation Areas"
Recreational Guide to the Kissimmee Waterway
Okee-Tantie Recreation Area
Lake Okeechobee

These guides are free if you write to:
Central and Southern Florida Flood Control District
3301 Gun Club Rd.
P.O. Box V
West Palm Beach, Fla. 33402

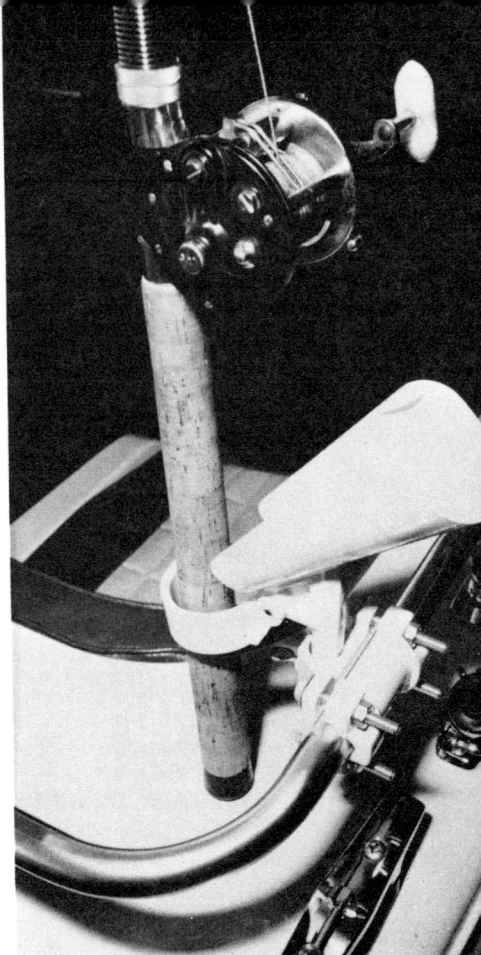

RAIL MOUNT FISHING ROD HOLDER

A new rail mount is now available for use with Tempo's two-position heavy-duty rod holder, which was designed especially for the sport-fishing enthusiasts and professionals who take their angling seriously. It can be installed easily on most standard tubular railings and is designed for quick removal of the rod holder when it is not in use.

Ruggedly made of die-cast aluminum alloy coated with a tough wear-resistant white enamel, Tempo's patented "open throat" design rod holder incorporates an exclusive drop-back ring that allows the angler to set his hook immediately when a fish strikes. This feature assures great success in hooking the fish solidly.

In the trolling position (left view in the photo) the rod nests firmly in the holder trough, where it is retained by the "ring" in the up position. When a fish strikes, the angler pulls back, setting the hook. The ring then automatically drops to a horizontal position, allowing the rod to be removed instantly from the holder with ease.

With the rod holder ring set in the horizontal position (right view in photo), the unit can be used as a rod retainer when not fishing. This position also permits the rod to be returned to the trolling position quickly after baiting or rigging up. The holder is completely open on top, which gives the fisherman one-hand control and makes the rod easily and quickly removable from the trolling position. The new 974 RM Rail Mount sells for $4.95. For more information write to:

Tempo Products Co.
6200 Cochran Rd.
Cleveland (Solon), O. 44139

THE STREAMSIDE TYER KIT

The Streamside Tyer Kit is a small, custom-hand-crafted leather fly tying kit, complete with all the tools and materials—vise, scissors, bobbin, dubbing, furs, hackle, cement, and other items needed to tie complete flies in the field. The kit is so well organized that everything is at your fingertips. There is a unique dubbing pod/page that handles eighteen individual colors of fur and measures out the right amount for use. Also a hook storage area, where hooks are kept in sized order ready for immediate use. Three Zip-lock storage pages of clear plastic are removable for replacement or can be added to for increased capacity. The Streamside Tyer Kit retails for $59.95 and is available from:
**Laggies Fish Catching Co.
7059 Varna Ave.
North Hollywood, Calif. 91605**

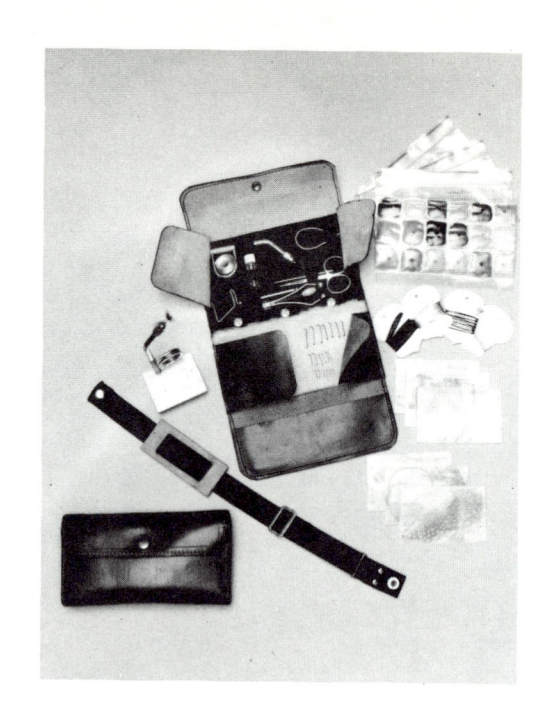

FISH THE ROUGH WATER

Many fly fishermen fishing for trout with dry flies pass up the shallow, broken water or rapids and concentrate mainly on the pools, deep holes, and calm, flat stretches. But you can have excellent dry fly fishing in the whitewater rapids, especially if they are studded with rocks. Trout often lie in the deeper, quieter pockets in such water and will rise to the dry fly. You can approach such feeding stations in rough water closer than in the calmer waters and make fairly short casts. The best dry flies for such fishing are the fan wings, bivisibles, spiders, variants, and Wulffs in sizes from 8 to 12. These larger sizes are easier to see and follow in the rough water and also float better and longer.

FISH THE SHADOWS

When the day is bright and sunny, fishing often falls off because most fish shun bright light and go deeper. But you can often have good fishing on such days if you fish the shadows. Trout will often lurk in the shadows created by overhanging rocks, ledges, banks, brush, trees, and bridges. Bass will be found under lily pads, hyacinths, logs, ledges, and trees. Panfish such as crappies, white bass, and bluegills will hang around under lily pads, logs, stumps, tree roots, docks, and bridges. Cast your lure, fly, or bait into such shadows, and the fish will often strike. If the shadows cover a wide area you may run into a group or school of fish and catch more than one out of such a spot.

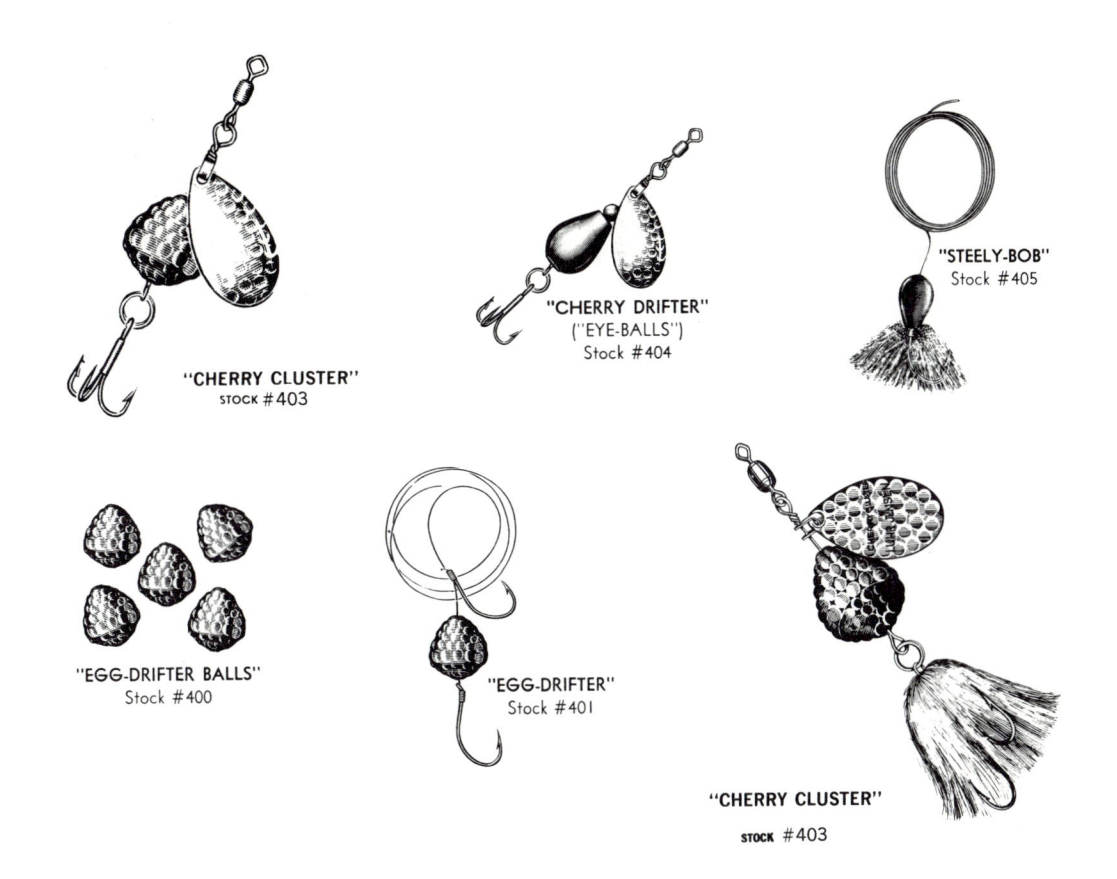

STEELHEAD LURES

Luhr Jensen and Sons, Inc., makes many lures for steelhead fishing, such as their Egg-Drifter Balls, Cherry Drifter, Cherry Cluster, Steely-Bob, and Shrimp-Louie baits. The Egg Drifters come plain as balls for rigging, or you can get them already snelled and rigged with a hook for immediate fishing. The other lures have spinners in hammered nickel or brass finishes. They also make many other spinners, spoons, and flies for steelhead, trout, and coho salmon fishing, as well as multiple-spinner rigs for lake trolling. Their catalog costs $.50 and can be obtained from:

Luhr Jensen and Sons, Inc.
P.O. Box 297
Hood River, Ore. 97031

ILLINOIS FISHING GUIDE

The purpose of this guide is to help the angler realize more fully the opportunities available for sport fishing in Illinois. All of the Department of Conservation fishing areas are included, together with a complete directory of streams and lakes in every county where sport fishing may be enjoyed. There are twenty drawings showing the most important sport species in Illinois. There are also maps and charts showing boat-access areas built with state boating act funds. The guide can be obtained from:

Dept. of Conservation
Div. of Fisheries
605 State Office Bldg.
Springfield, Ill. 62706

215

HOW TO FIND FISH—AND MAKE THEM STRIKE

The book *How to Find Fish—and Make Them Strike* by Joseph D. Bates, Jr., is a volume that deals with the basic principles: How do you find fish? How do you provoke them to strike a lure or bait? The book doesn't tell you how to cast or tie knots. It does tell you how to catch more fish, because after you read it you'll be fishing over fish instead of over empty water, and you'll be fishing with the right lure or bait and giving it the right action.

To write this book, author Joe Bates teamed up with angler-photographer Rex Gerlach. Rex photographed actual lake and stream situations, and Joe explained how to fish them, using diagrams on the photos to indicate holding and feeding water. In addition, Joe obtained some unusual split-vision photo-drawings that show both the surface and bottom structure of lakes. Combined with the information on water temperature and its effects on fishing, structure holds the key to success in lake fishing.

Next, you learn how to fish the water where the fish are, how to appeal to their senses with the right bait or lure under all kinds of conditions, and how to give it the kind of action that brings strikes. On bright days or dull days, in spring, summer, or fall, you'll know where to fish and what to fish with.

The book covers fishing for trout, bass, walleyes, pickerel, pike, muskies, and panfish. *How to Find Fish—and Make Them Strike* sells for $8.95 and is published by:
Harper & Row, Publishers, Inc.
10 East 53rd St.
New York, N.Y. 10022

SPIN FISHING RECORDS

Some amazing catches of freshwater and salt-water fish have been made on spinning tackle and light lines since these reels became popular with anglers in this country. A 19-lb., 4-oz. large-mouth bass was caught on 8-lb. line. A 32-lb., 4-oz. pike was caught on 4-lb. line. A 67-lb., 15-oz. muskellunge was caught on 10-lb. line. A 28-lb., 3-oz. brown trout was caught on 8-lb. line, and a 22-lb. steelhead was taken on 4-lb. line.

In salt water there have been such catches as a 57-lb., 1-oz. striped bass on 10-lb. line. A 17-lb., 4-oz. bluefish was caught on 6-lb. line. A 60-lb., 8-oz. channel bass was taken on 12-lb. line. A 112-lb., 8-oz. California black sea bass was caught on 10-lb. line. A 64-lb. white marlin was caught on 6-lb. line. A 183-lb., 7-oz. striped marlin was caught on 10-lb. line. And a 312-lb., 3-oz. black marlin was taken on 12-lb. line.

Many more equally outstanding catches have been made on spinning tackle, and such records are kept by the International Spin Fishing Association. They publish a *World Record Book* of such spin fishing catches, and it can be obtained for $.50. They also accept individuals and fishing clubs as members. And you can get a record application card if you catch a fish on spinning tackle you think will beat their present record in a certain line class. All this information and an application card can be obtained from:
International Spin Fishing Assn.
P.O. Box 81
Downey, Calif. 90241

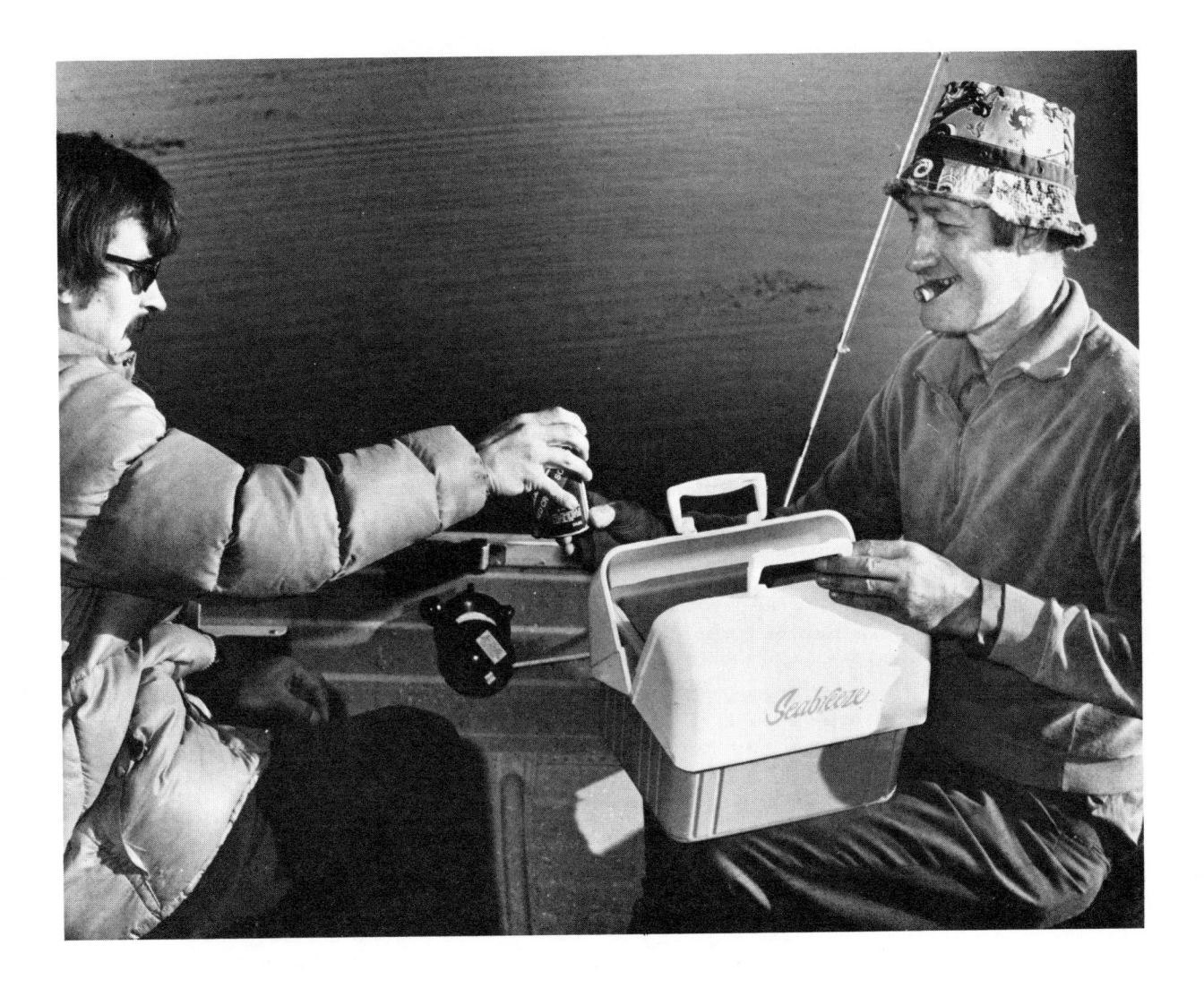

SEABREEZE MINI-COOLER

The Seabreeze Mini-Cooler by Covey is as handy as a fisherman's tackle box and about the same size, making it ideal for taking along in a boat. It has a unique lid that opens like a clam shell and stays right on the cooler so it cannot be misplaced or dropped overboard.

For keeping drinks and food cold for up to eight hours, the Seabreeze Mini-Cooler has polyurethane insulation sandwiched between its tough pebble-grain-finished blue exterior and smooth one-piece inner liner that resists stains and odors.

Separate the handles and each side of the cooler lid pivots open; swing them together and special locking cams keep it closed tight for longer cooling. Although small, the Mini-Cooler can hold twelve king-size bottles or two six-packs with plenty of room for ice and sandwiches. For more information write to:

Covey Corp.
P.O. Box 1317
Houston, Tex. 77001

BAITS IN A SUPERMARKET

You can buy many different kinds of baits in any supermarket or grocery store. Bread, rolls, or biscuits can be kneaded and formed into doughballs of various sizes for panfish, carp, and catfish. Ordinary flour and cornmeal can also be mixed with water and heated to make doughball baits. Cheese can be used as bait for panfish and catfish. Canned corn kernels make a good bait for carp in fresh water and flounders in salt water. Shrimp can also be used for many salt-water fish and for catfish in fresh water. Marshmallows cut into tiny cubes can be used for trout and panfish. And various vegetables and whole grains such as barley, lima beans, green peas, potatoes, carrots, and parsnips can be soaked or parboiled and used for carp. Beef, pork, liver, and other meats can be cut into strips or small chunks and used for catfish. Even a small piece cut from a cake of white laundry soap has been used for catfish.

BIG BASS ON A BROKEN ROD

Buddy Morse decided to try his luck in a lake near his home at the Country Club of Miami. So he put a Rapala lure on the end of his line and cast it out. There was a big splash as a fish went after the lure, but it missed. Buddy cast out again, and this time the fish grabbed the plug. It jumped three times and ran off 25 ft. of line and then ran toward shore, and just then the rod tip broke. Then the rod came apart at the ferrule, and Buddy fought the fish with half a rod. Finally, he succeeded in landing it, and when he weighed it, the bass pulled the scale down to 11 lbs., 6 ozs.!

FISH WITHOUT WATER

Although most freshwater and salt-water fish need water to survive, the remarkable lungfishes of Africa, Australia, and South America can live even if the stream or river in which they are found dries up completely. They merely burrow into the clay or mud bottom, curl up, breathe air with the lungs they possess, and await the wet or rainy season, which will fill the stream or river with water again. While in this state, the lungfish have been shipped to various parts of the world in lumps of dry clay, then chiseled out and put into a tank of water, where they became active again!

FISHING WITH STREAMERS

When using streamer or bucktail flies in a stream or river, retrieve them much faster when they are moving with the current or across the current. But when you are retrieving them against the current, move them much slower and even stop or pause every so often to imitate a minnow or small fish struggling against the current.

SHRINKING FISH

After being caught, fish shrink slightly in weight because of the evaporation of moisture. This weight loss is very small, but may be important when fishing in tournaments, or for prizes or pools or for a record. So weigh a fish officially as soon as possible, or keep it in water or covered with wet rags or burlap to minimize this weight loss.

FISHING WESTERN WATERS

The large-size paperback *Fishing Western Waters* by Morie Morrison covers fishing in most of the western states from British Columbia to California. A native of California, the author has fished all over the world but especially in the western states about which he writes. He describes the lakes and streams and rivers an angler will find from the Rocky Mountains west. He tells about the fish and their senses, fishing tackle, lures, and baits. He tells how to fish the streams, rivers, and lakes. He covers the trout, salmon, steelhead, and other fishes caught in western waters. And he recounts the fishing you'll find in each state. *Fishing Western Waters* sells for $2.95 and is published by:
Chronicle Books
870 Market St.
San Francisco, Calif. 94102

ELECTRIC FISH SCALER

This electric fish scaler lifts fish scales from any fish quickly and cleanly without cutting the skin. It is fast, clean, and safe, and is power driven. The working end of this tool revolves and deflects all scales downward, without cutting into the fish or causing injury to the user's hands. It is ruggedly built and sufficiently durable for commercial use, but is reasonably priced for the sport fisherman who catches a lot of fish and wants to ease the chore of scaling and cleaning them. The scaler head has a superhard coating and is impregnated with Teflon. It is very easy to clean and keep clean. It is highly resistant to salt water and rusting. The electric fish scaler comes in three models. The cheapest one, retailing for $13.50, has no motor and is plugged into an electric drill. The other two models, selling for $35.00 and $41.50, have their own motors. For more information write to:
Bear Paw Tackle Co., Inc.
Bellaire, Mich. 49615

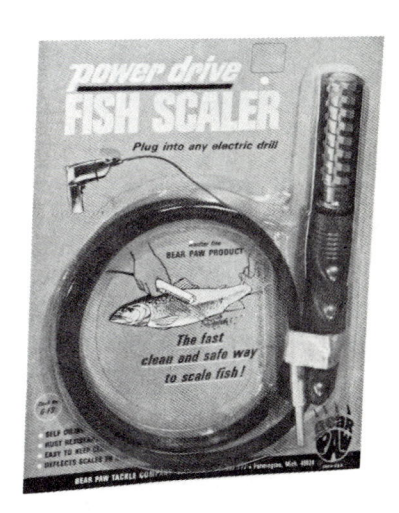

ORVIS FLY FISHING SCHOOLS

The Orvis Fly Fishing Schools have been held for over ten years at Manchester, Vermont, and have proven very popular with anglers who are beginners and want to learn how to fly cast and fish. And they are also attended by more advanced students who want to polish their skills. The three-day sessions offer meals, room at a mountain lodge, casting lessons, and practice at the Orvis trout ponds, with expert instructors at your elbow. You get a tour of the Orvis rod factory and free use and tryout of the Orvis fly rods. You get a three-day Vermont fishing license to fish the evening rises on the lovely Battenkill. There are illustrated lectures on tackle and fly selection, stream entomology, and knot tying. The Orvis Fly Fishing Schools are held during April, May, June, July, and August. For specific dates and more information write to:

Orvis Fly Fishing School
10 River Rd.
Manchester, Vt. 05254

GLASTRON T-172 BASS BOAT

Glastron T-172 Bass Boat boasts two live fish-wells fore and aft, with circulating pump and thru-hull drains, two adjustable folding seats that swivel 360 degrees, and a cushioned pilot seat. There's room for everything—deep storage under elevated platforms, under the pilot's seat, in the bow and under the port bench seat. The hull is self-draining, with cut-pile carpet. There's a plexiglas windshield with handrails, space for trolling motor with flush-mounted outlet, and a 12-v./24-v. switch. There are easy-access mounts for anchor winches, two locking glove boxes, rod locker, and a custom console with a built-in 18-gal. fuel tank and battery storage. The V-172 takes outboard power to 115 hp. and is available in blue or burgundy with white. For more information contact:
Glastron Boat Co.
P.O. Box 9447
Austin, Tex. 78766

WHITE BASS AND CRAPPIE FISHING BOOKLETS

Two excellent booklets—*Crappie—A Fish for All Seasons* and *White Bass—A Fish for Tomorrow*—have been published by the Gapen Tackle Company. Dan Gapen, president of the company, felt that many species of fish are neglected by anglers, with too much pressure on such fish as trout, bass, and muskies. So he inaugurated a series of booklets dealing with these "lesser" species. The first booklet was on carp fishing, reviewed earlier in this catalog. The booklets mentioned above in this paragraph deal with crappies and white bass, and other booklets in the series will cover other neglected species. Each of these booklets sells for $2.00 and can be obtained from:

Gapen Tackle Co.
Big Lake, Minn. 55309

FISH GET THE "BENDS"

Deep-sea divers are often afflicted with an illness called the "bends." It occurs when dissolved nitrogen enters the diver's bloodstream and then expands when he returns to the surface. Although it can be prevented, when it does occur the bends is a painful and sometimes fatal illness.

Strange as it seems, fish can also have the bends. According to the fishing department at Mercury Marine, biologists have learned that under certain thermal-water conditions fish actually develop gas bubbles in their blood.

The problem was observed during research being conducted at a large southeastern lake to learn the effects of hot-water discharge from nuclear power plants on fish and aquatic plant and insect life.

Scientists discovered that fish captured in hot water often had a condition known as "pop-eye." Gas bubbles had formed behind their eyes, causing them to protrude from the head. And in some cases the fish were blind from the loss of both eyes. Evidently, when the fish moved from cold water to the thermal-discharge area, they became exposed to the gas-bubble disease.

Fisheries biologists seeking the cause of the bubbles concluded that an excess amount of dissolved nitrogen was being released in the hot water from the power plant and then absorbed by the fish. Nitrogen supersaturation, as the condition is called, caused the fish to experience a condition similar to the "bends" suffered by divers when they surface quickly from deep water.

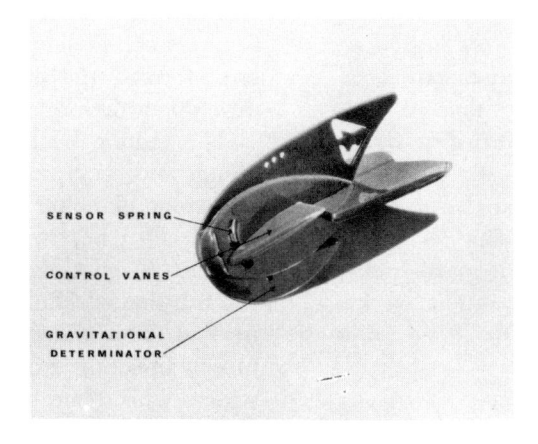

THERMALFINDER DIVING PLANE

The same principle used in home and automobile thermostats is used in a unique new device designed for trolling fishing lures at specific temperature levels in the thermocline.

Called the Thermalfinder, this 1-oz. diving plane has a large rear fin for stability and two smaller control vanes connected to a bimetal sensor spring inside, preset for specific temperatures. As the temperature changes, the spring contracts or expands, altering the angle of the Thermalfinder's control vanes and causing it to dive or rise to the proper water-temperature range.

Attached to a short leader on a triple swivel ahead of the lure, the Thermalfinder is designed for a maximum trolling speed of 3 mph. In addition to its vertical rudder, the Thermalfinder also has a small loose metallic weight (gravitational determinator) inside the molded plastic body to maintain precise balance while trolling.

The Thermalfinder comes in three color-coded models: green for cold water below 50 degrees (lake and rainbow trout and salmon), blue for midrange of 50 to 65 degrees (brook, brown and steelhead trout, walleye and northern pike), and yellow for 60-to-75-degree water (bass, sunfish, crappies, and muskies).

Retail-priced at $14.95, the Thermalfinder is available from:
Aquadene Sales, Inc.
P.O. Box 26236
Salt Lake City, Ut. 84125

DEPTH AND SPEED

When choosing a fishing lure you have to consider the depth it can be worked at and the speed that brings out the best action and that the fish want at a given time. Some lures can be worked at various depths, but others are designed for surface use or shallow-running depths or for deep-water fishing. Some lures can be used at different speeds, but most of them work best at a certain speed. And, of course, some fish will hit faster-moving lures than others. And on certain days a varied retrieve will work better than a straight one-speed retrieve. So expert anglers experiment all the time, fishing different depths and trying different speeds until they find the combination that works best and interests the fish.

TROUT IN LAKES

Trout in most lakes usually do not stay put in one spot when feeding. They have no current to bring food to them, so they have to cruise around searching for it. So here the best procedure is to choose a good spot on shore or in a boat and stay put until you see a trout come cruising by. Then you can cast your lure or fly well ahead of it so that it crosses the path of the fish. Of course, this works best in clear water, mountain lakes, or shallow water near shore where you can see the fish more readily. You can also locate trout toward evening on many lakes when they dimple the surface while feeding on hatching flies and you can cast to such rises.

NATIONAL FRESHWATER FISHING HALL OF FAME

The National Freshwater Fishing Hall of Fame is a nonprofit organization that will be dedicated to the conservation and sport of fishing throughout the world. It will construct and maintain a Hall of Fame and Museum where the history of fishing and angling achievements can be portrayed. The idea of a Hall of Fame was spawned in 1960, and ten years later five persons—Bob Kutz, Erv Gerlach, Bud Nelson, Oscar Treland, and Quentin Johnson—formed the organization and began developing the project.

The Fishing Hall of Fame grew both in design and scope as the founders met for numerous planning sessions. The Museum was deemed necessary; and then to add a sparkle of something special, the five-story-tall fish-shaped Hall of Fame building was devised. This will be a likeness of a giant musky breaking from a sparkling pool of water. This "big fish" will measure 160 feet from tail to mouth. The history of fishing will be told inside the "big fish" building.

Casting ponds, demonstration areas, and open-air shelters will be featured on the grounds to accommodate group and individual instruction on subjects such as fly tying, rod and reel repair, the food cycle of fish, and water quality improvement.

The founders of the Fishing Hall of Fame had set a five-year construction timetable with Phase One—the completion and opening of the Administration Reception Center in 1975, with the rest to be finished by 1980. Total cost will be over $1.5 million, and funds will come from individuals, clubs, and companies. The National Freshwater Fishing Hall of Fame is located in Hayward, Wisconsin. For more information contact:

The Fishing Hall of Fame
Wisconsin Ave.
Hayward, Wis. 54843

NATIONAL FRESHWATER FISHING HALL OF FAME · HAYWARD, WISCONSIN   RICHARD EVJEN ASSOCIATES · ARCHITECTS

MAXIMA FISHING LINES

Maxima monofilament fishing lines are popular with many freshwater and saltwater anglers and come in various types and strengths and colors. Their Super Soft foam-green monofilament, originally designed for freshwater fishing, has received the acclaim of both freshwater and saltwater anglers for its fine performance on all types of reels. Super Soft is immune to temperature changes because of a new chemical that has been added, and it will stay soft on your reel for many months of heavy use.

Their Chameleon monoline changes color. It contains chemical reagents that absorb the rays of light but do not reflect them. Thus the line is less visible to fish. These chemicals also make this line change color in water and daylight. And Chameleon mono is not affected by temperature extremes like many lines. For more information or a brochure write to:

Bruce B. Mises, Inc.
1122 S. Robertson Blvd.
Los Angeles, Calif. 90035

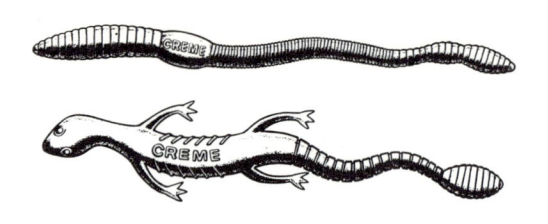

FISHING WITH PLASTIC LURES

The Creme Lure Company, which originated the plastic worm that has now become the No. 1 lure in the country for bass, has published a very helpful guide on fishing with these lures. Called *Tips and Techniques from the Creme Tester Staff*, the booklet has contributions from many expert anglers who tell how to use plastic worms, grubs, lizards, and other plastic lures most effectively. The booklet also shows and describes the various worms and lures made by the company. It costs $1.00 and can be obtained from:

Creme Lure Co.
P.O. Box 87
Tyler, Tex. 75701

PRACTICAL FISHING KNOTS

Practical Fishing Knots by Lefty Kreh and Mark Sosin is a thorough and practical guide to better knots for lines and splices of all kinds for fishing—freshwater and saltwater fly fishing, spinning, bait casting, and even boating knots. The easy-to-understand tying directions are illustrated with line drawings and photographs showing each stage of the tie. *Practical Fishing Knots* also shows how to buy, store, and get maximum benefit from nylon monofilament. Learn special uses for wire and a score of other knot secrets that will help you hold the fish you hook whatever the size. *Practical Fishing Knots* sells for $5.95 and is published by:

Crown Publishers, Inc.
419 Park Ave. S.
New York, N.Y. 10016

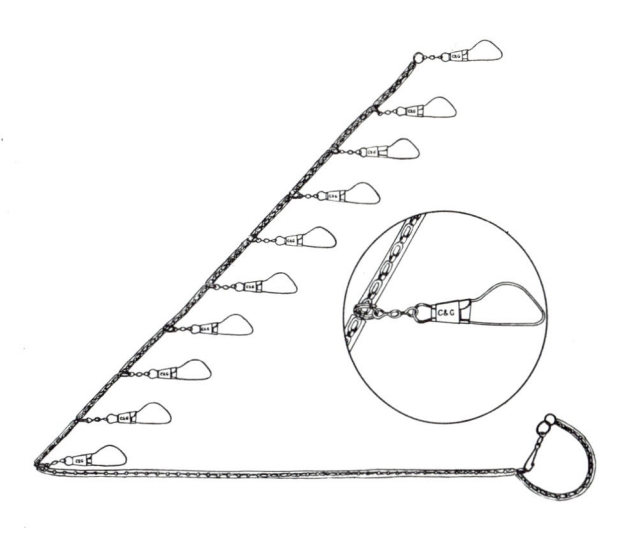

FLY CASTING FROM THE BEGINNING

This is a concise, informative booklet written by Jim Green, who is a rod designer and master fly caster and fisherman. He tries to explain the complex sport of fly fishing as simply as possible so that any beginner can learn the fundamentals. He covers the tools of the fly fisher such as the rod, reel, line, leader, and flies. Then he deals with the fly-casting basics, showing how to cast with a fly rod so that you can reach the fish and present the fly naturally. He covers dry fly fishing, wet fly fishing and nymph fishing in streams, rivers, and lakes. *Fly Casting from the Beginning* sells for $2.00 and is available from:
Fenwick
P.O. Box 729
Westminster, Calif. 92683

CHRIS' DELUXE FISH STRINGER

Chris' Deluxe Fish Stringer lives up to its name and is a high-quality product that will stand up and not fail you when you need it. In fact, this stringer is guaranteed, and any defective stringer will be replaced at no charge. This stranger is made of solid brass, and is encased in plastic tubing to give extra durability, reduce noise, protect hands, and prevent marring of your boat. It has ten swiveled, heat-treated stainless-steel hooks with double safety locks. The chain is solid brass and is 6 ft. long and tests 200 lbs. The stringer is rustproof in salt water or fresh water. It sells for $8.95 and is made by:
C & G Tackle Mfg. Co., Inc.
1343 N. 108 E. Ave.
Tulsa, Okla. 74116

FLIES

The book *Flies* by J. Edson Leonard was published many years ago and has become a classic in its field. It is an encyclopedic treatment of twenty-two hundred fly patterns covering dry flies, wet flies, nymphs, streamers, bucktails, salmon flies, bass bugs, and salt-water flies. The author tells about the origin, natural history, and parts of each fly. He tells how to tie the flies and goes into hooks, tools, and materials needed for fly tying. The book is illustrated with color and black-and-white illustrations. It sells for $9.95 and is published by:
A. S. Barnes & Co., Inc.
P.O. Box 421
Cranbury, N.J. 08512

LUNKER

The book *Lunker* by Bob Underwood is the result of a major effort to study the freshwater bass in its natural element and surroundings and find out what makes the fish behave the way they do. The author went down with scuba gear, light meters, thermometers, a portable recorder, and cameras, while a friend fished for bass from a boat above him. Some seventeen hundred hours later, Bob Underwood discovered exactly what kinds of cover, food, light, water temperature, bottom structure, noise, current, and weather motivate bass to seize a lure.

Bob Underwood doesn't tell you anything about what boat or rod or reel or line to use. He figures that if you're a bass fisherman, you have your own favorites. And they'll work better for you than anything he could recommend. But he does tell you about lure retrieves and the best ways to make the bass hit. He covers spinner baits, crankbaits, noisemakers, spoons, plastic worms, bugs, and streamers. He also has informative tips on live baits—the striped siren, the caledonian, and the golden shiner. He lets you in on how blackbirds and pickerelweed can lead you to bass concentrations. If you like after-dark fishing, he has hints for you.

Bob Underwood, a longtime resident of Florida, has fished in most of the United States, so his combined knowledge and research have resulted in a valuable book for the bass fisherman. *Lunker* sells for $12.95 and is published by:
McGraw-Hill Book Co.
1221 Ave. of the Americas
New York, N.Y. 10020

LURES FROM YARN

You can make inexpensive lures by using a skein of knitting yarn, which comes in various colors. Cut short lengths and tie one strand around a small hook for crappies, bluegills, perch, or other panfish. You can cut longer lengths and tie several strands around jig heads, hooks on spoons, and plugs, and use these for bass, pickerel, walleyes, and pike.

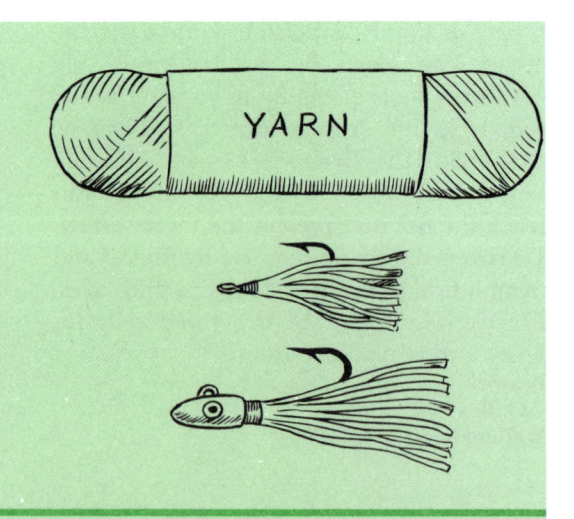

LOCATING TROUT SPOTS IN A STREAM

The quickest way to learn the best holding and feeding spots used by trout in a stream is to examine and study it during the summer when the water is low. By walking along the bank you can see the holes, boulders, big rocks, sunken trees, undercut banks, and other good spots that are hard to see when the water is high. You can even draw rough maps and make notes of these spots so that you can consult them when the water rises later on or next spring.

SILVERLINE KODIAK BASS BOAT

Bass fishermen who want to get quickly from one spot to another will appreciate Silverline's Kodiak 17T. Introduced originally as out outboard rated for up to 120 hp., the new Kodiak is available in a stern-drive model also with 120-hp. and 140-hp. engine options.

While the family may enjoy skiing behind the Kodiak, Silverline designed it with the fisherman in mind. It has two swivel seats with armrests, a helmsman seat, 6-ft. illuminated, lockable dry storage compartments with rod holders, a front storage compartment, two live bait wells with an aeration system, an outlet for an electric trolling motor, fore and aft courtesy lights, and forward side handrails. Also standard are chrome running lights and deck hardware; teak step pads; horn; rack and pinion steering; a built-in, gauged fuel system; flotation foam; and a removable windshield that facilitates storage in low-overhead enclosures.

The stern-drive model also includes full instrumentation, with speedometer, bilge pump, and blower and an insulated icebox. The Kodiak's centerline is 16 ft., 10 in.; beam, 76 in.; bow depth, 25 in.; approximate weight, 1,050 lbs.; and maximum load capacity, 1,365 lbs.

For more information write to:
Silverline, Inc.
2300 12th Ave. S.
Moorhead, Minn. 56560

FISH-N-FLOAT MARKER KIT

This marker kit is for marking topographic features of lakes, rivers and bays—plus your favorite "hot spot" or fishing hole so you can locate it whenever you want to. It is an excellent orientation system when shoreline and landmarks aren't visible. And if you are trolling and get a hit or a fish, you can quickly throw one overboard to mark the spot. The kit includes six plastic markers in bright red and yellow, with nylon line and an instruction sheet and helpful hints. For more information write to:
Lowrance Electronics, Inc.
1200 E. Skelly Dr.
Tulsa, Okla. 74128

OKIEBUG FISHING TACKLE

This company sells a varied line of fishing tackle for the bass fisherman and other anglers. They carry the well-known brands of fishing rods, reels, lines, lures, hooks, tackle boxes, fishing clothes, knives, depth/fish finders, electric motors, bass boat equipment, and many accessories. They also have lead molds for jigs, lure-making component parts, and rod-making parts. Their big catalog showing all this fishing tackle costs $1.00 and can be obtained from:
Okiebug Distributing Co.
3501 S. Sheridan Rd.
Tulsa, Okla. 74145

ELECTRIC MOTOR HOLD-DOWN

This Super Boomer electric motor hold-down was actually developed through tournament use by the pros who fish for bass and demand fast boats and everything fastened down securely. This sturdy strap holds the electric motor secure when not in use. The motor rests on resilient rubber cushion provided with the Super Boomer. A quick-release latch locks or releases at a simple flick of the wrist. For more information write to:
Byrd Industries, Inc.
201 Rock Industrial Park Dr.
Bridgeton, Mo. 63044

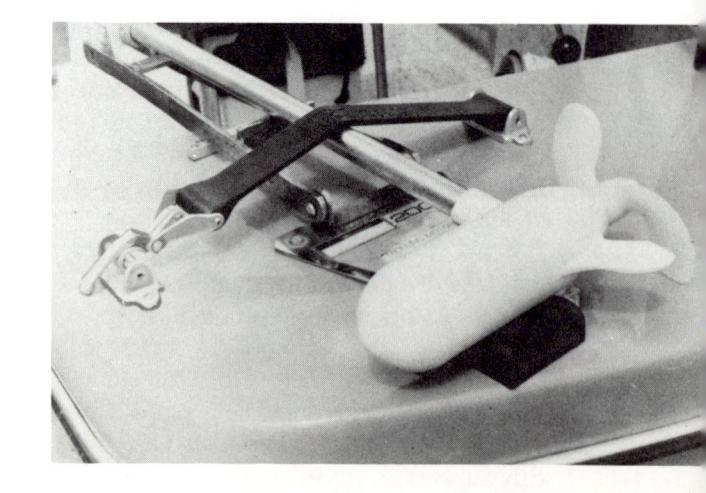

ADVANCED BASS TACKLE AND BOATS

The book *Advanced Bass Tackle and Boats* by A. D. Livingston covers almost the entire field of equipment used by the modern black-bass fisherman. "I've never seen a bassman who wasn't interested in tackle," says Livingston, "and some of us are almost fanatical about the subject!" One reason is that no other form of fishing makes use of such a huge array of equipment. *Advanced Bass Tackle and Boats* gives America's thirty million bass anglers the detailed, up-to-the-minute information they need on gear, tackle, and boats.

Inside this book you'll find six chapters on space-age rods, highly engineered reels, modern lines, hot new lures, and terminal tackle. Another three chapters are devoted to fish-finding aids such as sonar depth finders, CdS light-intensity meters, electronic temperature indicators, and oxygen monitors, along with fishing maps and an extensive list of sources of hard-to-find maps. Still another four chapters cover bass-fishing boats and delve into design, construction, motors, accessories, and the less-expensive smaller boats. And there are many tips on buying and using the right equipment for your kind of fishing. *Advanced Bass Tackle and Boats* sells for $9.95 and is published by:

J. B. Lippincott Co.
E. Washington Sq.
Philadelphia, Pa. 19105

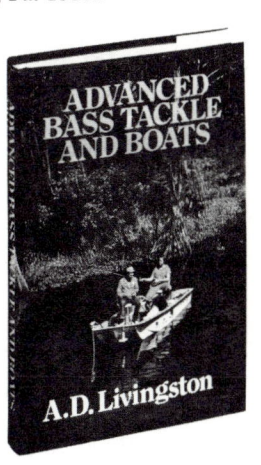

FLY FISHERMAN'S BOOKCASE AND TACKLE SERVICE

This company sells almost anything the freshwater or salt-water fly fisherman needs to fish the streams, rivers, lakes, ponds, and ocean. They sell many different kinds of fly rods made of Fiberglas and graphite. They also have fly-rod blanks and the component parts needed for making the finished rod. They carry a big selection of fly reels for freshwater and salt-water fishing. They also have the fly lines to match. Their selection of flies is varied and complete. Or you can get tools and materials from them to tie your own flies. And you can find most of the old and recent books on fly fishing and fly tying in their catalog. For their catalog write to:

Fly Fisherman's Bookcase
Rte. 9A
Croton-on-Hudson, N.Y. 10520

UNIVERSAL VISE CORPORATION

The Universal Vise Corporation sells fly-tying tools such as vises, lights, bobbins, pliers, scissors, clips, tweezers, fly-tying kits, hooks, thread, body materials, dubbing materials, winging materials, necks or hackle, and everything else needed to tie flies. They have a catalog that can be obtained for $.75 from:

Universal Vise Corp.
22 Main St.
Westfield, Mass. 01085

HEDDON 3200 BAIT-CASTING REEL

The new Heddon 3200 bait-casting reel has been made as free from backlash as possible, and this results in longer casts with lighter lures. It has a patented clutch system, automatic centrifugal drag system, calibrated spool tension, fingertip star drag, 4.1 to 1 gear ratio, precision steel ball bearings and helical gears, and a large, heavy-duty crank handle. For more information write to:

James Heddon's Sons
Dowagiac, Mich. 49047

REBEL LURES

The Rebel lures are noted for their fish-getting qualities and are widely used in fresh water and salt water for many gamefish. They make such types as the Popper, Floater, Bonehead Popper, Minnow, Humpback, Super-R, and others. These are available in the popular silver finishes as well as other colors. Their catalog costs $1.00 and is available from:

Rebel Division—Plastics Research and Develop. Corp.
P.O. Box 1587
3601 Jenny Lind Rd.
Fort Smith, Ark. 72901

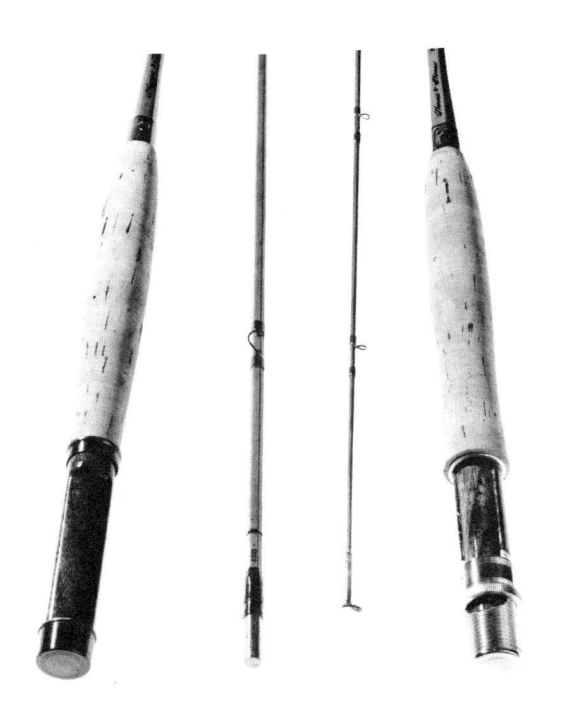

NORTH CAROLINA INLAND FISHING WATERS

The book *Catalog of the Inland Fishing Waters of North Carolina* lists all the freshwater lakes, rivers, and waters in that state. It gives a description of the streams, rivers, and lakes, including water conditions and fish populations. It also tells whether the fishing is done from shore or by wading or from boats, and if boat access and rentals are available. There are sectional maps of the state, and color illustrations of the most popular freshwater fishes. The book sells for $4.85 and is published by:
The Graphic Press, Inc.
418 S. Dawson St.
Raleigh, N.C. 27603

THOMAS & THOMAS RODMAKERS

The Thomas & Thomas Company makes handcrafted fly and salmon rods the old way—from split bamboo. Their Individualist and Classic fly rods are made from exceptional, aged Tonkin bamboo—from a vintage stock acquired over thirty years ago. All Individualist rods can be ordered with either a varnished finish or with the T & T impregnated, buffed, permafinish. They offer nickel silver ferrules and many reel seat and grip options. Their trout rods are made in lengths from 6 ft. to 9 ft. Their salmon rods are available in lengths from 8 ft. to 14 ft. for a double-handed rod. It takes several weeks to several months to get a finished rod. This shop also repairs bamboo rods and sells many other tackle items for the fly fisherman. For their catalog write to:
Thomas & Thomas Co.
22 Third St.
Turners Falls, Mass. 01376

THE CONVERSE GUIDE FOR THE OUTDOORSMAN

The Converse Guide for the Outdoorsman is a paperback packed with information for the angler, camper, hunter, and outdoorsman. The fishing section covers about half of the book and deals with such topics as how to catch trout, steelhead and salmon *facts,* locating landlocks, bass, pike and pickerel, perch, bullheads and catfish, natural baits, how to weigh fish, cleaning and keeping fish, bait hookups, fishing knots, and other tips and hints about fishing. There is also information on better wading, care of boots and waders, what to wear while fishing, and information about other clothing and gear. The rest of the book deals with hunting and a catalog section of some of the boots, waders, parkas, and other clothing made by Converse. The book sells for $1.75 and can be obtained from:
Converse Rubber Co.
55 Fordham Rd.
Wilmington, Mass. 01887

THE FISHES OF KENTUCKY

The book *The Fishes of Kentucky* by William M. Clay is mostly for fisheries biologists, aquatic biologists, and ichthyology students, but anglers and serious amateurs will also find this a valuable reference to the fishes of Kentucky and nearby states. It covers some 201 species illustrated by drawings and photos. Each fish is described, giving its range, distribution, and life history. *The Fishes of Kentucky* is 416 pages long and sells for only $3.00 per copy from:

Dept. of Fish and Wildlife Resources
Capitol Plaza Tower
Frankfort, Ky. 40601

BUILDING FISHING RODS

If you want to make your own fishing rods, there's a brochure put out by Fenwick that is very helpful. It has step-by-step instructions and illustrations showing how to put together a fly rod, casting rod, or trolling or boat rod. It gives tips on how to install ferrules and reel seats, add grips and handles, how to wind on the guides, and how to finish the rod. The brochure also shows the various kinds of rod blanks and component parts sold by this company. *Building Fishing Rods* is available for $.25 from:

Fenwick
P.O. Box 729
Westminster, Calif. 92683

Part Two

Salt-water Tackle and Fishing

Rods, reels, lines, lures, baits, hooks, sinkers, snaps, swivels, floats, other terminal gear, tackle boxes, clothing, fishing boats, outboard motors, fish finders, other accessories, fishing tips and hints, fishing facts, fishing spots, clubs and organizations, fishing books, booklets, guides, catalogs, brochures, and other publications

PFLUEGER SPINNING REELS

Pflueger offers several spinning reels suitable for light and for heavy salt-water fishing from boats or surf. They have a full range of drag assemblies and multidisk drags. Most of the reels have smooth ball-bearing operation. Gear ratios of 3.5 to 1 are found on the larger models. These hold up to 200 and 250 yds. of 20-lb.-test line. For their catalog showing these and other reels and tackle they make write to:
Pflueger Sporting Goods Div.
P.O. Box 185
Columbia, S.C. 29202

HOW TO CATCH SALT-WATER FISH

The book *How to Catch Salt-water Fish* by Bill Wisner is a big 584-page guide to fishing for most of the species found along the Atlantic Coast. The author covers the 23 most popular species, giving information on where, when, and how to catch them. The geographical distribution, feeding patterns, and seasonal migrations of each fish are dealt with. He also goes into the best fishing tackle, rigs, hooks, lures, and baits for each fish, how to present your bait or lure to these fish, and how to play and land the fish. There is a wealth of advice on the best techniques for bottom fishing, trolling, drifting, surf casting, top fishing, jigging, jetty fishing, and almost every salt-water method used to catch the fish covered in the book. *How to Catch Salt-water Fish* sells for $8.95 and is published by:
Doubleday & Co., Inc.
501 Franklin Ave.
Garden City, N.Y. 11530

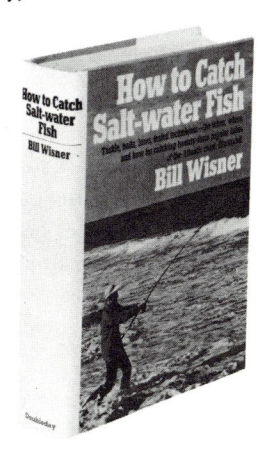

SUGAR-CURED BAIT

You can sugar cure your own mackerel (or other fish) to use as bait by filleting them, then spreading them on a newspaper. Now get some anise oil and brush the fillets with it. Then cover them with a mixture of salt and sugar and put them in a jar or jug for future use. Such sugar-cured fish can be used when fishing from the beaches in surf, jetties, or from boats for many salt-water species.

239

INTERNATIONAL GAME FISH ASSOCIATION

This organization, known to most salt-water anglers as the IGFA, was founded back on June 7, 1939, at a meeting attended by Michael Lerner, Dr. William K. Gregory, Van Campen Heilner, and Francesca LaMonte. Up until then there was no real clearinghouse for marine angling records, information, regulations, and ethics.

The purposes of the IGFA were spelled out as follows: to encourage the study of gamefishes for the sake of whatever pleasure, information, or benefit it may provide; to keep the sport of marine game fishing ethical; to make IGFA rules acceptable to the majority of salt-water anglers; to encourage the sport both as a recreation and as a potential source of scientific data; to place such data at the disposal of as many people as possible; and to keep attested and up-to-date charts of world record marine fishes.

For many years membership in the IGFA was limited to fishing clubs and scientific institutions. Then early in 1973, under the leadership of President William K. Carpenter and Executive Vice President Elwood K. Harry, the IGFA expanded its goals and began an extensive reorganization program. Various membership categories were established so that individuals and clubs could help support the association (which until that time had been privately funded) and its expanded work as an active representative for anglers throughout the world.

As a result many individuals and clubs joined, and today the IGFA salt-water records are internationally recognized, and the angling rules published in the annual *World Record Marine Fishes* booklet are not only accepted for all world record catches, but have also been adopted for use in major fishing events and tournaments throughout the world.

If you would like to join the IGFA or enter a record salt-water catch, you can write for the proper forms and rules and find out the various membership categories by writing to:

International Game Fish Assn.
3000 E. Las Olas Blvd.
Fort Lauderdale, Fla. 33316

EVER CATCH A LAFAYETTE?

You've probably caught a "Lafayette" if you have ever caught the small fish called the "spot" found along the Atlantic Coast especially from Virginia south. The name "Lafayette" was given to the fish by New Yorkers when the spot suddenly appeared in great numbers in 1824 when the great French patriot Lafayette visited this country.

BIG MARLIN ON THIN LINE

One of the most outstanding catches on light tackle was made by Edwin D. Kennedy of New Jersey. He hooked and boated a 244-lb. black marlin at Piñas Bay, Panama, on 6-lb. line! He tried for six days and broke off three times, but finally hooked the big marlin, which fought for 18 min. and jumped at least 15 times during the battle.

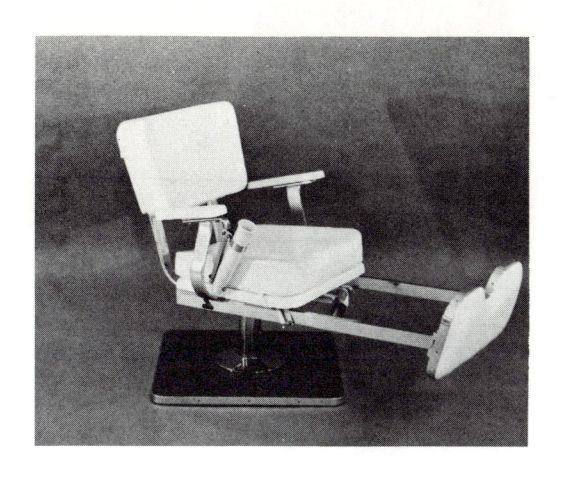

POMPANETTE FISHING CHAIR

An all-occasion fishing chair? If you've never heard of such a thing it is quite understandable. The seatmakers for the boating industry, Pompanette, Inc., just developed it.

The new Pompanette 9-ORC answers virtually every demand a serious deep-sea angler can make. The outstanding feature is that the cushioned back is easily and quickly removable, allowing the angler plenty of added fighting room while battling an oversized fish.

A standard chair has a removable footrest. A headrest is a $55 option. The chair can be flush-mounted on a stainless-steel pedestal, or it can be offered in its "Q" form, on a four-legged stainless-steel and molded base for portability.

"The great thing about the 9-ORC is its versatility," says Pompanette president Bud Hudnall. "It is perfect for the cockpit of a large sportfishing boat, yet it is equally ideal for the popular 18-to-24-ft. open fishing boats."

The 9-ORC has a 180-degree turning capability and a 39-in. maximum radius. The height from deck to chair seat is 17 in. In addition to all of its other features, the reclining-back model is extremely comfortable, making fishless days a little more tolerable.

The 9-ORC retails for $556.55 and can be ordered from any Pompanette dealer. For more information you can write to:
Pompanette, Inc.
1515 S.E. 16th St.
Fort Lauderdale, Fla. 33316

PORK RIND IN SALT WATER

There are many ways you can use pork rind baits and strips in salt-water fishing. They are especially effective when used for such fish as striped bass, bluefish, tarpon, snook, cobia, and similar species. The Uncle Josh Bait Company even makes an extralong "Big Boy" strip, which is 10 in. in length and can be used when trolling for sailfish, marlin, school tuna, barracuda, and dolphin. Pork strips of various sizes and lengths can also be added to spoons, jigs, spinners, plugs, nylon eels, and other lures. To find out about these pork rind strips and baits send $.25 for their catalog to:
Uncle Josh Bait Co.
Fort Atkinson, Wis. 53538

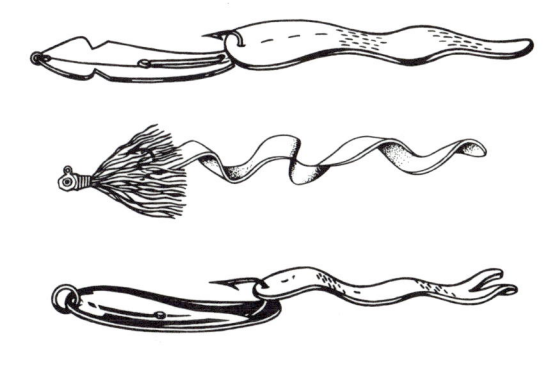

FISH THE OIL RIGS

Some of the best fishing in salt water is found around the oil rigs that are now common in the Gulf of Mexico off Louisiana. The base or supports of these platforms are encrusted with moss, algae, barnacles, and mussels. They also provide shade and hiding places. This attracts crabs, shrimp, and small fish, which in turn bring the larger gamefish.

These oil rigs can be fished by trolling so your lines and lures swing near the piles supporting the platforms. Or you can drift near them and cast out lures or baits. Or you can let down a bottom rig with a bait as you drift along. Some of the best fishing takes place at night near the rigs.

Some of the fish you'll catch around the oil rigs in the Gulf of Mexico include king mackerel, Spanish mackerel, bonito, cobia, bluefish, pompano, snappers, and spadefish.

WANDERING FISH

It is well known that Pacific salmon make long journeys during their migrations and spawning runs. One salmon tagged in Alaskan waters was caught 44 days later in a Siberian stream and had swum 1,300 miles. But Pacific albacore make even longer journeys than that. An albacore tagged in California was caught 324 days later by a Japanese fisherman 450 miles off Tokyo. The fish had crossed the Pacific Ocean and had traveled a total distance of 4,724 airline miles! And a giant bluefin tuna tagged off the Bahamas was recaptured off Bergen, Norway, only 50 days later. It was estimated that this speedy swimmer crossed the Atlantic Ocean at close to the rate of 100 miles per day!

THE COMPLETE BOOK OF THE STRIPED BASS

The Complete Book of the Striped Bass by Nicholas Karas lives up to its title as one of the best and most up-to-date books written about this popular gamefish. The author is a well-known outdoor writer who fishes almost everywhere but who has especially pursued the striper in most of the waters where this fish is found. The book consists of three parts. The first part deals with the biology and habits and management of the striped bass. It covers its distribution and migrations, reproduction, growth, and feeding. It tells about the striper in fresh water and is concerned with the conservation and future of the fish. The second part of the book gets down to fishing methods and techniques, covering fishing from shore, surf, piers, jetties, bridges, and boats. There is a chapter on fly-rodding for striped bass. It also deals with chumming and night fishing. The third part of the book covers the fishing tackle and lures, baits, and accessories needed to catch stripers. Bass fishing boats and beach buggies are covered and even striped-bass cookery. *The Complete Book of the Striped Bass* sells for $10 and is published by:
Winchester Press
460 Park Ave.
New York, N.Y. 10022

TUBE ALOU

The Garcia Tube Alou is a tough, surgical rubber version of the well-known Alou Eel. It has an action head like the eel, which gives it a lively wiggle. It comes in three weights, from 1½ ozs. up to 6 ozs., and in red or black colors. It is used for striped bass, bluefish, king mackerel, barracuda, and other salt-water gamefish. For more information write to:
The Garcia Corp.
326 Alfred Ave.
Teaneck, N.J. 07666

WAHOO

There are many kinds of game fish in tropical salt waters and most of them put up a good fight, but for sheer power, speed, and endurance it is hard to beat the wahoo. This long, slim member of the mackerel family, which is fairly common in Bermuda and the Bahamas and is also caught in Florida, likes to prowl the edges of reefs and dropoffs where it seeks smaller fish, and here it is best to troll your lures.

Luckily, the wahoo is no real heavyweight—most fish will range from 15 to 60 lbs. So despite the fish's speed and power, you can use fairly light tackle, with lines testing from 12 to 25 lbs. But no matter which outfit you use, don't forget to use a wire leader and avoid shiny swivels or snaps. They'll hit and cut your line with their sharp teeth if attracted by bright swivels or even bubbles in the water.

Wahoo will hit various lures such as white feathers, nylon jigs, metal squids, spoons, whole mullet, balao (ballyhoo), and strip baits. The whole-fish baits or strip baits can be trolled from outriggers 90 to 115 ft. behind the boat. These baits should be trolled fast so that they skip on top or ride just below the surface. Feather lures, jigs, and metal lures can be trolled on flat lines from 30 to 50 ft. back. Wahoo will often come close behind the boat and even hit the teasers.

When hooked, a wahoo will usually make three or four long runs at a fast speed, then run back toward the boat, often resulting in slack line and a lost fish. The angler has to be alert and let the fish run on a light drag, then reel fast to regain any slack line.

Wahoo make delicious eating fresh or smoked, but that's an extra bonus after the thrilling fight.

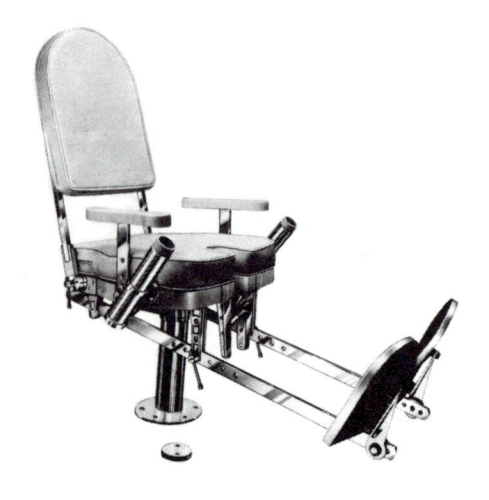

LEE'S FIGHTING CHAIR

Lee's fighting chair is now made of Fiberglas with seats 2 in. thick and all hardware of solid brass and triple chrome plate. The arms are easily adjusted to four positions and are completely removable. The footrest adjusts to over fifty positions and features a new, anodized aluminum footboard curved with nonslip surface. The back is adjustable to any angle and completely removable. The chair is only 150 lbs. in weight and is noted for its comfort and quietness—it does not rattle in operation. The rod holders, which are optional, are the striking type in which the fish can be struck while the rod is in the holder. For more information about this fighting chair and outriggers, outrigger holders, rod holders, gimbals, and other boat fishing equipment, write to:
Lee's Tackle
2185 N.W. 34th Ave.
Miami, Fla. 33142

ROD' R CHART-MATE TUBE

Expensive fishing rods and valued charts can be given excellent protection from the weather and soiling when stowed in these lightweight plastic Rod' r Chart-Mate tubes with end closures.

Handy for these and many other uses, the tubes are made of high-quality marine plastic that won't crack and are provided with tight-fitting, molded-end caps. With the caps in place on the tube it will float if dropped in the water. The watertight closure keeps rods or charts dry in any weather.

Rod' r Chart-Mate tubes are available in four sizes: 2 in. diameter by 49 in. long, 3 in. by 36 in., 4 in. by 36 in., and 4 in. by 60 in. All are white with red caps. Suggested retail prices at marine stores range from $5.95 to $10.95 each, depending on the size. For more information write to:

**Beckson Mfg., Inc.
P.O. Box 3336
Bridgeport, Conn. 06605**

GETTING RID OF SHARKS

Salt-water fishermen are often bothered by sharks near a boat when they are fishing and would like to get rid of them. One good method is to get some of the larger Clorox or other plastic bleach containers and tie a strong rope to the handle. Then tie a hook on a short wire leader to the rope and bait this with a small whole fish or a big chunk of fish and throw it overboard, near the shark. The shark will usually grab the bait, swallow it, and get hooked. Then it will panic and move away from the scene with the plastic float.

BIG AMBERJACK ON A FLY ROD

Big amberjack are tough on any tackle and put up a long, stubborn fight. So you can imagine what Steve Chappell was up against when he hooked a big amberjack on a fly rod. He was fishing over an old shipwreck off Key West, Florida, when the fish grabbed his fly. A storm approached as Chappell fought the big amberjack. Finally, after an hour and forty-five minutes, it was boated. Later, when weighed, it went 73 lbs.!

MEXICO FISHING

The book *Fishing the Coast and Lakes of Northeast Mexico* by Stan Slaten is a detailed account of fishing both the fresh and salt waters of this section of Mexico. A large section of the book concencentrates on fishing the lakes and reservoirs for black bass. But there are also sections on fishing in salt-water passes and bays for sea trout, snook, and tarpon. *Fishing the Coast and Lakes of Northeast Mexico* sells for $8.75 in hardcover and for $5.75 in softcover and is published by:
Cordovan Corp.
5314 Bingle Rd.
Houston, Tex. 77018

FISHERMAN'S LOG

Now you can keep your fishing records in these handsome "Fisherman's Logs" to record all the necessary information for your future reference and pleasure. It gives the date, locality, weight, time, weather, water conditions, temperature, length, rod, reel, line, leader, lure, number of fish killed, number of fish released, and other comments. The logs—one for fresh water and the other for salt water are 9 in. by 6 in. and contain 64 pages bound in a heavy cover. The freshwater log has a trout on the cover, while the salt-water log has a sailfish. Specify which when ordering. They sell for $5.95 postpaid and can be obtained from:
Sporting Logs
P.O. Box 193
Wellesley, Mass. 02181

LOST SWORDFISH

Swimmers at the New Silver Beach in Falmouth, Massachusetts, were surprised to see a huge fish finning close to shore. Two police officers then arrived in a boat and fired their revolvers at the fish, wounding it, and then threw a rope around its tail. Then they dragged it up on the beach. When it was dressed out and weighed, the swordfish went 280 lbs.!

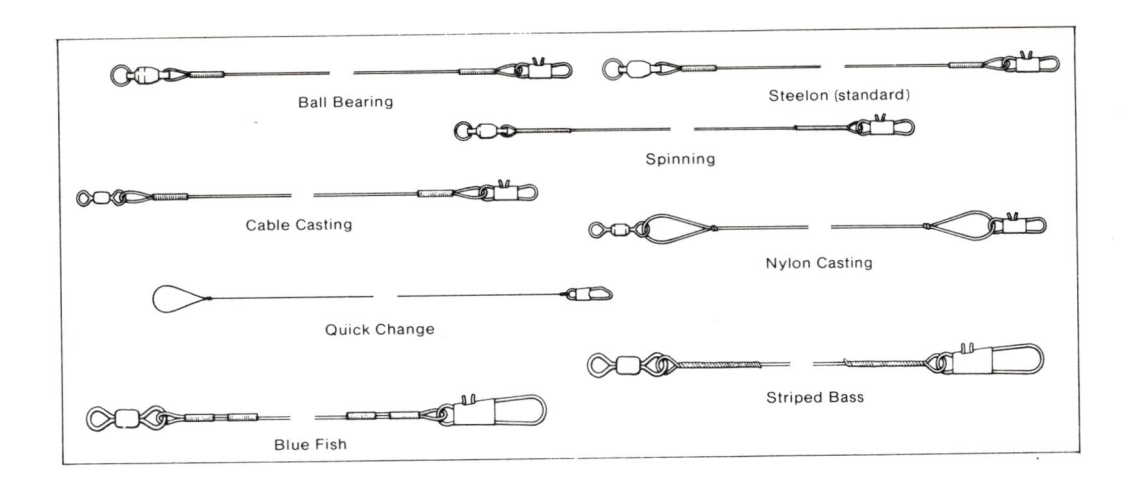

BERKLEY STEELON LEADERS

Berkley and Co. of Spirit Lake, Iowa, makes many fine fly leaders and casting and trolling leaders as well as other fishing tackle. Their Steelon leaders have a steel core covered with clear nylon and are widely used for pike and muskies in fresh water and striped bass, bluefish, king mackerel, Spanish mackerel, barracuda, and other fish in salt water. They come in various lengths, from 6 in. up to 72 in., and test from 20 lbs. to 60 lbs. For their catalog or more information about these leaders write to:

Berkley and Co.
Spirit Lake, Ia. 51360

WATCH OUT FOR TARPON!

Any angler who fishes for tarpon knows that these fish will often leap high into the air again and again when hooked, and sometimes they even jump into a boat. One Texas angler was fishing in the Gulf of Mexico and was just drifting lazily in a skiff. Then, without warning, a 7-ft. tarpon jumped out of the water, struck the man a tremendous blow, and knocked him overboard. When he managed to swim back to the boat, he found the tarpon lying on the bottom of it. Later the man found out he had suffered four broken ribs and a wrenched spine.

CATCHING SQUID

You can often catch squid for bait in New England waters in places under a light or lamp shining into the water. Bridge or pier or dock lights are good spots for this at night. The light attracts small baitfish, and this in turn attracts the squid that move in to feed on the small fish. You can make up a snagging rig with a treble hook to catch the squid. They will often go for the bare hook and weight, but you can also snag a baitfish and leave it on the hooks. When a squid wraps its tentacles around the bait and hook you can jerk and impale it on the hooks.

JOHN EMERY FLY REEL

The John Emery fly reel is a big-game salmon, tarpon, offshore and billfish fly reel with a single action and direct positive retrieve. It weighs 13½ ozs., with the inside of the spool 1 3/16 in., diameter of the inside spool rim 3 7/8 in., and diameter of the outside spool rim 4 3/8 in. The line capacity of this fly reel is 600 yds. of 30-lb. Gudebrod GT dacron plus WF 13 F sw fly line. It will hold even more line with thinner and lighter backing and fly lines.

This fly reel features a radical one-piece machined concept—the entire spool and frame (including main shaft and housings for drag dogs) machined from bar stock aluminum alloy. A large-diameter cork disk drag plate machined from aluminum bar stock gives exceptionally smooth and powerful drag. Twin dogs governing drag disk (one more than other reels) operate without tricky "hair" springs. An outside flanged spool allows extra drag control by palming. The entire reel can be taken down without tools by removing the drag knob. Extra spools are available and are very easy to change. Hard Coat black anodized finish eliminates fish-scaring glare and is far more durable than any other finish on the market. The reel runs on stainless-steel ball bearings of advanced design. Available in either right- or left-hand wind, it can be converted in minutes. For more information about this reel write to:

John Emery Reels
7770 Sunset Dr.
Miami, Fla. 33143

LARGEST SALT-WATER FISH

Salt-water anglers seeking "monsters of the deep" go after tuna, marlin, and sharks. Bluefin tuna over 1,000 lbs. have been caught on rod and reel and are believed to reach 2,000 lbs. Blue marlin over 1,000 lbs. have also been caught. And black marlin up to 1,560 lbs. have been taken. Most anglers believe that black marlin over 2,000 lbs. will be caught sometime in the near future. White sharks or man-eaters reach a great size and have been caught up to 3,417 lbs. on rod and reel. They are believed to reach a length of 20 to 25 ft. and a weight of several thousand pounds.

But the biggest salt-water fish are not caught by anglers but have been harpooned. One of these is the basking shark, which reaches a weight of over 10,000 lbs. and a length of 30 ft. or more. The largest fish in the world, however, is the whale shark. One 38-ft. specimen harpooned in Florida was estimated to weigh over 26,000 lbs. They are believed to reach a length of 50 ft. or more!

STRIPERS UNLIMITED

Stripers Unlimited is basically a service organization of dedicated striped bass fishermen that is devoted to promoting the striped bass as a gamefish and also to conserve this fish for future generations. The five main goals of this organization are:

1. To develop a fraternity of fishermen willing to help one another
2. To stop indiscriminate netting of striped bass
3. To develop legislation of benefit to sportfishermen
4. To curb pollution of striped bass waters
5. To develop more areas of public access

Stripers Unlimited provides information on striped bass fishing along the Atlantic Coast, giving the latest information on fish populations; the fishing; the best lures, baits, and methods; and the current hot spots. They send out regular monthly bulletins and publish an annual guidebook. Much of their work is devoted to striped bass hatching, rearing, stocking, and tagging, and learning new facts about this popular salt-water gamefish. Annual membership is $7.50, and you can send for an application blank and more information to:

Stripers Unlimited
P.O. Box 45
South Attleboro, Mass. 02703

WESTERN FISH KNIVES

The Western Cutlery Company makes these fish fillet and bait knives as well as many other kinds of fishing, hunting, camping, pocket, and general-purpose knives. The fish fillet knives have corrosion-resistant stainless-steel blades that stay bright and sharp. They have a full bevel grind for longer edge life. The handles are laminated hardwood that will not shrink, crack, or discolor under the roughest use. For their catalog showing these and other knives they make write to:

Western Cutlery Co.
5311 Western Ave.
Boulder, Colo. 80302

S-W769 SUPER FILLET - Overall 14" - Blade 9"

S-W766 FISH FILLET - Overall 11" - Blade 6"

S-W764 BAIT-CAMP KNIFE - Overall 9" - Blade 4½"

VIRGINIA SALT-WATER FISHING TOURNAMENT

The Virginia Salt-water Fishing Tournament was inaugurated in 1958 and has been a popular event with anglers who fish the waters of this state. Under the able direction of Claude Rogers, this tournament has grown and expanded and now includes 22 eligible species, which can be entered if they go over a minimum weight. The eligible fish range from blue marlin, which must weigh 250 lbs. or more, to the small spot, which must be 15 ozs. or more. Plasticized plaques, in full color and hand-lettered with the angler's name, the species, and the weight are given to those who catch fish in the Citation class. In the 1975 Tournament 5,034 citations were awarded for outstanding catches in the annual 7-mo. contest.

All requests about this tournament should be addressed to:
**Virginia Salt-water Fishing Tournament
Claude Rogers, Director
25th and Pacific Aves.
Virginia Beach, Va. 23451**

TROLLING FOR GROUPER

Grouper are usually caught in southern waters by bottom fishing from an anchored or drifting boat. Here a bottom rig with sinker and a big hook are used with small live fish or cut fish as bait. But you can also catch grouper by trolling slowly with your boat using small barracuda, Spanish mackerel, or king mackerel rigged with two or three hooks. You can also use a feather lure and rig three hooks behind it in tandem, then take a fillet from a mullet and impale it on the hooks. These baits and rigs should be trolled very slowly down deep, using weighted lines or wire lines. The best spots for grouper include coral reefs, rock bottoms, and along dropoffs.

WEIRD CATCHES

A fishhook is supposed to catch fish, but often it snags some weird and unusual objects. Anglers have caught their own and other people's lost fishing tackle, watches, bracelets, diamond rings, eyeglasses, false teeth, and similar items. One angler fishing from a party boat in the ocean off New Jersey hooked and brought in a 12-lb. lobster!

GREATEST BONEFISH CATCH

The late Joe Brooks, one of the top fly fishermen of his time, once caught forty-six bonefish on flies in a single day! He fished with a fly rod and a pink shrimp fly from 9 a.m. to sunset and caught twenty-four bonefish in the morning and another twenty-two in the afternoon. The catch was made at the Isle of Pines, Cuba, in the days before Castro.

BONITO BOATS

The Bonito boats are designed for professionals who are able to stay at work when the amateurs and runabouts head for home. They are owned and used by many fishing guides who take anglers out inshore and offshore for a wide variety of saltwater species.

The boats are designed by fishing professionals like Captain Dick Lema for their own exacting requirements, unusual stiffness from huge double longitudinals, excess strength in massive Fiberglas construction, water tightness from three molded sections, and a hull design providing comfort, stability, and safety under the most severe conditions. This boat keeps moving fast in choppy and rough seas that slow other boats down considerably.

The Open Model is the ultimate open fishing boat, with a length of 25 ft., 8 in. and an 11-ft., 1-in. beam. A high, flared bow and broad, nonskid working areas combine with 6,000-lb. displacement and efficient power train to produce both speed and fishing comfort. It also has urethane foam flotation under the sole, large scuppers, very heavy deck hardware, lockable rod stowage under the forward platform, live bait well, six rod racks, and two rod holders.

They also make a smaller Lema 20 I/O Model in the same design, with a length of 19 ft., 8 in. and a beam of 8 ft., 4 in. And they have a Cuddy Model, which is an honest working cruiser without sacrifice of fishing performance. It has two berths with custom cushions, a marine head, two cabin lights, and 5 ft., 9 in. in headroom available in the cuddy cabin. Forward is a 2-ft.-by 2-ft. translucent hatch; aft are teak sliding hatch and louvered doors. The full windshield has two vents, and all deck hardware is heavy chrome on brass or stainless steel. For more information about these fishing boats write to:

Bonito Boat Corp.
Mumford Rd.
Narragansett, R.I. 02882

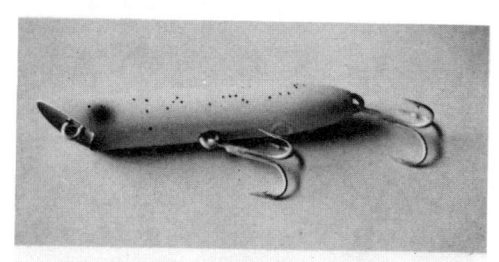

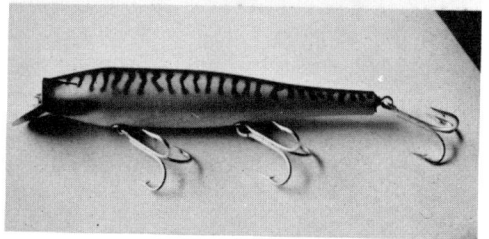

STAN GIBBS PLUGS

Stan Gibbs has fished from the surf and boats for striped bass, bluefish, and other salt-water fish for many years. And through these years he has developed and designed some highly effective plugs that are preferred by most expert anglers. His popping-type plug is one of the earliest designs, has great buoyancy, and can be worked at all speeds, from the slowest to the fastest. His slim Pencil Popper raises fish when other plugs fail and can be worked in a wide variety of movements with rod action and reeling. His Polaris plug is also a popper with a bomber-type body that casts great distances. They also make a Swimmer and a Darter. Most of these plugs are available in different sizes and weights. Stan Gibbs plugs are made from wood because this offers the optimum characteristics for castability, flotation, and hydrodynamic action. For their catalog describing these lures write to:
Stan Gibbs Lures, Inc.
35 Old Plymouth Rd., R.F.D.
Buzzards Bay, Mass. 02532

BIG SALMON PARADISE

If you like to catch big king or chinook salmon, you can't pick a better place than Alaska during the spring and early summer months. The big chinooks usually start to run in May and continue during June and July. King salmon between 20 and 40 lbs. are common, and bigger ones are caught up to 50 and 60 lbs. A bit later on during July, August, and September, the smaller silver or coho salmon appear, and they run between 8 and 30 lbs. Many salmon derbies are held during these months, and big fish win big prizes. The best salmon fishing occurs in southeastern Alaska in the rivers, channels, and bays among the islands stretching from Ketchikan, Craig, Wrangell, Petersburg, and Sitka to Juneau. For more information about this salmon fishing you can write to:
Alaska Div. of Tourism
Alaska Office Bldg.
Juneau, Alaska 99801

SECRETS OF STRIPED BASS FISHING

The book *Secrets of Striped Bass Fishing* by Milk Rosko deals with all the methods and techniques used to catch this popular gamefish from most of the waters where it is found. Milt Rosko covers surf casting, trolling, jetty casting, fly casting, chumming, boat casting, lures, and natural baits. There is even a chapter on tackle maintenance, and another on where to go to catch stripers. His wife, June, even wrote a chapter on how to cook the striped bass. All in all, the book is a complete guide to striped bass fishing under all conditions and situations. *Secrets of Striped Bass Fishing* sells for $5.95 and is published by:
Macmillan, Inc.
866 Third Ave.
New York, N.Y., 10022

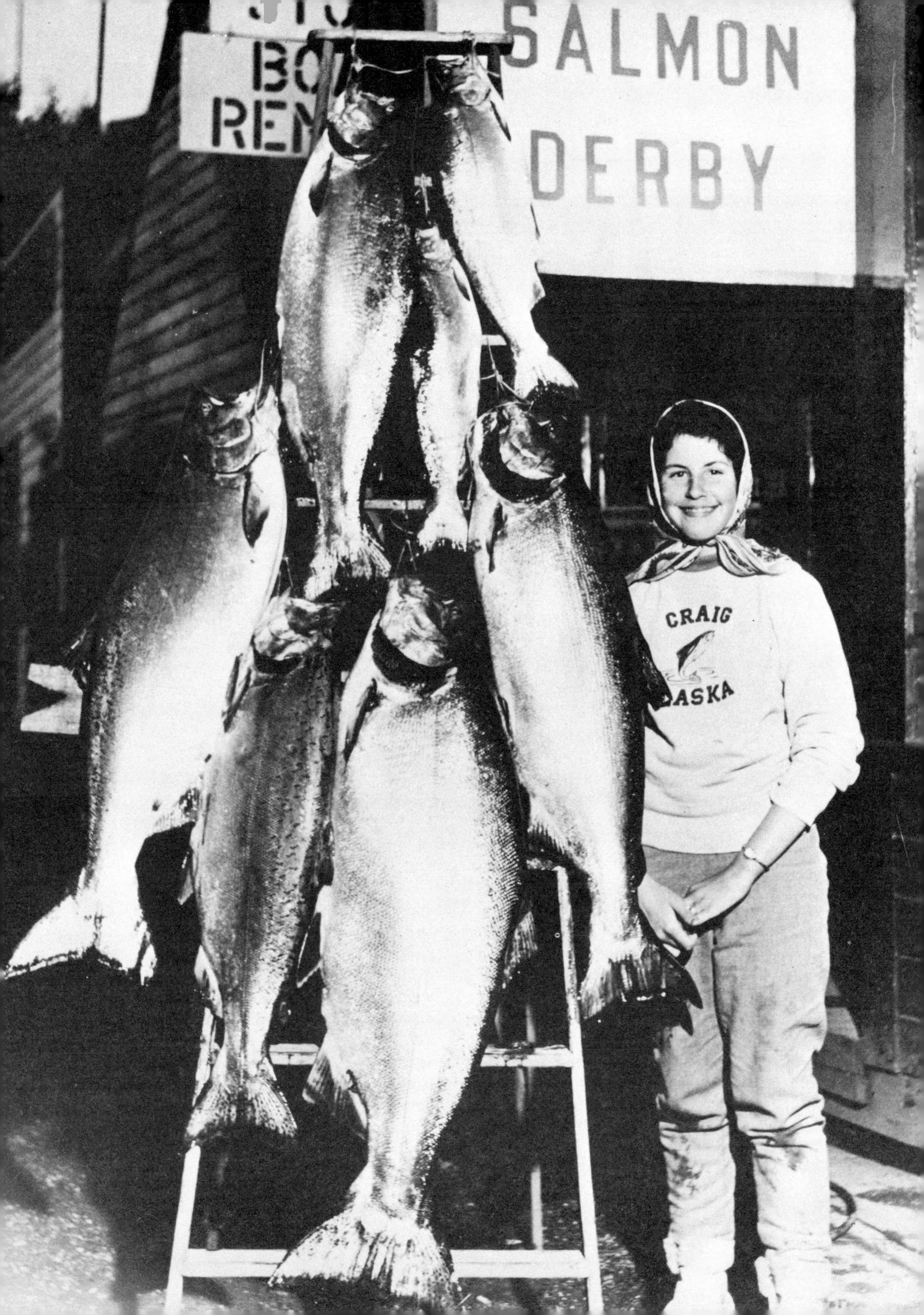
SALMON
DERBY
CRAIG

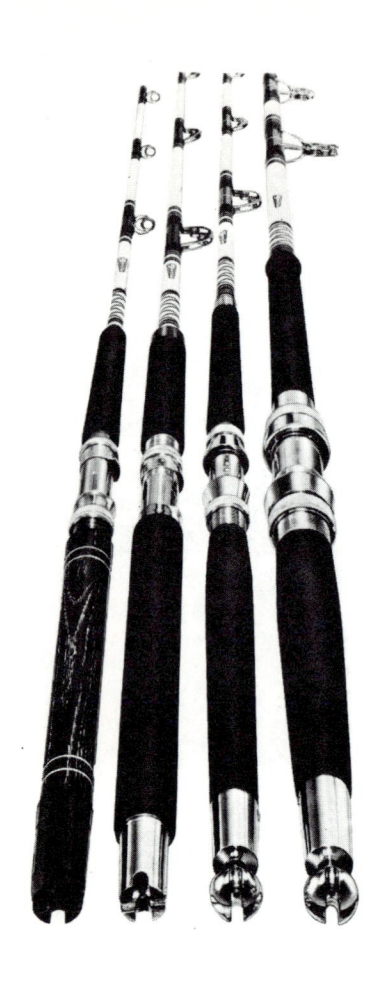

GARCIA TROLLING RODS

The Garcia big-game trolling rods range from special wire line trolling rods to heavy offshore rods for the biggest fish. They are made to conform fully to the specifications of the International Game Fish Association for the various classes from 12-lb.-test to 130-lb.-test lines. The wire line rods have tungsten carbide guides and tip-tops. The trolling rods have roller guides and tip-tops. They have Varmac heavy-duty reel seats. For more information about these rods write to:
The Garcia Corp.
329 Alfred Ave.
Teaneck, N.J. 07666

CALIFORNIA BARRACUDA

California barracuda are popular with the anglers fishing from the live-bait or party boats along the Pacific Coast. They will take a live or dead queenfish, anchovy, sardine, or strip bait. These are often used on a double-hook rig because barracuda have a habit of chopping a baitfish in half and eluding the front hook. For best results the bait used should be cast out and reeled in with some rod action soon after it hits the water. The barracuda will also hit lures such as plugs, spoons, metal lures, jigs, and feathers.

TARPON FISHING HOT SPOT

One of the best spots for tarpon is Boca Grande in Florida. Here in April, May, and June you are almost certain to see and catch some tarpon each day if you go out with one of the local fishing guides on his boat. One group of 13 anglers fishing there caught 170 tarpon during a 16-hr. period. Most of these fish were, of course, released to fight again. The tarpon caught at Boca Grande range from 30 to 150 lbs. and put up a good fight in the strong current and deep water in the inlet.

HOOKS AND TACKLE

The International Hook and Tackle Company carries one of the largest stocks of Mustad hooks in this country. They sell mostly to manufacturers and dealers who buy in large quantities. They also carry rods; reels; lines; parts for making spinners, spoons, and jigs; jig molds, and terminal tackle such as snaps, swivels, split rings, connecting links, and similar parts. They also have accessories such as fishing knives, scales, pliers, and fish stringers. For their catalog write to:
**International Hook and Tackle Co.
1830 S. Acoma St.
Denver, Colo. 80223**

MONTAUK STRIPER BUNKER SPOONS

These are the big spoons used when trolling to catch big striped bass, especially in New York and New Jersey waters. They come in three different lengths: 7¼ in., 8¼ in., and 10 in. They are made of stainless steel and have lead keels. You can get them painted in different colors on request. This company also makes tube lures, Gorilla rigs, and Coat Hanger and Umbrella rigs. For prices and more information write to:
**Julian Bait Co., Inc.
Rte. 36
Atlantic Highlands, N.J. 07716**

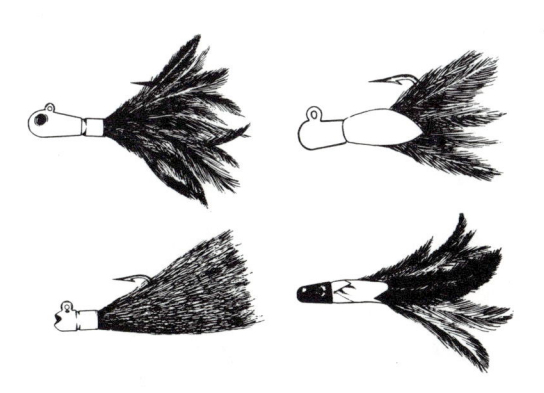

RAIL ROD HOLDER

The rail rod holder clamps on quickly on a rail of a fishing boat or flying bridge or anywhere else there is a rail. It comes in ⅞-in. or 1-in. sizes. The same company makes many other rod holders, gimbals, rod racks, and outrigger equipment. For more information or a catalog write to:
**Lee's Tackle
2185 N.W. 34th Ave.
Miami, Fla. 33142**

NO-ALIBI LURES

The No-alibi lures are well-known lures made by John C. Kremer. They are mostly jigs, feather lures, nylon eels, and spoons used for many salt-water fish from the small pompano up to dolphin, barracuda, king mackerel, and tuna. Their Smiling Bill series of jigs is very popular for striped bass and bluefish. The jigs and feathers come in many different sizes and weights and in solid or combination colors. For a catalog showing these lures write to:
**John C. Kremer
P.O. Box 3664
West Palm Beach, Fla. 33402**

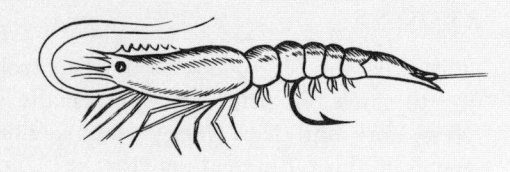

CATCH BONEFISH THE EASY WAY

Many articles and books written about bonefish stress how difficult it is to catch bonefish. This may be true when using fly rods and flies or even spinning tackle and lures. But you can also catch bonefish the easy way by using bait. Here is one of the best baits—a live shrimp hooked, as shown above in the drawing. Then you cast it out and let it lie on the bottom. Here it is often a good idea to chum with pieces of shrimp or crushed spiny lobster or cut-up conch. Let this chum stream toward the spot where your bait is lying. This is best done from an anchored boat during an incoming tide. But you can also wade a bonefish flat and cast your shrimp to fish that are sighted. But don't cast the shrimp too close! Instead, let it drop about 15 or 20 ft. in front and a few feet beyond the bonefish. Then reel in the bait so it settles on the bottom in the path of the bonefish where it can be seen and taken by the fish.

EARTHWORMS IN THE SALT

Ordinary garden worms, earthworms, or night crawlers usually used in freshwater fishing as bait can also be tried in salt water. They soon die in salt water but wiggle actively when first submerged and attract surf fish in Pacific waters. They have also been used successfully for flounders.

TEASING FISH

A highly effective way to attract and hook such fish as the amberjack, cobia, sharks, and even grouper is to use a live bait such as a blue runner, pinfish, or other small fish as a teaser. First, you have to locate a good spot such as a buoy, shallow reef, rocky patch, or sunken wreck where the fish are concentrated. Then you get a long pole and tie a short length of line to the end and thread the line through the back of a live baitfish, using no hook. Then start swishing the fish back and forth on top of the water so that it splashes and thrashes around. This should soon draw the big fish up to the surface to investigate, and after you have excited them enough, you can present a bait, lure, or fly with a hook in it and they will usually grab it quickly.

SPOONS FROM SPINNERS

You can easily make small spoon-type lures for casting or trolling from old or new spinner blades. All you have to do is place the hook eye and shank in the concave or dished-out side of the blade and then pour some molten lead to fill it to the edges. Then tie some feathers or bucktail hair around the hook and the lure is ready to use.

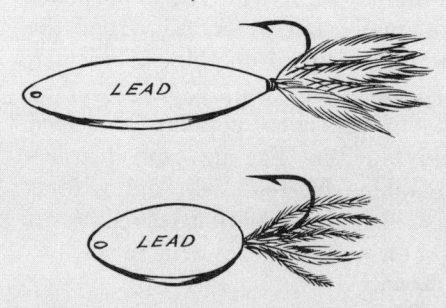

HOW TO RIG BAITS FOR TROLLING

The book *How to Rig Baits for Trolling* is a handy, easy-to-read guide showing how to rig a wide variety of baits for offshore trolling. There are step-by-step photos showing how to rig these baits from beginning to end. It covers such widely used baits as eels, squid, mullet, balao, flying fish, live fish, and strip baits. There are also tips in this book on how to use these rigged baits covering the number of lines to troll, distances from the boat, speed of the boat, courses to follow, hooking the fish, and the best hooks and leaders to use. The book sells for $1.95 and can be obtained from:
The Penn Fishing Tackle Mfg. Co.
3028 W. Hunting Park Ave.
Philadelphia, Pa. 19132

TAG A SHARK

Sharks are hated, feared, and despised by most people, and even most anglers shoot or lance or kill a shark after it has been brought up to a boat. But sharks, like most living things, play an important role in the ocean's ecology and should not be exterminated. Only a few species of sharks are considered dangerous to man, and even they rarely attack a human being. So if you fish for sharks or expect to catch many of them, you can contribute a great deal to our knowledge of these fish by tagging them and releasing them alive. By studying shark movements and migrations and growth, a great deal has already been learned about sharks. But a lot more research must be done before we fully understand sharks and their habits. You can help by tagging and releasing a shark when you fish for them or catch one while going after other fish. To get tags and more information on tagging sharks write to:
Jack Casey
Narragansett Sport Fisheries Marine Laboratory
P.O. Box 522-A
Narragansett, R.I. 02882

FLEXNET CASTING SHIRT

The Flexnet Casting Shirt is a waterproof garment for fishermen who want to fish in the rain or bad weather or around breaking waves. It can be worn while wading or from shore or in a boat. It has a drawcord hood, waterproof zipper, front pocket with snap closure, elasticized cuffs, raglan sleeve, and is extralong. It can be worn over hip boots or waders so that you have complete protection. For a catalog showing this and other protective clothing they make for fishermen and hunters write to:
Royal Red Ball
8530 Page Ave.
St. Louis, Mo. 63114

CALIFORNIA STRIPED BASS MAP

There's a striped bass fishing map available showing the best spots for this fishing in California bays and ocean. The price of this map is $.40. When ordering, ask for No. 41, "Striped Bass Angler's Guide." It can be obtained from:
Office of Procurement, Documents Div.
P.O. Box 20191
Sacramento, Calif. 95820

ALEE EELS

The Alee Eels are plastic eels that have a metal action head up front to give them the snaky movement of a swimming eel. They come in four sizes: The Alee Elver is 8 in. long with 5/0 head hook and 2/0 tail hook; the Alee Shoestring is 10 in. long and has a 6/0 head hook and 4/0 tail hook; the Alee Super Bass is 15 in. long and has an 8/0 head hook and 8/0 tail hook; the Alee Cow Killer is 18 in. long and has a 9/0 head hook and a 9/0 tail hook.

They also make an Alee Big Game Eel, which is designed for surface trolling offshore for white marlin, tuna, dolphin, sailfish, and other deep-water species. It comes in two sizes: a 12-in. model with two 8/0 hooks; and a 15 in. size, which has two 9/0 hooks. These eels have a bright-colored skirt up in front for added attractiveness. For their catalog showing these and other lures write to:
Gold Seal Industries, Inc.
P.O. Box 324
South Orange, N.J. 07079

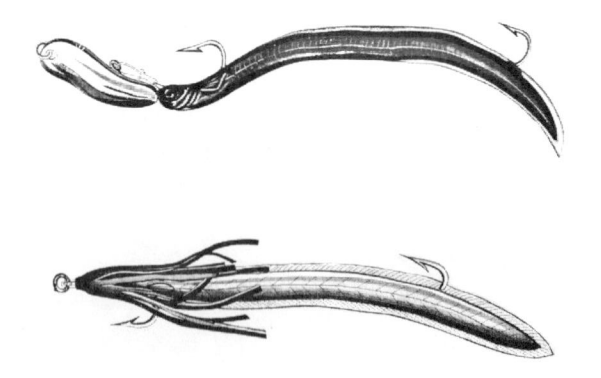

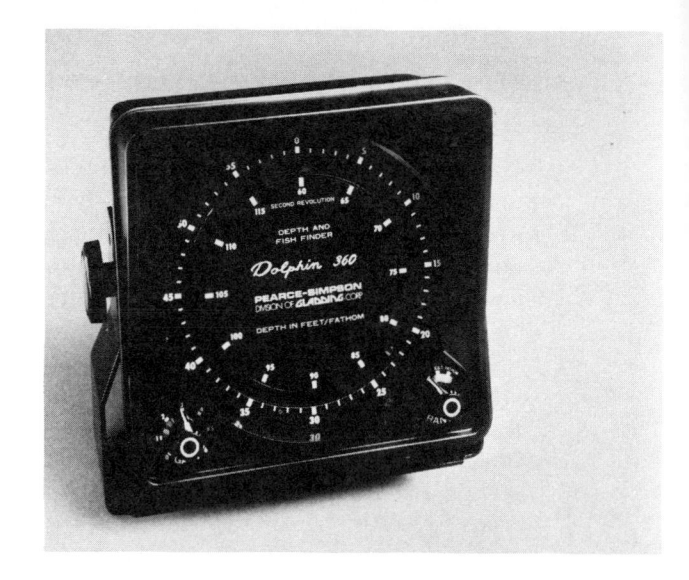

DOLPHIN 360 FISH/DEPTH FINDER

Pearce-Simpson has solved the problem of reading a fish/depth finder in bright sunlight. The Dolphin 360 features a removable sunshield, which snaps on the front of the unit.

The all-solid-state 60 ft./60 fath. Dolphin 360 was completely designed by practical marine electronics engineers for accuracy and versatility. On the 60-ft. scale, the 5½-in.-diameter dial provides detailed readings. On the 60-fath. scale, the Dolphin 360's readings are sharp and bright all the way down to 360 ft.

Even motor speed regulation is solid state for a reliable noise-free circuit. And the little details every boatman or angler will appreciate are there: plugs on the back of the indicator for transducer and power leads; versatile mounting on shelf, bulkhead or overhead; and knobs that are easy to turn (even with wet hands).

Choose between a bronze transducer for through-hull installation or a plastic transducer for transom mounting (stainless-steel mounting bracket supplied). Even the Dolphin 360's case is designed for long years of service. It's a high-impact material that won't rust, corrode, or break. For more information contact:
Pearce-Simpson Div. of Gladding Corp.
P.O. Box 520800, Biscayne Annex
Miami, Fla. 33152

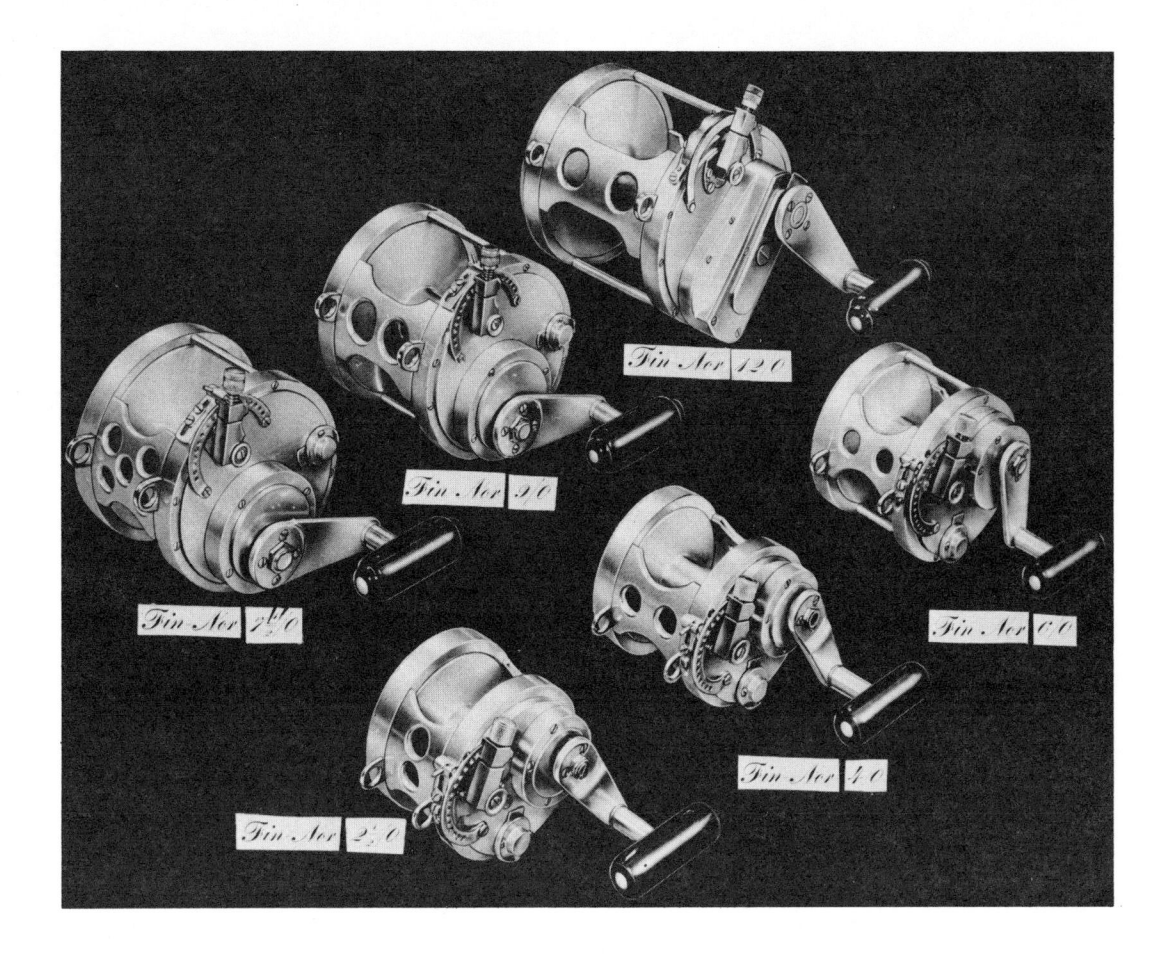

FIN-NOR BIG-GAME REELS

The Fin-Nor big-game reels are, of course, well known in any fishing port where anglers seek big swordfish, marlin, and tuna, which really test your tackle. It all started back in 1935 when some fishing guides and sportsmen stopped at Fred Greiten's Fin-Nor Machine Shop in Miami and asked him if he could build a fishing reel that could stand up under the strain of fighting the big marlin and tuna in the Bahamas. Fred went to work, and the result was the Fin-Nor big-game reel, which is still considered the finest offshore fishing reel on the market today.

All the parts of this reel are turned on a lathe, rather than being cast or stamped. The reel spool alone takes three hours to make by hand. As each aluminum part assumes its final shape, it is buffed and polished to a mirrorlike finish. Then it is anodized to twice the depth of standard finishes to protect it from corrosion for the life of the reel. Special stainless steels are selected for the smaller parts to provide great strength. Finally, as each reel is assembled, it is individually run in to assure perfect performance.

Each Fin-Nor trolling reel features an ultrafast drop-back, and a counterthrust braking mechanism. All are individually registered and guaranteed for the life of the reel against defects of materials and craftsmanship. Included is a permanent engraved nameplate. Every reel comes in a custom, shockproof carrying case built to take the rigors of tournament travel.

The Fin-Nor reels come in sizes from 2½/0 used with 12-lb.-to-20-lb.-test lines up to the largest 12/0 model used with 130-lb.-test lines. For more information about these reels and other tackle they make write to:

Tycoon/Fin-Nor
7447 N.W. 12th St.
Miami, Fla. 33126

FENWICK KONAHEAD

The Fenwick Konahead is an offshore trolling lure that can be rigged with a hook or can be trolled unrigged as a teaser. It has been very successful in raising and hooking marlin and large tuna. It has an indestructible body with contrasting Psychotail skirt. When trolled it breaks to the surface, then dives and swims in a fish-attracting manner. It is also made with a reflective and a nonreflective transparent head. The nonreflective head has a white insert, while the reflective head has a stamped-metallic insert that reflects light from all directions. The Konaheads are made in 7¾-, 11-, 13-, and 15½-in. sizes weighing from 2 ozs. to 16 ozs. Their catalog showing these and other lures and tackle they make costs $.25 from:
Fenwick
P.O. Box 729
Westminster, Calif. 92683

FIN-NOR FLY REELS

The Tycoon/Fin-Nor Corporation, which makes the famous big-game reels, also makes fly-fishing reels for salt water. It now has a No. 2 and a No. 3 antireverse Fly Reel. These incorporate all the features of their earlier fly reels plus an antireverse feature in which the handle does not turn while the fish is running. These reels use the Fin-Nor full-circle drag, which is easily adjustable with the preset knob located on the right-hand side of the reel. The crank has a double handle and is inset into the housing in order to eliminate tangling the line in the handle. The frame is made from one piece of aluminum bar stock, with no screws and no seams. The line capacity of the No. 2 fly reel is 200 yds. of 15-lb.-test backing plus 40 yds. of No. 9 fly line. The No. 3 fly reel capacity is 250 yds. of 20-lb.-test backing plus 40 yds. of No. 10 fly line. For more information about these and other fly reels write to:
Tycoon/Fin-Nor Corp.
7447 N.W. 12th St.
Miami, Fla. 33126

THE INTERNATIONAL OCEANOGRAPHIC FOUNDATION

This is a nonprofit organization chartered in 1953 by a Board of Trustees composed of outstanding scientists and laymen who are enthusiastic about the sea—our last great frontier on earth.

Members of the International Oceanographic Foundation find a common bond not only in the enjoyment of the sea, but also in encouraging and developing today's oceanographic exploration and scientific research. Through its publications, they exchange information about all forms of sea life—food and game fish, and the numerous other fascinating creatures of the high seas and shore—as well as ocean currents, the deep-sea floor, submarine detection, and the industrial applications of oceanography, to name just a few aspects of the exciting field of marine science. Members of the IOF receive a full-color bimonthly magazine *Sea Frontiers,* and the bimonthly question-and-answer series "Sea Secrets." They have various categories of membership, from member to patron. For more information about this organization you can write to:
The International Oceanographic Foundation
10 Rickenbacker Causeway, Virginia Key
Miami, Fla. 33149

FISHING IN CAPE MAY COUNTY

If you want to find out all about the saltwater fishing in New Jersey's Cape May County, drop them a line requesting this information and they'll send you maps, folders, guides, and reprints of fishing articles telling all about the striped bass, bluefish, weakfish, black drum, fluke, porgies, sea bass, and other fish caught in that area. Write to:
Dept. of Public Affairs
P.O. Box 365
Cape May Court House, N.J. 08210

ASHAWAY FISHING LINES

The Ashaway Line & Twine Company is one of the oldest fishing line manufacturers in the country. The company was founded by Captain Lester Crandall way back in 1824, and since then they have been making fishing line and twine for commercial and sport fishing. Today they specialize in braided nylon and Dacron lines for bait casting, trolling, squidding, and big-game fishing. Their big-game trolling lines are available in tests from 12 to 180 lbs. Their braided squidding line is popular in 25-, 36-, and 45-lb. tests. For their catalog showing these fishing lines write to:
Ashaway Line & Twine Co.
Ashaway, R.I. 02804

EELSKIN ON A PLUG

You can make a swimming plug even more effective by pulling an eelskin over it. To do this remove all the treble hooks and file a groove around the plug at the head just behind the metal lip. Then pull an eelskin turned inside out over the plug so that 3 or 4 in. of the tail of the skin extend beyond the end of the plug. Now tie the front part of the eelskin with line around the groove. Then replace the front but not the rear or tail treble hooks. To do this you have to cut or make slits in the skin where the hooks are attached. Treble hooks with open eyes that can be opened and closed with pliers are best for this job. Such an eelskin plug is deadly for big striped bass and bluefish in northern waters and for snook, barracuda, and tarpon in southern waters.

MULLET MEAN ACTION

Surf anglers and jetty and pier fishermen wait for the mullet to appear along the beaches each fall because they know these baitfish trigger some fast action. In northern waters the striped bass, bluefish, and weakfish come into the white water to feed on the mullet. Farther south, channel bass, bluefish, snook, tarpon, and jacks do the same, and anglers on the scene reap a harvest.

You can usually spot the mullet swimming on top of the water in small, compact schools rippling the surface or leaping out of the water, especially when chased by the larger gamefish. At such times you can cast surface plugs, underwater plugs, metal squids, and jigs into the breaking fish and enjoy some fast fishing.

LIVE EELS FOR BAIT

Although most anglers associate live eels with striped bass and use them mostly for these fish, you can also try the "snakes" for other fish with excellent results. Big bluefish will also go for the live eels, but here you'll have to use a two-hook rig, with one hook in the head and the other in the tail to prevent the blues from chopping the eel in half. Big weakfish will also go for the smaller-sized live eels when fished in the surf, inlets, and bays. A live eel also makes a top bait for big cobia in Chesapeake Bay and elsewhere. And you can also catch school tuna, dolphin, and sharks on live eels when fishing in deep water offshore.

BIG BLACK DRUM FROM THE SURF

When Gerald Townsend went surf fishing with his wife, Joan, off Cape Henlopen Point, Delaware, he was expecting to catch a few small sea trout or bluefish. He was using a line testing only 25 lbs. and baited his small hook with cut mullet for bait. He didn't have to wait too long for a bite, and when he set the hook he felt a real heavyweight on the end of his line. He fought the fish for 30 min. before he could finally beach it. When he saw the monster he knew he had the surf catch of his life. It was a huge black drum that later weighed 113 lbs., 1 oz., and this is now the official world record for the All-Tackle class in the IGFA records.

MINI-ON-DECK TACKLE BOX

This tackle box for sportfishing boats is available in all sizes, with prices quoted on your sketch and dimensions. You can have teak racks for hooks and lures, several drawers, and a teak-top cutting board for cutting bait or cleaning fish. The model shown is 31 in. high, 18¾ in. wide, 21¾ in. deep, and costs $500. For more information write to:
**Pompanette, Inc.
1515 S.E. 16th St.
Fort Lauderdale, Fla. 33316**

ORVIS SPINNING REELS

The Orvis Spinning Reels have been around for many years and are favored by many expert freshwater and salt-water anglers. They are especially popular with light-tackle fishermen who like to use a one-handed spinning rod and cast lures for bonefish, tarpon, snook, sea trout, striped bass, bluefish, dolphin, and other salt-water fish. Many professional fishing guides use this reel for their own fishing. There are several models to choose from, and most of them have a fast retrieve. Those intended for salt-water fishing have stainless-steel ball bearings, and the internal parts are stainless steel or plated with cadmium or chrome to provide maximum protection against prolonged exposure to salt. For their catalog showing these reels and other tackle they sell write to:
**The Orvis Co., Inc.
Manchester, Vt. 05254**

SEACRAFT SF 23 INBOARD

The SeaCraft SF 23 Inboard is designed as a fishing boat to run offshore to deep water at a fast speed, yet its open cockpit makes it ideal for inshore fishing and casting too. Although it has inboard power, SeaCraft has gone one step farther. They recessed the prop and rudder slightly into the deep V bottom, resulting in an outstanding ride with moderately shoal draft. It has a center console and is ruggedly built to take it under the toughest conditions. There's a 408-qt. forward storage compartment, two 20-qt. iceboxes, and 105-gal. fuel capacity. Other standard equipment includes an electric bilge blower, full engine instrumentation with electric fuel gauge, a 2.5-lb. dry chemical fire extinguisher, and a fuel filter with water separator. For their catalog or more information about this and other boats they make write to:
SeaCraft
P.O. Box 4040
Princeton, Fla. 33030

SALT-WATER CASTING REEL

The Garcia 10,000 C Ambassadeur reel is a larger addition to the family of salt-water Ambassadeur casting reels. They are popular with surf anglers and boat casters who want a reel that casts well and can also handle fast-running, active fish. It has a fast 4.2-to-1 ration when retrieving lures, but when a fish gets hooked it automatically changes down to a 2.5-to-1 ratio. If the fish turns and runs toward you, the reel shifts back to the faster-retrieve ratio again. The reel has a centrifugal brake that helps reduce backlashes. It also has stainless-steel bearings, and an extralarge spool capacity holding up to 475 yds. of 30-lb.-test Royal Bonnyl II line. For more information write to:
The Garcia Corp.
329 Alfred Ave.
Teaneck, N.J. 07666

CALIFORNIA HALIBUT

California halibut like a lively bait, so the best way to catch them is from a moving boat that gives the bait some action. Most anglers drift or slow-troll for these fish with a bottom rig and sinker and bait. When fishing from piers or jetties, however, your best bet is to use live baits such as anchovies, herring, sardines, or small queenfish. You can cast these out with a bottom rig and let the live baitfish swim around just off the bottom. If you are using dead baitfish, the best procedure is to cast out and reel in slowly along the bottom with slow lifts of the rod tip at regular intervals. If you feel a pickup or bite, lower your rod tip and give some slack line so the hablibut can swallow the bait.

GIRL BOATS BIG COD

Cathy Foote decided to go out for a day of codfishing on her father's party boat Sea Star out of Hampton, New Hampshire. When they got to the fishing grounds the other anglers around her started to haul in cod from 20 to 40 lbs., but Cathy just caught a small cusk. Then she lowered the big Norwegian jig to the bottom and started to work it up and down. Suddenly it seemed to hang up on a rock, but this rock had life and started to move off with the line. After a tough fight, which lasted 15 or 20 min., Cathy brought the fish to the surface. It was the biggest cod anyone on the boat had ever seen. They needed two gaffs to bring it aboard, and later it weighed 76 lbs.!

GOLDEN REGAL TROLLING REELS

Tycoon/Fin-Nor, which makes the well-known Fin-Nor big-game reels, also makes a less expensive Golden Regal reel for light-tackle trolling and fishing. These reels have a one-piece frame and spool, and endplates that are turned from solid aluminum bar stock for maximum strength and precision. All aluminum parts are polished and buffed to a mirrorlike finish, then anodized for enduring beauty. Critical parts are machined from stainless steel and Monel for extra strength. The Golden Regal reels have Fin-Nor's exclusive counterthrust breaking, fast-throw lever, preset drag tension, and high gear ratio for fast retrieve. They come in three models—the Golden Regal 20, the Golden Regal 30, and the Golden Regal 50—with the numbers indicating the test of the line recommended for each reel. For more information write to:
Tycoon/Fin-Nor
7447 N.W. 12th St.
Miami, Fla. 33126

SAMPO SWIVELS

Every angler, whether he fishes in fresh or salt water with lures, often runs into line twist. Whether casting or trolling with certain types of lures, line twist can be a problem and can weaken your line or make it hard to manage on the reel or during a cast. Anglers also like to use a snap on the end of the line to enable them to change lures or leaders quickly. The best swivels or snap swivels have ball bearings in order to turn freely under a strain or a weight on the end of a line. The Sampo people have been making such ball-bearing snaps and swivels for a long time, and several types, styles, and sizes are available. For more information write to:
Sampo, Inc.
Barneveld, N.Y. 13304

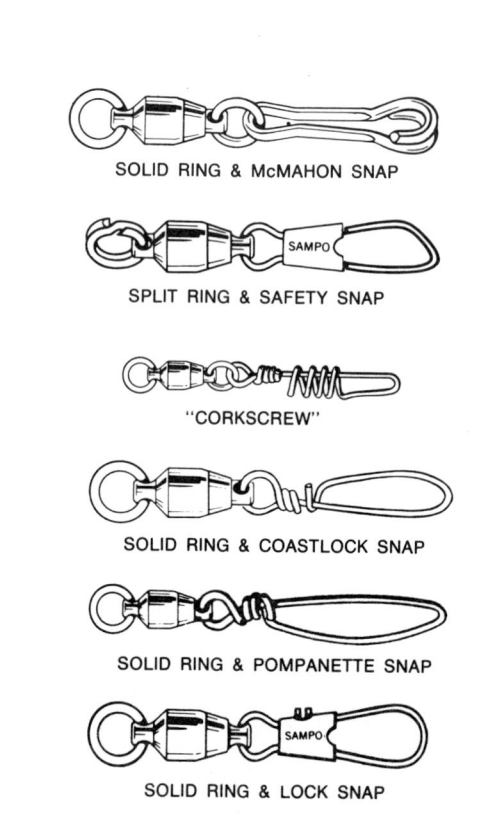

SOLID RING & McMAHON SNAP

SPLIT RING & SAFETY SNAP

"CORKSCREW"

SOLID RING & COASTLOCK SNAP

SOLID RING & POMPANETTE SNAP

SOLID RING & LOCK SNAP

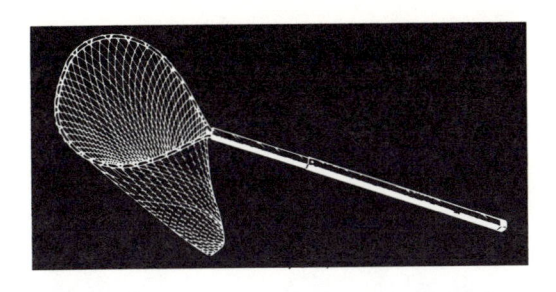

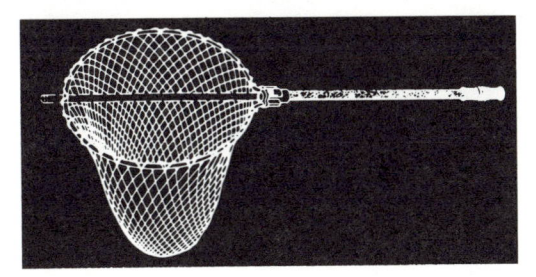

PEPCO NETS

This company carries one of the most complete lines of nets for all kinds of freshwater and salt-water fish and fishing. They have trout and salmon nets, jumbo landing nets, wading nets, boat nets, telescope nets, shovel nets, bait well and bait dealer nets, minnow nets, shrimp and smelt nets, crab nets, and other nets. They also have collapsible frame landing and trout nets and also several kinds of gaffs. For more information write to:

J. F. Pepper Co., Inc.
P.O. Box 445
Rome, N.Y. 13440

USEFUL SEA PESTS

When most salt-water anglers catch a crab, skate, dogfish, blowfish, sea robin, or bergall or cunner, they fume and curse or slash or squash the sea pest and kill it or throw it back overboard. But most of these unwanted sea pests can be put to good use instead of being wasted.

Crabs, for example, can be used as bait for various kinds of fishes. Or you can break them up into small pieces and scatter them around the boat or under a pier or bridge as chum.

If you catch a sea robin, skate, dogfish, or other fish you can cut strips from the white belly and use these to catch fluke or summer flounders. You can even try eating dogfish and skate wings. The same thing can be done with the puffers or blowfish you catch in northern waters. The meat in their tail sections is a delicacy and is even sold in the fish markets as "sea squab" or "chicken of the sea."

ADD COLOR TO YOUR BAITS

You can dye clams and mussels and other shellfish by putting the meats from them into a container and adding a teaspoonful or two of liquid food coloring. Usually yellow or red dyes are used. Then stir the contents and let them stand for a while. The length of time you let the mixture stand depends on how dark you want the clams or mussels to be. Then wash the baits and use them for flounders, cod, blackfish, porgies, croakers, and any other fish that take these baits.

CANDLES FROM FISH

There is a small, slender fish found in northern Pacific waters called the eulachon or candlefish. The reason for the latter name is that if you dry these fish and run a wick through them, you can light them like a candle.

CHUMMING IN SOUTHERN WATERS

Although chumming is done more often in northern waters for bluefish, tuna, mackerel, and weakfish, it can also be highly effective in southern waters. Chumming is the art of luring fish up to your boat by offering them a free handout in the hope that later on they will take your baited hook or lure. Chumming attracts fish near the boat, the scent and food excites them, and they start a feeding frenzy that makes them take a bait or lure more readily.

For example, you can anchor in a spot on the flats where bonefish or permit move in on the incoming tide. Cut up some conch, spiny lobster tail, or shrimp, and toss the pieces overboard so they drift out with the tide. Then bait a hook with a live shrimp and drift it out to any fish you see coming in to feed on the chum.

Various small fish such as menhaden, mullet, pilchards, pinfish, blue runners, and even grunts and snappers can be ground up or cut up into small pieces and tossed overboard. This will bring king mackerel, Spanish mackerel, cobia, and sharks up to your boat. Then a piece of the fish can be let out on a hook or you can cast lures into any fish near the boat. Such chumming and fishing can be done from an anchored or drifting boat.

Even so-called bottom species such as grouper, mangrove snappers, yellowtail snappers, and other fish will respond to chum and gather under the boat. Here it's a good idea to use a chum pot or chum bag. A chum pot can be bought or you can make it by forming a box or wire frame and covering it with wire mesh. A burlap bag or onion sack and netting material can also be used as a chum bag. Fill the pot or bag with ground-up fish or crushed clams or crabs or shrimp or even canned dog or cat food. Lower the chum pot or bag to the bottom on a rope. You may have to add a rock or some other weight inside to get it down deep enough and have it stay there in a tide. Every so often, raise and shake the pot or bag to release some chum. Then lower a baited hook near the chum pot or bag where the fish will usually congregate.

ANGRY MARLIN

Three anglers fishing off the coast of Mexico hooked a 500-lb. marlin that suddenly went berserk. The fish rammed the side of their boat, piercing a hole in it with its bill and leaving its lower jaw imbedded in the wood. The crazed fish then came back and struck the boat once more, this time breaking off its long bill. Finally, the pugnacious marlin minus jaw and bill took off for parts unknown.

SLACK LINE FOR TARPON

When fishing for tarpon with dead baits it is important to give the fish plenty of slack line when he picks up the bait. One way to do this is to cast your bait out and let it sink to the bottom, then strip off line from the reel and coil it on a seat or the floor of the boat. When you get a bite, let the tarpon take the coiled slack line so that he can swallow the bait. Then when the line straightens, set the hook hard.

SEA WATER TEMPERATURE INDICATOR

Dytek Laboratories has announced the availability of their revolutionary Sea Water Temperature Indicating System. Available previously only for commercial and tournament fishermen, the Model 703200 system is now available at $229 at leading marine dealers nationally. Based on the theory that most surface-feeding gamefish are caught in waters having narrow temperature bands, depending upon species of fish, the temperature-sensing system gives the angler a highly visible, three-digit temperature reading in tenths of a degree Fahrenheit. Solid-state circuitry accurately updates changing trends in surface-water temperature every 5 secs.

Fishermen know that most tuna, albacore, marlin, swordfish, and sailfish are caught at very defined times of the year. This is primarily because they are sensitive to seawater temperatures. Dytek Laboratories has done considerable research on the effects of water temperature and the presence of feeding fish and have found that it is not necessarily the absolute temperature but the relative temperature that affects the presence of these feeding fish. Research conducted by the United States Department of Fisheries in Honolulu with species of tuna have indicated that they can perceive variations in temperature to as little as .2° F. And when migrating, they will tend to stay within a body of water that is at a constant temperature. The fish may start their migration in water of a certain temperature. Then winds and currents will break the water into pockets. During their normal migration the fish will remain in these pockets unless pushed out by some unnatural force. As these pockets move along the Coast, these temperatures will slowly change.

Enter the sport fisherman with a Dytek Sea Water Temperature System, fishing southwest of San Diego for albacore. Bang! —a hit, he looks at his seawater temperature indicator: 72.8° F. Some 15 or 20 min. to boat his fish, he again looks at his temperature-indicating system (71.4° F.), throws his boat into gear, and at 72.8° F.— another hit! This type of fishing normally is done by throwing a buoy or marker; the Dytek system is more effective and saves a lot of buoys.

Dytek's Model 703200 System Indicator can be easily mounted on the dash or bulkhead and comes equipped with 24 ft. of cable and transducer. The temperature probe may be mounted through the hull, or an optional transom mount is also available. Using this system, it is recommended that the angler log the exact surface-water temperature and the location of every major gamefish taken on his boat. These data will show definite trends and lead to increased success on future fishing trips.

A free Sea Water Temperature Chart and descriptive literature is available from leading marine distributors or by writing to:
Dytek Laboratories, Inc.
110 Wilbur Pl.
Bohemia, N.Y. 11716

SOUTH CAROLINA FISHING GUIDE

One of the best fishing guides telling about the salt-water fishing in South Carolina is called *A Guide to Salt-water Sports Fishing in South Carolina*. It covers surf fishing, pier and bridge fishing, inshore, inlet, and sound fishing, offshore fishing, and bottom fishing. It gives artificial reef and offshore fishing locations. It tells which fishing tackle, baits, and lures to use. It covers coastal marinas, boat rental stations, campgrounds, and other facilities. It also tells about fishing tournaments and rodeos. It has several charts and maps pinpointing where fish are caught. This guide is well illustrated with black-and-white and color photos and drawings. There are color plates of the most popular salt-water species caught in South Carolina. *A Guide to Salt-water Sports Fishing in South Carolina* sells for $1.00 and is published by:

South Carolina Wildlife & Marine Resources Dept.
P.O. Box 12559
Charleston, S.C. 29412

BAIT TAIL FISHING

Bait Tail Fishing by Al Reinfelder was one of the first books written about fishing with the plastic-tail baits with lead heads. Al Reinfelder with his partner Lou Palmer helped create and develop the deadly Alou plastic eel with metal action head that is now so widely used for striped bass. Then he went on and made several bait tails with metal heads and plastic bodies and tails. These proved very effective lures in fresh and salt water, and now there are many variations on the market. Al tells in his book how to use the bait tails for striped bass, bluefish, weakfish, sea trout, channel bass or redfish, snook, tarpon, and even such bottom species as fluke or summer flounders. He tells how to use the bait tails around bridges, from piers, jetties, breakwaters, beaches, in rivers, canals, inlets, and from boats. *Bait Tail Fishing* sells for $6.95 and is published by:

A. S. Barnes & Co., Inc.
P.O. Box 421
Cranbury, N.J. 08512

HOPKINS "ST" LURES

Hopkins Fishing Lures, Inc., makers of the No Eql Lures, which have been used by surf anglers and boat anglers for many years, have now come out with what they call their ST lures. One of these has the same hammered body as the No Eql but has a plastic swimming tail on the hook to provide a twisted tail action. The other lure is a hammered jig head with a plastic curved tail on the hook. These lures can be obtained with amber, black, blue, chartreuse, pink, white, and yellow plastic tails and come in different weights. For their catalog or more information write to:

Hopkins Fishing Lures, Inc.
1130 Boissevain Ave.
Norfolk, Va. 23507

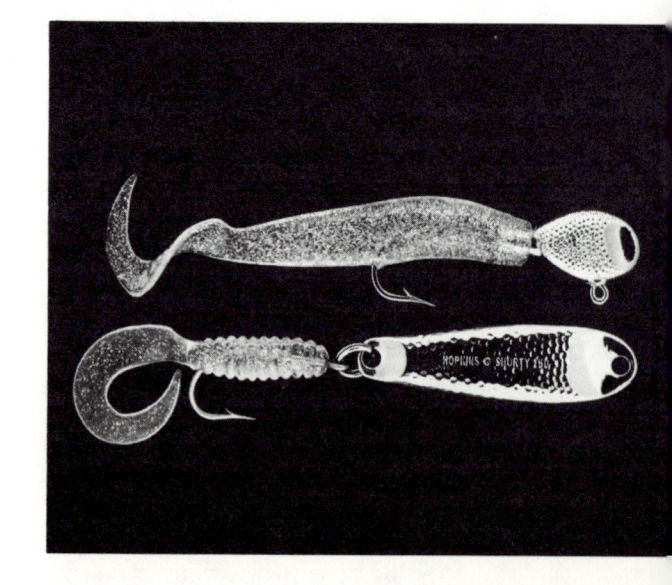

CONOLON CUSTOM DELUXE RODS

These Garcia spinning rods are designed for salt-water fishing and casting from boats and surf. The shorter models are 7 and 8 ft. in length, while the longer ones run up to 11 ft., 8 in. They also come in different actions, from medium-light to heavy. The rods have hard-chromed stainless-steel guides and ceramic Conoglide tip-tops. The grips and butts are covered with a special cork tape, and the reel seats are chrome over brass. For more information write to:
The Garcia Corp.
329 Alfred Ave.
Teaneck, N.J. 07666

ORVIS FLY REELS

The Orvis Company continues its tradition of making and selling fine fly reels ever since Charles F. Orvis invented the first ventilated fly reel back in 1874. For more than a hundred years the Orvis Company has steadily improved and precision-designed fly reels with the thrilling purring sound and reliable performance of superior machining.

From the new CFO fly reels pictured here through the less expensive but handsome Battenkill fly reels and the tough, top-quality "workhorse" utility Madison fly reels, the fly fisherman can select the reel to meet his specific needs. There are also special-function fly reels, such as the Orvis Magnalite Multipliers, with fast two-to-one retrieve; the rugged service reel; the Orvis salt-water single-action reel; and the champion Seamaster and the hand-built Bogdans, which are used for salt-water fly fishing. For their catalog showing these and other reels and fishing tackle they make write to:
The Orvis Co., Inc.
Manchester, Vt. 05254

ATTRACTING AMBERJACK

One good way to attract amberjack to a spot is to run your boat in tight circles over the water you plan to fish. Then wait until the disturbance dies down before you cast your lures or bait into the water.

HOLDING BAIT ON A HOOK

Rubber bands are a handy and neat way to keep soft baits such as clams, soft-shelled or shedder crabs, or delicate baitfish on a hook. Get the very thin rubber bands and simply snap them around the bait and hook a few times.

THE REEL THING

The Reel Thing is a simplified respooling device for every fisherman who respools his own fishing lines. Simple to use, it attaches to most all-smooth surfaces or may be glued on permanently. For larger spools of line you use the normal width or setting. For narrow spools you reverse the top slide. It will take up to 5½-in.-diameter spools of line. For more information write to:

**RedTack of America
P.O. Box 36
Downey, Calif. 90241**

LES DAVIS HERRING DODGER

Since its introduction more than forty years ago, the fame of this flasher has spread throughout the world. It is a standard flasher for both commercial and sport fishermen after Pacific salmon has proven an effective trolling flasher for many species of gamefish. The larger sizes are commonly used by salt-water fishermen, and the smaller sizes are used on lakes to bring in large rainbow trout, lake trout, coho, and other fish. The herring dodger gives off a flash and action like a school of live baitfish. It is rigged between the sinker and bait or lure to produce a darting action to the bait and gives an extra fish-attracting flash. It works equally well with trolling spoons or plugs or with natural baits such as smelt or herring or even large streamer flies. For their catalog showing all the models and sizes of the dodgers they make write to:

**Les Davis Fishing Tackle Co.
1565 Center St.
Tacoma, Wash. 98409**

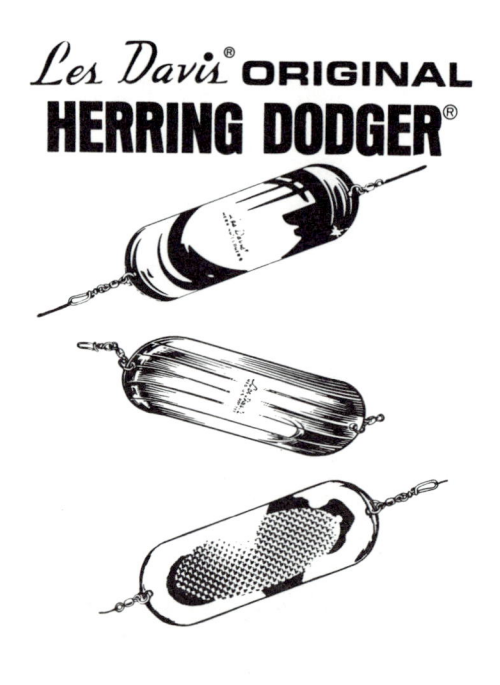

GRADY-WHITE BOATS

Grady-White Boats, Inc., of Greenville, North Carolina, have added four completely new models to their line, bringing the total to fifteen models between 17 and 21 ft. Complete specifications on these various models are available from:
Grady-White Boats, Inc.
P.O. Box 1527
Greenville, N.C. 27834

SINKER AND LURE MOLDS

Anglers in fresh and salt water who do a lot of fishing make their own sinkers and lures. You can obtain many molds and lure-making parts from the Midland Tackle Company. They have molds for making all types of sinkers such as the bank, pyramid, cannonball, dipsy or bell, pinch-on, split-shot, diamond, and trolling weights. They also have molds for making such lures as jigs and plastic lures.

If you want to make your own fishing rods for fresh or salt water you can also obtain graphite and Fiberglas blanks, reel seats, cork grips, ferrules, butts, guides, winding silk, and other rod components. And they also have such lure-making parts as plug bodies, jig heads, surgical and plastic tubing, spoon and spinner blades, clevises, split rings, and treble and single hooks. And they also carry fly-tying materials. For a free catalog write to:

Midland Tackle Co.
66 Rte. 17
Sloatsburg, N.Y. 10974

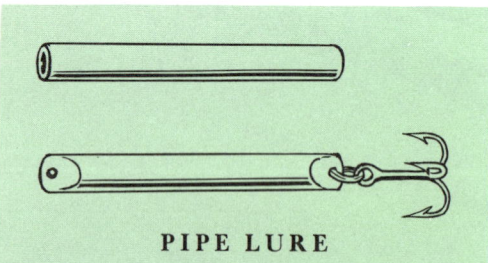

PIPE LURE

This pipe fishing lure can be made quickly and easily by taking a length of metal pipe, flattening both ends, drilling holes in each end, and adding a split ring and then a single or treble hook. By using pipes of different diameters and cutting them to various lengths you can make lures of almost any size or weight. To make them even heavier you can fill the pipe with hot lead after you flatten one end. Chrome-plated pipes can be used as they are, but copper or brass pipes can be sprayed or painted in various colors. These lures can be cast, trolled, or jigged for many salt-water species.

SPORT FISHING COURSE

North Carolina University at Raleigh has been offering a short five-day course in salt-water sport fishing for many years. It is usually held in June at Hatteras, North Carolina. The total cost of the five-day course is $300, and it includes room, group meals, all boats, fishing trips, and instruction by experts, tackle company representatives, and university staff members. Students stay in motels, and meals are served at local restaurants. Classes are held in a nearby community center, and fishing trips originate from the local docks, with charter boats participating. There are lectures and demonstrations, with special emphasis on such tackle as rods, reels, lines, lures, and baits. There are also casting exhibitions. Due to the nature of this course, enrollment is usually limited to about seventy persons. For more information write to:

Mr. Denis Jackson
Div. of Continuing Education
P.O Box 5125
Raleigh, N.C. 27607

PUMA ANGLER KNIFE

The Gutmann Cutlery Company makes many folding knives for fishing and hunting, as well as general-use and pocket knives. They also make sheath knives for hunting. Their Puma Angler Knife is a versatile utility knife that fishermen will find handy. It is rugged, ever-sharp, rust-resistant, lightweight, and compact. This knife has a special blade that scales fish and helps remove fish hooks easily. It will also saw through the bones of those big ones. It has a classic British hollow-ground cutting blade of stainless superkeen cutting steel. The knife folds to a handy 4¼-in. size and has individual safety locks for each blade. For a catalog showing this and other knives they make write to:
Gutmann Cutlery Co., Inc.
900 S. Columbus Ave.
Mount Vernon, N.Y. 10550

GEORGIA FISHING BOOKLET

This Is Georgia Fishing tells about the freshwater and salt-water fishing in the state of Georgia. This booklet has a section dealing with North Georgia reservoirs, Middle Georgia reservoirs, South Georgia reservoirs, trout streams, rivers, lakes, and small impoundments. The various freshwater and salt-water sport fish of Georgia are described and illustrated. There are also sections telling about the various facilities, fishing camps and areas, and launching ramps for both freshwater and salt-water fishing. You can obtain a copy of *This Is Georgia Fishing* from:
Dept. of Natural Resources
270 Washington St., S.W.
Atlanta, Ga. 30334

"CALIFORNIA OCEAN FISHING MAP"

This fishing map covers San Francisco, San Mateo, and Santa Cruz counties, and the Elkhorn Slough Area of Monterey County. It is a summary of ocean sport fishing, including a list of fishing areas, kinds of fish caught, best times of year to fish, and the gear and bait to use. It is available from:
Dept. of Fish and Game
1416 Ninth St.
Sacramento, Calif. 95814

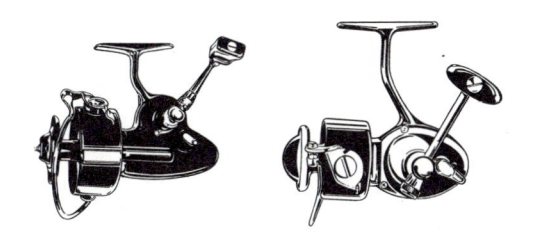

WRIGHT & MCGILL REELS

The Wright & McGill Company sells several models of spinning reels suitable for light salt-water, surf, and heavy salt-water fishing. Their two most popular brands are the Mediterranean and the Blue Pacific spinning reels. They have heavy-duty bail pickups with rustproof chromed line rollers. The gear ratios vary from 3.5 to 1 to 5.5 to 1, depending on the model. And they hold anywhere from 200 to 350 yds. of line, depending on the pound test used. Their catalog showing these reels and other fishing tackle they make costs $.25 from:
Wright & McGill Co.
P.O. Box 16011
Denver, Colo. 80216

BONEFISHING

While bonefish can be caught the year round in the Florida Keys, some months are better than others. During the winter months, windy days, rough and dirty water, and cold weather will often ruin the fishing. During a cold front the bones may leave the flats for several days. This is the time of year when most of the tourists and many anglers fish for them. But the fishing is better from April to October, when the water is calmer and warmer.

SNOOK IN SHALLOW WATER

When snook are cruising close to shore in shallow water they are extremely wary and spooky. Then it's a good idea to stand back away from the water's edge at least 30 or 40 ft. and do your casting from there. This is especially true when fishing for them in clear water along sandy beaches with no surf breaking. When there is a surf breaking or if the water is discolored or murky, you can fish closer. Or you can try fishing shallow-water spots at night.

BOTTOM FISHING WITH BAIT

When fishing on the bottom in deep water, a good general rule is to use big baits if you want big fish. A small bait will hook and catch more fish, but these will be smaller fish, which usually steal the bait quickly too. A big bait, on the other hand, gives you more fishing time, since you don't have to reel in as often as when you are using small baits. It takes more time to steal a big bait off the hook, and in the meantime a big fish may come along and grab it.

KASTMASTER LURE

The Aero-Dynamic Kastmaster is a scientifically designed metal lure with unusual flash appeal and action, and can be cast great distances. There are sizes for all freshwater and salt-water gamefish, from 1/12 oz. up to 3 ozs., and they come in chrome, copper, gold, and chrome/neon blue finishes. The lure can be used casting or trolling and is especially effective for striped bass, bluefish, channel bass, weakfish, mackerel, barracuda, snook, and tarpon. The Acme Tackle Company, which makes this lure, also makes many other spoons, metal lures, and jigs for freshwater and salt-water fishing. For their catalog showing all these lures send $.25 to:
Acme Tackle Co.
69 Bucklin St.
Providence, R.I. 02907

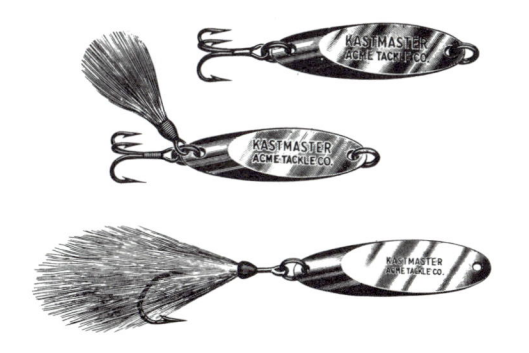

LFG 460 DEPTH SOUNDER

The Lowrance LFG 460 Depth Sounder is one of their Bluewater Pro models with a powerful highly sensitive unit that registers fish and extreme depths on any of three ranges: 0 to 60 ft., 0 to 180 ft., or 0 to 60 fath. (360 ft.) Preset the audible, adjustable alarm and the operator is alerted to the presence of fish, structure, or shallow water within range. Narrow and bright flashers, a patented light trap, and an extended sun shield make viewing easy. False signals from interference are eliminated with an adjustable suppressor. A heavy-duty, high-speed transducer mounts through the hull or on the transom. For more details about this and other depth sounders, write for their catalog, which costs $.25, to:
Lowrance Electronics, Inc.
12000 E. Skelly Dr.
Tulsa, Okla. 74128

SALTWATER FISHING IN WASHINGTON

Saltwater Fishing in Washington by Frank Haw and Raymond Buckley is a 200-page book with full-color photos of the 51 most commonly caught marine fishes taken by sportsmen in Northwest salt waters. The book also has over 100 black-and-white photos and illustrations. There is a detailed 42-page section that pinpoints Washington's 14 best salmon and bottom fishing areas. The species of fish, best fishing spots and periods, and other information are included, along with the fishing maps. There are big sections on knots, rigs, baits, and cleaning fish. The book sells for $4.95 and is published by:
Stan Jones Publishing Co.
3421 E. Mercer St.
Seattle, Wash. 98112

277

PROFILES IN SALT-WATER ANGLING

Since the beginning of time, man has been lured to the sea in search of fine fishing grounds. In the book *Profiles in Salt-water Angling*, George Reiger traces the history of the sport—its people, tackle, and techniques.

Through the words and deeds of the great men of ocean angling, Reiger details the development of salt-water fishing from a vocation to a sport. The book profiles such early salt-water fishing pioneers as Charles Frederick Holder, Geroge Farnsworth, Harlan Major, Van Campen Heilner, Tommy Gifford, and Michael Lerner. The book also covers such present-day masters of the sport as Frank Woolner, Johnny Cass, Lefty Kreh, Don Holm, Ray Cannon, and the late Al Reinfelder. There are also chapters on famous writers and personalities like Zane Grey and Ernest Hemingway, both of whom loved big-game fishing and caught many big fish.

George Reiger is an associate editor of *Field & Stream* magazine and has written other books and many magazine articles on fishing and conservation. Reiger personally interviewed many of the present-day masters of salt-water fishing who are written up in the book. Thoroughly researched, it is one of the first books to document the history of salt-water angling during the past 100 yrs. *Profiles in Salt-water Angling* sells for $14.95 and is published by:
Prentice-Hall, Inc.
Englewood Cliffs, N.J. 07632

ROD BELTS

Rod belts are used by surf anglers and boat anglers for fishing and fighting a fish when standing up. They are usually made from leather or plastic, strap around an angler's waist, and have a cup or butt rest into which the butt of the rod is inserted. This helps to take the strain off your arms when waiting for a bite or when fighting a good-sized fish for any length of time. Sampo, Inc., makes many different kinds and styles of surf rod belts, butt rests, and gimbal-type rod belts. For more information write to:
Sampo, Inc.
Barneveld, N.Y. 13304

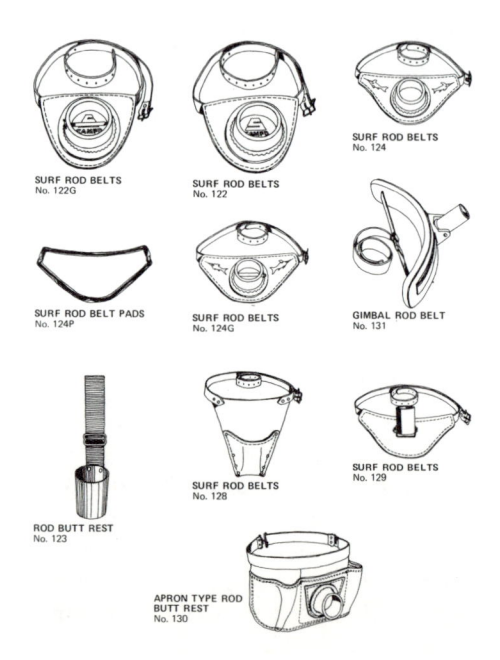

SURF ROD BELTS
No. 122G

SURF ROD BELTS
No. 122

SURF ROD BELTS
No. 124

SURF ROD BELT PADS
No. 124P

SURF ROD BELTS
No. 124G

GIMBAL ROD BELT
No. 131

ROD BUTT REST
No. 123

SURF ROD BELTS
No. 128

SURF ROD BELTS
No. 129

APRON TYPE ROD BUTT REST
No. 130

PFLUEGER SUPREME FLY REEL

The Pflueger large-sized Medalist reels have been used for salt-water fly fishing for many years. Now this company offers their Supreme deluxe single-action fly reel for heavy-duty freshwater or for salt-water fly fishing. It features a quick-take-apart spool and 360-degree drag. For more information write to:
**Pflueger Sporting Goods Div.
P.O. Box 185
Columbia, S.C. 29202**

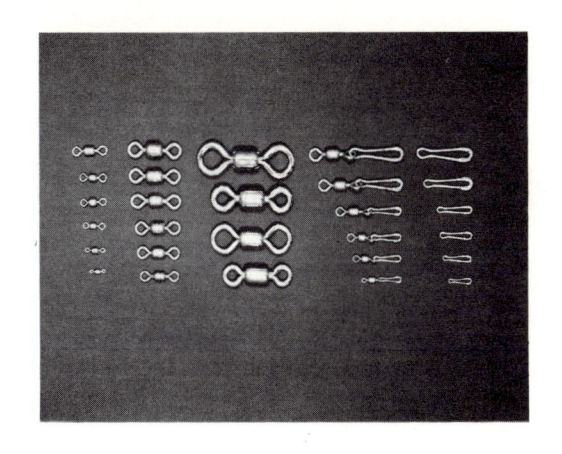

BERKLEY-MCMAHON SNAPS AND SWIVELS

These snaps, swivels, and snap-swivels are widely used in freshwater and salt-water fishing when casting or trolling. They make changing leaders and lures easy and quick. And they also help to prevent line twist when using lures that revolve and spin. The swivels come in size Nos. 10 to 11/0, while the snaps come in size Nos. 1 to 6. The snap-swivels come in size Nos. 10 to 4/0. They are made from brass, either nickel plated or in a black finish. They are sold in most fishing-tackle shops. For more information write to:
**Berkley and Co.
Spirit Lake, Ia. 51360**

BONEFISH AT NIGHT

Although most bonefish are usually caught in the daytime, these fish will also feed at night and can often be caught at daybreak and dusk, when it is quite dark. Long casts are not needed at such times because the bones are less wary and will approach and feed close to a wading angler or a boat. Chumming with cut shrimp or crabs or conch and using live shrimp for bait are the best ways to catch them in the dark.

GROUPER ON LURES

You can catch grouper on lures such as plug or jigs by fishing for them in shallow-water spots where they hang out. Rocky bottoms and coral reefs and ledges are good spots to try, and they can be spotted as darker patches or seen in clear water. You can drift over these and cast your lures, letting them sink or run deep, and when you get a hit or catch a fish you can anchor the boat and fish the spot thoroughly.

MODERN SALT-WATER SPORT FISHING

Modern Salt-water Sport Fishing by Frank Woolner is one of the best books ever written on salt-water fishing, bringing up to date most of the modern methods and techniques used in the briny. Frank Woolner, who is editor of the *Salt-water Sportsman* magazine is, of course, well qualified to write this book, and he went out of his way to make it the most comprehensive volume ever written. He covers fishing tackle such as rods, reels, lines, lures, and accessories. He also goes into detail about natural baits and rigs and how to use them. He covers bottom fishing, surf fishing, pier, jetty, and bridge fishing, inshore and offshore trolling, casting from shore and boats, and salt-water fly fishing. Frank also covers all the major salt-water fishes, from porgies to giant tuna as well as most of the important fishing spots in this country and abroad. The book is well illustrated with photos and runs 319 pages. *Modern Salt-water Sport Fishing* sells for $8.95 and is published by:
Crown Publishers, Inc.
419 Park Ave. S.
New York, N.Y. 10016

CRIMPING PLIERS AND LEADER MATERIAL

You can easily and quickly make your own wire leaders of any length and strength with these Berkley crimping pliers, tube sleeves, and Steelon wire leader material. You can buy these separately or get a kit that contains everything you need to make the leaders. The Steelon leader material comes in tests from 10 lbs. up to 120 lbs. And the tube sleeves come in different diameters for crimping the different strengths of leader material. For a catalog showing all these materials and other fishing tackle write to:
Berkley and Co.
Spirit Lake, Ia. 51360

280

EVERGLADES NATIONAL PARK FISHING

This is a fisherman's paradise in southern Florida, and thousands of local and visiting anglers come here every year to fish these productive waters. Here you can fish the winding creeks, the bays and channels in the mangrove back country even in the fall and winter and catch snook, tarpon, redfish, sea trout, snapper, and sheepshead. Or you can try the many islands and outside beaches, shorelines, and oyster bars for many of the same fish. Or you can run out to the Gulf of Mexico and fish these outside waters for Spanish mackerel, king mackerel, and other fish by casting or trolling. And you can try bottom fishing in the deeper holes and around rocks for grouper, mangrove snapper, sheepshead, and grunts.

The Everglades National Park, of course, is also noted for its birdlife and wildlife. While fishing here you'll see crocodiles, alligators, manatees, raccoons, bobcats, deer, and such birds as egrets, roseate spoonbills, wood storks, bald eagles, and ospreys. For more information about the Everglades National Park you can write to:

Chamber of Commerce
Everglades City, Fla. 33929

PLANO TACKLE BOX

The Plano No. 7420 Tackle Box is an extralarge box especially designed for large lures. There are two big trays that will take many of the lures used in salt-water casting and trolling. The box has double ABS latches, Stay-Dri ribs in eleven compartments, and 5 in. between the trays and the bottom for reels and other gear. There is also a pork rind holder and tackle rack for two Plano clear utility boxes. This tackle box is 19 in. long, 10¼ in. wide, and 9½ in. high. For a catalog or more information you can write to:
Plano Molding Co.
Plano, Ill. 60545

FLORIDA'S FISHIN' HOLES

An exciting new Florida sportfishing publication provides very complete information for the salt-water angler about Florida's fishing spots. Entitled *Florida's Charted Salt-water Fishin' Holes*, this book shows the exact location of more than five hundred charted inshore and offshore fishing spots around Florida's ocean and Gulf coastlines.

Authenticated by research conducted by the state of Florida and private sources, it describes each "fishin' hole," depth of the water, what species of fish are there, the season of the year each species can be caught, and what baits and lures are used to catch them.

Critics have acclaimed this publication as the "bible of Florida salt-water fishing," and "the most complete authority on salt-water fishing in Florida ever compiled."

The book contains 112 pages of charts and information printed in multicolor. *Florida's Charted Salt-water Fishin' Holes* sells for $3.00 and is available from:
Bureau of Maps
Drawer No. 5317
Tallahassee, Fla. 32301

PENN SPINFISHER REELS

The Penn Fishing Tackle Manufacturing Company makes a complete line of spinning reels for freshwater and salt-water fishing, from ultralight models to heavy-duty surf and salt-water reels. They feature stainless-steel mainshafts, stainless-steel bails, and multidisk Teflon drags. The 706 heavy-duty salt-water Spinfisher is also available with a manual pickup. Most of the reels have fast gear ratios, from 3.8 to 1 up to 5 to 1. And most of them are available in right-hand wind too. For more information about these and other fishing reels they make write for their catalog to:
The Penn Fishing Tackle Mfg. Co.
3028 W. Hunting Park Ave.
Philadelphia, Pa. 19132

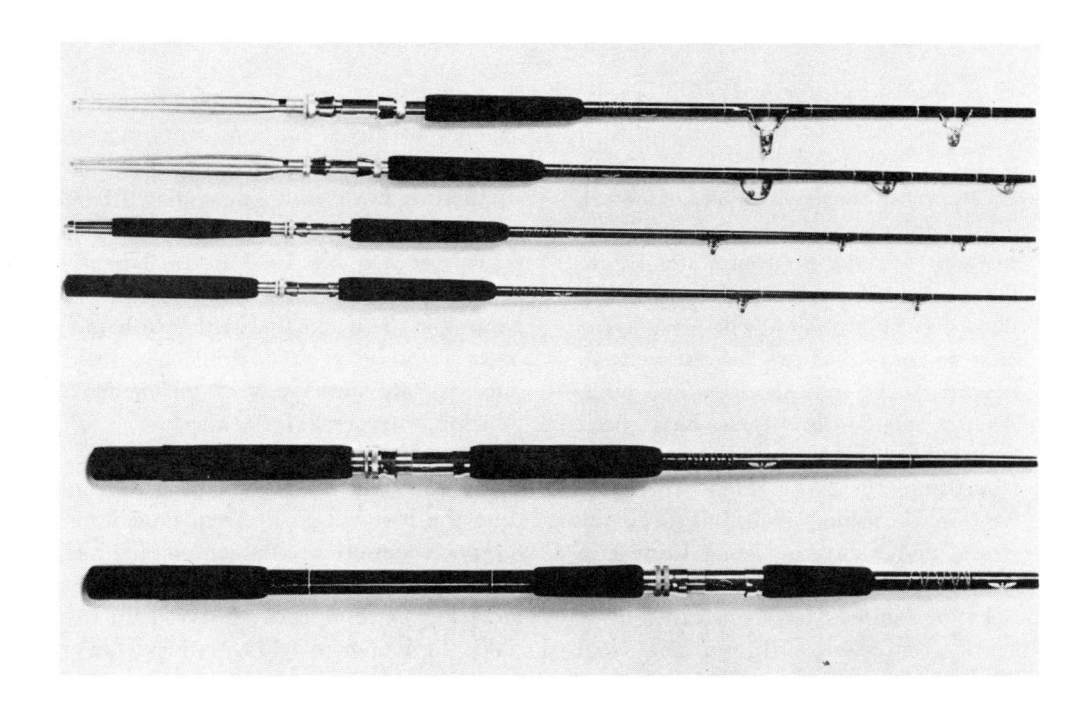

FENWICK SALT-WATER RODS

Fenwick makes a full line of salt-water surf, trolling, boat, and live-bait rods for a wide variety of fishing in the ocean. They have 15 Fiberglas models and several graphite rods to choose from covering almost every length, weight, and action. Their live-bait and jig rods range from 7 ft. to 9 ft. and handle lines testing from 12 lbs. to 60 lbs. Their surf spin sticks range from 9 ft. to 12 ft. and handle lines testing from 10 lbs. to 40 lbs. and weights from 1 oz. to 10 ozs. Their big-game offshore trolling rods come in the standard series with the regular butts or the deluxe series with stainless-steel butts and gimbals. These trolling rods are made for all classes of line, from 12 lbs. to 130 lbs. For their catalog showing these rods and other rods and fishing tackle, send $.25 to:
**Fenwick
P.O. Box 729
Westminster, Calif. 92683**

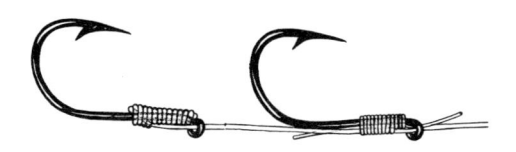

SALMON MOOCHERS

These salmon moochers are tied with a special knot that prevents a scored, weakened leader. They are rigged with stationary and sliding hooks so that you can adjust the hooks to fit the herring baits usually used with these rigs. They come in two- and three-hook rigs and with a treble hook. They also come in different leader strengths and hook sizes from Nos. 1/0 to 6/0. You can also get them on nylon-covered leaders testing 20 lbs. and 30 lbs. This company also carries trout and steelhead flies in dry, wet, nymph, streamer, and bucktail patterns. For their catalog write to:
**Poulsen Quality Flies
P.O. Box 13627
Portland, Ore. 97213**

SHARKS FROM SHORE AND PIERS

When most anglers think of shark fishing, they visualize a good-sized boat way out offshore in deep water where these marauders are usually found. But sharks, even big ones, will often come close to shore and can be caught from beaches, rocky shores, jetties, and piers. Anglers in South Africa have been catching big sharks up to a ton or more from shore for many years. There are now shark fishing clubs all over the world, and many are being formed in this country too.

In the United States you can fish for sharks from shore, surf, and piers from New England to the Gulf of Mexico and also along the Pacific Coast. The summer months are usually best, but sharks can be caught the year 'round in Florida and Caribbean waters.

To catch sharks this way you'll need strong tackle—heavy-surf rods with big reels filled with lines testing 50 to 80 lbs. are usually used. Some anglers use big-game trolling outfits with 6/0 to 12/0 reels filled with line testing from 80 to 130 lbs.

You need a big 10/0 to 16/0 hook with a long wire leader on the end of your line. This can be baited with almost any good-sized fish, but the bloody, oily ones such as menhaden, bluefish, mackerel, false albacore, and bonito are best. The big problem in shark fishing from shore or piers is getting the bait out away from land into deeper water. Here you can employ an inflated balloon or a plastic container or a big piece of cork or styrofoam to take the bait in a wind or tide. However, the surest way is to have someone in a boat take the bait and line out into deeper water.

You may have to wait a long time for a bite, but once you hook a big shark from shore or from a jetty or pier you'll have plenty of sport.

BARRACUDA ON PLUGS

Barracuda provide excellent sport, especially on light tackle, and one of the most thrilling and exciting ways to catch them is by casting a top-water or surface plug. Such plugs work best in the shallow, inshore waters on flats and along mangrove shores. When you see a barracuda, cast your plug 10 to 15 ft. beyond it and retrieve your plug in a fast, erratic action so that it passes a few feet in front of the 'cuda. Avoid casting too close to the fish, because this will spook it. And long casts will bring more strikes on the clear-water, shallow flats than short casts.

BIG FISH ON SMALL TACKLE

When Frank Oblak of Fort Lauderdale tried some jigging around Elliot Key, Florida, he was using a light spinning rod, small spinning reel filled with 4-lb.-test monofilament line. Suddenly he got a terrific strike and something big took off for the depths. After chasing the fish for 15 mi. and a battle lasting over 2 hrs., he finally got it close to the boat where it could be gaffed. It was an African pompano, which later weighed in at 23¼ lbs.! Anyone who has caught other members of the jack and pompano family knows what a great light-tackle catch this was.

PAINT YOUR SINKERS

Anglers fishing for flounders have found that they will attract and catch more fish if they paint their sinkers red. Red nail polish or lacquer is good for this. The same thing can be done when fishing for other fish in salt water, and here you can try brighter colors such as white, yellow, orange, or silver on your sinkers. Then when you raise and quickly lower your sinker it will flash and shine and attract fish to the scene. Then they will see the bait above the sinker and grab it.

THE FISH THAT FISHES

The angler fish is an accomplished fish catcher, as its name implies. It has a long dorsal spine for a fishing rod, and on the end is a permanent wormlike tissue that acts as the bait. When a small fish is attracted by this bait, it comes close to the angler's huge mouth, which suddenly opens wide and engulfs the unsuspecting prey. One deep-sea angler fish that lives in the dark depths even has such a lure or bait equipped with tiny hooks, and it is lit up to attract the smaller fish!

FISHWELLS UNLIMITED

This company makes fishwells that have a double wall, are easily maintained, corrosion-proof, porcelainlike, and have gleaming molded Fiberglas with a polyurethane foam core for triple insulation. The lids are handcrafted solid teakwood, with a clear, water-repellent Marine coating that brings out the wood beauty and protects from stains. The fastenings are all marine hardware. The ¾-in. drains can easily be adapted with a water-circulating pump, so the fishwell can accommodate live bait. The fishwells come in 36-in., 38-in., 44-in., 48-in., 60-in., and 64-in. lengths. They make two types: one with a lid hinged in the middle and that opens from either side, and another that opens from the front with the hinge in the back.

They also make dunnage boxes, baitwells, deck boxes, combination seats and fishwells, teak rod holders, tool racks, and deck chocks. They will also build a fishwell or baitwell to suit your special needs, and if you send in the dimensions and specifications, they will quote a price. For their folder showing these fishwells and boxes write to:
Fishwells Unlimited
4228 N.E. 6th Ave.
Fort Lauderdale, Fla. 33308

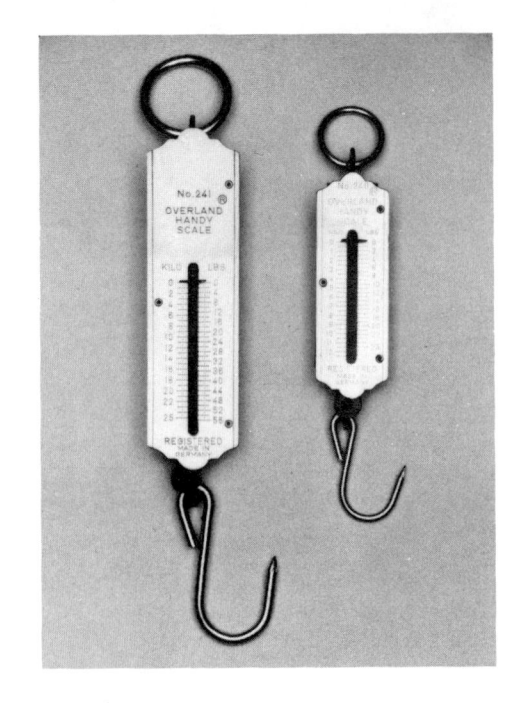

FISHERMAN'S FRIEND SCALES

The Overland Fisherman's Friend scales are designed primarily for weighing fish, but can be used to weigh almost anything. The hand scales come in 25-, 50-, and 100-lb. models and show the weights in pounds and kilos. For more information write to:
Syl-Mark Enterprises
P.O. Box 806
Northbridge, Calif. 91324

NEW GUIDE TO SALT-WATER FISHING

This is an eighty-page softcover book by Milt Rosko on how to fish in salt water for most of the species found along our coasts. He covers the salt-water fishing tackle used; the lures, baits, and rigs needed; and methods such as casting, trolling, chumming, and bottom fishing. The *New Guide to Salt-water Fishing* is one of the titles in the Lowrance Expert Anglers Collection and sells for $2.00. It is published by:
Lowrance Electronics, Inc.
12000 E. Skelly Dr.
Tulsa, Okla. 74128

FLY FISHING IN SALT WATER

Fly Fishing in Salt Water by Lefty Kreh is an up-to-date, complete guide to this growing sport practiced in bays, sounds, tidal rivers, inlets, surf, and even offshore. The name Lefty Kreh is known to most salt-water anglers as a man who is a real pro in all branches of salt-water fishing. But Lefty is partial to fly fishing, and his book covers everything you need to know to take part in this sporty method for all kinds of fish up to the sailfish and marlin. *Fly Fishing in Salt Water* sells for $9.95 and is published by:

Crown Publishers, Inc.
419 Park Ave. S.
New York, N.Y. 10016

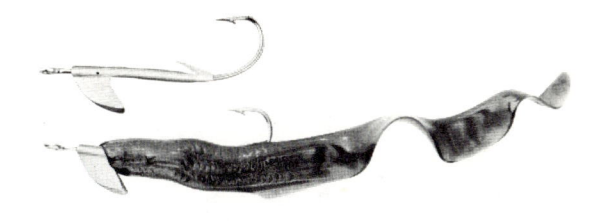

MEAN-O-EEL

The Mean-O-Eel is a new large-sized plastic eel designed for casting or trolling. It has a special plastic formula developed to resist throwing off when casting. The extralong shanked hook rides in the strike zone for surer hooking power on strikes. The weighted stabilizer head maintains perfect action trolling and retrieving. The lure comes in two sizes: an 8-in. body with 6/0 hook and weighing 1½ ozs., and a 10-in. body with a 9/0 hook and weighing 2½ ozs. The lure comes in seven colors, and replacement tails are available. The Mean-O-Eel can be used for striped bass, bluefish, snook, tarpon, cobia, and other salt-water fish. For more information write to:

Cordell Tackle, Inc.
P.O. Box 2020
Hot Springs, Ark. 71901

LOCATING POMPANO

Look for pompano in inlets or rivers entering the ocean. Good spots to fish here are the mouths of such waterways where waves are strong enough to create a surf to wash out the crabs, sand bugs, and other crustaceans the pompano feed on. Another good spot to fish for the pomps in the surf is where the waves crash and break over a sandbar and into a trough. Here pompano will be feeding along the inner edge or dropoff along the sandbar.

HOOKING PERMIT

Permit are never easy to entice to a hook, either with bait or lures. You'll usually hook more permit if you cast to a group or small school of fish rather than a single fish. A lone fish can take its time and be cautious and wary. But in a group or school there is competition as each fish tries to beat the other one to a bait or lure. Permit are usually more plentiful and tend to travel in groups more in deeper water around sunken wrecks than on the shallow flats.

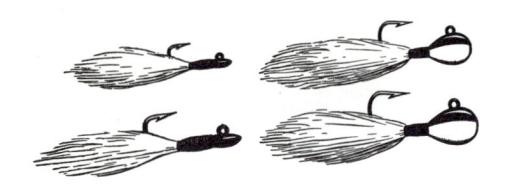

BILL UPPERMAN BUCKTAILS

Bill Upperman was one of the first to make jigs for freshwater and salt-water fishing. Their red-and-white flathead bucktail has been used for striped bass and other salt-water fish for many years. Their bucktails come in eight different sizes, from the small 1/13-oz. No. 4 hook model up to the 2-oz. 8/0 hook size. Besides red and white you can also get these bucktails in all-white, all-yellow, and all-black. For more information write to:
Bill Upperman
P.O. Box 1428
Atlantic City, N.J. 08404

OREGON SALT-WATER FISHING GUIDE

The *Oregon Salt-water Fishing Guide* is a 204-page book that is filled with practical how-to articles, pictures, charts, maps, and diagrams outlining specific techniques for catching and preparing salmon and bottom fish. There is also an article on striped bass fishing. The book contains full-color pictures of 51 species of fish most commonly caught from northwestern coastal waters. A 32-page, 2-color section details Oregon's 15 major salmon and bottom fish areas, from the Columbia's mouth to the Chetco River near the California border. Other highlights of the book include chapters on fishing methods, gear, cutting bait, cleaning, preparing and cooking fish, surf fishing, razor clam digging, and how to prepare salmon eggs for bait fishing. The book sells for $3.95 and is published by:
Stan Jones Publishing Co.
3421 E. Mercer St.
Seattle, Wash. 98112

BIG PERMIT ON LIGHT LINE

Mary Bartz was fishing with Captain Steve Huff on his Sea Ducer off Key West, Florida, with a light spinning outfit and 6-lb.-test line on her Orvis spinning reel. Suddenly the captain spotted a big permit, and Mary cast her small crab bait toward the fish. The permit inhaled the crab, and when Mary set the hook, the shallow water exploded and the fish headed straight for the boat. He stopped two feet from the boat, then turned suddenly and made a long, screeching run toward deep water. The fight continued for another 17 min. before the fish could be gaffed. The permit weighed 32½ lbs. and set records for 6-lb. line in the IGFA Women's Division and the IGFA 6-lb.-line class.

SPORTY CATFISH

Although most catfish are caught in fresh water, there are two kinds found in southern salt waters that can also be caught on rod and reel. The first one is the regular sea catfish, and this one is considered a pest and not much as sport or food. The other one, called the "Gafftopsail catfish," is a much more desirable species. It is found in bays, sounds, passes, along beaches, and in tidal rivers from the Carolinas south to Florida and the Gulf of Mexico. It can be caught on a wide variety of baits such as shrimp, small baitfish, and strips or chunks cut from larger fish. It will also hit lures such as underwater plugs, jigs, and metal lures. It puts up a tough fight and makes excellent eating.

SKIMMAR SEA SPORT BOAT

The Skimmar 15-ft. Sea Sport is a versatile runabout rated for a 55-hp. outboard, but a 40 is really all you need to scoot in a hurry to where the fish are. The Sea Sport has all the stability you could ask for in a 15-ft. boat. It's a safe working platform for grown men, and its advanced trihull wing design keeps its stability in tight, high-speed turns. It's a roomy, handy boat not only for fishing but also for many other uses. It is both wider and deeper than other trihulls that cost a lot more than the $1,195 asked for this boat with a console, seat, and steering. Without this console and seat and steering it sells for $995. For a color brochure showing this and other boats they make write to:

Aero-Nautical, Inc.
154 Prospect St.
Greenwich, Conn. 06830

GUDEBROD ROD FINISH

The Gudebrod Company has developed their "Hard 'n Fast" one-coat rod finish for modern fishing rods to use when building a new rod or when repairing or maintaining an old one. The luxurious, super-hard gloss finish gives a rod that custom look and holds the thread wrap and guides secure for years. It also gives the rod added strength when applied over the entire blank. Only one coat is required. The two-part mix develops just the right consistency for easy application with a natural hair brush. It can be applied in a matter of minutes and sets up fast, drying in 5 to 7 hrs. and reaching maximum hardness in 36 hrs. For more information write to:
Gudebrod Fishing Tackle
12 S. 12th St.
Philadelphia, Pa. 19107

ROD CADDY

This company makes a variety of rod cases to protect and carry freshwater and saltwater fishing rods. They have slim cases for one- or two-fly or spinning rods and extra-wide cases that hold eight to ten freshwater rods or four salt-water rods. Many of their cases are adjustable and can be extended up to 65 or 72 in. The cases are made from plastic or extraheavy fiber construction with polycoated exterior. For more information write to:
Rod Caddy Corp.
920 W. Cullerton St.
Chicago, Ill. 60608

ANGLER'S PAL ROD HOLDER

This rod holder is an adjustable type that features a wide variety of possible positions. It has a universal ball-locking device with "select position" locking knob and a removable base mount. A single screw easily removes the unit from the base for storage or to interchange mounts. The rod holder is also available with a permanent mount. It comes in two sizes: 7¾ in. deep and 10 in. deep. For more information write to:
Bystrom Bros.
2200 Snelling Ave., S.
Minneapolis, Minn. 55404

TRI-FIN LURES

The Tri-Fin Fishing Tackle Mfg. Corp. makes a large variety of tube and jig lures for salt-water fishing. Their Whiptail is very popular for weakfish, striped bass, and bluefish. It comes in weights from ⅛ oz. up to 3 ozs. in several colors. Their eel worm, eels, and rip eels have metal action heads and can be used in casting and trolling for striped bass and bluefish. Their twist tube lures come in short and long models from 5½ in. up to 18 in. Their Jig 'N Squid comes in various sizes and weights from ½ oz. up to 6 ozs. The Rip Whip comes in 2, 3, and 6 ozs. Most of these lures have tails or bodies of durable latex rubber. For more information write to:
Tri-Fin Fishing Tackle Mfg. Corp.
P.O. Box 80
Smithtown, N.Y. 11787

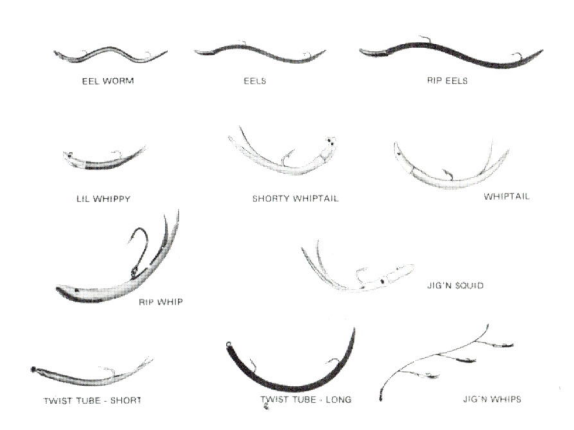

JUNIOR TARPON CHAMP

Ray Dee, who is only 14 yrs. old, has probably caught more tarpon, including big ones, than many anglers twice or three times his age. He started fishing only four years ago and caught 38 tarpon in a recent year, including a 101-lb. tarpon. In 1974 he caught a 134-lb. fish, and his latest catch was a 150-lb. tarpon, which he hooked in the Manatee River in Florida. It took 1½ hrs. to subdue this big silver king.

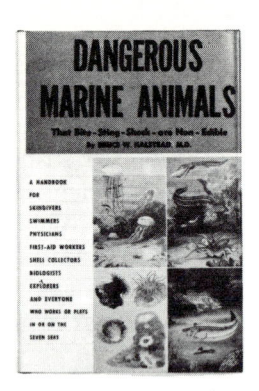

DANGEROUS MARINE ANIMALS

The book *Dangerous Marine Animals* by Bruce W. Halstead has been out for quite some time now, but it keeps on selling because it warns of the marine animals that bite, shock, sting, or are poisonous to eat. It is a valuable handbook for fishermen, skin divers, boaters, shell collectors, explorers, and everyone else who works or plays in or on the seven seas. It deals with such animals and fish as sharks, stingrays, barracuda, moray eels, sea snakes, scorpion fishes, puffers, and many others. It tells how to identify them, how to avoid them, how to treat their bites or poisons, and other information and precautions to take when exposed to their dangers. *Dangerous Marine Animals* sells for $5.00 and is published by:
Cornell Maritime Press, Inc.
P.O. Box 109
Cambridge, Md. 21613

TOUGH TUNA

When you tackle the big, tough bluefin tuna, you are really in for thrills and the unexpected. One angler hooked a giant tuna and fought it all night off Massachusetts. After 14 hrs. the rod broke and the line parted. But he got off easy compared to one of the longest battles with a fish on record. It happened in the early days of tuna fishing off Nova Scotia. A big tuna hit and got hooked on a Monday near Liverpool. The big 792-lb. tuna was finally boated on Thursday, 62 hrs. later! Everybody on board the yacht was exhausted taking turns fighting the fish, and the tuna had hauled the craft around for 200 mi.

TRIPLE CATCH

Dick Davis of the city of Portland, Oregon, was fishing in Hawaiian waters when he hooked and boated a 748-lb. marlin during a fishing tournament. But he had the hard luck to hook the fish after the stop-fishing signal, and his catch was disqualified for the contest. Then when he opened up the marlin he found a 65-lb. tuna inside, and the tuna had a 5-lb. bonito in its gullet!

CAMOUFLAGED FISH

Most fish change color to match the water, the bottom, or the surroundings. Thus if the water and bottom are dark, the fish tend to be darker in color. If the water is clear and the bottom is light, the overall body color of a fish will also be light. Some fish such as fluke or flounders will even show light and dark spots on their backs when lying on a pebble or gravel bottom.

HELEN-S VI PARTY BOAT

There are many "head" boats or "party" boats or "drift" boats along our coasts that take people out for a half-day or full day's fishing. But the Helen-S VI, located at Pompano Beach in Florida, is unusual in that it makes from three- to seven-day trips to the Bahamas, where all kinds of fish such as grouper, snappers, yellowtail, amberjack, tuna, and even wahoo are caught. They fish off Walker's Cay, Great Harbor, and Bimini, and the price includes hotel rooms, meals, and tackle and bait during the entire period. For information and schedules of the trips and prices write to:

Helen-S Fleet
Hillsboro Inlet (A1A)
Pompano Beach, Fla. 33062

NATIONAL COALITION FOR MARINE CONSERVATION

The National Coalition for Marine Conservation is an organization committed to the conservation of oceanic gamefish. They feel that unless immediate action is taken, gamefish stocks the world around are going to continue to melt away, so that sportfishing for many species will stop in the near future. Already there are once-prolific fishing grounds that no longer produce, and there are species in danger of possible extinction. The Coalition is striving to reverse these trends through political action in order to assure our grandchildren the kind of fishing that we remember in the best of the Good Old Days!

Some of the problems that concern this organization include protection of depleted species such as Atlantic salmon, blue marlin, striped marlin, swordfish, white marlin, tuna, striped bass, white sea bass, mako shark, and others. They are also concerned about pollution, oil spills, sewerage, fisheries management, coastal zone management, and marine biological research.

The Coalition publishes a monthly newsletter called *Right Rigger,* and the members of the organization receive a subscription to this publication. There are individual and club and company memberships open to this organization. For an application blank or more information write to:

National Coalition for Marine Conservation
P.O. Box 5131
Savannah, Ga. 31403

THE COMPLETE GUIDE TO SALT AND FRESH WATER FISHING EQUIPMENT

Bill Wisner's buying guide is an all-in-one package for fishermen throughout the country. Beginning with the rudiments of salt-water and freshwater fishing, the guide outlines basic angling methods and types and care of tackle and lures. Invaluable salt-water and freshwater tackle "Show Room" chapters describe what to look for when you buy, and picture in detail representative tackle available today. A special section on accessories includes the latest fishing fashions, electronic aids, and boat gear, all fully illustrated along with prices. The book sells for $10 and is published by:
E. P. Dutton & Co., Inc.
201 Park Ave. S.
New York, N.Y. 10003

MAKE-A-MOLD KIT

Now you can make your own molds for fishing lures with a revolutionary new silicone rubber mold kit. You can duplicate existing jigs and other metal lures or make new patterns and designs and turn out dozens and hundreds of lures at a fraction of the cost of store-bought ones. With this mold you simply place the lure to be duplicated in the supplied canister and pour in the silicone rubber. Shortly after, you have a mold ready to take lead. The complete kit will make three molds, which can be used over and over. The complete kit sells for $14.95 and is sold by:
**Fibber McGee's Closet
P.O. Box 88
Needham, Mass. 02192**

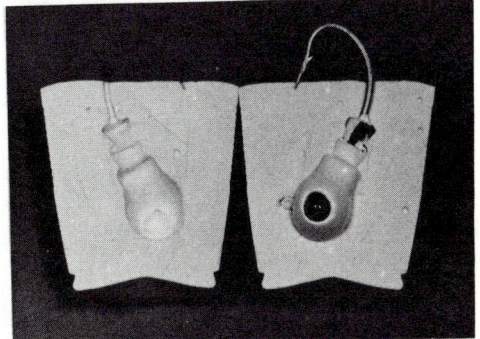

SALT-WATER FLY-FISHING HANDBOOK

The *Salt-Water Fly-Fishing Handbook* was written by Sam Nix, who has been a dedicated fly fisherman for over sixty years. In this book he tells in detail all he knows about the challenging sport of tackling big fish on fly tackle. He covers fly rods, lines, reels, leaders, and other equipment needed to get started in salt-water fly fishing. He names his favorite flies for salt-water fishing and tells you how to tie them. The author covers salt-water fly fishing from shore, jetties, and boats. He also gives the best spots along the West Coast, Florida, and in Mexico where you can catch fish with a fly rod. The book sells for $6.95 and is published by:
**Doubleday & Co., Inc.
501 Franklin Ave.
Garden City, N.Y. 11530**

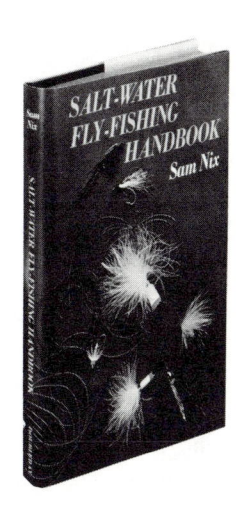

TOURNAMENT GIN POLES

The Tournament gin poles are made of stainless steel and of rugged construction throughout for easy boating of big-game fish. They have a Swing-out Arm bracket, retainer ring, and base plate, all constructed of cast bronze with chrome plating. The unit comes complete with rugged nylon pulleys and nylon rope. The standard pole sizes are 7 ft. and 10 ft. in length, but the poles are available in longer lengths upon request. This company also makes fighting and fishing chairs, outriggers, rod holders, a fishing harness, and various marine hardware products for boats. For their catalog showing the gin pole and the other products write to:
Tournament Marine Products
Commerce & Jackson Dr.
Cranford, N.J. 07016

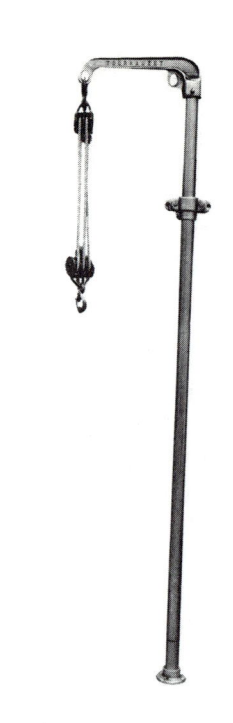

TRI-FIN REVERSE SQUID AND JIGS

Tri-Fin has come out with their new Jig 'N Tails, which are hair jigs that have brilliant coloration and no ties or tapes. There are two types: a slim-line flat-bottom jig and a pogyhead jig. They come in various weights, from ¼ oz. to 3 ozs., and in several colors.

Their Reverse Squid is an old lure that has been revived and improved and has brilliant coloration with a unique design so that it is more durable. It has rubber tentacles with a lifelike squid head and two hooks. It comes in 1-oz. and 3-oz. weights.

Their other lure is the Silverfish, which can be used like a diamond jig but which has a swimming action. It has a silver metal body and a rubber split tail. It can be cast or trolled or jigged and comes in 2-oz. and 3-oz. weights. For more information about these lures write to:
Tri-Fin Fishing Tackle Mfg. Corp.
P.O. Box 80
Smithtown, N.Y. 11787

MFG'S FISHIN' CAPRICE 19

For fishermen after the big ones, MFG's Fishin' Caprice 19 is the boat to consider. An outboard model rated up to 160 hp., the Fishin' Caprice 19 features a Fiberglas command console, upholstered helmsman swivel fishing chairs, rod racks, a raised Fiberglas forward casting platform with storage underneath, two chrome rod holders, and a Fiberglas fish box.

Other standard features include a bilge pump, cockpit courtesy light, self-bailing cockpit, bow and stern lights with fuse and three-position switch, chrome bow and stern cleats, bow lifting ring, stainless-steel bow rail, bow and stern eyes, mechanical steering, foamed-in-place flotation, and a built-in 36-gal. fuel tank.

Optional equipment includes a suntop, stainless-steel console grabrail, tinted windshield, and a reversible-back Fiberglas bench seat with storage. The Fishin' Caprice 19 has an 18-ft., 10-in. centerline, a 90-in. beam, and weighs approximately 1,500 lbs. For more information write to:
MFG Boat Co.
55 4th Ave.
Union City, Pa. 16438

BLUEWATER PRO 610 FLASHER-GRAPH

This Lowrance Flasher-Graph was designed for fish locating and navigating deep inland and oceanic waters. Use the Flasher alone for excellent signals of very deep targets. Switch on the Graph Recorder for detail printout of fish, structure, bottom conditions, and topography. The Flasher system registers on three scales: 0 to 60 ft., 0 to 180 ft., and 60 fath. (360 ft.). The Graph records on six ranges: 0 to 60 ft., 60 to 120 ft., 120 to 180 ft., 0 to 20 fath., 20 to 40 fath., and 40 to 60 fath. The unit offers a 24-in.-per-hr. printout for low-speed cruising and scouting plus an exclusive 144-in.-per-hr. printout for the high-speed fisherman. Completed printouts are automatically rolled and stored inside a case. It includes heavy-duty high-speed transducer, 25-ft. double-shielded cable, extra stylus, two rolls of graph paper, and a foul-weather cover. For a brochure or more information write to:
Lowrance Electronics, Inc.
12000 E. Skelly Dr.
Tulsa, Okla. 74128

DIAMOND RATTLESUB

This is a torpedo-shaped-type plug that can be either made to work fast and kick up a commotion on the surface, or reeled and worked slower just below the surface. It imitates a small mullet or similar baitfish. It has a sound chamber with a rattle. It has a plastic body, nickel-plated hardware, and comes in four colors and two sizes—½ oz. and ¾ oz. For their catalog showing this and other lures write to:
Strader Tackle, Inc.
P.O. Box 708
Havana, Fla. 32333

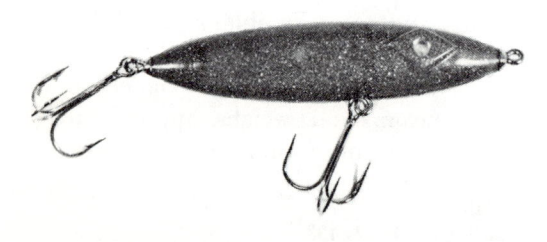

GLAS-GARD EYEGLASS HOLDER

This Glas-Gard eyeglass holder is just the thing for the active fisherman to keep his sunglasses or regular glasses in place when engaged in his favorite pastime. Of course, it is also handy for any person who takes part in watersports or any other sports. But fishermen are always losing sunglasses or regular glasses when they lean over the side to fight or gaff a fish. With this eyeglass holder you can move around and bend over as much as you want and the glasses will stay in place. For more information write to:
Seron Mfg. Co.
254 Republic Ave.
Joliet, Ill 60435

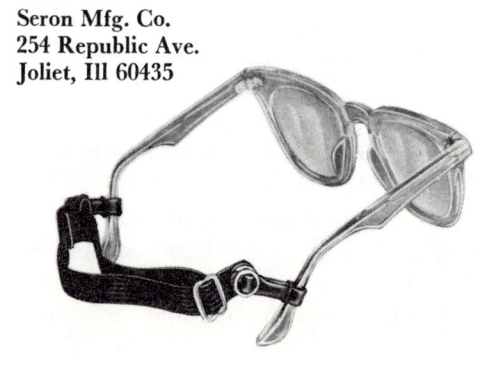

SURF FISHING WITH METAL LURES

There is an art to using metal squids, Hopkins lures, and other metal lures in the surf that comes only with plenty of practice. You have to make these lures look alive and irresistible to the fish. If you just cast out and reel in at a steady speed you may catch a few fish, but you'll get more if you vary your reeling and try different speeds. When surf fishing you have to contend with winds, currents, waves, and the backwash or undertow, which can help or hinder the action of a metal lure.

Take waves, for example, which can be big and strong and can toss your metal lure around so that it loses much of its effectiveness. Here the trick is to wait for a wave to curl over or break and then cast behind it. Then your line will be taut and the metal lure will have plenty of action. But if you cast in front of an incoming wave it will push your lure toward you faster than you can take up the slack line, and this will kill the action of the lure.

After a wave passes and the water rushes back to sea, it pulls on your lure. Then you slow down your reeling, because if you reel too fast the lure will spin or rise to the surface.

Winds can also affect the action of your metal lures, especially those that blow strong from either side and create a big "belly" in your line. Then you can't feel a strike, and you find it difficult to set the hook in a fish that does hit. And if you try to reel fast to take up the slack, the lure will rise to the top and skate on the surface of the water. When this happens try holding your rod tip low to keep most of the line in the water.

In rocky areas with shallow water, you can foul your metal lures in the rocks and weeds. Here you have to start reeling in fast as soon as the lure hits the water and keep reeling fast all the way in.

But when fishing from jetties or breakwaters, you can reel in slower and hold your rod tip down, almost touching the water. And keep your lure working right up to the rocks, because fish such as striped bass have a habit of following a lure and then hitting just before it disappears in the wash alongside the rocks.

When the water is clean and clear, reel your metal lures faster. When it is dirty or discolored, reel slower. Reel slower at dusk and daybreak and at night.

STRIPERS LIKE WHITE WATER

When fishing along rocky shores such as those found at Montauk, New York, in Rhode Island, and in parts of Massachusetts and Maine, you'll catch more striped bass by casting your lure into the white patches or wash around rocks and boulders and in the gullies and small coves along shore. It is surprising how a little white water will attract and hold stripers along such rocky shores. If you see such a small pocket or patch of white water, cast your lure just beyond it and reel it through the wash.

ROCK-AWAY SKIFF-TYPE OUTRIGGER

The Rock-Away skiff-type outriggers are compact and easily handled and are adjustable through 180 degrees fore and aft for trolling, cruising, and passing under bridges. Outboard trolling position is preset at 45 degrees, with an automatic locking cam when returned to a vertical position. They are made in four sizes for boats from 34 ft. to the smallest. They are solid cast bronze, machined, and heavily chrome-plated. For their catalog or more information about these and other outriggers, fighting and fishing chairs, rod holders, and other marine equipment write to:
Rock-Away Sport Fishing Equipment Co.
Yale and Myrtle Aves.
Morton, Pa. 19070

GRIZZLY LURES

This company makes many spoons, plugs, spinners, and other lures, including the well-known Andy Reeker spoon, which has been used for more than 50 yrs. for salmon along the Pacific Coast. It is now popular with freshwater fishermen trolling for coho salmon in the Great Lakes and other waters where these fish have been introduced. They also make the Spooner spoon, which has the same action as the Andy Reeker but comes with a treble hook instead of a single hook. They also make dodgers, plugs, spinners, and rudders. For a catalog showing their complete line of lures write to:
Grizzly, Inc.
P.O. Box 649
Vancouver, Wash. 98660

SEA TROUT IN THE SURF

You can often have good fishing for sea trout or southern weakfish in the surf and along the beaches of Virginia to Florida and the Gulf of Mexico. Look for deep sloughs or troughs that average at least 6 ft. of water. If the trough has deep water even at low tide, the sea trout will remain in it and you can have good fishing even during dead low water.

SNOOK FROM A BEACH

Snook often appear along sandy beaches of Florida's Gulf Coast and cruise up and down along the shoreline. Here you can cast a lure well ahead of the fish and a short distance beyond it and work it closer as the fish approaches. If you are using a floating plug, let it lie in the fish's path and then twitch it as the snook moves closer and spots it.

ROYAL RED BALL WADERS

Royal Red Ball makes two fishing waders for freshwater and salt-water fishermen. One is the McGinty Sportster Wader and the other is the Cahill Master Wader. Both have tops of the new Tuff-Guard material, which is a woven, nylon fabric bonded to rubber. It will not tear and is extremely high in snag and puncture resistance. When worn, Tuff-Guard feels more flexible and lightweight than previous all-rubber tops. The Cahill Master Wader is quick-drying and has a special inside/outside pouch. It has extra suspender buttons and extra belt loops for short men. It is reinforced in the crotch seams and is 100 per cent waterproof. For their catalog or more information about these waders and other hip boots and clothing they make for fishermen write to:

Royal Red Ball
8530 Page Ave.
St. Louis, Mo. 63114

BAIT FOR BIG WEAKFISH

An excellent bait for big weakfish is a live snapper (small bluefish) from 6 to 8 in. long. You can hook the snapper with a 2/0 treble hook. Two of the hooks are run through the upper jaw and the other one through the lower jaw. The live snapper can then be let out from an anchored or drifting boat. Usually no weight is needed, but if the current or tide is strong you can add a clincher sinker or egg sinker a few feet above the hook to get the snapper down deep enough.

BONITO AND ALBACORE ON FLIES

You can catch bonito and albacore on flies if you first chum with live baitfish such as anchovies, sardines, herring or pilchards to bring the school of fish up to the boat. Then you can cast a streamer or bucktail fly with a silver body or tinsel or Mylar to the feeding fish.

FAITHFUL FISH

No human husband can be more faithful to his wife than the deep-sea angler fish. This tiny, devoted male grasps the much larger female with its jaws somewhere along the body and never lets go. As time passes his skin fuses with her skin and her blood vessels connect with his blood vessels. True, he becomes more or less of a parasite. But the female angler fish is assured of a mate for life, with no divorce possible. When the female fish dies, the male dies with her!

TWO SHARKS ON ONE LINE

An angler fishing at Cox's Ledge from a party boat sailing out of Montauk, New York, had a bite and then a tough time bringing the fish in. When he got it near the surface he found he had two 100-lb. blue sharks on the same line. It seems that both sharks went after the same piece of bait. One got the hook and the other got tangled up in the line. Both sharks were gaffed and boated.

BIG COD

Cod in the old days reached big sizes, and during the 1800s many cod over 100 lbs. were caught by commercial fishermen. The heaviest cod on record is a 211½-lb. fish caught on a line trawl off Massachusetts in 1895. Since then with overfishing by many nations, the size of the cod caught has diminished. But sports fishermen still catch many cod over 50 lbs. The present IGFA rod and reel record is a 98-lb., 12-oz. cod caught by Alphonse Bielevich on June 8, 1969, at the Isle of Shoals off New Hamsphire.

SWEETEN THE JIG

When salt-water fish aren't hitting a plain jig, try adding a strip of squid or fish to the hook. Or take half of a small shrimp and put that on the hook. This usually works better than the unadorned jig, and you can reel and bounce it along the bottom even slower than the plain jig and catch not only gamefish but many "bottom" species.

BERKLEY SALT-WATER RIGS

These salt-water rigs are made in many types and lengths and with one or two droppers. They have the eyes for the hooks and snaps for the sinkers, and after the snelled hooks are added they are ready to use. The rigs are made from stainless-steel wire or nylon and can be used for many salt-water species. They are sold in most coastal fishing tackle shops. For more information you can write to:

Berkley and Co.
Spirit Lake, Ia. 51360

PIONEER TACKLE CO.

This company has a Powermaster extended-reel handle, which fits most of the popular Penn fishing reels. They come in two models and will give you a longer handle on many reels made by Penn. They also sell two spoon-type and jigging-type lures —one called the Jerry Jig, which comes in 4-in. and 6-in. lengths and weights from 1 oz. to 7½ ozs. This comes in chrome, red and white, blue and white, and yellow and green. And they have another spoon called the Hoowink, which comes in weights of 1¾ ozs. and 2¾ ozs. In addition to a flash, this lure also gives off a vibration or sound that attracts fish. For more information about the extended-reel handle or the lures write to:

Pioneer Tackle Co.
P.O. Box 1224
Reseda, Calif. 91335

AMERICAN LITTORAL SOCIETY

The American Littoral Society encourages the underwater study of shore life by direct observation of the occurrence and ways of fishes and other marine animals. They keep records of their observations and studies and publish these in their *Underwater Naturalist*. They also publish special booklets and newsletters with brief, up-to-date notes on the state of the ocean's edge and what's happening to affect it, plus information on marine science education and careers. Littoral Society members also make field trips, which are guided by qualified naturalists. Members can also participate in the Littoral Society's active volunteer fish-tagging program. The Society provides fish tags at cost and instructions on how to tag fish. It keeps records of all tagging information, records that inform fish taggers where their fish have been and how much they have grown. This is published in their magazine and made available to professional marine biologists. Individual membership in the Littoral Society is $10 a year, and they also have contributing, sustaining, supporting, and donor memberships. For more information write to:

American Littoral Society
Sandy Hook
Highlands, N.J. 07732

SETTING THE DRAG

There's a quick way to set your drag with fairly light tackle such as spinning, bait-casting, surf, and conventional tackle. All you do is rig your rod and string your fishing line through the guides. Then tighten your drag so that it doesn't slip at all. Next tie the end of your fishing line to a stationary object such as a tree, pole, or other solid support. Now raise your rod and pull back so that it assumes its maximum power bend—as far as it will go. Then back off your drag setting until the line just starts to slip off the reel while the rod tip is still bent to its maximum curve. Now you are ready to fish, and your drag setting will be safe enough to set the hook and let the fish run with the maximum tension being applied. Of course, if the fish runs off a lot of line, you should loosen the drag a bit.

STALKING REDFISH

The smaller channel bass called "redfish" in the South make a good substitute for bonefish when they are found feeding on the flats. They may not make long runs, but they put up a stubborn fight. They are also easier to catch, since they are nearsighted and are not as wary as the bones. With bonefish and permit you have to make your first cast count, but with redfish you usually get another chance to cast if the fish fails to see the lure or splash the first time. And you do have to cast close to a redfish and almost hit it on the nose to make it see your lure or bait.

TOUGH-LUCK SWORDFISH

Walter Bronston, Jr., of Mamaroneck, New York, had been fishing in tournaments for nine years without any luck. Finally, in his tenth year, he hooked a big swordfish that was successfully boated and later weighed at 455 lbs. by tournament officials. He had caught the biggest fish in the tournament, but then the judges found out that the fish had been hooked five minutes before the official start of the contest, and the big fish was disqualified!

PACIFIC SHEEPSHEAD

The Pacific sheepshead is usually found around rocks or over rocky bottoms, where it feeds on shellfish and crustaceans. It will take such baits as shrimp, crabs, lobster, mussels, and clams. You need fairly heavy tackle for this fish because it has a tough mouth and you have to set the hook hard. And as soon as the fish is hooked it has to be held or turned away from crevices or rocks toward which it will try to plunge and foul your line.

SNOOK HANGOUT

Look for snook at the mouths of small feeder or tributary streams and creeks, especially during an outgoing tide. Small baitfish, shrimp, crabs, and other marine foods that have been up these small streams during high tide start to leave them or get washed out when the tide drops, and snook wait for the tidbits at the creekmouths.

SUNSHINE POPPER PLUG

The Sunshine Popper plug is a plastic popping and darting plug with a struggling action when worked on top of the water that infuriates the killer instinct in striped bass, bluefish, and other fish. It has a twisting, struggling, crippled baitfish action that attracts and triggers stripers and blues to strike again and again. It brings up fish even on days when other lures don't work or when conditions aren't quite right. The plug is 5¼ in. long and weighs 1½ ozs. It has 3X strong Mustad Treble hooks firmly held in the body of the lure for those big fish that may hit. It comes in red, amber, and silver flash finishes and sells for $2.19 each. This company also sells other saltwater fishing tackle by mail and issues a catalog for $.25. For more information about the plug or their other tackle write to:

Ocean State Fishing Supplies, Inc.
P.O. Box 8043
Cranston, R.I. 02920

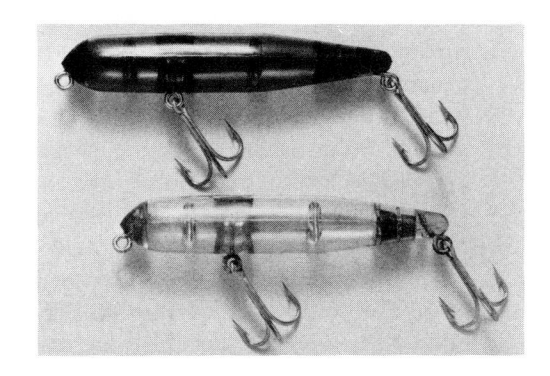

JIGGING RIG

The Alee Jigging Rig consists of three colored (silver, red, and black) teaser tubes rigged in tandem. The effect of this rig is that of a small, helpless band of baitfish swimming together. The method of using such a rig is very simple. A weight (sinker) is snapped on the terminal end, and the entire rig is lowered to the bottom. Then the rig is bounced up and down. It may also be worked to the surface to attract foraging gamefish at other levels. The secret of success with this rig is to keep it moving all the time. It can be fished from boats, bridges, piers, or even slow-trolled. It comes in two types: one with large 5/0 hooks and the other with smaller hooks. This rig can be used for bluefish, pollock, cod, king mackerel, mackerel, whiting, and sea bass. For their catalog showing this rig and other lures they make write to:

Gold Seal Industries, Inc.
P.O. Box 324
South Orange, N.J. 07079

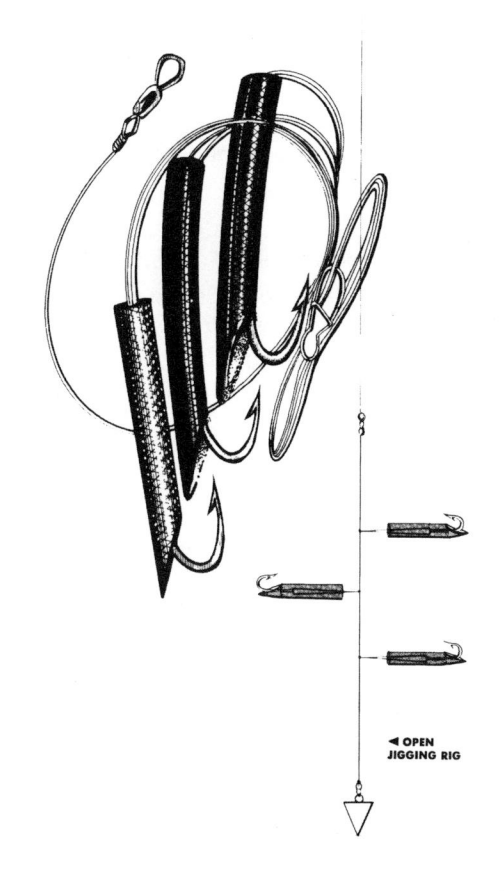

◄ OPEN JIGGING RIG

GRAB A SWORDFISH

Some anglers spend a lifetime trying to catch a swordfish on rod and reel and are still looking for their first one. But three "lucky" fishermen in the Gulf Stream off Fort Lauderdale, Florida, caught a big sword with their bare hands! They were trying out a new 35-ft. Bertram when they spotted what looked like a big "log" ahead of them. It turned out to be a swordfish sunning itself on top of the water. They moved in close to the fish, and one of the men, Greg McIntosh, grabbed the bill. The other men grabbed the fins, and they heaved the swordfish into the boat. Then they pinned the fish to the deck to hold him down while he thrashed, but not too wildly. Later on, when they weighed the swordfish, it went 298 lbs., and they cut it up into steaks and fed themselves and several friends.

SMALL BOY—BIG JEWFISH

Jimmy Lewis, son of Captain Bob Lewis, was fishing off Triumph Reef in Florida with a heavy outfit for big fish. He had a live pinfish on the hook for bait. This was grabbed by a mutton snapper, and Jimmy started to reel both fish in. Suddenly a big jewfish came up and swallowed the pinfish and the mutton snapper and got hooked itself on the 10/0 hook.

It took Jimmy 50 min. to hoist the big jewfish to the boat where it could be gaffed and tied up. When it was weighed later it pulled the scale down to 426 lbs. When Jimmy Lewis made this catch he was only 9 yrs. old and weighed a mere 74 lbs.!

BEST TIME FOR SEA TROUT

Sea trout or southern weakfish will bite most of the day, but the peak fishing periods usually occur at daybreak, dusk, and during the night. This is especially true if you want to catch the bigger "alligator" sea trout. Drifting on the flats or wading a lagoon during the above periods will give you a chance to hook more of these big sea trout. Use small popping and underwater plugs, jigs, and live shrimp under a cork.

MAKE IT A DOUBLE

When two anglers are fishing together, they can often catch more fish if they play on the competitive instincts of fish that travel in groups or schools. If one angler hooks a fish, the second angler should cast his lure or bait near the hooked fish. He will often hook a fish too and make it a double catch. Many fish follow a hooked fish and try to grab the bait or lure in the other fish's mouth. If you cast a lure or bait near the hooked fish, another one will usually grab it.

MAINE FOR THE BIG COD

If you want big codfish the place to go is Maine where giant cod are caught even during the summer months not many miles from shore. And sailing on a party boat or head boat such as those leaving Boothbay Harbor is your best bet if you want to catch a big cod. Here codfish weighing 74½ and 86 lbs. have been caught using big diamond jigs on the end of the line.

PET SPOON

The Pet Spoon made by Tony Accetta & Son has been around for quite a while but keeps on winning awards and honors for the number and size of the fish taken in both fresh and salt water. The assortment ranges from tiny freshwater sizes weighing a fraction of an ounce up to big spoons suitable for striped bass, barracuda, and other large salt-water fish. The Pet Spoon has a lifetime jewelry chrome finish and a hook that is replaceable. The spoons are made in six finishes and come plain or with feathers. For a brochure or more information write to:
Tony Accetta & Son, Inc.
932 Ave. E
Riviera Beach, Fla. 33404

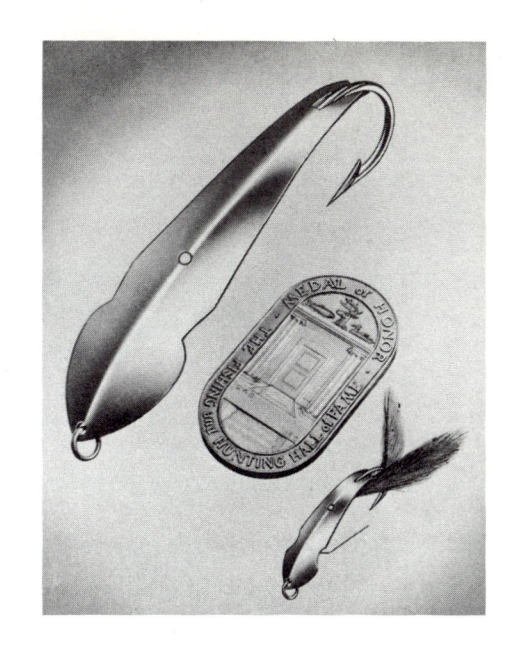

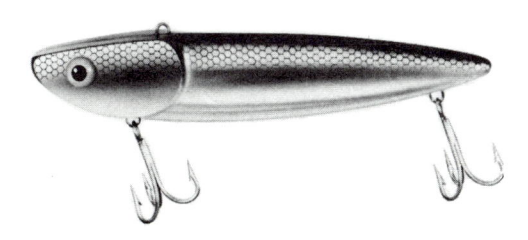

HAMMERHEAD

This salt-water lure called the Hammerhead is made by the Fred Arbogast Company, makers of many other fine freshwater and salt-water lures. It comes in two models; a floating type with a diving, erratic swimming action designed with the serious fisherman in mind, and a sinking one for deep trolling or casting over deep structures, dropoffs, reefs, and holes. It can also be used for casting and jigging deep obstructions. There are two sizes in both lures: a 5½-in.-long, 1-oz. one, and a 7½-in.-long, 2½-oz. one. The lures come in a variety of colors. For more information you can write to:
The Fred Arbogast Co., Inc.
313 W. North St.
Akron, O. 44303

JIG-A-DO SPOONHEAD EEL

The Jig-A-Do Spoonhead Eel is a plastic eel with an action head that makes it swim and look like a live eel. It can be cast or trolled for striped bass, bluefish, snook, and other salt-water species. This eel holds the bluefish world record of 31 lbs., 12 ozs. caught on it. It is rigged with a stainless-steel chain and comes in two sizes: 9 in. weighing 2 ozs., and 12 in. weighing 3¼ ozs. For a catalog or more information about this eel and other plastic lures write to:
Burke Fishing Lures
1969 S. Airport Rd.
Traverse City, Mich. 49684

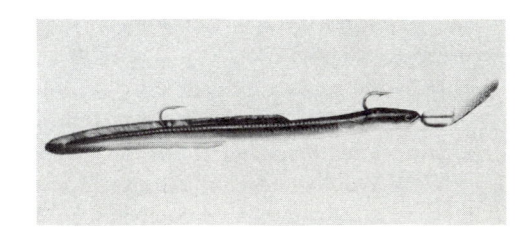

WEAKFISH ARE STRONG

There's nothing "weak" about a weakfish except its mouth, which is paper-thin and apt to tear and rip and have the hook pull out. But when it comes to hitting and taking baits, lures, and fighting, the common or northern weakfish is a real sportfish. They were scarce or even totally absent in many areas but have come on strong in recent years. From Cape Cod to the Carolinas they are running in numbers and good sizes.

Because of their weak mouths, light tackle and thin lines are best for these fish. And always bring a big landing net to haul in the big weaks and even the medium-sized ones. A light, one-handed spinning rod, small spinning reel filled with 6- or 8-lb.-test mono line will serve best. But some anglers like to use a light bay rod or bait-casting-type "popping" rod with reel to match. Here you can use a heavier 15-lb.-test line.

Weakfish will hit many lures such as underwater plugs, metal squids, spoons, and jigs. One of the most effective lures these days is an imitation shrimp jig with a soft, plastic tail. Although weakfish will hit this lure at various depths, it is most effective if allowed to sink to the bottom and is then retrieved slowly with some rod action.

Weakfish will also take natural baits such as sandworms, grass shrimp, edible shrimp, squid, shedder crab, small baitfish, and pieces of fish. These can be drifted out from a boat or bridge without any weight, or you can add a sinker and fish them on the bottom.

So try your skill and luck on weakfish this season. They are found in surf, inlets, bays, sounds, tidal rivers, and creeks, and run best from May to October.

MACKEREL AS BAIT

One of the most common and versatile baits you can use along the Atlantic Coast is the mackerel. Both the small "tinkers" and the bigger "Bostons" can be used. A small, whole mackerel on a hook can be used for fluke, bluefish, small striped bass, and school tuna. Live mackerel are best for the striped bass and school tuna. The larger mackerel can also be used live for big striped bass, giant tuna, marlin, and sharks. Or dead mackerel can be drifted out in a chum slick or trolled behind a boat for the same fish.

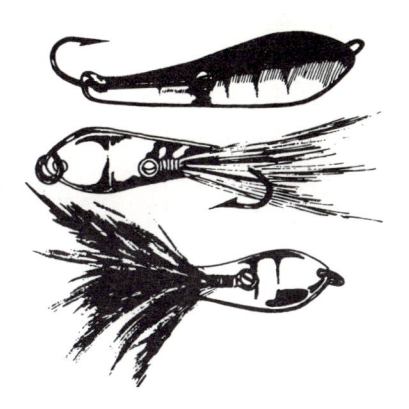

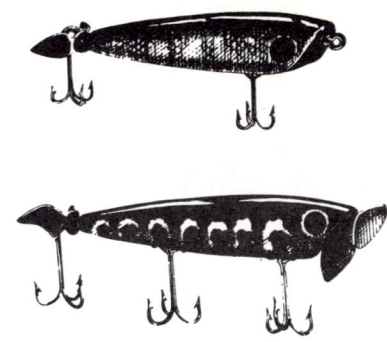

REFLECTO AND DALTON LURES

This company makes the well-known Reflecto spoon, which is used for many saltwater gamefish. They come in many sizes and finishes and colors, either plain or with feathers. They range in hook size from No. 6 to No. 9/0. They are widely used for such fish as striped bass, bluefish, channel bass, tarpon, snook, king mackerel, and barracuda. The other lures they make include the Dalton Special and the Dalton Twist, which are used for large-mouth bass, especially in Florida, but also in other states. They are surface lures that create a lot of fuss and commotion on top, bringing smashing strikes from bass. For a color brochure showing these lures write to:

Marine Metal Products Co., Inc.
1222 Range Ave.
Clearwater, Fla. 33515

MARYLAND SPORT FISHING TOURNAMENT

The Maryland Sport Fishing Tournament has now been running for twelve years and is popular with anglers who fish in the fresh and salt waters of that state. Most of the popular freshwater and salt-water species are eligible if they go over a minimum weight for that particular species. The tournament has a Chesapeake Bay Division and Atlantic Coast Division. The fish must be registered at an "Official Weighing Station," and a registration form must be legibly and completely filled out to be eligible for citations. There is no registration fee. The tournament begins on April 1 and ends on November 30. For more information about this tournament write to:

Bill Perry
Maryland Sport Fishing Tournament Office
Dept. of Natural Resources
Tawes State Office Bldg.
Annapolis, Md. 21401

INTERNATIONAL WOMEN'S FISHING ASSOCIATION

This association is made up of women members who are dedicated to fishing and participate actively in fishing for billfish and other species in fresh and salt water. The stated purposes of the organization are "to promote angling competition among women anglers, to encourage conservation, and to promote fishing tournaments of all kinds." They give monthly and yearly awards for outstanding fishing accomplishments. They have established a scholarship trust to help graduate students further their education in the field of marine sciences. They publish a monthly bulletin, *Hooks and Lines,* and an annual yearbook. For more information about this organization write to:

International Women's Fishing Assn.
P.O. Box 2025
Palm Beach, Fla. 33480

M-637	M-638	M-640	M-641
SSD MD	SSE ME	SRA SRME	SRC SRMC
M-639	M-642	M-644	M-646
SRT SRMT	SFSSE	SRFL	SSEL

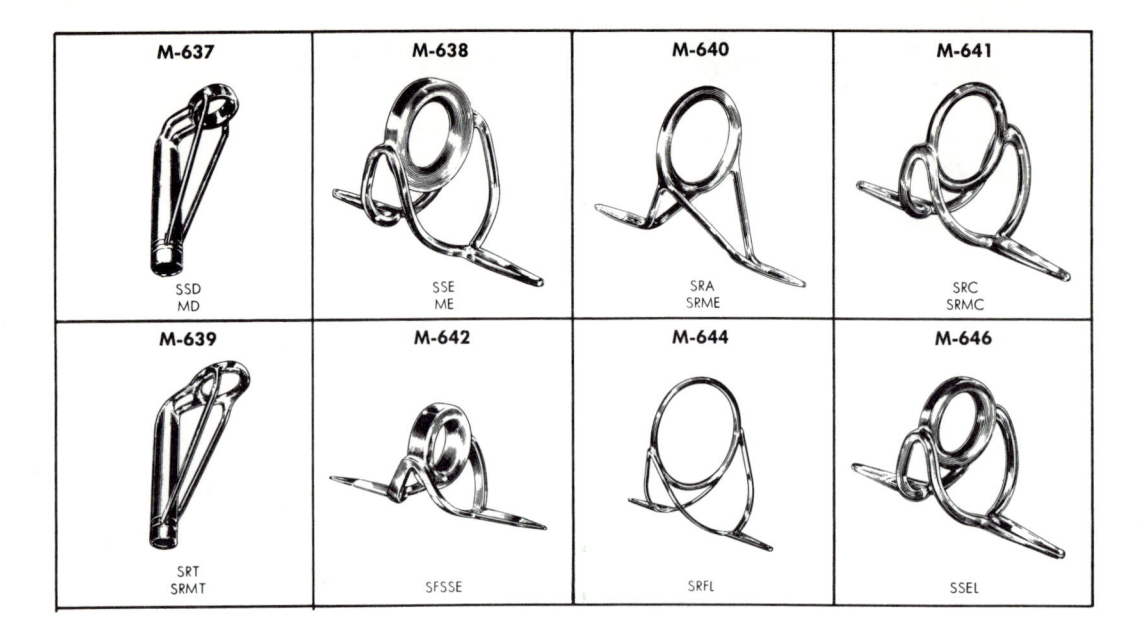

MILDRUM GUIDES

This company makes the well-known Mildrum guides used on spinning, casting, trolling, and big-game rods. The guides are made of Carboloy or stainless steel. The stainless steel is a nickel-bearing, nonmagnetic alloy to insure the greatest possible resistance to freshwater and salt-water corrosion. They also make guides with an inner ring of Mildrum Livesavers, which is an extremely hard ceramic that has been polished to a smooth finish. The guides come in a wide range of mountings for many types of rods. For more information or a catalog showing their complete line of fishing rod mountings write to:
Mildrum Mfg. Co.
East Berlin, Conn. 06023

LIFE VESTS AND BOAT CUSHIONS

The Gentex Corporation has been making life vests and preservers and boat cushions as well as special flotation jackets for a long time. They have several styles and types for fishermen, boaters, and water skiers. They come in various sizes to fit most people. Almost all of them are UL listed and Coast Guard approved. For more information send for their catalog to:
Gentex Corp.
Carbondale, Pa. 18407

Sportcoat

Boat Cushion

Seal Series

Mariner

WELLCRAFT 24-FT. AIRSLOT CONSOLE CABIN FISHERMAN

This is a new-concept boat that is a serious alternative to the big sportfishing machines. It has the soft, dry ride of an Airslot, the comfort of a cabin, and the walk-around advantage of a center-console fishing boat. All in one boat. Instead of a center console it has a center cabin with a walk-around deck, which makes it easy to work a fish, or go forward to tie a bow line. The cabin is fully enclosed and has two V-berths. A head is optional. There's a giant 11-ft.-by-6-ft. nonskid cockpit, big enough for you to mount a fighting chair. And two helm seats with a 180-degree swivel, so they double as fishing chairs. There's a bow seat, a big 4-ft. fish box, a live-bait well, teak trim, loads of storage space, and an optional Bimini top. The 24-ft. Airslot Fisherman weighs 4,600 lbs., has a full capacity of 122 gal., and takes up to a 280-hp. motor. For more information or a catalog write to:

Wellcraft Marine Corp.
8151 Bradenton Rd.
Sarasota, Fla. 33580

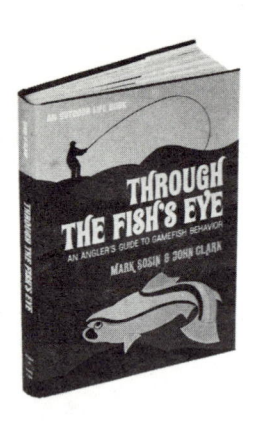

THROUGH THE FISH'S EYE

Why are fish so hard to figure? Simply because they think like fish—not like men. In this unique, fascinating new book you learn how fish live, think, and react, and how to predict them, outwit them, and land many more.

The more a fisherman knows about the behavior of fish, the better his chances of catching them. This is the basic premise of angling author Mark Sosin and ichthyologist John Clark, who collaborated on this truly unique book. While most fishing books focus on the fisherman, his tackle and techniques, this one concentrates on his quarry—the fish.

As the title suggests, the book explains what goes on under the surface while the angler is casting his bait or lure above. Starting with the basic anatomy and structure of a fish, the authors proceed to show how this specialized creature functions in its water environment—how it swims and feeds, how it uses its five senses, how it conceals itself with color and camouflage. While different species of fish may differ in particulars, in their general behavior all fish follow much the same pattern. Once the angler understands general modes of behavior common to all fish, specific traits of his favorite species will be more significant.

This is a science-oriented study of fish behavior put into simple words that every layman and angler can understand. *Through the Fish's Eye* by Mark Sosin and John Clark sells for $7.95 and is published by:

Harper & Row, Publishers, Inc.
10 East 53rd St.
New York, N.Y. 10022

SHRIMP TOUT TAIL

The Tout tails have earned a reputation as great fish-getters in fresh and salt water. They are especially favored for such fish as bass in fresh water and for sea trout, snook, jacks, redfish, and tarpon in salt water. The larger sizes with big hooks are best for big tarpon, especially when fishing at night. They come in many colors, weights, and hook sizes. You can buy them complete or just the heads, and add the tails to make the complete lure. For a catalog of all the colors and sizes in these and other lures they make write to:

The Boone Bait Co., Inc.
P.O. Box 571
Winter Park, Fla. 32789

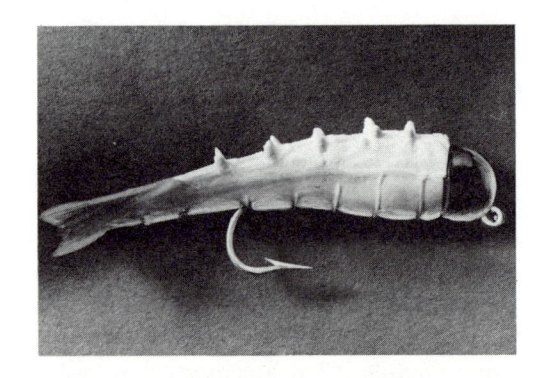

ANDE MONOFILAMENT LINE

The importers of this monofilament line made in Germany call it "The line of Champions," and this is based on the fact that over one hundred world-record fish have been caught on this line. It is used by many expert anglers in both fresh and salt water because they like its limpness and uniform diameter. It also has good knot strength and a minimum of stretch. It is available in pink, clear, gun-metal, and tournament green, and in tests from 2 to 400 lbs. It also comes in regular and premium finish, both of which are of the same quality, but the premium has a shiny finish and the regular has a dull or matte finish. You can buy it in ¼-, ½-, 1-, 2-, and 6-lb. spools. For more information write to:
Ande, Inc.
1500 53rd St.
West Palm Beach, Fla. 33407

THE SHARK SUCKER

The shark sucker, also called the remora, is a "free-loader" and "hitchhiker" that depends on other fish for a free ride and food. It has a suction disk on top of its head that enables it to attach itself to a smooth surface, such as the side of a ship, a whale, swordfish, marlin, shark, or turtle. It particularly likes sharks because they are sloppy eaters, and shreds of fish drift down so that the remora can grab them and also eat. The suction disk is so powerful that it is almost impossible to remove the remora from a fish by pulling on its tail. Natives in tropical waters have tied lines to the tails of remoras and released them in the water when a turtle is seen. The remora attaches itself to the turtle and they then haul both of them into the boat.

COCKTAIL BAIT

Using two or even three baits on the same hook often produces better than just one bait. Such "cocktails" offer a choice and also enable you to use one tough bait and a softer one. If the softer bait is stolen or lost you still have the tough bait left on the hook to attract and catch fish.

BOSTON WHALER MONTAUK 17

A boat designed for the avid fisherman, the Boston Whaler Montauk 17, has a reversible teak-backed pilot seat with room for two fishermen trolling aft while the helmsman stands. The Fiberglas console has two built-in lockable storage areas, stainless-steel grab rail with plexiglas windscreen, stainless-steel wheel, teak dash panel, and wiring harness with two switches and fuses. This company also makes many other models of the Boston Whaler. For a catalog or more information write to:
Boston Whaler, Inc.
1149 Hingham St.
Rockland, Mass. 02370

TEXAS FISHING BOOKS

Three paperback books that are excellent guides on fishing the coast, bays, and offshore waters in Texas for most of the fish found there in salt water are:

Fishing the Bays of Texas by Anton Husak $4.75
Fishing the Texas Coast Inshore and Offshore by A. C. Becker $4.50
Texas Salt-water Big 3 (covers sea trout, redfish, and flounders) by A. C. Becker $4.25

These books are available from:
Cordovan Corp., Publishers
5314 Bingle Rd.
Houston, Tex. 77018

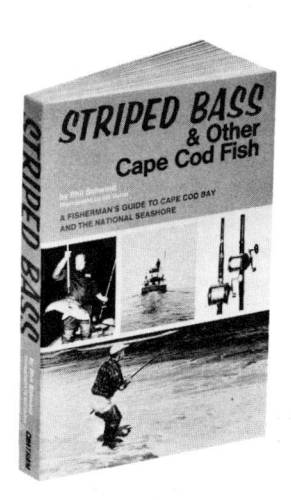

STRIPED BASS & OTHER CAPE COD FISH

The book *Striped Bass & Other Cape Cod Fish* by Phil Schwind covers the fishing in Cape Cod Bay, on Cape Cod, and along the National Seashore. The author spent most of his life as a commercial fisherman, charter boat skipper, and writer on Cape Cod, so he knows his waters and fishing. Some of the subjects, methods, and techniques and tackle he covers are:

> *When and where you'll catch what kinds of fish*
> *The art of spinning and free-spool surf casting*
> *The best rods, reels, lines, lures, and other gear*
> *Bottom rigs and bait for flounder, tautog, and cod*
> *How to make and fish eelskin rigs and skin plugs*
> *The ideal boat to own or charter*
> *Tips on expert boat handling and fish finding*
> *How to get results trolling for stripers and blues*
> *Why fishing for mackerel is fun for children*

The author also interviews three expert anglers on how to fish for striped bass and giant tuna. *Striped Bass & Other Cape Cod Fish* sells for $3.95 from:
The Chatham Press
143 Sound Beach Ave.
Old Greenwich, Conn. 06870

PENN FATHOM-MASTER

The Penn Fathom-Master is a device for deep trolling featuring a drag-brake control system, cable footage counter, and glass-reinforced Lexan Troller spool. Attached to the deck with base plate of reinforced nylon, the entire unit except the base plate is easily removed for storage when not in use. The handle does not revolve when weight is descending. The Fathom-Master is designed for both freshwater and salt-water use, and all parts are durable and corrosion-resistant. It comes with 200 ft. of 135-lb. stainless-steel cable and snap swivel. For more information about this trolling device write to:
Penn Fishing Tackle Mfg. Co.
3028 W. Hunting Park Ave.
Philadelphia, Pa. 19132

CATCHING MULLET

One of the best baits you can use in salt water for many species inshore and offshore is the mullet. Mullet can be bought dead or frozen in many fish markets and from bait dealers and tackle shops. A few dealers sell live mullet at times but at a very high price, so most fishing guides and anglers try to catch their own. You can sometimes snag a few mullet with lures or snagging rigs, or you can seine some mullet near shore in shallow water, especially at night. But the best way to catch mullet is by use of a "cast net," which is a circular net tied to a line in the center and with lead weights along the circumference or outer edge. When the net is thrown over a school of mullet it opens unbrellalike and sinks to the bottom, trapping any mullet under it. You can use the cast net from shore, piers, bridges, or bulkheads. The nets come in different diameters, and it takes quite a bit of practice before you become skilled in throwing one well enough to catch mullet.

RECORD KING MACKEREL

When Norton Thomton, a resident of Minnesota, arrived in the Florida Keys to do some fishing, he never expected to shatter the world record on rod and reel for king mackerel. But that is what he did when he hooked and boated a king mackerel that pulled the scale down to 90 lbs.! It was 5 ft., 11 in. long and was caught on a trolled ballyhoo from a 19-ft. private boat. It took 25 min. to subdue, and Thomton's catch is now the official all-tackle record in the IGFA record book.

ANGLERS SPECIALTIES

This company makes and sells various types of equipment for sportfishing boats. They have a complete line of fishing and fighting chairs, both permanent-mount and portable. They also have outrigger poles, outrigger holders, rod holders, custom tuna towers, and rod belts. For more information about these products write to:
Anglers Specialties, Inc.
676 W. 17th St.
Costa Mesa, Calif. 92627

GARCIA MITCHELL 302 REEL

The Garcia Mitchell 302 is a big, rugged salt-water spinning reel that is widely used by surf anglers and boat anglers for many kinds of fish. It has polished stainless-steel ball bearings and self-lubricating oilite bushings to deliver power with smoothness. It has a new anti-inertia brake; smooth, hard chromed line guide, and a large, folding handle. This reel will hold up to 400 or 500 yds. of 15-lb.-test monofilament line, depending on the brand used. Their combined *Fishing Annual and Catalog* showing this and other reels and tackle costs $1.50 and can be obtained from:
The Garcia Corp.
329 Alfred Ave.
Teaneck, N.J. 07666

PANDORA'S TACKLE BOXES

For years anglers fishing from boats, especially from the smaller craft, have had problems with lure and tackle storage. Ordinary tackle boxes are usually made for small freshwater lures, and the compartments are not big enough for salt-water lures. Now there's a tackle box designed specifically for the small- and big-boat fisherman. Called the Pandora's tackle box, it is hand-made by skilled craftsmen. Nothing but the finest-quality mahogany and marine plywood and brass, chrome, and stainless-steel hardware are used in the making of this box.

The standard Pandora's tackle box is 19 in. tall, 16 in. wide, and 16¾ in. deep. There are six drawers with five trays each that will hold big salt-water plugs and other lures. The box is also designed to be used as a seat if you place a U. S. Coast Guard-approved throw cushion on top. In addition to the standard tackle box they make, they will also custom-build a tackle box to suit your needs or to fill a special place in your boat. For this you send dimensions or plans and they'll send back a design and price. For more information write to:
Pandora's Tackle Boxes
P.O. Box 213
Chilmark, Mass. 02535

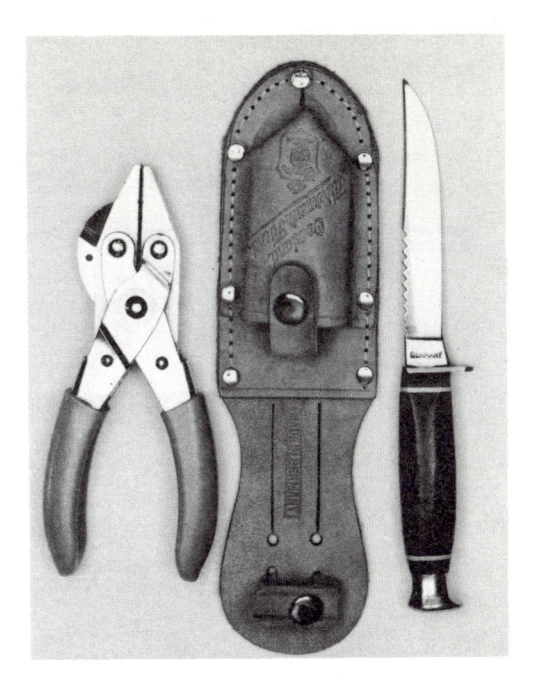

FISHING KNIFE AND PLIERS SET

The Overland Fisherman's Friend knife and pliers set is a combination that includes a 3½-in. blade knife with genuine leather handle and multipurpose pliers. A leather sheath comes with the set and holds both the knife and pliers and can be worn on a belt. For more information write to:
Syl-Mark Enterprises
P.O. Box 806
Northbridge, Calif. 91324

PROTECTING SURF REELS

If you want to protect your surf fishing reels from flying sand when they are on a beach buggy or when they are not being used on the beach, try covering them with a small plastic bag. Tie the opening of the bag around the reel leg or base. Then when the buggy is moving or the wind is blowing, your reel will be protected from flying sand.

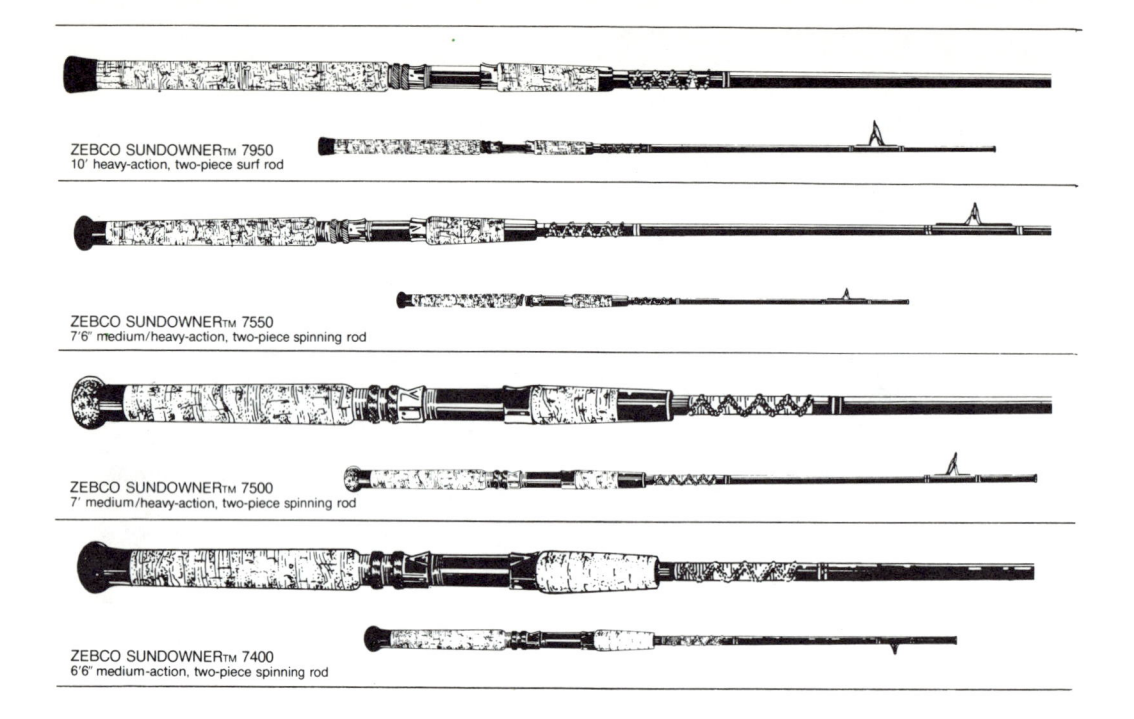

ZEBCO SUNDOWNER™ 7950
10' heavy-action, two-piece surf rod

ZEBCO SUNDOWNER™ 7550
7'6" medium/heavy-action, two-piece spinning rod

ZEBCO SUNDOWNER™ 7500
7' medium/heavy-action, two-piece spinning rod

ZEBCO SUNDOWNER™ 7400
6'6" medium-action, two-piece spinning rod

ZEBCO RODS

Zebco makes a full line of freshwater and salt-water spinning and spin-casting rods. The ones pictured here are their Sundowner rods, which include a surf rod of 10 ft. in heavy action and several shorter 7½-to-6½-ft. spinning rods for medium or light salt-water fishing. For their color catalog showing their full line of rods, reels, and other tackle write to:
Zebco Div.—Brunswick Corp.
P.O. Box 270
Tulsa, Okla. 74101

FORTY-EIGHT SHARKS ON ONE LINE!

Roy Lowe, a Florida Keys fishing guide, caught a great hammerhead shark 11 ft. long and weighing 900 lbs. Then when he opened up the female shark he found forty-seven young ones inside!

PANANGLING TRAVEL SERVICE

This is a complete booking and travel service to some of the best fishing spots throughout the world. They provide airline tickets, obtain hotel and fishing camp reservations, and take care of other details at no additional cost or service charge. Some of the places they can arrange fishing trips for include Canada, Alaska, Nicaragua, Costa Rica, Argentina, Labrador, Iceland, New Zealand, Mexico, and Panama.

They also publish a monthly newsletter called *The PanAngler,* which gives detailed information about the various fishing spots they service. A yearly subscription to *The PanAngler* costs $15. For more information about this newsletter and their travel service write to:
PanAngling Travel Service
180 N. Michigan Ave.
Chicago, Ill. 60601

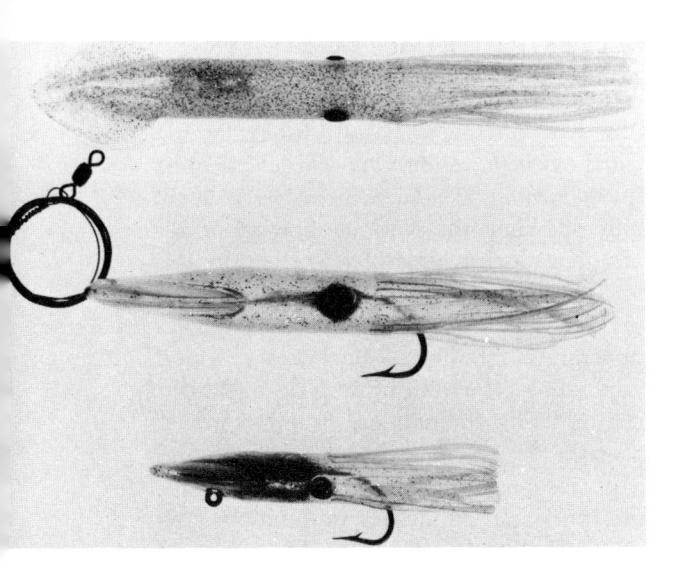

FENWICK PSYCHOSQUID

The Fenwick Psychosquid is a trolling lure that imitates a squid that most salt-water fish feed on. It can be used as a skip bait on top of the water, or it can be made to swim underwater. The baits come unrigged or rigged and in 4-in. and 6-in. sizes. If you add a weight at the head of the squid it can be used for casting too. This lure has been used for striped bass, bluefish, king mackerel, dolphin, and school tuna. For their catalog showing these and other lures and tackle send $.25 to:
Fenwick
P.O. Box 729
Westminster, Calif. 92683

FISH SALT-WATER NOVA SCOTIA

The little booklet *Fish Salt-water Nova Scotia* lists the seasons and spots where you can catch tuna, striped bass, cod, pollock, and sea trout. It also lists the charter-boat operators who can be hired at various spots to fish for these fish. The booklet is available from:
Dept. of Tourism
P.O. Box 456
1649 Hollis Street
Halifax, N.S.
Canada B3J 2R5

FISHING IN HAWAII

Hawaii is a chain of islands surrounded by deep water, and there is excellent salt-water fishing to be found the year 'round. There are no seasonal restrictions, no fishing limits, and no salt-water fishing licenses. They have such billfish as Pacific blue marlin, striped marlin, black marlin, sailfish, and swordfish. Then there are the yellowfin tuna, skipjack tuna, dolphin, wahoo, and bonitos. Shallow-water fishermen and bottom fishermen catch bonefish, jack crevalle, barracuda, amberjack, snappers, and scads. You can charter boats for offshore fishing. For more information about fishing Hawaii's salt waters write to:
Hawaii Visitors Bureau
2270 Kalakaua Ave.
Honolulu, Hawaii 96815

HARBEN FISH SCALER

The Harben fish scaler is a unique, one-piece precision design of aluminum alloy. It has seventy-two scalpel edges that will cleanly remove the scales from a fish quickly and neatly with no flying scales. It will stay bright always and will not rust or corrode. To use, you simply place the fish on a board or table with the head toward you. Then you scale by scraping from the tail toward you. To get rid of surplus scales you simply dip the scaler in water or hold it under a faucet. It is available in right-handed or left-handed models and sells for $1.49. For more information write to:
Harben Mfg. Co.
2101 N. Green Bay Rd.
Racine, Wis. 53405

SUCCESSFUL BLUEFISHING

The book *Successful Bluefishing* by Henry Lyman is the only book devoted entirely to this great gamefish. The author, who is publisher of the well-known *Salt-water Sportsman* magazine, has fished for and studied the bluefish for many years and has caught them in many parts of the world. In the book he covers the life cycle of the bluefish itself, the history of the fishery, the best fishing grounds, and the tackle and methods employed to catch them. Henry Lyman tells about catching and fishing for bluefish from the beaches in the surf in New England and elsewhere. He also covers fishing for blues from boats by trolling, casting, and chumming. A good portion of the book is devoted to the best rods, reels, lines, lures, baits, and fishing outfits to use when bluefishing. *Successful Bluefishing* sells for $10 and is published by:
**International Marine Publishing Co.
Camden, Me. 04843**

BRITISH COLUMBIA FISHING GUIDE

You can obtain a handy fishing guide called *British Columbia Tidal Waters Sport Fishing Guide,* which has a large map showing the various hot spots for salmon and what time of year the fishing is best for them. It also describes the various methods of fishing for salmon such as mooching, trolling, bucktailing, and stripcasting. It shows how to rig and hook herring baits for salmon fishing. And it gives the license requirements, seasonal and area closures, size limits, daily bag limits, and other restrictions and prohibitions governing the salmon fishery. This map and folder can be obtained from:
**Fisheries and Marine Service
Dept. of the Environment
1090 W. Pender St.
Vancouver, B.C.
Canada V6E 2P1**

LEISURE LIFE LURES

These are soft, plastic lures designed to look like natural fish or squid, which big gamefish like to feed on. They look, act, and feel alive and are completely rigged for immediate fishing. They have smaller lures imitating minnows, bullheads, small eels, and salamanders, many of which are rigged with a spinner in front of the plastic imitation itself. These are more suitable for freshwater or light salt-water fishing. But they also have larger-sized lures designed to imitate squid, mackerel, flying fish, needlefish, mullet, and other baits. These can be used offshore when trolling for such fish as sailfish, marlin, tuna, dolphin, and other big fish. For more information about these lures write to:
**U. S. Promotions, Inc.
P.O. Box 9721
North Hollywood, Calif. 91609**

CRUISERS ALBACORE FISHING MACHINE

Cruisers 19-ft. Albacore is a center-console fishing machine with an 18-ft., 11-in. center length, 90-in. beam, approximate weight of 1,600 lbs., and is rated for up to 175 outboard hp.

In addition to a pair of swivel/sliding helm seats, the Albacore includes such other features for the angler as two forward dry stowage compartments, lockable radio and tackle stowage compartments in the console, two removable aft bait wells, self-bailing cockpit, built-in storage for six rods, four rod holders, a smooth "nonsnag" gunwale design, and level foam flotation.

Other standard equipment includes a tinted plexiglas windscreen, 25-gal. foamed-in-place aluminum fuel tank with electric gauge, anchor/rope locker, batter stowage compartments, rack and pinion mechanical steering, switched and fused navigational lights, two 8-in. stern cleats, bow mooring bit, teak trim, electric trumpet horn, and bow rail of stainless steel.

Nearly thirty factory-installed options such as vinyl forward shelter covers and curtains, VHF radio, graph-type depth recorders, upholstered dual pilot seat/ice chest combination, and other fishing and cruising accessories are also available.

The vee-hull and deck are fog white, and the interior is amber gold. For more information about this and other boats they make write to:
Cruisers—Mirro Marine Div.
804 Pecor St.
Oconto, Wis. 54513

FISHING ATLASES AND MAPS

These fishing atlases and maps are complete guides to the areas covered, giving the species of fish found there and seasons and spots where they are caught. There are articles and tips on catching the different kinds of fish. The maps pinpoint the hot spots and the kind of fish caught there. The atlases have color plates showing the most popular fish caught in the areas covered. The following atlases are available:

Salt-water Sport Fishing and Boating in Virginia $7.44

Salt-water Sport Fishing and Boating in Maryland $7.44

The following maps are available at $2.47 each:

"Chincoteague-Assateague Fishing and Recreation Map"

"Virginia Beach Fishing Map"

"Ocean City Fishing Map"

"Chesapeake Bay Fishing Map, from the Bay Bridge to the Gooses"

"Cape Lookout to New Topsail Inlet Fishing Map"

"Wrightsville Beach, N.C., to Little River, S.C., Fishing Map"

"Middle Chesapeake Bay Fishing Map from the Patuxent River to Tangier Island"

"Lower Chesapeake Bay Fishing Map from Smith Point to Lynnhaven Inlet"

"Hatteras Offshore Fishing Chart"

These atlases and maps are published by:
Alexandria Drafting Co.
417 Clifford Ave.
Alexandria, Va. 22305

THE COMPLETE BOOK OF WEAKFISHING

The Complete Book of Weakfishing by Henry Lyman and Frank Woolner was written before the present upsurge in the weakfish population took place. These popular gamefish have returned to their former haunts and are now being caught along most of the Atlantic Coast. But despite its age, this book still has a lot of valuable information on how to catch both the northern or common weakfish and the southern or spotted weakfish, more often called the "sea trout." The authors go into the tackle, rods, reels, lines, lures, and baits used to fool weakfish in most of the waters where they are found. *The Complete Book of Weakfishing* sells for $5.95 and is published by:
A. S. Barnes & Co., Inc.
P.O. Box 421
Cranbury, N.J. 08512

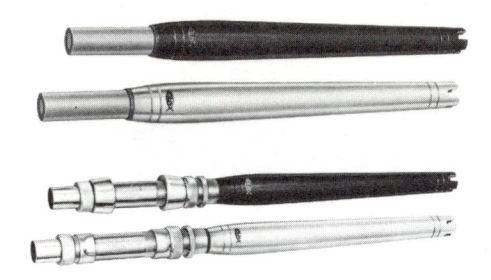

BIG-GAME TROLLING BUTTS

The AFTCO big-game trolling butts are made of high-strength, lightweight aluminum. They use a unique Swaging process, which puts extra thickness into the walls of the handle where the outside diameter is smallest. Where the handle is largest, the walls are thinner. Thus handle is uniformly strong from end to end without added weight. The special aluminum alloy is deeply anodized, making the butts impervious to salt-water corrosion, weather, and aging. They are available in six sizes for big-game rods in most of the line classes. For more information write to:
Axelson Fishing Tackle Mfg. Co., Inc.
1559 Placentia Ave.
Newport Beach, Calif. 92660

ANGLER'S NEWS

This is a weekly newspaper-type publication that gives the latest fishing information from Rhode Island to the Carolinas. It especially concentrates on the New Jersey–New York area and not only tells where the fish are running but also has articles on the "how to" end of the sport in both fresh and salt water. Such well-known writers as Milt Rosko, Lou Rodia, and Fred Walczyk contribute columns to the paper. They offer seasonal tips and advice about the fish that are running at the time as well as mentioning the spots where the action is taking place. You can subscribe to the *Angler's News* for $7.00 a year, and they can be written at:
Angler's News
330 Kennedy Blvd.
Bayonne, N.J. 07002

WHAT A CATCH!

Most offshore anglers consider themselves lucky if they catch one big billfish or a good mess of smaller fish during a fishing trip. But Sam Johnson hit the jackpot while fishing in the Gulf of Mexico out of Panama City, Florida. He caught 45 Spanish mackerel, 3 sailfish, a 60-lb. white marlin, a 150-lb. broadbill swordfish, and then topped it off with a 430-lb. blue marlin!

STIRRING UP TARPON

When tarpon are lurking under the mangroves, try stirring them up by taking a long pole and splashing with it along the edge of the mangroves. Then back off the boat a good distance and wait. This splashing often stirs up the tarpon, which move out from under the roots and leaves of the trees out of curiosity. Then you can cast lures or baits to them.

FIDDLER ON THE HOOK

Fiddler crabs make excellent bait for such fish as bonefish, sheepshead, and blackfish or tautog. You can often buy these crabs with the single big claw in coastal tackle shops or from bait dealers along the Atlantic Coast. You can also catch your own fiddler crabs in bays and inlets and tidal waterways along sandy shores. They can be herded against a trap made from two boards in the shape of a corner. The fiddlers can be kept alive for a long time without any water in a fairly large container if kept in a cool spot. When using fiddlers for bait remove the big claw and insert the hook into the hole that is left.

HOOKING PACIFIC SALMON

When using a natural bait such as a rigged herring while mooching or slow trolling for Pacific salmon, don't set the hook immediately. Usually the first indication of a bite means the salmon is fooling around with the bait. At this time drop back some slack line and let the fish mouth the bait, then set the hook.

BIG COBIA ON A FLY ROD

One of the largest cobia to be taken on a fly rod was caught by Ralph Delph of Miami, Florida. He was casting a streamer fly on the Gulf side of the middle Florida Keys when the big cobia grabbed his lure. Cobia on any tackle put up a long, stubborn fight, and when Delph finally subdued the fish and weighed it later, it went 69 lbs.!

PILOT FLASHER DEPTH SOUNDER

Unimetrics, Inc., introduces its all-new "Pilot" series of flashers/depth sounders/fish locators with many built-in features, such as all-solid-state with latest chip-integrated circuitry for superior reliability. They have built-in, interference-free, noise-blanking circuitry that eliminates false indications. They have a brilliant neon flasher with a high-intensity button for easy, instantaneous reading even in direct sunlight. An easy-to-read 6½-in.-by-6-in. bold dial face is recessed to insure glare-free operation. Other features include: separate on-off switch main control; 360-degree horizontal swivel and vertical rotation mounting; built-in depth alarm; heavy-duty, super-high-impact Cycolac plastic body; massive knobs for easy dismantling and storage; corrosion-resistant materials throughout; heavy-duty bronze transducer and all mounting hardware included with each model. All models operate on 12-v. DC negative ground with complete and positive reverse polarity protection. For their catalog or more information about these flashers/depth sounders/fish locators write to:
Unimetrics, Inc.
123 Jericho Tpk.
Syosset, N.Y. 11791

MODERN SALT-WATER FISHING

The book *Modern Salt-water Fishing* by Vic Dunaway is a complete manual of instruction for the coastal angler. From it he can learn techniques, systems, and procedures for all the many different salt-water specialties. The book gives step-by-step instruction in selecting and matching tackle, choosing baits and lures, rigging baits, leaders, and terminal tackle. Vic Dunaway then analyzes each particular type of angling and shows how to go about it in an efficient and productive manner. He gives the exact procedures for trolling, drifting, bottom fishing, jigging, and casting, both inshore and offshore. He covers pier, surf, and bridge fishing, using everything from light fly-fishing gear to heavy 130-lb. tackle. The author has had many years of fishing experience as fishing editor of the Miami *Herald* and present editor of *Florida Sportsman*. And most of the methods and techniques and lures he covers in the book are like the title implies: "modern" and "up-to-date." The book sells in paperback for $5.95 and is published by:
Stoeger Publishing Co.
55 Ruta Ct.
South Hackensack, N.J. 07606

EAGLE CLAW TROLLING REELS

The Wright & McGill Company has come out with a line of new trolling reels for fresh and salt water. Called the Blue Pacific 500 Series, their models range from small, level-wind types suitable for coho, lake trout, and salmon in fresh water and for light salt-water fishing, to the heavier models for offshore trolling for the smaller billfish such as sailfish and white marlin and also for school tuna and albacore. The reels feature full-range star-drag systems, spool and bearing tension adjustments, ball sealed lubrication ports, chrome plate brass spools, and durable stainless-steel-reinforced side plates. Their catalog showing these reels and other fishing tackle and hooks they make costs $.25 from:
Wright & McGill Co.
P.O. Box 16011
Denver, Colo. 80216

MINI TUNA TOWER

The Mini Tuna Tower was designed to fill a specific need for smaller boats of 7-to-10-ft. beams by affording the boater greater visibility and a platform from which to locate fish.

The tower is extremely strong and is built for long-lasting, hard use, with safety bracing around the standing platform. It can be equipped with a variety of controls for any engine, single or twin.

Patented construction gives the Mini Tuna Tower the versatility of adjusting to fit many different existing boats, and can be done by the boat owner himself with a great saving in both time and money. Using the dock or your own backyard and by following the simple, comprehensive instructions, the Mini Tuna Tower can be easily erected. All hardware is included and nothing else is required other than a few simple tools.

The Lay Down (Fold Down) feature, used when trailering or for low bridges, makes the Mini Tuna Tower superior to static, fixed affairs. With this feature your boat can be used for inland waterways or canals. It is also desirable for rack storage. The Mini Tuna Tower sells for $895. For more information write to:
Imperial Marine Equipment
7601 N.W. 66th St.
Miami, Fla. 33166

SINKER CARRIER

To store or carry sinkers in a tackle box, car, boat, or even at home, get some heavy wire like the coat hanger type and make a ring with an eye on one end and a catch on the other. Then slip your sinkers on the wire and close the ring. You can make a separate ring for each size sinker or carry assorted sizes on the ring.

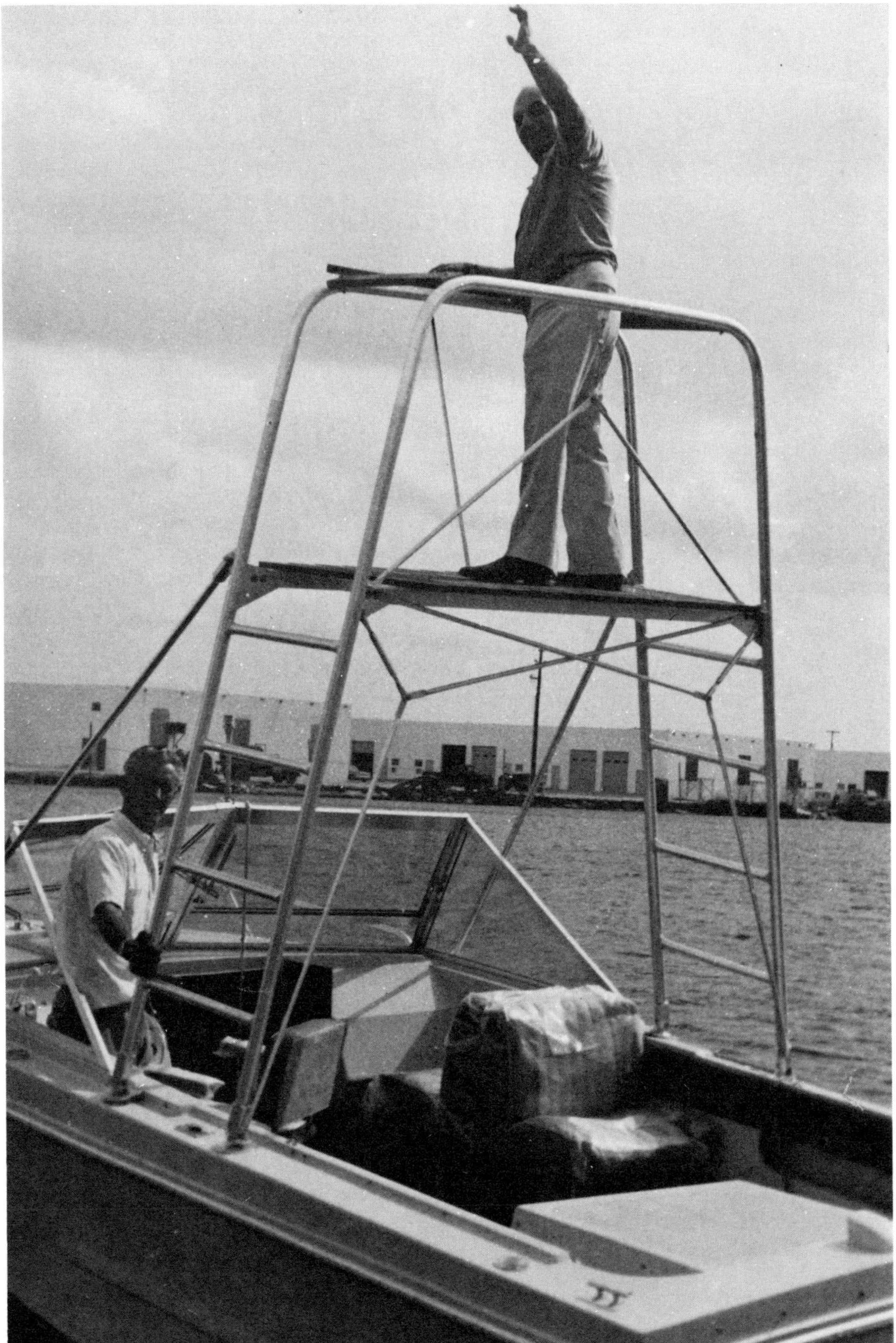

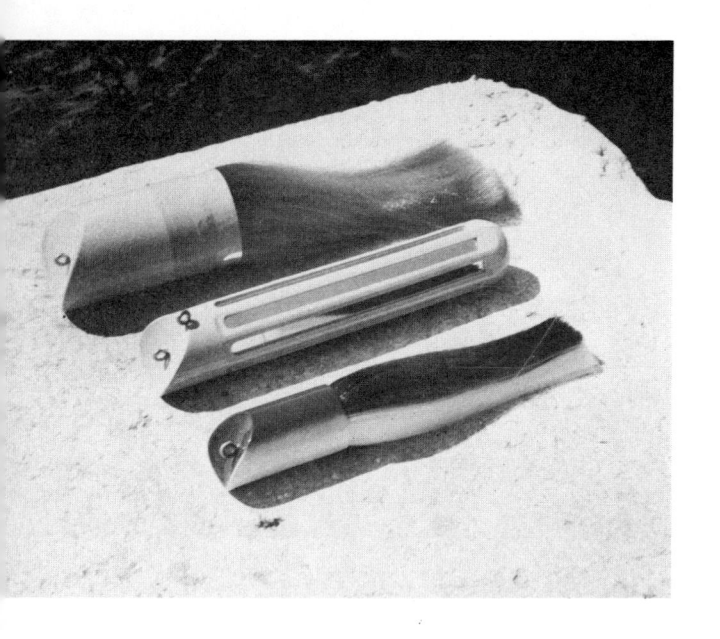

BOONE TEASERS

The Boone Bait Company makes many lures for freshwater and salt-water fishing, and they also make teasers for offshore trolling. They offer the standard-type teasers with plastic heads and undulating nylon tail that dart, dive, and provide surface action that brings up the big billfish. These teasers come in two sizes: 12 in. and 15 in. long, with the smaller one weighing 4 ozs. and the bigger one going almost 1 lb. in weight. They come in five color combinations. The other teasers they make are the Sundance and the Sea-Deucer. The Sundance teaser has eight glass-strip mirrors, runs just below the surface, and sends out brilliant rays and reflections. The mirrors on this teaser are replaceable. The Sundance is available in six colors. For their catalog showing these teasers and other lures they make write to:
Boone Bait Co., Inc.
P.O. Box 571
Winter Park, Fla. 32789

SUCCESSFUL STRIPED BASS FISHING

The book *Successful Striped Bass Fishing* by Frank T. Moss covers fishing for this popular salt-water gamefish along our Atlantic and Pacific coasts and in inland waters where they have been introduced. There are chapters on biology and the range of stripers in salt and fresh water. Illustrated chapters detail deep trolling with and without wire lines, how to fish selectively for record fish with "legitimate" tackle, where to go in various seasons of the year, how to rig hooks, leaders, live-bait rigs, and many other essential details. There are large sections on using such lures as bucktails, plugs, tube lures, plastic eels, and natural baits for striped bass. Although most of the book is devoted to boat fishing, there are sections on surf fishing too. Important contributions were made to the book by such well-known writers and striped bass fishermen as Charles R. Meyer, Larry Green, Herb Duerksen, Bob Hutchinson, Pete McClain, Mark Sosin, and the late Al Reinfelder. *Successful Striped Bass Fishing* sells for $12.50 and is published by:
International Marine Publishing Co.
Camden, Me. 04843

DOLPHIN 120 FISH/DEPTH FINDER

Now there's a fish/depth finder that's both inexpensive and as foolproof as a sensitive instrument can be—Pearce-Simpson's Dolphin 120.

Skilled marine electronic enigneers made the Dolphin 120 a rotating neon flasher type because they wanted to offer a versatile but sensibly priced unit. But in order to make it worthy of the Pearce-Simpson name, they first had to overcome the usual problems associated with flasher sounders. You won't find a dim bulb that's hard to read in bright sunlight. The Dolphin 120's bright red light and special sunlight-reflecting dial make reading easy under all conditions. And the large scale yields detailed readings on bottom type and structure, water depth, and fish in the area.

If you ever need servicing, plug-in transistors and solid-state circuitry make it easy. And don't worry about the printed circuit board—it's Pearce-Simpson's own special seagoing Fiberglas. Power doesn't stop at 120 ft. There's enough in the Dolphin 120 to go well beyond that depth if necessary.

Despite the economy price, the Dolphin 120 is sold complete with transducer and 25-ft. cable. For more information or literature write to:
Pearce-Simpson Div. of Gladding Corp.
P.O. Box 520800, Biscayne Annex
Miami, Fla. 33152

TOUGHENING MUSSELS

Mussels make good bait for many saltwater fish, but they are soft and easily come off the hook or are stolen by the fish. One way to toughen them is to open the shells and let them lie in the hot sun for a while. You can also dump the mussels into boiling water, then shut off the heat. This kills the mussels and opens the shells and at the same time toughens the meat. If all else fails, you can always wrap the mussels around a hook with fine thread.

TOUGH SURF ANGLER

Surf anglers are noted as a tough group who fish from slippery rocks and jetties, get washed overboard, fight the waves, and fish all night and in the rain and cold just to catch a striped bass, bluefish, or channel bass. One such surf angler was fishing Rhode Island's rocky shore when a big wave came rolling in, picked him up, and slammed him into some boulders and broke his leg. But as soon as the angler could hobble around he was back surf fishing again!

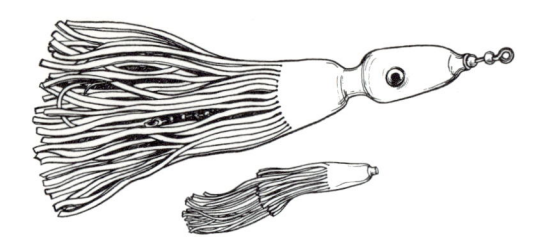

HOOCHY TAILS AND TROLLS

These Hoochy tails and trolls are made in many varieties, sizes, weights, and colors by the Weber Tackle Company. You can obtain them with weighted heads and hooks rigged on bead chains. Or you can get the tails or skirts alone and rig them yourself. They are made of flexible vinyl plastic for lively action in the water. The tails alone can also be added in front of a lure or a whole-fish bait being trolled offshore for big-game fish. Their catalog showing these and other lures and tackle they make costs $1.00. Write for it to:
Weber Tackle Co.
Stevens Point, Wis. 54481

J. LEE CUDDY FISHING ROD COMPONENTS

This company has one of the largest selections of fishing rod components in the country. They carry fishing rod blanks for fresh and salt water as well as reel seats, ferrules, guides, tips, cork handles and rings, butts, butt caps, winding thread, and everything else needed to build a finished rod. They handle Fiberglas blanks, both solid and tubular, as well as a complete line of graphite blanks. They also have many types of handles and adapters, and they sell fly lines and monofilament lines as well. Their catalog showing their complete line costs $3.00 and can be obtained from:
J. Lee Cuddy Associates, Inc.
450 N.E. 79th St.
Miami, Fla. 33138

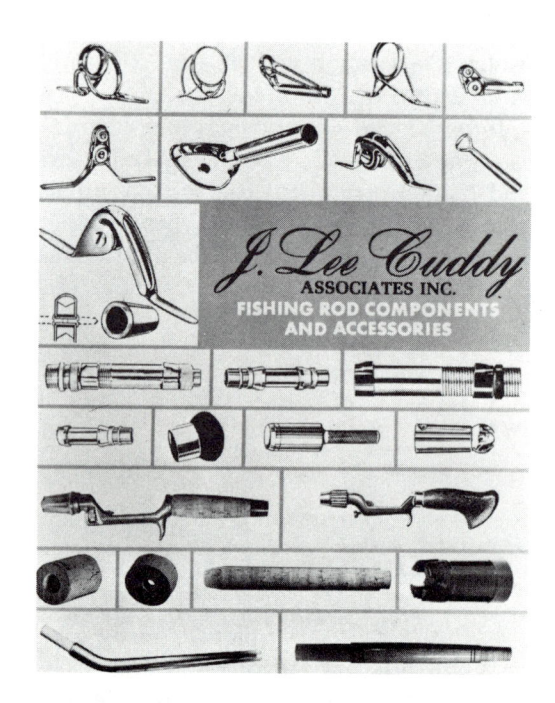

TROLLING TRICK FOR STRIPERS

When trolling for striped bass with more than one line, one good trick is to wait until you get a fish on. Then the other anglers should grab their rods and reel in slowly and give their lures some added rod action. On many occasions you'll hook a second or third striper this way. Striped bass, like many other fish, tend to follow a hooked member of a school and will hit lures being trolled or worked near the first fish.

STEURY 18-FT. OFFSHORE FISHERMAN

The Steury 18-ft. Offshore Fisherman has been designed for fishing in deeper waters and features a walk-around captain's stand with windshield and grab rail. It also has a glove box, large wet well, three dry storage boxes, bow rail, two trolling rod holders, courtesy lights, Destroyer wheel, hydrolift spray rails, bilge pump, twin eighteen-gal. fuel tanks, and captain's chair and bench. A Bimini top with side and aft curtains is optional. The list price of this boat is $2,695. For a catalog showing this and other boats they make write to:
Steury Corp.
310 Steury Ave.
Goshen, Ind. 46526

FISHERMAN PUBLICATIONS

These are very complete and informative fishing guides on catching some of the most popular game and bottom species in Atlantic waters. They are written and illustrated by many of the authors who are editors of or contributors to *The Fisherman* magazine. The first of the three guides that have been published so far is *Fishing for Fluke* by Scott Simons. It is actually the first book ever published on how to catch fluke. It has chapters on tackle, equipment, rigging up, natural baits, bottom formations, drifting, trolling, chumming, and artificials. It is 112 pages long and sells for $2.95 plus $.25 postage.

Another book is *Fishing for Weakfish* by Dr. William A. Muller; it is the latest guide to catching this popular fish since it has come back strong in recent years. There are chapters devoted to tackle, artificial lures, natural baits, methods and techniques, and an in-depth where-to-go section. It is 80 pages long and sells for $2.50 plus $.25 postage.

Dr. William A. Muller has also written another one for this series called *Fishing for Flounder,* which tells all about the tackle, rigs, baits, and methods used for these flatfish. It sells for $2.95 plus $.25 postage.

Other books planned in this series will deal with striped bass, cod, and other species usually caught along the Atlantic Coast. To obtain the complete list of their *Fisherman* books write to:

The Fisherman
P.O. Box 143
Deer Park, N.Y. 11729

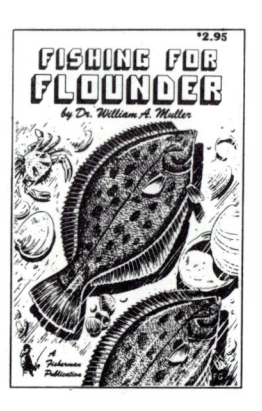

WATCH OUT FOR LADYFISH!

When a ladyfish hits a lure or bait and gets hooked, look out: It makes long runs and wild, twisting, gyrating leaps so fast that you can't keep up with them. They'll often run toward you so fast that even with a fast retrieve reel you can't take up the slack line.

The ladyfish is highly underrated as a gamefish. For its size it is one of the fastest and most spectacular fighters, making other fish look like slowpokes. Unfortunately, like the bonefish, which it resembles somewhat, the ladyfish isn't fit to eat, so few anglers deliberately fish for them.

But if you want top sport, get a light spinning or casting outfit, add a surface or underwater plug, spoon, jig, or similar lure, and cast it out where ladyfish are present. If the tide is right they'll hit again and again, and it is no problem to hook fish after fish. They like to hang around bridges, causeways, bays, inlets, and mouths of rivers and other shallow water spots with sand or mud bottoms. For best results work your lures fast and with plenty of rod action and you'll have no problem hooking ladyfish. Of course, you'll lose some during the runs and jumps. But there are always more ladyfish to oblige.

GARCIA NYLON SQUIDDING LINE

This is the line that is preferred by many surf anglers and casters when using conventional reels with revolving spools. It is made of DuPont nylon that is braided to give it precisely the proper amount of stretch and then permanently heat set it. It has a special "braided in" lubrication that helps eliminate internal friction, and special waterproofing reduces water absorption. It comes in two connected 50-yd. spools, six connected 50-yd. spools, or 1,000-yd. bulk spools in tests from 18 to 45 lbs. For more information write to:
The Garcia Corp.
329 Alfred Ave.
Teaneck, N.J. 07666

TARPON AND THE MOON

The best tarpon fishing usually occurs during the new-moon and full-moon periods when the tides and currents are the strongest. Around three or four days before the full moon and two or three days after, it is a good time to fish for tarpon. The same thing is true of other salt-water gamefish that feed on smaller fishes. During the full moon the strong tides and currents and rips trap the baitfish and make it easier for the larger fish to catch them.

VALENTINE FLY REELS

The Valentine fly reels are high-class precision products designed for fly fishermen who want something better than the average fly reel. The Valentine is made of tempered gold-anodized aluminum alloy, making it much stronger, lighter, and less brittle than a casting. The bearings are bronze, and the line guards are stainless steel. All parts are corrosion-resistant, making them ideal for salt-water use. The parts are hand-assembled without rivets, so the complete dissassembly is easy. An improved new friction brake utilizes a Teflon disk for cooler, smoother, and stronger infinitely variable drag. The Valentine fly reels are made in three sizes: Model No. 350 is 3½ in. in diameter, Model No. 375 is 3¾ in. in diameter, and Model 400 is 4 in. in diameter. The Model 400 holds a WF11F fly line and 300 yds. of 20-lb.-test line for backing, making it popular for those who fish for big, long-running, salt-water gamefish. For more information about these reels write to:
Val-Craft, Inc.
67 N. Worcester St.
Chartley, Mass. 02712

AQUA SCOPE DEPTH SOUNDERS

The Aqua Scope recording depth sounders give you accurate depth soundings as well as a permanent recording of individual and schools of fish at their actual depth and locality. You can even relate the size of the marking on the graph with the size and species of your catch. Moreover, the graphs help you to return to the exact location that has proved productive. Aqua Scope's high-resolution white-line or bottom-line discrimination circuit helps you to separate fish or plants on or close to the bottom from the actual bottom. They have reliable all-solid-state electronics that provide compactness, extremely low power drain, portability, and high performance. They make narrow-beam and wide-beam units sounding to depths of several hundred feet or more. For a folder describing these models write to:
Telisons International Corp.
Marine Products Div.
70751/2 Vineland Ave.
North Hollywood, Calif. 91605

POMPANETTE GAFFS

The Pompanette people are well known in the big-game and offshore fishing field for their fine fighting and fishing chairs, gin poles, fish boxes, outriggers and holders, fishing kites, deck hardware, and nautical furniture. They also make some excellent gaffs in different sizes and models from big flying gaffs to short, small-surf, and release gaffs. They have a big, handsome catalog showing these gaffs and their other products. The catalog costs $1.50 and can be obtained from:
Pompanette, Inc.
1515 S.E. 16th St.
Fort Lauderdale, Fla. 33316

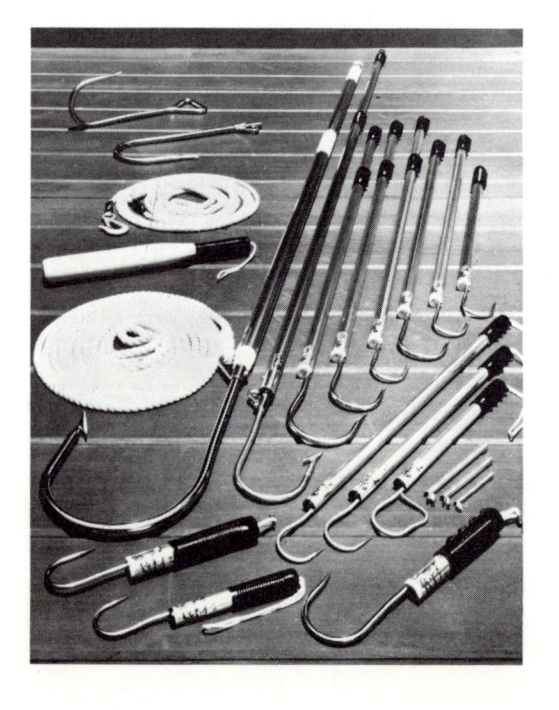

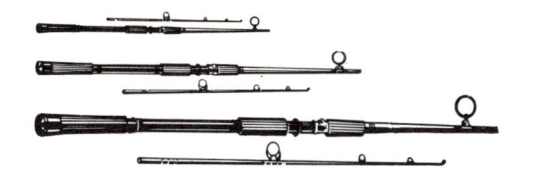

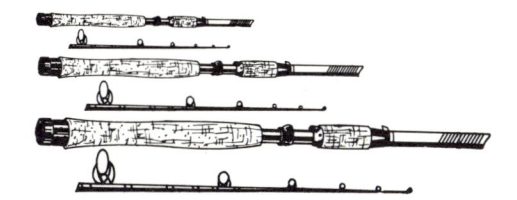

BLUE WATER TACKLE

This is a mail-order house that handles most of the fishing tackle and accessories needed for salt-water fishing from boats, shore, surf, piers, or any other place. They handle such well-known reels as the Fin-Nor, Penn, Garcia, Olympic, and Daiwa in big-game, trolling, surf, spinning, and casting models. They also have all kinds of rods for salt-water fishing. And they sell outriggers, rod holders, lines, leaders, snaps, swivels, hooks, rigs, lures, tackle boxes, knives, fishing harnesses, and various accessories. For their catalog showing all these items write to:
Blue Water Tackle
P.O. Box 438
Arlington, Mass. 02174

BALLYHOO FOR BAIT

Ballyhoo or balao make good bait, and while they can be bought in most southern tackle stores and from bait dealers, some anglers catch their own. This can be done offshore if you chum with oatmeal and then use tiny hooks baited with bits of shrimp. Most ballyhoo are used dead by rigging a whole one with a single or double hook and then drifting with it or trolling it on top of the water. But a live ballyhoo can also be used for sailfish with or without a float from a drifting boat.

MONSTER SNOOK

When Bill Hodges cast out a live shrimp from a seawall near Fort Pierce, Florida, he never expected to hook a snook that would prove to be one of the largest caught on rod and reel in United States waters. But that is what happened when he got a bite at daybreak and fought and landed a monster snook that later weighed in at 50 lbs., 12 ozs. This is less than 2 lbs. shy of the all-tackle record caught in La Paz, Mexico, in 1963. That snook weighed 52 lbs., 6 ozs.

FISHING FROM BOATS

The book *Fishing from Boats* by Milt Rosko covers almost everything you need to know to catch fish from boats in bays, sounds, inlets, surf, and offshore. Milt starts off with the different kinds of boats that are used for fishing, telling what kind of fishing they are best suited for. Then he goes into selecting the basic tackle, trolling, chumming, bottom fishing, boat casting, fighting, and boating your fish. Next there are detailed profiles of the boatman's fifty favorite species. There is even a glossary of boat-fishing terms at the end of the book. *Fishing from Boats* sells for $6.95 and is published by:
Macmillan, Inc.
866 Third Ave.
New York, N.Y. 10022

GIANT TUNA PARADISE

Prince Edward Island in Canada has jumped into the foreground in recent years as one of the top spots in the world for giant bluefin tuna. The fishing is relatively new and only started less than a dozen years ago. Since then big tuna going over 1,000 lbs. have been caught, and hundreds of tuna from 600 to 1,000 lbs. have been taken. There are charter boats available for this fishing, which runs from July to September. There is also fishing for cod, pollock, halibut, hake, and mackerel available in these waters. For more information about the tuna fishing write to:
Dept. of Environment and Tourism
P.O. Box 2000
Charlottetown, P.E.I.
Canada C1A 7N8

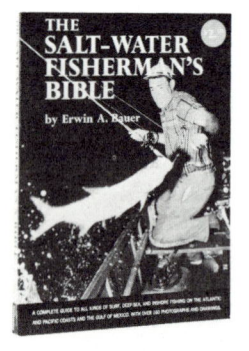

TWO MEN—ONE FISH!

Two anglers from Miami, Florida, were jigging off the Bahamas when both their rods went down and each thought he had a fish. But when they reeled in the 31-lb. grouper they saw that the fish had taken both their lures and they were hooked to the same fish!

THE SALT-WATER FISHERMAN'S BIBLE

The Salt-water Fisherman's Bible by Erwin A. Bauer is a complete guide to all kinds of fishing in the surf, inshore, bays, inlets, sounds, and offshore along the Atlantic, Pacific, and Gulf coasts. It covers most of the popular species such as striped bass, channel bass, weakfish, bluefish, tarpon, ladyfish, snook, bonefish, permit, swordfish, marlin, sailfish, dolphin, wahoo, mackerel, cobia, tuna, snappers, groupers, cod, pollock, porgies, fluke, flounders, yellowtail, albacore, sheepshead, salmon, and many others. The author also covers the fishing tackle, lures, and natural baits and rigs used in salt-water fishing. Some of the salt-water fishing hot spots are also covered, and there's even a chapter on how to cook salt-water fish, with thirty-eight recipes and advice on smoking fish. The book is well illustrated with line drawings and photos. It sells for $2.50 and is published by:
Doubleday & Co., Inc.
501 Franklin Ave.
Garden City, N.Y. 11530

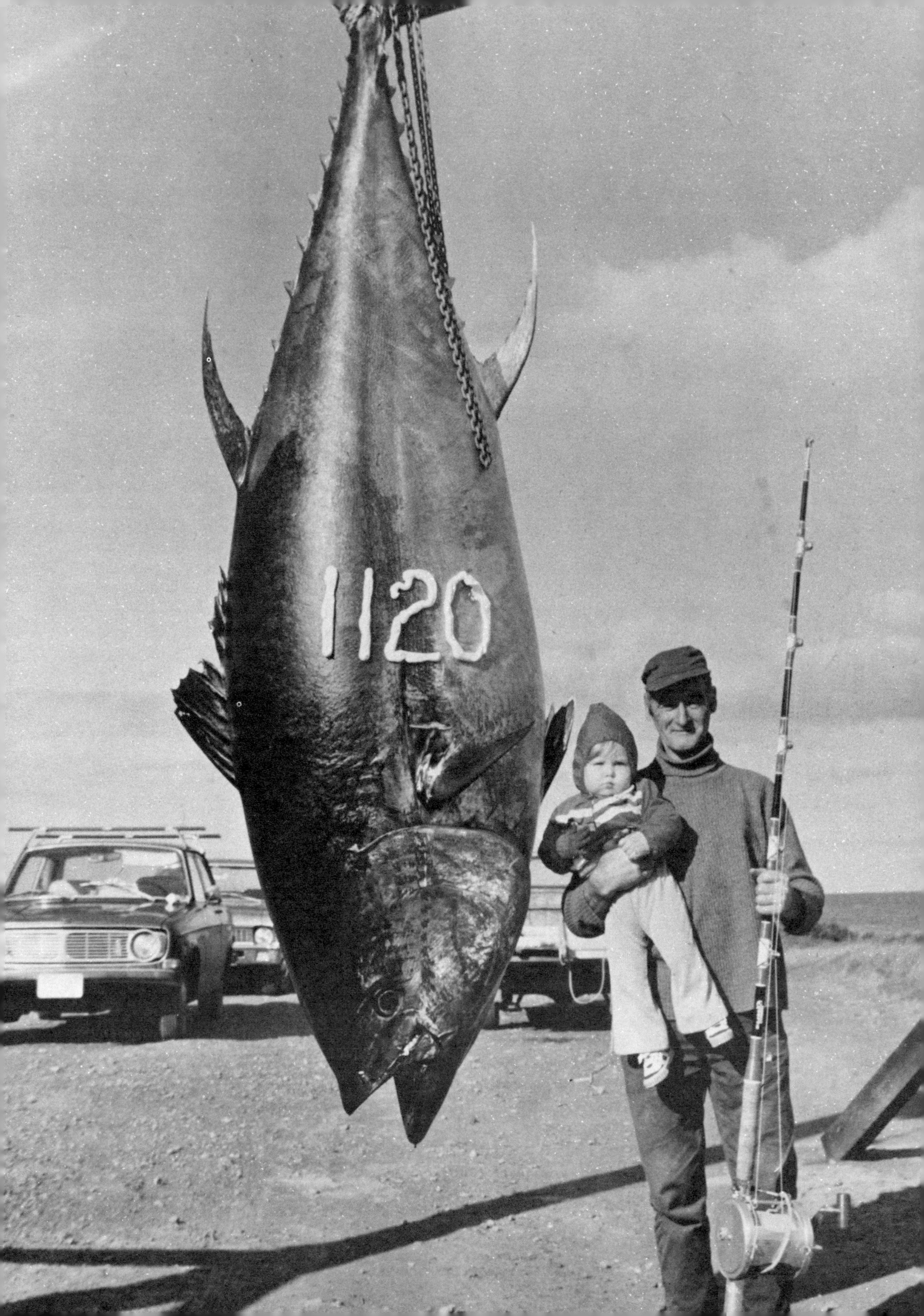
1120

FISH HAWK MARINE 1206

This electronic fishing aid offers the best of both fishing worlds. You can use the 60-ft. scale and range for close-up analysis of structure—or just slide the dial-face switch for deep search on the 180-ft. scale. It has a fine-line readout for detailed structure analysis. It has a long-life, bright-light signal bulb and nonglare face. It wires directly to the boat's 12-v. system. The electronics are sealed from rain and spray, and it has special protection against corrosion, rust, electrolysis, and mildew. This same company makes many other electronic fish aids for both fresh and salt water in a wide variety of models and price ranges. For a catalog or more information contact:
The Waller Corp.
4220 Waller Dr.
Crystal Lake, Ill. 60014

FISHING ROD HOLDERS

These fishing rod holders lock in three positions: center, left, or right. The rod is supported at a 45-degree angle. The holder is 6½ in. long, with 1⅞ in. inside diameter. The standard model locks in position with a stainless-steel lock screw. The charter model is designed to allow changing from one position to another simply by raising the holder and changing position. The shaft ring acts as a stop lock. This company also makes other marine hardware for fishing such as outrigger poles, outrigger holders, fish boxes, live bait tanks, downriggers, and a variety of boat hardware. For their catalog showing all of these write to:
R. C. Plath Co.
337 N.E. 10th Ave.
Portland, Ore. 97232

ROCK-AWAY SAILFISH CHAIR

The Rock-Away Sailfish Chair is a medium-to-heavy-duty fishing chair that has wide, comfortable proportions for sitting, yet is ruggedly functional for fishing. It has heavy castings throughout, 3-in.-diameter stanchion with oilite bearings. It can be deck-mounted with through deck mount, complete with cover for use when chair is removed, and all necessary hardware. It is available with or without the foot rest. It has one deluxe rod holder and one glass holder. For their catalog and more information about this and other fishing and fighting chairs, outriggers, and rod holders write to:
Rock-Away Sport Fishing Equipment Co.
Yale and Myrtle Aves.
Morton, Pa. 19070

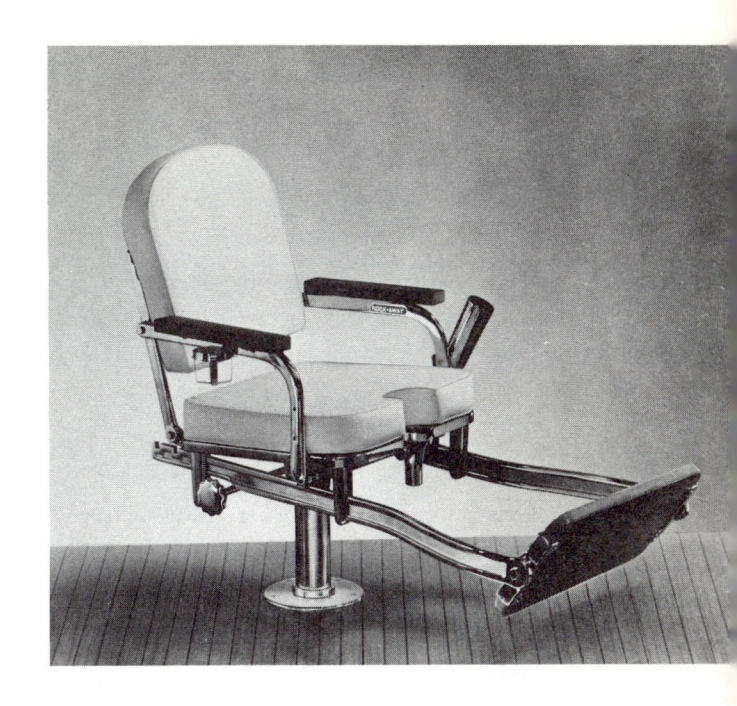

AL PFLUEGER'S FISHERMAN'S HANDBOOK

This is a paperback by a skilled angler, fish expert, taxidermist, and naturalist. The name "Pflueger" is, of course, known all over the world where big-game fish are caught and sent to be mounted at the Pflueger Marine Taxidermy plant in Florida. Al Pflueger, Jr., the author of this fishing handbook is the son of the man who founded the taxidermy company.

The *Fisherman's Handbook* covers all the important freshwater and salt-water species and tells where they are found, their habits, and how to catch them. It is profusely illustrated with color paintings by Russ Smiley and color photos of live fish from the Miami Seaquarium. *Al Pflueger's Fisherman's Handbook* sells for $5.00 and can be obtained from:
Russ Smiley
12000 N.W. 22nd Pl.
Miami, Fla. 33167

FISHES OF THE NORTHERN GULF OF MEXICO

This book is primarily an identification manual that will enable an angler to recognize almost any fish that he will catch in the shallow waters between central Florida and southern Texas in the Gulf of Mexico. Each species is illustrated with one or more identification diagrams. There are 522 diagrams of whole fish plus over 200 drawings of tooth, head, and fin details. Over 200 species are illustrated in color. Great care has been taken to make both the common names and scientific names agree with current usage. The book is 432 pages, hardbound, plastic-laminated color on the cover. *Fishes of the Northern Gulf of Mexico* by Jerry G. Walls sells for $9.95, $.50 for postage and is published by:
T.F.H. Publications, Inc.
211 W. Sylvania Ave.
Neptune City, N.J. 07753

PENN SURF REELS

The Penn Fishing Tackle Manufacturing Company has been making fine reels for many years. Their surf reels such as the Squidder and the Surfmaster are used by many expert and veteran surf casters when fishing for big fish. The surf reels all have precision ball bearings, triple chrome plating and one-screw take-apart for quick spool change. They are available in either metal or plastic spools. The reels hold anywhere from 200 to 400 yds. of line depending on the test being used. For more details about these and other reels they make send for their catalog to:
The Penn Fishing Tackle Mfg. Co.
3028 W. Hunting Park Ave.
Philadelphia, Pa. 19132

ALCEDO SPINNING REELS

The Alcedo spinning reels are well known as high-quality products and have been around for a long time. The Alcedo 2 C/S is popular as a light salt-water spinning reel. It weighs 11½ ozs. and has a gear ratio of four to one. It holds 350 yds. of 6-lb.-test monofilament and 200 yds. of 10-lb. test. It has 36 precision ball bearings and precision-machined helical gear drive resulting in a smooth operation. The double cam rollers close the bail pickup on ¼ handle turn. The bail is stainless steel, and the reel is anodized to prevent corrosion.

They also have two heavy-duty Alcedo salt-water spinning reels for surf and even offshore fishing. One is the Mark IV, which holds 700 yds. of 14-lb. test, and the other is the Mark V, which holds 600 yds. of 20-lb. test. Both reels have heavy-duty ball bearings, five multiplying, heat-treated helical gears, and a brake system that gives progressive braking—six full turns from free spool to full lock. The roller is diamond-ground agate. The finish is hard, anodized Sulumin. For more information about these Alcedo reels write to:
Continental Arms Corp.
697 Fifth Ave.
New York, N.Y. 10022

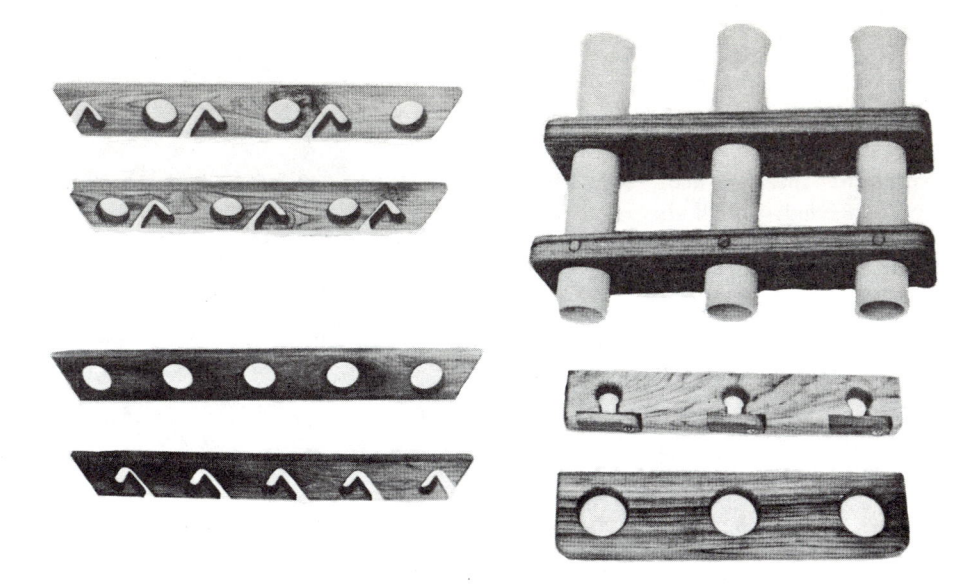

TEAK ROD HOLDERS

This company makes teak rod holders for mounting in a boat, mobile home, or camper. They are designed for secure stowage and keep rods and reels in place under the roughest sea or road conditions. The rod racks are available in teak or mahogany unfinished. Mounting boards and locking tabs are available. They have two-, four-, and six-rod holders from 8 in. to 23 in. in length. They also have a tournament rack for console mounting that has the strength of PVC and the beauty of teak. These come in two-, three-, and four-rod holders. And they make a lock-in rack designed to be used in the vertical or horizontal position. These come in two-, three-, and four-rod holders. They also make other teak accessories for boats such as galley racks, cup racks, glass racks, bottle racks, knife racks, and folding and fixed ladders. Their catalog costs $.50 and shows all these teak products. Write to:

Chips & Shavings
9410 N.E. 13th St.
Miami, Fla. 33126

SALTY BOOGIE

The Salty Boogie is a large-sized plastic plug designed for surf casting and saltwater trolling. It has a natural swimming motion and constantly vibrating action that appeals to striped bass, bluefish, channel bass, tarpon, snook, and other fish. It weighs 3 ozs., is 4½ in. long, and casts like a bullet. It comes in ten colors and sells for $3.00. For more information or their catalog showing this and other lures write to:

Whopper Stopper, Inc.
P.O. Box 1111
Sherman, Tex. 75090

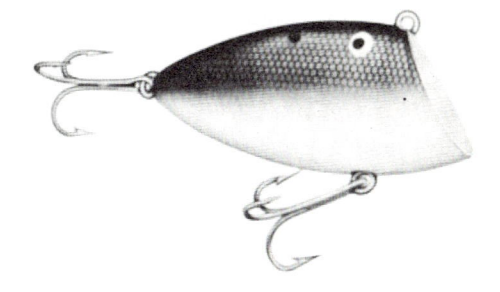

SURF BAG

Surf anglers who do a lot of fishing with lures such as metal squids, spoons, plugs, and plastic eels need a container that holds such lures and makes them available quickly when needed. To fill this need the Shoreline Products people designed a handy surf bag with a shoulder strap and belt loops so that it can be worn, leaving your hands free for casting and playing fish. There are two sizes: a ten-compartment bag that sells for $17.95, and a five-compartment bag that sells for $13.95. In addition to the metal-lined inner compartments there are outer pockets for metal squid or Hopkins lures. The bags are made and sold by:

Shoreline Products
P.O. Box 233
East Northport, N.Y. 11731

FLOATING SUNGLASSES

Fishermen are always dropping sunglasses overboard or are worried about doing so. Most sunglasses sink and are lost forever when this happens. But not the "Aqua-Mates," which are designed to float and are made by Foster Grant Co., Inc., one of the world's largest manufacturers of sunglasses.

The "Aqua-Mate" sunglasses are ruggedly constructed of a specially formulated lightweight and durable plastic. They also feature polarized lenses that are unsurpassed in dispelling glare and that enable a fisherman to see down into the water to spot obstacles and fish. They make several different types, and the glasses retail for $6.00 per pair with a carrying case that also floats. For more information write to:

Foster Grant Co., Inc.
Leominster, Mass. 01453

CONVERSE BOOTS AND PARKAS

The Converse Rubber Company is well known for their complete line of boots, waders, parkas, jackets, and other clothing, which are widely used by fishermen and hunters. They make several kinds of hip boots, pacs, and shoes. Their "Rod & Reel" boots come in regular and insulated models. They are lightweight and have a rubber surface and fabric lining with cleated crepe sole and molded heel. The women's boots come in sizes 5 to 10, and the men's boots come in sizes 6 to 14.

They also make a nylon parka pullover and trousers that are handy to keep in a car or in a boat or carry on a fishing trip in case it rains—or when riding in a boat that throws spray. It offers windproof, waterproof protection, combined with lightweight strength and comfort. The parka features a foldaway hood with drawstring, a stand-up collar, inside elasticized cuffs, side take-up cords, and a gusset-backed 9-in. zipper. The trousers are full cut with elasticized waist. This parka comes in Sherwood Green in sizes S-M-L-XL For their catalog showing the boots, parkas, and other clothing they make write to:

Converse Rubber Co.
55 Fordham Rd.
Wilmington, Mass. 01887

PEQUEAU RIGS

Pequeau Fishing Tackle, Inc. (pronounced "Peck-Way"), has been making rigs and tackle since 1902. Their rigs are widely used both for fresh and salt water. They make worm gangs, snelled hook spinners, panfish rigs, minnow rigs, salmon egg rigs, and trout rigs for freshwater use. For saltwater fishing they make tandem hooks, fluke rigs, mackerel rigs, codfish rigs, snapper rigs, flounder rigs, porgy rigs, bluefish rigs, striped-bass trolling rigs, bottom rigs, and surf rigs. They also carry a complete line of snelled hooks for all kinds of fish and fishing and many types of nylon-covered wire leaders. They also sell fishing rods, lines, lures, and accessories. For their catalog, which shows all these rigs and other tackle, write to:
**Pequeau Fishing Tackle, Inc.
Strasburg, Pa. 17579**

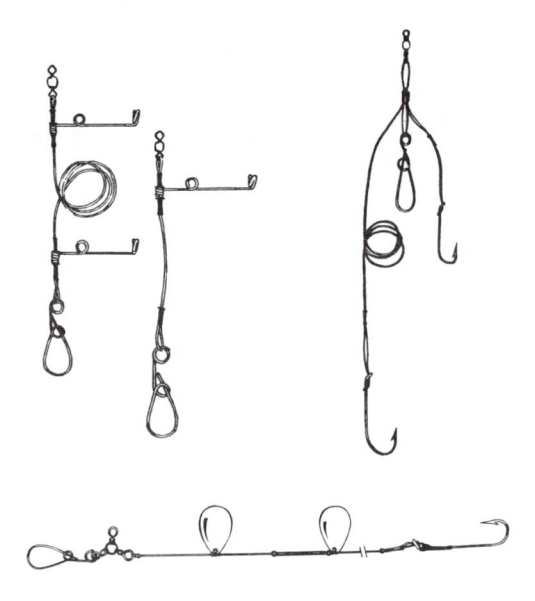

SHAKESPEARE SPORTFISHING RODS

Three new sportfishing rods for live-bait fishing or jigging have been added by Shakespeare. Primarily designed for West Coast yellowtail and albacore, these new rods can also be used for many kinds of fishing in other areas. The rods are one-piece design with heavy-duty Varmac reel seats and two locking rings. Large, comfortable Hypalon fore and rear grips for two-handed fighting of large fish are used on these rods.

The 6-ft. BWC 615 and 7-ft. BWC 616 rods have seven hard-chrome, wire-frame guides and tip-top. These two rods are equipped with casting guides for use with conventional casting reels. For use with open-face spinning reels, the 7-ft. BWS 617 has seven stainless-steel spinning guides and carbide tip-top. The lead and second guides are bridged. All three rods are constructed from tubular WonderGlass rod blanks in a rich brown. Dark brown winds over white complete the attractive appearance of these new Shakespeare sportfishing rods. For more information contact:
**Fishing Tackle Div.
Shakespeare Co.
P.O. Box 246
Columbia, S.C. 29202**

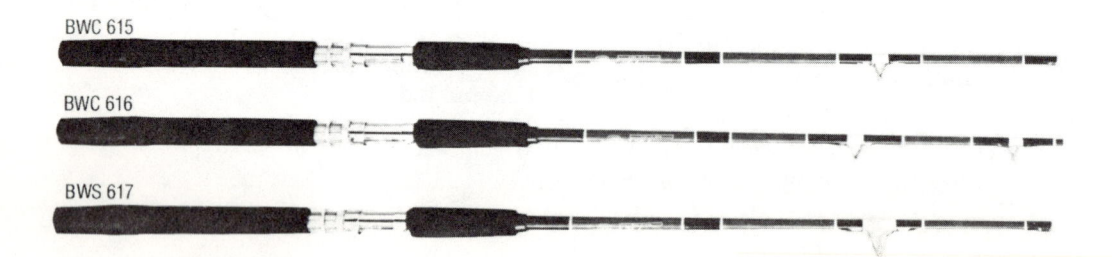

FISHING KITE

There has been a boom in kite fishing offshore, especially off Florida and other waters where sailfish, billfish, and sharks abound. On days when these fish won't take a bait that is trolled from an outrigger or a flat line, they will often hit a live bait suspended from a kite. Such baits as mullet, blue runners, small jacks, pinfish, and others can be made to swim on top of the water in a lively, attractive manner with a kite. Pompanette has a kite developed by Bob Lewis. It comes complete with the pole and reel and is ready to go. For more information write to:
Pompanette, Inc.
1515 S.E. 16th St.
Fort Lauderdale, Fla. 33316

THE SALT-WATER CRAFTSMAN

The book *The Salt-water Craftsman* by Anton Husak is full of all kinds of practical ideas and tips you can use in salt-water fishing, especially in Texas and along the Gulf Coast. He tells how to read the bays, how to locate and catch speckled trout and redfish, float wading, natural baits, oysters, and other shellfish, making your own nets, smoking and preserving your catch, and how to cook it. It is well illustrated with photos and how-to-do-it drawings. The book sells for $8.75 in hardcover and $5.75 in softcover. It is published by:
Cordovan Corp.
5314 Bingle Rd.
Houston, Tex. 77018

SUCCESSFUL OCEAN GAME FISHING

The book *Successful Ocean Game Fishing* by Frank T. Moss covers the entire field of inshore and offshore fishing in the salt waters of the United States and the Bahamas, the Caribbean, Mexico, and other parts of the world. Frank T. Moss was a charter-boat captain for many years at Montauk, New York, and a writer of fishing articles. He also rounded up some knowledgeable contributors who have written chapters for the book. They are Nelson Benedict, Vic McCristal, Mark Sosin, Milt Rosko, Charles Meyer, Harry Bonner, Norman Phillips, Larry Green, and Russell Tinsley. Together they cover such important subjects as choosing and equipping a sport fishing boat, trolling inshore and offshore, jigging, casting, choosing and using salt-water tackle, making leaders, rigging natural baits, kite fishing, and other methods and techniques.

Some of the fish covered in the book include the swordfish, marlins, tunas, sailfish, dolphin, yellowtail, kingfish, striped bass, and bluefish. The book is well illustrated with photos and line drawings showing how to tie knots and rig the baits as well as fishing tackle, equipment, and action fishing shots. *Successful Ocean Game Fishing* sells for $12.50 and is published by:
**International Marine Publishing Co.
Camden, Me. 04843**

CATHER'S SPOONS

J. T. Cather & Son, Inc., makes several kinds of spoons, including shad spoons and larger types. Their shad spoons come in No. 00, No. 0, and No. 1, and are either with plain hooks or with bucktail hair or feathers. They come in nickel or gold finishes. They also have a shad rig with a shad spoon on top and a jig on the bottom. Their Cather's spoons come in larger No. 2½, No. 3, and No. 4 sizes, with stronger 2/0, 5/0, and 7/0 hooks. These are popular for striped bass, bluefish, weakfish, redfish, and other fish. They also come in nickel or gold finishes with feathers of all-white, all-yellow, all-pink, or red and yellow and green and yellow. For a brochure showing these lures write to:
**J. T. Cather & Son, Inc.
6401 Pine Lane Dr.
Suitland, Md. 20023**

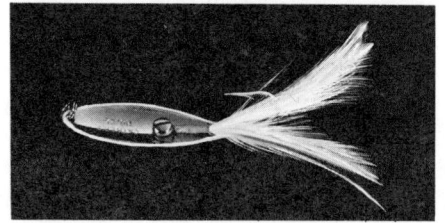

JOHNSON SEA-HORSE OUTBOARDS

The Johnson Outboards Company now offers their famous Sea-Horse motors in many models, from their small 2-, 4-, and 6-hp. engines to the big, powerful 115-, 135-, and 200-hp. models, with many different sizes in between. For a catalog giving more detailed information about all the outboards they make write to:

Johnson Outboards Co.
200 Sea-Horse Dr.
Waukegan, Ill. 60085

O'DONNELL ROD COMPANY

This company specializes in handmade rods built to the customer's specifications. They are all custom-made for fishermen who appreciate fine workmanship and a quality rod. If you are not sure exactly the type of rod you want, you can write them telling them what kind of fishing you plan to do, average weight and size of the fish you plan to catch, the lure or sinker weights you will be using, the line test, and the casting distance desired, and they'll suggest a rod and quote a price.

They make salt-water trolling rods, boat rods, surf rods, casting and popping rods, spinning and bait-casting rods, and fly rods. They can usually complete and ship a custom-made rod within three to four weeks from receipt of order. For more information and prices of their rods write to:

O'Donnell Rod Co.
107 Westfield Rd.
Holyoke, Mass. 01040

SURF FISHING

The book *Surf Fishing* by Vlad Evanoff deals with the branch of salt-water fishing that is both challenging and difficult. Here you will get a full course in this exciting form of angling. The book gives expert advice on reading the shoreline, the wind, the waves, and the weather, and how they affect surf fishing. Surf-fishing rods, reels, lines, and accessories are thoroughly covered. So are the various lures such as metal squids, spoons, other metal lures, surface and underwater plugs, jigs, rigged eels, plastic eels, and eelskin lures. There is also a chapter on natural baits covering bloodworms, sandworms, surf clams, crabs, sand bugs or fleas, shrimp, mullet, menhaden, eels, squid, and other baits, together with the rigs used with such baits.

There are also chapters on the techniques and ways of fishing sand beaches, rocky shores, jetties, and breakwaters. There is also information on the Atlantic and Pacific striped bass, channel bass, bluefish, weakfish, sea trout, pompano, blackfish, kingfish, pollock, black drum, Atlantic croaker, snook, tarpon, sharks and rays, spotfin croaker, yellowfin croaker, corbina, surf perch, rockfish, and salmon.

The chapter on the surf angler's workshop covers the making of surf-fishing lures and the care and repair of fishing tackle. Another chapter deals with dangers, manners, conservation, and sportsmanship. And at the end of the book there is a long section covering surf-fishing spots in each of the coastal states. *Surf Fishing* sells for $6.95 and is published by:
Harper & Row, Publishers, Inc.
10 E. 53rd St.
New York, N.Y. 10022

BEAD CHAIN MONEL SWIVELS

The Bead Chain Company has been making these Monel swivels and snaps for all kinds of fishing for many years. Each bead acts as a swivel and helps prevent line twist. The snaps are easy to open and close, and the metals used do not rust or corrode in salt water. The same company also makes many other kinds of casting and trolling leads and keel leads with the Bead Chain swivels. They also have flexible spinners in silver and gold on the Bead Chain swivels. For a catalog or more information write to:
Bead Chain Co.
Bridgeport, Conn. 06605

BEAD CHAIN Monel Swivels
"EVERY BEAD A SWIVEL"

ITEM NO.	LBS. TEST
PLAIN	
21	25
61	35
101	75
131	175
SINGLE SNAP	
22	25
32	30
62	35
645	45
102	75
132	120
LOCK TYPE SNAP	
62L	35
102L	75
132L	150
DOUBLE SNAP	
63	35
103	75

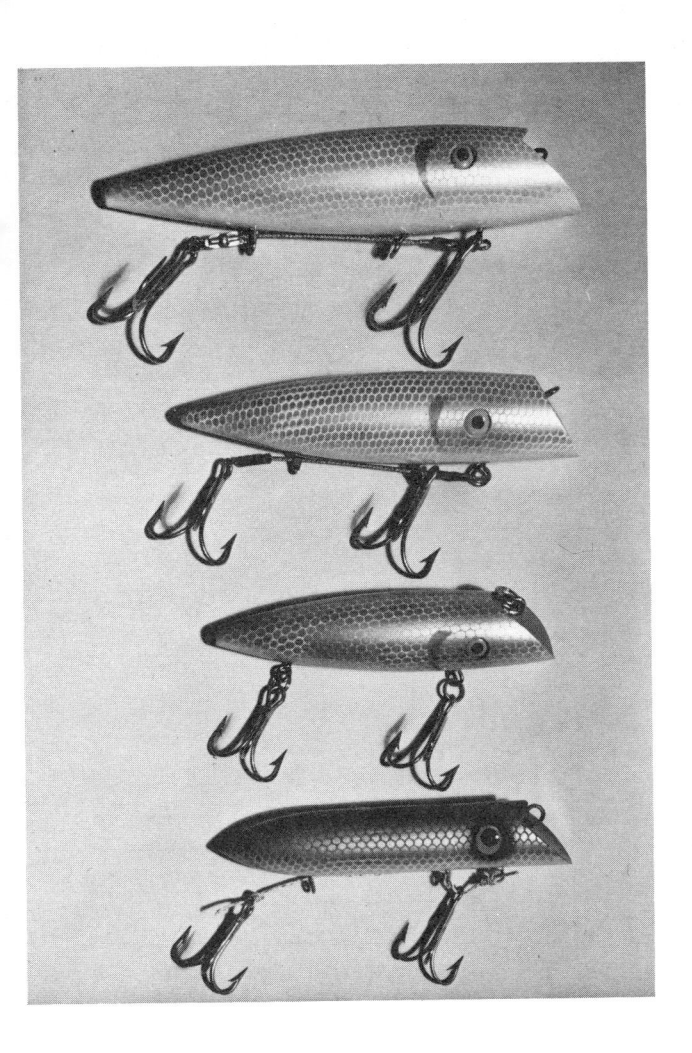

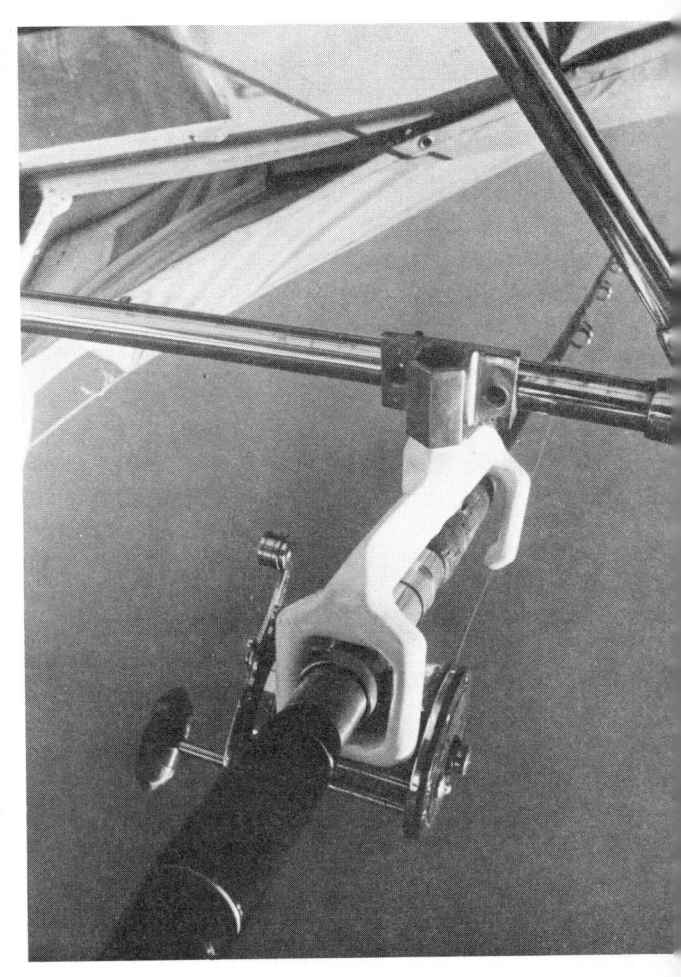

MARTIN PLUGS

The Martin plugs have been famous for many years and have been used in casting or trolling for good-sized fish such as Pacific salmon, striped bass, bluefish, tarpon, and other salt-water species. They come in four models, and three of them have the canit-lever hookup, with a direct line-to-fish hookup. When the fish is hooked, the body of the plug is released, permitting a direct pull on the line. The plugs are made in several sizes, from 3 to 7 in. in length, and in a dozen different finishes. For their catalog describing these and other lures and tackle they make, write to:

Martin Tackle and Mfg. Co.
512 Minor Ave. N.
Seattle, Wash. 98109

DOCKER FISHING ROD HOLDER

The Docker Fishing Rod Holder has a high-tensile aluminum body heavily coated with vinyl to absorb shock and protect the rod from mars and scratches. It is available in flush mount, side mount, or tubular mount in chrome or burnished finishes. This company also makes other marine and boating products, and you can get their catalog from:

Docker Marine
350 Gate 5 Rd.
Sausalito, Calif. 94965

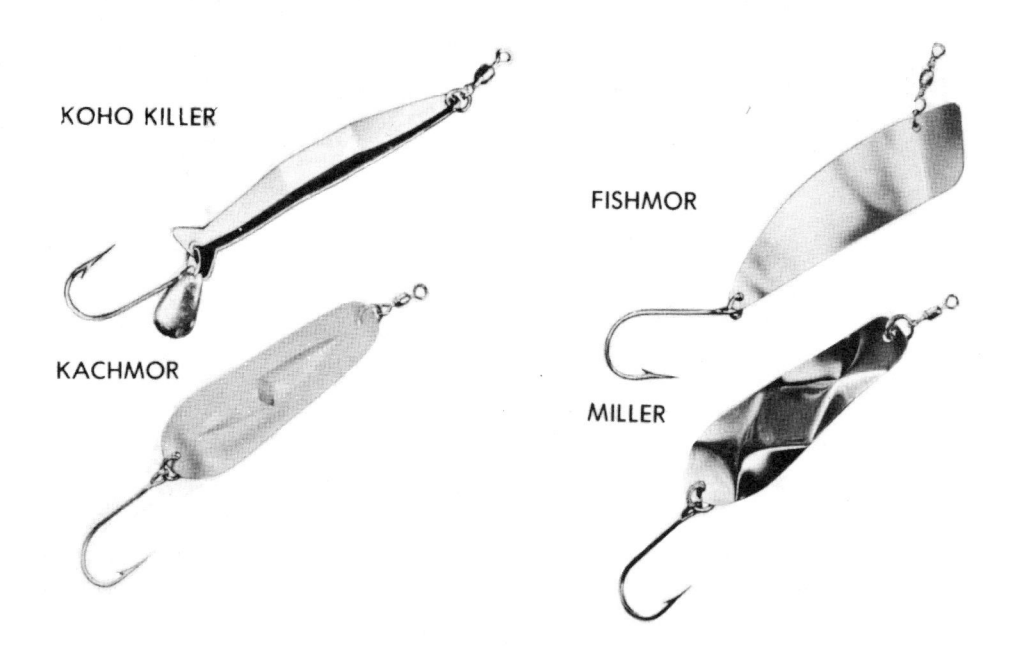

MARTIN SPOONS

The Martin Company specializes in lures used on the Pacific Coast for salmon and other fish in those waters. They make several spoons that are used by sports and commercial fishermen when trolling for silver or king salmon. Their Koho Killer comes in one 3-in. size and has a long, slim blade that imitates a candlefish in action. The Kachmor spoon has a diamond-shaped indentation that increases its crazy wobbling action and light flashes. The Fishmor spoon has a new design that makes it ride upright, causing a wild side-to-side action. And the Miller spoon has seven planes formed at distinct angles to each other to radiate strong light flashes down deep where few sun rays penetrate. The spoons come in various finishes and in three or four sizes, from 2⅛ in. to 5¼ in. For their catalog or more information about these and other lures and tackle they make write to:
Martin Tackle and Mfg. Co.
512 Minor Ave. N.
Seattle, Wash. 98109

CAPT. ANDY MCLEAN'S FISHING MATE

This is a paperback publication which comes out every year. and tells in detail how, when, and where to fish in Everglades National Park in Florida. Captain McLean covers fishing for snook, redfish, tarpon, sea trout, and other fish found there and in the Ten Thousand Islands area. There are sixteen pages of fishing charts of such great fishing spots as Marco Island, Horse to Indian Key, Chokoloskee area, Mormon to Lostman River, Highland Point to Shark River, Big Sable to East Cape, Whitewater Bay, and the Flamingo area. There are also many articles on such subjects as the wind, the moon, and fishing, the barometer and fishing, understanding the tides, trolling, working artificial lures, and bottom fishing. *Capt. Andy McLean's Fishing Mate* sells for $1.95 and is sold at many newsstands and tackle shops in southern Florida. It can also be obtained from:
Captain Andy McLean
5158 N.W. 32nd Ave.
Miami, Fla. 33142

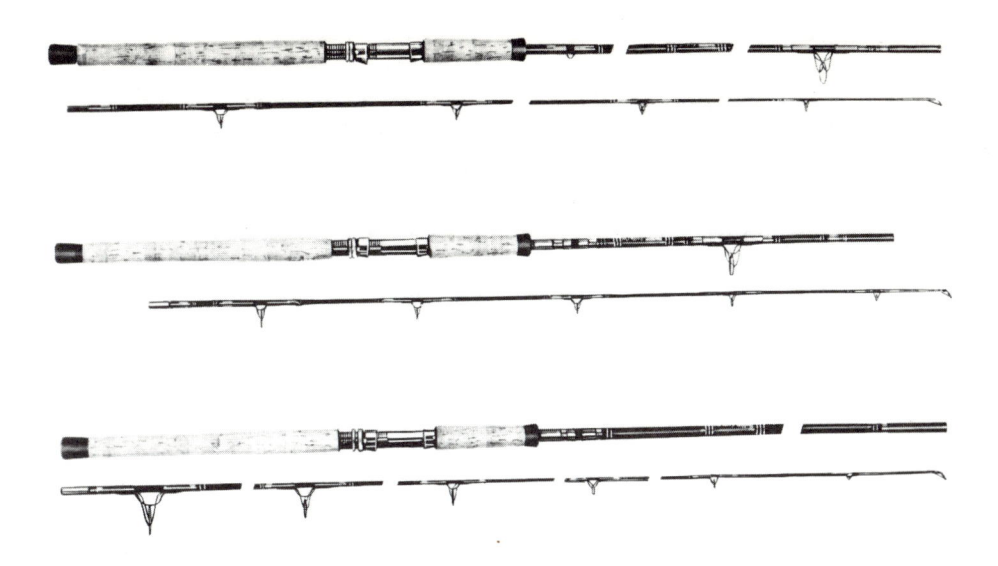

HEDDON SALT-WATER RODS

James Heddon's Sons makes a series of salt-water fishing rods for all kinds of fishing such as medium spinning, heavy spinning, surf fishing, and trolling models. Their "Silver Mark," "Brown Pal," and "Green Pal" spinning rods come in lengths from 8 to 10 ft. in two-piece models. They are made from Fiberglas. They have specie cork butts and foregrips, and corrosion-resistant ferrules, guides, and reel seats. They also have rubber butt caps.

Heddon also makes trolling rods and boat, bay, and pier rods from Fiberglas. Most of these have hardwood handle butts and heavy-duty guides, and some rods are wound with wire. The trolling rods have gimbal butts. For their catalog showing all these rods write to:
**James Heddon's Sons
Dowagiac, Mich. 49047**

TAURUS FLY REEL

The Taurus Fly Reel is a large-sized reel for salt-water fly fishing or big fish in fresh water. It is completely corrosion-proofed, incorporating the most advanced materials. It has a three-way antireverse knob opposite the handle; the knob can be set for right-hand, left-hand, or off. The drag control ring at the base of the grip handle adjusts line tension from very light to full brake. This reel will hold a WF-11 fly line plus 250 yds. of 20-lb. monofilament or braided line. For their catalog showing this and other reels write to:
**Feurer Bros., Inc.
77 Lafayette Ave.
North White Plains, N.Y. 10603**

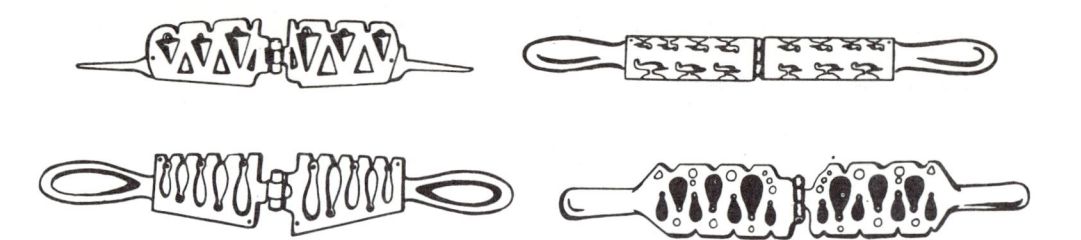

ALUMINUM SINKER MOLDS

This company sells several kinds of aluminum sinker molds for pouring your own lead sinkers. They have a mold for making bank sinkers, pyramid sinkers, egg sinkers, bass casting sinkers, and pinch-on sinkers. Each mold has several cavities for pouring sinkers of different sizes and weights. For more information write to:
Jorgensen Bros.
P.O. Box 69
Pleasanton, Calif. 94566

TAIL TEASER LURES

Tail teasers are a combination of a short, supersoft tail attached to a weighted jig head. They are made in two types: shrimp and split tail grub. They can be bought and used singly, or they can be obtained rigged in tandem, with two lures being used at the same time. These are rigged on 30-lb.-test Steelcore, 24 in. long. For their catalog or more information about these and other lures enclose $.50 and send it to:
Erwin Weller Co.
P.O. Box 3204
Sioux City, Ia. 51102

Rigged Shrimp

Rigged Split Tail Grub

SPEED UP FOR MARLIN

If you see a blue marlin following the bait being trolled but reluctant to strike, try speeding up so that the baits skip across the water in wild leaps. This will often excite the marlin into hitting the bait.

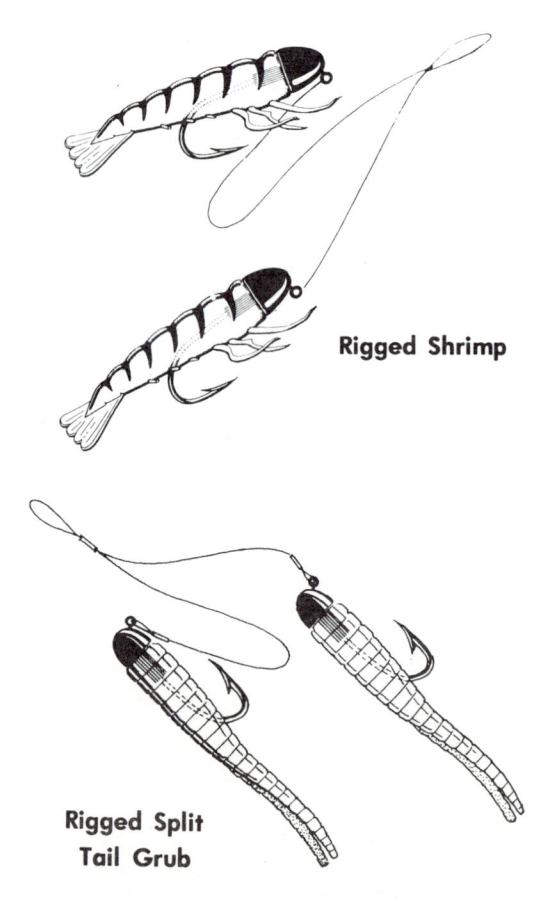

BAHAMAS FISHING

As anyone who has fished there knows, the Bahamas provide some of the world's best salt-water fishing. Located 50 mi. off the coast of Florida, this chain of islands stretches in a 750-mi. arc through 100,000 sq. mi. of the Atlantic Ocean. Here you'll find flats and inshore fishing for the famed bonefish and tarpon. In somewhat deeper waters you can look for grouper, snappers, amberjack, and kingfish. Tuna show up in May and June at Bimini and Cat Cay. And still farther offshore you'll run into sailfish, white marlin, blue marlin, dolphin, yellowfin, tuna, and wahoo. For a colorful and informative brochure *Bahamas Fishing*, write to:

Bahamas Tourist Office
200 S.E. First St.
Miami, Fla. 33131

GARCIA MITCHELL 600A REEL

The Garcia Mitchell 600A reel is one of the 600 Series of reels designed for casting and trolling in salt water. The sideplates are made of DuPont Delrin. There is heavy chrome plating on all exposed metal parts to help prevent corrosion. The reel has oversize bronze maingear and bushings. It has a free-spool control, anti-blacklash spool-tension control that adjusts for any lure or sinker weight. It has a metal spool and self-closing lubricating ports. The 600A holds 400 yds. of 30-lb. Royal Bonnyl II line. Their *Fishing Annual and Catalog* showing this and other reels and tackle costs $1.50 from:
**The Garcia Corp.
329 Alfred Ave.
Teaneck, N.J. 07666**

SHAKESPEARE 2540 SPINNING REEL

Shakespeare has expanded its popular 2500 spinning reel series with the addition of a new reel with larger line capacity. Designed for coho, lake trout, striped bass, and other long-running battlers, the new 2540 has a 3.5-to-1 gear ratio and 250-yd. capacity of 12-lb. mono. Equipped with an efficient spring-loaded multidisk drag, the 2540 has a ball bearing for smooth retrieve. Other features of the new reel include extrastrong precision gears, one-piece foldaway crank with large grip, and selective nonreverse. For more information about this and other spinning reels they make write to:
**Fishing Tackle Div.
Shakespeare Co.
P.O. Box 246
Columbia, S.C. 29202**

MAINE SALT-WATER FISHING

The following publications dealing with Maine salt-water fishing are available:

Catch Me is a brochure describing briefly and in general terms the salt-water sport fishing you'll find in Maine.

The Marine Sport Fishery in Maine contains several pages of salt-water fishing information.

Party Boat List is a listing of some of the party boats, head boats, and charter boats that are available at various ports along the Maine coast.

These publications can be obtained from:
**Dept. of Marine Resources
State House
Augusta, Me. 04333**

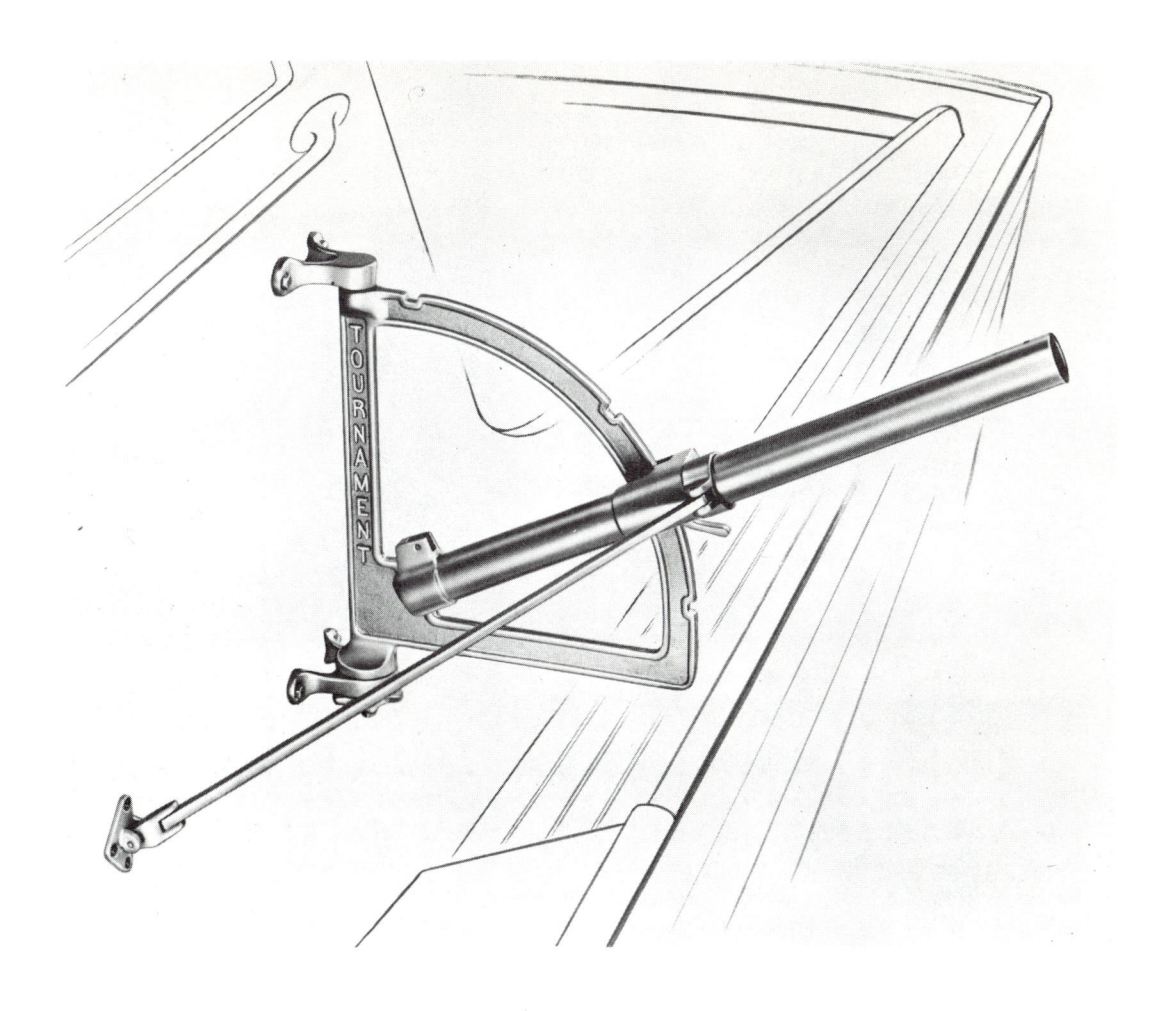

TOURNAMENT OUTRIGGERS

This company makes several types and styles of outriggers to fit on the deck or cabin of any size inboard or outboard. They are ruggedly constructed of cast bronze with heavy chrome plating and stainless-steel hardware. The simple cam handle permits the unit to be swung outboard for trolling or folded inboard. With the "Trigger-lock" feature the outrigger poles are positively locked in any of four positions. You can order just the socket or with the 15-ft. and 20-ft. telescoping poles. This company also makes fighting and fishing chairs, fishing harnesses, rod holders, and various marine hardware for boats. Their catalog showing these is available from:
**Tournament Marine Products
Commerce and Jackson Dr.
Cranford, N.J. 07016**

BIG SNOOK ON SEWING THREAD

Tom Grand is seventeen years old and he likes to fish. So he got an old rod and spinning reel and filled the reel spool with nylon sewing thread, which tested about 4 lbs. Then he baited his hook with shad and cast it out from the banks of the Dixie Canal in Dania, Florida. A big fish grabbed the bait and the battle was on. He had to follow the fish for a mile and even had to go on board a boat docked along the bank to fight the fish in the clear. Finally after a half hour he beached the fish, a big snook that later weighed in at 29 lbs., 8 ozs.!

FISH AROUND BRIDGES

Some of the best fishing in salt water takes place around bridges, either from boats or from the bridge itself. There is usually a strong tide or current under a bridge, and the supports act as buffers and also get covered with mussels and barnacles, which attract crabs, shrimp, and small baitfish and seaworms, which in turn attract the bigger fish.

You can troll from a boat around bridges for striped bass, bluefish, and weakfish in northern waters and for tarpon, snook, sea trout, and other fish in southern waters. Plugs, spoons, metal lures, jigs, plastic worms, and eels can all be used for this. Anglers fishing from the bridge itself can cast these lures into the tide or around the bridge supports. Here fishing is usually better at night than in the daytime.

Live baits such as menhaden, herring, mullet, pilchards, pinfish, and other small fish can also be used around bridges from a boat or from the bridge itself. Here the bait can be live-lined so it swims under the bridge, or you can use a float and let it move out in the tide or current.

And you can fish with other baits such as seaworms, clams, shrimp, crabs, cut fish, and squid under a bridge from a boat or from the structure itself. These baits can be let out in the tide with little or no weight, or you can use them on a bottom rig with a sinker.

The great thing about bridge fishing is that there is no charge for this fishing, and you can come and go as you please. However, tides do govern the fishing, and you have to find out which tides are best for the bridge and the fishing you plan to do. Try different tides and different times of the day or night to determine the best fishing periods.

STU APTE'S FISHING IN THE FLORIDA KEYS

Thousands of anglers who like to fish the Florida Keys and use light tackle will welcome this small but complete guide to fishing the Florida Keys and Flamingo. And no one could have written a better guide for this area than Stu Apte, a name known and respected by most expert and pro anglers throughout the world. Stu knows Florida Keys fishing like the back of his hand, because he has a home there, fishes every chance he gets, and has spent many years as a fishing guide in the Keys.

The book covers almost every important fish that is caught in the Florida Keys, and there are maps and charts that pinpoint the hot spots for each species. Special emphasis is placed on the tarpon, bonefish, permit, barracuda, and sailfish, which are light-tackle favorites with the author. There is also a list of marinas and tackle shops found throughout the Keys. This book is a must if you ever plan to fish the Florida Keys or Flamingo. It sells in many bookstores, tackle shops, and newsstands in Florida for $2.95. It is published by:
Windward Publishing, Inc.
P.O. Box 370233
Miami, Fla. 33137

FISHING CANOPY

A favorite of fishing boat owners, the Fishing Console Canopy affords protection from both sun and rain without cluttering the gunwhale. The Fishing Console Canopy allows for ample headroom with large area coverage. A brilliant idea, the console-style fishing design and the Fishing Console Canopy give you 360-degree fishability and 100 per cent use of the boat interior. Snagged or tangled fishing lines and anchor ropes are avoided, and since the Canopy is extremely strong, it can be used as a hand rail or windshield guard—thus eliminating guard rails and hand holds around the windshield. The price is $199.95. For more information write to:
Imperial Marine Equipment
7601 N.W. 66th St.
Miami, Fla. 33166

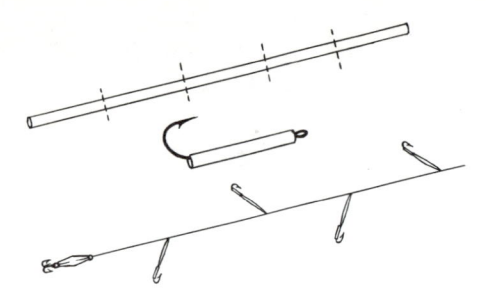

STRAW LURE

You can make a cheap but effective lure from a plain drinking straw such as the plastic ones used at soda fountains and that can be bought in any supermarket. They come in different colors and even with red, yellow, or orange stripes. Simply cut a straw into the length desired or needed and slip it over a hook. You can cut them short for small fish and longer for bigger fish. Use long-shank hooks for the longer straw lures. Then tie a single lure on the end of a line and use it with a fly rod or long pole. Or you can tie anywhere from two to five of the straw lures above a sinker or small diamond jig and cast and jig this rig for small bluefish, weakfish, mackerel, herring, and hickory shad.

CUSTOM MARINE RELEASE 26

The Custom Marine Release 26 is a fast, streamlined fishing boat that has a 200-mi. range and can run all day at up to a third of the fuel consumption of the larger cabin fishing boats. It has been ocean tested for two years and is a top-flight, no-nonsense pocket fisherman. The custom-hand-laid Fiberglas hull is designed specifically to provide high-speed running to offshore fishing waters. Inlaid teak decks and a sensibly designed control console highlight the uncluttered cockpit of the Release 26. The control console's position adjacent to the fighting chair creates an efficient fishing team between the helmsman and angler. The Twin Waukesha 302-cu.-in., 165-hp. engines produce a running speed of approximately 45 mph. economically. The Release 26 is big enough for the open seas, yet small enough for the open road. Easily trailerable, the pocket fisherman is a versatile craft that opens new horizons for the inshore and offshore angler. For a color brochure describing this boat more fully write to:

Custom Marine
P.O. Box 1768
Savannah, Ga. 31402

HILDE'S JERK JIGGER

The Jerk Jigger is made by the John J. Hildebrandt Corporation, famous for their line of spinners. This one, however, is a weighted lure designed for salt-water fishing by casting, trolling, or jigging. It has a wild, zigzag action when cast out and retrieved with plenty of rod action. You can also troll it and give it additional rod action, or you can lower it to the bottom and jig it up and down. It is very good for bluefish, mackerel, sea trout, blue runners, and jacks. For a complete catalog showing this and other lures write to:

John J. Hildebrandt Corp.
P.O. Box 50
Logansport, Ind. 46947

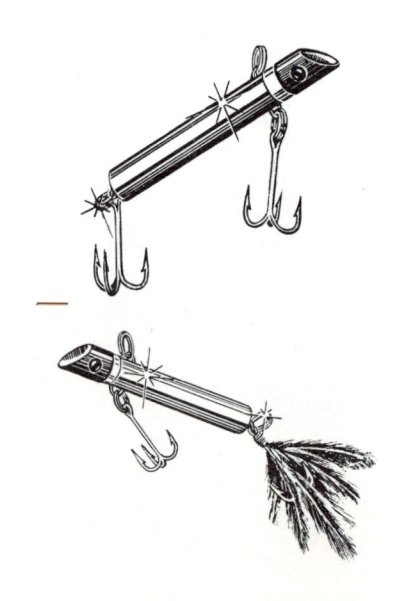

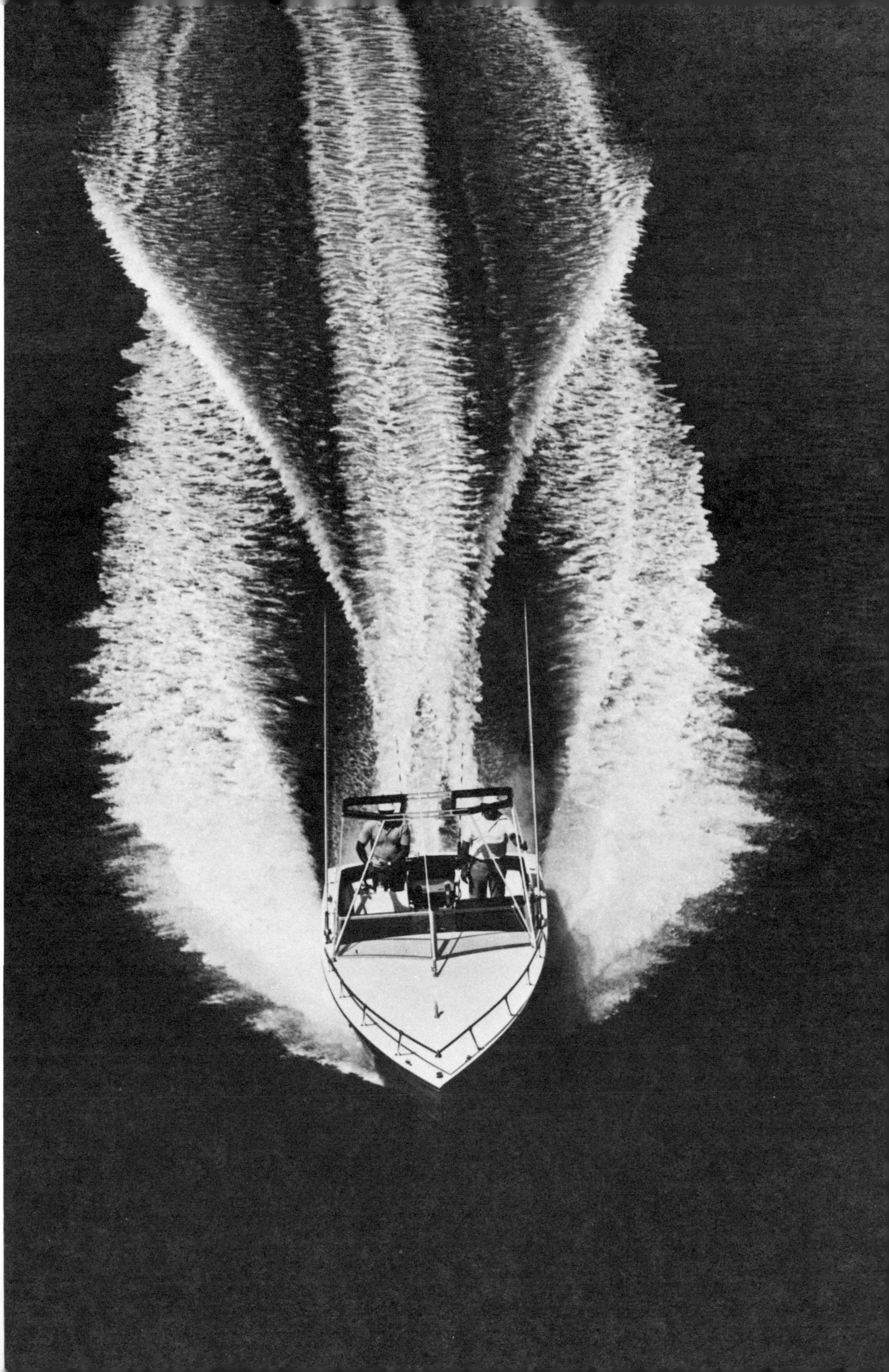

CREEK CHUB PLUGS

The Creek Chub Bait Company plugs are big and husky and are made to hold fish such as striped bass, bluefish, tarpon, snook, king mackerel, and other salt-water species. Such models as the Striper Strike, Straight Pikie, Jointed Pikie, Giant Jointed Pikie, and others are used by surf and boat anglers for the fish mentioned above. They also make a full line of smaller plugs for freshwater and salt-water fishing. Their catalog costs $.25 and shows these plugs and lures in color. Write to:

Creek Chub Bait Co.
Garrett, Ind. 46738

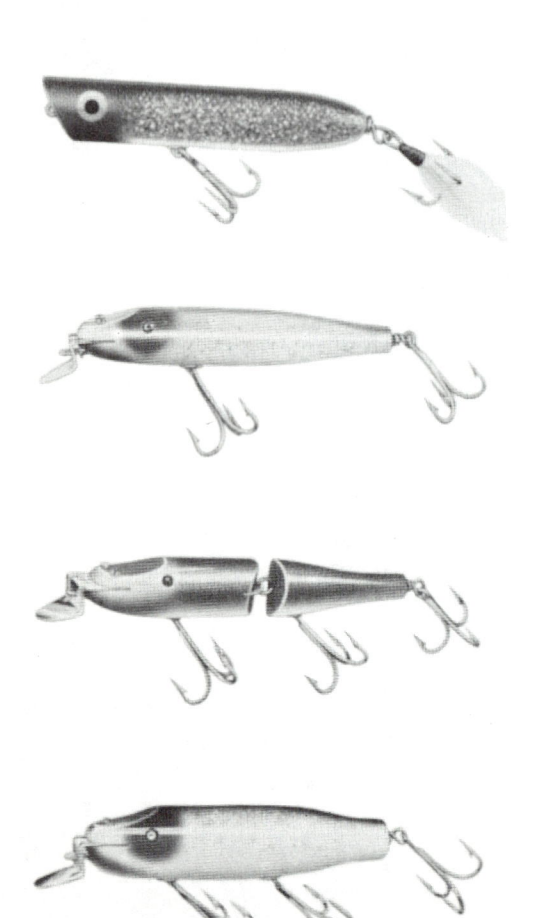

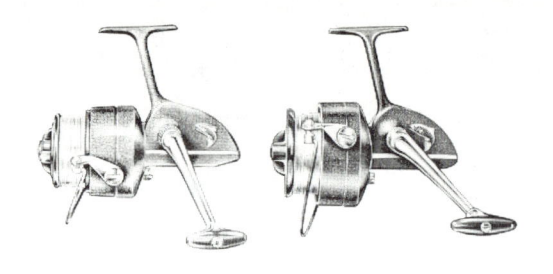

QUICK SPINNING REELS

The Quick spinning reels designed for salt-water fishing are popular with anglers seeking bonefish, snook, tarpon, sea trout, striped bass, bluefish, channel bass, and other salt-water species caught from shore, surf, and boats. They feature ball-bearing drive on the main shaft, stainless-steel bail with tungsten carbide line guides, self-lubricating handle bearings, all precision-machined gears, and handle conversion from right to left hand. They also have an adjustable bail release mechanism for softer or harder operation to suit special fishing needs. The reels are galvanically treated to resist corrosion. They also make fast-retrieve models for reeling in lures fast or taking in line fast when fighting speedy fish. These reels hold from 200 to 400 yds. of line, depending on what test or strength is used. For their catalog showing these and other reels and tackle they make send $.25 to:

Quick Corp. of America
620 Terminal Way
Costa Mesa, Calif. 92627

KEEPING LEADERS

If you fold your monofilament leaders like an accordion instead of coiling them, you'll find it easier to straighten them out when you need them. Use a rubber band to hold the folds of the leader together until it is used.

PENN TROLLING REELS

The Penn Fishing Tackle Manufacturing Company makes a complete line of offshore trolling and big-game fishing reels in a wide price range. Their Senator reel has been popular with anglers and charter-boat captains for many years and comes in sizes from 4/0 to 16/0 for all kinds of offshore fishing. They feature one-piece machined bronze spools, and in the larger models these run on aircraft-quality ball bearings for smoothness and long life. They also make three special fast-retrieve Senators in sizes 3/0, 4/0, and 6/0.

The Penn International Tournament trolling reels are higher priced and are made in sizes for all line classes from 20 lbs. to 130 lbs. They feature a machined aluminum frame and spool with floating disk drag design. They have a lever-action drag control that ranges over a 120-degree arc and provides a wide selection of stable drag adjustments. The preset drag automatically keeps drag tension within safe limits and prevents broken lines. These reels have heavy anodizing for corrosion resistance. For more information about these and other fishing reels they make send for their catalog to:

The Penn Fishing Tackle Mfg. Co.
3028 W. Hunting Park Ave.
Philadelphia, Pa. 19132

GREAT STRIPER CATCH

As any veteran long-time striper fisherman knows, these wary and temperamental fish do not come easy, especially when you try to catch a big one from the surf. But Frank Mitchell from Philadelphia doesn't think they are that hard to catch. He was surf fishing at Stone Harbor, New Jersey, only the second time in his life when he hooked and beached a 52-lb. striped bass and won the surf fishing tournament running at the time. Many a surf angler has fished a lifetime without catching such a big striper and would gladly give up a month's pay to do so.

FISHING FROM JETTIES

Jetties and breakwaters often provide good fishing, and many different kinds of salt-water fish can be caught from them. In northern Atlantic waters you'll catch striped bass, bluefish, weakfish, pollock, mackerel, blackfish or tautog, porgies, and summer flounders from them. In southern waters you'll catch redfish or channel bass, snook, tarpon, sea trout, jacks, Spanish mackerel, sheepshead, snappers, grouper, croakers, and spot. In Pacific waters anglers get salmon, halibut, greenling, ling cod, rockfish, and surf perch from the rock piles.

Fish such as striped bass, especially, will come close to the rocky jetties to feed at night. Here casting lures such as plugs, rigged eels, plastic eels, and jigs from the front or sides of the jetty will often produce. Work these lures right up to the rocks, since stripers will often follow a lure until it is about to disappear in the white water, and then they'll hit it. You'll catch bigger fish from the rocks than from the beach because you can cast to deeper water and more productive spots.

The higher, more recently built jetties and breakwaters can often be fished during the high tides. But the lower, older jetties are often covered by water at this time, and then you'll have to wait for low tide to fish them.

But jetties and breakwaters can also be dangerous to fish, and anglers have been swept off the rocks by big waves or injured themselves in falls on the slippery rocks. Certain precautions are necessary to fish them safely. First, it pays to have ice creepers or sandals with hob nails on your waders to give you better footing on the mossy or wet rocks. And bring along a gaff with a long handle to hoist the fish from the water when the waves are breaking. Fish with a buddy at all times in case either of you get into trouble. And always stand back or on a high rock where the waves can't reach you with their full force.

CHRONOMARINE TIDEWATCH

As every salt-water fisherman fishing from shore, surf, or boat knows, tides are very important and have a great bearing on when and where the fish will be biting. So every salt-water angler in the past has studied the local tide tables to find out when the tide was favorable for the area he was fishing.

Now there's a watch called the Chronomarine Tidewatch, which will give you the stage of the tide at a glance. The first setting of the Tidewatch is made at the exact time of either high tide or low tide on the day when it is first used. For this you consult local tide tables for your coastal area to find the correct times for that day.

The tidewatch will then indicate daily, under normal tide conditions for your coastal area, the average stage of the tides without further reference to the tide tables. The numerals on the right-hand side of the dial indicate progressively, in a clockwise direction, how many hours to low water; those on the left-hand side of the dial the number of hours to high water.

The Tidewatch sells for $45. You can obtain more information, including a little brochure, *An explanation of the Tides*, from the following company:
Regent Marine & Instrumentation, Inc.
1051 Clinton St.
Buffalo, N.Y. 14206

CORTLAND DACRON LINE

The Cortland "Greenspot" Dacron trolling line has distinctive greenspot markings and is popular with offshore and big-game fishermen. It is a shock-resistant, small-diameter trolling line that meets IGFA class specifications and is braided coreless for easy splicing, with a needle to avoid strength-sapping knots. It is made in tests from 12 lbs. to 130 lbs. and comes in 50-yd. and 100-yd. attached spools in boxes or on 500-, 800-, and 1,200-yd. single spools. For their catalog showing this and other freshwater and salt-water fishing lines write to:
Cortland Line Co.
Cortland, N.Y. 13045

363

LUCKY LUJON LURES

The "Lucky Lujon" lure made by the Louis Johnson Company is a versatile lure that can be used for casting, trolling, or jigging. This lure casts like a bullet because of its slim, compact "Nordic" design. It is especially deadly when it is lowered to the bottom and jigged up and down or reeled back fast with plenty of rod action. It can be used for striped bass, bluefish, weakfish, mackerel, salmon, yellowtail, king mackerel, sea trout, and many other salt-water species. The "Lucky Lujon" comes in four sizes, from a tiny ⅛-oz. model up to the big 2½-oz. size. It comes in chrome, brass, black-nickel, white-scale, blue-scale, yellow-scale, and green-scale finishes. For their catalog showing these and other lures they make write to:
Louis Johnson Co.
1547 Old Deerfield Rd.
Highland Park, Ill. 60035

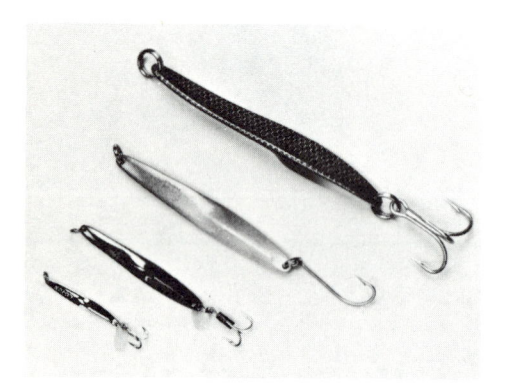

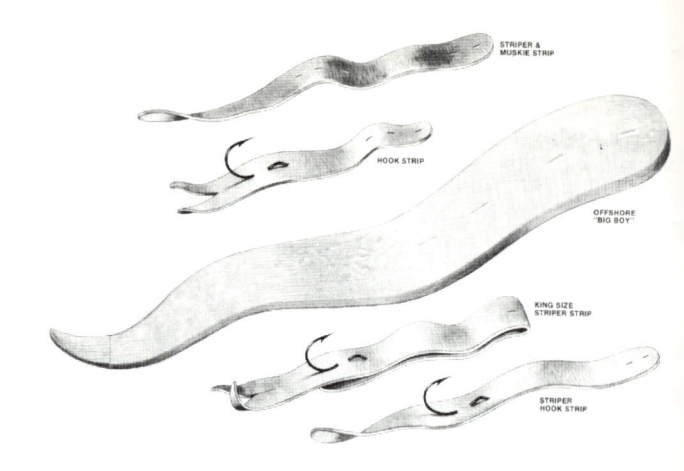

UNCLE JOSH PORK RIND

The Uncle Josh Bait Company has been making pork rind baits, strips, chunks, and eels for many years. Salt-water anglers find their baits great for using on metal squids, spoons, jigs, and other lures. They are especially popular for striped bass, and special strips are made for these fish with a hook in the tail for the short strikers or for extra insurance in hooking these fish. But their strips are also used for many other species. They even have a big 10-in. offshore Big Boy strip, which can be used for sailfish, marlin, and other deep-water fish. For their catalog showing these and other pork rind baits write to:
Uncle Josh Bait Co.
Fort Atkinson, Wis. 53538

TWO BLUES AT A TIME

Mrs. Joan Arruda was casting with a plug in the surf at Martha's Vineyard, Massachusetts, and hooked a fish. Then she suddenly felt a heavier weight, and her line took off in another direction. After a long, tough fight she worked the fish close to the beach and was surprised to see that she had two bluefish on the same lure! One was hooked on the front treble hook and the other on the rear treble. One bluefish later weighed 11 lbs., 12 ozs., and the other weighed 11 lbs., 11 ozs., for a total weight of 23 lbs., 7 ozs.

VIRGINIA SALT-WATER FISHING

You can obtain a folder called *Salt-water Sport Fishing in Virginia,* which tells about the salt-water fishing in that state. It has a map showing some of the best fishing spots. It has a list of the most popular species caught and gives methods, locations, seasons, baits, and lures for each fish. There is also a list of the charter boats available, small-boat rentals, and fishing piers in the state. You can get a copy of this fishing folder by writing to:
Virginia State Travel Service
Dept. of Conservation and Economic
 Development
911 E. Broad St.
Richmond, Va. 23219

MIAMI HERALD OUTDOOR GUIDE

This is an annual publication by the Miami *Herald* that gives a lot of information about fishing in the southern part of Florida. It has 105 salt-water fish in full color and freshwater fish in black-and-white illustrations. It gives tides, fishing spots, fish records, and fishing laws and regulations. There is information on knots, rigs, baits, and methods such as bottom fishing, surf fishing, casting, and trolling. The book sells for $2.00 at newsstands and tackle shops or by mail from:
The Miami Herald
Public Service Counter
1 Herald Plaza
Miami, Fla. 33101

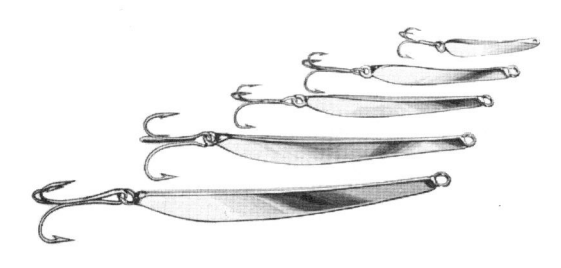

BRIDGEPORT VI-KE LURE

The Bridgeport Vi-Ke lure is a high-luster nickel-finish metal lure with a wild, erratic action that is popular for most salt-water species. It can be cast out and retrieved with rod action. Or you can troll it from a boat. Or it can be jigged by lowering it to the bottom and then working it up and down to catch cod, pollock, and other bottom species. It can also be jigged for mackerel. These lures come in many sizes, from ¼ oz. to 24 ozs. The same company also makes diamond jigs, metal squids, spoons, spinners, and other metal lures. For their catalog write to:
Bridgeport Silverware Mfg. Co.
65 Holland Ave.
Bridgeport, Conn. 06605

ROLLER GUIDES AND TIP-TOPS

The AFTCO stainless-steel roller guides and tip-tops come in many sizes and are available in both regular and heavy-duty models for use with all regular lines. They are the most widely accepted roller guides for salt-water trolling and fishing rods. The same models are also offered with specially hardened Rollers and Frames for use with wire lines. You can also use these hardened guides with any other type of line. They can be bought singly or in complete matched sets for winding on a rod. For more information write to:
Axelson Fishing Tackle Mfg. Co., Inc.
1559 Placentia Ave.
Newport Beach, Calif. 92660

MARINE GAME FISHES OF THE PACIFIC COAST

The Smithsonian Institution has reprinted a book on salt-water fishes that should be of interest to many anglers. The book is called *Marine Game Fishes of the Pacific Coast—Alaska to Ecuador* and is written by Lionel A. Walford. It has been reprinted in the original quarto format complete with thirty-eight colored plates and a new Introduction, additional records, and updating of the nomenclature by Lionel A. Walford. This classic was originally published in a limited edition in 1937, has long been out of print, and is considered a rarity, with copies selling for as much as $100. This new edition sells for $15 and is available from:

The Smithsonian Institution Press
Washington, D.C. 20560

NORTH CAROLINA FISHING GUIDE

A big, soft-covered book called *North Carolina Coastal Fishing & Vacation Guide* has articles by expert anglers telling how to catch more fish along the North Carolina coast in salt water. It also has directories of charter boats, party boats, sound, river, and ocean piers, marinas, hotels, motels, guides, information on each section of the coast, ferry schedules, and tide tables. There are also thirty-two pages of color maps of coastal and sound waters, with the best spots marked for the various kinds of fish caught in those waters. The guide sells for $3.00 and can be obtained from:

The Graphic Press, Inc.
P.O. Box 26808
Raleigh, N.C. 27611

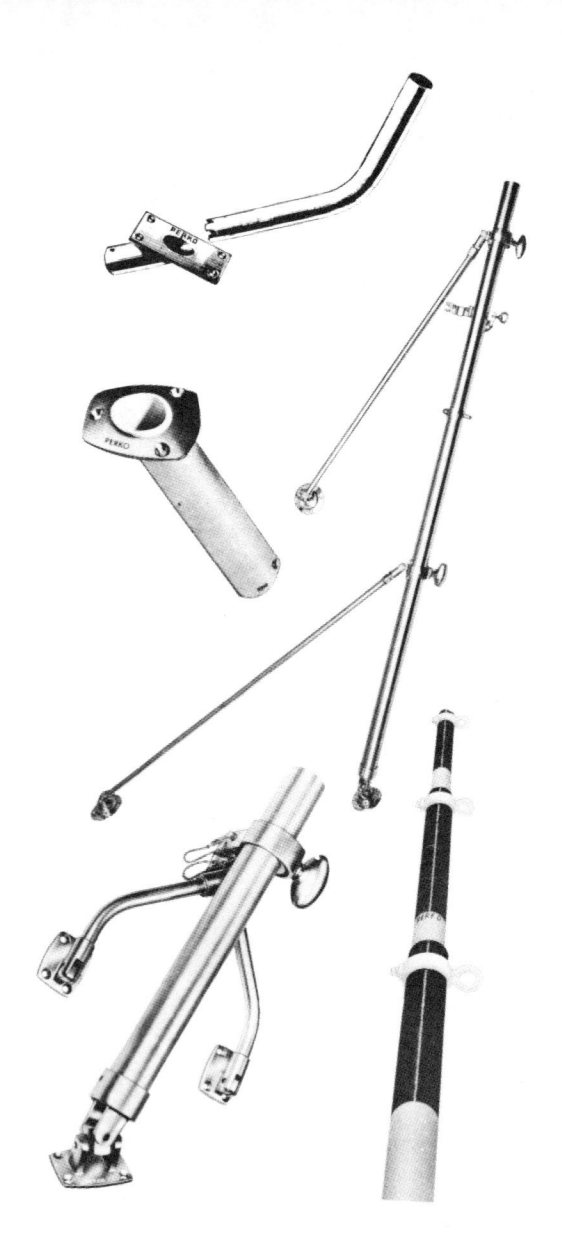

PERKO FISHING HARDWARE

This company makes such marine hardware and fishing equipment as outrigger poles, spreaders, telescopic Fiberglas outriggers, outrigger pole holders, rod holders, trolling pins or clips, and similar gear needed to outfit a sportfishing boat. Most of these are made from bronze, brass, or stainless-steel parts that are chrome-plated to prevent corrosion. For their catalog showing this marine equipment write to:

Perkins Marine Lamp & Hardware Corp.
16490 N.W. 13th Ave.
Miami, Fla. 33164

STRIPED BASS CHAMP

When it comes to catching striped bass consistently, especially in Maine waters, the name Bob Boilard stands out above the others. During the 14 years or so he has been fishing there, he has caught close to 15,000 stripers. In one year alone he caught 2,511 striped bass, for an average of 35 bass per trip! In fact, he has been so sure that he can catch stripers on almost every trip that when he took people out in his boat he guaranteed fish or no pay. Bob lives in Biddeford, Maine, and does most of his fishing in the Saco River and Bay.

Bob uses light tackle such as a 7- or 7½-ft. "popping" type rod with level-wind salt-water reel and 20-lb.-test line. For lures he likes a 7-in. plastic eel or worm with a lead head. He adds a 3- or 4-in. section of natural sandworm to the tail hook. He trolls these lures with two rods—one with a long line and heavier lure down deep, and the other rod with a shorter line and lighter lure at about middepth. Most of the stripers he catches this way in the Saco River are on the small side.

When Bob Boilard wants bigger stripers he heads out to the mouth of the Saco River or out into the bay and the ocean. Then he uses live mackerel or dead pogies and catches bigger stripers. He caught one going 52 lbs. this way on the same light tackle he uses when trolling for the smaller fish.

SAILFISH JACKPOT

Captain Buddy Carey was trolling six lines from his charter boat Sea Boots off Miami, Florida, when all of his lines were struck, and fish were hooked on all six of them! With only two anglers on the boat, the scene became a madhouse as they all rushed from line to line trying to fight the wild sails. The amazing thing was that although they lost three of the fish, they succeeded in boating the other three sailfish!

BIG TARPON

One of the biggest tarpon caught in recent years was taken by Gus Bell off Key West, Florida, from Captain Bob West's boat. The tarpon weighed 243 lbs. and beat the all-time Florida record of a tarpon of 218 lbs. Other tarpon going over 200 lbs. in weight have been caught in the Panuco River in Mexico. Tarpon going over 300 lbs. have been caught by commercial fishermen in nets.

BE ALERT FOR STRIPERS

When you are trolling surgical tubes, rigged eels, or plastic eels for striped bass, it pays to be alert and ready for a strike, even when you are letting out the line and lure. Many a striper will sock such a lure or bait as it is sinking toward the bottom. In fact, some anglers like to do this often by reeling in several feet, then letting the lure drop back again toward the bottom as they are trolling.

SHORE CHUMMING

When fishing from shore or the surf, a good way to attract fish to a spot is to wade out at low tide and lower some sacks of chum to the bottom, then fish that spot as the tide comes in. Or in rocky areas you can walk out at low tide and scrape mussels off the rocks and crush them, then fish the spot on the rising tide.

HUMAN FISH

The surf angler from Brooklyn was casting from the beach into the treacherous riptide at Far Rockaway, New York, but the striped bass or other fish weren't biting that day. Suddenly he heard a cry for help and saw a man in the water about 50 yds. offshore struggling against the fast current, which was carrying him out to sea. The surf angler made a cast over the man; his line landed just within reach, where the exhausted swimmer grabbed it and wrapped it around his arm. Then the angler slowly reeled in the swimmer toward shore and safety. On the beach the human fish, who weighed 180 lbs., unraveled the 36-lb.-test line from his arm and thanked his rescuer!

PROLIFIC COD

Many fish produce thousands of eggs when they spawn, but the cod spawns eggs by the millions. Even a small cod will produce a million eggs annually. And a big cod may have as many as 9 million eggs! One biologist figured that if all the eggs spawned by all the female cod in one season hatched and reached maturity, the oceans of the entire world would be a solid mass of cod.

AMF ROBALO 230

The AMF Robalo 230, with a deep-V hull and full foam flotation, is the queen of the Robalo center-console fishing fleet. It has an overall length of 23 ft., a beam of 8 ft., weighs 2,050 lbs., and has a fuel capacity of 90 gal. It is built for rough-water and bad-weather fishing. Equipped with Robalo's all-new center console, a new fish box aft, with optional live bait well to port, nonskid decks as on all Robalos, and the two-color inner liner to cut down glare, it is designed for boating and fishing pleasure. For more information and a catalog write to:
AMF Slickcraft Boat Div.
500 E. 32nd St.
Holland, Mich. 49423

LUPO LURES

This company makes several excellent lures for salt-water fishing that are especially popular with anglers fishing for striped bass, bluefish, tarpon, snook, cobia, and other salt-water species. They make a big "bunker" spoon, which is 10 in. long and is a great lure for big striped bass and bluefish when they are feeding on bunker, herring, or other large baitfish. They also make a popping plug, surface swimmer, and deep-trolling and casting plug. They make tube lures such as the "Action Eel" and "Silver Snake." They also have an umbrella rig with seven hooked lures. Their catalog showing these lures costs $.25 and can be obtained from:
Lupo Tackle, Inc.
37-22 28th St.
Long Island City, N.Y. 11101

SALT-WATER SPORT FISHING IN VIRGINIA

The booklet *Salt-water Sport Fishing in Virginia* was compiled by two outstanding Virginia anglers—Bob Hutchinson and Claude Rogers. It tells almost everything you have to know to fish in that state for surf, bay, inlet, inshore, and offshore species. It deals with channel bass, black drum, weakfish and sea trout, bluefish and striped bass, cobia, dolphin, marlin, tuna, flounder, croakers, and many others. The booklet also has a map showing the coast of Virginia. The booklet is available from:
Virginia State Travel Service
Dept. of Conservation and Economic
  Development
911 E. Broad St.
Richmond, Va. 23219

DEEP SIX DIVING SINKER

The Les Davis Deep Six Diving Sinker is designed to reach great depths, closer to the boat, with less line and without a heavy weight by using a planing action. It can be used with almost any underwater lures such as spoons, spinners, plugs, jigs, or natural baits such as smelt or herring. It can also be used with braided, monofilament, or wire lines. When trolling it dives and keeps the bait or lure at a certain level depending on your line, the current or tide, how much line you have out, and the weight and size of your lure. When a fish strikes it will plane to the surface. It is used in freshwater lakes for coho and lake trout and in salt water for Pacific salmon, striped bass, bluefish, king mackerel, and other fish that often feed deep. It is made in three sizes. For a catalog or more information write to:
Les Davis Fishing Tackle Co.
1565 Center St.
Tacoma, Wash. 98409

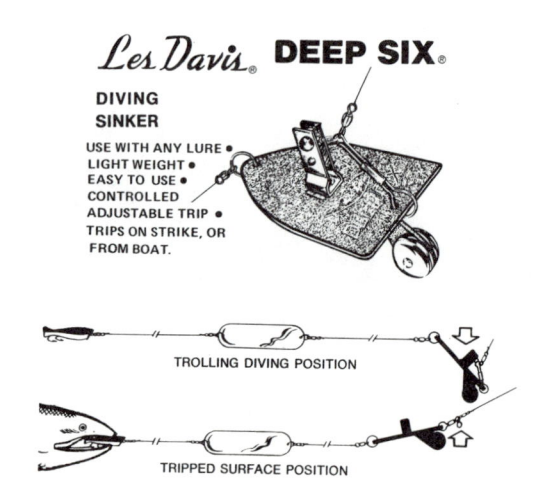

NANTUCKET BB-45 POPPER PLUG

The Nantucket BB-45 Popper Plug is an end product of six years of development and testing by fishermen around Nantucket Island on striped bass and bluefish. It can also be used for tarpon, snook, barracuda, jacks, and other fish in southern waters.

This plug is easy to work because of its shallow nose and concentrated rear weights. You can add or subtract the lead weights at will in seconds to adapt the plug to the tackle you are using and the fishing conditions encountered. The hollow construction of this plug also allows these same weights to rattle, thereby causing loud vibrations, which attract fish to the plug.

The rear, hollow cavity of this plug has been designed to accept chum. You simply chop up the bunker, squid, herring, mackerel, or other baitfish into tiny pieces and place these in the cavity.

This is easy and simple to do because all the hardware on the Nantucket BB-45 Popper Plug is interchangeable and held together with pins that can be removed quickly to take the lure apart. You can add single or different hook sizes or replace rusty or old hooks. You can even reverse the plug and use it the other way by placing the weights forward of the center pin.

This plug comes in clear, white, light blue, blue-and-white marble, and fluorescent orange. For more information write to:

Nantucket Ocean Products, Inc.
21 Upper Vestal St.
Nantucket, Mass. 02554

FISH CATCHES ANGLER

One angler fishing near Sarasota, Florida, from a bridge with a heavy clothesline hooked a big one, and then the line wrapped around his arm and yanked him from a height of 25 ft. into the water. He was pulled for half a mile, sometimes under, at other times on top of the water before a boat came alongside and cut him free. Then they pulled in a 260-lb. shark on the end of the line.

CALLING COBIA

Unlike most fish, noise seems to attract cobia up to a boat. So many anglers race their boat motors, stomp on the floor boards, beat the water with the rod tip, gaff, or pole, and create as much commotion as possible to attract the fish. Cobia are also attracted by sea turtles, rays, floating boxes, buoys, and other moving or stationary objects in the water.

CHANNEL BASS CHAMP

There are many so-called "experts" or "masters" when it comes to striped bass fishing. But when it comes to channel bass fishing, only a few men stand out as masters of this fish, and one of the best is Claude Rogers of Virginia. He has probably caught more big channel bass from the surf and boats than any other angler. Claude is director of the Virginia Salt-water Fishing Tournament and has played a big part in the development of new fishing methods and techniques and fishing spots in his state.

Claude helped perfect the "sight" fishing for channel bass in Magothy Bay and other waters of Virginia. He cruises around looking for channel bass lying or swimming just below the surface. Then he casts a Hopkins lure into them.

Claude has also explored almost all of the Barrier Island beaches of Eastern Shore Virginia and has caught many big channel bass from them, including the 60-lb. fish shown here caught off Smith's Island. He has also caught good-sized channel bass on a fly rod. Actually, Claude is a fine all-around angler who also fishes for tarpon, black drum, sea trout, striped bass, cobia, bluefish, and many other species found in Virginia and nearby states.

SALT-WATER SPORTSMAN

This is the magazine most salt-water anglers read when they want to keep informed about the latest developments in salt-water fishing. It covers the entire fishing scene along the Atlantic, Pacific, and Gulf coasts as well as Bermuda, the Bahamas, the Caribbean, and Mexico. Publisher Henry Lyman and Editor Frank Woolner are both skilled fishermen whose column "Tackle Talk" in the magazine gives the latest dope on salt-water rods, reels, lines, lures, baits, methods, and techniques. Some of the top salt-water anglers and outdoor writers contribute to the pages of this magazine. Month after month you'll see articles by such writers and fishermen as Lefty Kreh, Charles Waterman, Milt Rosko, Mark Sosin, Max Hunn, Chuck Garrison, Bob Stearns, Clint Hull, Al Ristori, and others of similar caliber in the *Salt-water Sportsman*. One of the most popular monthly features in the magazine is the "Coastal Fishfinder," which tells what fish are running where and covers the entire coastline from Maine to Florida and Texas, California, Mexico, Alaska, and Hawaii. A yearly subscription to the *Salt-water Sportsman* is $6.00 from:

Salt-water Sportsman
P.O. Box 6050
Marion, O. 43302

WADER LURE BOX

The wader lure box is ideal for the shore, surf, or wading angler who wants to carry fishing lures yet keep his hands free for casting, playing a fish, or landing one. It is made of rugged polypropylene and has compartments inside for the lures. This can be removed from the box for easy lure handling. You can wear this wader lure box over your shoulder or around your waist. For more information write to:

Woodstream Corp.
P.O. Box 327
Lititz, Pa. 17543

DWINDLING ACRES

This is a big mail-order house selling almost every kind of fishing tackle you can think of or need. They carry all kinds of fishing rods, reels, lines, lures, tackle boxes, knives, hooks, molds, rigs, lure-making parts, and various accessories. They issue a big catalog. Write to:

Dwindling Acres
P.O. Box 68
North Dartmouth, Mass. 02747

TEAK ROD HOLDERS

These teak rod holders are for boats or dens or other places where you want to store or hold your rods safely but have them available when needed. They can be mounted overhead or on the side of a boat. They are dipped in a long-life preservative for lasting beauty. They come in pairs for two rods, four rods, and six rods. The other items shown are teak knife and tool holders and teak mounting chocks for attaching fish wells and deck boxes on the deck of a boat. They also make fish wells and fish boxes. For more information about the teak rod holders and other marine products write to:
Dolphin Marine Products
1660 S.W. 13th Ct.
Pompano Beach, Fla. 33060

EVINRUDE'S 200-HP. V-6

Evinrude enters a new era of outboard power with the introduction of the first 90-degree V-6 cross-scavenged, two-cycle outboard put into production anywhere in the world. They claim it is the world's most powerful outboard. It combines the compact design of a 90-degree V with the power of six cylinders, resulting in outstanding performance. The Evinrude 200, available in a 20-in. transom model and a 25-in. transom model, features as standard equipment a built-in power trim and tilt unit. Only 2 in. wider than the V-4 and 2⅞ in. higher on the transom than the Evinrude 70 hp., this headliner of the Evinrude "fleet" is styled in satin silver and matte blue with Free Spirit piping. For more information contact:
Evinrude Motors
4143 N. 27th St.
Milwaukee, Wis. 53216

TUNA SINKS BOAT

When Charles Carson of Milford, Massachusetts, hooked a big tuna in the Rhode Island Tuna Tournament, he fought the fish for a half hour. Suddenly the tuna ran under the boat and evidently fouled the leader around the propellers, which loosened a plank. Then the boat started to sink fast. Another boat nearby removed the angler and other passengers just before the 40-ft. sport fisherman sank in 90 ft. of water!

CALIFORNIA OCEAN FISHING MAPS

There are four ocean fishing maps available giving detailed information about the salt-water fisheries resources off California's coast between Del Norte and San Diego counties, including how and where to fish, baits to use, and recreation facilities available. They are as follows:

51. "Del Norte, Humboldt, and Mendocino Counties"

52. "Marin and Sonoma Counties"

53. "San Francisco, San Mateo, and Santa Cruz Counties"

54. "Monterey and San Luis Obispo Counties"

Each of these guides costs $.40, and they should be ordered by name and number. They can be obtained from:
Office of Procurement, Documents Div.
P.O. Box 20191
Sacramento, Calif. 95820

FISHING IN NORTH CAROLINA

The booklet *Fishing in North Carolina* is a handsome publication that details the salt-water and freshwater fishing found in North Carolina. It covers surf and pier fishing for channel bass, bluefish, striped bass, sea trout, and whiting. It also covers inlet, bay, river, and sound fishing for channel bass, striped bass, flounder, mackerel, bluefish, cobia, and sea trout, and it describes the offshore fishing for marlin, sailfish, dolphin, amberjack, wahoo, barracuda, and tuna. The freshwater section deals with the lakes, reservoirs, rivers, and brackish waters where fishing is done for black bass, pickerel, trout, and panfish. For a copy of *Fishing in North Carolina* write to:
North Carolina Dept. of Natural Resources
P.O. Box 27687
Raleigh, N.C. 27611

DARK BLAZER LIGHT

For the fisherman who does night fishing or travels or camps out a lot, this Dark Blazer all-weather floating lantern can solve many lighting problems. This Model 511 features a Super II Reflector System that theoretically produces 77 per cent more candlepower for a much brighter beam. A four-way switch gives the user a choice of Off, Beam Only, Flasher Only, or Beam and Flasher, with an interior warning flasher to illuminate the front of the rod case for emergencies. The 120-degree swivel stand locks up out of the way when not in use and is removable. The high-impact case is bright red. For more information about this light write to:
Nicholl Bros., Inc.
1204 W. 27th St.
Kansas City, Mo. 64108

MIRROLURES

The Mirrolures are plastic plugs that come in many styles and models and are used for freshwater and salt-water fish. They are made from tough plastic that stands up well in salt water when used for striped bass, bluefish, sea trout, tarpon, snook, mackerel, and other gamefish. The plugs are made in a wide variety of finishes and colors and in sizes from tiny $\frac{1}{16}$-oz. models to larger 1- and 2-oz. weights. For a color brochure showing these and other plugs write to:

L. & S. Bait Co., Inc.
150 E. Bay Dr.
Largo, Fla. 33540

MISTER TWISTER EEE-LLL

Mister Twister's new EEE-LLL combines the fish-catching appeal of a delectable food with the living-lure action of the famous Mister Twister tail. The Mister EEE-LLL has already been the downfall of a horde of salt-water species and even some big fish of the freshwater variety.

The EEE-LLL comes in three lengths: 7, 9, 11 in. and in nine colors. It comes unrigged (plain), rigged, and rigged with a faceplate. It features extra strong hooks and stainless-steel cable rigging. For more information about these lures write to:

Mister Twister, Inc.
P.O. Drawer 996
Minden, La. 71055

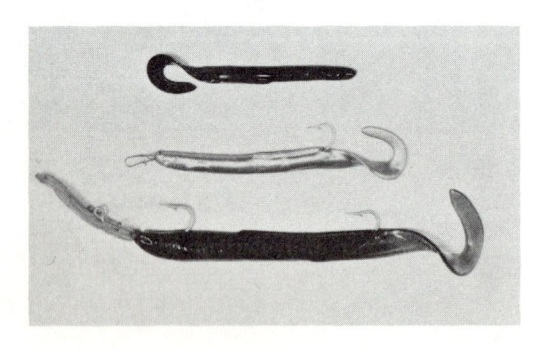

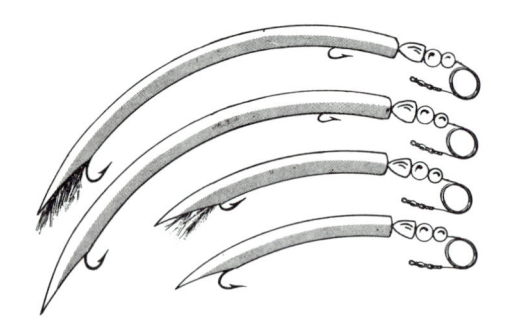

J. T. SURGE LURES

The Jeros Tackle Company, Inc., offers these J. T. Surge Lures made of heavy surgical rubber tubing on a long leader and swivel to help prevent twisting of the line when trolling. They come in several sizes and are available with or without weighted heads. This company is one of the largest suppliers of all kinds of fishing rigs, hooks, lines, snaps, swivels, spreaders, wire leaders, clam rakes, creels, nets, knives, and lures. They do not sell direct to the consumer but only to dealers and distributors. They will send their catalog to these dealers or distributors, who should write to:

Jeros Tackle Co., Inc.
111 16th St.
Brooklyn, N.Y. 11215

FISH FILLET KNIFE

The G-96 Magnum Fillet Knife has a long, razor-sharp blade that is formulated from a unique, rustproof steel that combines all the edge-holding properties of high-carbon steel with the durability of stainless steel. It will not rust and will hold its edge through long and repeated use. This professional-style fillet knife can be used with ease by both the casual weekend fisherman and the commercial or professional fisherman.

The transparent fingergrip handle is nonslip and permanently bonded to the full heavy-steel tang of the blade. There are no rivets to loosen. The handle cannot absorb water, and its gripping qualities actually improve with use. Each knife has its own contour-molded plastic sheath that holds it snug to prevent loss. It will not absorb fish odors and will stay clean and dry while affording full protection to the razor-sharp blade. Each G-96 Magnum Fillet Knife is fully guaranteed, and a certificate of guarantee is enclosed with each knife. The knife has a blade length of 9 in. and a handle length of 5 in. and sells for $12.95. It is sold by Jet-Aer Corporation, which also has other fishing and hunting knives. For more information write to:

Jet-Aer Corp.
100 Sixth Ave.
Paterson, N.J. 07524

RHODE ISLAND FISHING

The following two publications are available about Rhode Island salt-water fishing. The first one is *Rhode Island Salt-water Sport Fishing* and tells when, where, and how to fish for white marlin, tuna, swordfish, striped bass, bluefish, weakfish, porgies, mackerel, blackfish or tautog, cod, pollock, and flounders.

The other folder is *Rhode Island Party and Charter Boat Association* and lists the charter boats and party boats sailing from various Rhode Island ports. Both leaflets can be obtained from:

Rhode Island Dept. of Economic Development
1 Weybosset Hill
Providence, R.I. 02903

SOUTH CAROLINA FISHING PIERS AND BOATS

There's a helpful folder called *Marine Angler's Guide to Fishing Piers and Boats in South Carolina*. It gives a list of the various fishing piers found in the state and also the names, addresses, and phone numbers of the party boats and charter boats. There is also a list of spots and marinas where you can rent boats for a day's fishing in an inlet, bay, sound, river, or ocean. You can obtain this booklet from:

S. C. Wildlife and Marine Resources Dept.
Recreational Fisheries Section
P.O. Box 12559
Charleston, S.C. 29412

STRIPER ATOM PLUGS

The Striper Atom plugs are well known to thousands of surf anglers and boat fishermen along the Atlantic Coast. They are widely used for striped bass and bluefish and weakfish. They can also be used in southern waters for tarpon, snook, sea trout, and other fish. They make a large and junior Swimmer, a Reverse Atom, a Talking and Spit 'N Striper swiper popper, a Reactor plug, a Mackerel plug, and several spin-size types. Most of these plugs are available in several colors and different weights and sizes. For more information write to:
Atom Mfg. Co., Inc.
880 Washington St.
South Attleboro, Mass. 02703

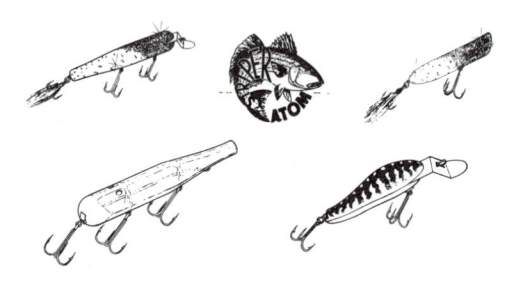

LAND OF GIANT MARLIN

If you want to catch a big black marlin, the place to go is Cairns, Australia, where fish over 1,000 lbs. are caught in large numbers every year. In 1975, for example, a total of 37 black marlin weighing over 1,000 lbs. were caught between September 30 and November 27. The largest fish that year was caught by Neville Green of Sydney, who boated a 1,367-lb. black marlin. Jo-Jo Del Guerico of Fort Lauderdale, Florida, caught and released as many as 58 black marlin in 13 days of fishing the same year, and lost one near the boat that was estimated between 1,500 and 2,000 lbs.!

SHARK SAFARI

The book *Shark Safari* by Captain Hal Scharp is the result of years of study, research, and practical experience with sharks both for sport and science. Hal Scharp has been a charter-boat captain in the Florida Keys for many years and has caught hundreds of sharks for both sport and research. He has also studied and assisted many marine laboratories in their studies of shark behavior and the utilization of sharks for medical science and commerce. The book covers the biology and behavior of sharks, the shark danger, sport fishing for sharks, and the value of sharks as food and for various products. *Shark Safari* sells for $9.95 and is published by:
A. S. Barnes & Co., Inc.
P.O. Box 421
Cranbury, N.J. 08512

WESMAR SS80 SCANNING SONAR

A fish-finding sonar for all sports fishermen has been developed by WESMAR (Western Marine Electronics) in Seattle, Washington. Until now, WESMAR scanning sonar equipment has only been available in much larger models to the international fishing industry. Unlike depth sounders that require that the boat pass directly over fish for detection, the WESMAR SS80 scanning sonar searches a circle measuring up to 1,000 feet underwater surrounding your boat.

Thus the SS80 is ideal for trolling, casting, and live-bait fishing in fresh or salt water. With skillful use of the SS80, single fish may be located. Whether the bottom is hard or soft can also be ascertained with the SS80. Of course, this is valuable information for the fisherman searching for the bottom conditions preferred by his specific quarry.

On its large 5 in. CRT (cathode-ray tube) screen, the SS80 shows fish, underwater objects, and bottom features in range, depth, and relative bearing from the boat. Employing an 8½-degree beam of ultrasonic sound, the unit operates at selectable ranges of 50, 100, 250, and 500 ft. Sent through the water by a transducer, the search beam can be tilted at any angle in the water. After a beam strikes a fish or other object, some of the sound energy echoes back to the transducer, where it is received and converted into electrical energy. The targets are then displayed at the console on the easily readable CRT screen. The SS80 is also equipped with an audio speaker, so that the fisherman, while he is cruising, will not have to constantly watch the CRT screen to know when fish are detected. For more information contact:
WESMAR Marine Systems Div.
905 Dexter Ave. N.
P.O. Box C19074
Seattle, Wash. 98109

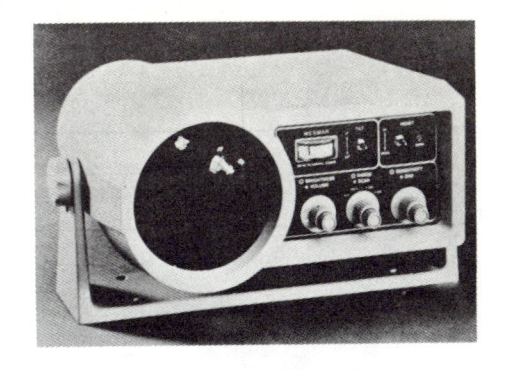

HIGH-LEAPING FISH

Fish have been known to leap amazing distances and heights. The champion leaper in fresh water is the salmon, which has cleared waterfalls 18 ft. high. But salt-water fish can leap even higher and greater distances. Tarpon have been known to leap 18 ft. into the air and cover an arc of 30 ft. The mako shark leaps 20 ft. into the air. King mackerel or kingfish have been seen leaping higher than the outriggers on a sportfishing boat. One observer estimated that a king mackerel can reach a height of 30 ft. or more above the water!

379

MASTEREEL

The Mastereel is a fairly large spinning reel designed for salt-water fishing. It has a full bail pickup, but can be converted to manual pickup. There's a slide-type antireverse button and a patented quadrant-drag brake. It is anodized to prevent corrosion. This reel holds 350 yds. of 10-lb.-test line, 200 yds. of 15-lb.-test line, and 185 yds. of 20-lb.-test line. For more information or their catalog showing this and other reels, write to:
Feurer Bros., Inc.
77 Lafayette Ave.
North White Plains, N.Y. 10603

SPORTFISHING FOR SHARKS

The book *Sportfishing for Sharks* is the combined effort of Captain Frank Mundus and Bill Wisner. Captain Frank Mundus pioneered sport fishing for sharks at Montauk, New York, right after World War II, and many record shark catches were made from his charter boat. Bill Wisner has been the editor of fishing magazines, is a newspaper outdoor columnist, and is author of many fishing books. Together they have written one of the most complete books on fishing for sharks with rod and reel.

The book starts off with a general history and introduction to the shark family, then goes into the fishing tackle needed for sharks, accessory gear, boat gear, shark baits, chum, presentation of the baits, and other details, methods, and techniques. Then they deal with the individual species of sharks such as the mako, blue shark, brown shark, dusky, white shark, tiger shark, hammerheads, and others. The book winds up telling about sharks as food, their other uses, and even how to prepare the skin, teeth, and jaws. *Sportfishing for Sharks* by Captain Frank Mundus and Bill Wisner sells for $10.95 and is published by:
Macmillan, Inc.
866 Third Ave.
New York, N.Y. 10022

TEASING WITH A TEASER

When you have a billfish such as a marlin behind a teaser but it shows little or no interest in the baits being trolled near it, here's a trick that often works. Try yanking the teaser out of the water and hauling it in as quickly as possible so the fish can't get it. The surprised or frustrated fish will often start searching for the teaser and come up on and take a trolled bait as a substitute.

LOCATING BONEFISH

Bonefish like to feed on small crabs, so they will usually be found feeding on flats, where such crabs are plentiful. Flats with grass or weeds are better than bare flats because they have more hiding places for the crabs. Likewise, creeks or shores that are lined with mangroves attract bonefish because here, too, crabs, shrimp, and other crustaceans are abundant, and bonefish cruise around looking for them.

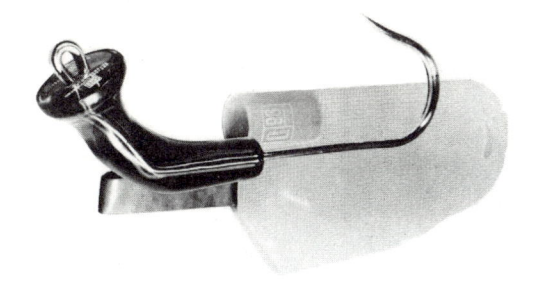

G-96 MARINER SURF GAFF

This gaff has been designed for the surf fisherman or shore fisherman who wants to be sure to land his catch. Each gaff comes with its specially designed plastic holder, which enables the surf or shore fisherman to wear the gaff on his belt. It remains within easy reach for immediate use. Each gaff has the unique sure-grip, nonslip handle that is molded into the tempered stainless-steel hook that passes through the handle and ends in a steel loop. The handle is 6 in. long, and the overall length of the gaff is 13 in. The gaff sells for $10.95 and can be obtained from:

Jet-Aer Corp.
100 Sixth Ave.
Paterson, N.J. 07524

DUAL RANGE RECORDER/FLASHER

Ray Jefferson has introduced a Dual Range Recorder/Flasher Depthsounder that charts bottom topography, finds fish, and reads depths down to 300 ft. The new Model 5300 is designed for both deep-sea and freshwater fishing and navigation; it traces, on a moving chart, the contour of the bottom under the boat. The unit gives simultaneous flashing-light indication of bottom conditions and shows all intervening objects and fish. It's perfect for making a permanent record of bottom conditions along a particular course for navigation and safety, for navigating in shoal waters, locating underwater debris, and charting the best fishing areas.

As a recorder, the Model 5300 records down to 150 ft. in three 50-ft. ranges in the X1 position, or from 0 to 300 ft. in three 100-ft. ranges in the X2 position. The chart records at 24 in. per hour.

As a flasher, the Model 5300 helps the skipper to navigate safely and to check his course against his charts. The flasher section shows underwater topography and all intervening objects, including fish. The 4-in.-diameter high-intensity neon flasher reads from 0 to 150 ft., or from 0 to 300 ft., depending on the range selected. For additional information contact:

Ray Jefferson
Main and Cotton Sts.
Philadelphia, Pa. 19127

DRIFT FOR DOLPHIN

If you can't locate any dolphin by trolling offshore, try shutting off the engine of your boat and drift. Dolphin will often be attracted to the boat as they are drawn by other floating objects.

381

NORTH CAROLINA BLUE MARLIN
by Joel Arrington

When Dr. Fulton Katz of Wheaton, Maryland, landed a 1,128-lb. blue marlin off Hatteras on June 5, 1975, it underscored the pre-eminence of the waters off North Carolina's Outer Banks for blue marlin fishing in the Atlantic. The catch occurred less than a year after Jack Herrington set the IGFA all-tackle record off Oregon Inlet, just a few miles north of Hatteras, with a 1,142-lb. blue.

As background, the largest Pacific blue in the record book weighed 1,153 lbs. and was caught off Guam in 1969. There is a 1,100-lb. blue that stands as a record in the men's 130-lb. class from off Mauritius in 1966. The other Pacific records fall below the 1,000-lb. mark.

Before Herrington's and Katz's catches, it was reasonable to believe that Atlantic blues rarely if ever grew to a half ton, notwithstanding reports of experienced skippers and anglers of very large fish seen or hooked and lost off the Bahamas and the Virgin Islands. No fish over 845 lbs. had been caught.

Ernest Hemingway's "The Old Man and the Sea" had its genesis in a tale recounted in one of Hemingway's stories in Esquire many years ago about a Cuban peasant fisherman who caught a white marlin on a hand line and was bringing it in when suddenly it was seized by an unseen leviathan. The fisherman in his small boat was towed by the giant fish for two days and a night, or something like that, before the smaller fish was released and the Cuban pulled up a battered but uncut white marlin over 6 ft. long. It had been held crosswise in the mouth of a toothless fish—to wit, a giant marlin.

Papa's embellishment of that story helped him win the Nobel Prize and renewed the hopes of marlin fishermen of someday boating a blue marlin in the Atlantic larger than anyone had even seen or most had even imagined. Well, Jack Herrington did that on an ordinary charter boat in Oregon Inlet, a boat just like one you or I could charter. If Katz's catch had weighed 15 lbs. more, he would have done it again less than a year later out of Hatteras. His catch is now the official men's 80-lb. class record in the IGFA record book.

SALMON SPOONS

Some of the best spoons for salmon trolling in Pacific waters are made by Luhr Jensen and Sons, Inc. They are located in the heart of the salmon country in Oregon and have had many years of experience and know-how in making lures that catch coho and chinook salmon. They also make dodgers and flashers that are rigged in front of baits and lures and trolled for salmon. Their salmon spoons in chrome or brass range up to 5 or 6 in. and are rigged with big, strong 6/0 or 7/0 hooks. For their catalog showing these and other lures they make send $.50 to:

Luhr Jensen and Sons, Inc.
P.O. Box 297
Hood River, Oreg. 97031

ACTION MASTER DODGER

This Riviera Action Master Dodger is a completely new and unique concept in a fish attractor. It is perfectly balanced to achieve a consistent lifelike action. It also has strategically located holes that create a sonic sound that entices fish from great distances. It is available in a chrome-plated finish and several solid and edge-accented colors. For more information write to:

Riviera Mfg., Inc.
3859 Roger Chaffee Blvd., S.E.
Grand Rapids, Mich. 49508

NYLON STOCKING FOR CHUM

If you haven't got a chum pot or bag, you can use an old nylon stocking for this purpose. Just put a rock or other weight inside, add the chum, and tie the opening with a line and lower it to the bottom. The chum oils and scent will ooze out of the stocking and attract fish to the scene.

LOOK FOR TWO FISH

Blue marlin often travel in pairs, so if you hook one, keep on trolling in the same area and try for its "mate" or the other fish. The same thing is often true of swordfish. If you see a swordfish on top and lose it or it doesn't respond to your bait, keep on searching in the same area for another fish.

SHAMROCK 20 BOAT

The Shamrock 20 is a truly flexible boat with the economy and dependability of an inboard engine, the maneuverability of old-time tested designs, and the incredibly strong shamite-filled keel that protects the prop and rudder even when she's beached. This also enables her to ride up and over logs or other underwater obstructions, with little chance of damage, giving her unique shallow-water performance. This means that you can go fishing in the back bays, on the flats or up shallow creeks as well as in the usual deep waters where inboards perform so well.

The Shamrock 20 has a 185-hp. Pleasure Craft marine engine, a conversion of the popular Ford 302, and a Borg-Warner transmission. She is capable of 40 mph. and has a range of 170 mi. per tank of regular gas. She averages less than 6 gal./hr. at 30 mph.

The decks all have effective nonskid surfaces. The custom-built Fiberglas fuel tank is fitted below decks, is easily accessible, and will not rust or corrode. The engine and fuel compartments are completely vented, exceeding all Coast Guard regulations. The hull is designed along the lines of offshore boats noted for their seakeeping abilities.

There are four teak rod racks under the gunwale, 20 cu. ft. of wet or dry storage with two hatch covers, and a fish box under the helm seat.

They also make a Shamrock 20 Cuddy Cabin boat along the same lines but with a big, forward cabin that has two 6½-ft. bunks, full headroom, and a convenient marine head. For more information about these boats write to:

Shamrock Marine, Inc.
P.O. Box 1095
Cape Coral, Fla. 33904

DRIFTING FOR FISH

A good way to locate and catch fish is by drifting in your boat and letting out anywhere from two to six lines with baits, depending on the size and length of the boat. Or you can shut off the motor and drift through feeding schools of striped bass, bluefish, channel bass, mackerel, dolphin, tarpon, sea trout, and other fish, and cast lures into them.

A drifting boat doesn't frighten fish like a moving or trolling boat, especially when the fish are feeding on the surface or in shallow water. You'll often hook fish close to the boat when drifting.

You can drift with small live fish or dead whole fish anywhere from just below the surface to many feet down. Or you can put on a bottom rig with sinker and bait the hook and drag this along the bottom, from the moving boat.

Drifting can be done over most bottoms, but is usually most effective over large areas such as banks, rock bottoms, coral reefs, and shellfish beds. Once you find a good spot you can throw over a marker buoy and keep drifting over the same spot as long as the fish bite.

Drifting is best when there's some wind or enough tide to move the boat. The boat shouldn't move too fast or too slowly for best results. So drift along, save gas, and work in lowering or raising anchors and catching more fish.

Index

Accetta, Tony, 307
Acme Tackle Co., 4, 277
Advanced Bass Fishing (Weiss), 61
Advanced Bass Tackle and Boats (Livingston), 231
Adventurer Tackle Boxes, 90
Aero-Nautical, Inc., 289
African pompano, 284
Alabama, booklets and folders on, 61, 109
Aladdin Laboratories, Inc., 4, 168
Alaska, 23; booklet on, 125; salmon in, 252
Alaska Sport Fishing Guide, 125
Albacore, 24, 336; on flies, 302; migrations of, 242
Alee Eels (plastic eels), 258
Alee Jigging Rig, 305
Alexandria Drafting Co., 176, 185, 322
All About Fishing Reels (American Fishing Tackle Manufacturers' Assn.), 12
All About Fishing Rods (American Fishing Tackle Manufacturers' Assn.), 12
Allied Sports Co., 74, 92
Alligator gar, 2, 36
Al Lindner's Bassin' Facts, 212
Allyn, Rube, 45
Al Pflueger's Fisherman's Handbook, 339
Al's Goldfish Lure Co., 50
Alumaweld Co., 90
Aluminum sinker molds, 352
Amberjack, 20, 256, 319; attracting, 271; caught on a fly rod (story), 245
American Bass Fisherman (magazine), 137
American Fishing Tackle Manufacturers' Assn., 12
American Fly Fisher (magazine), 150
American Institute of Bass Fishing (AIBF), 196
American Littoral Society, 303

American Sportsman's Club, 42
Ames, Francis H., 23
AMF Slickcraft Boat Div., 369
Anchor for boats: bracket for, 158; electric device for raising and lowering, 133; plastic jug, 120
Ande, Inc., 313
Angler, The (magazine), 144
Angler fish, 285; faithfulness of, 302
Angler Publications, 144
Angler's Calendar and Fishing Handbook, The, 57
Angler's Guide (to Saskatchewan), 106
Angler's Guide to Eastern Nevada, 136
Angler's Guide to Lakes Mead, Mohave, and the Colorado River, 136
Angler's Guide to Lake Tahoe, 136
Angler's Guide to Northeast Nevada, 136
Angler's News, 323
Angler's & Shooter's Bookshelf, 147
Anglers Specialities, Inc., 316
Animals, fish named after, 36
Apte, Stu, 357
Aquabug International, Inc., 99
Aquabug motors, 99
Aquadene Sales, Inc. 223
Aqua-Mate sunglasses, 342
Aqua Scope depth sounders, 334
Arapaima, 2
Arbogast Co., Inc. (Fred), 52, 170, 307
Archer fish, 44
Arctic char, 98
Arndt & Sons, Inc., 142, 146
Arnold Tackle Co., 67
Arrow Glass Boat & Mfg. Corp., 3
Arrow-Lock hook, 7
Arruda, Joan, 364
Art of Plug Fishing, The (Circle), 152

Ashaway Line & Twine Co., 261
Atherton, John, 144
Atlantic salmon, 13, 20, 82
Atlantic Salmon, The (Wulff), 195
Atlantic Salmon Flies and Fishing (Bates), 74
Atom Mfg. Co., Inc., 378
Auto Track II Down Rigger, 40
Axelson Fishing Tackle Mfg. Co., Inc., 323, 365

Bahamas Fishing, 353
Bailey, Dan, 174
Bailey, John, 174
Bait: adding color to, 267; Bomber Co., 185; books on, 131; bottom fishing rig, 16; bottom fishing with, 276; bucket trolling, 12; cages for, 10, 191; canteen for, 104; casting second bait or lure near, 306; chewing gum, 120; crickets, 164; eels for, 262; fiddler crab, 324; Fin processed, 142; freshwater, 26, 30, 36, 39, 48, 58, 75, 101, 108, 114, 120, 142, 146, 154, 164, 172, 176, 185, 191, 205, 210, 218; holding on a hook, 271; holding with rubber bands, 114; leech, 48; lump of sugar, 101; macaroni (for carp), 108; minnows, 30, 36, 102, 210; pork rind, 39, 172, 241, 364; salmon eggs, 58, 92; salt-water, 239, 241, 302, 308, 313, 324, 335, 364; sandwich lunch, 146; scented, 154; sugar-cured, 239; in a supermarket, 218; teasing fish and, 256; toughening up mussels for, 329; useful sea pests, 267; using spinners for, 195; worms, 26, 36, 104, 115, 256. *See also* under names of fish; Lures; Plugs
Baitfish (Ohio Dept. of Natural Resources), 55

Bait Tail Fishing (Reinfelder), 270
Ballyhoo, for bait, 335
Bamboo rods, 14, 37, 233
Bank type sinker molds, 187
Barnes & Co., Inc. (A. S.), 195, 227, 270, 322, 378
Barracuda, 309, 319; bait for, 241, 254, 262; in California, 254; leaders for, 247; on plugs, 284
Bartz, Mary, 288
Bashline, L. James, 122, 144
Basking shark, 248
Bass, 44, 56, 66, 67, 162; bait for, 66, 70, 164, 210; boat for, 3, 135, 221, 229; books on, 19, 26, 45, 61, 130, 173, 181, 252; bugs for, 179; in cold weather, 51; deadly spinner for, 206; in farm ponds, 44; float fishing for, 32; Florida maps, 119; fly rods for, 128; follow-up for, 184; in the "forest" areas, 151; hangout, 180; hiding places of, 214; leaping into boat (story), 146; lures for, 4, 8, 40, 43, 52, 64; at night, 204; popularity of, 54; school courses for, 42, 196; spinners for, 12; spot for fishing, 120; wading for, 76; why pros catch more, 118; world's record (weight), 54. *See also* types of bass
Bass Anglers Sportsman Society (BASS), 20, 37, 212
Bass Boss tackle boxes, 50
Bass Buddy Float clothing, 159
Bass bug, 179
Bass Fisherman's Bible, The (Bauer), 26
Bass Fishing (Gooch), 173
Bass Fishing (McKinnis), 181
Bass Fishing in New England (Elliot), 82
Bassmaster Fishing Annual, 20
Bassmaster Magazine, 20
Bass Structure Fishing—Kerr Reservoir, 185
"Bass Structure Fishing—Lake Anna" (map), 176
"Bass Structure Fishing—Lake Gaston" (map), 176
"Bass Structure Fishing—Occoquan Reservoir" (map), 176
Bass Structure Fishing—Santee-Cooper Lakes, 185
"Bass Structure Fishing—Smith Mountain Lake" (map), 176
Bates, Joseph D., Jr., 20, 45, 74, 216
Batfish, 36
Bauer, Erwin A., 1, 26, 336
Bauer, Parker, 1
Bead Chain Co., 348
Bead chain Monel swivels, 348

Bean, Inc. (L. L.), 157
"Bear Creek" (map), 131
Bear Paw Tackle Co., Inc., 16, 219
Becker, A. C., 25, 314
Beckson Mfg., Inc., 245
Beginner's luck, 112
Bell, Gus, 368
Bell sinker mold, 187
Bell with clip for rod, 149
Belts for rod, when standing up, 278
"Bends," the, 222
Benedict, Nelson, 346
Berger, Tisdall, Clark, and Lesley, Ltd., 62
Bergh, Kit, 189
Berkley and Co., 34, 162, 173, 247, 279, 280, 303
Berkley-McMahon snaps and swivels, 279
Berkley salt-water rigs, 303
Berkley Steelon leaders, 247
Best Ways to Catch More Fish in Fresh and Salt Water (Evanoff), 180
Bevin-Wilcox Line Co., 141
Bicarbonate of soda, 124
Bielevich, Alphonse, 302
Big Jim plug, 50
Big Jon, Inc., 88
Big-O lure, 101
Black bass, 24, 37, 66; greedy (story), 194; hangout, 180; "jump" fishing for, 112; in tidewaters, 202
Black crappies, 60
Black drum, official world record for, 262
Blackfish, bait for, 324
Black marlin, 216, 248
Black Max 115-hp. motor, 71
Blaisdell, Harold, 82
Blanton, Dan, 144
Blue catfish, 2
Bluefin tuna, 248, 336; migrations of, 242
Bluefish, 20, 24, 216, 308, 309, 336, 346; bait for, 262; book on, 320; leaders for, 247; plug for, 341; two, caught at the same time, 364
Bluegills, 13, 18, 228; bait for, 164; bottom fishing rig for, 16; hiding places of, 214; lures for, 34; plastic minnow bait, 70; on plastic worms, 108; spot for fishing, 120; technique for catching, 128
Blue marlin, 248, 323; IGFA record, 382; in pairs, 383
Bluewater Pro 610 Flasher-Graph, 298
Blue Water Tackle Co., 335
Blue Water tackle equipment, 335
Boards: for cleaning fish, 51; for filleting, 54
Boarfish, 36
Boating Access to Virginia Waters, 96
Boats: Alumaweld, 90; aluminum, 29, 84; AMF Robalo 230, 369; anchors, 120, 133, 158; Avon inflatable, 102; Bonito Co., 251; book on fishing from, 336; Boston Whaler Montauk 17, 314; canopy, 357; chairs, 241, 244, 339; Crestliner, 154; Cruisers 19-ft. Albacore, 321; cushion for, 136, 310; Custom Marine Release 26, 358; Electric Feather Pirouge, 28; EPP-12-SB, 62; Fabuglas, 75; Fisher Marine, 9; freshwater, 3, 8, 10, 21, 28, 29, 53, 58, 62, 75, 83, 84, 90, 101, 135, 154, 170, 176, 201, 221, 229; Glastron T-172 Bass, 221; Grady-White, 273; inflatable, 102; Lowe, 171; McKenzie drift, 90; Meteor bass, 3; MFG's, 10, 297; Mirro-Craft, 83; MonArk flat-bottom, 201; for parties, 293, 354; Polar Craft, 21; Rhyan-Craft, 84; salt-water, 251, 264, 273, 289, 293, 297, 311, 314, 316, 321, 326, 331, 358, 369, 384; SeaCraft SF 23 Inboard, 264; Shambrock 20, 384; Silverline Kodiak bass, 229; Skeeter bass, 135; Skimmar 15-ft. Sea Sport, 289; specialty equipment for, 316; Steury Bass, 177; Steury 18-ft. Offshore Fisherman, 331; Stump Knocker, 58; Super Bass, 10; tower for, 326; Water Strider DDC marine, 9; Wellcraft 24-ft. Airslot Console Cabin, 311. *See also* Canoes; Motors
Bodmer's Fly Shop, Inc., 153
Boilard, Bob, 313, 367
Bomber Bait Co., 185
Bonefish, 20, 24, 98, 319, 332, 336; bait for, 324; best time to fish, 276; catching at night, 279; easy way to catch, 256; forty-six caught in a single day, 250; locating, 380
Bonito, 24, 319; on flies, 302
Bonito Boat Corp., 251
Bonner, Harry, 346
Book of Florida Fishing, The (Lewis), 45
Books and publications: freshwater fishing, 1, 13, 14, 16, 18, 19, 20, 23, 25, 26, 29, 30, 37, 38, 45, 47, 52, 61, 64, 67, 69, 70, 72, 73, 74, 82, 92, 95, 96, 106, 109, 113, 115, 119, 122, 123, 126, 130, 131, 134, 135, 136, 137, 140, 143, 144, 152, 154, 160,

389

162, 168, 172, 179, 180, 185, 186, 188, 195, 196, 203, 212, 216, 219, 222, 226, 227, 228, 231, 233, 234; rare and out-of-print, 61, 147; salt-water fishing, 239, 243, 246, 252, 256, 257, 275, 277, 278, 279, 280, 288, 292, 294, 295, 303, 309, 312, 314, 315, 316, 319, 322, 328, 332, 336, 339, 346, 348, 354, 357, 365, 366, 370, 375, 377, 378, 380. *See also* names of books; guides; magazines; newspapers; publications
Boone Bait Co., Inc., 7, 63, 312, 328
Boots and parkas, 343
Boston Whaler, Inc., 314
Boulder Mountain Lakes Booklet, 119
Bream, 64; bait for, 164; lures for, 40
Bridge fishing, 356
Bridgeport Silverware Mfg. Co., 365
British Columbia Tidal Waters Sport Fishing Guide, 320
Bronston, Walter, Jr., 304
Brooks, Joe, 113, 250
Brook trout, 13, 69, 73, 118, 134, 142
Brook Trout in Ohio, 55
Browning, Bill, 122
Browning Co., 188
Brown trout, 13, 73, 118, 134, 142, 216
Brown Trout in Ohio, 55
Bruce B. Mises, Inc., 226
Buchner, Jay and Kathy, 34
Buckets, for minnow, 12, 140
Buck Knives, Inc., 152
Buckley, Raymond, 277
Buck's Baits, 168
Bucktails, 288
Bud Lilly's Trout Shop, 67
Buffalo fish, 13, 36
Building Fishing Rods, 234
Bullard, Gene, 25, 119
Bullfrog Marina, Colo., 42
Bullheads, 13, 36
Bullheads in Ohio, 55
Buoys, 138
Burke Fishing Lures Co., 58, 64, 159, 198, 307
Busey, Dick, 186
Butterfly fish, 36
Byrd Industries, Inc., 110, 230
Byrd Universal rod holders, 110
Bystrom Bros., 291

Cadieux, Charles L., 188
Cahill Master Wader, 301
Cairns, Australia, 378
Calculator, 175
Calendar, angler's, 57
California, 5, 23; barracuda in, 254; books on, 198; Florida bass in, 66; guides on, 119; halibut in, 265; ocean fishing maps, 275, 375; striped bass map, 258; trout of, 69; trout maps, 131
California black sea bass, 216
California Steelhead Fishing, 119
California Trout Fishing, 119
Camillus Cutlery Co., 156
Camillus knives, 156
Canada, 72, 144; big pike in, 80; tuna in, 336. *See also* names of provinces
Candles from fish, 267
Cannon, Ray, 278
Cannonball molds, 187
Canoes: Carleton pack, 53; Chipewyan pack, 53; paddling for landlocked salmon, 175; Pelican (12-ft. squareback), 62; Rushton pack, 53. *See also* Boats
Canopy, boat, 357
"Cape Lookout to New Topsail Inlet Fishing Map," 322
Cape May County, N.J., 261
Capt. Andy McLean's Fishing Mate, 350
Carey, Capt. Buddy, 368
Carleton pack canoe, 53
Carp, 13; on artificial flies, 157; bait for, 108, 154, 218; flies for, 157; scented lures for, 2
Carpenter, William K., 240
Carp in Ohio, 55
Carson, Charles, 374
Case knives, 116
Case & Sons Cutlery Co. (W. R.), 116
Casey, Jack, 257
Cass, Johnny, 278
Catalog of the Inland Fishing Waters of North Carolina, 233
Catches, weird objects, 66, 250
Catching Great Lakes Salmon and Trout, 55
Catch Me, 354
Catch More Bass (Fagerstrom), 126
Catch More Trout (Siberian Salmon Egg Co.), 92
Catfish, 2, 13, 18, 36, 64; bait for, 154, 218; jugging for, 118; scented lures for, 2
Catfish and How to Know Them, 154
Cather & Son, Inc. (J. T.), 346
Caviar, types of, 148
Caxton Printers, Ltd., 23
Chairs: for boats, 241, 244, 339; convertible (for picnic and fishing), 28
Channel bass, 20, 24, 262, 309, 336; champion catches of, 372; plug for, 341
Channel catfish, 18
Chappell, Steve, 245

Chatham Press, 95, 315
Cheezette eggs bait, 92
Chelsea Products Co., 69
"Chesapeake Bay Fishing Map, from the Bay Bridge to the Gooses," 322
Chest and hip waders, 208
"Chincoteague-Assateague Fishing and Recreation Map," 322
Chinook salmon, 252; flies for, 5; lures for, 4
Chipewyan pack canoe, 53
Chips & Shavings, 341
Chris' Deluxe Fish Stringer, 227
Chroma-Glo Water Demon hook, 62
Chronicle Books, 119, 198, 203, 219
Chronomarine tidewatch, 363
Chubs, 13
Chum, nylon stocking for, 383
Chumming, 268; from shore, 368
Circle, Homer, 1, 152
Cisco Kid Tackle, Inc., 112
Clamp-type sinker molds, 187
Clark, John, 312
Claudio Rod Co. (F. M.), 165
Clay, William M., 234
Cleaning boards, 51
Clear water, fishing in, 9
Clift, John, 130
Clipped minnow plugs, 187
Clothing, 61; Bass Buddy float, 159; jacket patch, 42; life vest, 121, 310; shirts for bad weather, 257; vests, 162, 174, 310; waders, 197, 208, 301
Cobia, 256, 268, 336; on a fly rod, 324; how to catch, 371
Cod, 20, 336; in Maine, 306; 76-lb. weight catch, 265; sizes of, 302; spawning of, 368
Coho knife, 15
Coho salmon, 82, 98; hooks for, 62; in Lake Michigan, 110; lures for, 4; spoons for, 19; trolling for, 50, 160
Coho Salmon in Ohio, 55
Colorado, bass fishing school in, 42
Color changes in fish, 292
Columbia Sportswear Co., 162
Combination rods and reels, 18, 203
Complete Book of Casting, The (Gerlach), 64
Complete Book of the Striped Bass, The (Karas), 243
Complete Book of Weakfishing, The (Lyman and Woolner), 322
Complete Fly-tier, The (Cross), 144
Complete Guide to Salt and Fresh Water Fishing Equipment, The (Wisner), 294
Connecticut, booklet on, 180
Continental Arms Corp., 340

Converse Guide for the Outdoorsman, The, 233
Converse Rubber Co., 197, 233, 343
Converse waders, 197
Convertible fishing chair, 28
Cooler (for drink and food), 182, 217
Cordell Tackle, Inc., 101, 287
Cordes, Ron, 57
Cordovan Corp., Publishers, 130, 246, 314, 345
Coren's Rod & Reel Service, 10
Cornell Maritime Press, Inc., 292
Cortland fly outfit, 208
Cortland Line Company, 3, 46, 67, 147, 184, 208
Cotton Cordell Tackle Co., 101
Covey's convertible chest cooler, 182
Covey Corp., 182, 217
Cowfish, 36
Crab bait, 267
Crandall, Capt. Lester, 261
Crappie—A Fish for All Seasons (Gapen), 222
Crappies, 13, 64, 114; bait for, 176; bottom fishing rig for, 16; hiding places of, 214; lures for, 34, 40; plastic minnow bait, 70; spot for fishing, 120; in the summer season, 164; trolling for, 60
Creative Fishing (Farmer), 8
Creek Chub Bait Co., 129, 360
Creme Lure Company, 226
Crestliner Division of AMF, 154
Crimping pliers, 280
Cross, Reuben R., 144
Crown Publishers, Inc., 19, 35, 130, 136, 160, 172, 226, 280, 287
"Crown Valley" (map), 131
Cruisers—Mirror Marine Div., 321
Cushions, boat, 136, 310
Cushion sinker mold, 187
Custom handle rod, 63
Custom-made fly rods, 165
Custom Marine, 358
Cutthroat trout, 69, 162

D. D. E. Loop A Line eyelet, 193
Dale Clemens Custom Tackle, 48
Dalrymple, Byron, 47
Dance, Bill, 19, 37
Dangerous Marine Animals (Halstead), 292
Dark Blazer all-weather floating lantern, 375
Dart Mfg. Co., 150
Davis, Dick, 292
DBI Books, Inc., 122
"Dead Lakes" (Florida bass map), 119
Dee, Ray, 291
Deep Trolling by Williams, 19

Del Guerico, Jo-Jo, 378
"Del Norte, Humboldt, and Mendocino Counties" (map), 375
Delong Lures, Inc., 199
Delong plastic worms, 199
Delph, Ralph, 324
Depth finders, 22, 36, 258, 329
Depth sounders, 72, 92, 277, 325, 334, 381
Dickey, Charley, 181
Dillon Press, Inc., 189
Dipsy-Doodle swivel sinker mold, 187
Docker Fishing Rod Holder, 349
Docker Marine, 349
Dogfish, 36; as bait, 267
Dog salmon, 36
Dolly Varden trout, 69
Dolphin, 20, 24, 319, 320, 336, 346; drifting for, 381; pork rind for, 241
Dolphin depth finders, 258, 329
Dolphin Marine Products, 374
Double bait gripper (snelled hook spinner), 12
Double carlisle (snelled hook spinner), 12
Doubleday & Company, Inc., 13, 26, 140, 180, 188, 239, 295, 336
Downey, Earl, 45
Downriggers (trolling unit), 209; portable transom mount for, 88
Drag, setting, 304
Drifting for fish, 384
Dry-fly spray and leader sink, 191
Dual Range Recorder/Flasher Depthsounder, 381
Duerksen, Herb, 328
Dumb fish (that don't learn), 184
Dunaway, Vic, 325
Du Pont de Nemours & Co. (E. I.), 43
Dutton & Co., Inc. (E. P.), 61, 294
Dutton-Lainson Co., 158
Dwindling Acres, 373
Dytek Laboratories, 269
Dytek Sea Water Temperature System, 269

Eagle claw hooks, 173
Eagle ray (fish), 36
Early Bird Worm Bedding, 26
Earthworms. *See* Worms
Eason, Al, 25
Eels, 13; for bait, 262; Jig-A-Do lure, 64; scientific investigations of, 148
Eelskin on a plug, 262
Eggleston, Max, 130
Electric catfish, 44
Electric eel, 44
Electric fish scaler, 219
Electric fish smoker, 72

Electric ray, 44
Electric winch anchor bracket, 158
Electronic fish-finder, 39
Elephant fish, 36
Elliot, Bob, 82
Emco Specialties, Inc., 28
"Emigrant Basin" (map), 131
Eppinger Mfg. Co. (Lou J.), 72, 98
Erwin Weller Co., 12, 352
ESB, Inc., 67
Eska Co., 35
Eska motors, 35
Esterbrook, Gary L., 61
Eulachon (or candlefish), 267
Evanoff, Vlad, 13, 24, 131, 179, 180, 348
Everglades Chamber of Commerce, 281
Everglades Holiday Park, 64, 146
Everglades National Park, 281, 350
Evinrude Anglers Club, 73
Evinrude Motors, 73, 374
Evinrude 200-hp. V-6 motor, 374
Explanation of the Tides, An, 363
Eyeglass holder, 298
Eyelets, 193

Fabuglas Co., Inc., 75
Factory Distributors, 182
Fagerstrom, Stan, 126, 144
Fallfish, 13
Falls Bait Co., Inc., 30
Family Waters Sports in Big Wyoming, 47
Farmer, Charles J., 8
Farnsworth, George, 278
Feldmann Engineering & Mfg. Co., Inc., 8, 85
Fellegy, Joe, 189, 212
Felt sole kit, 153
Fenwick Co., 106, 142, 227, 234, 260, 283, 319
Fenwick Fly Fishing Schools, 211
Ferguson, Paul, 186
Feurer Bros., Inc., 351, 380
Fibber McGee's Closet, 295
Field & Stream (magazine), 36, 70, 278
Filleting a fish, how to, 105
Filleting boards, 54
Fillet knives, 15, 204, 249, 377
Films, free, 98, 177, 203
Fin & Feather Mfg. Co., 28
Fireside Angler, Inc., 38
Fish culture, 66
Fisherman (magazine), 332
Fisherman Co., 332
Fisherman's Fall (Haig-Brown), 172
Fisherman's Spring (Haig-Brown), 172
Fisherman's Summer (Haig-Brown), 172

Fisherman's Winter (Haig-Brown), 172
Fisher Marine, Inc., 9
Fishes of Kentucky, The (Clay), 234
Fishes of the Northern Gulf of Mexico (Walls), 339
Fishes of Utah, 119
Fish Freshwater Nova Scotia, 98
Fish Hawk 500 meter, 22
Fish Hawk Marine 1206 scale, 338
Fish Hawk 204 finder, 113
Fishing (Bates), 20
Fishing Alabama's Bays and Tidal Streams, 109
Fishing Alabama's Small Streams, 109
Fishing and Camping in East Tennessee, 185
Fishing Annual (Eppinger Mfg. Co.), 72
Fishing Annual and Catalog (Garcia Corp.), 52, 100, 316, 354
Fishing Console Canopy, 357
Fishing Facts (magazine), 18, 30
Fishing for Flounder (Muller), 332
Fishing for Fluke (Simons), 332
Fishing for Weakfish (Muller), 332
Fishing from Boats (Rosko), 336
Fishing Holes of Texas (Wilke), 130
"Fishing Hole, The" (TV show), 50, 181
Fishing in America (Waterman), 156
Fishing in Kansas Lakes and Reservoirs, 137
Fishing in Kentucky, 92
Fishing in Manitoba, 73
Fishing in Michigan, 55
Fishing in North Carolina, 375
Fishing in the Florida Keys (Apte), 357
Fishing Nebraska, 69
Fishing Saskatchewan, 106
Fishing Tennessee, 185
Fishing the Bays of Texas (Husak), 314
Fishing the California Wilderness (Hayden), 198
Fishing the Coast and Lakes of Northeast Mexico (Slaten), 246
Fishing the Midge (Koch), 144
Fishing the Mississippi, 64
Fishing the Oregon Country (Ames), 23
Fishing the Texas Coast Inshore and Offshore (Becker), 314
Fishing Tips (Cisco Kid Tackle, Inc.), 112
Fishing Western Waters (Morrison), 219
Fishing with Natural Baits (Evanoff), 131
Fishing with Small Fry (Freeman), 203
Fish Lo-K-Tor, 202
Fishmor spoon, 350
Fish n' Fillet cleaning board, 51
Fish-n-Float marker kit, 230
Fish pond, building your own, 8
Fish Salt-water Nova Scotia, 319
Fish the Impossible Places (Pobst), 144
Fish Tracker depth sounder, 74
Fishwells Unlimited, 286
Flat bank sinker molds, 187
Flat diamond bank mold, 187
Flat snagless sinker molds, 187
Flexnet Casting Shirt, 257
Flies: Adams, 122; bonito and albacore on, 302; books on, 196; Boulder, 189; Brown Bivisible, 122; for carp, 157; for chinook salmon, 5; Dan Bailey's, 189; divided-wing, 31; Gallatin, 189; hackle, 31; hair-bodied, 31; hair-wing, 31; High Country, 34; Light Cahill, 122; Madison, 189; by mail-order, 38; Marabou streamer, 108; March Brown, 122; Orvis, 31; parachute, 31; pocket-size organizer for, 25; Poulsen Quality, 283; Quill Gordon, 122; Royal Coachman, 122; for small-mouth bass, 194; spider, for trout, 57; terrestrial, 31; thorax-type, 31; for trout, 122, 156, 189; tying your own, 30; Weber, 182; Yellowstone, 189. See also under names of fish
Flies (Leonard), 227
Flikker Rigs, 67
Flipgun fish hook remover, 192
Float fishing, 32
Float Fishing on the Sipsey River (state of Alabama), 109
Floating sunglasses, 342
Floats, types of, 85
Florida: bass maps, 119; books on, 45, 186, 212, 282; guide to, 134. See also Everglades
Florida bass, 184; in California, 66
Florida Fisherman's Handbook, The, 186
Florida Fishes (Allyn), 45
Florida Keys, guide to, 357
Florida Publishing Co., 186
Florida's Charted Salt-water Fishin' Holes, 282
Florida's Fishing Grounds (Moe), 45
Florida Sportsman (publication), 325
Florida Wildlife Federation, 134
Flounder, 23, 336; bait for, 256; book on, 332
Fluke, 336

Fly and the Fish, The (Atherton), 144
Fly boxes, 168
Fly Casting from the Beginning (Green), 227
Fly File, 25
Fly Fisherman's Bookcase, 231
Fly Fishing for Bass and Panfish (Scientific Anglers), 25
Fly Fishing in Salt Water (Kreh), 287
Fly-fishing school sessions, 19
Fly Fishing Strategy (Swisher and Richards), 160
Flying fish, 44
Fly lines. See Lines
Fly reels. See Reels
Fly Rod Fishing Made Easy (Cortland Line Co.), 67, 208
Fly rods. See Rods; names of fly rods
Fly-tying Materials (Leiser), 35
Folding knife, 46
Folding scissors, 107
Fong, Michael, 144
Food and Game Fishes of the Texas Coast, 154
Foote, Cathy, 265
Forest areas, 151
Foster Grant Co., Inc., 342
4-sided pyramid sinker mold, 187
Fox, Charles K., 144
Fox shark, 36
Freeman, Jim, 203
"French Canyon" (map), 131
Fresh, keeping fish, 202
Freshet Press, 144
Freshwater Fisherman's Bible, The (Evanoff), 13
Freshwater Fishes of New Hampshire (Scarola), 29
Freshwater Fishes of Texas, 154
Freshwater Fishing and Hunting in Virgina, 185
Freshwater Fishing in Hawaii, 18
Freshwater Fishing in Texas (Tinsley), 130
Frogfish, 36

Gaffs, 334, 381
Gafftopsail catfish, 288
Gaines Co., 56
Gallager Co. (A. J.), 196
Gapen, Dan, 222
Gapen Tackle Co., 222
Garcia bait-casting reel,
Garcia Bass Fishing School, 42
Garcia Corp., 52, 100, 109, 126, 243, 254, 265, 271, 316, 333, 354
Garrison, Chuck, 373
Gary L. Esterbrook (bookstore), 61
Gasaway, Dick, 42
Gene Bullard Custom Rods, Inc., 25, 119

Gentex Corp., 310
Georgia, booklet on, 275
Gerber knives, 115
Gerber Legendary Blades Co., 115
Gerlach, Erv, 224
Gerlach, Rex, 64, 216
Gibbs, Jerry, 122
Gifford, Tommy, 278
Gladding Aqua-Float boat cushion, 136
Gladding Corp., 69, 121, 134, 136, 209, 258, 329
Gladding International Sport Fishing Museum, 69
Gladding South Bend life vest, 121
Glas-Gard eyeglass holder, 298
Glastron Boat Co., 221
Globe Float Co., 192
G-96 Magnum Fillet Knife, 377
G-96 Mariner Surf Gaff, 381
Golden trout, 69
Gold Seal Industries, Inc., 258, 305
Goosefish, 36
Grady-White Boats, Inc., 273
Grand, Tom, 355
"Granite Creek" (map), 131
Graphic Press, Inc., 233, 366
Graphite fly reels, 46
Grassi, Jim, 144
Grayling, 98
Great Fishing Tackle Catalogs of the Golden Age (Melner and Kessler), 130
Great Outdoors Publishing Co., 45
Green, Jim, 227
Green, Larry, 137, 144, 328, 346
Green, Seth, 66
Gregory, Dr. William K., 240
Greiten, Fred, 259
Grey, Zane, 278
Grizzly, Inc., 300
Grouper, 268, 336; on lures, 198, 279; trolling for, 250
Grove, Alvin R., 144
Gudebrod Bros. Silk Co., Inc., 123
Gudebrod Fishing Tackle Co., 23, 290
Guide to Fun in Florida, 134
Guide to Salt-water Sports Fishing in South Carolina, A, 270
Gutmann Cutlery Co., Inc., 275

Haig-Brown, Roderick L., 172
Halstead, Bruce W., 292
Hamilton, Carl, 46
Hank Roberts Co., 47, 48
Harben fish scaler, 319
Harben Mfg. Co., 319
Harmony Enterprises, Inc., 121
Harper & Row, Publishers, Inc., 24, 113, 216, 312, 348
Harry, Elwood K., 240
Hatcheries, 66
"Hatteras Offshore Fishing Chart," 322
Haw, Frank, 277
Hawaii: freshwater fishing in, 18; salt-water fishing, 319
Hayden, Mike, 198
Heath Co., 36
Heddon, James, 77
Heilner, Van Campen, 240, 278
Helen-S Fleet, 293
Helen-S VI party boat, 293
Hemingway, Ernest, 278
Henshall, Dr. James A., 54
Herring dodger, 272
Herrington, Jack, 382
Herter's, Inc., 82
Hi & Dry fly flotant, 100
High Country Flies Co., 34
Hildebrandt Corp. (John J.), 115, 358
Hilde's Jerk Jigger, 358
Hille Co. (E.), 166
Hills, John Waller, 144
Hines, Bob, 188
Hip boots, replacing worn felt on, 153
History of Fly Fishing for Trout, A (Hills), 144
Hodges, Bill, 335
Hofschneider Corp., 178
Hogfish, 36
Holder, Charles Frederick, 278
Holland, Don, 140
Holm, Don, 23, 278
Holt, Rinehart & Winston, Inc., 73, 156
Hoochy tails and trolls, 330
Hooks, 31, 62, 67, 255; adding a strip of squid or fish to, 302; Arrow-Lock weedless, 7; Chroma-Glo Water Demon, 62; for coho salmon, 62; Eagle Claw, 173; flipgun remover, 192; holding bait on, 271; keeping sharp, 21; Mustad, 255; salmon moochers, 283; two or three baits on, 313
Hooks and Lines (International Women's Fishing Assn.), 309
Hopkins Fishing Lures, Inc., 270
Horsefish, 36
Houndfish, 36
How to Catch California Trout, 119
How to Catch Fish in Fresh Water (American Fishing Tackle Manufacturers' Assn.), 12
How to Catch Fish in Fresh Water (Johnson Reels, Inc.), 203
How to Catch Fish in Salt Water (American Fishing Tackle Manufacturers' Assn.), 12
How to Catch Salt-water Fish (Wisner), 239
How to Field Dress Game & Fish (Gerber Legendary Blades), 115
How to Find Fish—and Make Them Strike (Bates), 216
How to Fish for Bass (Smith), 45
How to Fish for Bass (Zuber), 130
How to Fish for Snook (Downey), 45
How to Rig Baits for Trolling, 257
How to Wrap a Rod with Gudebrod, 123
Hubs Chub Lures Co., 10
Hudnall, Bud, 241
Huff, Capt. Steve, 288
Hui, Stan, 174
Hull, Clint, 373
Humminbird Mark-IV depth sounder, 92
Hunn, Max, 373
Hunter's & Fisherman's Ontario/Canada, The, 144
Hurley, Ray, 174
Husak, Anton, 314, 345
Hutchinson, Bob, 328, 370

Ice drills, 8
Ice fishing, 162; shelters, 121; tackle, 67
Ice skimmer, 85
Idaho, 67; booklet on, 175
Idaho Lakes and Reservoirs, 175
Ideal Fishing Float Co., 99
Illinois, guide to, 215
Imperial Marine Equipment, 326, 357
Indiana, guide on, 143
Inflatable boats, 102
Inland Marine Co., 102
Inline troller sinker molds, 187
International Game Fish Assn. (IGFA), 240, 254
International Hook and Tackle Co., 255
International Marine Publishing Co., 320, 328
International Oceanographic Foundation, 261
International Spin Fishing Assn., 216
International Women's Fishing Assn., 309
IPCO, Inc., 54, 60, 204
Isaac Franklin Co., Inc., 165
Izaak Walton League of America, 55

Jabsco Products ITT, 102
Jack crevalle (fish), 319
Jacket patch, 42
Jackson, Denis, 274
James Heddon's Sons, 35, 77, 78, 168, 351
Janes, Edward C., 82
Jefferson, Ray, 131, 164, 381
Jerk Jigger, 358
Jeros Tackle Co., Inc., 376
Jet-Aer Corp., 377, 381
Jetties, fishing from, 362
Jewfish, 306

Jiffy, lures in a, 148
Jiffy Hand Ice Drill, 8
Jiffy ice skimmer, 85
Jiffy Power Ice Drill, 8
Jigging rig, 305
Jigs: adding cloth or plastic strips to, 66; catching more fish on, 210
John C. Kremer Co., 255
Johnny Reb lectranchor, 133
Johnny Reb Mfg. Co., 133
Johnson, Quentin, 224
Johnson, Sam, 323
Johnson Outboards Co., 347
Johnson Reels, Inc., 170, 203
Johnson Rod-Reel Combos, 203
Johnson Sea-Horse Outboard motors, 347
Jorgensen Bros., 352
Joy of Fishing, The (Rand McNally & Co.), 174
Jugging for catfish, 118
Julian Bait Co., Inc., 255
Jump fishing, 112
"Juniper Lake" (Florida bass map), 119

Kansas, booklet on, 137
Karas, Nicholas, 243
Karp, Dr., 148
Katz, Dr. Fulton, 382
Kennedy, Edwin D., 240
Kentucky, books on, 92, 234
Kerr Reservoir, 206
Kessler, Hermann, 130
Kicker (metal wobbler), 178
Kimble, R., 150
Kingfish, 346; leap of, 379
King mackerel, 268, 281, 309; leap of, 379; 90-lb. record catch, 368
King salmon, caught by eight-year-old (28-lb. fish), 108
Kite fishing, 345
"Klamath River" (map), 131
Klamath River Fishing, 119
K-Mac & Co., 107, 159
Knife Know-how (Buck Knives, Inc.), 152
Knight, John Alden, 169
Knight, Mrs. Richard Alden, 169
Knives, 15, 115, 152, 156, 249; Case, 116; fillet, 15, 204, 249, 377; folding, 47; and pliers set, 317; puma angler, 275; Swiss Army, 15
Knots, 226
Know Your Fishing Baits (Zuber), 130
Know Your Fishing Boats (Zuber), 130
Koch, Ed, 144
Kokanee salmon, 82
Kokanee trout, 73
Konizeski, Dick, 14
Kreh, Lefty, 57, 278, 287, 373

Kremer, John C., 255
Kutz, Bob, 224

L. & S. Bait Co., Inc., 376
Ladyfish, 336; catching, 332
"Lafayette" fish, 240
Laggies Fish Catching Co., 100, 214
Lake and Stream Information (Indiana Dept. of Natural Resources), 143
Lake Berryessa Fishing, 119
"Lake George" (Florida bass map), 119
Lake Jackson, Fla., 80; bass map for, 119
"Lake Kissimmee" (Florida bass map), 119
Lakeland Industries, 143
Lake Michigan, coho salmon in, 110
"Lake Okeechobee" (Florida bass map), 119
Lake Okeechobee (guide), 212
Lakes that disappear, 80
"Lake Tahoe" (map), 131
"Lake Talquin" (Florida bass map), 119
"Lake Tohopikaliga" (Florida bass map), 119
Lake trout, 13, 73, 98, 184; bait for, 147; hooks for, 62; lures for, 4, 198; spoons for, 19; trolling for, 50, 160
LaMonte, Francesca, 240
Landlocked salmon, 2, 13, 82; near smelt, 2; paddling a canoe for, 175; spoons for, 19; trolling for, 50, 160
Lantern, all-weather, 375
Large-mouth bass, 13, 18, 19, 20, 73, 134, 216; lures for, 40; plastic worms for, 15
Large-mouth Bass in Ohio, 55
Largest freshwater fish, 2
Largest salt-water fish, 248
Laycock, George, 1
Lazy Ike Corp., 141
Leader-Keeper, 205
Leaders, 100, 247; keeping, 205, 360; tying to the lure, 70
Leader straightener, 100
Leather gifts, 98
Lee Cuddy Associates, Inc. (J.), 330
Lee's fighting chair, 244
Lee's Tackle Co., 244, 255
Leiser, Eric, 35
Leonard, J. Edson, 227
Leonard Fly-Fishing School, 19
Leonard Rod Co. (H. L.), 19
Lerner, Michael, 240, 278
Les Davis Fishing Tackle Co., 272, 370
Les Davis Herring Dodger, 272
Let's Go Freshwater Fishing in Virginia, 96

Lew Childre & Sons, Inc., 107, 135, 190
Lewis, Bob, 345
Lewis, Gordon, 45
Lewis, Jimmy, 306
Lew's Fiberglas telescopic poles, 190
LFP 300 Fish Lo-K-Tor, 39
Life vest, 121, 310
Lightning, strike by (story), 178
Lights for night, 114
Lilly, Bud and Greg, 67
Limit Mfg. Corp., 138
Lindner, Al, 212
Lindy Rigs, 67; tips on using, 48
Lindy tails (plastic worms), 15
Lines: Ande monofilament, 313; Ashaway, 261; Berkley, 77; Bevin-Wilcox, 141; big fish on small lines, 284; Cortland 333, 147; Dacron, 261, 363; fish catches (story), 371; fluorescent color, 43; by mail-order, 38; Maxima, 226; nylon squidding, 333; Nylorfi, 3; Perlene (Perlex), 141; Pop-Up automatic tip-up for, 79; Royal Bonnyl II, 109; Scientific Anglers, 94; sinking and sink-float fly, 184; Stren (fluorescent), 43; swimming rescue with (story), 316
Lionfish, 36
Lippincott Co., 231
Lisk-Fly Mfg. Co., 34
Live bait cages, 10
Livewell Aerator Kit, 102
Livingston, A. D., 137, 231
Livingston, David, 58
Locating freshwater fish, 46
Logs, 246
Long, Evelyn, 186
Loop A Line Co., 193
Louis Johnson Co., 78, 364
Lowe, Roy, 318
Lowe Line Boats, 171
"Lower Chesapeake Bay Fishing Map from Smith Point to Lynnhaven Inlet," 322
Lowrance Electronics, Inc., 1, 39, 46, 175, 202, 230, 277, 286, 298
Luck versus skill, 166
Luhr-Jensen Down-Rigger, 40
Luhr Jensen & Sons, Inc., 40, 215, 383
Lungfish, 218
Lunker (Underwood), 228
"Lunker" lake trout, 144
Lupo Tackle, Inc., 370
Lure and Love of Trout Fishing, The (Grove), 144
Lure Life foil, 150
Lure of Fishing, The (Lazy Ike Corp.), 104

Lures: Acme, 4, 277; Arbogast, 52, 170, 307; "banana" type, 52; Bee Bug, 56; beer can, 118; Big George, 87; Big-O, 101; Bonehead, 232; box for, 373; Boy Howdy, 101; Bridgeport Vi-Ke, 365; bright colored, 80; Burke Co., 58, 64, 159, 198, 307; Bush Bug, 56; "Candy Yazz," 91; cans as, 118; changing, 156; Cherry Cluster, 215; Cherry Drifter, 215; Chopstick, 101; Chug Bug, 13; Chugger Spook, 77; Cisco Kid, 112; Cohokie, 129; color, size, or action of, 68; components, 143; Cordell, 101, 287; Cotton's Crab, 101; Crazy Tail, 101; Creek Chub, 129; Crippled Killer, 38; Dalton, 309; Di-Dapper, 205; Dorado, 52; from a drinking straw, 358; Dying Flutter, 77; Dynamite, 56; Egg-Drifter Balls, 56; Fat Face, 56; Fatso, 13; Feisty, 91; Fenwick, 260, 319; Floater, 232; Floozy Spinner Bait, 91; fluorescent, 80; Flutter-Fin, 43; foil finish, 150; freshwater, 2, 4, 6, 8, 13, 15, 18, 23, 30, 34, 37, 38, 40, 43, 50, 52, 56, 58, 64, 68, 70, 77, 82, 84, 87, 91, 101, 104, 112, 118, 128, 137, 138, 140, 141, 148, 150, 152, 156, 157, 159, 167, 168, 170, 172, 178, 179, 194, 195, 198, 199, 200, 205, 215, 226, 232; Froggie, 56; Fuzz Bug, 56; Gaines, 56; Garcia Tube Alou, 243; Gay Blade, 101; George, 87; Grizzly, 300; grouper on, 279; Gudebrod fireback, 23; Hairy Hank, 56; Hairy Mary, 56; Hammerhead, 307; Hartig's, 172; Hawaiian Wiggler, 170; Hawg Hunter, 50; Heddon, 77, 168; Hellbender and Hellraiser, 6; holder for, 104; Hopkins "ST," 270; "Hot 'N' Tot," 13; how many to carry, 194; Hubs Chub, 10; Hula Poppers, 170; Humpback, 232; Huzzy, 91; injured minnow, 129; J. T. Surge, 376; in a jiffy, 148; Jig-A-Do (eel), 64, 307; Jig-A-Lo (saltwater), 91; Jitterbug, 170; Jointed Darter, 129; Kastmaster, 277; Kinzua Country, 56; kit for making, 167; Konahead, 260; Lazy Ike, 104, 141; lead-bodies jig, 56; Leisure Life, 320; Lil Corky drifter, 18; Li'l Tubby, 141; Lisk, 34; Little George, 87; Lucky Lujon, 364; Lupo, 370; making your own, 30, 138, 167; 179; Marathon Scrappy, 140; "mini," 82; Minnow, 232; Mouse, 129; Mr. Whiskers, 56; "N," 84; Nasty, 91; Nikie, 129; No-alibi, 255; one fish on two (story), 336; Pico, 178; Pikie, 129; pipe, 274; plastic worms, 15, 37, 58, 66, 159, 182, 199; Plunker, 129; Pole Kat, 34; Popper, 232; Punkin Seed, 77; "R" series, 195; Rabble Rouser, 205; Rapala, 105, 157, 218; Rebel, 195, 232; Red Eye, 178; Red Fin, 101; Reflecto, 309; River Runt, 77; Rogers, 50; Roo-Tur, 205; Rouster, 205; salt-water, 243, 255, 258, 259, 270, 274, 277, 279, 287, 291, 299, 300, 307, 309, 319, 320, 328, 351, 358, 364, 365, 369, 376; scented, 2; Sea-Deucer teaser, 328; Shady Lady, 91; Shiner Minnow, 13; Shrimp-Louie, 215; Sinking Red Fin, 101; Sin-Sation, 40; Skunk Nymph, 34; Snagproof, 152; soda can, 118; Sonar, 77; Sonic, 77; speed and depth, 224; spin-tail, 200; Spook, 77; Spottie, 56; Sputterbug, 170; Sputterfuss, 170; Steelhead, 215; Steely-Bob, 215; Streaker, 129; Stream Cleaner, 56; Suick, 8; Sundance teaser, 328; Super George, 87; Super-R, 232; Super Shad, 101; Super Threadfin, 38; surf fishing with, 299; Surf Shiner, 101; Tadpolly, 77; tail teaser, 352; Tar Heel Ant, 34; teaser, 328, 352, 380; Thin-fin, 13; Threadfin Shad, 38; Tiny Tim, 129; Torpedo, 77; Trailer Bug, 56; Tri-Fin, 291; tying leader to, 70; Vibra Tail, 101; Viper, 129; Whiz Bang, 13; Wiggle Wart, 13; Wig-Wag, 58, 198; Worth's Musky, 137; from yarn, 228; Zara, 77. *See also* Bait; Spoons; Streamers; Plugs; types of lures; under names of fish
Lyman, Henry, 320, 322, 373
Lyons, Nick, 57

McClain, Peter, 328
McClane's New Standard Fishing Encyclopedia, 73
McCristal, Vic, 346
McGinty Sportster Wader, 301
McGovern, Frank, 150
McGraw-Hill Book Co., 228
McIntosh, Greg, 306
Mack, Tony, 137
Mackerel, 20, 244, 336; as bait, 308; bait for, 239; leaders for, 247

McKinnis, Jerry, 50, 181, 196
McLean, Capt. Andy, 350
Macmillan, Inc., 16, 252, 336, 380
McQuaig, Baxley, Jr., 150
Magazines. *See* names of magazines
Mail-order houses, 38, 48, 82, 166, 231, 373
Maine: cod in, 306; publications on, 38, 354
Mains, Paul, 186
Major, Harlan, 278
Make-a-Mold kit, 295
Make Your Own Fishing Lures (Evanoff), 179
Mako shark, leap of, 379
Mangrove snappers, 268
Manitoba, 80; literature on, 73
Mann, Tom, 196, 212
Mann's Bait Co., Inc., 87
Man vs. Muskie (Nat. Muskie Assn.), 72
Marathon Bait Co., 140
Marathon Rubber Products, 61
"Marble Mountains" (map), 131
"Marin and Sonoma Counties" (map), 375
Marine Angler's Guide to Fishing Piers and Boats in South Carolina, 377
Marine Game Fishes of the Pacific Coast—Alaska to Ecuador (Walford), 366
Marine Metal Products Co., Inc., 309
Marine Sport Fishery in Maine, The, 354
Marker Buoys, 138
Marker kits, 230
Marlin, 20, 24, 320, 336, 346; in Australia, 378; caught on 6-lb. line, 240; pork rind for, 241; pugnacious kind, 265; 65-lb. tuna inside, 292; speeding up for, 352
Martin, Roland, 196
Martin Reel Co., Inc., 143, 199, 211
Martin Tackle and Mfg. Co., 160, 349, 350
Martin Travel Set, 199
Martin Trolls, 160
Maryland Sport Fishing Tournament, 309
Mean-O-Eel (plastic eel), 287
Melner, Sam, 130
Merc 1150 motor, 71
Mercury Marine, 60, 71, 165, 222
Mercury outboard motors, 71, 165
Mexico, books on, 246
Meyer, Charles R., 328, 346
Meyers, Dave, 144
Meyers Industries, Inc., 29
MFG Boat Co., 10, 297
Michigan Fish and How to Catch Them, 55

"Middle Chesapeake Bay Fishing Map from the Patuxent River to Tangier Island," 322
Midland Tackle Co., 274
Migration runs, 242
Mildrum guides, 310
Mildrum Mfg. Co., 310
Mini-on-Deck tackle box, 263
Mini Tuna Tower for boats, 326
Minn Kota Mfg. Co., 161
Minn Kota motors, 161
Minnows: adding weight to, 36; buckets for, 12, 140; catching, 30; clipped plugs, 187; keeping alive, 102; plastic, 15, 30, 70; tying weedless hook on, 210
Mirro-Craft Co., 83
Mississippi Commission Lakes, 64
Mississippi Game Fish, 64
Mister Twister, Inc., 40, 376
Mister Twister's EEE-LLL, 376
Mitchell, Frank, 361
Mit-Shell Co., 72
Model "90" fish thermometer, 164
Modern Salt-water Fishing (Dunaway), 325
Modern Salt-water Sport Fishing (Woolner), 280
Modern Talking Picture Service, Inc., 177
Moe, Martin, 45
Molds, making your own, 295; *See also* Sinker molds
MonArk Boat Co., 201
Monel swivels, 348
"Mono Creek" (map), 131
Montana, 67; book on, 14
Montanan's Fishing Guide, The (Konizeski), 14
"Monterey and San Luis Obispo Counties" (map), 375
Moore, W. E., 212
Morrison, Morie, 219
Morse, Buddy, 218
Moses, Fred, 181
Moss Frank T., 328, 346
Motors. *See* names of motors
Mountain Press Publishing Co., 14
Mudskipper, 149
Muller, Dr. William A., 332
Mullet, 262; best way to catch, 316
Mundus, Capt. Frank, 380
Murray, Bobby, 196
Museum of American Fly Fishing, 150
Muskellunge, 2, 13, 24, 73, 134, 216; booklets on, 72; caught from a dock, 52; on a fly rod, 194; how to fool, 23; how to hook more, 120; lure for, 8, 64, 137; spoons for, 19, 52
Muskellunge Fishing in Ohio, 55
Mussels, toughening up for bait, 329
Mustad hooks, 255

My Buddy tackle box, 116

Nantucket Ocean Products, Inc., 371
Narragansett Sport Fisheries Marine Laboratory, 257
National Coalition for Marine Conservation, 294
National Freshwater Fishing Hall of Fame, 224
National Muskie Assn., 72
Nauheim, Bob, 5, 57, 144
Nebraska, booklet on, 69
Nelson, Bud, 224
Nemes, Sylvester, 95
Nets, 165, 267; wood frame, 56
Net weight molds, 187
Nevada, booklets on, 136
New England, books on, 82
New Guide to Black Bass Fishing (Circle), 1
New Guide to Panfish Fishing (Laycock), 1
New Guide to Salmon and Trout Fishing (Bauer), 1
New Guide to Salt-water Fishing (Rosko), 286
New Guide to Walleye and Sauger Fishing (Bauer), 1
New Hampshire Fishing & Hunting, 29
New Jersey Trout Guide, 193
New Mexico Fishing Waters, 25
New York, map and information on, 153
Nicholl Bros., Inc., 375
Night fishing for bass, 204
Night Fishing for Trout (Bashline), 144
Night lighting, 114
Nitrogen supersaturation, 222
Nix, Sam, 295
Norman Mfg. Co., Inc., 84
Normark Corp., 51, 105, 157
North Carolina, books on, 233, 366, 375
North Carolina Coastal Fishing & Vacation Guide, 366
North Carolina University, 274
Northern Pike Fishing (Bergh), 189
North Sierra Trout Fishing, 119
Northwoods Publishing Co., Inc., 30
No-snag sinker molds, 187
Nova Scotia, booklets on, 98, 319

Oberlin Canteen Co., 104, 132, 191
Oblak, Frank, 284
"Ocean City Fishing Map," 322
Ocean State Fishing Supplies, Inc., 305
O'Donnell Rod Co., 347
Ohio, publications on, 55
Oil rigs, trolling near, 242

Okee-Tantie Recreation Area, 212
Okiebug Distributing Co., 230
Okiebug tackle, 230
Oklahoma, leaflets about, 18
Old Town Canoe Co., 53
Olsen Knife Co., 14
101 Best Fishing Trips in Oregon (Holm), 23
1001 Fishing Tips and Tricks (Evanoff), 24
Ontario, 80; booklet on, 144
"Orange/Lochloosa" (Florida bass map), 119
Oregon, 146; books on, 23; salt-water guide to, 288
Orvis, Charles F., 271
Orvis Co., Inc., 31, 109, 263, 271
Orvis Fly Fishing School, 220
Outdoor Life (magazine), 36
Overland Fisherman's Friend knife and pliers set, 317
Oxfish, 36
Oxmoor House, 181

Pacific Coast sturgeon, 2
Pacific North (Holm), 23
Pacific salmon: hooking, 324; migrations of, 242; spoons for, 19
Pacific sheepshead, 304
Padre Island Co., 178
Paducah Tackle Co., Inc., 91
Palenske, R. H., 188
Palmer, Lew, 144
Palmer Mfg. (C.), 187
Palmer sinker molds, 187
Pal rod holder, 291
PanAngler, The (newsletter), 318
PanAngling Travel Service, 318
Pandora's Tackle Boxes Co., 317
Panfish, 20, 23, 24, 44, 64, 67, 228; bait for, 154, 164, 218; float fishing for, 32; hiding places of, 214; lures for, 34, 52; plastic minnow bait, 30; spinners for, 12
Panfishing in Texas (Tinsley), 130
Parkas, 343
Parrotfish, 36
Party Boat List (along Maine coast), 354
Pelican canoe, 62
Penn Fathom-Master trolling device, 315
Penn Fishing Tackle Mfg. Co., 257, 282, 315, 340, 361
Penn surf reels, 340
Penn trolling reels, 361
Pepco nets, 267
Pepper Co., Inc. (J. F.), 267
Pequeau Fishing Tackle, Inc., 344
Pequeau rigs, 344
Perch, 228; lures for, 34, 40; in 10 to 50 ft. deep water, 194
Perkins Marine Lamp & Hardware Corp., 366

Perko fishing hardware, 366
Permit fish, 287, 336; IGFA Women's record catch, 288
Perrine fly boxes, 168
Perry, Buck, 168
Pete Test's Compleat Angler, 153
Pfeiffer, Boyd, 136
Pflueger, Al, Jr., 339
Pflueger Marine Taxidermy, 339
Pflueger Sporting Goods Div., 239, 279
Phil Bart Inventions, 205
Phillips, Norman, 346
Phillips Fly & Tackle Co., 38
Pickerel, 13, 24, 64; areas for (Atlantic Coast), 150; float fishing for, 32; plastic minnow bait, 70; skittering for, 57; weedless minnow bait for, 210
Pickerel in Ohio, 55
Pigfish, 36
Pike, 13, 20, 24, 73, 98; books on, 189; in Canada, 80; easy catch (story), 68; fly rods for, 2; lures for, 4, 8, 52, 64, 198; spinners for, 12; spoons for, 19, 52; weedless minnow bait for, 210
Pilot flasher depth sounder, 325
Pinch-on sinker molds, 187
Pioneer Tackle Co., 303
Piranhas, 172
Plano Molding Co., 44, 282
Plano tackle boxes, 44, 282
Plastic bottles and containers, 108
Plastic eels, 258, 287, 307
Plastic fish box, 182
Plastic lures, fishing with, 226
Plastic minnows, 30, 70
Plastics Research & Development Corp., 32, 138, 166, 232
Plastic worms, 15, 37, 58, 66, 159, 182, 199; bluegill on, 108; book on, 37; choosing and rigging, 159; hooking bass on, 66. *See also* Worms
Plastilite Corp., 70, 85
Plastilite floats, 85
Plath Co. (R. C.), 338
Pliers, 63; crimping, 280; and knife set, 317
Plugs: adding cloth or plastic strips to, 66; barracuda on, 284; Big Jim, 50; for bluefish, 341; Bump 'N' Grind, 23; Creek Chub, 360; crippled minnow, 187; darter, 131; Deep Jim, 50; Diamond Rattlesub, 298; eelskin on a, 262; Little Jim, 50; Martin, 349; Maverick, 23; Middle Jim, 50; Mirrolures, 376; Nantucket BB-45 Popper, 371; Salty Boogie, 341; for snook, 341; Stan Gibbs, 252; Striper Atom, 378; Sunshine Popper, 305; for tarpon, 341
Pobst, J. Richard, 144

Polar Craft Mfg. Co., 21
Pollock fish, 336
Pompanette, Inc., 241, 263, 334, 345
Pompanette chair, 241
Pompanette gaffs, 334
Pompano fish, locating, 287
Popular Utah Fishing Waters, 119
Porcupine fish, 36
Porgies, 336
Pork rind bait, 241, 364; making strips tastier, 39; in salt water, 241; ways to use, 172
Powerscopic Corp., 6
Practical Black Bass Fishing (Sosin and Dance), 19
Practical Fishing Knots (Sosin), 226
Practical Fly Fisherman, The (McClane), 70
Prentice-Hall, Inc., 70, 131
Prince Edward Island, 336
Profiles in Salt-water Angling (Reiger), 278
Pro Filleting Knife, 204
Proven Fishing Methods and How to Fillet Fish (Normack Corp.), 105
Public Access Areas (in Alabama), 61
Public Access to Connecticut Fishing Waters, 180
Public Fishing Waters in Central Ohio, 55
Public Fishing Waters in Northeastern Ohio, 55
Public Fishing Waters in Northwestern Ohio, 55
Public Fishing Waters in Southeastern Ohio, 55
Public Fishing Waters in Southwestern Ohio, 55
Puyans, Andre, 144
Pygmy dwarf goby, 80

Quebec, 80
Quick Corp. of America, 129, 158, 360

Rabbit fish, 36
Rabble Rouser Lures Co., 205
Raccoon perch, 36
Rail rod holder, 213, 255
Rainbow trout, 13, 18, 69, 73, 142, 162, 184
Rainbow Trout in Ohio, 55
Raising Earthworms for Profit (Shields), 115
Rambler 12/24 electric motor, 32
Rand McNally & Co., 174
Rangeley Region Sports Shop, 56
Ranger Tackle Co., Inc., 38
Rapala, Lauri, 157
Rapala cleaning and skinning board, 51
Ratfish, 36

Ray-O-Vac Fishing Tackle Division, 15, 67
Rebel Bass'N Box, 138
Rebel electric motors, 166
Rebel Lures Co., 195, 232
Recreational Guide to the Kissimmee Waterway, 212
"Recreational Map of the Everglades Conservation Areas," 212
Recreation on TVA Lakes, 109
Redfish, 281; stalking, 304
RedTack of America, 186, 272
Reed Tackle Co., 30
Reel holder, wall-mounted, 60
Reels: Alcedo, 340; Ambassadeur, 52, 265; Berkley, 173; Blue Pacific, 71; Bretton spinning, 211; Century/Citation, 170; Commander, 170; Cortland graphite fly, 46; Eagle Claws, 71, 326; Fin-Nor, 259, 260, 266; Freline Spinning, 71; Garcia, 52, 100, 316, 354; Gladding South Bend, 134, 209; Golden Regal, 266; Heddon, 35, 232; Jerry Jig, 303; John Emery, 248; Johnson, 170, 203; Lew Childre, 107; by mail-order, 38; Martin Automatic, 143, 199, 211; Mastereel spinning, 380; Orvis fly, 271; Orvis spinning, 263, 288; Penn, 282, 340, 361; Perrine automatic, 4; Pflueger spinning, 239; Pflueger supreme, 279; President 1980 casting, 125; protecting, 317; Quick reel, 129, 369; Record, 186; repairs, 10; Sabra, 170; Scientific Anglers, 153; 710, 170; Shakespeare spinning, 354; speed spool casting, 107; spin-casting, 35; System, 153; Taurus, 351; Valentine, 333; Wright & McGill, 275; Zebco, 7. *See also* Rod-reel combinations; Spinners
Reel Thing (respooling device), 272
Regent Marine & Instrumentation, Inc., 363
Reiger, George, 278
Reinfelder, Al, 270, 278, 328
Respooling device, 272
Return to the River (Haig-Brown), 172
Rhode Island Party and Charter Boat Assn., 377
Rhode Island Salt-Water Sport Fishing, 377
Rhode Island Tuna Tournament, 374
Rhyan-Craft Boat Mfg. Co., 84
Richards, Carl, 160
Richey, David, 122
Right Rigger (newsletter), 294

397

Ring Rod Holder, 27
Ristori, Al, 373
River Never Sleeps, A (Haig-Brown), 172
Riviera Action Master Dodger, 383
Riviera downriggers, 209
Riviera Mfg., Inc., 209, 383
Rock-Away Fishing Equipment Co., 339
Rock-Away Sport Fishing Equipment Co., 300
Rock bass, 13, 134
Rockfish, 23
Rocky Mountains, 75
Rod belts, 278
Rod Caddy Corp., 290
Rod cases, 290
Rod holders, 27, 100, 213, 255, 291, 338, 349, 374; teak, 341, 374; wall-mounted, 60
Rodia, Lou, 323
Rod keeper, wall piece, 69
Rod-Klip Co., 149
"Rodman Reservoir" (Florida bass map), 119
Rod' r Chart-Mate tubes, 245
Rod-reel combinations, 18, 203
Rods: Ambassadeur casting, 126; bamboo, 14, 37, 233; for bass, 128; bell for, 149; belt for, when standing up, 278; Berkley, 34, 162; book on, 67; broken, fish caught on (story), 218; Browning, 188; building your own, 25, 234; Bullard, 25, 119; Claudio, 165; cobia on, 324; complete outfit, 208; components, 330; Conolon custom deluxe, 271; Cortland outfit, 208; custom handle, 63; custom made, 165; Eagle Claw, 88; Fenwick HMG Graphite, 142; Fenwick salt-water, 283; Fenwick Voyageur, 106; Garcia trolling, 254; gloss finish for, 290; guides for, 310; Heddon, 78, 351; Lew Childre, 135; by mail-order, 38; making your own, 30; musky on, 194; O'Donnell, 347; Orvis fly, 109; pack (broken down in several sections), 162; pack model (System 6), 68; for pike, 2; Quick Finessa, 158; repairs, 10; Scientific Anglers, 161; Shakespeare, 96, 344; storing, 69; telescopic, 6; Thomas & Thomas Co., 233; Trimarc, 95; using two, 166; Uslan, 37; Voyageur fly, 106; Zebco, 318
Rogers, Claude, 370, 372
Roller guides and tip-tops, 365
Rosko, Milt, 16, 252, 286, 323, 336, 346, 373
Rough water, fishing in, 214

Round flat sinker molds, 187
Royal Red Ball Co., 257, 301
Rube Allyn's Fishermen's Handbook, 45
Rushton, J. Henry, 53
Rushton pack canoe, 53

Sailfish, 20, 24, 320, 336, 346; catch of three (at same time), 368; pork rind for, 241
Salmon, 23, 56, 86, 98, 162, 336; in Alaska, 252; best spoons for, 383; flies for, 5, 189; lure for, 198
"Salmon and Steelhead" (map), 131
Salmon eggs: as bait, 58, 92; "red" caviar from, 148
Salmon Fishing in the Northeast (Janes), 82
Salmon moochers (hooks), 283
Salmon spoons, 383
Salt-water Craftsman, The (Husak), 345
Salt-water Fisherman's Bible, The (Bauer), 336
Saltwater Fishing in Washington (Haw and Buckley), 277
Salt-Water Fly-Fishing Handbook (Nix), 295
Saltwater Jig-A-Lo lure, 91
Salt-water rigs, 303
Salt-water Sport Fishing and Boating in Maryland, 322
Salt-water Sport Fishing and Boating in Virginia, 322
Saltwater Sport Fishing in Virginia (Hutchinson and Rogers), 370
Salt-water Sport Fishing in Virginia (State Travel Service), 365
Salt-water Sportsman (magazine), 280, 373
Sampo, Inc., 266, 278
Sampo Swivels, 266
Sand Diego Bass Lakes Fishing, 119
"San Francisco, San Mateo, and Santa Cruz Counties" (map), 375
Santee-Cooper Reservoir, 206
Sargent & Co., 63
Saskatchewan, 80; publications on, 106
Sawgrass Recreation Park, 64
Scad, 319
Scaler, 219, 319; in an emergency, 63
Scales, 286
Scaling, 23
Scarola, John F., 29
Scharp, Capt. Hal, 378
Schmidt, Johannes, 148
Schools and school courses, 196, 211, 220, 274; for bass fishing,

42; to become a better angler, 146; for fly-fishing, 19
Schweibert, Ernie, 57
Schwind, Phil, 315
Scientific Anglers, 25, 68, 94, 153, 161
Seabreeze Mini-Cooler, 217
SeaCraft Co., 264
Sea dragon, 36
Sea Frontiers (magazine), 261
Sea mink, 36
Sea perch, 23
Sea raven, 36
Sea robin, 36, 267
Sea trout, 24, 281; best time for, 306; lure for, 198; in the surf, 300
Sea Water Temperature Chart, 269
Sebago Trolls, 50
Secrets of Striped Bass Fishing (Rosko), 252
Seidel Co. (T. R.), 191
Selph's Cricket Ranch, 164
Sentry Oxygen Monitor, 131
Seron Mfg. Co., 298
"700" dry-fly spray, 191
Shad, 13, 20, 23, 162
Shad Fishing (Pfeiffer), 136
Shadows, fishing in, 214
Shakespeare Co., 24, 96, 125, 344, 354
Shallow water: hiding places (freshwater fish), 128; slow-trolling lure for, 52; snook in, 276
Shamrock Marine, Inc., 384
Sharks, 248, 256, 268; book on, 380; forty-eight on one line, 318; getting rid of, 245; from shore and piers, 284; tagging and releasing, 257; two caught on one line, 302
Shark Safari (Scharp), 378
Shasta Lake Fishing, 119
Sheepshead, 13, 36, 281, 336; bait for, 324
Sheldon's, Inc., 15
Shellcracker fish, 195
Shelters, ice-fishing, 121
Sherman, Bernie, 144
Shields, Earl B., 115
Shields Publications, 115
Shore chumming, 368
Shoreline Products, 342
Shrimp tout tail, 312
Shrinking fish, 218
Siberian Salmon Egg Co., 92
Silence and stealth when fishing, 200
Silverline, Inc., 229
Simons, Scott, 332
Sinker and lure molds, 187, 274, 352
Sinkers: Gremlin, 94; Les Davis Deep Six Diving, 370; painting,

285; Stingray Trolling, 99; storing or carrying, 326; wrap-around, 130
Sisley, Nick, 122, 137
"600" leader sink, 191
Skate bait, 267
Skeeter Products, 135
Skipjack, 319
Skittering, 57
Slaten, Stan, 246
Slaymaker, S. R., II, 122
Slip (egg-shaped) sinker mold, 187
Smallest fish in the world, 80
Small-mouth bass, 13, 15, 18, 19, 20, 73, 134; flies for, 194; lures for, 40; plastic worms for, 15
Smelt, landlocked salmon and, 2
Smiley, Russ, 339
Smith, Paul A., 45
Smith River, Calif., 5
Smithsonian Institution Press, 366
Smoker, portable electric, 72
Snagproof Mfg. Co., 152
Snapper, 281, 319, 336; lure for, 198
Sneaking up, 206
Snook, 20, 24, 281, 309, 336; bait for, 262; from a beach, 300; caught on sewing thread, 355; hangout for, 304; largest caught, 335; plug for, 341; in shallow water, 276
Soft-hackled Fly, The (Nemes), 95
Solana Studios, 203
Solunar Tables, 169
Sonar, fish-finding, 379
Sosin, Mark, 19, 122, 226, 312, 328, 346, 373
South Carolina, publications on, 270, 377
South Dakota's Angler's Almanac, 123
Southern Guide Fishing Maps, 119
Spanish mackerel, 268, 281, 323; leaders for, 247
Special Catch and Release Trout Streams (West Va. Dept. of Natural Resources), 78
Speckled trout, lures for, 40
Spider fish, 36
Spider fly, skating for trout, 57
Spinfishing (Strung and Rosko), 16
Spin fishing records, 216
Spinners: adding cloth or plastic strips to, 66; Aglia, 15; Black Fury, 15; Colorado, 115; Comet, 15; Flicker, 115; Giant Killer, 15; Hilde's, 115; Idaho, 115; Indiana, 115; June Bug, 115; Kriss Spoon, 15; Mepps, 15; Musky Killer, 15; Plastic Mino, 15; Shad-King, 115; single bait gripper, 12; snelled hook, 12; spoons from, 256; Swing-King, 115; Trolling Fly, 15; using as bait, 195; Weller's Bob-It, 12; Willow Leaf, 115. *See also* Reels; under names of fish
Spinning reels. *See* Reels
Splake, 73
Split-shot mold, 187
Spoonplug, 168
Spoonplugging Lesson, A (Perry), 168
Spoons: adding cloth or plastic strips to, 66; Al's Goldfish, 50; for bass (in cold weather), 51; Cather's, 346; for coho salmon, 19; Dardevle, 72, 98; Kachmor, 350; Koho Killer, 350; for lake trout, 19; for landlocked salmon, 19; Martin, 350; Miller, 350; Montauk striper bunker, 255; muskies on, 19, 52; for Pacific salmon, 19; Pet, 307; for pike, 19, 52; for salmon, 383; silver minnow, 78; from spinners, 256
Sportfishing for Sharks (Mundus and Wisner), 380
Sport Fishing in New York State, 153
Sport Fishing Institute, 176
Sport Fishing U.S.A. (Bureau of Sport Fisheries and Wildlife), 134
Sport Fish of Oklahoma, 18
Sporting Logs, 246
Sportmate pliers, 63
Sports Afield (magazine), 36
Sportsman's Guide to Game Fish (Dalrymple), 47
Spot for fishing: making your own, 120; trout, in a stream, 288; trying different kinds of, 194
Squid, catching, 247
Squirrel fish, 36
Stackpole Books, 8, 152
Stan Gibbs Lures, Inc., 252
Stan Jones Publishing Co., 162, 277, 288
State-owned and -managed Public Fishing Lakes (in Alabama), 61, 109
Stearns, Bob, 373
Steelhead, 13, 23, 69, 86, 162; float fishing for, 32; locating, 143; using bright-colored lures, 80
Steelon leader material, 280
Steury Corp., 177, 331
Stingray Trolling Sinker, 99
Stoeger Publishing Co., 64, 325
Stone Wall Press, 82
Storm Mfg. Co., 13
Strader Tackle, Inc. 298
Stratton & Terstegge Co., 116
Streamer Fly Tying and Fishing (Bates), 45
Streamers, fishing with, 218
Streamside Anglers Co., 136
Streamside Tyer Kit, 214
Stringers, 227; rope and braid, 70
Striped bass, 20, 23, 24, 216, 308, 309, 336, 346; angler's organization, 249; bait for, 262, 364; book on, 328; California map, 258; champion catches of, 367; good locations for, 206; leaders for, 247; lure for, 64; near white water, 299; plug for, 341; trolling trick for, 330
Striped Bass & Other Cape Cod Fish (Schwind), 315
Striped marlin, 216
Striper Fish, catching, 361, 368
Stripers Unlimited, 249
Striper—The Super Fish (Clift), 130
Strung, Norman, 16, 122
Sturgeon, 2, 13, 23, 134, 162; bait for, 146; on hook and line, 146; weight and size of, 2
Successful Bluefishing (Lyman), 320
Successful Ocean Game Fishing (Moss), 346
Successful Striped Bass Fishing (Moss), 328
Suckers, 13, 124
Suick Lure Co., 8
Sunglasses, 342; holder for, 298
Super Boomer electric motor hold-down, 230
Superbug motors, 99
Surf bags, 342
Surf Fishing (Evanoff), 348
Swallows, watching, 44
Sweney, Fred, 188
Swisher, Doug, 160
Swiss Army knife, 15
Swivels, 266, 348
Swordfish, 24, 304, 323, 336, 346; caught with bare hands, 306; caught by police officers (story), 246; in pairs, 383
Syl-Mark Enterprises, 286, 317
System 6 Pack Rod, 68

Tackle boxes, 44, 50, 90, 96, 116, 138, 263, 282, 317, 335; for sportfishing boats, 263
Tackle equipment: books on, 196; Dale Clemens, 48; Hank Roberts, 48; ice fishing, 67; mail-order, 48; making your own, 30, 138; Okiebug, 230; saltwater fishing, 255
Tackle Mfg. Co., Inc. (C & G), 227
Tackle satchel, 169
Tagging and releasing fish (for scientific research), 257
Tarpon, 20, 24, 98, 281, 309, 336;

399

bait for, 262; at Boca Grande, Fla., 254; good time to fish, 333; junior champ catch (1974), 291; leaps of, 247, 379; lure for, 198; over 200 lbs., 368; plug for, 341; slack line for, 268; stirring up, 323
Tautog, bait for, 324
Taxidermists, 212
Taylor Co., Inc. (N. A.), 138
Teak rod holders, 341, 374
Teaser lures, 328, 352; teasing with, 380
Telescopic fishing rods, 6
Telescopic poles, 190
Telisons International Corp., 334
Tempo Products Co., 27, 213
Tennessee, booklets on, 185
Texas, books on, 154, 314
Texas Fisherman, The, 25
Texas Menhaden Fishery, The, 154
Texas Salt-water Big 3 (Becker), 314
T.F.H. Publications, Inc., 339
T. H. E. Co., 174
T. H. E. Fishing Vests, 174
There He Is! (Dance), 37
Thermalfinder diving plane, 223
Thermometers, 164
This Is Georgia Fishing, 275
This Wonderful World of Trout (Fox), 144
Thomas & Thomas Co., 233
Thomas Y. Crowell Co., Inc., 47
Thomton, Norton, 368
Through the Fish's Eye (Sosin and Clark), 312
Tidewatch, 393
Tidewater areas, black bass in, 202
Tidewater Publishers, 173
Tigerfish, 36
Tiger shark, 36
Tiger trout, 118
Tinsley, Russell, 25, 130, 346
Tips and Techniques from the Creme Tester Staff, 226
Tips on Rod Building (Bullard), 25
Toadfish, 36
To Cast a Fly (Scientific Anglers), 25
Tom Mann's Secrets of the Bass Pros, 212
Tony Accetta & Son, Inc., 307
Topwater Fishing (Eggleston), 130
Toughness, fisherman, 329
Tournament gin poles, 296
Tournament Marine Products, 296, 355
Tournament outriggers, 355
Tout tails, 312
Tower for boats (to locate fish), 326
Townsend, Gerald and Joan, 262

Travel set, 199
Travel-Troler electric motor, 35
Treland, Oscar, 224
Tri-Fin Fishing Tackle Mfg. Corp., 291, 296
Tri-Fin Reverse Squid and jigs, 296
Trimarc Corp., 95
"Trinity Alps" (map), 131
Trinity River Fishing, 119
Trolling bait bucket, 12
Trolling butts, 323
Trolling sinker molds, 187
Trophies, mounting, 212
Trout, 23, 24, 44, 56, 67; bait, 92, 154, 164; books on, 113, 181; California maps, 131; caught by jumping in icy water (story), 118; cruising for food, 224; fall season, 120; fishing close to the bottom, 181; flies and size for, 122, 156, 189; float fishing for, 32; importance of first cast, 146; locating spot, 228; lures, 40; most difficult kind to catch, 142; net for, 56; an opening day of season, 124; spider fly skating for, 57; spinners for, 12; spring season, 122; trolling for, 160. See also kind of trout
Trout Fisherman's Bible, The (Holland), 140
Trout Fishermen's Digest, The (ed. Richey), 122
Trout Fishing (Brooks), 113
Trout Fishing (Dickey and Moses), 181
Trout Fishing in New England (Blaisdell), 82
Trout of California, 69
Trout Streams of Oklahoma, 18
Trout Unlimited, 86
Tubby Tackle, Inc., 141
Tucker Duck and Rubber Co., 198
Tucker "Fish-N-Float," 198
Tuna, 24, 308, 319, 320, 336, 346; in Canada, 336; migrations of, 242; pork rind for, 241; sinks boat (story), 374; toughness of, 292
2-In-1 Globe Bobber, 192
Tycoon/Fin-Nor Corp., 259, 260, 266

Umco Tackle Box, 96
Uncle Josh Bait Co., 58, 154, 172, 178, 241, 364
Underwater Naturalist (American Littoral Society), 303
Underwood, Bob, 228
Unimetrics, Inc., 325
U. S. Promotions, Inc., 320
Universal Transom Mount, 88
Universal Vise Corp., 232
"Upper Bishop Creek" (map), 131

Upperman, Bill, 288
Upperman bucktails, 288
Uslan Rods Co., 37
Utah Division of Wildlife Resources, 119
Utah Fishing and Hunting Guide, 119

Val-Craft, Inc., 333
Vermont Fisheries Annual, 61
Vermont Guide to Fishing, 61
Vests, 162, 174, 310
Vexilar, Inc., 22
Vexilar Fish Scout depth finder, 22
Virginia, publications on, 96, 365, 370
"Virginia Beach Fishing Map," 322
Virginia Salt-water Fishing Tournament, 250, 372
Vlchek Plastics Co., 90
Von Schlegell, Fritz, 208

Wader lure box, 373
Wading and casting, 76
Wahoo, 24, 319, 336; how to catch, 244
Walczyk, Fred, 323
Walford, Lionel A., 366
Walking fish, 149
Waller Co., The, 338
Waller Corp., 22, 113
Walleyes, 13, 24, 73, 98, 134; books on, 189; float fishing for, 32; hooks for, 62; lures for, 4, 64, 198; plastic minnow bait, 70; plastic worms for, 15; spinners for, 12; in the summer season, 86; tempting with leeches, 48
Walleyes and Walleye Fishing (Fellegy), 189
Walls, Jerry G., 339
Walton's Thumb knife, 47
Washington State, 146; books on, 162, 277
Washington State Fishing Guide, The, 162
Water: finding depth and temperature indicator (sea water), 269; oxygen content of, 22, 131; temperature indicator (sea water), 269; thermometer, 164
Water Cricket "natural" insects, 147
Water Gremlin Co., 94
Waterman, Charles, 156, 186, 373
Ways of Game Fish, The (Cadieux and Williams), 188
Weakfish, 20, 24, 336; bait for, 302; book on, 322; strength of, 308
Weber, Sharon, 98
Weber Tackle Co., 182, 330
Weedless Arrow-Lock hook, 7

400

Weedless Jig-A-Lo lure, 91
Weir & Son, 14
Weiss, John, 61
Wellcraft Marine Corp., 311
Wesmar Marine Systems Division, 379
Wesmar SS80 scanning sonar, 379
West, Capt. Bob, 368
Western Cutlery Co., 249
Western fish knives, 249
"West Virginia Stream Map," 78
West Virginia Trout Fishing Guide, 78
West Yellowstone, Mont., 67
Whale shark, 248
White bass, 13, 114; bottom fishing rig for, 16; hiding places of, 214; "jump" fishing for, 112; lures for, 34
White Bass—A Fish for Tomorrow (Gapen), 222
White Bass in Ohio, 55
White crappies, 60, 134
Whitefish, 13, 162; bait for, 75
White marlin, 216, 323
White perch, 13; bottom fishing rig for, 16; plastic minnow bait, 70
White sharks, 248
White sucker, 134
Whiz Bang lure, 13
Whopper Stopper, Inc., 6, 341
Why Fish Carp? (Gapen Tackle Co.), 135
Wig-Wag plastic worms, 58
Wilke, L. A., 25, 130
Williams, Larry, 137
Williams, Russ, 188
Williams Gold Refining Co. of Canada Ltd., 19
Williams spoons, 19
Winchester Press, 243
Windward Publishing, Inc., 357
Wisconsin Muskellunge Waters, 134
Wisconsin Streams, 134
Wisconsin Trout Streams, 134
Wisconsin Walleye Waters, 134
Wisner, Bill, 239, 294, 380
Wolffish, 36
WonderTroll motors, 24, 117
Wood frame trout net, 56
Woodstream Corp., 12, 50, 140, 169, 373
Woodworth, Melissa, 108
Woolner, Frank, 278, 280, 322, 373
World Record Book (International Spin Fishing Assn.), 216
World Record Marine Fishes (International Game Fish Assn.), 240
Worm Bedding pulp, 132
Worms: as a business, 36; canteen for, 104; Jig-A-Do lure, 64; keeping alive (for long periods), 26; raising for profit, 115; for salt-water fishing, 256. *See also* Plastic worms
Worth Co., 42, 43, 62, 79, 137, 167
Worth lure-making kit, 167
Worth's Pop-Up magnetic tip-up, 79
Wrap-around sinkers, 130
Wright & McGill Co., 71, 173, 275, 326
"Wrightsville Beach, N.C., to Little River, S.C., Fishing Map," 322
Wulff, Lee, 195
Wyoming Fishing Guide, 47

Yakima Bait Co., 18
Yarn, lures from, 228
Yellowfin tuna, 319
Yellow perch, 13, 16
Yellowstone National Park, 67
Yellowtail, 268, 336, 346
Yum-Yum plastic worms, 182
Yurgealitis, Bill, 194

Zak Tackle Mfg. Co., 192
Zebco Division (Brunswick Corp.), 7, 18, 318
Zebco outdoor films, 177
Zimmerlee, David, 66
Zuber, Jerry, 130